# Palgrave Studies in African and Development Economics

Series Editor
Arkebe Oqubay
British Academy Global Professor
SOAS University of London
London, UK

This series provides a wide-ranging analysis of African economics, development economics, and global transformation. Combing theoretical and empirical evidence, it offers thoughtful and policy relevant insight to the economic challenges and opportunities seen within the developing world. It engages with emerging and topical debates, including issues relating to sustainable development, food security, and the green transition, to make sure countries in Africa and the developing world are included in these important discussions.

Ibrahim Nandom Yakubu
Editor

# Public Debt and Economic Resilience in Africa

## Strategies for Sustainable Growth and Fiscal Stability

palgrave
macmillan

*Editor*
Ibrahim Nandom Yakubu
School of Business
University for Development Studies
Tamale, Ghana

ISSN 3004-9601 ISSN 3004-961X (electronic)
Palgrave Studies in African and Development Economics
ISBN 978-3-032-25834-2 ISBN 978-3-032-25835-9 (eBook)
https://doi.org/10.1007/978-3-032-25835-9



This Palgrave Macmillan imprint is published by the registered company Springer Nature Switzerland AG
The registered company address is: Gewerbestrasse 11, 6330 Cham, Switzerland

# Contents

**Part I Foundations of Public Debt and Fiscal Stability in Africa** 1

**1 The Economics of Debt in Africa: Stakes for Fiscal Stability and Growth** 3
Ibrahim Nandom Yakubu
*1.1 Introduction* 3
*1.2 Conceptualizing Public Debt and Fiscal Stability* 6
*1.3 Historical Evolution of Debt in African Economies* 13
*1.4 Theoretical Perspectives on Debt and Growth* 20
*1.5 Economic Rationale for Public Borrowing* 20
*1.6 Challenges and Risks of Rising Debt Levels* 26
*1.7 Policy Implications for Fiscal Management* 28
*1.8 Conclusion* 31
*References* 32

**2 Drivers of Public Debt Accumulation in African Economies: Insights from Panel Data Analysis** 37
Yazidu Ustarz
*2.1 Background* 37
*2.2 Stylised Facts on Debt Dynamics in Africa* 39
*2.3 Literature Review* 43
*2.4 Methodology* 48
*2.5 Analysis of Findings and Discussions* 52
*2.6 Conclusion and Policy Recommendations* 56
*References* 56

**3 Measuring What Matters: Context-Specific Debt Sustainability Metrics for Sub-Saharan Africa** 61
Ibrahim Nandom Yakubu and Muazu Ibrahim
*3.1 Introduction* 61
*3.2 Conventional Indicators of Debt Sustainability* 65
*3.3 Limitations of Standard Debt Metrics* 71
*3.4 Context-Specific Metrics for SSA* 75
*3.5 Alternative Approaches and Models* 79
*3.6 Policy Relevance of Revised Indicators* 82
*3.7 Conclusion* 85
*References* 86

**4 Fiscal Rules and Debt Sustainability in Ghana: An ARDL Bounds Testing Approach** 91
Mubarik Salifu
*4.1 Introduction* 91
*4.2 Literature Review* 93
*4.3 Methodology* 96
*4.4 Data Analysis and Discussion of Findings* 100
*4.5 Conclusions and Policy Recommendations* 105
*Appendix* 109
*References* 110

**Part II Debt Management Strategies and Global Dynamics** 113

**5 Examining the Effectiveness of Debt Restructuring Mechanisms in African Countries** 115
Mohammed Ridwan Saani, Ibrahim Nandom Yakubu, and Abdulai Iddrisu
*5.1 Introduction* 115
*5.2 Overview of Debt Restructuring Instruments* 117
*5.3 Historical Cases of African Debt Restructuring* 124
*5.4 Outcomes and Lessons Learned* 129
*5.5 Multilateral and Bilateral Roles* 134
*5.6 Policy Challenges and Future Reforms* 134
*5.7 Conclusion* 137
*References* 141

6 **Global Economic Shocks and Debt Vulnerability in African Economies** 149
Khadijah Iddrisu
*6.1 Introduction* 149
*6.2 Debt Evolution and Vulnerabilities in Africa* 151
*6.3 Evidence on Global Economic Shocks and Debt Vulnerability* 154
*6.4 Coping Mechanisms and Policy Responses* 158
*6.5 Future Outlook* 161
*6.6 Conclusions* 163
*References* 164

7 **Evaluating the Effectiveness of Concessional Loans in Reducing Debt Stress in Africa** 171
Khadijah Iddrisu
*7.1 Introduction* 171
*7.2 Debt Stress in Africa* 173
*7.3 Overview of Concessional Loans* 175
*7.4 Evaluating the Effectiveness of Concessional Loans* 180
*7.5 Challenges of Using Concessional Loans: What Can Be Done* 183
*7.6 Conclusion* 186
*References* 188

8 **Islamic Sovereign Bonds (Sukuk) and Debt Sustainability in Africa: Emerging Trends and Policy Options** 193
Abdul-Hamid Abdul-Wahab and Ibrahim Nandom Yakubu
*8.1 Introduction* 193
*8.2 Principles and Structures of Sukuk* 195
*8.3 Global and African Trends in Sukuk Issuance* 204
*8.4 Sukuk for Infrastructure and Debt Diversification* 210
*8.5 Comparative Analysis with Conventional Bonds* 213
*8.6 Regulatory and Institutional Requirements* 216
*8.7 Opportunities and Risks in Sukuk Adoption* 219
*8.8 Conclusion and Recommendations* 221
*References* 223

Part III Innovative Financing, Social Dimensions, and Governance in Debt Management 231

9 Climate Financing: Innovative Tool for Debt Management in Africa 233
Khadijah Iddrisu
*9.1 Introduction* 233
*9.2 Climate Finance in Africa* 235
*9.3 Mechanism of Climate Financing for Debt Management* 239
*9.4 Opportunities and Benefits for Africa* 242
*9.5 Challenges and Future Prospects for Africa* 246
*9.6 Conclusion* 250
*References* 251

10 Economic Globalization, Institutions, and Debt Dynamics: Evidence from Sub-Saharan Africa 255
Mohammed Ridwan Saani, James Atta Peprah, Mark Armah, and Kwadwo Ankomah
*10.1 Introduction* 255
*10.2 Literature Review* 258
*10.3 Methodology* 260
*10.4 Discussion of Empirical Results* 262
*10.5 Conclusions and Policy Recommendations* 268
*Appendix 1 (Table 10.5)* 268
*References* 270

11 Public Debt, Corruption Control, and Economic Growth Dynamics in Africa 275
Mohammed Ridwan Saani, Abdul-Malik Abdulai, and Munira Muhammed Alhassan
*11.1 Introduction* 275
*11.2 Literature Review* 278
*11.3 Methodology of the Study* 281
*11.4 Data Analysis and Discussion* 284
*11.5 Conclusions and Recommendations* 289
*References* 290

**12 Driving Inclusive Development Through Borrowing in Africa: The Urgency for Asymmetric Analysis** 297
Emmanuel Issifu Fuseini, Muazu Ibrahim, and Ustarz Yazidu
*12.1 Introduction* 297
*12.2 Literature Review: The Sovereign Debt and Development Prospects Relationship* 300
*12.3 Methodology* 304
*12.4 Findings* 307
*12.5 Conclusion* 324
*Appendix* 325
*References* 326

**13 Integrating ESG Considerations into Public Debt Management in Africa: A Pathway to Responsible and Sustainable Borrowing** 331
Osman Issah, Khadijah Iddrisu, and Ibrahim Nandom Yakubu
*13.1 Introduction* 331
*13.2 ESG in Public Finance: Concepts and Relevance* 333
*13.3 Debt Landscape in Africa: Risks, Opportunities, and ESG Gaps* 335
*13.4 Innovative ESG Tools and ESG-Driven Debt Management Strategies* 338
*13.5 Lessons from Other Continents and Implication for African Countries* 343
*13.6 Conclusion* 347
*References* 349

**Part IV Risks, Volatility, and Debt Sustainability** 353

**14 Debt Overhang and Private Investment in Sub-Saharan Africa: Crowding Out or Complementarity?** 355
Emmanuel Issifu Fuseini
*14.1 Introduction* 355
*14.2 Literature Review* 359
*14.3 Methodology* 365

*14.4 Empirical Results* 369
*14.5 Conclusion* 377
*References* 378

**15 Public Debt and Exchange Rate Volatility in Africa: Implications for Trade and Investment** 383
Khadijah Iddrisu, Simplice A. Asongu, and Richard Stephens Cromwell
*15.1 Introduction* 383
*15.2 Public Debt and Exchange Rates in Africa* 385
*15.3 Channels Linking Public Debt and Exchange Rate Volatility* 393
*15.4 Implications for Trade and Investment* 395
*15.5 Conclusions* 400
*References* 401

**16 The Role of Commodity Price Volatility in Public Debt Sustainability in Resource-Dependent African Countries** 405
Khadijah Iddrisu, Moses Dumayiri, Richard Takyi Opoku, and Felix Owusu Gyebi
*16.1 Introduction* 405
*16.2 Commodity Price Volatility in Africa* 407
*16.3 Channels of Transmission to Public Debt Sustainability* 411
*16.4 Policy and Institutional Responses* 414
*16.5 Why Some of These Policy and Institutional Responses Fail?* 420
*16.6 Conclusions* 422
*References* 423

**Index** 429

# Notes on Contributors

**Abdul-Malik Abdulai** is an associate professor in the Department of Economics of the School of Economics at the University for Development Studies, Ghana. His research interest includes macroeconomics, labor economics, and migration-related studies.

**Abdul-Hamid Abdul-Wahab** is Lecturer in Finance in the Department of Finance, School of Business at the University for Development Studies (UDS), Ghana. He previously served as Head of the Department of Business Analytics and MIS within the same school. Dr. Abdul-Wahab holds a PhD in Business Administration specializing in Islamic Finance, an MSc in Finance, and a Bachelor of Business Administration (Finance) from the International Islamic University Malaysia. He has over a decade of academic and professional experience spanning higher education, international financial infrastructure, and global standard-setting institution. Prior to his current role, he worked with the Society for Worldwide Interbank Financial Telecommunication (SWIFT) and the Islamic Financial Services Board (IFSB), the global standard-setting body for Islamic finance headquartered at the Central Bank of Malaysia. At the IFSB, he contributed to several high-level regulatory and industry initiatives in collaboration with international stakeholders, including the World Bank, the International Monetary Fund, and the Islamic Development Bank. His work included contributions to the Islamic Financial Services Industry (IFSI) Stability Reports, the development of regulatory standards for Islamic banking and capital markets, and case studies for the Facilitating the Implementation of IFSB Standards (FIS) workshops. He also participated in technical workshops on the Core Principles for Islamic Finance Regulation (Banking Sector), the Revised Capital Adequacy Standard for Institutions Offering Islamic Financial Services (IIFS), and the Guidance Note on Quantitative Measures for Liquidity Risk Management. Dr. Abdul-Wahab's research focuses on Islamic finance and sustainable finance, within the context of the Middle East and Africa. He is a member of the International Council of Islamic Finance Educators (ICIFE).

**Kwadwo Ankomah** is a lecturer in the Department of Applied Economics, School of Economics at the University of Cape Coast, Ghana. He specializes in risk management, behavioral finance, corporate finance, and microfinance.

**Mark Kojo Armah** is an Economist and a professor in the Department of Applied Economics, School of Economics at the University of Cape Coast, Ghana. He specializes in development economics, econometrics, and public policy, with a strong focus on applied econometric methods in policy analysis and economic development research.

**Simplice A. Asongu** holds a PhD from Oxford Brookes University and is the Lead Economist and Director of the African Governance and Development Institute in Cameroon. He is also an Adjunct Professor at the University of Cape Town and affiliated with several institutions across Africa and the UK as a supervisor and research associate. He serves as an associate editor for key journals and specializes in inclusive economic development, ICTs, education, poverty reduction, and innovation policy, with extensive expertise in economic and social policy.

**Richard Stephens Cromwell** is a researcher with a strong academic background and diverse expertise. He holds an MPhil in Finance and a BSc in Banking and Finance, and is a PhD candidate in Petroleum and Energy Studies at the University of Cape Coast (UCC), Ghana. His research interests encompass banking, finance, economics, and petroleum and energy studies, reflecting a multidisciplinary approach to addressing complex economic and financial issues. Beyond academia, Richard serves as a consultant in business and research, providing analytical support and strategic guidance to organizations and individuals across various sectors.

**Moses Dumayiri** is a lecturer at the University of Business and Integrated Development Studies (UBIDS), Ghana. His expertise lies in financial economics, applied financial econometrics, time series analysis, and financial networks, with a strong focus on quantitative financial research.

**Emmanuel Issifu Fuseini** is a PhD candidate in Business Administration with a focus on finance and an adjunct lecturer at the University for Development Studies, Ghana. Emmanuel holds a Master of Commerce and is a member of the ICA-Ghana. Emmanuel is an AMIE Mentee for the 2025/2026 academic year. Emmanuel's primary research interest revolves around the nexus among fiscal policy, debt, institutions, technology, finance, and growth. Emmanuel has written in reputable international journals like *Information Technology for Development*, *Journal of Global Information Technology Management*, and *Journal of Financial Economic Policy*, among others.

**Felix Owusu Gyebi** is a lecturer in the Accountancy Department at Koforidua Technical University, Ghana. He holds a PhD in Finance from Simon Diedong Dombo University of Business and Integrated Development Studies (SDD-UBIDS) and an MPhil in Finance from the University of Professional Studies, Accra, Ghana. A member of the Institute of Chartered Accountants, as well as chartered in economics and taxation, his research focuses on economic development and foreign capital flows. He contributes to academic and policy discourse on finance and development through teaching and scholarly work.

**Muazu Ibrahim** is an Economist with the Global Debt and Macro Unit, Economic Prosperity (EP) Global Practice, where he works on debt policy, including review of debt sustainability analysis (DSAs) and contributing to macroeconomic surveillance. Prior to joining the World Bank, he worked for the African Development Bank (AfDB), United Nations Economic Commission for Africa (UNECA), and the United Nations Industrial Development Organization (UNIDO). He also had a stint in academia, having taught at the School of Business, University for Development Studies (UDS), Ghana. Muazu holds a PhD in Economics and Finance from the University of the Witwatersrand, Johannesburg, South Africa, and an MSc in Development Economics from the School of Oriental and African Studies (SOAS), University of London, UK. His research areas include macroeconomics and development finance.

**Khadijah Iddrisu** is a lecturer at the Islamic University College, Ghana, with over five years of academic and professional experience. She also lectures part-time at Simon Diedong Dombo University of Business and

Integrated Development Studies (SDD-UBIDS) and serves as a consultant for the African Export Import Bank. Additionally, she is a research associate on the prestigious Reynolds & Gifford PRI Grant project, where she currently coordinates the African cohort. Dr. Iddrisu holds a PhD and an MPhil in Finance, a BSc in Accounting, and an Executive Mini MBA in Corporate Governance and Financial Management. Her research interests lie at the intersection of finance, economics, sustainability, inclusivity, foreign capital, and economic development, merging scholarly insight with real-world relevance. With her multifaceted expertise and commitment to advancing knowledge, Dr. Iddrisu is a valuable asset to her institutions and the broader academic community.

**Abdulai Iddrisu** holds a PhD in Finance from the University of Ghana. He is a lecturer in the Department of Finance at the University for Development Studies (UDS), Ghana. His research expertise lies in efficiency and productivity analysis, with a strong focus on Data Envelopment Analysis (DEA). He applies both the CCR (Constant Returns to Scale) and BCC (Variable Returns to Scale) models to evaluate institutional productivity and performance across sectors. His scholarly interests span financial performance analysis, operational efficiency, and quantitative research methods in finance.

**Osman Issah** is a senior lecturer and head of the Accounting Department at the University for Development Studies, Ghana. He holds a BA in Economics, an MSc in Economics and Finance, and is a member of ACCA. His research interests span business administration, accounting scholarship, and financial economics. With a strong academic and professional background, he contributes to advancing financial education and research, playing a key role in developing future professionals in accounting and finance in Ghana.

**Munira Alhassan Muhammed** is Lecturer in Economics in the Department of Economics, School of Economics at the University for Development Studies, Ghana. She is pursuing a PhD in Development Economics at the SDD University of Business and Integrated Development Studies. Her research interests encompass development economics, financial economics, and behavioral economics. She holds an MPhil in Economics from the University of Ghana.

**Richard Takyi Opoku** is a lecturer in the Department of Banking and Finance at the Islamic University College, Accra, Ghana. His research interests span financial economics, global commodity markets, asset pricing, macroeconomic fundamentals, and financial market dynamics.

**James Atta Peprah** is Professor of Economics and Finance in the Department of Applied Economics, School of Economics at the University of Cape Coast, Ghana. He is the former Dean of School of Economics at the same university. He holds a PhD in Economics, an MPhil in Economics, and a Bilingual MBA in Banking and Finance. His areas of research include development economics and finance, financial market and institution in developing countries, microfinance, economic growth and development, as well as small- and medium-scale enterprise (SMEs) development. James is the principal editor of *Financial Sector Development in Ghana Exploring Bank Stability, Financing Models, and Development Challenges for Sustainable Financial Markets*, a book published by Palgrave Macmillan. He has also written a number of research articles that focus on SMEs, microfinance, and poverty in Ghana, Sub-Saharan Africa, and Africa. He teaches courses in economics and finance at the undergraduate and graduate levels. James Peprah has rich experience in consultancy services as well.

**Mohammed Ridwan Saani** is Lecturer in Economics in the Department of Economics, School of Economics at the University for Development Studies, Ghana. He is currently pursuing a PhD in Economics at the University of Cape Coast. His research interests encompass financial economics, labor economics, and development economics. He holds an MPhil in Economics from the University of Ghana.

**Mubarik Salifu** is a senior lecturer in the Department of Economics at the University for Development Studies, Ghana. He serves as the Deputy Director in charge of the Third Trimester Field Practical Program (TTFPP) and Community-Based Education and Service (COBES) within the Directorate of Community Relations and Outreach Programmes (DCROP). Dr. Salifu holds a PhD in Economics and a BA in Economics from the University of Cape Coast, Ghana, as well as an MPhil in Economics from the University of Ghana, Legon, Ghana. Throughout his academic career, he has contributed to research projects as a team member and has written peer-reviewed articles in esteemed journals. Dr. Salifu has actively participated in numerous international conferences, workshops, and training sessions across Africa, serving as a panelist, presenter, or discussant. His research interests include financial and monetary economics, development economics, health economics, and poverty studies, with a specific focus on developing and transitioning economies. He possesses strong communication and teamwork skills and is known for his diligence and ability to work effectively under pressure in multicultural environments. Dr. Salifu is proficient in statistical software packages such as STATA, EViews, and SPSS.

**Yazidu Ustarz** holds an MPhil in Finance from the University of Ghana and a PhD in Development Finance from the University of Stellenbosch Business School, South Africa. He is a senior lecturer and head in the Department of Finance at the University for Development Studies, Tamale, Ghana. Dr. Ustarz's research interests cover financial development, foreign capital inflows, sectoral growth, and international trade, among others. Dr. Ustarz has written in a number of reputable journals including *The Journal of International Trade and Economic Development*, *Cogent Economics and Finance*, *African Journal of Economic and Management Studies*, and *Agricultural and Food Economics*, among others.

**Ibrahim Nandom Yakubu** is a lecturer in the School of Business at the University for Development Studies (UDS), Ghana, and holds a PhD in Banking and Finance. His research interests include inclusive finance, financial markets, corporate governance, sustainability, and financial technology (FinTech). With a strong quantitative orientation, he has written extensively in peer-reviewed journals and contributed to numerous academic books in finance. He also serves as an editor of several scholarly volumes on topics such as fintech and financial inclusion, green finance, and regulatory innovation, contributing to ongoing academic discourse on contemporary issues in finance and development. Dr. Yakubu is a recipient of the prestigious 2022 Emerald Literati Award for Outstanding Paper, recognizing his impactful scholarly work. Beyond academia, he is an experienced consultant with expertise in institutional capacity assessments and applied research for civil society organizations and development partners in Ghana. He is a member of the African Accounting and Finance Association (AAFA) and serves as an associate editor for the *Review of Business Management (RBGN)* and the *Cureus Journal of Business and Economics.*

# List of Figures


| | | |
|---|---|---|
| Fig. 2.1 | Total external debt stocks for SSA (US$ billion). Source: Author's construction based on the World Bank (2024) | 40 |
| Fig. 2.2 | Composition of African's creditors—2023. Source: Author's based on data from UNCTAD, 2025 | 41 |
| Fig. 2.3 | Outstanding Eurobond Debt to GDP ratio for SSA Countries—2023. Source: Author's based on Development Reimagined (2024) | 42 |
| Fig. 2.4 | Debt service, expenditure on health and education as a percentage of total government spending. Source: Author's construct based on data from https://data.one.org/analysis/african-debt | 42 |
| Fig. 3.1 | Evolution of public debt in SSA. Source: World Bank (2025) | 63 |
| Fig. 3.2 | Median debt service-to-GDP in SSA. Source: Authors' computation based on data from the LIC DSF database as of end-June 2025 | 64 |
| Fig. 3.3 | External risk of debt distress in SSA. Source: World Bank (2025) | 70 |
| Fig. 3.4 | PPG external debt composition by creditor category. Source: Authors' computation based on data from the International Debt Statistics (IDS) of the World Bank | 73 |
| Fig. A1 | Stability test | 109 |
| Fig. 6.1 | External debt (% GNI) in Africa, 2000–2023, by country. (Source: Authors' Construct based on data from World Development Indicators of the World Bank) | 153 |
| Fig. 7.1 | RDB concessional loans in Africa, 2000 to 2023, by country. Notes: RDB is Regional Development Banks. Source: Author's Construct based on data from World Bank's World Development Indicators | 177 |

Fig. 7.2 RDB concessional loans in Africa 2023, by country. Notes: RDB is Regional Development Banks. Source: Author's Construct based on data from World Bank's World Development Indicators 178
Fig. 7.3 IMF concessional loans in Africa, 2000 to 2023, by country. Source: Author's Construct based on data from World Bank's World Development Indicators 178
Fig. 8.1 Trends in public debt-to-GDP ratios in developing economies. Source: Were (2025) 194
Fig. 8.2 Structure of *Ijara sukuk*. Source: Kusuma and Silva (2014) 199
Fig. 8.3 Structure of *Murabaha sukuk*. Source: Kusuma and Silva (2014) 200
Fig. 8.4 Structure of *Mudaraba sukuk*. Source: Kusuma and Silva (2014) 201
Fig. 8.5 Structure of *Musharaka sukuk*. Source: Kusuma and Silva (2014) 202
Fig. 8.6 Structure of *Wakala sukuk*. Source: Kusuma and Silva (2014) 203
Fig. 8.7 Structure of *Salam sukuk*. Source: Kusuma and Silva (2014) 203
Fig. 8.8 Structure of *Istisna sukuk* (combined with a forward lease arrangement) 204
Fig. 8.9 Structure of hybrid *sukuk*. Source: Razak et al. (2019) 205
Fig. 8.10 Global sukuk issuances and outstanding (2004–2024) (USD in billion). Source: IFSB (2025) 205
Fig. 8.11 Sukuk issuances by issuer type (2024). Source: IFSB (2025) 206
Fig. 8.12 Regional distribution of sukuk issuances in 2024. Source: IFSB (2025). Note: Gulf Cooperation Council (GCC), East Asia and Pacific (EAP), Europe and Central Asia (ECA), Middle East and North Africa (MENA excluding GCC), South Asia (SA), Sub-Saharan Africa (SSA) 207
Fig. 8.13 Sustainability and green sukuk issuances (2017–2024). Source: IFSB (2025) 208
Fig. 9.1 Climate finance flow in Africa, 2019/2020 and 2021/2022, by actor. Source: Author's Construct based on Data from Meattle et al. (2022, 2024) 236
Fig. 9.2 Instrument of climate finance in Africa, 2019/2020 and 2021/2022. Source: Author's Construct based on Data from Meattle et al. (2022, 2024) 236
Fig. 11.1 Trend graphs of public debt and GDP for the top 10 indebted countries in Africa 285
Fig. 13.1 Trend in public debt in Sub-Saharan Africa (2004 to 2026) by subgroup. Source: Adapted from the IMF 335

Fig. 13.2 Sub-Saharan African countries with debt (% GDP) levels above 55% in 2024. Source: Adapted from the IMF 336
Fig. 15.1 Trend in gross government debt (2000 to 2022). Source: Authors' construction based on data from UNCTAD (2023) 386
Fig. 15.2 Gross government debt in Africa 2022, by country. Source: Authors' construction based on data from UNCTAD (2023) 387
Fig. 15.3 Creditor composition of external debt in Africa (2010 and 2021). Source: Authors' construction based on data from UNCTAD (2023) 387
Fig. 15.4 Public debt components in some African countries. Notes: The data reflect 2021 figures, except for Morocco and Senegal, where 2020 data is used. Source: Authors' construction based on data from Raga et al. (2022) 389
Fig. 15.5 Trend in international trade in Africa (1999 to 2022), by components. Notes: Total merchandise and services were computed by the author using data for Eastern and Southern and Western, and Central Africa. Source: Authors' construction based on data from World Bank's World Development Indicators 395
Fig. 16.1 Trend in natural resource rent in Africa (2000 to 2021). Source: Authors' construct based on data from World Development Indicators 410
Fig. 16.2 In-country natural resource rent in Africa (2000 to 2021). Source: Authors' construct based on data from World Development Indicators 410
Fig. 16.3 Trend and estimates in Angola's export (1990 to 2030). Notes: The dataset covers actual values for 1990–2020, while figures for 2021–2030 represent projections. Source: Authors' construct based on data from Cao et al. (2022) 411
Fig. 16.4 Average (pro)cyclicality in SSA, resource dependent and rich versus other countries (2000–2016). Source: Authors' construct based on data from Herrera et al. (2019) 413
Fig. 16.5 Average (pro)cyclicality in SSA versus other region (2009–2016). Source: Authors' construct based on data from Herrera et al. (2019) 413

# List of Tables


| | | |
|---|---|---|
| Table 1.1 | Core concepts of public debt and fiscal stability in Africa | 8 |
| Table 1.2 | Selected African countries—debt sustainability metrics (2023–2024) | 10 |
| Table 1.3 | Theoretical perspectives on debt and growth | 21 |
| Table 2.1 | Top African countries with the highest debt from China | 43 |
| Table 2.2 | Summary of variables and data sources | 49 |
| Table 2.3 | Summary of statistics | 51 |
| Table 2.4 | Determinants of debt accumulation (economic factors): MMQREG and OLS approach | 53 |
| Table 2.5 | Determinants of debt accumulation (demographic and structural factors): MMQREG and OLS approach | 54 |
| Table 2.6 | Determinants of debt accumulation (institutional and political factors) | 55 |
| Table 3.1 | IMF–World Bank thresholds based on LIC DSF | 70 |
| Table 3.2 | Context-specific debt sustainability metrics for SSA | 76 |
| Table 4.1 | Descriptive statistics of variables | 100 |
| Table 4.2 | Results of Unit Root Test (ADF and PP) | 100 |
| Table 4.3 | Results of bounds test for cointegration | 101 |
| Table 4.4 | Estimated long-run results | 102 |
| Table 4.5 | Estimated short-run results | 104 |
| Table 4.6 | Residual and stability tests results | 105 |
| Table 5.1 | Roles of multilateral institutions, bilateral creditors, and private lenders in African debt restructuring | 135 |
| Table 5.2 | Key policy challenges and reform proposals for improving African debt restructuring | 138 |
| Table 6.1 | Current public debt landscape in Africa | 153 |
| Table 7.1 | Proxy of debt stress | 173 |

| | | |
|---|---|---|
| Table 7.2 | Difference between concessional and non-concessional loans | 176 |
| Table 8.1 | Common *sukuk* structures | 198 |
| Table 8.2 | Sovereign sukuk issuances from select countries | 211 |
| Table 8.3 | Conventional bonds vs. sukuk | 215 |
| Table 9.1 | Trend in international sources of climate finance in Africa, 2011 to 2021 | 238 |
| Table 10.1 | Descriptive statistics of variables | 263 |
| Table 10.2 | Correlation matrix with variance inflation factor analysis | 264 |
| Table 10.3 | GMM results: effect of globalization on public debt | 265 |
| Table 10.4 | GMM results: Effect of institutional quality on globalization and debt nexus | 267 |
| Table 10.5 | List of countries covered in the sample | 268 |
| Table 11.1 | Definitions of variables | 283 |
| Table 11.2 | Descriptive statistics of variables | 284 |
| Table 11.3 | Panel unit root tests | 286 |
| Table 11.4 | Moderation effect of corruption on the GDP and debt relationship | 287 |
| Table 12.1 | Summary of variables definition, measurement, and sources | 305 |
| Table 12.2 | Descriptive statistics | 309 |
| Table 12.3 | Panel cointegration test | 310 |
| Table 12.4 | Symmetric effect of sovereign borrowing and servicing cost on inclusive human develoment | 312 |
| Table 12.5 | The asymmetric effect of sovereign borrowing and debt servicing cost on inclusive human development | 313 |
| Table 12.6 | Symmetric effect of sovereign borrowing on inclusive human development dimensions | 314 |
| Table 12.7 | The asymmetric effect of sovereign borrowing on Inclusive human development dimensions | 315 |
| Table 12.8 | Symmetric effect of sovereign debt servicing cost on inclusive human development dimensions | 316 |
| Table 12.9 | The asymmetric effect of debt servicing cost on inclusive human development dimensions | 317 |
| Table 12.10 | Panel stationarity test Variables | 318 |
| Table 12.11 | Testing for slope heterogeneity | 320 |
| Table 12.12 | Testing for weak cross-sectional dependence (CSD) | 320 |
| Table 14.1 | Summary of data and variables | 366 |
| Table 14.2 | Descriptive statistics | 369 |
| Table 14.3 | Relationship between debt overhang and sectoral infrastructural investment | 371 |
| Table 14.4 | Diagnostic test | 372 |
| Table 14.5 | Correlation Matrix | 373 |

# List of Boxes


| | | |
|---|---|---|
| Box 1.1 | Ghana's Domestic Debt Exchange (2022–2023) | 11 |
| Box 1.2 | Zambia's Default and Common Framework Negotiations | 12 |
| Box 5.1 | Nigeria's 2005 Paris Club Agreement | 119 |
| Box 5.2 | Zambia and the G20 Common Framework | 120 |
| Box 5.3 | Impact of HIPC/MDRI on African Debt Burdens | 121 |
| Box 5.4 | Ghana's 2023 Eurobond Exchange | 122 |
| Box 5.5 | Ghana's Domestic Debt Exchange Programme (DDEP) | 123 |
| Box 5.6 | Seychelles Debt-for-Nature Swap | 124 |
| Box 6.1 | HIPC Initiative and MDRI | 151 |
| Box 6.2 | African Monetary Fund a Means to Minimise Debt Vulnerability in Africa | 160 |
| Box 6.3 | Some Examples of Financial Market Deepening in Africa | 162 |
| Box 7.1 | Senegal Secured a Concessional Loan from the IMF | 181 |
| Box 7.2 | Concessional Loans Contribute to Fiscal Space in Rwanda | 182 |
| Box 9.1 | Climate Action Window at COP29 to Promote Fight Against Climate Change | 237 |
| Box 9.2 | Seychelles Used Debt-for-Climate Swap to Manage High Public Debts | 239 |
| Box 9.3 | Nigeria Issued Africa's First Sovereign Green Bonds | 240 |
| Box 9.4 | Gabon Applied Blended Finance for Kinguélé Aval Hydropower | 241 |
| Box 9.5 | Egypt's Green Bond Was Oversubscribed | 242 |
| Box 9.6 | Gabon Debt-for-Nature Swap Protect the Climate and Biodiversity | 244 |
| Box 9.7 | Corporate Green Bond Innovation Boost Domestic Capital | 245 |
| Box 9.8 | The Sun Exchange Enhance Trust in Climate Finance | 248 |

| | | |
|---|---|---|
| Box 13.1 | Kenya Borrowed for Prestige Infrastructure Without Considering ESG | 338 |
| Box 13.2 | Mozambique Allocates Funds to Address Crisis | 339 |
| Box 13.3 | Reactive Borrowing Amid Climate and Governance Fragility | 339 |
| Box 15.1 | Kenya's Involvement in Domestic Borrowing | 388 |
| Box 15.2 | CFA Franc Zone Reforms | 389 |
| Box 15.3 | Debt Sustainability of Chad and Ghana Under Different Exchange Rate Regimes | 391 |
| Box 15.4 | Currency Depreciation and Debt Service Spira in Nigeria | 392 |
| Box 15.5 | Currency Mismatch and Fiscal Compression | 394 |
| Box 15.6 | African Continental Free Trade Area (AfCFTA) | 397 |
| Box 16.1 | Establishment of Stabilisation Fund in Ghana | 415 |
| Box 16.2 | Botswana's Mineral Revenues, Expenditure and Savings Policy | 416 |
| Box 16.3 | Sudan Used Dual Exchange Rate System to Manage Scarce Foreign Exchange | 417 |
| Box 16.4 | Establishment of the Africa Mining Vision Initiative | 418 |
| Box 16.5 | The Role of International Institutions in Some African Countries | 419 |
| Box16.6 | Procyclicality in Zambia | 421 |

PART I

# Foundations of Public Debt and Fiscal Stability in Africa

CHAPTER 1

# The Economics of Debt in Africa: Stakes for Fiscal Stability and Growth

*Ibrahim Nandom Yakubu*

## 1.1 Introduction

Public debt has emerged as a central economic concern across Africa in the twenty-first century. The continent has endured multiple external shocks that have eroded fiscal buffers and compelled governments to rely more heavily on borrowing. The 2008 global financial crisis, the COVID-19 pandemic, and the ongoing Russia–Ukraine war have all exposed Africa's structural vulnerabilities, disrupting growth, curtailing revenues, and pushing governments into higher debt (International Monetary Fund (IMF), 2023; Zida et al., 2025). By mid-2025, sub-Saharan Africa's public debt-to-GDP ratio averaged more than 60%, while debt servicing

I. N. Yakubu (✉)
School of Business, University for Development Studies, Tamale, Ghana
e-mail: ibrahim.yakubu@uds.edu.gh



I. N. Yakubu (ed.), *Public Debt and Economic Resilience in Africa*, Palgrave Studies in African and Development Economics,
https://doi.org/10.1007/978-3-032-25835-9_1

consumed over 40% of government revenues in many countries.[1] This drastically reduced the fiscal space available for critical development spending.

Globally, debt burdens have climbed to historical levels. As of 2024, worldwide public debt stood at approximately 102 trillion US dollars, with nearly one-third held by developing countries (ONE Campaign, 2025). Africa accounts for a growing share of this global burden. The continent's public debt stock reached 1.8 trillion US dollars in 2022, representing a 183% increase since 2010 and rising much faster than GDP.[2] By 2024–2025, many African states continued to face elevated borrowing costs. Sixty-one developing countries worldwide, many of them African, were spending at least 10% of their revenues on interest payments on debts.[3] Such high debt-servicing obligations create binding constraints on governments' ability to meet the Sustainable Development Goals, particularly in health, education, and infrastructure (Zida et al., 2025).

The risks associated with this debt trajectory are pronounced. IMF projections suggested that sub-Saharan Africa's public debt could decline marginally from 60.1% of GDP in 2023 to about 56.8% in 2025.[4] However, more recent estimates indicate that debt instead stabilized at around 58% of GDP in 2025, while fiscal deficits are projected to widen to 3.2% of GDP in 2026, reflecting persistent fiscal pressures rather than meaningful consolidation (Adigun, 2026; Ple, 2026). Yet, this adjustment will occur against a backdrop of high borrowing costs, limited access to markets, and difficult fiscal choices. Moreover, governance weaknesses amplify this challenge. A recent audit in Senegal revealed off-book borrowing that pushed its debt-to-GDP ratio to nearly 119%.[5] This discovery led the IMF to suspend access to funding until transparency and accountability measures were strengthened.

Beyond headline numbers, the composition of Africa's debt has shifted in ways that have increased its vulnerability. Whereas concessional loans from multilateral and bilateral donors once dominated, the 2010s saw a

[1] https://www.undp.org/sites/g/files/zskgke326/files/2025-05/implication_of_imf_ssa_outlook_april_2025_insights_2-1.pdf

[2] Read more here: https://unctad.org/publication/world-of-debt/regional-stories

[3] https://twn.my/title2/finance/2025/fi250701.htm

[4] https://www.imf.org/en/Publications/REO/SSA/Issues/2025/04/25/regional-economic-outlook-for-sub-saharan-africa-april-2025

[5] https://www.afronomicslaw.org/category/african-sovereign-debt-justice-network-afs-djn/sovereign-debt-news-update-no-140-senegals

surge in commercial borrowing through Eurobonds and syndicated loans (Shah et al., 2025). Between 2010 and 2020, at least nineteen African countries issued Eurobonds, raising billions of dollars to finance infrastructure projects (Development Reimagined, 2024). While these issuances broadened financing sources, they also came with higher interest rates and shorter maturities than concessional debt. At the same time, China and other non-Paris Club lenders became major creditors, financing large-scale infrastructure projects across the continent. By 2020, private creditors accounted for about 40% of sub-Saharan Africa's external debt, complicating debt restructuring efforts when crises emerged.[6]

Regional disparities also characterize Africa's debt landscape. Resource-rich economies, such as Angola, Nigeria, and Zambia, experienced sharp increases in debt when commodity prices collapsed, while more diversified economies, such as Kenya and Côte d'Ivoire, borrowed heavily to fund infrastructure expansion (UNCTAD, 2025). Fragile and conflict-affected states, including Sudan and Mozambique, face acute debt distress amid their weak institutional capacities. Conversely, some countries, particularly in the West African Economic and Monetary Union (WAEMU), have managed debt within regional convergence criteria, but remain exposed to external shocks (IMF, 2025). These differences underscore the need for tailored policy approaches rather than one-size-fits-all solutions.

The stakes in Africa's debt surges are high. Borrowing enables governments to finance essential development projects, build infrastructure, and support social services. However, excessive reliance on debt undermines fiscal stability, erodes investor confidence, and poses long-term risks to economic sovereignty (Ngundu & Cilliers, 2025). The erosion of fiscal space also limits governments' ability to respond to new challenges, such as climate change, demographic pressures, and rising social demands. African policymakers must, therefore, walk a careful line, using debt as a strategic tool for growth while preventing it from becoming a structural hindrance to development and macroeconomic stability (Were, 2024a).

This chapter argues that Africa's public debt sustainability is fundamentally shaped by the interaction between domestic fiscal governance and global financial architecture, such that borrowing can support growth and stability only when underpinned by credible institutions, transparent debt management, and an international system aligned with long-term fiscal resilience.

[6] https://media.afreximbank.com/afrexim/Debt-Burden-in-Africa-and-the-Caribbean-_2025.pdf

The chapter is sectioned as follows: Section 1.2 clarifies the conceptual foundations of public debt and fiscal stability. Section 1.3 traces the historical evolution of African debt, from the debt crises of the 1980s and 1990s to the debt relief initiatives of the 2000s and the renewed borrowing surge of the 2010s and beyond. Section 1.4 reviews theoretical perspectives linking debt and economic growth. Section 1.5 examines the rationale for public borrowing in Africa, while Sect. 1.6 analyzes the risks posed by rising debt burdens. Section 1.7 explores policy implications for fiscal management, and Sect. 1.8 concludes with reflections on balancing debt and development in Africa's evolving economic landscape.

## 1.2 Conceptualizing Public Debt and Fiscal Stability

### *1.2.1 Defining Public Debt and Key Concepts*

Public debt, or sovereign debt, refers to the accumulated financial obligations of a government resulting from borrowing to cover fiscal deficits (Arslanalp et al., 2019). These obligations may take the form of treasury bills, bonds, syndicated loans, concessional loans, or guarantees. In the African context, the composition of public debt is especially important because it shapes vulnerability to exchange rate volatility, refinancing risk, and fiscal shocks.

Public debt in Africa takes multiple forms, and its implications for fiscal health depend not only on the size of liabilities but also on their structure. *Gross public debt* measures the total liabilities of the government without netting out financial assets.[7] This indicator is commonly reported in international statistics and is often used in debt sustainability analyses. *Net public debt*, in contrast, provides a clearer picture of fiscal exposure by deducting liquid assets, such as sovereign wealth funds or foreign reserves. However, many African countries lack the institutional capacity to consistently compile and report net debt figures (Were, 2024b).

Debt can be classified as domestic or external. *Domestic debt* refers to liabilities contracted within the country, usually denominated in local currency and held by residents.[8] *External debt* is contracted from foreign creditors and denominated in foreign currencies, primarily in US dollars

[7] https://www.elibrary.imf.org/downloadpdf/display/book/9781616352486/ch05.pdf
[8] https://www.nber.org/system/files/working_papers/w13946/w13946.pdf

or euros. The balance between domestic and external debt is critical in Africa. Domestic debt reduces currency mismatches but may crowd out private-sector borrowing if domestic financial markets are shallow (Bai et al., 2024; United Nations, 2024). External debt, while sometimes concessional, exposes governments to foreign exchange risks and global financial cycles. Another crucial dimension is the burden of *debt service*, which shows how much government revenue is absorbed by repayments. In countries such as Nigeria and Kenya, servicing costs consume disproportionate shares of revenues, leaving little space for development spending.[9]

To summarize, Table 1.1 outlines the main concepts of public debt, showing their definitions, key metrics, and policy relevance.

### 1.2.2 Fiscal Stability and Debt Sustainability

Fiscal stability refers to the government's ability to meet its expenditure and debt obligations in a manner that does not disrupt economic growth, undermine social spending, or trigger macroeconomic crises.[10] In practice, fiscal stability is achieved when governments maintain sufficient fiscal space to respond to shocks while ensuring that borrowing remains consistent with the long-term repayment capacity. In the African context, fiscal stability is particularly important because of high exposure to external shocks, narrow revenue bases, and relatively shallow domestic capital markets (African Development Bank, 2025).

Debt sustainability is closely linked to fiscal stability and commonly assessed using internationally recognized indicators. The most frequently cited measure is the debt-to-GDP ratio, which compares the total public debt stock to the size of the economy. While there is no universal threshold, ratios above 60%–70% of GDP in low- and middle-income countries are often associated with heightened risk.[11] The International Monetary Fund (IMF) and World Bank's Debt Sustainability Framework (DSF) provides tailored thresholds based on a country's policy and institutional strength.[12]

[9] See the case of Nigeria: https://apanews.net/nigeria-debt-servicing-costs-hit-4-1-of-gdp/

[10] https://www.imf.org/external/pubs/ft/pam/pam55/pam55.pdf

[11] https://unctad.org/publication/world-of-debt/regional-stories#:~:text=In%20fact%2C%20in%202020%20there,threshold%20in%202022

[12] For more information on the Debt Sustainability Framework (DSF) of the World Bank, visit: https://www.worldbank.org/en/programs/debt-toolkit/dsf

**Table 1.1** Core concepts of public debt and fiscal stability in Africa

| *Concept* | *Definition* | *Key metrics* | *Policy relevance* |
|---|---|---|---|
| Gross public debt | Total liabilities of the general government, including both domestic and external debt, guaranteed debt, and arrears | • Debt-to-GDP ratio (%)<br>• Debt-to-revenue ratio (%)<br>• Debt per capita | High gross debt levels can undermine fiscal stability, raise borrowing costs, and trigger fiscal consolidation or debt restructuring |
| Net public debt | Gross public debt minus government financial assets such as deposits, reserves, or sovereign wealth funds | • Net debt-to-GDP (%)<br>• Net debt-to-revenue (%) | Provides a more accurate measure of fiscal vulnerability, showing the real debt burden after accounting for liquid assets |
| Domestic debt | Borrowing sourced from residents, usually denominated in local currency and raised through treasury bills, bonds, or other domestic instruments | • Share of domestic debt in total (%)<br>• Domestic interest payments as % of revenue | Reduces foreign exchange risk but may crowd out private sector credit and raise domestic interest rates |
| External debt | Liabilities owed to non-residents, often in foreign currency, including multilateral, bilateral, and commercial obligations | • External debt-to-exports (%)<br>• External debt-to-GDP (%)<br>• Short-term external debt-to-reserves (%) | Increases exposure to exchange rate risk and global financial volatility; requires prudent external borrowing policies |
| Debt service | Total annual obligations (principal + interest) required to meet debt commitments | • Debt service-to-revenue ratio (%)<br>• Interest payments-to-revenue (%)<br>• Debt service-to-exports (%) | High debt service ratios reduce fiscal space for social and capital spending, constraining growth and development priorities |

Source: Author's compilation based on Bua et al. (2014), Committee for a Responsible Federal Budget (2025), and Institute for Government (2024)

Another critical metric is interest payments as a share of government revenue. High ratios suggest that fiscal resources are absorbed by debt servicing rather than productive investments or social spending. In Nigeria, interest payments exceeded 90% of federal revenues in 2022, highlighting an acute fiscal strain.[13] In Ghana, debt service costs absorbed more than half of the government revenues in 2023, forcing a domestic debt exchange.[14] Such figures demonstrate that even when debt-to-GDP ratios appear moderate, fiscal stability can be undermined if revenues are insufficient to cover debt service obligations.

Debt-to-export ratios are particularly relevant for Africa, given the reliance on external borrowing and export earnings for foreign exchange. Countries with high external debt relative to exports face repayment challenges during commodity price downturns, as witnessed in Zambia and Angola during the 2014–2016 oil and copper price slump (AFRODAD, 2017). Similarly, when exchange rates depreciate, external debt burdens can escalate quickly, leading to fiscal distress.

Regional organizations have also introduced convergence criteria aimed at safeguarding fiscal stability. The West African Economic and Monetary Union (WAEMU) requires member states to maintain a fiscal deficit below 3% of GDP and a debt-to-GDP ratio below 70% (Gammadigbe, 2025). The East African Community (EAC) sets a 50% debt-to-GDP ceiling.[15] While these thresholds help promote discipline, they are often breached during crises, underscoring the difficulty of enforcing regional rules in the face of national fiscal pressure. Table 1.2 reports debt sustainability indicators for selected African countries.

[13] https://www.brookings.edu/articles/fiscal-policy-options-for-growing-out-of-debt-evidence-from-nigeria/

[14] https://mofep.gov.gh/sites/default/files/reports/economic/2023-Annual-Public-Debt-Report.pdf

[15] https://ipfglobal.or.ke/wp-content/uploads/2023/10/Policy-Brief-2-EAC-Convergence.pdf

**Table 1.2** Selected African countries—debt sustainability metrics (2023–2024)

| *Country* | *External debt distress risk* | *Overall debt distress risk* | *Public debt as % of GDP (approximated)* | *Notes* |
|---|---|---|---|---|
| Ghana | High | High | 84% | Under IMF program; restructuring underway |
| Kenya | High | High | 70.2% | Rising domestic debt; fiscal consolidation needed |
| Ethiopia | In distress | In distress | 57% | Debt restructuring ongoing; foreign exchange (FX) constraints |
| Zambia | In distress | In distress | 120% | External debt restructuring in progress |
| Nigeria | Moderate | Moderate | 37% | Low revenue-to-GDP ratio; rising domestic debt |
| Angola | Moderate | Moderate | 84.9% | Oil-dependent; debt stabilizing post-COVID |
| Egypt | Moderate | Moderate | 92% | High debt service burden; FX pressures |
| Rwanda | Moderate | Moderate | 67% | Strong fiscal management; moderate risk |
| Senegal | Moderate | Moderate | 75% | Eurobond exposure; fiscal reforms ongoing |
| Mozambique | High | High | 100% | Fragile macro context; high debt burden |

Source: Author's compilation based on IMF (2025), UNCTAD (2025), and Nairametrics (2023)

### 1.2.3 *Linking Debt and Stability in Africa*

The relationship between public debt and fiscal stability in Africa is multifaceted and depends on more than just debt ratios. Fiscal stability is shaped by the structure of liabilities, the cost of servicing them, institutional credibility, and the quality of economic governance (Mupunga & Ngundu, 2020). Countries can sustain relatively high debt levels if borrowing is long-term, concessional, and directed toward productive investment.

Conversely, even moderate debt levels may destabilize economies when revenues are weak, borrowing is costly, or hidden liabilities emerge (Were, 2024b).

Ghana and Zambia illustrate the fragility that arises when debt service obligations overwhelm fiscal resources. In Ghana, debt servicing absorbed more than half of the government revenue by 2022, prompting the government to launch a domestic debt exchange program to restructure local bonds. While this reduced near-term pressure, it severely disrupted banks and pension funds and triggered macroeconomic instability (see Box 1.1). Zambia, on the other hand, became the first African country to default during the COVID-19 pandemic when it could not service its $17 billion debt. The complexity of its creditor mix, including the large share owed to China and private bondholders, delayed restructuring under the G20's Common Framework, prolonging economic uncertainty and investment stagnation (see Box 1.2).

**Box 1.1 Ghana's Domestic Debt Exchange (2022–2023)**

By 2022, Ghana's debt service consumed over half of government revenues and public debt reached nearly 88% of GDP. Mounting pressures from high interest costs, currency depreciation, and inflation forced the government to launch a Domestic Debt Exchange Program (DDEP) in December 2022. This involved restructuring about $14 billion in local bonds by reducing coupon rates, extending maturities, and deferring payments. The program eased short-term liquidity stress but severely disrupted domestic financial institutions. Banks, insurance firms, and pension funds, which held large volumes of government securities, faced significant losses, raising risks to financial sector stability. Inflation surged above 50% and the cedi depreciated by over 40% in 2023, eroding household welfare. Ghana secured a $3 billion IMF program in May 2023 to stabilize the economy, tied to fiscal consolidation and reforms. The episode illustrates how high debt service costs, rather than debt levels alone, can destabilize an economy and force painful domestic restructuring.

Source: Ministry of Finance (2023); Africa Centre for Energy Policy (2024)

**Box 1.2 Zambia's Default and Common Framework Negotiations**
Zambia defaulted in November 2020 on its Eurobond obligations, becoming the first African sovereign to do so during the COVID-19 pandemic. With $17 billion in total debt, including 42% owed to private creditors and significant loans from China, restructuring was complex. The government applied for relief under the G20 Common Framework, but protracted negotiations exposed the framework's weaknesses in coordinating diverse creditors. By 2021–2022, uncertainty and fiscal tightening weighed heavily on growth, while currency depreciation and inflation worsened social hardship. In June 2023, Zambia reached a deal with bilateral lenders, including China, to restructure $6.3 billion, followed by agreements with Eurobond holders to extend maturities and reduce near-term payments. While the agreements restored some fiscal breathing space, delays prolonged instability, weakened investor confidence, and deepened social costs. Zambia's case shows that creditor composition and lack of transparency can exacerbate crises, making restructuring processes as critical to fiscal stability as debt levels themselves.

Source: Asala (2024) and FindevLab (2024)

The other cases highlight different trajectories. Côte d'Ivoire has managed relatively high debt levels by adhering to the WAEMU fiscal rules and channeling borrowing into infrastructure with strong growth potential, helping maintain investor confidence.[16] Kenya, however, shows that even debt levels near regional averages can generate instability when debt service consumes two-thirds of revenues, forcing painful trade-offs in health, education, and social spending.[17] These examples underscore that debt stability in Africa is more than meeting numerical thresholds—it is about the interaction among debt structures, fiscal capacity, and institutional strength.

[16] https://www.ecofinagency.com/finance/2404-46678-cote-d-ivoire-raises-cfa454-2bn-in-record-regional-bond-auction

[17] https://cytonn.com/topicals/review-of-kenyas-1

## 1.3 Historical Evolution of Debt in African Economies

The trajectory of Africa's public debt reflects the continent's interaction with global financial cycles, domestic policy choices, and development financing needs. From the borrowing surge of the 1970s to the debt crises of the 1980s, the sweeping relief initiatives of the 2000s, and the renewed reliance on international markets in the 2010s, Africa's debt story is cyclical and deeply tied to its development path. Understanding this history is essential to appreciating today's fiscal vulnerabilities.

### *1.3.1 The 1970s–1980s Debt Crisis*

The origins of Africa's modern debt challenges can be traced to the borrowing boom of the 1970s and subsequent crisis of the 1980s. In the aftermath of independence, most African governments adopted ambitious development plans aimed at industrialization, infrastructure expansion, and modernization of agriculture.[18] These plans were financed through external borrowing, which was made attractive by abundant global liquidity following the oil shocks of 1973 and 1979. The recycling of "petrodollars" by international banks created a surge in lending to developing countries, including those in Africa, often on favorable terms and with limited scrutiny (Greene & Khan, 1990).

During this period, Africa's external debt sharply increased. Between 1970 and 1982, sub-Saharan Africa's total external debt grew from approximately \$11 billion to more than \$140 billion (Ezenwe, 1993). Loans were often contracted at variable interest rates, making them highly sensitive to changes in global financial conditions. Many governments also borrowed heavily against expected commodity revenues, assuming that rising oil, copper, cocoa, and coffee prices would sustain repayment capacity.

The optimism proved short-lived. By the early 1980s, a combination of global and domestic shocks triggered a full-blown debt crisis. The second oil shock of 1979 raised import costs dramatically, while the global

[18] Read more in Background to the African Debt Crisis, available at: http://www.fondad.org/uploaded/African%20Debt%20Revisited/African%20Debt%20Revisited-Chapter%20I.pdf

recession in the early 1980s reduced demand for African exports.[19] Commodity prices collapsed; copper, a key export for Zambia, lost more than half of its value, while cocoa and coffee prices also slumped. At the same time, the US Federal Reserve, under Chairman Paul Volcker, raised interest rates sharply to combat inflation, leading to a surge in global borrowing costs. For African countries, this meant rising debt service obligations at a time when export revenues were collapsing.

By 1986, Africa's average debt-to-GDP ratio exceeded 100%, and debt service consumed nearly 30% of export earnings in sub-Saharan Africa.[20] Several countries, including Zambia, Côte d'Ivoire, and Nigeria, experienced payment arrears and defaults and were forced into repeated rescheduling agreements with creditors. The crisis eroded fiscal stability, leading to what came to be known as the "lost decade" for development in Africa.

The international response took the form of Structural Adjustment Programs (SAPs) designed by the IMF and the World Bank. In exchange for debt rescheduling and limited relief, African countries had to implement austerity measures, such as reducing public spending, liberalizing trade, devaluing currencies, and privatizing state-owned enterprises. While the SAPs restored some fiscal discipline, they often undermined social development.[21] Spending on education, health, and social services fell sharply, exacerbating poverty and inequality. The focus on stabilization and liberalization often came at the expense of long-term structural transformation, leaving many African economies highly dependent on commodity exports and vulnerable to external shocks.

The legacy of the 1970s–1980s debt crisis was profound. This created a persistent debt overhang that discouraged private investment and forced many governments into cycles of borrowing, arrears, and rescheduling. It also highlighted the vulnerability of African economies to external conditions, especially their dependence on commodity prices and global financial cycles. Most importantly, it set the stage for the eventual recognition in the 1990s that traditional rescheduling and adjustment were insufficient, leading to the creation of the Heavily Indebted Poor Countries (HIPC) Initiative in 1996.

[19] http://www.fondad.org/uploaded/African%20Debt%20Revisited/African%20Debt%20Revisited-Chapter%20I.pdf

[20] https://yawboadu.substack.com/p/the-1980s-and-1990s-african-debt

[21] https://www.policycenter.ma/publications/addressing-africas-persistent-debt-problem

### 1.3.2 *Debt Relief and the HIPC/MDRI Era (1996–2006)*

By the mid-1990s, Africa's debt crisis had reached unsustainable levels. Many countries faced what economists described as a "debt overhang," where high debt burdens discouraged investment and trapped economies in cycles of arrears, rescheduling, and stagnation (Ezenwe, 1993). Traditional mechanisms, such as Paris Club reschedulings, offered temporary breathing space but failed to address the scale of the problem. Recognizing this, the World Bank and the International Monetary Fund (IMF) launched the Heavily Indebted Poor Countries (HIPC) Initiative in 1996.

HIPC targeted the world's poorest and most debt-distressed countries, the majority of them in Africa.[22] Its aim was to reduce external debt to sustainable levels, provided governments implemented macroeconomic reforms and adopted poverty reduction strategies. However, the initial framework was criticized as too narrow and slow. In response, the Enhanced HIPC Initiative was introduced in 1999, which increased the depth of relief and tied debt cancellation more explicitly to poverty reduction spending, especially in education, health, and infrastructure.

Building on this momentum, the Multilateral Debt Relief Initiative (MDRI) was launched in 2005.[23] MDRI went further by canceling 100% of eligible debts owed to the IMF, the World Bank's International Development Association (IDA), and the African Development Fund (ADF). This represented a historic breakthrough: for the first time, multilateral institutions granted full cancellation rather than rescheduling. By 2006, dozens of African countries, including Uganda, Mozambique, and Tanzania, had seen their external debts reduced by more than half.

The impact of these initiatives was significant. Sub-Saharan Africa's average debt-to-GDP ratio fell from over 100% in the early 1990s to about 35% by 2008. Debt service obligations, which had absorbed more than 20% of export earnings in the mid-1990s, dropped to below 10% after MDRI. This created much-needed fiscal space, allowing governments to redirect resources toward social and development programs. For instance, Uganda increased primary health care and education spending, Ghana

[22] Read more here: https://www.imf.org/en/About/Factsheets/Sheets/2023/Debt-relief-under-the-heavily-indebted-poor-countries-initiative-HIPC

[23] For more information on Multilateral Debt Relief Initiative, visit: https://www.imf.org/external/np/exr/mdri/eng/index.htm

expanded access to basic schooling, and Mozambique invested heavily in rural infrastructure.

Despite these gains, HIPC and MDRI were not without criticism. Conditionalities tied to debt relief, such as structural reforms and fiscal austerity, were seen as limiting policy autonomy. Furthermore, some countries emerged from relief still vulnerable due to weak domestic revenue mobilization, corruption, and dependence on commodity exports. As a result, while debt levels fell, underlying structural weaknesses in African public finance remained unaddressed.

Nevertheless, the initiatives marked a turning point in international policy. They acknowledged that excessive debt burdens could undermine development, legitimizing debt cancellation as part of the development agenda. They also underscored the principle that relief should be linked to poverty reduction. Yet, the subsequent build-up of debt in the 2010s revealed the temporary nature of these gains. Without stronger fiscal frameworks, diversified economies, and prudent borrowing strategies, many African countries once again slid into debt distress.

Overall, the HIPC and MDRI initiatives transformed Africa's debt landscape in the 2000s, providing substantial fiscal relief and enabling new investment in development priorities. Their legacy is mixed; while they delivered immediate benefits and set new norms for global debt policy, they fell short of securing long-term debt sustainability for many African economies.

### *1.3.3 Renewed Borrowing and the Eurobond Era (2010s)*

The 2010s marked a turning point in Africa's debt landscape. Following the significant reductions achieved through the HIPC and MDRI initiatives in the late 1990s and the early 2000s, many African economies entered the new decade with comparatively low debt burdens and renewed fiscal optimism. Average debt-to-GDP ratios fell by around 35% by 2008, and rapid growth buoyed by high commodity prices, expanding urban markets, and relative macroeconomic stability enhanced investor confidence.[24] This environment paved the way for African states to re-enter international capital markets on a scale not seen since the borrowing boom of the 1970s.

[24] https://www.imf.org/-/media/Websites/IMF/imported-flagship-issues/external/pubs/ft/reo/2008/AFR/eng/_sreo0408pdf.ashx

The combination of lower debt levels and strong global demand for yield encouraged international investors to view African sovereign bonds as attractive frontier assets. For African governments, tapping these markets offered a chance to mobilize substantial resources quickly, diversify away from concessional aid, and demonstrate integration into the global financial system. Countries such as Ghana, Nigeria, and Kenya became regular issuers, often framing access to Eurobonds as a symbol of financial maturity.[25]

Between 2010 and 2019, at least nineteen African countries issued Eurobonds, raising more than $130 billion (Icyeza, 2021). Ghana, one of the earliest entrants, raised $750 million in 2007 and continued to issue bonds in subsequent years.[26] Kenya debuted in 2014 with a $2 billion bond and then returned to the market several times. Côte d'Ivoire, Senegal, and Ethiopia also became notable issuers. Coupon rates ranged from 6% to 9%, substantially higher than those on concessional loans; however, governments valued the flexibility and speed of issuance.[27]

Eurobond proceeds were often used to finance large infrastructure projects in transport, energy, and communications, as well as to refinance existing debts. Kenya directed part of its 2014 Eurobond to road, rail, and energy investments,[28] while Côte d'Ivoire utilized funds for post-conflict reconstruction and infrastructure modernization. However, in some cases, the proceeds were diverted toward recurrent expenditures or plugging fiscal deficits, raising concerns about long-term returns.

Parallel to Eurobond issuance, China emerged as the single largest bilateral lender to Africa. Through the Belt and Road Initiative, Chinese state-owned banks extended loans for railways, ports, power plants, and telecommunications, particularly in countries such as Angola, Kenya, and Ethiopia. Between 2000 and 2019, Chinese loans to Africa amounted to more than $150 billion, with cumulative commitments reaching $182 billion by 2023.[29] Unlike traditional concessional financing, many of these loans were tied to resource-backed agreements or project-specific con-

[25] https://cytonn.com/topicals/sub-saharan-africa-ssa-6

[26] https://afrodad.org/sites/default/files/presentation/Africa-in-International-Bond-Market.pdf

[27] https://developmentreimagined.com/wp-content/uploads/2024/06/Final-Africa-Eurobond-Report-May-2024.pdf

[28] https://www.imf.org/external/pubs/ft/scr/2014/cr14302.pdf

[29] https://www.bu.edu/gdp/2024/08/21/relative-risk-and-the-rate-of-return-chinese-loans-to-africa-database-2000-2023/

tracts. Other non-Paris Club creditors, including India, Turkey, and Gulf states, also expanded their roles, financing infrastructure and energy projects. This diversification gave African governments more bargaining power but introduced greater complexity in debt management and restructuring. Unlike the Paris Club arrangements, which offered coordinated frameworks, non-traditional creditors often negotiated bilaterally, and contract terms were less transparent.

The 2010s borrowing boom transformed Africa's debt profile, shifting from concessional, long-term loans to commercial, market-based instruments. This created new vulnerabilities. Interest payments as a share of government revenues doubled in many countries between 2010 and 2019, while shorter maturities of Eurobonds heightened rollover risks. When global conditions tightened and commodity prices fell after 2014, several countries, including Zambia and Ghana, experienced fiscal stress. Thus, although renewed access to markets and diversified financing expanded Africa's fiscal space in the short run, it laid the foundation for renewed debt distress in the 2020s. The Eurobond era demonstrated both the opportunities and the perils of financial globalization for African economies.[30]

### *1.3.4 Debt Resurgence and Crisis Episodes (2020s)*

The 2020s witnessed a sharp reversal in Africa's debt fortunes. After nearly two decades of relative stability following HIPC and MDRI debt relief, African countries entered a new decade with higher but still manageable debt levels. However, the outbreak of the COVID-19 pandemic in 2020 precipitated an unprecedented fiscal shock, pushing many economies into renewed debt distress (Chandler, 2020).

The pandemic disrupted economic activity across the continent (Anyanwu & Salami, 2021). Lockdowns and border closures suppressed production and trade, while collapsing global demand sharply reduced export revenues. Commodity exporters such as Nigeria, Angola, and Zambia faced a dramatic fall in oil and mineral prices, while tourism-dependent economies such as Mauritius, Seychelles, and Kenya saw revenues evaporate.[31] At the same time, governments were forced to increase

[30] https://www.un.org/osaa/sites/www.un.org.osaa/files/docs/2118580-osaa-eurobonds_policy_paper_web.pdf

[31] https://www.commoditymonitor.org/2023/01/30/16463/

spending on public health, social protection, and economic stimulus. This twin effect of lower revenues and higher expenditures widened fiscal deficits and necessitated large-scale borrowing.

The consequences were visible in the debt ratios. Sub-Saharan Africa's average public debt-to-GDP ratio rose from about 30% in 2010 to nearly 60% by 2022.[32] Several countries exceeded traditional sustainability thresholds: Ghana's debt-to-GDP rose above 85% in 2022, Kenya's surpassed 67% by 2024, while Mozambique's and Zambia's debts exceeded 100%.[33] Importantly, the burden of debt service grew even faster. By 2022, interest payments absorbed more than 40% of revenues in many countries, and in Nigeria, the ratio exceeded 80%, leaving almost no room for discretionary spending.[34]

Global financial conditions amplified these vulnerabilities. As advanced economies tightened monetary policy in response to inflationary pressures from the Russia–Ukraine war, international borrowing costs rose sharply (Organisation for Economic Co-operation and Development (OECD), 2022). African Eurobond issuers faced soaring yields that effectively shut them out of markets. For instance, Ghana lost access to Eurobond financing in 2021,[35] while Kenya postponed a planned issuance in 2022 due to unfavorable rates.[36] Currency depreciations compounded the problem: the Ghanaian cedi and Nigerian naira both lost more than 30% of their value in 2022–2023, magnifying the cost of servicing foreign-currency-denominated debt.[37]

The result was a wave of debt distress episodes. Zambia became the first African country to default during the pandemic, halting payments on $17 billion in external debt in 2020 (Business Insider Africa, 2025). Ghana followed in 2022 with domestic debt exchange and suspension of external debt servicing. Ethiopia requested restructuring under the G20's Common Framework, while Mozambique continued to struggle with legacy hidden

[32] file:///C:/Users/USER/Downloads/REOAFREA2023-S002_IMG_PDF.pdf

[33] https://academic.oup.com/book/60608/chapter/524385502?login=false

[34] https://malala.org/news-and-voices/nigerian-girls-are-bearing-the-impacts-of-national-debt

[35] https://dmarketforces.com/ghana-market-conditions-stop-eurobond-plan-local-bond-yields-peak/#google_vignette

[36] https://www.elibrary.imf.org/downloadpdf/journals/002/2024/316/article-A001-en.pdf

[37] See for the case of Ghana: https://www.trade.gov/market-intelligence/ghana-currency-depreciation

loans. In North Africa, Tunisia and Egypt faced rising borrowing costs that strained fiscal positions.[38] According to the IMF and World Bank (2023), by mid-2023, thirteen African countries were at high risk of debt distress, and seven were already in distress.[39]

These developments underscore the fragility of Africa's fiscal stability in the 2020s. Debt ratios alone do not capture the full picture; it is the combination of elevated servicing costs, limited market access, and external shocks that has driven instability. The pandemic revealed how quickly fiscal space can evaporate when economies rely heavily on external borrowing, have weak domestic revenue bases, and face global volatility. Unless addressed through stronger fiscal reforms, enhanced debt transparency, and more effective international coordination, the continent risks repeating the debt crises of previous decades under more complex and costly circumstances.

## 1.4 Theoretical Perspectives on Debt and Growth

The academic debate on the debt–growth relationship has evolved over decades, producing a range of theories that highlight both the opportunities and risks of public borrowing. Classical and Keynesian economists stress the growth-enhancing role of debt when used productively, while modern theories, such as debt overhang and crowding out, emphasize the dangers of excessive indebtedness. Other perspectives, such as Ricardian equivalence, challenge whether debt has any effect. The synthesis of these approaches suggests that the relationship is fundamentally non-linear: beneficial at moderate levels, but harmful once thresholds are breached. Table 1.3 synthesizes the major theoretical positions.

## 1.5 Economic Rationale for Public Borrowing

Public borrowing is not inherently a sign of fiscal irresponsibility. On the contrary, economic theory and practice recognize multiple legitimate reasons for governments, especially in developing regions such as Africa, to rely on debt financing. Borrowing can help accelerate growth, stabilize economies during downturns, spread costs fairly across generations, and

[38] https://unctad.org/publication/world-of-debt/regional-stories

[39] Read more here: https://www.imfconnect.org/content/imf/en/annual-meetings/calendar/open/2024/04/16/183749.html

**Table 1.3** Theoretical perspectives on debt and growth

| *Theory/perspective* | *Core argument* | *Main proponents* | *Explanation and mechanisms* | *Implications for Africa* |
|---|---|---|---|---|
| Neoclassical growth view | Debt can support growth at moderate levels by easing capital shortages and financing public goods | Robert Solow (1956) | In the neoclassical tradition, growth depends on capital accumulation, labor, and technology. Developing countries often face capital scarcity, limiting investment. Public borrowing helps bridge this gap by funding infrastructure, health, and education to expand productivity. If funds are invested in high-return sectors, an increase in GDP can outpace the borrowing costs | Particularly relevant for Africa, where domestic savings are low and infrastructure gaps are wide. The success of this view depends heavily on the institutional capacity to allocate debt productively |
| Keynesian perspective | Deficit-financed spending can stimulate growth during recessions or demand shortfalls | Richard Musgrave (1959) | Keynesian theory emphasizes the role of aggregate demand. Borrowing allows governments to increase spending during downturns, offsetting private sector retrenchment, and stimulating output and employment. The countercyclical role of debt can prevent deeper recessions and support recovery | For African economies, where cyclical shocks are frequent, debt-financed stimuli can stabilize growth. However, a weak fiscal space limits the scope for sustained Keynesian borrowing without risking solvency |

(*continued*)

**Table 1.3** (continued)

| *Theory/ perspective* | *Core argument* | *Main proponents* | *Explanation and mechanisms* | *Implications for Africa* |
|---|---|---|---|---|
| Debt overhang hypothesis | Excessive debt discourages private investment and slows growth | Paul Krugman (1988) | Once debt becomes unsustainably high, investors expect higher future taxes or default risk. This expectation discourages private investment because the returns may be appropriated for debt service. The result is reduced capital formation, lower productivity, and slower long-run growth | Highly applicable to Africa, where repeated debt crises have discouraged both domestic and foreign investment. Excessive borrowing can perpetuate a cycle of low growth and rising debt |
| Crowding-out effect | Government borrowing competes with private sector credit, raising interest rates and reducing private investment | Robert Barro (1974); Elmendorf & Mankiw (1999) | Public debt competes for scarce financial resources, particularly in shallow banking systems. Large government borrowing raises interest rates and reduces funds available to the private sector. This weakens entrepreneurship, limits SME access to finance, and reduces overall growth potential | A major challenge in African economies is that the domestic capital markets are small. Heavy domestic debt issuance can crowd out private borrowers, constraining private-sector-led growth |

(*continued*)

**Table 1.3** (continued)

| *Theory/ perspective* | *Core argument* | *Main proponents* | *Explanation and mechanisms* | *Implications for Africa* |
|---|---|---|---|---|
| Ricardian equivalence | Debt and taxation are neutral for growth since households anticipate future taxes and adjust savings | David Ricardo (1820); Robert Barro (1974) | If households are perfectly rational and forward-looking, they save more in response to government borrowing, and expect higher taxes in the future. This offsets the stimulative effect of debt, making fiscal deficits irrelevant for growth | Rarely holds in Africa due to low household savings, limited financial literacy, weak financial inclusion, and large informal sectors. In practice, debt has real short- and long-run effects on African economies |
| Debt Laffer curve | The debt–growth relationship is non-linear: Beneficial at low levels, harmful at high levels | Paul Krugman (1988); Jeffrey Sachs (1989) | The debt Laffer curve illustrates that there is an optimal debt level. Below the threshold, borrowing can stimulate growth and is repayable; above this threshold, rising debt reduces repayment capacity and investor confidence. Identifying the precise tipping point is difficult and context-specific | For African economies, thresholds are likely lower than those in advanced economies (estimated at around 50–60% of GDP, and even lower in fragile states). Breaching these levels can quickly erode fiscal stability and growth prospects |

Source: Author's compilation

contribute to building stronger domestic financial systems. What matters is not whether governments borrow, but how and for what purpose. When debt is aligned with productive investment and sustainability, it can be a powerful tool for development. This section outlines the key rationales for public borrowing in the African context.

### 1.5.1 Financing Developmental Investment Needs

One of the strongest justifications for borrowing is the need to address a continent's massive infrastructure and human capital deficits. Africa requires between \$130 and \$170 billion annually in infrastructure investment, with a financing gap estimated at \$68–108 billion (African Union Development Agency, 2025). Reliance on current tax revenues alone would make it impossible to close these gaps. Borrowing allows governments to make front-load investments in transport, energy, education, and health infrastructure, thereby accelerating development. In neoclassical growth theory, capital-scarce economies are encouraged to borrow externally to augment domestic savings and expand their capital stock, provided that the funds are allocated to high-return projects.[40] If this condition is met, the resulting increase in productivity and fiscal revenues can outweigh borrowing costs, making debt a catalyst for long-term growth.

### 1.5.2 Intergenerational Equity and the "Golden Rule"

Another rationale is grounded in the principles of fairness and efficiency. Large-scale infrastructure projects yield benefits over decades, and it is equitable that future generations, who will also use these assets, will share their costs (Sesele, 2025). By financing such long-lived assets with debt, governments can avoid overburdening taxpayers. This reflects the "golden rule" of public finance, which suggests that borrowing should be limited to investment rather than current consumption.[41] In practice, this principle means that issuing long-term bonds to build a highway, port, or power plant spreads costs across generations, aligning financing with the duration of benefits. While not all borrowing in Africa conforms to this rule, it provides a guiding framework for sustainable fiscal policy.

### 1.5.3 Fiscal Smoothing and Macroeconomic Stabilization

African economies are highly exposed to shocks, particularly because of their narrow tax bases and dependence on volatile commodity exports. In downturns, revenues collapse as expenditure needs increase. Public borrowing serves as a countercyclical tool that allows governments to

[40] https://scispace.com/pdf/the-neoclassical-growth-model-and-twentieth-century-r5v3aihbzi.pdf

[41] https://www.jstor.org/stable/1054956

maintain spending without resorting to sudden tax hikes or severe expenditure cuts (Jalles et al., 2024). During the COVID-19 pandemic, for example, many African governments borrowed to finance medical supplies, vaccine imports, and social protection programs, despite falling revenues (Osakede & Adeleke, 2022). This rationale aligns with Keynesian theory, which emphasizes deficit spending during recessions to sustain aggregate demand and mitigate economic contraction. When managed prudently, borrowing during bad times and consolidating during good times help stabilize debt over the business cycle.

### 1.5.4 Leveraging Concessional Financing

Access to concessional loans from multilateral institutions and bilateral partners provides another strong rationale for borrowing. These loans are typically offered at interest rates well below market levels, often with grace and long maturity periods. The embedded grant element makes concessional debt cheaper than raising domestic taxes or issuing commercial bonds (Abor, 2023). Using such financing for high-priority projects can deliver significant growth payoffs at minimal fiscal costs. Following the debt relief of the 2000s, many African countries regained creditworthiness and responsibly re-entered concessional and semi-concessional borrowing to close infrastructure gaps.[42]

### 1.5.5 Supporting Domestic Financial Market Development

Government borrowing plays a catalytic role in building domestic capital markets. The issuance of government securities, particularly in local currencies, creates a benchmark yield curve, provides safe assets for banks and pension funds, and facilitates the development of secondary markets (Lartey & Li, 2018; Danquah & Osei Adu, 2025). In many African economies, government bonds form the backbone of the financial market infrastructure, enabling private firms to subsequently access capital markets (Kodongo et al., 2023). While this rationale is more indirect, it underscores the fact that borrowing can provide long-run institutional benefits beyond immediate fiscal needs.

[42] https://institute.global/insights/economic-prosperity/a-new-debt-deal-for-africa-breaking-the-vicious-cycle

## 1.6 Challenges and Risks of Rising Debt Levels

While borrowing can be a legitimate and even necessary tool for financing development, Africa's recent debt surge has brought significant risks that threaten fiscal stability, macroeconomic management, and long-term growth. Unlike advanced economies with deep financial markets and reserve currencies, African countries face tighter constraints: investor confidence can waver quickly, external shocks are more disruptive, and debt service burdens can overwhelm limited fiscal revenues. As public debt ratios rose sharply in the 2020s, so did the incidences of debt distress, defaults, and restructuring episodes across the continent. These trends highlight that the challenge is no longer simply whether governments can borrow, but whether they can sustain their obligations without undermining growth and social investment. This section examines the principal risks associated with rising debt levels in Africa.

### *1.6.1 Debt Sustainability and Default Risk*

One of the foremost concerns is whether African countries can sustain their debt burdens. By late 2023, the IMF and World Bank classified nearly twenty African nations as either at high risk of debt distress or already in distress.[43] Defaults and restructurings, such as Zambia in 2020 and Ghana in 2022, underscore the severity of the problem. Unlike advanced economies, which can sustain debt ratios above 100% of GDP, many African borrowers face distress at far lower levels because of their weaker revenue bases, limited investor confidence, and shallow domestic markets. The immediate consequence of deteriorating debt metrics is loss of access to international capital markets. Between 2022 and 2023, countries such as Ghana, Egypt, and Tunisia were effectively locked out of bond markets as yields surged to unsustainably high levels, forcing governments to rely on emergency IMF support or painful fiscal adjustments.[44]

[43] Read more here: https://acetforafrica.org/?smd_process_download=1&download_id=64880

[44] https://african.business/2022/06/finance-services/african-countries-face-rollover-risk-as-bonds-mature

### 1.6.2 *Rising Debt Servicing Burden*

Even in countries that have not defaulted, the fiscal costs of servicing debt have escalated sharply. Between 2010 and 2023, the average share of interest payments in Africa's government revenues more than doubled, rising from 6.5% to over 16%. In extreme cases, Nigeria devoted over 90% of its federal revenues to debt service in 2022 (Egboboh, 2023), while Ghana spent over one-third of its revenues on interest in the years leading up to default.[45] Alarmingly, nearly half of African countries now allocate more resources to interest than to health care, and in some cases, even more than to education.[46] This crowding-out effect reduces the fiscal space for investment in human capital and infrastructure, perpetuating a cycle in which high debt leads to low growth, which in turn makes debt even harder to sustain.

### 1.6.3 *Exposure to External Shocks and Currency Risks*

A growing share of Africa's debt is denominated in foreign currencies, mainly U.S. dollars and euros. This creates vulnerability to exchange rate depreciation and external shocks. Between 2010 and 2022, Africa's external debt rose from 19% to nearly 29% of GDP, while the external debt-to-exports ratio surged from 75% to 140%.[47] This indicates that many countries must devote a significant share of export revenues to service external debt, leaving them exposed to commodity price fluctuations and global demand downturns. Depreciating currencies amplify the local-currency cost of repayment, while rising global interest rates since 2022 have increased the refinancing costs. With a wave of Eurobond maturities due between 2024 and 2028, many African governments risk default if they cannot refinance at sustainable rates.[48]

[45] https://www.elibrary.imf.org/view/journals/002/2024/334/article-A002-en.xml

[46] Read more here: https://www.telegraph.co.uk/global-health/climate-and-people/africa-spending-more-on-interest-than-health-as-debt-crisis/

[47] https://unctad.org/publication/world-of-debt/regional-stories#:~:text=As%20a%20percentage%20of%20GDP%2C,servicing%20costs

[48] https://www.policycenter.ma/publications/addressing-africas-persistent-debt-problem

### 1.6.4 Complex Creditor Landscape and Restructuring Challenges

The structure of African debt has shifted away from reliance on a few official creditors toward a diverse mix of private bondholders, commercial banks, China, other non-Paris Club states, and multilaterals. By 2021, private creditors held about 44% of Africa's external debt.[49] This creditor diversity complicates restructuring efforts, as negotiations must balance the interests of multiple actors. The G20's Common Framework was designed to coordinate relief, but its implementation has been slow and fragmented. Zambia's restructuring process illustrates these challenges: protracted negotiations between Paris Club members, China, and private bondholders delayed resolution and prolonged economic uncertainty. The absence of a comprehensive sovereign bankruptcy mechanism means that heavily indebted countries often face prolonged fiscal stress and uncertainty before an agreement is reached.

### 1.6.5 Social and Political Risks

Beyond fiscal metrics, rising debt generates social and political costs. As debt servicing crowds out social expenditure, governments are often forced into austerity measures, including subsidy cuts, delayed wages, or tax increases. These measures can erode living standards, fuel inequality, and trigger social unrest. Politically, high debt reduces fiscal autonomy, leaving governments with limited flexibility to pursue developmental priorities or to respond to crises. In effect, debt overhang can trap countries in a cycle of low growth, social discontent, and political instability.

## 1.7 Policy Implications for Fiscal Management

Africa's rising debt levels demand an urgent and carefully calibrated policy response. The challenge for policymakers is not only to restore fiscal sustainability but also to ensure that debt continues to function as an instrument for development rather than a constraint on growth. Sound policies must therefore strike a balance between fiscal prudence and developmental needs, addressing short-term vulnerabilities while laying the foundation for long-term stability. Presented below are some of the key domestic

[49] https://unctad.org/publication/world-of-debt/regional-stories

and international measures that can help African countries manage the risks of rising debt more effectively and place their economies on a sustainable trajectory.

### 1.7.1 *Strengthening Fiscal Governance*

Credible fiscal frameworks are essential for building investor confidence and preventing excessive debt accumulation. This involves adopting and enforcing fiscal rules such as deficit and debt ceilings, which many African regions already include in their convergence criteria (e.g., a 3% GDP deficit limit and a 60% GDP debt ceiling). For these rules to work, however, they must be supported by robust legal and institutional arrangements, independent fiscal councils, and transparent reporting practices. Fiscal discipline should also extend beyond the central government to include state-owned enterprises and contingent liabilities, which often escape scrutiny but can destabilize public finances if left unchecked. Macroeconomic stability, reflected in low inflation and stable exchange rates, complements fiscal prudence by helping debt ratios decline through growth rather than austerity.

### 1.7.2 *Enhancing Domestic Resource Mobilization and Expenditure Efficiency*

Sustainable fiscal management requires reducing reliance on debt by raising more domestic revenues and spending more efficiently. Many African countries mobilize a relatively low share of tax revenues compared to their emerging market peers, leaving them with limited fiscal space to fund development priorities.[50] Expanding the tax base, closing loopholes, improving tax administration, and gradually integrating the informal economy can increase fiscal capacity without stifling growth. On the expenditure side, rigorous project appraisal and cost–benefit analysis should guide borrowing decisions, ensuring that debt-financed investments yield high returns. Governments must also curb wasteful spending, such as untargeted subsidies or redundant bureaucracy, and strengthen anti-corruption measures. Stronger public financial management, transparent procurement, and independent audits can raise the productivity of

[50] https://www.undp.org/sites/g/files/zskgke326/files/2025-05/implication_of_imf_ssa_outlook_april_2025_insights_2-1.pdf

every borrowed dollar, improve the debt-to-growth ratio, and ease long-term sustainability concerns.

### 1.7.3 Professionalizing Debt Management

Proactive and professional debt management can mitigate the many risks associated with borrowing. Governments must maintain a balanced portfolio between domestic and external debt and prioritize local currency instruments to reduce exchange rate exposure. Lengthening maturities helps avoid rollover risks, while issuing bonds in domestic markets deepens financial systems and mobilizes local savings. Transparency is critical: publishing timely, comprehensive debt data can strengthen investor confidence and provide early warnings of risk. Countries should avoid excessive reliance on non-concessional or high-interest loans, reserving them only for projects with clear and measurable economic returns. Where feasible, hedging strategies or sinking funds can smooth repayment pressures. Institutionalizing debt management through dedicated offices and clear strategies enhances negotiating capacity, reduces hidden liabilities, and ensures that borrowing decisions are guided by long-term sustainability considerations.

### 1.7.4 International Support and Debt Architecture Reform

Restoring sustainability also requires international cooperation. Many African countries will continue to rely on concessional financing and grants to meet their development needs without falling into unsustainable debt cycles. Multilateral development banks and bilateral partners can help by expanding concessional lending windows and ensuring that commercial lending to vulnerable countries does not exacerbate risks. Mechanisms for debt relief and restructuring also require reform. The G20's Debt Service Suspension Initiative (DSSI) provided temporary relief during the COVID-19 pandemic, but more enduring solutions are required. The G20 Common Framework has been slow and fragmented, suggesting the need for clearer rules, timelines, and principles for burden-sharing among creditors, including private bondholders and non-Paris Club lenders such as China. In extreme cases of unsustainable debt, partial cancellation similar to the HIPC and MDRI initiatives of the 2000s may be necessary, but this time is linked to governance reforms that prevent renewed debt spirals.

### *1.7.5 Addressing the Cost of Capital*

One structural challenge is Africa's disproportionately high cost of borrowing relative to fundamentals. African sovereigns often pay double-digit interest rates, even when their debt levels are lower than those of advanced economies. Addressing this requires innovative international initiatives, such as guarantee mechanisms or refinancing facilities that can substitute expensive commercial debt for long-term, lower-cost financing. Proposals for a "New Debt Deal" envision development banks or G20-backed facilities that could buy back or insure African debt, lower interest rates, and extend maturities in exchange for commitments to fiscal reforms and transparency. Such measures could provide a breathing space for countries caught in a high-debt, low-growth trap.

## 1.8 Conclusion

The dynamics of public debt in Africa reveal its potential as a tool for development and its dangers as a source of instability when mismanaged. Over the past decades, the continent has experienced successive cycles of borrowing booms, crises, and relief, each leaving lessons relevant today. From the heavy borrowing of the 1970s and the ensuing debt crises of the 1980s, through the HIPC and MDRI relief initiatives of the late 1990s and the early 2000s, to the resurgence of Eurobond-financed debt in the 2010s, African countries have grappled with the dual challenge of mobilizing resources for development while maintaining fiscal stability. The COVID-19 pandemic and the global financial tightening of the 2020s once again exposed the fragility of African debt positions, with many economies pushed into distress as revenues collapsed and servicing costs soared. Theoretical perspectives demonstrate that debt can support growth at moderate levels when used productively for infrastructure, education, health, and other high-return investments and that excessive borrowing triggers debt overhang, crowds out private investment, and undermines long-term growth prospects. Empirical evidence from countries such as Ghana, Zambia, and Nigeria illustrates that sustainability is determined not only by debt ratios but also by the structure of debt, strength of fiscal institutions, and quality of governance. High levels of debt service have already begun to erode the fiscal space, with many African states spending more on interest than on health and education, thereby constraining human capital development and worsening inequality. The risks are further compounded by currency mismatches, volatile global capital markets, and the increasingly complex creditor landscape, in which the involvement of private bondholders and non-Paris Club lenders complicates restructuring processes. These realities underscore that debt sustainability in Africa is not merely a technical matter of ratios and thresholds, but a question of institutional credibility, transparency, and prudent policy choices. Addressing this challenge requires decisive domestic reforms and supportive international engagement. Domestically, African governments must adopt enforceable fiscal rules, broaden tax bases, strengthen public financial management, and ensure that borrowed funds are allocated to projects with clear developmental returns. Professional debt management, greater transparency, and a balanced mix of domestic and external borrowing are also essential to reduce exposure to shocks and rebuild market confidence. Internationally, creditors and multilateral partners must expand access to concessional finance, coordinate debt relief more effectively, and address the structural problem of Africa's disproportionately high borrowing costs, which leaves the continent trapped in a high-debt, low-growth equilibrium. Innovative mechanisms, such as guarantee schemes or a "new debt deal" for Africa, could help refinance expensive debt with longer-term, cheaper instruments while tying relief to governance reforms that safeguard sustainability. Ultimately, the conclusion that emerges is that debt in Africa is neither inherently good nor inherently bad; it is a double-edged instrument that can either propel development or deepen fragility, depending on how it is managed. The stakes are particularly high in the current decade, as demographic pressures, climate change, and global uncertainty intensify financing needs. If governments, with the support of the international community, can transform borrowing into a credible, transparent, and growth-oriented strategy, debt can become the foundation for resilience and inclusive progress. If not, the risk is a return to cycles of crisis and austerity that undermine Africa's aspirations for sustainable development.

## References

Abor, J. Y. (2023). Financing infrastructure development in Africa: The role of national development banks. In *The changing role of national development banks in Africa* (pp. 125–143). Springer. https://link.springer.com/chapter/10.1007/978-3-031-38639-8_6

Adigun, O. (2026). IMF projects Sub-Saharan Africa fiscal deficit at 3.2% in 2026. https://nairametrics.com/2026/04/18/imf-projects-sub-saharan-africa-fiscal-deficit-at-3-2-in-2026/

Africa Centre for Energy Policy. (2024). *An assessment of the impact of the Domestic Debt Exchange Program (DDEP) on Ghana's pensions sector.* https://acep.africa/wp-content/uploads/2024/10/An-Assessment-of-the-Impact-of-the-Domestic-Debt-Exchange-Program-DDEP-on-Ghanas-Pensions-Sector-September-2024.pdf

African Development Bank. (2025). *Africa's performance and outlook.* https://www.afdb-org.kr/wp-content/uploads/2025/02/2025_meo_-_complete_enversion_05.02.2025.pdf

African Union Development Agency. (2025). New report calls for unlocking $170 billion annually to meet Africa's infrastructure needs. https://www.nepad.org/news/new-report-calls-unlocking-170-billion-annually-meet-africas-infrastructure-needs

AFRODAD. (2017). *Impacts of fluctuating commodity prices on government revenue in four selected countries in the SADC region.* https://www.afrodad.org/sites/default/files/publications/IMPACTS-OF-FLUCTUATING-COMMODITY-PRICES_SYNTHESIS-REPORT_POLICY-BRIEF.pdf

Anyanwu, J. C., & Salami, A. O. (2021). The impact of COVID-19 on African economies: An introduction. *African Development Review, 33*(Suppl 1), S1.

Arslanalp, S., Bergthaler, W., Stokoe, P., & Tieman, A. F. (2019). *Concepts, definitions and composition. Sovereign debt: A guide for economists and practitioners* (pp. 56–101).

Asala, K. (2024). Zambia declared in default of debt repayment to creditors. https://www.africanews.com/2020/11/18/zambia-declared-in-default-of-debt-repayment-to-creditors/

Bai, Y., Xu, J., & Jin, C. (2024). The crowding-out effect of government debt: A loan financing-based perspective. *Borsa Istanbul Review, 24*(5), 1059–1066.

Bua, G., Pradelli, J., & Presbitero, A. F. (2014). Domestic public debt in low-income countries and structure. *Review of Development Finance, 4*(1), 1–19.

Business Insider Africa. (2025). 4 African countries on the brink of debt default. https://africa.businessinsider.com/local/markets/4-african-countries-on-the-brink-of-debt-default/pfhwh84.

Chandler, B. (2020). COVID-19 & African debt: Further distress or the beginning of a new paradigm. *The Mo Ibrahim Foundation.* https://mo.ibrahim.foundation/sites/default/files/2020-06/debt-distress-covid19.pdf

Committee for a Responsible Federal Budget. (2025). Q&A: gross debt versus debt held by the public. https://www.crfb.org/papers/qa-gross-debt-versus-debt-held public

Danquah, D. A., & Osei Adu, K. (2025). Effects of lending rates and financial development on loan portfolio in sub-Saharan Africa. *Future Business Journal, 11*(1), 227.

Development Reimagined. (2024). Africa's Eurobond. https://developmentreimagined.com/wp-content/uploads/2024/06/Final-Africa-Eurobond-Report-May-2024.pdf

Egboboh, C. (2023). Debt servicing gulped 106% of FG's revenue in 2022. https://businessday.ng/news/article/debt-servicing-gulped-106-of-fgs-revenue-in-2022/

Ezenwe, U. (1993). The African debt crisis and the challenge of development. *Intereconomics, 28*(1), 35–43.

FindevLab. (2024). *The road to Zambia's 2020 sovereign debt default.* https://findevlab.org/wp-content/uploads/2023/12/The-Road-to-Zambias-2020-Sovereign-Debt-Default-vf.pdf

Gammadigbe, V. (2025). Tax transition in the Waemu zone: Analysis of the effects on fiscal deficit. *Public Finance Review*, 10911421251345008.

Greene, J. E., & Khan, M. S. (1990). *The African debt crisis* (AERC Special Paper No. 3). African Economic Research Consortium. https://idl-bnc-idrc.dspacedirect.org/server/api/core/bitstreams/399c96bf-fa7f-4966-af59-c6194d65f731/content

Icyeza, P. (2021). *Summer in the field: Bond, Eurobond: Tracking African Eurobonds issued between 2006–2021.* https://www.bu.edu/gdp/2021/10/22/bond-eurobond-tracking-african-eurobonds-issued-between-2006-2021/.

IMF. (2025). *Regional economic outlook: Sub-Saharan Africa.* https://www.imf.org/en/Publications/REO/SSA/Issues/2025/04/25/regional-economic-outlook-for-sub-saharan-africa-april-2025

Institute for Government (2024). *What are the different ways to measure public debt?* https://www.instituteforgovernment.org.uk/explainer/measure-public-debt

International Monetary Fund. (2023). *Debt dilemmas in sub-Saharan Africa: Some principles and trade-offs.* https://www.imf.org/-/media/Files/Publications/REO/AFR/2023/October/English/debt-note2.ashx

Jalles, J. T., Kiendrebeogo, Y., Lam, R., & Piazza, R. (2024). Revisiting the countercyclicality of fiscal policy. *Empirical Economics, 67*(3), 877–914.

Kodongo, O., Mukoki, P., & Ojah, K. (2023). Bond market development and infrastructure-gap reduction: The case of sub-Saharan Africa. *Economic Modelling, 121*, 106230.

Lartey, V. C., & Li, Y. (2018). Zero-coupon and forward yield curves for government of Ghana bonds. *SAGE Open, 8*(3), 2158244018800786.

Ministry of Finance. (2023). *Update on Ghana's domestic debt exchange programme.* https://www.mofep.gov.gh/press-release/2022-01-31/update-on-ghanas-domestic-debt-exchange-programme

Mupunga, N., & Ngundu, T. (2020). *Escalating public debt levels and fiscal responses in sub-Saharan African countries.* AERC. https://aercafrica.org/wp-content/uploads/2020/04/Research-paper-385.pdf

Nairametrics. (2023). Nigeria's debt service-to-revenue ratio rises to 112%. https://nairametrics.com/2023/05/17/nigerias-debt-service-to-revenue-ratio-rises-to-112-in-2022-cbn/

Ngundu, M., & Cilliers, J. (2025). *Indebted and underfunded*. https://futures.issafrica.org/blog/2025/Indebted-and-underfunded

OECD. (2022). Impacts of the Russian invasion of Ukraine on financial market conditions and resilience. In *Assessment of global financial markets*. OECD Publishing.

ONE Campaign. (2025, March 11). *African debt*. https://data.one.org/analysis/african-debt

Osakede, U. A., & Adeleke, O. K. (2022). Government borrowing, infrastructure and human development in Africa: A panel threshold approach. In *Financial crises, poverty and environmental sustainability: Challenges in the context of the SDGs and COVID-19 recovery* (pp. 81–92). Springer International Publishing.

Ple, L. (2026). In sub-Saharan Africa, public debt stabilises but vulnerabilities increase. https://economicresearch.bnpparibas.com/Media-Library/en-US/Saharan-Africa-public-debt-stabilises-vulnerabilities-increase-1/27/2026,c44631

Sesele, M. (2025). Infrastructure as an asset class: A critical literature review and case study analysis. In *Development and Investment in Infrastructure in developing countries: A 10-year reflection* (pp. 91–100). CRC Press.

Shah, S. S. A., Dickinson, D., Tao, K., Wang, C., & Zhang, L. (2025). The heterogenous threshold effects of public debt on economic growth: Empirical evidence from developing countries. *Open Economies Review, 36*(1), 243–280.

UNCTAD. (2025). *A world of debt 2025*. https://unctad.org/publication/world-of-debt

United Nations. (2024). *Tackling domestic debt sustainability challenges in Africa*. https://www.un.org/en/desa/tackling-domestic-debt-sustainability-challenges-africa

Were, M. (2024a). *Sub-Saharan Africa faces an alarming debt burden that could hinder progress on sustainable development goals*. https://www.wider.unu.edu/publication/sub-saharan-africa-faces-alarming-debt-burden-could-hinder-progress-sustainable

Were, M. (2024b). *Emerging public debt challenges in sub-Saharan Africa* (No. 2024/36). WIDER Working Paper. https://www.econstor.eu/handle/10419/298086

World Bank. (2023). *Unlocking the development potential of public debt in sub-Saharan Africa*. https://www.worldbank.org/en/results/2023/12/15/unlocking-the-development-potential-of-public-debt-in-sub-saharan-africa

Zida, I., Ouedraogo, I., & Sawadogo, R. (2025). Effects of public debt on income inequality in sub-Saharan Africa: exploring the direct and indirect transmission channels. *Economic Change and Restructuring, 58*(5), 83.

CHAPTER 2

# Drivers of Public Debt Accumulation in African Economies: Insights from Panel Data Analysis

*Yazidu Ustarz*

## 2.1 Background

Public debt dynamics has long been of concern to policymakers because of their implications for economic stability and welfare, particularly in developing countries. There has, however, been renewed interest in the face of the financial crisis of 2008/2009 and the recent novel COVID-19 (Kose et al., 2021). These events have worsened the already bad fiscal imbalances in these countries (Klutse et al., 2023) as they have depressed earnings from international trade and critical sources of inflow such as foreign direct investment (FDI), cross-border lending, and the international capital market. The inability to generate the necessary inflows from these sources means that developing countries will have to resort to public borrowing to meet the increasing demand for infrastructure, health

Y. Ustarz (✉)
Department of Finance, School of Business, University for Development Studies, Tamale, Ghana
e-mail: uyazidu@uds.edu.gh



I. N. Yakubu (ed.), *Public Debt and Economic Resilience in Africa*, Palgrave Studies in African and Development Economics,
https://doi.org/10.1007/978-3-032-25835-9_2

education, and other welfare needs (Sinha et al., 2011). The situation is even more dire for African countries that primarily rely on primary commodities in international trade, which is considered volatile and was severely affected by these international crises (Baban & Greene, 1992).

Even before the financial crisis, many African countries' exposure to mounting debt was glaring, necessitating the adoption of the Highly Indebted Poor Countries (HIPC) programme in the early 2000s. For instance, of the 39 countries that subscribed to the HIPC initiative, 34 were from Africa, representing over 87% (Benson, 2022). After the programmes, African countries' debt levels drastically reduced. After a decade, however, most African countries are back to their pre-HIPC levels or even worse. This calls for a critical analysis of what could be driving these persistent debt levels in Africa. Understanding these varied drivers is crucial for proposing appropriate policies to address these debt levels, given their devastating impact on the economy and welfare of the population.

The concerns about high debt accumulation stem from the fact that evidence on how it positively impacts growth and welfare remains contentious both from theory and empirical literature. While the classical and the neoclassical schools of thought believe that public debt is detrimental to growth and the welfare of future generations through reduced investment capital, modern Keynesians, however, argue that moderate government debt could stimulate growth and welfare (Ncanywa & Masoga, 2018). From an empirical perspective, African countries have been affected by rising debt levels, particularly as a number of African countries have access to the international capital market, thereby increasing their vulnerabilities both domestically and internationally. Given these complex dynamics, recent studies are re-examining the various factors driving these debt levels and the channels through which they affect the welfare of African countries. This chapter seeks to uniquely contribute to the literature by disaggregating the drivers of public debt into economic, demographic, structural, political, and institutional factors. This approach allows policymakers to assess the varied impacts of these factors on public debt, which helps in formulating policies to uniquely target these factors.

The rest of the section is presented as follows: Section 2.2 provides stylised facts on the debt situation in Africa, while the literature review is presented in Sect. 2.3. The methodology for the study is contained in Sect. 2.4, with Sect. 2.5, capturing the results and discussion of findings. The chapter concludes with and offers policy recommendations in Sect. 2.6.

## 2.2 Stylised Facts on Debt Dynamics in Africa

Post-independence, most African countries inherited an economic structure bequeathed to them by colonial masters, which was largely commodity-dependent. Successive governments had attempted to reposition their economies through industrialisation by implementing an import substitution policy to add value to their primary products for domestic consumption and export (Acheampong & Vitenu-Sackey, 2024; Soludo, 1998). Financial institutions were established to support the operations of these industries with a specific policy directive for directing credit to key targeted industries. For instance, in Ghana, a number of financial institutions were established to support the industrialisation agenda, including the Agricultural Credit and Cooperative Bank in 1965 and the National Investment Bank in 1963 with specific mandates (World Bank Group, 2016). The industries, though successful in promoting local ownership and entrepreneurship and some drive in manufacturing output, were short-lived due to several factors, including a lack of international competitiveness (Soludo, 1998). Hence, African countries continued to rely largely on a few primary commodities through international trade. The volatile commodity prices and oil shocks in the 1970s were occasioned by the Yom Kippur War between Israel on the one hand and Egypt and Syria on the other hand in 1973. The 1979 oil crisis resulted from the Iranian Revolution, which disrupted the global supply of oil from Iran. These events drove the oil price to increase from US$3.35 at the beginning of 1970 to reach $32.5 by the close of 1970, representing an increase of more than 870% (Hammes & Wills, 2005). These events pushed the import bills of most African countries and worsened their finances, resulting in higher borrowing (Simson, 2019). In the 1980s, faced a global recession and further depressed earnings from primary commodities, and growth stagnated. With little earnings from these commodities, African countries had to resort further to borrowing. The continent also faced severe drought, which affected lives and properties, as well as the economic capacity of most countries. A number of countries were unable to service their outstanding debt obligations as a result of the series of crises (International Monetary Fund, 1989).

The 1990s through the 2000s saw the launch of debt relief initiatives led by the World Bank and the IMF to provide some relief to heavily indebted poor countries. The result was a massive reduction in the debt portfolio of African countries. Furthermore, the Multilateral Debt Relief

Initiative (MDRI) was introduced in 2005 to further reduce the debt levels of vulnerable countries.[1] As a result of the intervention, the general government's gross debt reduced from a high level of 65.3% to about 32.5% in 2008. It began to increase from 2013, and by 2019, it had reached 60.6%. Following the novel Covid-19 in 2020 and its attendant fiscal challenges, Fig. 2.1 further rose to 70.6% of GDP, almost 10 percentage points higher than the HIPC level (Commodore & Awuah, 2024).

Post 2000, there was a significant shift in the debt dynamics of African countries, as most African countries began to access the international capital market thanks to a breakthrough by Ghana in 2007. Ghana sourced $750 million in 2007, although South Africa was the first to issue it in 1995 (Chuku & Yenice, 2022). As demonstrated in Fig. 2.1, the external debt stock for sub-Saharan African (SSA) countries alone increased by over 153% between 2010 and 2023 (from $341 billion to $864 billion) (World Bank, 2024).

By August 2020, 21 African countries were able to access the international capital market and issue Eurobonds to the tune of $155 billion. By 2021, Eurobond constituted 58% of African's private credit.

Traditionally, African countries rely heavily on Official Aid to supplement domestic revenue. This major source has dwindled and is also

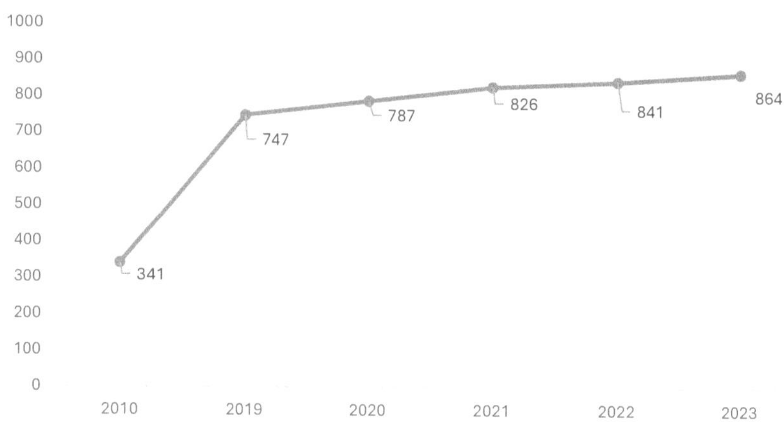


**Fig. 2.1** Total external debt stocks for SSA (US$ billion). Source: Author's construction based on the World Bank (2024)

[1] https://www.worldbank.org/en/topic/debt/brief/hipc

associated with a lot of uncertainty, forcing African countries to borrow externally to augment the little domestic revenue (Friedrich-Ebert-Stiftung, 2023). The Covid-19 crisis and the Russian-Ukrainian conflict further complicated the debt situation for African countries as earnings from international trade were severely affected. Thus, there was a shift from multilateral and bilateral institutions to private debt, which comes at a higher cost. For instance, as of the end of 2023, 42% of Africa's debt was from private creditors, as indicated in Fig. 2.2.

As of the end of 2023, some African countries have accumulated Eurobonds as high as 24% of their GDP, as indicated in Fig. 2.3.

These external debts come with the annual ritual of debt servicing. For instance, the annual debt servicing of the government's debt increased from $20.4 billion in 2000 to reach $67.5 billion in 2022. Indeed, in some countries, over 30% of their foreign exchange earnings are used to service their external debt (Commodore & Awuah, 2024). The implication is that resources will have to be spent on service debt at the expense of key developmental initiatives. As captured in Fig. 2.4, the total debt services as a percentage of government total expenditure is higher than that of health services from 2009 to 2024. Indeed, in countries such as Angola, Egypt, and Gabon, debt service is higher than both education and health.

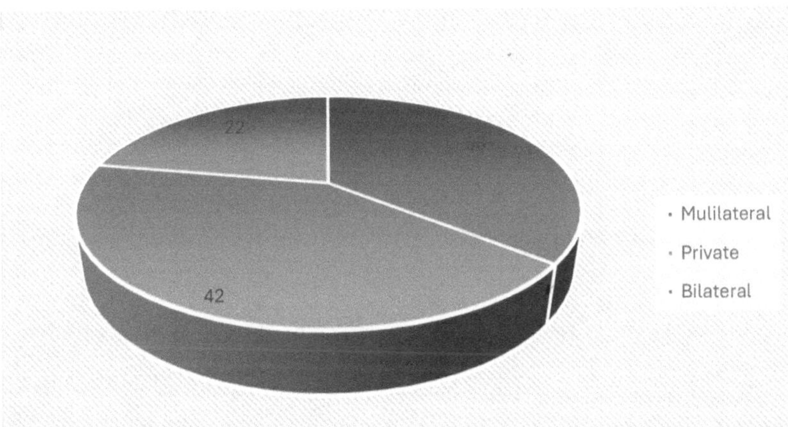


**Fig. 2.2** Composition of African's creditors—2023. Source: Author's based on data from UNCTAD, 2025

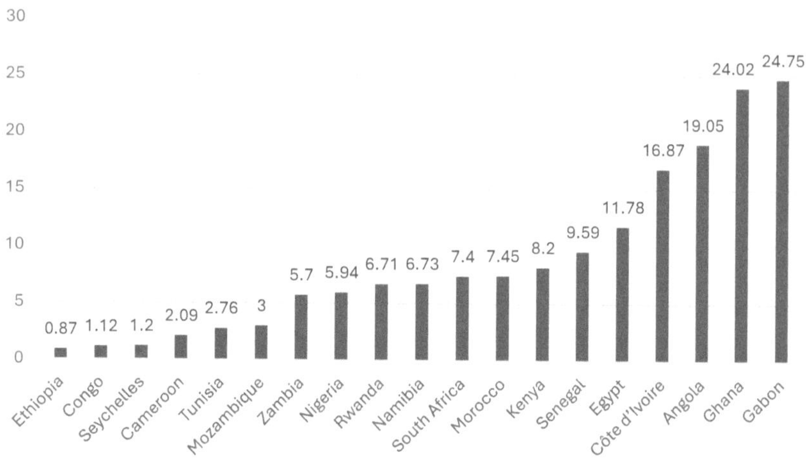


**Fig. 2.3** Outstanding Eurobond Debt to GDP ratio for SSA Countries—2023. Source: Author's based on Development Reimagined (2024)

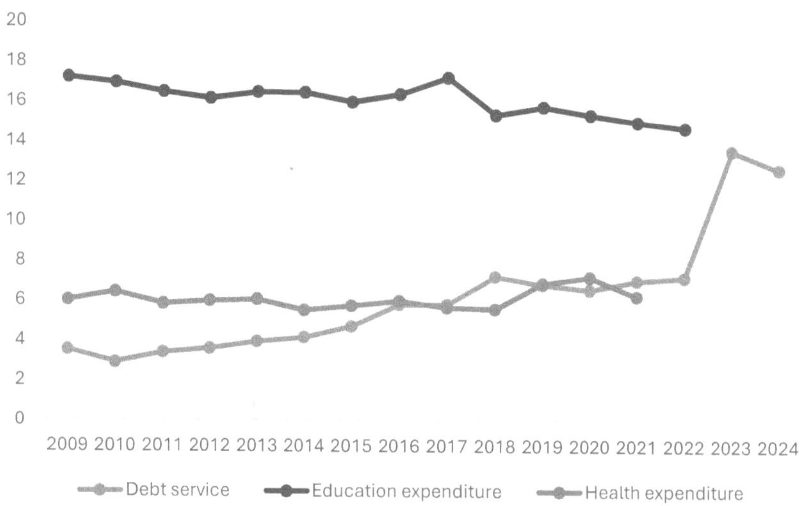


**Fig. 2.4** Debt service, expenditure on health and education as a percentage of total government spending. Source: Author's construct based on data from https://data.one.org/analysis/african-debt

**Table 2.1** Top African countries with the highest debt from China

| *Country* | *Amount ($ billion)* |
|---|---|
| Angola | 17.8 |
| Ethiopia | 6.5 |
| Egypt | 6.3 |
| Zambia and | 6 |
| Kenya | 6 |
| South Africa and | 3.5 |
| Cameroon | 3.5 |
| The republic of Congo | 3.2 |
| The Democratic Republic of Congo | 2.9 |

Source: Author's based on Data from: https://www.aa.com.tr/en/economy/africa-makes-up-over-half-of-all-countries-with-highest-debt-to-china/3594478#

China has also emerged as a major source of debt for African countries. China has become the largest bilateral holder of Africa's debts. As of 2023, its public holdings of African external debt stood at $62 billion, while the private holdings were around $23 billion.[2] Of the 20 countries highly indebted to China, 11 are from Africa, as shown in Table 2.1.

Besides these issues, many African countries have experienced episodes of political instability, which have affected private investment and deprived them of external inflows. Weak institutional qualities and governance have also been responsible for the state of debt in Africa (World Bank, 1994).

The stylised fact shows that African countries have over the years experienced episodes of debt accumulation with its attendance consequences on welfare spending such as education and health. It is therefore important for the study to uncover the various factors that give rise to the persistently high debt levels in Africa.

## 2.3 Literature Review

Various theoretical arguments have been made regarding why governments accumulate debt. Classical economists favour taxes to public debt accumulation, as they argue that it only crowds out private investment and saddles the nation with debt servicing. The Keynesians, on the other hand, believe that in times of economic downturns, the government could resort to moderate borrowing in order to stimulate economic growth. Thus,

[2] https://data.one.org/analysis/african-debt

they assert that economic depression could push the government to increase public debt to restore the economy towards an equilibrium point (Keynes, 2018). The neoclassical posits that public debt is derived from the inability of the government to raise the needed revenue, resulting in fiscal imbalance. Hence, to correct the imbalance, the government resorts to borrowing to compensate for the shortfall. This is typical of African countries, where government revenue is inadequate to address the developmental needs of the economy. Alesina and Tabellini (1986) advanced the political economy theory position that political pressures and electoral cycles could drive the fiscal deficit higher. The situation could be worse where state institutions are too weak to ensure that the fiscal deficit is kept within a manageable limit. The fiscal deficit in Africa tends to be extremely high in election years compared to other years, as incumbent governments try to maintain their grip on power. In election years, governments tend to be reluctant to increase taxes to raise the needed revenue while at the same time wanting to increase expenditure in an attempt to fulfil campaign promises to be retained in power. This leaves borrowing as the only option to meet increasing needs while lowering tax revenue.

Others argue that persistent borrowing by African countries is a result of some structural challenges with the fundamentals of their economies (United Nations Conference on Trade and Development, 2016). The dependency theory suggests that the world economic arrangement, in which developing countries turn to focus on the export of primary commodities, puts their economies at a disadvantage, as earnings from these commodities turn out to be volatile and with little diversification in the export base (Prebisch, 1950). Thus, when earnings from exports fall unexpectedly, it affects government external inflows, resulting in an increase in borrowing to support the economy. Moreover, most developing countries have a significant proportion of economic activities operating within the informal sector, which adversely affects domestic revenue mobilisation. The modern macrofinancial perspective presented by Reinhart and Rogoff (2010) asserts that increasing financial integration offers both opportunities and threats to developing countries. While this allows them to borrow from the international capital market, they are also exposed to various risks including interest and exchange rate risks. Due to poorer institutional qualities and weak fundamentals, developing countries have lower sovereign risk, which increases their borrowing cost.

In addition, the theory of tax smoothing advanced in a seminal paper by Barro (1979) and extended by Lucas and Stokey (1983) offers a foundational understanding of how fiscal cyclicality could drive government debt. According to Barro (1979), governments should maintain a stable tax rate while they borrow in times of economic shocks and exceptional circumstances such as war, which increases expenditure. The debt is expected to be repaid when the situation normalises by raising revenue incrementally through tax or controlling expenditure. Thus, Lucas and Stokey (1983) extended the framework into a general equilibrium one with uncertainty by arguing that the government can smoothen taxes not just in good times but also in good and bad times by issuing state-contingent debt instruments with a higher repayment when in a good state and less when the economy is in a bad state.

Alesina and Perotti (1995), however, argue that governments accumulate debt based on political considerations which further the interests of the ruling class. Unlike Barro (1979), where the decision to borrow is as a result of economic considerations, borrowing as a result of a high budget deficit is largely driven by political gains facilitated by weak institutional structures. According to them, politicians benefit by running high budget expenditure, especially in an election year, to enhance their electoral success, even at the expense of economic reasoning. Indeed, the increase in expenditure comes with lowering taxes to create a picture of economic well-being. The result is that the country is confronted with a high-deficit post-election cycle. Unfortunately, most voters, particularly in developing countries, fail to notice the future economic implications, as they overestimate the benefits of the increase in expenditure and underestimate the possible tax implications of the action. The situation is exacerbated when the institutional framework necessary to ensure fiscal discipline and rules are weak.

The theoretical review provides a foundation to enhance the understanding of how various factors drive public debt. On the empirical front, various factors have been argued to be key drivers of public debt, although there is no unanimity in the literature on these set factors and the direction of their effects (Cifuentes-Faura & Simionescu, 2024). While some studies are conducted at the country and cross-country levels, others are based on regional and income groups. Based on the objectives of the study, these studies have employed varied methodological approaches, such as threshold models to account for asymmetric effects, cross-sectional dependence models to account for common cross-sectional effects, GMM to address endogeneity, and ARDL to address small sample size and stationarity conditions, among others.

The empirical literature is discussed along certain key thematic areas. The drivers of public debt could be grouped into economic, demographic, structural, political, and institutional factors.

### *2.3.1 Macroeconomic Factors*

Several macroeconomic indicators have been identified as key determinants of public debt, with results varying depending on the level of study and methodological approaches. The factors examined include fiscal, socio-economic, and political factors (Cifuentes-Faura & Simionescu, 2024).

Studies have identified macroeconomic fundamentals such as growth, interest rate, domestic credit, government expenditure, and private investment inflation as key determinants of debt accumulation. When countries experience economic downturns, it affects government revenue for development purposes. Hence, the government resorts to borrowing to make up for the shortfall (Sasmal & Sasmal, 2020). Economic growth has been one of the widely studied variables in relation to public debt, with varied findings. Azolibe (2021) provided macroeconomic determinant evidence focusing on HIPC, with results pointing to government expenditure, corruption, aid dependency, population growth, and unemployment as positive drivers of debt. Economic growth and international reserves were, however, found to have a negative impact. Sinha et al. (2011) demonstrated that the determinants of public debt could vary significantly among different income groups. While economic growth, expenditures of the central government, and education were key drivers in both income groups, inflation and FDI were only significant in driving debt among low-income groups. Underdeveloped financial systems make it difficult for developing countries to be able to.

Reinhart and Rogoff (2010) suggested the existence of a threshold effect of 90%. In other words, debt above this threshold exerts a negative impact on growth. Égert (2015), however, suggested that the threshold could be lower than suggested by Reinhart and Rogoff (2010), and it varies significantly across countries and income groups. Baum et al. (2013) examine selected countries from the Eurozone using a dynamic threshold model and find the impact to be significant only in the short run, below a threshold of 67%. Their findings enrich the literature on the relationship between debt and growth, both in times of crisis and growth, given the sample period from 1990 to 2010.

### 2.3.2 Political and Institutional Factors

Political institutions tend to resort to excessive borrowing, particularly in election years, to enhance their chances of retaining power. Hence, in election years, the government run excessively high fiscal budget deficit, which is largely funded through borrowing accumulation (Persson & Svensson, 1989). The issue is compounded when institutional regimes turn to be very weak and incapable of setting and adopting fiscal rules to keep fiscal deficit within a manageable limit.

### 2.3.3 Structural Factors

A section of the literature also considered the structural factors that fundamentally affect the ability of developing countries to raise needed revenue. Historically, these countries have relied on primary commodities with little diversification. Earnings from these commodities are volatile; hence, a shortfall will mean additional borrowing to support developmental projects (Da & Diarra, 2023; Majumder et al., 2021). Additionally, the informal nature of these economies affects their ability to generate the required revenue, necessitating the need to borrow to support development. Further, countries with deep local financial markets can raise capital in the domestic currency at a relatively lower cost than external sources. It also helps reduce debt servicing costs as the risk of foreign exchange rate mismatch is eliminated (Eichengreen & Hausmann, 1999).

### 2.3.4 Social and Demographic Factors

Other studies have focused on the social determinants of public debt. Social factors such as inequality, unemployment, and population could impact public debt by increasing fiscal expenditure and creating economic stability. Using a panel of 158 countries from 2000 to 2019, Carrera and de la Vega (2021) demonstrated that income inequality adversely affects public debt.

### 2.3.5 Recent Studies on the Determinants of Public Debt in Africa

Several studies have focused on Africa. Appiah-Kubi et al. (2022) using a GMM and instrumental variables show that, government consumption and tax revenue to have a dampening effect on public debt, while corruption increases public debt accumulation. Hlongwane and Daw (2022) provided results on the South African economy based on a regime-switching model for the period from 1990 to 2020. The results reveal that macroeconomic factors, including inflation, government, and unemployment, significantly impact debt accumulation. Musah (2023) considered macro determinants of public debt in Ghana using the ARDL. He found trade, investment, interest payments, and government expenditure to be positive drivers of public debt. Nikolaidou and Okwoche (2023) focused on the role of governance and macroeconomic indicators using a sample of 38 SSA countries. The quality of governance and economic growth were found to have a dampening effect on debt, while political instability had a magnifying effect on debt. Abotsi (2023) concentrated on governance in an extended sample of 45 African countries between 1996 and 2019. The study finds that various governance indicators have a negative effect on debt. They also found that economic growth and government revenue have an inverse relationship with public debt, while government expenditure and investment increase public debt.

## 2.4 Methodology

This section presents the discussion on the variable, data source, and empirical approaches to analyse the determinants of debt accumulation in Africa.

### *2.4.1 Variables and Data Sources*

A panel dataset of 38 countries in sub-Saharan Africa is sourced from reputable international organisation databases, including the World Bank (WB) data centre World Development Indicators (WDI) and Worldwide Governance Indicators (WGI), spanning 2006 to 2023. The sample size of 38 and the timeframe are due to missing data on some countries in the sources. In addition, data on public debt are sourced from the International Monetary Fund (IMF).

To determine the drivers of debt accumulation in Africa, the dependent variable is denoted by public debt, measured by the percentage of government debt to GDP (see Table 2.2). This approach of measuring public debt is well rooted in the empirical literature (Abubakar et al., 2025; Acar & Öztürk, 2025).

**Table 2.2** Summary of variables and data sources

| *Variables* | *Construct* | *Measurement* | *Sources* |
|---|---|---|---|
| Public debt | pudebt | Debt instruments, central government, per cent of GDP | IMF |
| Remittance | remit | Personal remittances, received (% of GDP) | |
| Financial integration | finin | Sum of stock of total assets and liabilities/GDP | Milesi-Ferretti, 2024 |
| Health | health | Health; life expectancy at birth (years) | WDI, WB |
| Aid | aid | Net official development assistance and official aid received (current US$) | WDI, WB |
| Population | popnuw | Population, total | WDI, WB |
| Trade openness | trade | Trade (% of GDP) | WDI, WB |
| Inflation | inflation | Inflation, consumer prices (annual %) | WDI, WB |
| GDP growth rate | econs | GDP growth (annual %) | WDI, WB |
| Government expenditure | govexp | General government final consumption expenditure (% of GDP) | WDI, WB |
| Terms of trade | barterterm | Terms of trade adjustment (constant LCU) | WDI, WB |
| Exchange rate | exchrate | Price level ratio of PPP conversion factor (GDP) to market exchange rate | WDI, WB |
| Control of corruption | concurpt | Control of corruption: Percentile rank | WDI, WB |
| Government effectiveness | goveff | Government effectiveness: Percentile rank | WGI, WB |
| Political stability | polista | Political stability and absence of violence/terrorism: | WGI, WB |
| Regulatory quality | rq | Regulatory quality: Percentile rank | WGI, WB |
| Rule of law | rl | Rule of law: Percentile rank | WGI, WB |
| Voice and accountability | voacc | Voice and accountability: Percentile rank | WGI, WB |
| Urbanisation | urban | Urban population (% of total population) | WGI, WB |
| Healthcare | health | Health; life expectancy at birth (years) | WDI, WB |
| Standard of living | standlv | Gross National Income Per Capita (2021 PPP$) | WDI, WB |
| Education | edu | Mean years of schooling (years) | WDI, WB |
| Digitisation | digit | Mobile cellular subscriptions (per 100 people) | WDI, WB |

The drivers or determinants of public debt accumulation are grouped into three key dimensions: economic, institutional, and political, and demographic, and structural factors. The factors in the economic dimension are financial integration, aid, remittances, GDP growth, exchange rate, inflation, trade openness, terms of trade, and FDI, as shown in Table 2.2. The motivation for employing these determinants from an economic perspective is based on some existing empirical works (Aimola & Odhiambo, 2021; Chhabra et al., 2023; Delessa et al., 2024; Marozva & Magwedere, 2025). Institutional and political factors are grounded in the work of Kaufmann et al. (2010) on the six indicators of robust public governance dynamics: "control of corruption, rule of law, regulatory quality, government effectiveness, voice and accountability, and political stability" (Kaufmann et al., 2010).

The proposed drivers of debt accumulation from demographic and structural perspectives include healthcare, education, population, urbanisation, digitisation, and standard of living. These factors have been utilised in prevailing empirical studies to determine macroeconomic outcomes (see, e.g. Bose & Banerjee, 2025; Fuseini, 2025). Table 2.3 provides further details of the variables and data sources.

### 2.4.2 *Empirical Strategy*

With regard to the objective of this study, it employed the quantile regression approach as initially espoused by Koenker and Bassett (1978). However, recent developments have modified Koenker and Bassett's (1978) seminal work. For instance, Machado and Santos Silva (2019) and Rios-Avila (2022) extended quantile regression by integrating the moment condition to compute quantile regression based on the method of moments. Based on the purpose of this study, the study posits in Eq. (2.1) that the public debt accumulation (pudebt) is a function (*f*) of the economic factors (EF), Institutional and political factors (IPF) and demographical and structural factors (DSF)

$$\text{Pudebt} = f\left(\text{EF,IPF,DSF}\right) \tag{2.1}$$

Following the argument on the robustness of the MMQREG approach, Eq. (2.2) is mathematically expressed to show the method of moment condition

**Table 2.3** Summary of statistics

| *Variable* | *Obs* | *Mean* | *Std. dev.* | *Min* | *Max* |
|---|---|---|---|---|---|
| pudebt | 684 | 56.01248 | 49.70136 | 7.276108 | 471.5262 |
| aid | 684 | 9.58E + 08 | 9.36E + 08 | 2.09E + 07 | 1.14E + 10 |
| finin | 683 | 1.192502 | 0.789644 | 0 | 6.1201 |
| barterterm | 660 | 105.8822 | 18.62495 | 64.9 | 199.2 |
| health | 684 | 59.87286 | 6.155182 | 14.665 | 76.059 |
| remit | 684 | 4.206098 | 5.581851 | 0 | 37.9371 |
| digit | 683 | 60.82466 | 33.80751 | 2.152569 | 174.0251 |
| edu | 684 | 4.568866 | 1.845792 | 0.98 | 8.930847 |
| standlv | 684 | 3143.384 | 1890.306 | 688.3473 | 9694.499 |
| urban | 684 | 38.86543 | 14.87911 | 9.617 | 76.401 |
| voacc | 684 | 30.67397 | 17.26435 | 0.469484 | 79.12621 |
| rl | 684 | 24.47879 | 16.95225 | 0.469484 | 75 |
| rq | 684 | 23.98196 | 14.54992 | 0.471698 | 60.84906 |
| polista | 684 | 27.6812 | 18.55859 | 0.471698 | 80.18868 |
| concurpt | 684 | 26.61532 | 19.45627 | 0 | 82.38095 |
| exchrate | 684 | 0.420867 | 0.099702 | 0.172549 | 0.935284 |
| fdi | 683 | 4.423164 | 8.494683 | −17.2921 | 103.3374 |
| termstrade | 611 | 3.35E + 10 | 1.10E + 12 | −5.75E + 1 | 1.97E + 13 |
| govexp | 594 | 14.05866 | 6.769978 | 2.047121 | 43.48232 |
| econs | 684 | 3.836315 | 5.112682 | −46.0821 | 21.45206 |
| inflation | 666 | 11.12103 | 34.49328 | −16.8597 | 557.2018 |
| trade | 612 | 62.20826 | 26.82733 | 2.473729 | 165.0489 |
| pogrow | 684 | 2.537241 | 0.938613 | −5.41591 | 5.589722 |

$$\in\left[\left(\gamma - I\left(y_{\text{it}} \le X_{\text{it}}^{T}\beta(\gamma)\right)\right)X_{\text{IT}}\right] = 0 \tag{2.2}$$

From Eq. (2.2), as an alternative to reducing the loss function as in the conventional quantile approach, the MMQREG addresses the moment condition. Equation (2.2) suggests that the residual from the $\gamma$th Quantile estimation, weighted by the explanatory variables, should have an anticipated value of zero, which is similar to the OLS assumptions; however, at the selected quantile $\gamma$.

Empirically, the study specified (2.3), (2.4), and (2.5) for EF, IPF, and DSF, respectively, to compute the MMQREG based on the variables in the study.

$$Q_\gamma\left(\text{Pudebt}\right)_{\text{it}} = \beta_0\gamma + \beta_1\gamma\text{aid}_{\text{it}} + \beta_2\,\gamma\,\textit{finin}_{\text{it}} + \beta_3\gamma\text{remit}_{\text{it}} + \beta_4\gamma\text{inflation}_{\text{it}} + \beta_5\gamma\text{trade}_{\text{itit}} + \beta_6\gamma\text{econs}_{\text{it}} + \beta_7\gamma\text{govexp}_{\text{it}} + \beta_8\gamma\text{barterterm}_{\text{it}} + \beta_9\gamma\,\textit{fdi}_{\text{it}} + \beta_{10}\gamma\text{exchrate}_{\text{it}} + \varepsilon_{\text{it}} \tag{2.3}$$

$$Q_\gamma\left(\text{Pudebt}\right)_{\text{it}} = \beta_0\gamma + \beta_1\gamma\text{concurpt}_{\text{it}} + \beta_2\,\gamma\text{goveff}_{\text{it}} + \beta_3\gamma\text{polista}_{\text{it}} + \beta_4\gamma rq_{\text{it}} + \beta_5\gamma rl_{\text{itit}} + \beta_6\gamma\text{voacc}_{\text{it}} + \varepsilon_{\text{it}} \tag{2.4}$$

$$Q_\gamma\left(\text{Pudebt}\right)_{\text{it}} = \beta_0\gamma + \beta_1\gamma\text{edu}_{\text{it}} + \beta_2\,\gamma\text{standlv}_{\text{it}} + \beta_3\gamma\text{health}_{\text{it}} + \beta_4\gamma\text{urban}_{\text{it}} + \beta_5\gamma\text{digit}_{\text{itit}} + \beta_6\gamma\text{popnum}_{\text{it}} + \varepsilon_{\text{it}} \tag{2.5}$$

where $\gamma$ denotes the quantile number, and in this study, we use the 25th, 50th, and 75th quantiles. $\beta$ represents the coefficients at either the 25th, 50th, and 75th quantiles. $i$ and $t$ represent the country and time, respectively. Based on the recent extension by Rios-Avila (2022), we opt not to use either fixed or random effects.

## 2.5 Analysis of Findings and Discussions

### 2.5.1 *Descriptive Statistics*

To examine the properties of the variables used in the study, descriptive statistics were run, and the results are captured in Table 2.3. Public, as the dependent variable, has a mean of about 56% but displays a lot of variation across countries, with a minimum value of about 7% and a maximum of about 471%. The independent variables also show varied characteristics.

### 2.5.2 *Determinants of Public Debt*

The results of the study are presented in a disaggregated manner, capturing the sub-categories of drivers of public debt.

*Economic Determinants of Public Debt*
The results from the quintile of the method of moments quintile regression are displayed in Table 2.4. The model performance shows that over 27% of the variations in the dependent variables are accounted for by the explanatory variables, with the F-statistic being significant. This further

**Table 2.4** Determinants of debt accumulation (economic factors): MMQREG and OLS approach

| | (1) | (2) | (3) | (4) | (5) | (6) |
|---|---|---|---|---|---|---|
| VARIABLES | location | scale | qtile_25 | qtile_50 | qtile_75 | OLS |
| aid | −3.24e − 09** | −1.33e − 09 | −2.07e − 09* | −2.85e − 09** | −3.90e − 09** | −3.24e − 09** |
| | (1.38e − 09) | (1.12e − 09) | (1.07e − 09) | (1.20e − 09) | (1.80e − 09) | (1.40e − 09) |
| finin | 12.58*** | 3.338* | 9.625*** | 11.60*** | 14.22*** | 12.58*** |
| | (2.393) | (1.891) | (2.071) | (2.149) | (3.024) | (2.416) |
| remit | 0.584* | 0.578* | 0.0713 | 0.413 | 0.867* | 0.584* |
| | (0.335) | (0.299) | (0.234) | (0.276) | (0.443) | (0.339) |
| inflation | 0.270** | 0.161*** | 0.128 | 0.223** | 0.349*** | 0.270** |
| | (0.116) | (0.0533) | (0.104) | (0.111) | (0.132) | (0.118) |
| trade | 0.105 | 0.0951 | 0.0206 | 0.0767 | 0.151 | 0.105 |
| | (0.100) | (0.0972) | (0.0420) | (0.0744) | (0.143) | (0.101) |
| econs | −0.918*** | −0.289 | −0.661*** | −0.832*** | −1.059** | −0.918*** |
| | (0.315) | (0.237) | (0.178) | (0.260) | (0.421) | (0.318) |
| govexp | 0.363 | 0.451* | −0.0371 | 0.229 | 0.584 | 0.363 |
| | (0.283) | (0.256) | (0.157) | (0.222) | (0.385) | (0.285) |
| barterterm | −0.00619 | 0.00307 | −0.00891 | −0.00710 | −0.00468 | −0.00619 |
| | (0.0683) | (0.0595) | (0.0479) | (0.0571) | (0.0915) | (0.0690) |
| fdi | 0.0518 | −0.249 | 0.273 | 0.126 | −0.0707 | 0.0518 |
| | (0.283) | (0.265) | (0.175) | (0.225) | (0.388) | (0.286) |
| exchrate | −87.97*** | −32.26 | −59.38*** | −78.43*** | −103.8*** | −87.97*** |
| | (21.06) | (20.47) | (9.445) | (15.56) | (29.52) | (21.27) |
| Constant | 63.52*** | 16.14** | 49.21*** | 58.74*** | 71.45*** | 63.52*** |
| | (7.956) | (6.526) | (6.205) | (6.883) | (10.32) | (8.034) |
| Observations | 569 | 569 | 569 | 569 | 569 | 569 |
| F (10, 558) | | | | | | 13.46 |
| Prob>F | | | | | | 0.0000 |
| R-squared | | | | | | 0.266 |

Robust standard errors in parentheses

*** $p < 0.01$; ** $p < 0.05$; * $p < 0.1$

reinforces the model performance. Robust standard error was used to account for any possible heteroscedasticity effect. These results indicate that aid has a negative effect on public debt. Thus, an increase in aid results in a reduction in public debt across quintiles. Aid is a major source of resources to African countries, and hence, a reduction in aid could spark borrowing to make up for the shortfall. In addition, economic growth displays a negative effect; as the economy grows, more resources are available to the economy and, hence, there is no need to resort to borrowing. These results are in line with the findings of Azolibe (2021) and part of the results of Abotsi (2023). Financial integration is significant in driving public debt, which is a result of increasing access to the international capital market. Inflation is also shown to have a positive effect on borrowing, as it erodes economic gains and increases the cost of living, thereby necessitating further government expenditure. Finally, the real exchange rate poses a negative effect on debt, signifying that, as real exchange rate increases, it reduces the real burden of domestic debt, thereby improving fiscal space and consequently the need for further borrowing.

*Demographic and Structural Determinants of Public Debt*

The demographic factors captured in Table 2.5 show that education and health contribute positively to the level of debt in Africa, while an improvement in the standard of living drives down the level of debt. Education and health are key developmental issues captured in the SDGs; hence, African countries allocate significant proportions of their budget to these sectors, leading to an increase in debt levels, as noted by Sinha et al. (2011). Digitalisation comes with efficiency gains and cost reduction; hence, the variable exerts a downward effect on debt, in line with the observation of Tsvirko (2021). Increasing urbanisation calls for an increase

**Table 2.5** Determinants of debt accumulation (demographic and structural factors): MMQREG and OLS approach

| | *(1)* | *(2)* | *(3)* | *(4)* | *(5)* | *(6)* |
|---|---|---|---|---|---|---|
| VARIABLES | location | scale | qtile_25 | qtile_50 | qtile_75 | OLS |
| edu | 3.587*** | 3.394*** | 0.758 | 2.448*** | 5.020*** | 3.587*** |
| | (1.072) | (1.152) | (0.496) | (0.738) | (1.492) | (1.077) |
| standlv | −0.00679*** | −0.00497*** | −0.00265*** | −0.00512*** | −0.00889*** | −0.00679*** |
| | (0.00120) | (0.00112) | (0.000662) | (0.000899) | (0.00167) | (0.00120) |
| health | 2.479*** | 1.493*** | 1.234*** | 1.977*** | 3.109*** | 2.479*** |
| | (0.455) | (0.501) | (0.150) | (0.303) | (0.695) | (0.458) |
| urban | 0.716*** | 0.274* | 0.487*** | 0.624*** | 0.832*** | 0.716*** |
| | (0.155) | (0.154) | (0.0897) | (0.117) | (0.216) | (0.156) |
| digit | −0.162** | −0.324*** | 0.108*** | −0.0531 | −0.299*** | −0.162** |
| | (0.0709) | (0.0667) | (0.0300) | (0.0518) | (0.106) | (0.0712) |
| popnum | −1.18e − 07** | 1.49e − 08 | −1.30e − 07*** | −1.23e − 07*** | −1.11e − 07 | −1.18e − 07** |
| | (5.19e − 08) | (5.35e − 08) | (2.05e − 08) | (3.61e − 08) | (7.35e − 08) | (5.22e − 08) |
| Constant | −102.7*** | −52.78** | −58.74*** | −85.02*** | −125.0*** | −102.7*** |
| | (24.00) | (26.67) | (8.230) | (15.91) | (35.97) | (24.12) |
| Observations | 683 | 683 | 683 | 683 | 683 | 683 |
| F(6, 676) | | | | | | 21.78 |
| Prob.>F | | | | | | 0.0000 |
| R-squared | | | | | | 0.142 |

Robust standard errors in parentheses

*** $p < 0.01$; ** $p < 0.05$; * $p < 0.1$

in infrastructure such as energy, housing, and security, among others. As a result, it exerts a positive effect on public debt. However, contrary to expectations, the population shows a negative effect on debt. This requires further assessment.

*Institutional and Political Determinants of Public Debt*

Regulatory quality and voice and accountability have been shown to dampen public borrowing (see Table 2.6). This shows that when citizens are involved in the governance process and regulatory institutions are working, it puts the government in check and reduces wastage. These findings are supported by Abotsi (2023) and partially by Nikolaidou and Okwoche (2023). Control of corruption, however, showed a positive effect on debt, contrary to expectations.

**Table 2.6** Determinants of debt accumulation (institutional and political factors)

| | (1) | (2) | (3) | (4) | (5) | (6) |
|---|---|---|---|---|---|---|
| VARIABLES | location | scale | qtile_25 | qtile_50 | qtile_75 | OLS |
| concurpt | 0.787*** | 0.585*** | 0.258** | 0.577*** | 1.042*** | 0.787*** |
| | (0.185) | (0.133) | (0.123) | (0.152) | (0.238) | (0.186) |
| goveff | 0.435 | 0.547* | −0.0597 | 0.238 | 0.673 | 0.435 |
| | (0.307) | (0.296) | (0.182) | (0.233) | (0.432) | (0.309) |
| polista | 0.119 | 0.00121 | 0.118 | 0.119 | 0.120 | 0.119 |
| | (0.145) | (0.136) | (0.0774) | (0.107) | (0.197) | (0.145) |
| rq | −1.769*** | −1.472*** | −0.438** | −1.240*** | −2.411*** | −1.769*** |
| | (0.319) | (0.299) | (0.173) | (0.238) | (0.461) | (0.321) |
| rl | 0.344 | 0.255 | 0.113 | 0.252 | 0.455 | 0.344 |
| | (0.273) | (0.267) | (0.151) | (0.199) | (0.373) | (0.274) |
| voacc | −0.666*** | −0.527*** | −0.189* | −0.476*** | −0.895*** | −0.666*** |
| | (0.224) | (0.198) | (0.111) | (0.166) | (0.313) | (0.225) |
| Constant | 77.34*** | 47.89*** | 34.01*** | 60.11*** | 98.21*** | 77.34*** |
| | (6.028) | (5.304) | (3.289) | (4.620) | (9.112) | (6.059) |
| Observations | 684 | 684 | 684 | 684 | 684 | 684 |
| F (6, 677) | | | | | | 10.33 |
| Prob.>F | | | | | | 0.0000 |
| R-squared | | | | | | 0.114 |

Robust standard errors in parentheses

*** $p < 0.01$; ** $p < 0.05$; * $p < 0.1$

## 2.6 Conclusion and Policy Recommendations

Public debt poses a critical challenge to the development of developing countries, including African countries. This has many policy implications regarding welfare and development. This study contributes to the literature by adopting a disaggregated approach to examine the determinants of public debt. Using the quintile method of moment, this study examines the varied impact of economic, demographic, structural, institutional, and political factors on public debt dynamics in Africa using a panel of 38 African countries from 2006 to 2023. The results show that economic factors account for more variations in public debt than other factors, as captured by the R-squared value. In terms of the individual effect, aid, economic growth, and exchange rate as economic factors had a negative effect, while financial integration and inflation displayed a positive effect. With respect to demographic and structural factors, health, education, and urbanisation emerged as key drivers of public debt, while digitalisation showed a negative effect. Finally, regulatory quality and voice and accountability as institutional factors exhibited downward pressure on debt. The varied findings mean that policymakers will have to take into account the varied impact of these factors on public debt. Countries. Achieving macroeconomic stability and improving institutional quality can contribute to maintaining sustainable and moderate levels of public debt.

## References

Abotsi, A. K. (2023). Influence of governance indicators on public debt accumulation in Africa. *Journal of Economic and Administrative Sciences*, (ahead-of-print).

Abubakar, A. B., McCausland, W. D., & Theodossiou, I. (2025). Do debt relief and fiscal rules improve public debt sustainability? The experience of sub-Sahara African countries. *Journal of Policy Modeling, 47*(1), 166–186. https://doi.org/10.1016/j.jpolmod.2024.06.007

Acar, O., & Öztürk, N. (2025). The role of public debt in economic growth: The case of Türkiye (2000–2024). *Journal of Finance Letters (Maliye ve Finans Yazıları), 40*(123), 188–209.

Acheampong, T., & Vitenu-Sackey, P. A. (2024, October 10). *Industrialisation in Africa: Leading countries and reasons for their success.* Africa Policy Research Institute. https://afripoli.org/industrialisation-in-africa-leading-countries-and-reasons-for-their-success

Aimola, A. U., & Odhiambo, N. M. (2021). Public debt and inflation: Empirical evidence from Ghana. *Development Studies Research, 8*(1), 1–13. https://doi.org/10.1080/21665095.2021.1872392

Alesina, A., & Perotti, R. (1995). The political economy of budget deficits. *IMF Staff Papers, 42*(1), 1–31. https://doi.org/10.2307/3867336

Alesina, A., & Tabellini, G. E. (1986). A positive theory of fiscal deficits and government debt in a democracy. National Bureau of Economic Research.

Appiah-Kubi, S. N. K., Malec, K., Phiri, J., Krivko, M., Maitah, K., Maitah, M., & Smutka, L. (2022). Key drivers of public debt levels: Empirical evidence from Africa. *Sustainability, 14*(3), 1220.

Azolibe, C. B. (2021). Determinants of external indebtedness in heavily indebted poor countries: What macroeconomic and socio-economic factors matter? *The American Economist, 66*(2), 249–264.

Baban, R.C. and Greene, M. J. E. (1992). *The export performance of sub-Saharan Africa, 1970-19+ L69390: A survey.* International Monetary Fund. IMF Working Papers, 1992(055), A001. Retrieved September 27, 2025, from https://doi.org/10.5089/9781451847567.001.A001

Barro, R. J. (1979). On the determination of the public debt. *Journal of Political Economy, 87*(5), 940–971. https://doi.org/10.1086/260807

Baum, A., Checherita-Westphal, C., & Rother, P. (2013). Debt and growth: New evidence for the euro area. *Journal of International Money and Finance, 32*, 809–821.

Benson, E. A. (2022, August 12). These 34 African countries are on the heavily indebted poor countries list according to the World Bank. *Business Insider Africa.* https://africa.businessinsider.com/local/markets/these-34-african-countries-are-on-the-heavily-indebted-poor-countries-list-according/prtlq90

Bose, S., & Banerjee, S. (2025). Social spending and fiscal policy in India: Towards an alternate macro-fiscal framework integrating human development. National Institute of Public Finance and Policy.

Carrera, J., & de la Vega, P. (2021). The impact of income inequality on public debt. *The Journal of Economic Asymmetries, 24*, e00216.

Chhabra, M., Giri, A. K., & Kumar, A. (2023). *What shapes economic growth in BRICS? Exploring the role of institutional quality and trade openness.* Economic Papers. https://doi.org/10.1111/1759-3441.12378

Chuku, C., & Yenice, M. Y. (2022). Eurobonds, debt sustainability and macroeconomic performance in Africa: Synthetic control experiments. *International Economics, 172*, 368–388.

Cifuentes-Faura, J., & Simionescu, M. (2024). Analyzing the importance of the determinants of public debt and its policy implications: A survey of literature. *Public Finance Review, 52*(3), 345–375.

Commodore, R., & Awuah, G. B. (2024, November 19). *The changing nature of debt in Africa.* African Center for Economic Transformation. https://acetforafrica.org/research-and-analysis/insights-ideas/the-changing-nature-of-debt-in-africa/

Da, D., & Diarra, M. (2023). Effect of international commodity price shocks on public finances in Africa. *Public Finance Review, 51*(2), 236–261. https://doi.org/10.1177/10911421221137426

Delessa, K., Alemu, T., & Bane, J. (2024). Remittances inflow and economic growth nexus in sub-Saharan Africa: Do institutional quality and macroeconomic stability matter? *Heliyon, 10*(3). https://doi.org/10.1016/j.heliyon.2024.e25690

Development Reimagined. (2024, May 28). *Africa & Eurobonds: How many Eurobonds does Africa have and how might it impact their budgets in the future?* Development Reimagined. Retrieved September 23, 2025, from https://developmentreimagined.com/africa-and-eurobonds-how-many-eurobonds-does-africa-have-and-how-might-it-impact-their-budgets-in-the-future/

Égert, B. (2015). The 90% public debt threshold: The rise and fall of a stylized fact. *Applied Economics, 47*(34–35), 3756–3770.

Eichengreen, B., & Hausmann, R. (1999). *Exchange rates and financial fragility.* NBER Working Paper No. 7418. National Bureau of Economic Research. https://doi.org/10.3386/w7418

Friedrich-Ebert-Stiftung (2023). *The African Union and the G20: How African states can achieve collective agency.* (FES Briefing Paper). PG 10 Friedrich-Ebert-Stiftung. https://library.fes.de/pdf-files/bueros/fesua/19365-20231010.pdf

Fuseini, E. I. (2025). *Institutional quality-banking efficiency nexuses in Africa. How does ICT moderate?* (pp. 1–25). Information Technology for Development. https://doi.org/10.1080/02681102.2025.2460157

Hammes, D., & Wills, D. (2005). Black gold: The end of Bretton woods and the oil-price shocks of the 1970s. *The Independent Review, 9*(4), 501–511.

Hlongwane, N. W., & Daw, O. D. (2022). *Determinants of public debt in South Africa: A regime-switching approach* (p. 113203). MPRA Paper.

International Monetary Fund. (1989). *The external debt problem of sub-Saharan Africa.* International Monetary Fund (IMF), Working Paper 89/23. https://www.elibrary.imf.org/view/journals/001/1989/023/article-A001-en.xml

Kaufmann, D., Kraay, A., & Mastruzzi, M. (2010). *The worldwide governance indicators: Methodology and analytical issues.* World Bank Policy Research, Working Paper 5430, 1682130. http://ssrn.com/abstract

Keynes, J. M. (2018). The general theory of employment, interest, and money. Springer.

Klutse, S. K., Sági, J., & Kiss, G. D. (2023). The role of COVID-19 in worsening the debt sustainability in developing economies–The case of Ghana and Kenya. *Regional Science Policy & Practice, 15*(6), 1259–1276.

Koenker, R., & Bassett, G. (1978). Regression Quantiles. *Econometrica, 46*(1), 33–50. JSTOR. https://doi.org/10.2307/1913643

Kose, M. A., Nagle, P., Ohnsorge, F., & Sugawara, N. (2021). *Global waves of debt: Causes and consequences.* World Bank Publications.

Lucas, R. E., Jr., & Stokey, N. L. (1983). Optimal fiscal and monetary policy in an economy without capital. *Journal of Monetary Economics, 12*(1), 55–93. https://doi.org/10.1016/0304-3932(83)90049-1

Machado, J. A. F., & Santos Silva, J. M. C. (2019). Quantiles via moments. *Annals: In Honor of Roger Koenker, 213*(1), 145–173. https://doi.org/10.1016/j.jeconom.2019.04.009

Majumder, M. K., Raghavan, M., & Vespignani, J. L. (2021). Impact of commodity price volatility on external debt: The role of exchange rate regimes. *Applied Economics, 53*(57), 6626–6640.

Marozva, G., & Magwedere, M. R. (2025). Uncertainty, FDI inflows, and financial market development: Empirical evidence. *Economies, 13*(6), 147. https://doi.org/10.3390/economies13060147

Milesi-Ferretti, Gian Maria (2024). The External Wealth of Nations Database, The Brookings Institution (based on Lane, Philip R. and Gian Maria Milesi-Ferretti, 2018, The External Wealth of Nations Revisited: International Financial Integration in the Aftermath of the Global Financial Crisis).

Musah, I. (2023). An empirical investigation of macroeconomic determinants of public debt in Ghana. *Cogent Economics & Finance, 11*(2), 2285625.

Ncanywa, T., & Masoga, M. M. (2018). Can public debt stimulate public investment and economic growth in South Africa? *Cogent Economics & Finance, 6*(1). https://doi.org/10.1080/23322039.2018.1516483

Nikolaidou, E., & Okwoche, P. (2023). Determinants of government debt in sub-Saharan African countries: The role of conflict, governance, and economic factors. *Peace Economics, Peace Science and Public Policy, 29*(2), 145–170.

Persson, T., & Svensson, L. E. (1989). Why a stubborn conservative would run a deficit: Policy with time-inconsistent preferences. *The Quarterly Journal of Economics, 104*(2), 325–345.

Prebisch, R. (1950). *The economic development of Latin America and its principal problems.* United Nations, Economic Commission for Latin America.

Reinhart, C. M., & Rogoff, K. S. (2010). Growth in a time of debt. *American Economic Review, 100*, 573–578.

Rios-Avila, F. (2022). *MMQREG: Stata module to estimate quantile regressions via method of moments* [Computer software]. https://EconPapers.repec.org/RePEc:boc:bocode:s458750.

Sasmal, J., & Sasmal, R. (2020). Public debt, economic growth and fiscal balance: Alternative measures of sustainability in the Indian context. *Global Business Review, 21*(3), 780–799.

Simson, R. (2019). Africa's lost decades, 1974–1994. In M. Jerven (Ed.), *The economic history of Africa: An introduction (African economic history network textbook)*. African Economic History Network. https://www.aehnetwork.org/textbook/africas-lost-decades-1974-1994/

Sinha, P., Arora, V., & Bansal, V. (2011). *Determinants of public debt for middle income and high income group countries using panel data regression*. University Library of Munich, Munich Personal RePEc Archive (MPRA) Paper 32079. https://mpra.ub.uni-muenchen.de/32079/

Soludo, C. C. (1998). 10 Africa: Industrialization strategy in the context of globalization. In *Trade reform and regional integration in Africa*. International Monetary Fund. Retrieved September 27, 2025, from https://doi.org/10.5089/9781557757692.071.ch010

Tsvirko, S. (2021, June). Digital technologies for prudent public debt management. In *International conference on comprehensible science* (pp. 108–117). Springer International Publishing.

UNCTAD. (2025). *A world of debt: It is time to reform*. UNCTAD. https://unctad.org/publication/world-of-debt

United Nations Conference on Trade and Development. (2016). *Economic development in Africa report 2016: Debt dynamics and development finance in Africa*. UNCTAD.

World Bank. (1994). *Adjustment in Africa: Reforms, results, and the road ahead*. Oxford University Press.

World Bank. (2024). *International debt report 2024*. World Bank. https://hdl.handle.net/10986/42444

World Bank Group. (2016). *Ghana's development finance institutions: Review of current status and principles for reform*. World Bank. http://hdl.handle.net/10986/30215

CHAPTER 3

# Measuring What Matters: Context-Specific Debt Sustainability Metrics for Sub-Saharan Africa

*Ibrahim Nandom Yakubu and Muazu Ibrahim*

## 3.1 Introduction

Debt remains a pivotal yet paradoxical instrument for countries in sub-Saharan Africa (SSA). On the one hand, public borrowing is an indispensable source of financing for infrastructure, social programs, and structural transformation (Adeve & Karabou, 2022; Gallagher et al., 2024). On the other hand, unsustainable debt burdens can undermine fiscal space, trigger macroeconomic instability, and reverse hard-won development gains. More recently, Atta-Mensah and Ibrahim (2024) find that unbridled debt accumulation above certain estimated thresholds does not lower income inequality, indicating that the income inequality–reducing impact of debt holds at lower levels of debt. They conclude that while debts serve as additional financing options for countries, they could also contribute to increasing income inequality. Debt sustainability, therefore, is not merely

I. N. Yakubu (✉) • M. Ibrahim
School of Business, University for Development Studies, Tamale, Ghana
e-mail: ibrahim.yakubu@uds.edu.gh; imuazu@uds.edu.gh



I. N. Yakubu (ed.), *Public Debt and Economic Resilience in Africa*, Palgrave Studies in African and Development Economics,
https://doi.org/10.1007/978-3-032-25835-9_3

a technical measure but a central concern for economic governance and social development. It generally refers to a government's capacity to meet current and future debt service obligations in full without recourse to exceptional financing or default while maintaining growth and macroeconomic stability (Hakura, 2020). In practice, debt sustainability is assessed through a combination of quantitative indicators, forward-looking projections, and stress tests that estimate the likelihood of distress under different scenarios.

Historically, the assessment of public debt sustainability has revolved around conventional benchmarks, particularly the public debt-to-GDP ratio. A ratio of 60% has often been cited as a prudential ceiling, drawing from the Maastricht criteria for European economies, and subsequently applied to emerging and developing countries.[1] Yet, the debt experience of SSA economies over the past decade reveals that such one-size-fits-all thresholds can be misleading. As shown in Fig. 3.1, public debt in SSA has experienced a dramatic surge over the past decade, nearly doubling to reach an estimated US$688 billion in 2024, twice the level recorded in 2014. External borrowing dominates this expansion, accounting for approximately two-thirds of the total public debt across the region. Domestic debt markets have also grown substantially, particularly following the COVID-19 pandemic, when many SSA countries faced reduced access to international capital markets amid rising global interest rates and weakening credit conditions. However, domestic obligations remain a small component of the region's overall debt burden, with external financing continuing to drive debt accumulation. The expansion of domestic debt markets accelerated in the post-pandemic period, as many SSA countries faced reduced access to international capital markets because of rising global interest rates and deteriorating credit conditions.

While debt has played a crucial role in closing SSA's financing gap, its rapid growth has intensified concerns about sustainability. The burden of debt service has escalated sharply. As shown in Fig. 3.2, domestic debt service in SSA has consistently exceeded external debt service since 2014, with the gap widening sharply in recent years. Median domestic debt service peaked at 4.7% of GDP in 2024—more than double external debt service obligations—largely driven by expanded domestic borrowing and increasing reliance on shorter-term, higher-cost instruments. This shift

[1] Read more here: https://www.bundesbank.de/en/statistics/public-finances/maastricht-deficit-and-debt-level/maastricht-deficit-and-debt-level-793140

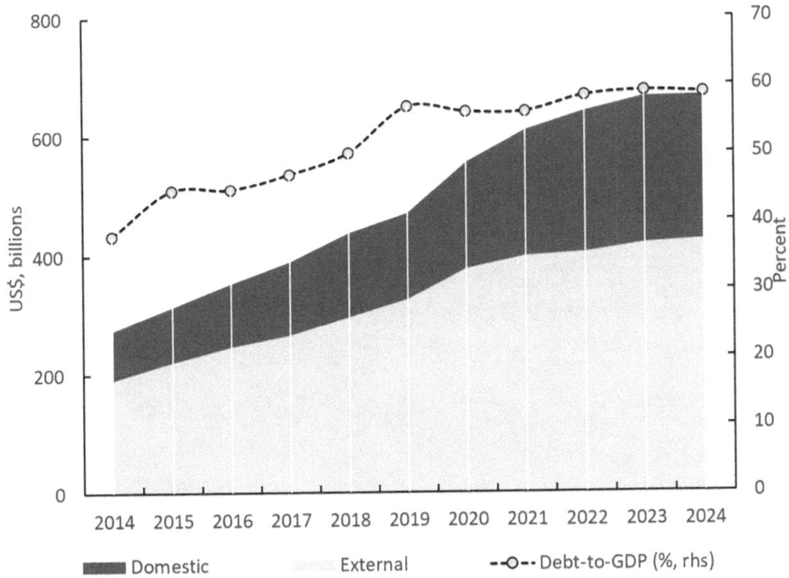


**Fig. 3.1** Evolution of public debt in SSA. Source: World Bank (2025)

represents a double-edged sword. While local debt market development has enhanced financing flexibility and reduced external vulnerabilities, it has also elevated fiscal risks. Governments now face higher interest burdens that strain public finances and an increased risk of crowding out private investments. At the same time, higher debt service obligations squeeze out resources for health, education, and infrastructure (Dryden & Volz, 2025). Alarmingly, more than half of SSA countries now spend more on interest payments than on health care, underscoring the opportunity cost of debt.[2] For example, the Tony Blair Institute for Global Change estimates that Ghana's interest payments absorbed roughly 26% of government revenues in 2023 compared to only 3% in France, even though Ghana's debt-to-GDP ratio was relatively lower. This contrast highlights a critical insight: headline debt ratios, while useful, may fail to capture the true burden of debt, which is a function of not only its size but also its cost, structure, and fiscal capacity. These realities underscore that debt

[2] https://drgr.org/files/2025/09/DRGR-Africa-Debt-Crisis.pdf#:~:text=burden%20has%20been%20worsened%20by,per%20year%20%E2%80%93%20with%20over

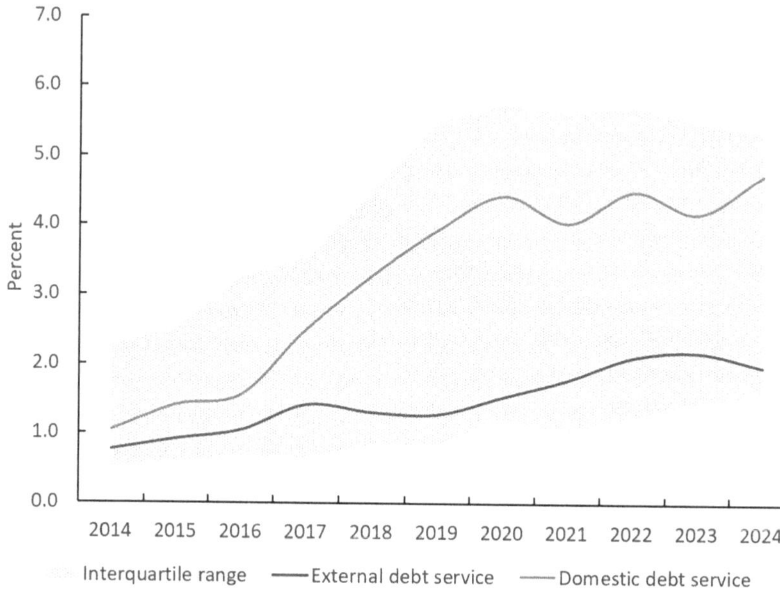


**Fig. 3.2** Median debt service-to-GDP in SSA. Source: Authors' computation based on data from the LIC DSF database as of end-June 2025

sustainability in SSA cannot be adequately understood using debt-to-GDP metrics alone.

SSA economies also face unique structural constraints, such as narrow export bases, dependence on volatile commodities, shallow domestic capital markets, and pressing development financing requirements (Gallagher et al., 2024). Applying conventional debt sustainability metrics rigidly, without accounting for these factors, risks misdiagnosing debt risks or prescribing inappropriate policy responses (Anajama & Nyamudzanga, 2025). These limitations potentially underscore the need for context-sensitive diagnostics to assess debt sustainability.

This chapter argues for a fundamental rethinking of debt sustainability metrics in SSA. Section 3.2 reviews the conventional indicators and their theoretical basis. Section 3.3 explores their limitations, particularly in low-income and commodity-dependent contexts. Section 3.4 proposes context-specific indicators that better capture SSA's realities, while Sect. 3.5 discusses innovative approaches and models for assessing sustainability.

Section 3.6 highlights the policy relevance of adopting improved indicators, especially for fiscal planning and debt relief negotiations. Finally, Sect. 3.7 concludes with key recommendations for integrating these rethought indicators into policymaking. The overarching objective is to move beyond simplistic debt thresholds toward a more nuanced, forward-looking approach that allows economies in SSA to borrow responsibly for development without falling into debt distress.

## 3.2 Conventional Indicators of Debt Sustainability

Assessing public debt sustainability traditionally relies on a set of quantitative indicators designed to measure a country's debt burden relative to its economic size, output, and repayment capacity. These indicators serve as early warning tools for policymakers and international financial institutions. They are widely used because of their simplicity, data availability, and ease of cross-country comparability. However, their interpretation must be cautious, as it offers a partial view of the complex debt dynamics at play. This section provides an overview of the key traditional debt sustainability indicators.

### *3.2.1 Present Value of Total Public Debt-to-GDP Ratio: The Headline Indicator*

The debt-to-GDP ratio remains the most widely used indicator of debt sustainability, expressing the total stock of public debt as a share of gross domestic product (GDP) and offering a broad measure of a country's debt burden relative to the size of its economy (Were, 2024). Policymakers frequently rely on threshold values as reference points for assessing whether debt is sustainable. The well-known 60% debt-to-GDP benchmark, first introduced under the European Union's Maastricht criteria, is often applied, sometimes uncritically, to developing and emerging economies (Vîntu, 2025).

While such benchmarks provide a useful yardstick, they are not absolute scientific limits. Debt sustainability ultimately depends on country-specific factors, such as fiscal capacity, revenue mobilization, interest rate dynamics, and long-term growth prospects (Anajama & Nyamudzanga, 2025). Crossing these benchmarks, however, can have immediate repercussions by eroding investor confidence, prompting credit rating downgrades, and increasing sovereign borrowing costs (Gallagher et al., 2024). In many SSA countries, debt-to-GDP ratios have risen rapidly since the mid-2010s, with several countries exceeding 70% or even 80% levels that have historically been associated with elevated risk of debt distress and vulnerability to external shocks.[3] This underscores the importance of looking beyond numerical thresholds and adopting a more comprehensive approach that incorporates other metrics not explored in current debt sustainability frameworks (DSF), including the efficiency of public investment.

#### 3.2.2 *Debt-Service-to-Revenue and Interest Burden Indicators*

In addition to stock measures such as debt-to-GDP, debt sustainability analysis also considers indicators of debt service, which capture the government's ability to meet its debt obligations given its fiscal resources.[4] The debt-service-to-revenue ratio compares the total public debt service (interest plus principal repayments) to government revenues. A high ratio implies that debt obligations absorb a large share of fiscal capacity, crowding out social spending and investment. The Debt Sustainability Framework for Low Income Countries (LIC DSF) of the World Bank and International Monetary Fund (IMF) uses indicative thresholds, which are linked to a country's debt-carrying capacity when analyzing its risk of external debt distress. These thresholds are indicative limits above which the risk of debt distress is considered elevated (IMF and World Bank, 2018). The threshold for public and publicly guaranteed (PPG) external debt service to revenue is set at 14% for countries with weak debt-carrying capacity, 18% for countries with medium debt-carrying capacity, and 23% for countries with strong debt-carrying capacity. Thus, countries with stronger capacity benefit from higher thresholds and vice versa.

A closely related measure, the interest-to-revenue ratio, isolates the share of revenues absorbed by interest payments alone (Mehrotra & Sergeyev, 2021). This indicator is particularly useful for gauging debt affordability over the medium term because interest is a non-discretionary expenditure that must be paid regardless of fiscal pressures. Persistently

[3] https://www.imf.org/-/media/Files/Publications/REO/AFR/2024/October/English/text.ashx

[4] For a detailed explanation of debt servicing, visit https://www.firecapitalmanagement.com/finance-101/understanding-debt-servicing-cost-an-essential-indicator-for-fiscal-policy

high interest burdens can crowd out productive investment, create liquidity stress, and even precipitate fiscal crises if left unchecked.[5]

Credit rating agencies and investors closely monitor these serviceability ratios because they provide early warning signals of potential repayment difficulties. A rising interest-to-revenue ratio can trigger credit rating downgrades, leading to higher borrowing costs and a self-reinforcing cycle of fiscal stress.[6] When combined with other indicators, such as the ratio of external debt service to export earnings or the share of short-term debt in total obligations, these metrics provide a more comprehensive picture of debt vulnerability than stock measures alone. For SSA economies, where export earnings and government revenues are often volatile, monitoring serviceability indicators is essential for anticipating liquidity pressures and designing timely corrective measures.

### 3.2.3 Present Value (PV) of PPG External Debt Indicators: Exports as the Denominator

For PPG external debt, analysts often use exports rather than GDP as the denominator, reflecting the fact that external obligations are often repaid in foreign currency.[7] The external debt-to-exports ratio measures the total outstanding PPG external debt against annual export earnings, serving as a key solvency indicator. Historically, under the Heavily Indebted Poor Countries (HIPC) Initiative, the PV of external debt at or above 150% of exports was considered unsustainable, meeting an eligibility criterion for debt relief.[8]

Equally important is the PPG external debt-service-to-exports ratio, which measures actual foreign currency payments due each year relative to export receipts. This indicates liquidity pressure: the higher the share of export earnings consumed by external debt payments, the greater the risk of reserve depletion and default.[9] The World Bank–IMF's thresholds

[5] https://www.elibrary.imf.org/view/journals/002/2024/334/article-A002-en.xml

[6] https://www.analystinterview.com/article/debt-service-coverage-ratio-its-critical-role-in-shaping-credit-ratings

[7] https://unstats.un.org/unsd/nationalaccount/docs/External_debt_statistics_guide.pdf

[8] Read more here: https://www.imf.org/external/pubs/ft/exrp/debt/eng/#:~:text=The%20debt%2Dto%2Dexports%20target%20is%20now%20150%20percent,with%20the%20eligibility%20thresholds%20reduced%20as%20follows:

[9] https://www.imf.org/external/pubs/ft/eds/eng/guide/file4.pdf

range from 10% to 21% of exports, depending on the country's debt-carrying capacity.[10] Several SSA countries, including Chad, Ethiopia, Ghana, and Zambia, have breached these levels in recent years, leading to debt service standstill or restructuring.[11]

### *3.2.4 Debt Dynamics and Primary Balance Requirements*

Beyond static ratios, debt sustainability analysis also examines debt dynamics, including the primary balance needed to stabilize debt at a given level. The debt-stabilizing primary balance considers the interest rate on debt, the real growth rate of the economy, and the initial debt stock. When interest rates exceed growth rates, which is common in many countries in SSA, a large primary surplus is required to prevent debt ratios from increasing (Aboagye, 2025). Conversely, strong growth can allow higher debt levels to be sustained, even with modest deficits. Atta-Mensah and Ibrahim (2020) argue that with the interest rate–growth differential as the main driver of overall debt dynamics, SSA countries need to maintain high real growth rates in order to ensure debt sustainability.

Indeed, stress testing forms a core part of the DSF (Cömert et al., 2024). Debt sustainability analysis projects debt trajectories under baseline macroeconomic conditions and tests their resilience by simulating shocks such as economic growth, primary balance, exports, currency depreciation, and other flows (e.g., current transfer and FDI).[12] In addition, other tailored stress tests are applied to countries exposed to a set of specific risks. These risks include natural disasters, volatile commodity prices, and market financing pressures.

Stress tests are designed to identify potential vulnerabilities before they manifest as crises. For instance, a country is assessed as having a low risk of external debt distress if none of the PPG external debt burden indicators breach their respective thresholds under the baseline or most extreme stress test. However, if none of the PPG external debt burden indicators breach their thresholds under the baseline, but at least one indicator breaches its threshold under the stress tests, then the country is rated as at

[10] https://www.elibrary.imf.org/view/journals/001/2023/079/article-A001-en.xml#:~:text=,used%20to%20assess%20debt

[11] https://afrodad.org/sites/default/files/publications/Afrodad%20Debt%20Restructuring%202082024.pdf

[12] https://www.imf.org/external/pubs/ft/dsa/

a moderate risk of external debt distress. Given the high risk of external debt distress, any PPG external debt burden indicator should breach the threshold even under the baseline.

For countries with durable and sustained market access, the IMF assesses their debt sustainability using the Sovereign Risk and Debt Sustainability Framework for Market Access Countries (MAC SRDSF), which incorporates probabilistic benchmarks, including Gross Financing Needs (GFNs) and sovereign bond spreads, to examine rollover risk and investor sentiment.[13] These approaches provide a forward-looking assessment of whether a country's fiscal position is robust enough to withstand adverse scenarios and continue meeting its obligations without resorting to disruptive adjustment measures.

### 3.2.5 *The IMF–World Bank Debt Sustainability Framework (DSF) for Low-Income Countries (LIC DSF)*

International financial institutions have formalized these metrics within the LIC DSF. The DSF combines multiple indicators in a comprehensive risk assessment. It focuses on five key ratios: PV of PPG external debt-to-GDP, PV of external debt-to-exports, PPG external debt service-to-exports, PPG external debt service-to-revenue, and PV of total public debt-to-GDP. Each of these indicators is compared against capacity-adjusted thresholds that depend on a country's assessed debt-carrying capacity, which is based on the World Bank's Country Policy and Institutional Assessment (CPIA) score, country-specific factors (real growth rate, remittances, and import coverage of reserves), and external conditions (world growth). Table 3.1 summarizes the indicative thresholds used under the LIC DSF.

Countries breaching these thresholds under baseline or stress-test scenarios are classified as being at high risk of debt distress or in distress. Recent data from the World Bank show that SSA's debt distress peaked in 2021 and continues to pose significant challenges to fiscal stability and development, despite some improvement. As shown in Fig. 3.3, risk levels in the region reveal a troubling trend: the number of SSA countries either experiencing debt distress or facing high risk has nearly tripled over the past decade, rising from 8 in 2014 to 23 in 2025. This means that almost

[13] https://www.imf.org/en/About/Factsheets/Sheets/2023/imf-world-bank-debt-sustainability-framework-for-low-income-countries

**Table 3.1** IMF–World Bank thresholds based on LIC DSF

| *Indicator* | *Strong debt-carrying capacity (if composite indicator (CI) < 2.69)* | *Medium debt-carrying capacity (if CI is 2.69 ≤ CI ≤ 3.05)* | *Weak debt-carrying capacity (if CI is ≤ 3.05)* |
|---|---|---|---|
| PV of external debt-to-GDP | 55% | 40% | 30% |
| PV of external debt-to-exports | 240% | 180% | 140% |
| External debt service-to-exports | 21% | 15% | 10% |
| External debt service-to-revenue | 23% | 18% | 14% |
| PV of total public debt-to-GDP | 70% | 55% | 35% |

Source: IMF and World Bank (2018)

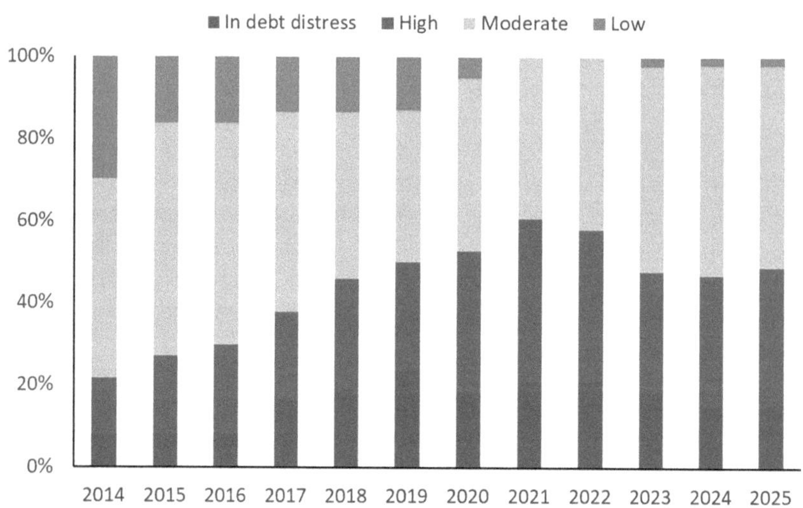


**Fig. 3.3** External risk of debt distress in SSA. Source: World Bank (2025)

half (49%) of all SSA countries now fall into this vulnerable category. Several interconnected factors have driven this deterioration. These include the lasting impact of borrowing during crisis periods, chronic shortfalls in revenue collection, an increasing shift toward non-concessional financing from sources outside traditional multilateral institutions, and inadequate debt management systems (World Bank, 2025). The multitude of factors that explain the risk of debt distress underscores the significance of designing multifaceted debt metrics to help improve debt policy and debt management.

### *3.2.6 Revised IMF–World Bank LIC DSF*

In response to mounting pressure from debtor countries and evidence of recurring debt crises, the IMF and World Bank overhauled the LIC DSF.[14] The revised DSA lengthened projection horizons, incorporated more rigorous stress tests, and introduced a composite index to capture the debt-carrying capacity. Crucially, it expanded its focus to include total public debt, thereby acknowledging the growing role of domestic borrowing in SSA economies.

For market-access countries, including those in SSA, the IMF introduced the MAC SRDSF in 2021.[15] This framework places greater emphasis on market signals, fiscal stress tests, and debt profile indicators, such as spreads and Gross Financing Needs (GFN). The revisions represent a shift toward probabilistic and risk-based analysis, acknowledging that debt sustainability is not binary but a matter of likelihood under varying scenarios.[16] Nonetheless, even these updated frameworks remain largely liability-focused and do not systematically incorporate the asset side or social spending needs (Gill & Pinto, 2024).

## 3.3 Limitations of Standard Debt Metrics

Conventional indicators are widely used because they are simple and comparable across countries. However, they have important limitations, especially in developing countries, where their structural features, financing terms, and development needs differ markedly from those assumed in standard frameworks. This section synthesizes the main critiques.

[14] https://ieg.worldbankgroup.org/evaluations/world-banks-role-and-use-low-income-country-debt-sustainability-framework/chapter-2-low

[15] https://www.imf.org/en/Publications/DSA/sovereign-risk-and-debt-sustainability-analysis-for-market-access-countries

[16] https://g24.org/wp-content/uploads/2023/09/Jeromin-Zettelmeyer_MAC-DSA-Presentation-to-G24.pdf

#### 3.3.1 *Ignoring the Purpose of Debt and the Asset Side*

Headline ratios provide a static snapshot of liabilities and often overlook what the borrowed resources finance (Guzman, 2018; Zucker-Marques et al., 2024). A debt-to-GDP ratio does not distinguish between loans used for productive investment, such as power and transport infrastructure, and borrowing for recurrent spending or consumption. This can create an anti-investment bias, as countries borrowing for development may look as risky as those borrowing for less productive uses, even when the former can yield growth and revenue to service debt over time (Zucker-Marques et al., 2024). The standard DSA treats debt uniformly as a liability and does not bring public assets into the balance sheet (Wang & Xu, 2022). Ignoring the asset side can overstate risk, where debt finances infrastructure and human capital that expand future fiscal capacity. Assessments should examine how debt is used and whether it builds national balance-sheet strength rather than relying solely on debt-to-GDP limits.

#### 3.3.2 *Affordability, Borrowing Costs, and Exchange Rate Risk*

Indicators based on stocks do not reflect the cost of carrying that stock. Two countries can have similar debt-to-GDP ratios but face very different interest burdens if risk premia differ. SSA sovereigns often pay higher coupons than advanced economies due to their ratings, perceived risk, and market sentiment (Olabisi & Stein, 2024). Thus, a lower debt ratio can still coincide with high interest-to-revenue burdens, as illustrated by the cases of Ghana and France.[17] Standard metrics also understate currency risk. With a large share of external debt in foreign currency, depreciation can quickly raise the domestic-currency value of debt and debt service, pushing ratios off track. For instance, Ethiopia's 2024 depreciation significantly increased the local currency debt ratios.[18] Volatility in commodity prices similarly affects revenues and exports, making static thresholds less reliable in SSA.

[17] https://institute.global/insights/economic-prosperity/a-new-debt-deal-for-africa-breaking-the-vicious-cycle

[18] https://ethiopianpolicy.com/2025/01/21/ethiopias-public-debt-surges-as-currency-depreciation-continues/

### 3.3.3 Composition and Terms Matter

Not all debt is equal. Risk differs by maturity, currency, interest structure, and creditor type. Two countries with the same debt-to-GDP ratio may face very different rollover and liquidity risks if one relies on short-term external commercial instruments, while the other relies on long-term concessional loans (Ngundu & Cilliers, 2025).

The composition of PPG external debt in SSA has shifted significantly over the past decade, with private and multilateral creditors playing an increasingly prominent role. Between 2014 and 2023, international bond issuance by SSA countries doubled, while multilateral lending grew by 128% (Fig. 3.4). This evolving structure reflects efforts to diversify financing sources amid a decline in bilateral concessional flows following the HIPC era. While market-based instruments offer increased access to capital, they also expose countries to heightened refinancing risks and sensitivity to global interest rate cycles.

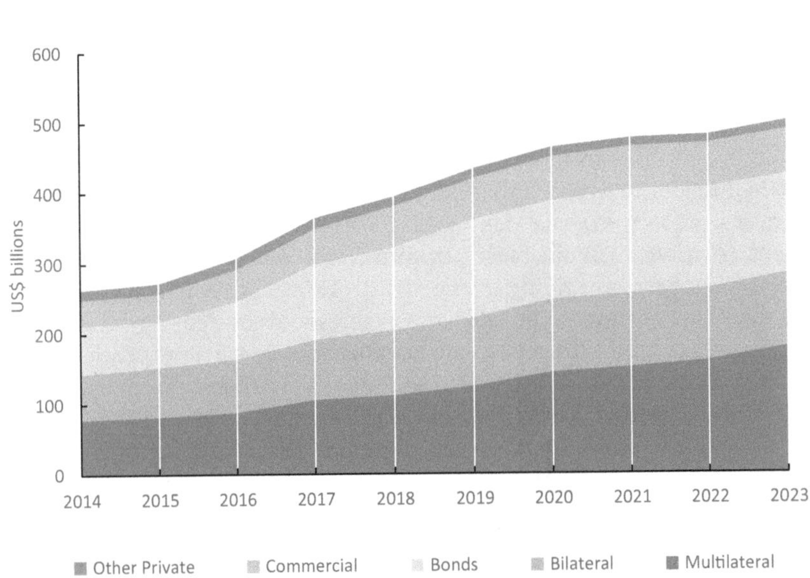


**Fig. 3.4** PPG external debt composition by creditor category. Source: Authors' computation based on data from the International Debt Statistics (IDS) of the World Bank

Commercial debt typically has higher coupons and shorter tenors. Simple stock ratios do not reveal maturity bunching, interest rate resets, or currency mismatches that drive crisis risk. In short, context matters, and composition should be explicit in sustainability assessments.

#### *3.3.4 Incomplete Coverage and Hidden Obligations*

Conventional indicators often exclude contingent liabilities and some parts of the broader public sector. State-owned enterprises (SOEs) may accumulate large debts, sometimes guaranteed, that fall to the central government once distress emerges (Horn et al., 2024). Mozambique's hidden-debt episode is a well-known cautionary case.[19] Focusing narrowly on central government liabilities can be misleading; guaranteed debt, SOE obligations, public–private partnership (PPP) commitments, and subnational borrowing can all pose fiscal risks.[20] Weak debt transparency in some countries means that certain loans, supplier credits, or PPP liabilities are omitted from official data, understating the true burden and delaying corrective action. Better coverage and disclosure are crucial for an accurate understanding of debt sustainability.

#### *3.3.5 Uniform Thresholds and Projection Bias*

One-size-fits-all thresholds are not appropriate for all regions (Raga, 2024). Evidence suggests that debt tolerance differs by structural characteristics. In SSA, external debt levels of 60–80% of GDP have been sufficient to trigger sustainability concerns, whereas some Latin American economies have historically tolerated 120–150% before default (Gallagher et al., 2024). Although the DSF adjusts thresholds by debt carrying capacity based on the CPIA and other macroeconomic variables, critics argue that the proxy can be imperfect and the calibrations appear optimistic (Graf Von Luckner, 2024; Fernando, 2025). Outcomes of the LIC DSF are sensitive to assumptions on growth, fiscal effort, and financing costs. If projections are overly optimistic, countries can be judged sustainable in theory until the debt crisis materializes. This optimism bias has been identified as a factor behind the underestimation of distress probabilities.

[19] Read more here: https://blogs.worldbank.org/en/africacan/mozambiques-hidden-debts-turning-crisis-opportunity-reform

[20] https://www.elibrary.imf.org/view/journals/002/2024/008/article-A002-en.xml

### 3.3.6 *Developmental Blind Spots and Climate Risk*

Standard indicators focus on solvency and liquidity but rarely integrate development needs and human impacts.[21] The desire of governments in SSA to spend on infrastructure, education, health, and security creates tension between servicing debt and meeting basic needs. Metrics seldom quantify the opportunity cost of debt service, such as foregone social spending or climate resilience (Arko, 2024). Traditional DSAs have not systematically incorporated Sustainable Development Goals (SDGs) financing gaps or the rising costs of climate adaptation.[22] As a result, assessments may either set sustainability thresholds too low relative to development needs or penalize the necessary investment when financed by borrowing. Enhanced DSAs that embed climate scenarios often find more countries on unsustainable paths than official DSAs suggest.

## 3.4 Context-Specific Metrics for SSA

The experience of SSA economies over the past two decades has made it clear that conventional debt sustainability indicators, while useful, are insufficient for capturing the continent's fiscal realities and development imperatives. Static benchmarks such as debt-to-GDP often mask the true repayment burden, especially in economies with narrow tax bases, volatile export earnings, and high infrastructure needs (Dryden & Volz, 2025). Many SSA countries have entered debt distress at levels well below the "safe" thresholds set in global debt frameworks, whereas others have sustained higher ratios without crisis due to concessional financing and robust growth prospects (Ebatamehi, 2025).

In response, scholars, policymakers, and regional institutions have called for context-specific debt metrics that integrate fiscal capacity, external vulnerability, social priorities, and long-term development goals. These refined indicators not only provide a more accurate measure of solvency and liquidity positions but also help policymakers make better decisions about borrowing, investment, and fiscal adjustment. Table 3.2 summarizes a comprehensive set of proposed SSA-tailored metrics, highlighting their rationale, methodological approach, and practical policy insights.

[21] https://www.un.org/en/desa/5-things-you-should-know-about-financing-sustainable-development

[22] https://unctad.org/publication/financing-sustainable-development-report-2024

**Table 3.2** Context-specific debt sustainability metrics for SSA

| *Metric/approach* | *Concept and methodology* | *Rationale for SSA* | *Policy implications* |
|---|---|---|---|
| Debt-to-revenue ratio | Calculates total public debt relative to annual government revenues rather than GDP. Revenue includes tax and non-tax income, and provides a direct measure of repayment capacity | Many SSA countries have low tax revenue-to-GDP ratios (often below 15%); therefore, debt-to-GDP ratios can understate the fiscal burden. This ratio reflects the state's actual ability to mobilize resources to service debt | Encourages reforms to broaden the tax base and enhance revenue collection; helps set more realistic debt limits tied to fiscal capacity rather than economic size alone |
| Net debt-to-public assets (sovereign balance sheet approach) | Net debt = gross public debt minus sovereign assets (e.g., resource wealth, public enterprises, financial reserves). Requires valuation of infrastructure and natural resource assets | Differentiates between productive debt that builds national wealth and unproductive debt. Encourages a shift from purely liability-focused analysis to net worth assessment | Promotes transparency of public sector balance sheets; incentivizes investment in infrastructure and human capital that raises long-term fiscal capacity |
| Smoothed or shock-adjusted debt ratios | Uses multi-year moving averages of GDP or exports (e.g., 3–5 years) or calculates debt ratios under adverse commodity price or growth scenarios | Reduces distortion from temporary booms (commodity windfalls) or busts (pandemic shocks). Avoids procyclical misclassification of debt sustainability risk | Supports countercyclical borrowing and spending policies; discourages premature fiscal tightening triggered by short-lived shocks |
| Net external debt/exports | Estimates external debts net foreign reserves before comparing to export earnings. This can also be expressed relative to the total foreign exchange inflows (exports + remittances) | Provides a clearer picture of external solvency by recognizing liquidity buffers. Important for economies that maintain high reserves or receive substantial remittance inflows | Rewards countries with prudent reserve accumulation; helps guide reserve adequacy policy and manage external borrowing in line with FX buffers |

(*continued*)

**Table 3.2** (continued)

| *Metric/approach* | *Concept and methodology* | *Rationale for SSA* | *Policy implications* |
|---|---|---|---|
| Debt-service-to-social spending ratios | Compares debt service to combined expenditure on health, education, and social protection | Reveals the opportunity cost of debt servicing in terms of forgone human development spending | Strengthens the case for debt relief, restructuring, or concessional financing, where debt undermines the delivery of essential services and SDG progress |
| Debt per capita/poverty-adjusted ratios | Expresses debt as a liability per head or adjusts GDP downward to reflect the taxable, formal share of the economy | Accounts for population size and poverty levels when judging sustainability. Ensures that assessments reflect the capacity to generate revenues per citizen, not just total GDP | Informs equitable fiscal adjustments and intergenerational burden-sharing; supports differentiated thresholds for low-income versus middle-income economies |
| Gross financing needs (GFN) indicator | Computed as the sum of the primary deficit, debt service (both interest and amortization), and realization of explicit and implicit contingent liabilities, less interest revenue | Identifies short-term liquidity risks that stock measures (like debt-to-GDP) cannot capture. Particularly relevant for countries with large short-term domestic debt or Eurobond maturities approaching | Guides debt managers to extend maturities, pre-finance redemptions, and smooth amortization profiles to reduce rollover risk |
| Interest-rate and currency-risk indicators | Measures the share of variable-rate debt, foreign currency debt, and computes average interest cost. Can include stress tests under global interest rate hikes or currency depreciation | SSA sovereigns are highly sensitive to global financial conditions and exchange rate swings, which can quickly raise servicing costs and inflate debt ratios | Encourages development of local-currency bond markets, fixed-rate issuance, and use of hedging instruments to reduce vulnerability |

(*continued*)

**Table 3.2** (continued)

| *Metric/approach* | *Concept and methodology* | *Rationale for SSA* | *Policy implications* |
|---|---|---|---|
| Climate- and SDG-adjusted debt space | Adjusts debt thresholds based on climate vulnerability indices and SDG financing gaps. Can involve upward adjustment when debt finances resilience projects or downward adjustment when climate risks require fiscal buffers | Recognizes that fiscal space must account for future adaptation needs and development goals. Avoids labeling development-oriented borrowing as unsustainable when it supports long-term growth and resilience | Supports mobilization of concessional climate finance, debt-for-climate swaps, and blended finance instruments. Aligns debt policy with Agenda 2063 and SDG objectives |
| Growth-linked or dynamic solvency metrics | Evaluates whether the actual primary balance is sufficient to stabilize or reduce the debt ratio given the interest-growth differential ($r$—$g$) | Offers a forward-looking, country-specific solvency test. Countries with strong growth can sustain higher debt; those with low growth need fiscal surpluses just to stabilize debt | Promotes growth-friendly fiscal strategies; helps identify when adjustment must focus on boosting growth rather than cutting spending |
| Export-concentration-adjusted debt ratios | Adjusts debt-to-exports by weighing exports based on diversification measures (e.g., Herfindahl index) | Highlights vulnerability of countries reliant on a single commodity or market. Angola's and South Sudan's debt risks are magnified by oil dependence | Encourages export diversification strategies, industrial policy, and regional trade integration to improve debt-carrying capacity |
| Regional or growth-adjusted thresholds | Uses SSA-specific convergence criteria (e.g., WAEMU's 70% debt-to-GDP rule) or links thresholds to expected growth and interest rate conditions | Aligns sustainability assessments with regional realities and integration agendas. Avoids applying benchmarks designed for advanced economies with very different fiscal structures | Prevents premature fiscal consolidation that could derail growth; ensures debt targets support investment-led development |

Source: Authors' compilation based on insights from Dryden and Volz (2025), Harcourt (2025), UNDP (2025), and Laws et al. (2025)

## 3.5 Alternative Approaches and Models

Debt sustainability in SSA can no longer be assessed using a single lens. The recurrent debt crises over the past two decades have shown that relying solely on conventional debt-to-GDP thresholds or static indicators often fails to predict distress or guide timely policy responses. Many SSA countries have entered debt distress despite appearing sustainable, while others have carried higher debt levels without crisis, largely due to differences in financing terms, governance, and growth trajectories (Ugwunta, 2025). This mismatch has prompted rethinking how debt sustainability can be measured and monitored. Alternative approaches seek to capture the complexity, uncertainty, and developmental context of SSA debt dynamics. The alternative approaches move beyond purely liability-focused analysis to incorporate risk probabilities, the value of public assets, market sentiment, governance quality, and social costs of debt service. This section discusses several innovative approaches.

### 3.5.1 *Stochastic and Scenario-Based Approaches*

A key innovation in recent years has been the application of stochastic simulations and scenario-based analyses to debt dynamics (Hela, 2019; Papaoikonomou, 2025). Rather than relying solely on baseline projections, this approach models the probability distribution of future debt outcomes by incorporating historical volatility in key variables, such as growth, interest rates, and exchange rates. The result is a spectrum of possible debt-to-GDP paths, providing policymakers with a more nuanced understanding of risk (Cottarelli, 2024).

Scenario-based approaches allow countries to test their resilience under specific shocks (Alcidi & Daniel, 2018), for instance, a prolonged drop in commodity prices, a global interest rate hike, or a climate-related disaster. These methods are particularly relevant for SSA economies exposed to terms-of-trade volatility and extreme weather events. Some recent proposals recommend integrating climate scenarios into standard DSAs, enabling governments to assess how droughts, floods, or adaptation spending might alter debt trajectories (Njoroge et al., 2024; Dryden & Volz, 2025). However, the supplement to the 2018 Guidance Note on the World Bank-IMF LIC DSF clarifies when climate change risks and climate investments have to be explicitly taken into consideration in the DSA as well as introducing general considerations on the incorporation of climate-linked debt instruments (IMF and World Bank, 2024). While considerations of climate change are acknowledged in the LIC DSF, a more rigorous approach that highlights vulnerabilities is needed to inform the design of climate-contingent debt instruments or fiscal buffers.

### 3.5.2 *Sovereign Balance Sheet and Net Worth Models*

A more radical departure from traditional practice is the sovereign balance sheet approach, which evaluates debt sustainability in terms of net worth rather than gross liabilities (Yeyati & Sturzenegger, 2023). This method accounts for public assets—financial holdings, infrastructure, and natural resources—and compares them to total liabilities, including public debt and contingent obligations. In this method, debt is considered sustainable if the net worth is stable or improving over time.

This approach is particularly compelling in SSA, where much of public borrowing has been used to finance infrastructure.[23] If borrowing leads to productive assets that generate future growth and revenues, the resulting improvement in public net worth can justify a higher level of debt. Conversely, when borrowing is used for consumption or unproductive subsidies, public net worth declines, signaling a less sustainable path. Variants of this approach also model the relationship between debt-financed investment and GDP growth using incremental capital–output ratios, effectively examining whether the growth dividend of new investment exceeds the cost of servicing the debt (Ali et al., 2023).

### 3.5.3 *Composite Debt Vulnerability Indexes*

Several researchers have proposed the creation of composite indices that synthesize multiple dimensions of sustainability into a single vulnerability score (Doemeland et al., 2022; Geda, 2025; Schlegelmilch et al., 2025). Such indices might combine debt stock ratios, debt service metrics, institutional quality, external buffers, and measures of economic diversification. This holistic perspective can overcome the limitations of focusing on a single indicator, such as debt-to-GDP, which can misrepresent actual risk. Composite measures also allow differentiation between countries with similar debt levels but very different fundamentals (Assa & Meddeb,

[23] https://www.bu.edu/gdp/2025/05/27/debt-sustainability-analysis-as-if-development-really-mattered/

2021). For example, a country with strong governance, deep financial markets, and diversified exports might safely carry higher debt than a fragile state with limited fiscal capacity. Regional development banks have experimented with these indices as early warning systems, and they could be refined further to guide concessional finance allocation or trigger automatic restructuring clauses (Mourchid & Filali, 2024).

### 3.5.4 *Market-Based and State-Contingent Indicators*

Market signals can also play a role in debt sustainability assessments. Eurobond spreads, credit ratings, and credit default swaps (CDS) provide real-time indications of investor perceptions of default risk (Bouabdallah et al., 2017). Persistent high yields, for instance, may suggest that markets view debt as unsustainable even before official DSAs indicate distress (Oduk & Mithia, 2025). In addition, innovative state-contingent debt instruments (SCDI), such as GDP-linked bonds or natural disaster clauses, change the risk profile of sovereign debt. Payments to such instruments automatically adjust downward in the event of growth shocks or disasters, thereby reducing the probability of default. A comprehensive sustainability analysis should recognize these instruments' risk-sharing features and allow for higher "safe" debt levels in countries that have adopted them.

### 3.5.5 *Institutional and Governance-Adjusted Approaches*

Another alternative is to incorporate governance, transparency, and historical default experience directly into sustainability models (Jousten, 2025). Countries with weak public financial management or a track record of hidden debt scandals may have lower effective debt tolerance because borrowing is less likely to translate into productive investment (Amankwah et al., 2018; Soko, 2022). Conversely, countries with robust institutions and credible fiscal rules may carry higher debt without triggering investor panic (Willems & Zettelmeyer, 2022). Adjusting debt thresholds for institutional quality would align sustainability analysis more closely with real-world risk.

### 3.5.6 *People-Centered and Development-Sensitive Frameworks*

Civil society organizations and SSA think tanks have called for debt sustainability assessments that explicitly consider human development outcomes.[24] This perspective argues that debt becomes unsustainable if servicing it forces governments to slash essential social spending below a minimum floor. A "people-centered" framework might include metrics such as debt service relative to health or education budgets, or require participatory debt audits to ensure borrowing is aligned with national priorities. This approach reframes debt sustainability not merely as a fiscal calculation but as a measure of whether debt supports or undermines development goals.[25]

## 3.6 Policy Relevance of Revised Indicators

Revising debt sustainability metrics is far more than a technical or academic exercise; it is a cornerstone of effective economic governance. In SSA economies, the adoption of context-sensitive and multidimensional debt indicators can transform how governments make borrowing decisions, design fiscal rules, and interact with creditors and development partners. Improved metrics provide policymakers with early warning signals, help set prudent borrowing limits, and ensure that debt remains a catalyst for development rather than a barrier. This section explores the policy applications of revised indicators.

### *3.6.1 Informing National Debt Management and Fiscal Policy*

One of the most direct applications of revised debt indicators is in the design of Medium-Term Debt Management Strategies (MTDS) and fiscal frameworks. By integrating ratios such as debt-service-to-revenue, external debt-service-to-exports, and interest-to-revenue into borrowing strategies, governments can calibrate their debt portfolios more prudently by choosing a mix of domestic and external borrowing, concessional and non-concessional financing, and fixed versus floating interest structures. For example, if the debt-service-to-revenue ratio approaches a critical threshold, policymakers might prioritize concessional loans, lengthen maturities to reduce rollover risk, or take measures to boost revenue collection. Similarly, fiscal policy rules can be redesigned to complement these indicators by establishing interest-payment caps or expenditure rules

[24] https://afrodad.org/news-events/news/afrodad-coordinates-other-civil-society-organisations-call-debt-justice-collective

[25] https://www.csis.org/analysis/finding-paths-sustainable-development-africa

that prevent crowding out of priority spending. Importantly, revised metrics can also reveal when a country is under-utilizing its borrowing capacity, allowing policymakers to take on productive debt for infrastructure and climate adaptation, where future growth prospects justify it. This proactive approach enables countries to pursue their development objectives without compromising their long-term sustainability.

### 3.6.2 *Strengthening Early-Warning Systems and Preventive Action*

A more comprehensive set of debt indicators also serves as an effective early-warning mechanism, allowing governments and regional institutions to intervene before fiscal stress materializes into a full-blown crisis. By monitoring a broader dashboard, including short-term debt maturity profiles, Gross Financing Needs (GFN), and reserve adequacy, authorities can detect vulnerabilities early and take preventive action. For instance, if indicators show rising short-term refinancing risks or a sharp increase in debt service to revenue, policymakers might opt for debt reprofiling, preemptive fiscal adjustment, or concessional refinancing to smooth future payment obligations. Regional organizations such as the African Union, the UN Economic Commission for Africa (UNECA), and the African Development Bank (AfDB) could institutionalize such monitoring through peer review mechanisms, setting "red line" indicators that trigger policy dialogue or technical assistance. This type of early intervention could help avoid painful defaults and maintain market confidence, saving governments from later costlier crisis responses.

### 3.6.3 *Enhancing Transparency and Accountability*

Revised debt indicators, when publicly reported, can significantly improve debt transparency and accountability. Publishing metrics such as debt-service-to-social-spending ratios, contingent liabilities of state-owned enterprises, and guarantees under PPPs enable legislators, civil society, and the public to better understand the fiscal trade-offs involved in borrowing. Transparent reporting makes it easier to scrutinize whether new borrowing aligns with national priorities and delivers measurable benefits. The experience of Mozambique's hidden debt crisis has underscored the importance of including all liabilities—explicit and contingent—in sustainability assessments.

According to the World Bank (2025), while public debt data in SSA is accessible in nearly 80% of the countries with instrument coverage improving between 2023 and 2024, significant transparency gaps persist. Over half of countries disclose nothing about recent loan agreements, and the share of countries with completely inaccessible debt data increased from 13% to 18% during this period. Enhanced metrics should encourage governments to adopt comprehensive debt reporting practices, strengthen parliamentary oversight, and prevent the accumulation of off-balance sheet obligations that could later destabilize public finances. International initiatives, including the World Bank's Sustainable Development Finance Policy (SDFP), are already incentivizing such reforms by linking concessional financing to improved disclosure, making transparency both a domestic and global expectation.

### 3.6.4 *Guiding International Support and Debt Relief*

Context-sensitive metrics also shape how international support, debt relief, and restructuring are designed and delivered. During negotiations under frameworks such as the G20 Common Framework, revised indicators that highlight the human development cost of debt, such as interest-to-health spending ratios or debt-service-to-SDG financing gaps, can justify deeper relief and more concessional terms. They can also support the case for innovative financing mechanisms, such as debt-for-nature or debt-for-SDG swaps, showing clearly how reduced debt service could free fiscal space for climate adaptation or social investment. Moreover, multilateral programs such as those of the IMF can integrate these metrics into conditionality, setting realistic targets that stabilize key ratios without undermining social protection or growth. This approach balances fiscal consolidation with development imperatives, ensuring that post-restructuring debt levels are genuinely sustainable and aligned with long-term objectives.

### 3.6.5 *Aligning Debt with Development Strategies*

Finally, the revised debt indicators help integrate debt management into the broader framework of national development planning. By linking borrowing decisions to infrastructure gaps, export diversification goals, and climate adaptation needs, governments can better sequence projects and align debt accumulation with the expected returns from investment. This forward-looking approach allows policymakers to justify borrowing when indicators show sufficient fiscal space or delay projects when key ratios signal vulnerability. Such communication can also improve public trust, as citizens see evidence-based decision-making that balances development ambitions with fiscal prudence. Over time, the consistent use of these metrics can foster a culture of disciplined borrowing, attract investor confidence, and ensure that debt contributes positively to structural transformation and inclusive growth.

## 3.7 Conclusion

Like many developing countries, SSA faces debt sustainability challenges that require a fundamental rethinking of the indicators and frameworks used to assess public debt. Conventional metrics, such as debt-to-GDP, while simple and widely applied, provide an incomplete picture of fiscal vulnerability because they ignore key dimensions, such as revenue capacity, debt composition, external liquidity buffers, and the developmental context in which borrowing takes place. Many SSA countries enter distress at debt levels far below global "safe" thresholds, while others sustain higher ratios when they benefit from concessional financing, export growth, or effective debt management. This shows that debt sustainability is a dynamic, probabilistic concept rather than a static rule.

This chapter highlights the limitations of standard debt indicators, including their failure to capture the purpose of debt, the cost of servicing it, and the risks arising from contingent liabilities, exchange rate volatility, and the creditor mix. It proposes context-specific metrics, including fiscal capacity, social trade-offs, and external solvency buffers (net external debt/exports). It also presents alternative approaches, such as sovereign balance sheet models, stochastic simulations, and composite vulnerability indexes, which integrate assets, risk probabilities, and development needs into sustainability analysis. Revising these metrics will inform national borrowing strategies, guide fiscal rules, shape debt relief negotiations, and support early warning systems that help prevent crises.

In conclusion, rethinking debt sustainability metrics is crucial for ensuring that debt remains a tool for growth rather than a drag on development. SSA policymakers, creditors, and international institutions must adopt more nuanced, forward-looking, and development-sensitive approaches that align debt management with the continent's structural transformation goals, climate resilience agenda, and pursuit of SDGs.

Integrating these improved indicators into policy and practice allows SSA to balance the need to mobilize resources for development with the imperative to safeguard long-term fiscal stability and protect future generations from recurring debt crises.

## References

Aboagye, A. Q. (2025). Stress testing Ghana's debt sustainability analysis. *Athens Journal, 11*(2), 179–196.

Adeve, K. A., & Karabou, E. F. (2022). Public debt and development sustainability issues in the West African Economic and Monetary Union (WAEMU). *Cogent Economics & Finance, 10*(1), 2079177.

Alcidi, C., & Daniel, G. R. O. S. (2018). *Debt sustainability assessments: The state of the art.* https://www.europarl.europa.eu/RegData/etudes/IDAN/2018/624426/IPOL_IDA(2018)624426_EN.pdf

Ali, A. A., Mengoub, F. E., Arbouch, M., Azaroual, F., Bourhriba, O., Jai, Y. E., & Mandri, B. (2023). *Morocco—Beyond debt: Sustainable pathways to higher growth* (No. 2343). Policy Center for the New South.

Amankwah, G., Ofori-Abebrese, G., & Kamasa, K. (2018). An empirical analysis of the sustainability of public debt in Ghana. *Theoretical Economics Letters, 8*(11), 2038–2054.

Anajama, C., & Nyamudzanga, L. (2025). Rethinking debt sustainability and inclusive development in sub-Saharan Africa: A systematic review. *Development, 67*, 1–11.

Arko, T. (2024). *Climate finance, debt and economic dependency in Africa.* https://unu.edu/inra/article/climate-finance-debt-and-economic-dependency-africa

Assa, J., & Meddeb, R. (2021). *Towards a multidimensional vulnerability index.* United Nations Development Programme. Retrieved April 14, 2023.

Atta-Mensah, J., & Ibrahim, M. (2020). Explaining Africa's debt: The journey so far and the arithmetic of the policymaker. *Theoretical Economics Letters, 10*, 409–441.

Atta-Mensah, J., & Ibrahim, M. (2024). Towards achieving the Sustainable Development Goals (SDGs): The impact of debts on income inequality in Africa. *Applied Economics and Finance, 11*(1), 1–12.

Bouabdallah, O., Checherita-Westphal, C. D., Warmedinger, T., De Stefani, R., Drudi, F., Setzer, R., & Westphal, A. (2017). Debt sustainability analysis for euro area sovereigns: A methodological framework (Occasional Paper 185). *ECB.* https://papers.ssrn.com/sol3/papers.cfm?abstract_id=2950979

Cömert, H., Düzçay, G., & Öncü, T. S. (2024). *Navigating debt sustainability: An in-depth analysis of the IMF's debt sustainability framework and its critique.*

https://www.networkideas.org/wp-content/uploads/2024/12/03_2024.pdf

Cottarelli, C. (2024). *Assessing the debt sustainability analysis methodology in the EU's new economic governance framework*. https://www.europarl.europa.eu/RegData/etudes/IDAN/2024/764180/IPOL_IDA(2024)764180_EN.pdf

Doemeland, D., Estevão, M., Jooste, C., Sampi Bravo, J. R. E., & Tsiropoulos, V. (2022). *Debt vulnerability analysis: A multi-angle approach* (No. 9929). The World Bank.

Dryden, A., & Volz, U. (2025). *Africa's vicious cycle of debt and climate change*. https://drgr.org/files/2025/09/DRGR-Africa-Debt-Crisis.pdf#:~:text=burden%20has%20been%20worsened%20by,per%20year%20%E2%80%93%20with%20over

Ebatamehi, S. (2025). Top 10 countries leading the charge in debt restructuring in Africa 2025. https://www.africanexponent.com/top-10-countries-leading-the-charge-in-debt-restructuring-in-africa-2025/

Fernando, J. (2025). *Global financial governance and debt sustainability in the global south*. Global South Perspectives, Southern Voice. https://southernvoice.org/wp-content/uploads/2025/05/Financial-governance-GS-GSP-Article-Fernando-2025.pdf

Gallagher, K. P., Ramos, L., Were, A., & Marques, M. Z. (2024). Debt distress and climate-resilient development in sub-Saharan Africa. *Journal of African Economies, 33*(Supplement_2), ii8–ii25.

Geda, A. (2025). Fundamental drivers of African debt and the debt sustainability assessment framework: A tale of two Tales. https://media.afreximbank.com/afrexim/APRWPS202503_The-Two-Tales-of-African-Debt-Examining-Fundamental-Drivers-and-Debt-Sustainability-Assessment-Frameworks.pdf

Gill, I., & Pinto, B. (2024). *Making the market access countries' debt sustainability framework relevant for emerging markets*. World Bank.

Graf Von Luckner, C. (2024). *Lifting the hood of the LIC-DSF to revamp its accuracy and transparency*. Finance for Development Lab. https://findevlab.org/wp-content/uploads/2024/10/FDL-_Policy-Note-18_The-Debt-Sustainability-Framework-for-Low-Income-Countries_Oct24.pdf

Guzman, M. (2018). *The elements of sovereign debt sustainability analysis*. Centre for International Governance Innovation. https://www.cigionline.org/static/documents/documents/Paper%20No.196web.pdf

Hakura, D. (2020). *What is debt sustainability?* https://www.imf.org/en/Publications/fandd/issues/2020/09/what-is-debt-sustainability-basics

Harcourt, S., Rivera, J., & Robertson, F. (2025). *Overview of African debt*. https://data.one.org/analysis/african-debt

Hela, B. K. H. (2019). *Public debt sustainability assessment: A stochastic approach for Tunisia*. https://mpra.ub.uni-muenchen.de/93892/

Horn, S., Mihalyi, D., Nickol, P., & Sosa-Padilla, C. (2024). *Hidden debt revelations* (No. w32947). National Bureau of Economic Research.

International Monetary Fund and World Bank (2018). *Guidance note on the bank-fund debt sustainability framework for low income countries* (IMF Policy Paper and WB Board Report). International Monetary Fund and World Bank.

International Monetary Fund and World Bank. (2024). *Supplement to 2018 guidance note on the Bank-Fund debt sustainability framework for low income countries.* International Monetary Fund and World Bank.

Jousten, A. (2025). Debt sustainability analysis methodology in the EU's new economic governance framework: An assessment. *In-depth Analysis* https://www.europarl.europa.eu/RegData/etudes/IDAN/2025/764183/IPOL_IDA(2025)764183_EN.pdf

Laws, A., Lemaire, T., & Spatafora, N. (2025). How to stabilize Africa' debt. https://www.imf.org/en/News/Articles/2025/07/08/cf-how-to-stabilize-africas-debt

Mehrotra, N. R., & Sergeyev, D. (2021). Debt sustainability in a low interest rate world. *Journal of Monetary Economics, 124*, S1–S18.

Mourchid, L., & Filali, A. F. (2024). Developing vulnerability index for MENA region. *African Scientific Journal, 3*(25), 1342–1342.

Ngundu, M., & Cilliers, J. (2025). Indebted and underfunded. https://futures.issafrica.org/blog/2025/Indebted-and-underfunded

Njoroge, P., Kenewendo, B., & Dryden, A. (2024). Unleashing Africa's green growth: Why debt relief is essential for climate resilience. https://drgr.org/news/unleashing-africas-green-growth-why-debt-relief-is-essential-for-climate-resilience/

Oduk, J., & Mithia, C. (2025). Debt sustainability analysis: Re-evaluating debt sustainability analyses in the context of hegemonic power and sovereign debt restructuring. *Development, 67*, 1–13.

Olabisi, M., & Stein, H. (2024). Do African countries still pay more to borrow? Evidence for 2006-22. *Journal of African Trade, 11*(1), 3.

Papaoikonomou, D. (2025). Stochastic debt sustainability analysis: A methodological note. https://papers.ssrn.com/sol3/papers.cfm?abstract_id=5220735

Raga, S. (2024). *An appraisal of debt sustainability analyses amid multiple crises.* Friedrich-Ebert-Stiftung eV. https://library.fes.de/pdf-files/international/21183.pdf

Schlegelmilch, J., Jain, G., Kamau, A., Kruczkiewicz, A., & Balkaran, T. (2025). *Climate Finance Vulnerability Index (CliF-VI).* https://clifvi.org/wp-content/uploads/2025/06/Climate-Finance-Vulnerability-Index-Technical-Methodology.pdf

Soko, B. (2022). *Debt management and governance in Africa.* Friedrich-Ebert-Stiftung Africa, Union Cooperation Office. https://library.fes.de/pdf-files/bueros/fes-ua/19364.pdf

Ugwunta, O. D. (2025). Africa's debt paradox: Why borrowing has not delivered growth. https://panafricanreview.com/africas-debt-paradox-why-borrowing-has-not-delivered-growth/

UNDP. (2025). *Navigating the debt crisis: Reforming the common framework for African countries.* https://www.undp.org/sites/g/files/zskgke326/files/2025-08/undp-working_paper_series-navigating_the_debt_crisis_7_aug_2025.pdf

Vîntu, D. (2025). *Maastricht criteria and public debt.* Munich Personal RePEc Archive. https://mpra.ub.uni-muenchen.de/125712/

Wang, Y., & Xu, Y. (2022). Debt restructuring in Africa: Building public assets and addressing bottlenecks for low-carbon economic transformation. *Open Journal of Business and Management, 13*(3), 20–36.

Were, M. (2024). *Sub-Saharan Africa faces an alarming debt burden that could hinder progress on sustainable development goals.* https://www.wider.unu.edu/publication/sub-saharan-africa-faces-alarming-debt-burden-could-hinder-progress-sustainable

Willems, T., & Zettelmeyer, J. (2022). Sovereign debt sustainability and central bank credibility. *Annual Review of Financial Economics, 14*(1), 75–93.

World Bank (2025, October). *Pathways to job creation in Africa* (Africa's Pulse, No. 32). World Bank. https://doi.org/10.1596/978-1-4648-2296-4

Yeyati, E. L., & Sturzenegger, F. (2023). *A balance sheet approach to fiscal sustainability.* https://cepr.org/voxeu/columns/balance-sheet-approach-fiscal-sustainability

Zucker-Marques, M., Gallagher, K. P., & Volz, U. (2024). Debt Sustainability Analysis as if Development Really Mattered. *Development, 67*(3), 158–166.

CHAPTER 4

# Fiscal Rules and Debt Sustainability in Ghana: An ARDL Bounds Testing Approach

*Mubarik Salifu*

## 4.1 Introduction

Ghana's economic landscape has long been characterized by a paradox of immense natural resource wealth juxtaposed with persistent fiscal instability and recurrent public debt crises. Despite being endowed with abundant resources such as gold, cocoa, and oil, the country has experienced cyclical debt build-ups, often necessitating intervention from international financial institutions like the International Monetary Fund (IMF). For instance, by 2022, Ghana's public debt-to-GDP ratio had soared to over 90%, culminating in a loss of international market access and a default on its external debt obligations (IMF, 2023). This recurring pattern underscores the profound challenges facing fiscal governance in resource-rich developing economies, where commodity revenue volatility often fuels

M. Salifu (✉)
Department of Economics, School of Economics, University for Development Studies, Tamale, Ghana
e-mail: smubarik@uds.edu.gh



I. N. Yakubu (ed.), *Public Debt and Economic Resilience in Africa*, Palgrave Studies in African and Development Economics,
https://doi.org/10.1007/978-3-032-25835-9_4

procyclical policies, leading to unsustainable debt trajectories (Frankel et al., 2013).

In response to these challenges, fiscal rules, defined as permanent numerical constraints on budgetary aggregates such as the deficit, debt, or expenditure have emerged as a key institutional mechanism to promote fiscal discipline and anchor debt sustainability (Symansky & Kopits, 1998). The theoretical underpinnings for such rules are rooted in addressing the problems of time inconsistency and the common-pool resource dilemma in fiscal policy. Kydland and Prescott (1977) demonstrated that policymakers, in the absence of pre-commitment devices, have incentives to prioritize short-term political gains over long-term fiscal stability, resulting in a deficit bias and escalating public debt. Fiscal rules serve as such a commitment device, helping to mitigate these inefficiencies and foster credibility (Debrun et al., 2009).

Ghana's own tryst with fiscal rules includes the 2011 Fiscal Responsibility Law and the more recent 2018 Fiscal Responsibility Act, which aimed to curb deficits and stabilize debt. However, the effectiveness of these rules has been mixed, often undermined by election-related spending, exogenous shocks, and structural vulnerabilities (Aryeetey & Kanbur, 2017). The efficacy of fiscal rules in enhancing fiscal performance is well documented in the context of advanced economies (Heinemann et al., 2018). In contrast, their function and success in commodity-dependent countries such as Ghana are comparatively under-researched and likely influenced by distinct contextual factors.

Existing studies on Ghana have often focused narrowly on fiscal deficits or primary balances, leaving a critical gap in directly linking fiscal rules to public debt dynamics, the ultimate indicator of sustainability. Moreover, the volatile relationships between fiscal policy, inflation, growth, and terms of trade in such economies necessitates an empirical approach capable of capturing both short-run fluctuations and long-run equilibrium relationships. The Autoregressive Distributed Lag (ARDL) bounds testing approach, pioneered by Pesaran et al. (2001), is particularly suited to this context, as it accommodates variables with different orders of integration and provides robust estimates amidst structural breaks and limited data, common features in developing economies.

This research fills this gap by analyzing the impact of fiscal rules on Ghana's public debt sustainability using annual data for the period

1990–2024. By employing the ARDL methodology, the study examines how fiscal rules, alongside macroeconomic variables such as inflation, GDP growth, and cocoa prices, influence Ghana's debt-to-GDP ratio in both the short and long run. The findings offer critical insights into the design and implementation of fiscal institutions in resource-dependent economies and contribute to the broader discourse on fiscal governance and debt sustainability in Sub-Saharan Africa.

## 4.2 Literature Review

### *4.2.1 Theoretical Underpinnings of Fiscal Rules*

The adoption of fiscal rules as instruments of fiscal policy finds its theoretical foundation in addressing two fundamental problems in public economics: time inconsistency and the common-pool resource dilemma. The seminal work of Kydland and Prescott (1977) on rules versus discretion demonstrated that policymakers without pre-commitment mechanisms have rational incentives to prioritize short-term political gains over long--term optimal plans, leading to a systematic deficit bias and unsustainable debt accumulation. This theoretical framework was extended to fiscal policy by Symansky and Kopits (1998), who argued that fiscal rules serve as crucial commitment devices that help governments overcome this time inconsistency problem by binding current and future administrations to predetermined fiscal paths.

Complementing this perspective, the common-pool resource theory, articulated by von Hagen and Harden (1994), provides additional theoretical justification for fiscal rules. This approach argues that national revenues represent a common pool from which various political actors (ministries, legislators, interest groups) seek to draw benefits. While the advantages of spending are concentrated among specific groups, the costs in the form of higher taxes or increased debt are distributed across the entire population. This fragmentation of budgetary decision-making leads to a "tragedy of the commons" scenario, resulting in excessive deficits and debt accumulation. Fiscal rules address this collective action problem by imposing aggregate constraints on the budgetary process, thereby internalizing the costs of public spending and forcing greater coordination among competing interests (Debrun et al., 2009).

### 4.2.2 Empirical Evidence on Fiscal Rules Effectiveness

A substantial body of empirical research has investigated the effectiveness of fiscal rules in promoting fiscal discipline and debt sustainability. Cross-country studies have generally found that well-designed fiscal rules are associated with improved fiscal outcomes. Fabrizio and Mody (2006) demonstrated that strong budgetary institutions could effectively counteract political indiscipline, leading to lower deficits, particularly in countries with weaker governance structures. More recently, a comprehensive meta-regression analysis by Heinemann et al. (2018) consolidated findings from numerous studies and confirmed that fiscal rules have a statistically significant constraining effect on fiscal policy, reducing budget deficits by an average of 0.5 to 1 percentage points of GDP.

However, the literature consistently emphasizes that the effectiveness of fiscal rules is highly heterogeneous and context-dependent. Key determinants of success include: (1) design features rules that are simple, transparent, and flexible enough to accommodate economic shocks tend to be more durable and effective (Schaechter et al., 2012); (2) enforcement mechanisms are associated with the presence of strong, independent fiscal councils to monitor compliance and provide objective analysis, which significantly enhance credibility (Debrun & Kinda, 2017); and (3) political and institutional environment rules are more likely to succeed in countries with strong legal systems, high-quality bureaucracy, and broad political consensus around fiscal sustainability (IMF, 2022).

Using ARDL approach for the period 1990–2022, Saani et al. (2024) identified a long-term negative correlation between public debt and inflation in Ghana. Their research proposes that fostering job creation and countering this effect can be achieved by promoting investments in infrastructure and agriculture. Aryeetey and Kanbur (2017) provide a comprehensive analysis of Ghana's economic development, including its fiscal management challenges. They document the country's historical pattern of procyclical fiscal policy, where commodity booms lead to expenditure increases that become unsustainable when prices decline. Their work highlights the institutional weaknesses that have undermined fiscal discipline in Ghana, including limited technical capacity for revenue forecasting and strong political pressures for spending.

Debrun et al. (2009) examined the impact of fiscal rules on fiscal performance in OECD and emerging market economies. They found that rules-based fiscal frameworks are associated with stronger fiscal performance, particularly when supported by independent monitoring institutions. Their research suggests that the combination of numerical rules and independent fiscal councils creates a powerful institutional arrangement for constraining fiscal discretion.

Using simultaneous equation models to correct for endogeneity in a 27-year panel of 43 Sub-Saharan African countries, Nabieu et al. (2021) provided evidence of a dual effect of fiscal rules, they significantly strengthen fiscal performance while dampening economic growth. The study concludes that expenditure rules exert the strongest influence on these variables.

Also, Alagidede et al. (2018) employ annual data spanning 1967–2013 and a sample splitting approach to examine the threshold level of Ghana's fiscal deficit and its impact on the country's economic growth. Our finding reveals an optimal fiscal deficit of 7.6% of GDP. They found that the impact on economic growth of fiscal deficit is negative regardless of the sample splitting. However, this evidence shows that this effect is only statistically significant above the threshold. Although, the impact of fiscal deficit on growth is less clear and debatable, we document that fiscal deficit significantly hurts growth when the level exceeds the threshold.

### 4.2.3 *The Challenge of Procyclicality in Commodity-Rich Developing Economies*

A particularly relevant strand of literature for the Ghanaian context focuses on the fiscal challenges specific to developing and commodity-exporting nations, where procyclical fiscal policy represents a persistent problem. Contrary to standard Keynesian prescription, which recommends countercyclical policies (saving during booms and spending during busts), these countries often increase expenditure during economic upswings and are forced to contract during downturns, thereby amplifying economic volatility (Frankel et al., 2013; Ilzetzki & Végh, 2008).

This procyclical bias is driven by several interconnected factors: revenue volatility, heavy reliance on volatile commodity revenues makes it difficult to distinguish between permanent and temporary income shocks, leading to unsustainable spending increases during price booms; secondly, borrowing constraints, during downturns, market access often evaporates, forcing austerity, while during booms, improved creditworthiness makes it easy to borrow and spend; and thirdly, political economy pressures, there are intense demands to spend windfall revenues immediately on popular projects, wages, or subsidies, making it politically costly to save (Alesina et al., 2008).

Ghana exemplifies this phenomenon. Several studies have shown that windfalls from cocoa, gold, and oil have historically led to large public sector wage increases and subsidy bills rather than productive investment or savings, leaving the economy vulnerable to commodity price corrections (Aryeetey & Kanbur, 2017; Ossowski & Halland, 2016). This pattern has contributed significantly to the country's debt sustainability challenges, with public debt reaching unsustainable levels multiple times over the past three decades.

### 4.2.4 *The Fiscal-Inflation-Debt Nexus*

The relationship between fiscal policy, inflation, and debt sustainability represents another critical dimension of the literature. The Tanzi-Olivera effect posits that high inflation can erode the real value of government tax revenue due to collection lags (the time between the accrual of a tax liability and its payment to the treasury) (Olivera, 1967; Tanzi, 1978). This self-reinforcing mechanism can worsen fiscal deficits, potentially leading to a fiscal dominance regime where monetary policy is subjugated to financing government debt. Conversely, moderate inflation can act as an implicit tax on nominal government debt, reducing its real value (Reinhart & Rogoff, 2009). The net effect of inflation on debt sustainability is thus an empirical question, contingent on the structure of the economy, the tax system, and the composition of public debt.

## 4.3 Methodology

This section presents the theoretical framework on the relationship between the variables under consideration; the various statistical tools used for analysis of the results. Annual data spanning from 1990 to 2024 was obtained from World Development Indicators (WDI) website and IMF World Economic Outlook Database. First and foremost, a statistically descriptive assessment of the variables was carried out. Secondly, a test for stationarity was conducted by employing the Augmented-Dicky-Fuller (ADF) and Phillips-Perron (PP) (Dickey & Fuller, 1979) tests for all the series. The ARDL method was then applied after the bound test for cointegration was completed. The lags of all variables were selected using the Akaike Information Criterion (AIC).

### 4.3.1 Empirical Model Specification

For the purpose of this study, an ARDL estimation procedure is implemented. The ARDL is employed due to its effectiveness in managing varying degrees of integration and its perceived superiority over the conventional or well-known cointegration models, such as the Engle Granger (Engle & Granger, 1987), Johansen test (Johansen & Juselius, 1990), and Phillip-Ouliaris test, which can simultaneously estimate short- and long-run estimates (Işık et al., 2013). The ARDL model has the benefit of simultaneous estimation of short- and long-run parameters. When the series are I (0), I (1), or a mix of the two, ARDL can be used. Pesaran (1997) and Ouattara et al., (2004) state that ARDL cannot be applied in cases where any variable is stationary at I (2) since the results will be erroneous.

We begin by implicitly specifying the effect of fiscal rules on debt sustainability as follows in equation (1) where debt sustainability is specified as a function of the fiscal rule (FR), inflation (INF), economic growth rate (GDP), and Commodity prices (CP):

$$DGDP = f\left(FR, INF, GDP, CP\right) \tag{4.1}$$

Where $DGDP = Debt - to - GDP$ ((% of GDP) (for debt sustainability)

FR: FISCAL_RULE_DUMMY, thus, a dummy variable taking 1 for years a fiscal rule was in place, 0 otherwise.
*INF* = *Inflation* rate (Annual inflation rate (%)).
GDP: GDP_GROWTH, Annual GDP growth rate (%).
CP: Commodity prices (Cocoa): Real Cocoa price (or export revenue) in USD, a proxy for terms-of-trade shocks.

Equation (1) can then be further explicitly specified to follow equation (2).

$$DGDP_t = \alpha_0 + \alpha_1 FR_t + \alpha_2 INF_t + \alpha_3 GDP_t + \alpha_4 CP_t + \varepsilon_t \tag{4.2}$$

The ARDL models to be estimated are specified as follows in equations (3) and (4):

$$\Delta DGDP_t = \beta_0 + \beta_1 PB_{t-1} + \beta_2 FR_{t-1} + \beta_3 INF_{t-1} + \beta_4 GDP_{t-1} + \beta_5 CP_{t-1} + \sum_{i=1}^{n} \gamma_1 \Delta DGDP_{t-i} + \sum_{i=1}^{q} \gamma_2 \Delta FR_{t-i} + \sum_{i=1}^{q} \gamma_3 \Delta INF_{t-i} + \sum_{i=1}^{q} \gamma_4 \Delta GDP_{t-i} + \sum_{i=1}^{q} \gamma_5 \Delta CP_{t-i} + \varepsilon_t \quad (4.3)$$

In equation 3, $\Delta$ represents the difference operator, $\beta_0$ denotes the intercept term $\beta_1$ to $\beta_5$ estimates the long-run parameters whiles $\gamma_1$ to $\gamma_5$ are the short run coefficients. n reports the lags for debt-to-GDP (debt sustainability) and q reports the lags for the regressors. To determine the short run coefficients, the error correction model (ECM) is then established. The ECM function can be stated as follows:

$$\Delta DGDP_t = \sum_{j=1}^{n} \alpha_1 DGDP_{t-j} + \sum_{j=1}^{n} \alpha_2 FR_{t-j} + \sum_{j=1}^{n} \alpha_3 INF_{t-j} + \sum_{j=1}^{n} \alpha_4 GDP_{t-j} + \sum_{j=1}^{n} \alpha_5 CP_{t-j} + \theta ECM_{t-j} + \mu_t \quad (4.4)$$

where $\theta$ is the ECM coefficient, which is essentially expected to be strongly negative and controls the rate of adjustment to long-run equilibrium. The error correction term known as ECM takes into account the model's long-run representation (Darko, 2016). The ECM provides a metric for the speed of adjustment to the long-run. Following the estimation of the long- and short-run coefficients, the model is subjected to pertinent diagnostic and stability tests to make sure it is stable, devoid of serial correlation, and heteroskedasticity.

### 4.3.2 *Variable Description and Measurement*

The dependent variable for this analysis is public debt sustainability, measured by the ratio of gross government debt to Gross Domestic Product (GDP). This metric is a central indicator of a country's fiscal health and its capacity to service its obligations without resorting to excessive inflation, default, or destabilizing fiscal adjustment. A rising Debt-to-GDP ratio signals increasing vulnerability and potential unsustainability, while a stable or declining ratio suggests a more sustainable fiscal trajectory. This measure is the standard benchmark used by international institutions, rating agencies, and empirical studies, such as those by Reinhart and Rogoff (2010), to assess sovereign solvency risk and fiscal space.

The independent variable of interest remains the binary fiscal rule dummy. This variable is coded as 1 for years in which a formal, binding fiscal rule was operational and actively targeted, and 0 for periods characterized by the absence or explicit abandonment of such rules. This classification includes years under International Monetary Fund (IMF) programs with strict debt and deficit performance criteria, as well as periods when domestically legislated rules like the Fiscal Responsibility Act (2018) were in effect. The expected sign on this coefficient is negative, hypothesizing that the presence of a fiscal rule is associated with a lower Debt-to-GDP ratio. This expectation is grounded in theory, which posits that rules enforce discipline and curb deficit financing, thereby slowing the accumulation of debt (Heinemann et al., 2018).

To isolate the effect of the fiscal rule from other fundamental drivers of debt dynamics, several control variables are incorporated. The primary balance, expressed as a percentage of GDP, is included as a key determinant. A higher primary surplus directly reduces the government's financing need and contributes to a lower debt stock, suggesting a negative relationship with the Debt-to-GDP ratio. This captures the direct fiscal effort channel separate from the institutional effect of the rule itself. The annual growth rate of real GDP is also controlled for. Its expected sign is negative, as stronger economic growth expands the denominator (GDP), thereby mechanically improving the debt ratio and enhancing the government's capacity to manage its debt burden, a relationship emphasized in debt dynamics literature (Escolano et al., 2014).

Furthermore, the annual inflation rate is added to the model. The expected sign is ambiguous. On one hand, higher inflation can erode the real value of existing nominal debt, potentially leading to a lower real debt burden, a phenomenon known as the nominal channel. On the other hand, high inflation often triggers macroeconomic instability, increases borrowing costs, and can be a consequence of fiscal dominance, ultimately undermining debt sustainability. A variable for commodity terms of trade is also critical for an economy like Ghana. An improvement in the terms of trade is expected to have a negative sign, as rising prices for key exports like gold, cocoa, and oil boost national income (GDP) and government revenues, which can be used to pay down debt or avoid new borrowing, thus improving the Debt-to-GDP ratio (Grigoli et al., 2014).

## 4.4 Data Analysis and Discussion of Findings

A descriptive analysis of the variables was done to show the distribution and trends among them. In Table 4.1, the descriptive statistics show that Ghana's Debt-to-GDP ratio has averaged 58.5% over the sample period, with significant volatility (standard deviation of 18.4), ranging from a low of 25.5% to a high of 98.8%. This wide fluctuation is characteristic of commodity-dependent economies prone to terms-of-trade shocks and procyclical fiscal policies (Frankel et al., 2013).

### *4.4.1 Stationarity Test*

Prior to ARDL estimation, the stationarity properties of the variables were tested using the Augmented Dickey-Fuller (ADF) and Phillips-Perron (PP) tests. The results (Table 4.2) are critical for validating the ARDL approach. Also, to avoid producing spurious regression results which

**Table 4.1** Descriptive statistics of variables

| *Variables* | *Obs* | *Mean* | *Std. Dev* | *Min* | *Max* |
|---|---|---|---|---|---|
| Debt to GDP | 35 | 58.5 | 18.413 | 25.5 | 98.8 |
| FISCAL_RULE_DUMMY | 35 | 0.514 | 0.507 | 0 | 1 |
| INFLATION | 35 | 20.369 | 12.986 | 4.865 | 59.462 |
| GDP_GROWTH | 35 | 5.207 | 2.425 | 0.514 | 14.047 |
| COCOA | 35 | 2157.673 | 1148.515 | 903.906 | 7390.564 |

**Source:** Author's Construct, 2025

**Table 4.2** Results of Unit Root Test (ADF and PP)

| *Variables* | *ADF* | | *PP* | |
|---|---|---|---|---|
| | *Levels* | *First* | *Levels* | *First* |
| Debt to GDP | - | −5.039*** | | −5.099*** |
| FISCAL_RULE_DUMMY | - | - | - | - |
| INFLATION | −3.756*** | - | −3.7620*** | |
| GDP_GROWTH | −3.842*** | - | −3.837*** | - |
| COCOA | | −5.389*** | - | −5.508*** |

Note: ***, represent significance at 1% level

**Source:** Author's Construct, 2025

could be used for analysis and consequently for making economic decisions, it is desirable to conduct stationarity test of the series. Therefore, the unit root test was conducted.

The outcomes of the unit root tests for each variable are shown in Table 4.2. The unit root tests indicate that the debt series is integrated of order one I(1), while other variables exhibit mixed orders of integration. However, FISCAL_RULE_DUMMY is inherently stationary. This mix of I(0) and I(1) variables precludes the use of traditional cointegration tests but makes the ARDL bounds testing approach the ideal methodology. Thus, applying the ARDL model makes sense because all the variables were of orders I (0) and I (1), and it reliably confirms that there are no I (2) series (Pesaran et al., 2001).

### 4.4.2 *Bound Test for Cointegration*

The first step in the ARDL approach is to test for the existence of a long-run relationship using an F-test on the lagged levels of the variables. The computed F-statistic is 14.56 (Table 4.3). Comparing this to the critical value bounds provided by Pesaran et al. (2001). At the 5% significance level, the I(1) upper bound is 3.49. Since 14.56 > 3.49, the null hypothesis of no cointegration is soundly rejected and therefore, providing strong evidence for a long-run cointegrating relationship among the variables. This confirms that fiscal rules, inflation, growth, and commodity prices collectively influence Ghana's debt trajectory in a stable equilibrium relationship. Cointegration demonstrates that the variables move together over the long run, despite likely short-term oscillations. We estimated the long run coefficients of the model using the ARDL technique once the cointegration of the variables are established.

**Table 4.3** Results of bounds test for cointegration

| *F-Statistic* | *Significance level* | *I(0)* | *I(1)* |
|---|---|---|---|
| 14.56 | 10% | 2.2 | 3.09 |
| | 5% | 2.56 | 3.49 |
| | 1% | 3.29 | 4.37 |

I(0) and I(1) are respectively the stationary and non-stationary bounds

**Source:** Author's estimation, 2025

**Table 4.4** Estimated long-run results

| *Variable** | *Coefficient* | *Std. error* | *t-Statistic* | *Prob.* |
|---|---|---|---|---|
| FISCAL_RULE_DUMMY(−1) | −136.9084 | 58.61949 | −2.335544 | 0.0275 |
| INFLATION(−1) | −5.942465 | 2.548813 | −2.331464 | 0.0277 |
| GDP_GROWTH | −12.47110 | 4.223004 | −2.953134 | 0.0066 |
| COCOA(−1) | 0.008325 | 0.010503 | 0.792652 | 0.4352 |
| C | 300.2885 | 94.45394 | 3.179206 | 0.0038 |

**Source:** Author's estimation, 2025

From Table 4.4, the empirical data shows a long-run correlation between the variables. Table 4.4 shows a large, negative, and statistically significant coefficient (−136.91) for fiscal rules. This strongly suggests that the presence of a formal fiscal rule is associated with a substantially lower Debt-to-GDP ratio in the long run. This result empirically validates the theoretical foundations of fiscal rules as commitment devices designed to mitigate the problems of time inconsistency and the common-pool resource dilemma (Kydland & Prescott, 1977; Symansky & Kopits, 1998). By binding policymakers to pre-defined fiscal paths, rules help overcome the rational incentive to prioritize short-term political gains over long-term fiscal stability, thereby curbing deficit bias and anchoring debt sustainability (Debrun et al., 2009). The magnitude of the coefficient underscores the potential power of institutional constraints. This finding aligns with cross-country evidence, such as the meta-analysis by Heinemann et al. (2018), which concluded that well-designed fiscal rules significantly constrain fiscal policy, reducing budget deficits by an average of 0.5 to 1 percentage point of GDP. In the Ghanaian context, this supports the argument made by Aryeetey and Kanbur (2017) that while the framework of the Fiscal Responsibility Law was sound, its effectiveness hinges on stronger enforcement and political commitment.

Also, the negative relationship between inflation and debt (−5.94) supports the "inflation tax" hypothesis, whereby higher inflation erodes the real value of nominal government debt (Reinhart & Rogoff, 2009).

In Ghana, historical episodes of high inflation (averaging 20.37% over the sample period, with peaks up to 59.46%) have coincided with nominal debt reductions, though this comes at the cost of macroeconomic instability (Saani et al., 2024). This aligns with the Tanzi-Olivera effect in reverse, where inflation aids debt sustainability in nominal terms but may exacerbate fiscal dominance if it stems from monetizing deficits (Olivera, 1967;

Tanzi, 1978). Empirical studies on African economies, including Ghana, corroborate this nexus, showing a long-term negative correlation between public debt and inflation (Saani et al., 2024; Abradu-Otoo et al., 2022).

Table 4.4 further revealed a significant negative coefficient (−12.47) between GDP growth and debt, this confirms the fundamental debt dynamics equation where higher economic growth dilutes the debt-to-GDP ratio. With an average growth rate of 5.21% over 1990–2024, periods of robust growth (up to 14.05%) have historically buffered against debt build-ups, emphasizing the need for growth-oriented policies in commodity-dependent nations (Carrère & de Melo, 2012). This finding echoes literature on Sub-Saharan Africa, where sustainable growth is pivotal for debt management (Amankwah et al., 2018). This underscores the importance of growth-friendly policies for debt sustainability, as emphasized in numerous IMF country reports on Ghana.

However, the results in Table 4.4 show that commodity prices (cocoa prices) were found to be statistically insignificant coefficient (0.008) which suggests that commodity price shocks do not have a direct long-run impact on debt sustainability. This reflects Ghana's procyclical fiscal behavior, where commodity windfalls (cocoa prices averaging \$2157.67, with volatility up to \$7390.56) are often expended on immediate consumption rather than saved, perpetuating vulnerability to terms-of-trade shocks (Frankel et al., 2013; Ilzetzki & Végh, 2008; Ossowski & Halland, 2016). Despite cocoa's role as a key export, this insignificance underscores the failure to distinguish permanent from transitory revenues, a common issue in resource-rich economies (Alesina et al., 2008; Aryeetey & Kanbur, 2017).

### *4.4.3 Short-Run Dynamics*

From Table 4.5, as expected, the ETC"CointEq (−1)" has a negative coefficient and is statistically significant at 1%. The short-run results reveal how variables interact during transitional periods. The error correction term measures the rate of adjustment from the short run to the long run. From Table 4.5, the error correction term (−0.256) is statistically significant and indicates that approximately 25.6% of any deviation from long-run equilibrium is corrected within 1 year. This moderate speed of adjustment suggests that while shocks to debt sustainability persist, policy interventions can effectively steer the economy back toward equilibrium. Also, the results in Table 4.5 further revealed the complex dynamics of

**Table 4.5** Estimated short-run results

| *Variable* | *Coefficient* | *Std. error* | *t-Statistic* | *Prob.* |
|---|---|---|---|---|
| COINTEQ* | −0.256186 | 0.022727 | −11.27253 | 0.0000 |
| D(DGDP(−1)) | 0.042906 | 0.093819 | 0.457327 | 0.6536 |
| D(DGDP(−2)) | −0.297338 | 0.107016 | −2.778435 | 0.0134 |
| D(DGDP(−3)) | 0.146523 | 0.065320 | 2.243140 | 0.0394 |
| D(FISCAL_RULE_DUMMY) | −5.907483 | 1.827227 | −3.233032 | 0.0052 |
| D(FISCAL_RULE_DUMMY(−1)) | 30.98203 | 3.307026 | 9.368548 | 0.0000 |
| D(FISCAL_RULE_DUMMY(−2)) | 22.26263 | 3.060037 | 7.275282 | 0.0000 |
| D(FISCAL_RULE_DUMMY(−3)) | 19.59189 | 2.480778 | 7.897477 | 0.0000 |
| D(INFLATION) | 0.038162 | 0.078767 | 0.484492 | 0.6346 |
| D(INFLATION(−1)) | 0.683130 | 0.143336 | 4.765939 | 0.0002 |
| D(INFLATION(−2)) | 0.596620 | 0.126230 | 4.726454 | 0.0002 |
| D(COCOA) | 0.002068 | 0.001268 | 1.630654 | 0.1225 |
| D(COCOA(−1)) | −0.009775 | 0.002712 | −3.604133 | 0.0024 |
| D(COCOA(−2)) | 0.006121 | 0.002600 | 2.353995 | 0.0317 |
| D(COCOA(−3)) | 0.010102 | 0.002973 | 3.398156 | 0.0037 |
| R-squared | 0.960367 | Mean dependent var | | 0.967742 |
| Adjusted R-squared | 0.925689 | S.D. dependent var | | 13.38754 |
| S.E. of regression | 3.649461 | Akaike info criterion | | 5.733380 |
| Sum squared resid | 213.0971 | Schwarz criterion | | 6.427245 |
| Log likelihood | −73.86739 | Hannan-Quinn criter | | 5.959562 |
| F-statistic | 27.69329 | Durbin-Watson stat | | 1.972456 |
| Prob(F-statistic) | 0.000000 | | | |

**Source:** Author's estimation, 2025

fiscal rules in the short run (with both negative and positive significant coefficients) likely reflect the implementation context of rules in Ghana.

This pattern suggests an initial debt-reducing impact upon rule adoption, followed by temporary increases, potentially reflecting a "J-curve" effect where rules are often implemented amid crises, leading to short-term adjustment costs before long-term benefits emerge (Debrun et al., 2009). In Ghana, rules like the 2018 Fiscal Responsibility Act were enacted during high-debt periods (e.g., post-2016 elections), where initial enforcement involves austerity measures that may temporarily elevate borrowing needs before stabilizing debt (Osei et al., 2013; IMF, 2023). This aligns with empirical evidence from OECD and emerging markets, where fiscal rules' short-run effects are heterogeneous due to implementation lags and political resistance (Debrun et al., 2009; Heinemann et al., 2018). The positive lagged coefficients may also capture procyclical overrides,

**Table 4.6** Residual and stability tests results

| *Method* | *F-Statistic* | *Prob* |
|---|---|---|
| Serial correlation | 1.221801 | F(2, 9) = 0.3393 |
| Heteroscedasticity | 0.645642 | F(19, 11) = 0.8060 |
| Normality (Jarque-Bera) | 3.975503 | 0.137003, Normal |
| CUSUM | Within 5% critical region | Stable |
| CUSUMSQ | Within 5% critical region | Stable |

**Source:** Author's construct, 2025

such as frequent target modifications or weak enforcement, undermining immediate discipline (Aryeetey & Kanbur, 2017; Schaechter et al., 2012).

Finally, the lagged effects of inflation and cocoa prices indicate that their impacts on debt sustainability operate through complex transmission mechanisms that unfold over multiple periods. This finding emphasizes the importance of dynamic analysis rather than static relationships when examining fiscal sustainability in developing economies.

### 4.4.4 *Residual and Stability Diagnosis*

The Breusch-Pagan residual test for heteroskedasticity, the Jarque-Bera test for normality, and the LM test for serial correlation are used in this investigation. Table 4.6 revealed that the probability values of the F statistic were higher than the usual significance level of 5%, implying that the data is normally distributed and that the model is free from serial correlation and heteroskedasticity issues. The CUSUM and CUSUMSQ, which are shown in figures A and B at the Appendix, are typically used to confirm the stability of the parameters. Models estimated at the 5% level of significance are shown to be stable since all of the blue lines fall inside the boundaries.

## 4.5 Conclusions and Policy Recommendations

### 4.5.1 *Conclusions*

This study set out to investigate the role of fiscal rules in shaping public debt sustainability in Ghana, using the ARDL bounds testing approach to capture both long-run equilibria and short-run dynamics over the period 1990–2024. The empirical findings offer several important insights that advance the understanding of fiscal governance in resource-dependent developing economies.

First, the results provide robust evidence that fiscal rules exert a significant and debt-reducing effect in the long run. The strongly negative and statistically significant coefficient for the fiscal rule variable provides empirical confirmation for theoretical propositions, indicating that such rules act as credible mechanisms for committing to fiscal discipline. They assist policymakers in resolving the challenges of time-inconsistent preferences and the common-pool resource problem. This result carries special significance for Ghana, a country with a documented tendency for procyclical fiscal policies and election-driven spending cycles. It confirms that well-designed institutional constraints can effectively curb the inherent bias toward deficits and establish a foundation for sustainable debt, even in a climate of political pressure.

The short-term results illustrate that the influence of fiscal rules is not instantaneous but evolves through intricate temporal pathways. The mixture of negative and positive coefficients in the short run implies that the adoption of rules is frequently associated with initial economic adjustments. In Ghana's experience, fiscal rules are often instituted in response to fiscal distress, which may explain why their early effect could include temporary fiscal pressures before the benefits of consolidation are realized in the long term. The error correction term's value, indicating a moderate adjustment speed, reinforces that deviations from the fiscal equilibrium are persistent. This highlights the critical need for unwavering policy implementation and supporting structural reforms to ensure the rules' effectiveness. Economic growth emerged as a key determinant of debt sustainability, confirming that higher growth rates dilute debt ratios and expand fiscal space. Similarly, the long-run negative association between inflation and debt suggests the presence of an "inflation tax" mechanism, where price increases reduce the real value of outstanding nominal debt. However, this finding should be interpreted cautiously, as reliance on inflationary erosion is neither sustainable nor costless, given its destabilizing effects on macroeconomic performance, investment, and welfare.

The study underscores the limits of commodity dependence in securing fiscal sustainability. Cocoa prices, despite their historical importance to

Ghana's export base, were found to exert no significant long-run effect on debt sustainability. This outcome reinforces the argument that procyclical fiscal responses to commodity windfalls such as wage increases and subsidies, have undermined the potential stabilizing role of resource revenues. The result reflects a broader challenge in resource-rich economies, where volatility in terms-of-trade often translates into debt accumulation rather than debt reduction.

### 4.5.2 *Policy Recommendations*

Based on the empirical results, this study proposes a multi-faceted policy framework to advance debt sustainability in Ghana.

Firstly, enhancing the legal and institutional architecture of fiscal governance is imperative. This requires implementing clear statutory debt limits, incorporating carefully calibrated escape clauses for legitimate economic shocks, and establishing consequential enforcement procedures. The credibility of this framework depends on robust oversight institutions, particularly an independent fiscal council endowed with technical autonomy and mandatory public disclosure requirements. Secondly, to counteract the cyclical volatility of commodity earnings, formal counter-cyclical instruments should be institutionalized. Establishing sovereign wealth or stabilization funds, alongside fiscal rules based on structural budget balances, would enable the sequestration of revenues during price upswings to create buffers for economic downturns. This strategy is vital for mitigating the procyclical expenditure patterns that have persistently disrupted fiscal discipline. Thirdly, fiscal consolidation must be underpinned by structural reforms that stimulate economic expansion. Strategic public investment in infrastructure, education, and economic diversification is crucial, as robust growth naturally alleviates debt pressures while creating fiscal space for priority development expenditures. Fourthly, although inflationary dynamics may provide temporary debt relief, deliberate reliance on this mechanism is economically detrimental. A sustainable approach necessitates policy coordination to maintain price stability through sound monetary policy, concurrent with steadfast fiscal adjustment. Finally, technical capacity for debt management requires strengthening through the development of domestic capital markets, enhanced transparency in debt reporting, and active liability management. Furthermore, cultivating cross-political and societal consensus on the principles of fiscal responsibility is essential for the enduring legitimacy and effectiveness of these rules.

In summary, while fiscal rules represent a powerful institutional innovation for Ghana, their success is contingent upon a synergistic policy environment. A comprehensive strategy that integrates credible institutions, counter-cyclical buffers, growth-friendly reforms, and prudent macroeconomic management provides the most viable pathway to durable debt sustainability and economic resilience.

### *4.5.3 Recommendations for Further Studies*

While this study has provided valuable insights into the role of fiscal rules in promoting debt sustainability in Ghana, it also opens avenues for further research. First, the analysis employed a national-level time series framework, which, although suitable for identifying long- and short-run relationships, may obscure important subnational and institutional heterogeneities. Future studies could adopt disaggregated approaches, such as examining the impact of fiscal rules on debt dynamics across different sectors of the economy where fiscal pressures and institutional capacities vary considerably. Second, this study focused primarily on the presence or absence of fiscal rules, operationalized through a binary dummy variable. While this approach captures the broad effect of rules, it does not fully account for differences in the design, scope, and enforcement of fiscal rules over time. Subsequent research could employ more nuanced indicators, such as fiscal rule indices that incorporate dimensions of coverage, legal basis, enforcement mechanisms, and escape clauses, to provide a deeper understanding of how rule design features influence fiscal outcomes.

# Appendix

See Fig. A1.

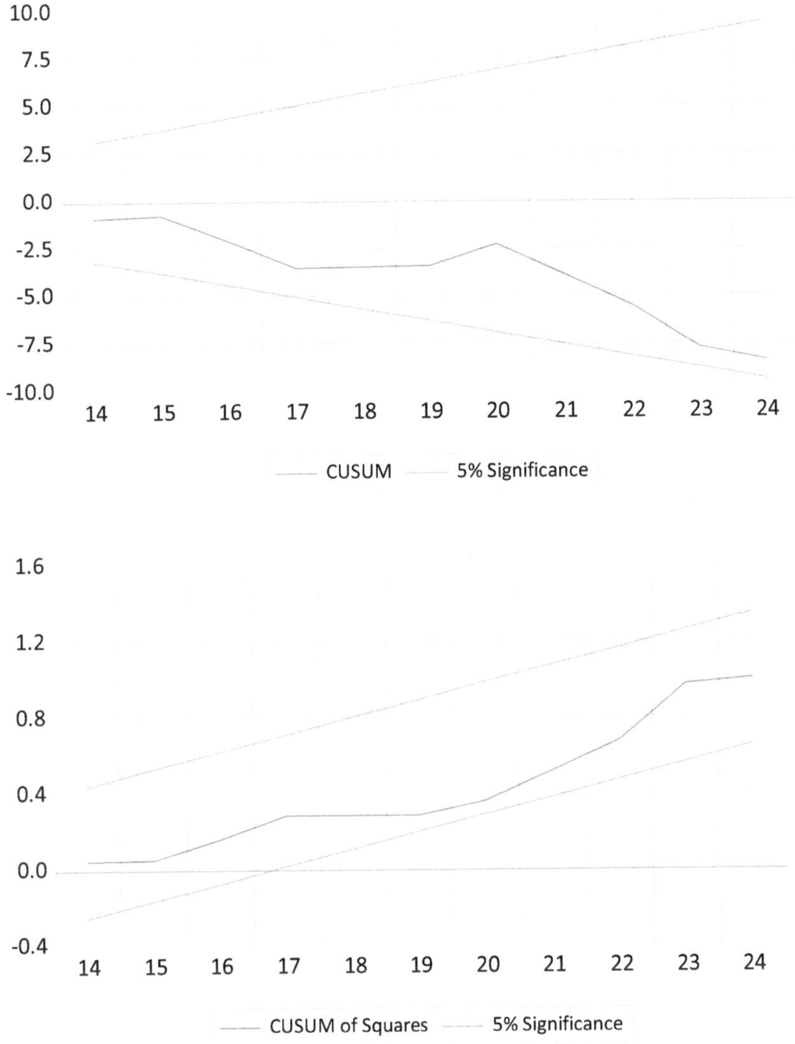


**Fig. A1** Stability test

## References

Abradu-Otoo, P., Acquaye, I., Addy, A., Akosah, N. K., Attuquaye, J., Harvey, S.,... & Nalban, V. (2022). Quarterly Projection Model for the Bank of Ghana. International Monetary Fund.

Alagidede, P., Mensah, J. O., & Ibrahim, M. (2018). Optimal deficit financing in a constrained fiscal space in Ghana. *African Development Review, 30*(3), 291–303.

Alesina, A., Campante, F. R., & Tabellini, G. (2008). Why is fiscal policy often procyclical? *Journal of the European Economic Association, 6*(5), 1006–1036.

Amankwah, G., Ofori-Abebrese, G., & Kamasa, K. (2018). An empirical analysis of the sustainability of public debt in Ghana. *Theoretical Economics Letters, 8*(11), 2038–2054.

Aryeetey, E., & Kanbur, R. (Eds.). (2017). *The economy of Ghana sixty years after independence.* Oxford University Press.

Carrère, C., & De Melo, J. (2012). Fiscal spending and economic growth: some stylized facts. World Development, 40(9), 1750-1761.

Darko, E. A. (2016). Growth impact of government consumption, transfer and interest payments in Ghana [PhD thesis, University of Cape Coast].

Debrun, X., & Kinda, T. (2017). Strengthening post-crisis fiscal credibility: Fiscal councils on the rise–a new dataset. *Fiscal Studies, 38*(4), 667–700.

Debrun, X., Hauner, D., & Kumar, M. S. (2009). Independent fiscal agencies. *Journal of Economic Surveys, 23*(1), 44–81.

Dickey, D. A., & Fuller, W. A. (1979). Distribution of the estimators for autoregressive time series with a unit root. *Journal of the American Statistical Association, 74*(366a), 427–431.

Engle, R. F., & Granger, C. W. (1987). Co-integration and error correction: Representation, estimation, and testing. *Econometrica, 55*(2), 251–276.

Escolano, M. J., Kolerus, M. C., & Ngouana, M. C. L. (2014). *Global monetary tightening: Emerging markets debt dynamics and fiscal crises.* International Monetary Fund.

Fabrizio, S., & Mody, A. (2006). Can budget institutions counteract political indiscipline? *Economic Policy, 21*(48), 690–739.

Frankel, J. A., Vegh, C. A., & Vuletin, G. (2013). On graduation from fiscal procyclicality. *Journal of Development Economics, 100*(1), 32–47.

Heinemann, F., Moessinger, M. D., & Yeter, M. (2018). Do fiscal rules constrain fiscal policy? A meta-regression-analysis. *European Journal of Political Economy, 51*, 69–92.

Ilzetzki, E., & Végh, C. A. (2008). *Procyclical fiscal policy in developing countries: Truth or fiction?* (No. w14191). National Bureau of Economic Research.

International Monetary Fund (IMF). (2023). *Ghana: 2023 article IV consultation and request for an extended credit facility arrangement.* IMF Country Report No. 23/168.

Işık, T., Ayhan, E., Uyarel, H., Tanboğa, İ. H., Kurt, M., Uluganyan, M., Ergelen, M., & Eksik, A. (2013). Association of neutrophil to lymphocyte ratio with presence of isolated coronary artery ectasia.

Johansen, S., & Juselius, K. (1990). Maximum likelihood estimation and inference on cointegration—With appucations to the demand for money. *Oxford Bulletin of Economics and Statistics, 52*(2), 169–210.

Kydland, F. E., & Prescott, E. C. (1977). Rules rather than discretion: The inconsistency of optimal plans. *Journal of political economy, 85*(3), 473–491.

Nabieu, G. A. A., Bokpin, G. A., Osei, A. K., & Asuming, P. O. (2021). Fiscal rules, fiscal performance and economic growth in Sub-Saharan Africa. *African Development Review, 33*(4), 607–619.

Olivera, J. H. (1967). Money, prices and fiscal lags: A note on the dynamics of inflation. *PSL Quarterly Review, 20*(82), 258–267.

Osei, R. D., Asem, F., & Domfe, G. (2013). The political economy dimensions of macroeconomic management of aid in Ghana (No. 2013/106). WIDER Working Paper.

Ossowski, R., & Halland, H. (2016). *Fiscal management in resource-rich countries: Essentials for economists, public finance professionals, and policy makers.* World Bank Publications.

Ouattara, A., Boccara, G., Kockler, U., Lecomte, P., Leprince, P., Leger, P., Riou, B., Rama, A., & Coriat, P. (2004). Remifentanil induces systemic arterial vasodilation in humans with a total artificial heart. *Anesthesiology, 100*(3), 602–607.

Pesaran, M. H. (1997). The role of economic theory in modelling the long run. The economic journal, 107(440), 178–191.

Pesaran, M. H., Shin, Y., & Smith, R. J. (2001). Bounds testing approaches to the analysis of level relationships. *Journal of Applied Econometrics, 16*(3), 289–326.

Reinhart, C. M., & Rogoff, K. S. (2009). *This time is different: Eight centuries of financial folly.* Princeton University Press.

Reinhart, C. M., & Rogoff, K. S. (2010). Growth in a time of debt. *American economic review, 100*(2), 573–578.

Saani, M. R., Abdulai, A. M., & Salifu, M. (2024). Inflation, public debt and unemployment nexus in Ghana. An ARDL analysis. *Cogent Economics & Finance, 12*(1), 2345296.

Schaechter, M. A., Kinda, M. T., Budina, M. N., & Weber, A. (2012). *Fiscal rules in response to the crisis: Toward the "Next-Generation" rules: A new dataset.* International Monetary Fund.

Symansky, S., & Kopits, G. (1998). Fiscal policy rules, IMF Occasional Paper, 162. *International Monetary Fund: Washington DC.*

Tanzi, V. (1978). Inflation, real tax revenue, and the case for inflationary finance: Theory with an application to Argentina. *Staff Papers-International Monetary Fund*, 417–451.

Von Hagen, J., & Harden, I. (1994). National budget processes and fiscal performance. *European Economy Reports and Studies, 3*(1994), 311–418.

PART II

# Debt Management Strategies and Global Dynamics

CHAPTER 5

# Examining the Effectiveness of Debt Restructuring Mechanisms in African Countries

*Mohammed Ridwan Saani, Ibrahim Nandom Yakubu, and Abdulai Iddrisu*

## 5.1 Introduction

Public debt levels in African countries have surged over the past decade, renewing concerns about debt sustainability and the urgent need for effective restructuring mechanisms. By 2024, at least 23 African nations were classified as being in or near debt distress, with several already defaulting or entering formal debt restructuring negotiations (Egiyi, 2025). The region's total debt burden has surpassed USD 1.8 trillion, and a significant share of government revenues is now absorbed by debt service obligations. For instance, interest payments by African governments rose from

M. R. Saani (✉)
School of Economics, University for Development Studies, Tamale, Ghana
e-mail: msaani@uds.edu.gh

I. N. Yakubu • A. Iddrisu
School of Business, University for Development Studies, Tamale, Ghana



I. N. Yakubu (ed.), *Public Debt and Economic Resilience in Africa*, Palgrave Studies in African and Development Economics,
https://doi.org/10.1007/978-3-032-25835-9_5

approximately 6.5 percent of revenue in 2010 to an average of 16.7 percent by 2023, reflecting the mounting cost of borrowing (Mathebula, 2023). These escalating debt service commitments reduce fiscal space for essential public investment in infrastructure, health, education, and social protection, thereby constraining inclusive economic growth and undermining progress toward the Sustainable Development Goals (SDGs) (Epaphra & Mesiet, 2021). Against this backdrop, sovereign debt restructuring, defined as the renegotiation of debt terms with creditors to restore solvency and ensure fiscal sustainability, has emerged as a vital policy instrument for African governments seeking to avert financial crises and maintain macroeconomic stability (Xafa, 2023).

African countries have a long and complex history of engaging in debt relief and restructuring initiatives. During the late 1990s and 2000s, the Heavily Indebted Poor Countries (HIPC) Initiative and the Multilateral Debt Relief Initiative (MDRI) provided more than USD 100 billion in debt cancellation to 37 low-income countries, 31 of which were in Africa (Owusu, 2019). These globally coordinated programs, led by the International Monetary Fund (IMF) and the World Bank, significantly reduced debt ratios, eased interest burdens, and created fiscal space for poverty-reduction programs and investment in human development (Balima & Sy, 2021). However, despite these successes, debt vulnerabilities re-emerged across much of the continent during the 2010s. This resurgence was driven by a combination of factors: renewed borrowing from private and non-traditional bilateral lenders, falling commodity prices, currency depreciations, climate-related fiscal shocks, and governance and transparency challenges in debt management (Nadabo & Alkasim, 2025). By the mid-2020s, approximately half of African low-income countries had returned to a high risk of debt distress or outright default. The COVID-19 pandemic further intensified these pressures by shrinking domestic revenues, elevating health and social expenditures, and triggering tighter global financial conditions (Naseer et al., 2023). In response, initiatives such as the G20 Debt Service Suspension Initiative (DSSI) temporarily deferred debt service payments in 2020–2021, offering short-term liquidity relief but leaving the deeper solvency challenges unresolved (Bello, 2024).

Importantly, today's debt challenges are unfolding in a very different macroeconomic and geopolitical context compared to earlier debt crises. Global interest rates have risen to multi-decade highs following aggressive monetary tightening in advanced economies, sharply increasing the cost of refinancing for African sovereigns (Mosley & Rosendorff, 2023b). Currency depreciation in several African economies has amplified external debt burdens denominated in foreign currency, while inflationary pressures have eroded real incomes and heightened social vulnerabilities (Coulibaly et al., 2024). At the same time, Africa stands at the cusp of major economic transformation opportunities, including the African Continental Free Trade Area (AfCFTA), digitalization of economies, and the energy transition toward renewables (Nchake, 2025). To leverage these opportunities, African governments require sustainable financing frameworks and debt levels that do not crowd out productive investment. Effective debt restructuring mechanisms are therefore not merely tools for crisis management but also critical enablers of long-term economic recovery, private sector confidence, and structural transformation (Petrukha et al., 2024).

This chapter critically examines the evolution, design, and effectiveness of debt restructuring mechanisms in African countries. Section 5.2 provides an overview of the main instruments and frameworks for sovereign debt restructuring, ranging from traditional Paris Club negotiations to market-based bond exchanges and innovative debt-for-nature swaps. Section 5.3 presents a historical review of major African debt restructuring episodes, highlighting country experiences and contextual drivers. Section 5.4 evaluates the outcomes of these restructuring efforts, identifying both successes and persistent challenges, and distills lessons for future practice. Section 5.5 assesses the role of multilateral institutions and bilateral partners, including the IMF, World Bank, Paris Club, China, and private bondholders, in shaping the trajectory of African debt workouts. Section 5.6 discusses key policy challenges and proposes reforms to enhance the timeliness, fairness, and developmental impact of debt restructuring mechanisms. Finally, Section 5.7 concludes by reflecting on the broader implications for Africa's fiscal governance and the need for a more resilient and equitable global debt architecture that can support sustainable economic development on the continent.

## 5.2 Overview of Debt Restructuring Instruments

Sovereign debt restructuring in Africa takes multiple forms and relies on a diverse set of instruments designed to restore debt sustainability while minimizing disruption to economic recovery. Restructuring typically involves altering the original contractual terms—extending maturities, lowering interest rates, applying haircuts, or swapping existing obligations for new instruments with more favorable profiles (Gelpern & Powell,

2023). The mix of tools chosen depends on the country's debt portfolio (domestic versus external, concessional versus commercial) and creditor composition (official bilateral, multilateral, or private) (Mosley & Rosendorff, 2023a). African countries have frequently used several of these instruments simultaneously as part of comprehensive debt workouts. This section examines the main categories of restructuring instruments with practical examples.

### 5.2.1 *Official Bilateral Debt Restructuring*

Official bilateral restructuring refers to debt owed directly to other governments, which historically made up a large share of African external public debt (Imosemi & Taiwo, 2016). For much of the post-independence period, the Paris Club has served as the primary platform for negotiating such debt treatments. The Paris Club's procedures brought together debtor governments and official creditors in a coordinated forum, providing standardized agreements that initially focused on rescheduling debt service over extended maturities (Ocampo & González, 2025). As the debt crisis deepened in the late 1980s and 1990s, the Paris Club progressively moved toward more concessional solutions, such as the Naples Terms (1994), which allowed up to a 67 percent reduction in the net present value of eligible debt, and the Cologne Terms (1999), which increased debt relief to 90 percent or more for countries qualifying under the Heavily Indebted Poor Countries (HIPC) Initiative (Chuku, 2024). These agreements were almost always linked to IMF-supported adjustment programs and were designed to restore a sustainable debt trajectory while encouraging fiscal and structural reforms (Committeri et al., 2021). Nigeria's landmark 2005 Paris Club deal demonstrates the transformative potential of these agreements in allowing countries to escape cycles of serial rescheduling and return to macroeconomic stability (see Box 5.1).

Beyond the Paris Club, the creditor landscape has shifted considerably over the past two decades, with emerging bilateral lenders, particularly China, becoming dominant players in African infrastructure financing (De Kluiver, 2023). This diversification has complicated debt resolution efforts

**Box 5.1 Nigeria's 2005 Paris Club Agreement**

Nigeria's 2005 Paris Club deal remains one of the largest and most comprehensive bilateral debt relief operations in African history. At the time, Nigeria's external debt stock had risen to over USD 35 billion, much of it owed to Paris Club creditors, creating a cycle of arrears and serial rescheduling that constrained fiscal policy and undermined investor confidence. After years of macroeconomic reforms, improved fiscal management, and a sustained campaign of engagement with creditors, Nigeria negotiated a landmark deal that cancelled USD 18 billion of debt (about 60 percent of its eligible obligations) and required a USD 12 billion upfront cash payment to clear arrears. This dual approach of debt buyback and cancellation reduced Nigeria's external debt stock by nearly USD 30 billion. The agreement not only improved Nigeria's debt sustainability indicators dramatically but also restored market confidence, allowing the country to focus on development priorities such as infrastructure and social services.

**Source**: Okonjo-Iweala (2007)

because many of these new creditors are not Paris Club members and have different lending practices, collateral arrangements, and approaches to restructuring (Gelpern & Powell, 2023). To address these coordination challenges, the G20 launched the Common Framework for Debt Treatments in 2020, which aims to bring both Paris Club and non-Paris Club official creditors to the negotiating table under a unified process, working in tandem with IMF and World Bank debt sustainability analyses. Zambia's ongoing restructuring under the Common Framework provides an important test case for this new mechanism and highlights both its promise and its limitations (see Box 5.2).

While the Common Framework has succeeded in aligning major official creditors, including China and traditional Paris Club members, its slow pace, complex negotiation dynamics, and uncertain treatment of private creditors have drawn criticism from debtor countries and observers

**Box 5.2 Zambia and the G20 Common Framework**
Zambia became the first African country to default during the COVID-19 pandemic, missing a Eurobond coupon payment in late 2020. The country applied for treatment under the G20 Common Framework, a mechanism designed to coordinate official bilateral creditors—including Paris Club members and major non-Paris Club lenders such as China—alongside multilateral institutions. Zambia's case was closely watched globally because it represented the first real test of the Common Framework's ability to deliver timely and comprehensive solutions. After prolonged negotiations, Zambia reached an agreement with its official creditor committee in June 2023 to restructure USD 6.3 billion of bilateral debt, which included extending maturities, lowering interest rates, and linking repayments to the country's economic performance. The deal unlocked much-needed IMF support but took more than two years to finalize, highlighting persistent challenges of slow timelines and difficulties securing comparable treatment from private creditors.

**Source**: Bowers & Low (2023) and IMF (2023)

(Ballard-Rosa et al., 2024). The Zambian experience underscores the need for reforms to make official bilateral restructuring more timely, transparent, and predictable, especially given the urgent liquidity pressures faced by many African economies in the aftermath of the COVID-19 pandemic and global interest rate hikes (Mathebula, 2025).

### 5.2.2 *Multilateral Debt Relief Initiatives*

Multilateral creditors such as the IMF, World Bank, and African Development Bank generally maintain preferred creditor status, meaning they are usually repaid in full. However, significant multilateral debt relief has been provided through collective initiatives such as the Heavily Indebted Poor Countries (HIPC) Initiative and the Multilateral Debt Relief Initiative (MDRI) (Jose Maliakal, 2024). Together, these programs reduced debt-to-GDP ratios in participating African countries from over 80 percent on average to around 30 percent by 2007, freeing fiscal space for poverty-reducing expenditure (see Box 5.3). More recently, the G20 Debt Service Suspension Initiative (DSSI) offered temporary relief during

**Box 5.3 Impact of HIPC/MDRI on African Debt Burdens**

The HIPC and MDRI initiatives transformed the debt landscape of Africa. Between 1996 and 2008, thirty African countries benefited from deep, irrevocable debt relief amounting to over USD 100 billion. The programs were conditional on governments implementing macroeconomic stabilization measures, governance reforms, and poverty-reduction strategies. The fiscal space created by HIPC and MDRI allowed governments to significantly boost social spending. For instance, Ghana was able to abolish school fees for basic education, contributing to a surge in primary school enrollment, while Mozambique redirected savings to fund critical infrastructure and health services. Debt service as a percentage of government revenue dropped dramatically, with some countries seeing reductions of up to 80 percent. However, many of these countries subsequently re-accumulated debt due to fresh borrowing from international markets and bilateral creditors, underscoring the importance of complementary debt management strategies to avoid repeated crises.

**Sources**: IMF (2019)

the COVID-19 crisis by deferring about USD 12.9 billion in debt service, demonstrating the feasibility of coordinated emergency measures even if they did not reduce debt stocks (Horas et al., 2025).

### 5.2.3 *Commercial Debt Restructuring*

The rise of commercial borrowing since the early 2000s, particularly through Eurobond issuances, has created new challenges for African debt restructuring. Negotiations with private creditors often involve bond exchange offers or consent solicitations, with collective action clauses (CACs) serving as a crucial legal tool to bind minority holdouts once a qualified majority agrees (Prenestini, 2021). Ghana's 2023 international bond restructuring demonstrates the importance of CACs (see Box 5.4). Earlier experiences, such as Côte d'Ivoire's 1998 Brady bond conversion, show how commercial bank loans were historically restructured through market-based solutions (Morrissey & Kleiman, 2025).

**Box 5.4 Ghana's 2023 Eurobond Exchange**
Ghana's Eurobond restructuring followed its declaration of a moratorium on external debt payments in late 2022. The exchange covered approximately USD 13 billion of outstanding Eurobonds. The government offered investors new bonds with longer maturities, lower interest rates, and reduced near-term cash flow demands. Participation exceeded 90 percent, a figure made possible by the presence of enhanced CACs that allowed collective decisions to bind all bondholders. This exchange significantly reduced Ghana's gross financing needs for 2023–2026 and was instrumental in securing IMF Board approval for a USD 3 billion Extended Credit Facility arrangement. While it provided immediate liquidity relief, the restructuring also extended the maturity profile of debt, implying that Ghana's debt service obligations remain high over the long term, requiring sustained fiscal discipline.

**Source**: Dzawu (2024) and Sandra (2025)

### 5.2.4 *Domestic Debt Operations*

Domestic debt has grown to represent a significant share of public debt portfolios in many African countries, reflecting efforts to deepen local capital markets and reduce reliance on external financing. However, when overall debt becomes unsustainable, governments may be compelled to restructure domestic obligations as part of a comprehensive debt workout (Igberi et al., 2016). Domestic debt operations typically involve exchanging or reprofiling local-currency bonds, treasury bills, and other instruments to extend maturities, lower interest rates, or provide grace periods (Gelpern & Powell, 2023). These exercises are politically and economically sensitive because they affect domestic stakeholders directly—banks, pension funds, insurance companies, and retail investors—and can disrupt financial intermediation if poorly managed (Mbalyohere & Lawton, 2018). For this reason, successful operations usually require extensive stakeholder consultations, legal frameworks to support enforceability, and complementary measures such as liquidity support for affected financial institutions. Ghana's 2023 Domestic Debt Exchange Programme (DDEP) illustrates both the necessity and risks of such operation (see Box 5.5).

**Box 5.5 Ghana's Domestic Debt Exchange Programme (DDEP)**
Faced with debt service consuming over 70 percent of government revenue, Ghana launched the DDEP in early 2023 to restructure roughly GHS 130 billion (USD 10 billion) in domestic bonds. The government offered new instruments with lower coupon rates and extended maturities, aiming to cut interest costs and create fiscal space. After multiple extensions and stakeholder consultations, about 85 percent of eligible bonds were tendered. The exchange imposed significant losses on domestic financial institutions, leading to declines in bank profitability and capital buffers. The Bank of Ghana responded with liquidity injections and a program to recapitalize affected banks. While the DDEP was successful in reducing interest burdens, it also highlighted the social and economic trade-offs of domestic debt restructuring, particularly its impact on household savings and pension funds.

**Source**: Ministry of Finance (2023) and Fitch (2023)

### 5.2.5 *Innovative Instruments and Debt Swaps*

African debt restructurings are increasingly exploring innovative instruments that link debt relief to economic performance or development outcomes. State-contingent debt instruments (SCDIs) tie debt service to GDP growth, commodity prices, or other indicators, providing automatic countercyclical relief in downturns (Masamba, 2024). Similarly, debt-for-nature and debt-for-development swaps exchange partial debt cancellation for commitments to invest in conservation, climate adaptation, or social programs (Radhakrishnan et al., 2025). The Seychelles 2015 debt-for-nature swap is a pioneering African example (see Box 5.6).

**Box 5.6 Seychelles Debt-for-Nature Swap**

Seychelles, a small island developing state with high debt and fragile marine ecosystems, executed a groundbreaking USD 21.6 million debt-for-nature swap in 2015 with support from The Nature Conservancy and bilateral creditors. The arrangement involved buying back external debt at a discount using a combination of donor funds and concessional financing. The savings were redirected into a locally managed trust fund tasked with financing marine conservation and sustainable fisheries management. This deal enabled Seychelles to designate 30 percent of its exclusive economic zone as marine protected areas, improve its fiscal sustainability, and position itself as a global leader in blue finance. The transaction later paved the way for Seychelles' issuance of the world's first sovereign blue bond, which mobilized an additional USD 15 million for ocean-related projects.

**Source**: The Commonwealth (2020) and Gerretsen (2020)

## 5.3 Historical Cases of African Debt Restructuring

Africa's debt restructuring history offers valuable lessons on the effectiveness of different mechanisms in restoring solvency and fiscal space. The early 2000s HIPC and MDRI initiatives delivered sweeping multilateral debt relief, cutting debt ratios and freeing resources for poverty reduction. Landmark bilateral deals, such as Nigeria's 2005 Paris Club agreement, demonstrated the potential of ad hoc arrangements (Gelpern, 2016). Post-conflict restructurings like Côte d'Ivoire's combined multilateral and commercial solutions, while governance failures triggered crises in Mozambique and the Republic of Congo. More recent COVID-19-era restructurings in Zambia, Ghana, and Chad highlight both the promise and the limitations of the G20 Common Framework (Vague, 2023). This section explores these episodes in detail, presenting each case to illustrate how various restructuring instruments have been applied and what outcomes they have produced.

### 5.3.1 HIPC/MDRI Era (2000s): Coordinated Multilateral Relief

The early 2000s witnessed an unprecedented wave of debt forgiveness through the HIPC Initiative and MDRI. In total, 30 African countries qualified for relief, with most reaching the HIPC "completion point" by 2004–2006 (Jose Maliakal, 2024). This milestone triggered irrevocable debt stock reductions and, in the case of MDRI, full cancellation of eligible multilateral debts owed to the IMF, IDA, and the African Development Fund. Countries such as Tanzania, Mozambique, Ghana, Cameroon, and Uganda had the bulk of their external obligations wiped out, dramatically improving their solvency indicators (Sembene, 2021). For example, Ghana's external debt stock fell by more than half after reaching completion point in 2004, while Mozambique received approximately USD 2 billion in debt forgiveness—over 70 percent of its total debt—by 2006. The program required governments to demonstrate sound macroeconomic management and to channel the resulting fiscal space into poverty-reducing expenditure, such as education and health services (Rodriguez Torres, 2023).

HIPC/MDRI is widely credited with restoring debt sustainability for many African low-income countries and enabling an expansion in social spending and investment in infrastructure. However, not all heavily indebted countries benefited at the time. Conflict-affected states such as Sudan and Somalia were unable to participate until much later due to arrears and political instability. Somalia, for instance, only reached the HIPC Decision Point in 2020 and Completion Point in 2023, unlocking approximately USD 4.5 billion in debt relief (Mohamud, 2025). This highlights the importance of political stability and arrears clearance in accessing coordinated multilateral debt relief. The HIPC era thus set a historical benchmark, showing that deep, coordinated debt reduction could reset debt trajectories—yet it also raised the challenge of how to maintain debt sustainability in the long term (Chuku et al., 2023).

### 5.3.2 Nigeria's 2005 Paris Club Deal: A Landmark Bilateral Arrangement

Nigeria's 2005 Paris Club agreement stands out as one of Africa's most significant bilateral debt restructuring successes. By the early 2000s, Nigeria had accumulated more than USD 30 billion in Paris Club debt, much of it dating back to the 1980s and 1990s, despite multiple rescheduling (Fatima & Olasunkanmi, 2023). The debt overhang constrained fiscal policy and deterred investment. Buoyed by a return to democracy, macroeconomic reforms, and windfall oil revenues, Nigeria mounted a sustained diplomatic and technical campaign for debt relief, arguing that its debt burden was unsustainable despite not qualifying for HIPC due to its oil income status (Okorie, 2023). In October 2005, a breakthrough agreement was reached: 60 percent of Nigeria's eligible debt was cancelled outright (USD 18 billion), while the remaining 40 percent (USD 12 billion) was repaid using accumulated oil savings. By April 2006, Nigeria had fully cleared its Paris Club obligations, becoming the first sub-Saharan African country to completely exit bilateral debt to official creditors (Joseph et al., 2024).

The results were transformative. Nigeria's debt-to-GDP ratio plummeted from about 60 percent to under 20 percent, annual debt service payments dropped sharply, and the country regained fiscal autonomy to invest in infrastructure and poverty reduction. The deal demonstrated that ad hoc bilateral negotiations, if backed by strong political commitment and fiscal resources, could yield substantial debt relief even outside the HIPC framework. However, Nigeria's unique oil revenues and fiscal space made such a deal difficult to replicate elsewhere in Africa (Póra, 2021).

### 5.3.3 Côte d'Ivoire: Post-Conflict Restructuring and Market Re-Entry

Côte d'Ivoire offers an instructive example of a country that underwent multiple phases of restructuring, combining bilateral, multilateral, and commercial debt operations. During the 1980s and 1990s, Côte d'Ivoire repeatedly rescheduled its debt through Paris Club agreements and restructured commercial loans under the London Club (Van Mourik, 2025). In 1998, it participated in a Brady Plan operation, converting USD 2.4 billion of commercial bank loans into Brady bonds. However, a civil conflict in the early 2000s led to new arrears and a sovereign default by 2004 (Burdekin & Sweeney, 2021). After peace was restored, Côte d'Ivoire entered the HIPC process, achieving Completion Point in 2012 and receiving approximately USD 6.5 billion in debt cancellation from official creditors, including France, its largest bilateral lender. The country also restructured its defaulted Eurobonds in 2010 and again in 2011 after an election-related crisis, before successfully returning to international capital markets with a Eurobond issuance in 2014 (Valadier et al., 2021). Côte d'Ivoire's experience highlights the importance of a comprehensive approach that combines bilateral, multilateral, and commercial debt treatment, as well as political stabilization, to restore market access and economic confidence (Arhin, 2024).

### 5.3.4 *Emerging Stresses in the 2010s: Commodity Price Shocks and Governance Failures*

Following HIPC/MDRI, many African countries began a new phase of borrowing—this time tapping domestic markets, contracting infrastructure loans from China, and issuing Eurobonds to finance ambitious development agendas (Tang & Pan, 2024). Initially, this "borrowing for growth" strategy was sustainable, supported by high growth rates and favorable global liquidity conditions. However, from 2014 onward, a collapse in commodity prices exposed fiscal vulnerabilities in resource-dependent economies such as Angola, Nigeria, and Zambia. Debt service burdens surged, exchange rates depreciated, and fiscal deficits widened (Tyson, 2021).

Governance failures also contributed to debt crises. Mozambique's "hidden debt" scandal is a prominent case: In 2016, the government disclosed USD 1.4 billion in previously undisclosed, state-guaranteed loans—equivalent to over 10 percent of GDP (Brown, 2025). This triggered a sovereign default on its Eurobond, suspension of IMF financing, and a deep economic crisis. Mozambique ultimately restructured its Eurobond in 2019, securing a partial write-down, extending maturities, and adding a GDP-linked payment clause that ties future repayments to natural gas revenue performance. While the restructuring improved short-term liquidity, it left Mozambique with continued debt vulnerabilities and highlighted the costs of weak debt transparency (Gumel & dos Santos Chivurre, 2024).

The Republic of Congo (Brazzaville) faced similar issues, defaulting in 2016 amid low oil prices and opaque oil-backed loans. It later negotiated debt relief from Chinese creditors and traders, though limited disclosure of terms raised concerns about comparability and fiscal risks (Smith, 2021). These episodes show that debt crises in Africa are no longer confined to low-income countries but can affect resource-rich, middle-income economies when transparency and fiscal discipline weaken (Fosu & Gafa, 2023).

### 5.3.5 *Zambia's Default and the Common Framework (2020–2023)*

Zambia became emblematic of Africa's contemporary debt crisis when it defaulted on a Eurobond coupon in November 2020, becoming the first African sovereign to default in the pandemic era (Mizes & Donovan, 2022). Years of heavy borrowing, combined with falling copper prices, currency depreciation, and rising debt service costs, had rendered its public external debt—estimated at over USD 12 billion—unsustainable (Thegeya, 2025). Zambia requested treatment under the G20 Common Framework in early 2021, initiating a complex negotiation process involving bilateral creditors (including China and Paris Club members), multilateral institutions, and private bondholders (Chelwa et al., 2024).

By June 2023, Zambia reached an agreement with its official creditor committee to restructure USD 6.3 billion of bilateral debt, including maturity extensions up to 20 years and interest rate reductions (Grigorian & Bhayana, 2024). Parallel negotiations with private bondholders resulted in an agreement-in-principle in 2024 targeting an NPV haircut of about 50 percent. Despite this progress, the drawn-out process—lasting nearly 3 years—inflicted significant economic costs, including currency depreciation, elevated inflation, and reduced investor confidence (Loewald et al., 2025). Zambia's case highlights both the value of creditor coordination under the Common Framework and the urgent need to accelerate decision-making to limit economic damage during default periods (Kaluba, 2025).

### 5.3.6 *Ghana's Comprehensive Restructuring (2022–2024)*

Ghana represents a more recent case of comprehensive restructuring involving domestic and external debt. By 2022, Ghana's debt-to-GDP ratio had surpassed 100 percent, and the country had lost access to international capital markets. In December 2022, Ghana announced a suspension of external debt payments, followed by the launch of a Domestic Debt Exchange Programme (DDEP) in early 2023 (Grigorian & Vessereau, 2024). The DDEP achieved approximately 85 percent participation, significantly reducing near-term interest costs but imposing losses on domestic banks and pension funds, which required liquidity and recapitalization support (James, 2024).

On the external side, Ghana requested treatment under the G20 Common Framework and secured a memorandum of understanding in January 2024 to restructure USD 5.4 billion in bilateral debt. Negotiations with Eurobond holders led to an exchange in September 2024 covering approximately USD 13 billion, achieving over 90 percent participation and delivering a 30–40 percent principal haircut (Note, 2024). Ghana's experience is notable for the speed of execution—roughly 1 year from default to bond deal—and for combining domestic and external restructuring into a single comprehensive strategy. The process was politically challenging but is expected to restore debt sustainability and enable renewed IMF support (Abotebuno Akolgo, 2023).

### 5.3.7 *Chad's Common Framework Experience (2021–2022)*

Chad was the first country to conclude a restructuring under the G20 Common Framework. The agreement, finalized in November 2022, involved rescheduling approximately USD 3 billion in official and commercial debt, much of its oil-backed loans from Glencore (Steadman et al., 2023). Rather than providing a reduction in principal, the deal mainly reprofiled payments and introduced a contingency clause requiring creditors to reconvene if oil prices fell sharply. While this approach alleviated immediate liquidity pressures and unlocked IMF disbursements, it left Chad's debt stock largely unchanged and highly sensitive to oil price volatility (Mathebula, 2025). Critics argue that the restructuring "kicked the can down the road," postponing rather than resolving Chad's debt sustainability problem. The case underscores the challenge of balancing short-term liquidity relief with the need for lasting debt reduction in commodity-dependent economies (Egiyi, 2025).

## 5.4 Outcomes and Lessons Learned

The diverse experiences of African debt restructurings provide rich insights into what these mechanisms achieve, where they fall short, and what lessons policymakers can draw for future crises. Evaluating effectiveness requires addressing critical questions: Did the restructuring restore debt sustainability, or was relief temporary? Did it support economic growth, public investment, and poverty reduction? What unintended consequences arose, including moral hazard or financial sector stress? This section synthesizes these outcomes across multiple dimensions, including debt sustainability, economic growth, social spending, timing and adequacy of relief, creditworthiness, and governance, highlighting key lessons for designing more effective sovereign debt workouts.

### 5.4.1 *Restoration of Debt Sustainability: Temporary or Durable?*

The central objective of any restructuring is to place public debt on a sustainable path. African experiences show that many operations achieved this goal in the short term but failed to guarantee long-term solvency. The HIPC/MDRI initiatives of the early 2000s decisively reduced debt burdens: On average, participating countries' debt-to-GDP ratios fell by about two-thirds by 2006, and debt service obligations were slashed to levels not seen in decades. For much of the late 2000s, these countries enjoyed moderate debt ratios and fiscal space for development spending (De Marchi, 2022).

However, a decade later, debt vulnerabilities had resurfaced. The median public debt-to-GDP ratio among 35 post-HIPC African countries more than doubled between 2012 and 2022, rising from roughly 27 percent to over 50 percent (Narnor, 2023). Debt service-to-revenue ratios also nearly doubled, reflecting heavier interest burdens. By 2023, the IMF classified 18 African economies as being in or at high risk of debt distress. This relapse demonstrates that one-off debt relief, while effective at crisis resolution, is not sufficient to ensure lasting sustainability (Dalio, 2022). Key drivers of re-accumulation included optimism bias during the high-growth 2000s, new access to private and non-Paris Club financing, and successive external shocks—commodity price collapses, the global financial crisis, and COVID-19—that weakened fiscal balances (Makin & Layton, 2021). The lesson is clear: Restructuring must be paired with durable fiscal rules, prudent borrowing strategies, and better shock absorbers (e.g., contingency reserves, countercyclical buffers) to avoid a repeat cycle of "relief followed by relapse."

### 5.4.2 *Economic Growth and Investment Outcomes*

Debt relief is often justified on the grounds that it removes the "debt overhang," stimulating investment and growth. Evidence from Africa suggests that this effect is real but modest and not always sustained. IMF studies indicate that growth in HIPC beneficiaries was about 0.7 percentage points higher, on average, in the 5 years after completion than before (Marcelino & Hakobyan, 2014). This likely reflects a combination of restored investor confidence, reduced debt service, and higher public investment. Indeed, many countries accessed capital markets for the first time post-HIPC (e.g., Ghana in 2007, Senegal in 2009), signalling regained creditworthiness.

Yet long-term growth performance has been uneven. After an initial acceleration in the 2000s, growth slowed from 2011 onward even as public spending remained high, suggesting that fiscal space was not always used productively (Ferry & Raffinot, 2019). In some cases, governments borrowed heavily for infrastructure, but projects yielded low returns or suffered from cost overruns and corruption. This weakened the expected growth dividend and contributed to renewed debt distress. The key lesson is that debt relief must be coupled with strong public investment management, improved governance, and structural reforms that enhance productivity—otherwise countries risk falling into a "borrow–grow–default" cycle that periodically requires new rounds of restructuring.

### 5.4.3 *Social Spending and Poverty Reduction*

A major rationale for debt relief is to create fiscal space for poverty reduction. The HIPC framework explicitly required countries to monitor and increase Poverty-Reducing Expenditures (PREs). Initially, this worked: Education's share of government budgets rose from about 15 to 18 percent, and several countries eliminated user fees for primary education, boosting enrolment. However, gains were uneven and often not sustained. Health spending remained broadly flat as a share of GDP (around 1.5–2 percent) over two decades, and some countries diverted fiscal space to subsidies, military spending, or patronage.

The re-emergence of high debt service burdens in the 2010s once again squeezed social spending. By the early 2020s, over 30 African countries were spending more on external debt service than on health. In countries like Ghana, Kenya, and Malawi, interest payments consumed 20–26 percent of revenue—more than their entire health budgets.[1] These outcomes suggest that unless restructuring achieves deep, durable reductions in debt

[1] Read more here: https://institute.global/insights/economic-prosperity/a-new-debt-deal-for-africa-breaking-the-vicious-cycle

service, the poverty dividend is short-lived. Future operations must right-size debt burdens to ensure governments can maintain adequate funding for health, education, and social protection without continually sliding back into arrears.

### 5.4.4 *Timing and Adequacy: Avoiding "Too Little, Too Late"*

African experience highlights a recurrent problem: Restructurings are often delayed until debt crises are full-blown and reserves are depleted, resulting in higher economic and social costs. Zambia's 2020 default and 3-year negotiation under the G20 Common Framework illustrates this challenge. Prolonged uncertainty led to inflation, currency depreciation, and reduced investor confidence, worsening the economic toll. Earlier, pre-emptive engagement might have contained the crisis at lower cost.

In addition, relief has sometimes been insufficient, leaving countries with debt levels still vulnerable to shocks. IMF research shows that "shallow" restructurings based on optimistic growth assumptions frequently lead to repeat defaults. Recent African cases have moved toward deeper relief: Ghana and Zambia's external bondholders accepted roughly 50 percent NPV haircuts—well above the historical emerging market average of around 37 percent—reflecting recognition of the severity of current crises (Savage, 2023). The policy takeaway is that restructurings should be both timely and comprehensive: Delay only increases adjustment costs, while underestimating the scale of relief needed risks setting the stage for another round of distress.

### 5.4.5 *Creditworthiness and Market Re-Entry*

Another measure of success is whether a country regains access to international capital markets on reasonable terms. Some countries have done so quickly—Nigeria issued a Eurobond by 2011, just 6 years after its Paris Club exit, and Côte d'Ivoire tapped markets by 2014 after its HIPC completion (Nwankwo, 2023). Others have remained excluded for long periods, as in the cases of Sudan and Zimbabwe, where unresolved arrears and political risks keep them locked out of international finance.

Even where re-entry occurs, ratings often remain speculative-grade for years, keeping borrowing costs high. Sovereigns that achieve orderly, collaborative restructurings—engaging bondholders early and securing high participation—tend to regain market trust faster. The use of collective action clauses in recent African bond restructurings has been helpful in maintaining creditor relations. The broader lesson is that regaining creditworthiness depends not only on debt reduction but also on credible post-restructuring policies that signal a commitment to fiscal discipline and reform.

### 5.4.6 *Moral Hazard and Responsible Borrowing*

A recurring concern is whether debt relief encourages reckless future borrowing. Evidence from Africa suggests that while governments did borrow more after HIPC, this reflected development financing needs and the availability of cheap credit, rather than a calculated expectation of future bailouts.[2] Nonetheless, the post-HIPC borrowing surge highlights the need for stronger safeguards: Transparent debt reporting, parliamentary oversight, and regional debt convergence criteria (such as those in WAEMU and CEMAC) can help anchor responsible borrowing. International creditors can reinforce these incentives by linking relief to governance improvements, as was done under HIPC completion point triggers that required public financial management reforms.

### 5.4.7 *Procedural Lessons: Coordination, Fairness, and Speed*

The process of restructuring itself has yielded important procedural lessons. Coordination among diverse creditors is essential to achieve equitable burden-sharing and avoid free-riding. Past HIPC experiences were undermined by holdout litigation, prompting legal reforms such as the United Kingdom's Debt Relief (Developing Countries) Act of 2010, which prevented vulture funds from suing HIPC countries for full repayment in UK courts. In the current era, the challenge is integrating new creditor classes—especially China—into coordinated processes. Zambia's Common Framework case shows that this is possible but time-consuming; clearer rules on comparability of treatment and faster decision-making procedures are needed (Essers & Cassimon, 2023).

Private creditor participation remains voluntary, leaving gaps in relief—as demonstrated by the limited effectiveness of the DSSI, which excluded

[2] https://www.afrodad.org/sites/default/files/publications/Afrodad%20Debt%20Restructuring%202082024.pdf

bondholders. Constructive engagement with bondholder committees and the use of collective action clauses, as seen in Ghana's 2024 bond exchange, represent progress toward more orderly outcomes. The overarching lesson is that the global sovereign debt architecture still lacks a comprehensive, binding mechanism; outcomes depend on creditor cooperation and debtor diplomacy, making reforms to streamline and depoliticize the process a priority for the future.

## 5.5 Multilateral and Bilateral Roles

The outcome of debt restructurings in Africa is shaped not only by debtor governments' policies but also by the actions of a diverse constellation of external stakeholders. Multilateral institutions, bilateral creditors, and private investors collectively determine the scope, depth, and speed of debt relief. Their roles are complementary but not always perfectly aligned. While the IMF and World Bank set analytical benchmarks and provide interim financing, bilateral and private creditors must deliver the actual debt treatment needed to restore sustainability. Table 5.1 maps these key actors, outlining their primary instruments, influence, contributions, and constraints.

## 5.6 Policy Challenges and Future Reforms

The persistent shortcomings in Africa's sovereign debt resolution processes underscore the need for systemic reform. Delays in negotiations, insufficient debt reduction, fragmented creditor participation, and governance gaps have repeatedly prolonged crises and undermined development gains. These challenges are not merely technical but have real socio-economic costs—depleting fiscal space, crowding out health and education spending, and eroding public trust. At the same time, they present an opportunity for innovation: from legal reforms and new contractual clauses to climate-linked financing instruments and stronger domestic debt governance. Table 5.2 presents the key policy challenges and the principal reforms to build a faster, fairer, and more development-friendly debt restructuring architecture for African countries.

**Table 5.1** Roles of multilateral institutions, bilateral creditors, and private lenders in African debt restructuring

| *Actor/group* | *Role and instruments* | *Influence on debt restructuring* | *Strengths/ contributions* | *Challenges/ constraints* |
|---|---|---|---|---|
| **IMF (International Monetary Fund)** | Provides macroeconomic programs (ECF, SBA), Debt Sustainability Analyses (DSA), bridge financing, and policy conditionality | Sets the debt relief "envelope" via DSAs; program approval signals reform commitment and unlocks other financing | Credible and independent arbiter; offers emergency funding to stabilize reserves during negotiations | DSAs sometimes contested by creditors; program conditionality can be politically sensitive; financing assurances requirement can delay disbursement |
| **World Bank (IDA) & AfDB** | Provide concessional loans, grants, and policy advice; support initiatives like HIPC/ MDRI and Debt Reduction Facility buybacks | Encourage creditors to act; offer development financing to ensure social spending continues post-restructuring | Long-term development focus; concessional funding offsets fiscal pressure; grants can fund debt buybacks | Maintain "preferred creditor" status and do not take haircuts, shifting more burden onto others; constrained balance sheets limit scope for relief |
| **Paris Club (Traditional bilateral creditors)** | Negotiates standardized rescheduling/ forgiveness terms (Toronto, Naples, Cologne); provides venue for coordinated bilateral relief | Aggregates creditors, ensures comparability of treatment, and sets precedent for other lenders | Transparent, tested procedures; progressively more concessional terms; quick decision-making | Membership excludes key emerging creditors (China, India, Gulf states); influence declining as share of debt falls |

(*continued*)

**Table 5.1** (continued)

| *Actor/group* | *Role and instruments* | *Influence on debt restructuring* | *Strengths/ contributions* | *Challenges/ constraints* |
|---|---|---|---|---|
| **China and other non-Paris club bilaterals** | Provide infrastructure and resource-backed loans; now participate in DSSI and G20 Common Framework | Critical for comprehensive solutions due to large share of debt (approximately 12 percent owed to China) | Willingness to co-chair creditor committees; offers maturity extensions and grace periods | Prefers maturity reprofiling over haircuts; coordination with Paris Club and private creditors can be slow; limited transparency of loan terms |
| **G20 Common Framework (CF)** | Formal platform aligning Paris Club and non-Paris Club creditors to negotiate jointly | Creates a single negotiation forum and links official relief to comparable private creditor treatment | Historic inclusion of China and India in collective process; aims to unify terms across creditors | Very slow processes (18–30 months in cases like Zambia, Chad); lacks legal tools to compel private participation; opaque timelines |
| **Private creditors (bondholders, banks, traders)** | Hold approximately 43 percent of Africa's external debt; restructure via bond exchanges, consent solicitations, or loan renegotiations | Their participation is crucial for comprehensive debt relief and IMF program approval | CACs and bondholder committees facilitate collective negotiation; can deliver large NPV reductions | Participation is voluntary; may delay until default; free-riding problem (as seen during DSSI); require strong incentives or IMF programs to agree |

(*continued*)

**Table 5.1** (continued)

| *Actor/group* | *Role and instruments* | *Influence on debt restructuring* | *Strengths/ contributions* | *Challenges/ constraints* |
|---|---|---|---|---|
| **African Union (AU) and regional institutions** | Advocate for reforms; propose Pan-African Credit Rating Agency; coordinate African Debt Action Plan | Amplify African voice in global forums; shape discourse on fairness and transparency | Push for systemic reform; encourage debt data transparency and faster resolution | Limited enforcement power over global creditors; rely on consensus-building and diplomacy |
| **Regional Development Banks (AfDB, Afreximbank)** | Provide bridge loans, liquidity support, and technical assistance | Help countries avoid disorderly defaults and finance critical imports during crises | Quick-response financing; support negotiation capacity through facilities like ALSF | Loans can add to debt burden if not coordinated with restructuring strategy; also claim preferred status, limiting relief burden-sharing |

**Source**: Authors' compilation

## 5.7 Conclusion

The analysis of debt restructuring in Africa demonstrates that while significant progress has been made in building frameworks such as the HIPC/ MDRI initiatives, the G20 Debt Service Suspension Initiative, and the Common Framework, Africa's debt challenges remain persistent and cyclical. The chapter showed that restructurings have often been delayed, partial, or overly optimistic in their assumptions, leading to renewed debt vulnerabilities within a decade. While Ghana's comprehensive domestic and external restructuring and Zambia's Common Framework agreement signal a maturing architecture, they also highlight the costs of protracted negotiations, including currency depreciation, investor flight, and social hardship. Moreover, creditor coordination remains imperfect, particularly with the rise of non-Paris Club bilateral lenders and private bondholders who hold a large share of Africa's external debt. Without reforms, Africa

**Table 5.2** Key policy challenges and reform proposals for improving African debt restructuring

| *Policy challenge* | *Description and implications* | *Illustrative cases/evidence* | *Proposed reforms and future directions* |
|---|---|---|---|
| **1. Slow and sequential restructuring (delays in action)** | Debt restructurings in Africa often occur several years after debt distress becomes evident, which worsens the economic and social costs of the crisis. Negotiations are usually sequential—first with official bilateral creditors (governments and multilateral institutions), followed by private creditors (bondholders, commercial banks). This back-to-back approach creates prolonged stalemates, erodes investor confidence, and forces countries to continue using scarce foreign currency reserves to service debt, leaving little for essential imports | Zambia defaulted in 2020 but did not finalize its debt restructuring agreement until mid-2023, during which time the currency depreciated sharply, inflation rose, and poverty increased. Ethiopia requested Common Framework treatment in 2021 but had yet to reach a deal by late 2024, worsening fiscal stress and slowing recovery | • Establish parallel negotiation tracks so that talks with official and private creditors take place simultaneously rather than sequentially.<br>• Introduce automatic standstills on debt service and legal actions when a country requests restructuring under International Monetary Fund (IMF) supervision.<br>• Include standstill clauses in bond contracts and secure their recognition in major legal jurisdictions such as the United Kingdom and New York to protect debtor countries from lawsuits during negotiations |
| **2. Inadequate debt relief (insufficient reduction)** | Some restructurings focus only on rescheduling payments rather than reducing the debt stock, leaving countries with high debt burdens that remain vulnerable to external shocks and risk falling back into distress | Chad's 2022 debt treatment merely deferred payments without reducing the principal or interest, leaving the country vulnerable to a decline in oil prices. Ghana's restructuring, though substantial, still leaves its debt-to-gross-domestic-product ratio at approximately 55 percent and interest payments consuming over 20 percent of government revenue | • Base restructuring terms on conservative debt sustainability analyses that incorporate stress tests for low growth or commodity price shocks.<br>• Target a manageable debt-service-to-revenue ratio, such as below 10 percent, to ensure fiscal space for essential development spending.<br>• Expand concessional refinancing options through institutions like the International Development Association (IDA) and the World Bank to replace expensive commercial debt with long-term, low-cost financing |

| | | | |
|---|---|---|---|
| **3. Limited participation of private creditors** | Private creditors now hold roughly 43 percent of Africa's external public debt, yet their participation in restructurings is voluntary and often delayed, weakening burden-sharing and prolonging crises | During the Debt Service Suspension Initiative (2020–2021), private creditors did not suspend any payments, while official creditors deferred approximately 13 billion US dollars—effectively allowing public resources to flow to bondholders instead of supporting crisis response | • Pass legislation in major jurisdictions (United Kingdom, New York, European Union) to require private creditor participation in restructurings endorsed by the IMF or the Group of Twenty (G20).<br>• Improve debt transparency through full disclosure of loan terms, collateral arrangements, and debt registries to build trust and speed up negotiations.<br>• Promote the use of bondholder committees and collective action clauses to secure high participation and prevent holdouts |
| **4. Complex and fragmented creditor landscape** | African countries now borrow from a wide range of creditors—traditional Paris Club members, China, Gulf states, hedge funds, commodity traders, and regional banks—making coordination difficult. Loans backed by commodities or project revenues create additional complexity and can result in preferential treatment for some creditors, undermining fairness | Zambia's restructuring involved lengthy negotiations to reconcile the positions of Chinese lenders, Paris Club members, and international bondholders. Collateralized loans from commodity traders and Chinese policy banks often received priority payments, complicating comparability of treatment with other creditors | • Standardize state-contingent clauses in loan agreements so that debt service automatically adjusts to economic shocks (e.g., GDP-linked or disaster-linked clauses).<br>• Develop principles for collateral treatment to ensure creditors with collateral share restructuring burdens equitably.<br>• Deepen regional financial markets and support initiatives like an African Stability Mechanism to reduce dependence on volatile international markets |

(*continued*)

Table 5.2 (continued)

| | | | |
|---|---|---|---|
| **5. Linking debt relief with development and climate goals** | High debt service burdens crowd out spending on the Sustainable Development Goals and climate adaptation, leaving African countries under-invested in green and resilient infrastructure | In 2023, more than 30 African countries spent more on debt service than on public health. The Seychelles debt-for-nature swap illustrates how debt treatment can be tied to conservation and development objectives | • Expand debt-for-climate and debt-for-nature swaps that redirect debt service savings into climate-resilient investments.<br>• Mainstream climate-resilient debt clauses that allow payment deferrals after natural disasters.<br>• Integrate debt restructuring with global climate finance initiatives such as the Bridgetown Initiative and Special Drawing Rights reallocation for resilience |
| **6. Weak domestic debt management and governance** | Poor debt recording, weak legal frameworks, and limited parliamentary oversight contribute to repeated cycles of unsustainable borrowing and hidden liabilities | Mozambique's "hidden debt" scandal revealed 1.4 billion US dollars in previously undisclosed loans in 2016, triggering a default and undermining public trust. Kenya and Ghana have faced repeated debates over rising debt ceilings and transparency | • Strengthen public debt management offices with capacity to assess risks and report transparently to legislatures and the public.<br>• Enact fiscal responsibility laws that cap debt accumulation and require parliamentary approval for new borrowing.<br>• Increase reliance on concessional loans and grants for development financing to avoid high-interest commercial debt that raises future debt distress risks |

**Source**: Authors' compilation based on Sokpoh and Kessler (2023), Commodore and Awuah (2024), and Gwaindepi (2025).

risks continuing the cycle of relief, relapse, and restructuring, undermining fiscal credibility and long-term development goals.

Moving forward, African governments, multilateral partners, and creditors must work toward a more timely, equitable, and development-oriented debt resolution system. Policy reforms should institutionalize parallel negotiations with official and private creditors to shorten timelines and reduce uncertainty. Automatic standstill clauses, recognized by major legal jurisdictions, would protect scarce resources during negotiations and prevent litigation from holdout creditors. Future restructurings must deliver debt service relief deep enough to restore fiscal space, supported by conservative debt sustainability analyses and stress-tested assumptions. Legal reforms, such as extending anti-vulture fund legislation and enforcing private sector participation, would enhance fairness and comparability of treatment. Finally, debt restructuring must be better aligned with Africa's development and climate objectives through instruments like debt-for-climate swaps and climate-resilient debt clauses, while African countries strengthen domestic debt management, transparency, and accountability to prevent a recurrence of unsustainable debt buildups. Together, these measures can transform debt restructuring from a reactive crisis tool into a proactive enabler of economic resilience and sustainable growth.

## References

Abotebuno Akolgo, I. (2023). Ghana's Debt crisis and the political economy of financial dependence in Africa: History repeating itself? *Development and Change, 54*(5), 1264–1295. https://doi.org/10.1111/dech.12791

Arhin, J. K. (2024). *Promoting Ghana beyond aid policy within ECOWAS economic integration: Challenges and prospects.* https://uniselinus.education/sites/default/files/2025-03/jonas%20kofi%20arhin.pdf

Balima, H., & Sy, A. (2021). IMF-supported programs and sovereign debt crises. *IMF Economic Review, 69*(2), 427.

Ballard-Rosa, C., Mosley, L., & Rosendorff, B. P. (2024, April, 3). Paris club restructuring and the rise of China. *Manuscript, University of North Carolina at Chapel Hill.* https://www.peio.me/wp-content/uploads/PEIO16/submission_124.pdf

Bello, M. (2024). *Re-imagining sovereign debt in international law through the lens of socio-economic rights.* Pretoria University Law Press.

Bowers, G., & Low, E. T. (2023). Implications of Zambia's sovereign debt restructuring. https://www.columbiathreadneedle.com/en/se/institutional/insights/implications-of-zambias-sovereign-debt-restructuring/

Brown, K. J. (2025). Why hide? Africa's unreported debt to China. *The Review of International Organizations, 20*(1), 1–32. https://doi.org/10.1007/s11558-023-09513-4

Burdekin, R. C., & Sweeney, R. J. (2021). The evolution of sovereign debt default: From the thirteenth century to the modern era. *The Journal of European Economic History (JEEH), 50*(2), 9–56.

Chelwa, G., Kaulule, N. S., & Renzio, P. D. (2024). External forces and Zambia's permanent debt crisis. *Development, 67*(3–4), 248–259. https://doi.org/10.1057/s41301-025-00431-z

Chuku, C. (2024). Wholesale debt relief: Do LICs need a new package? *Journal of African Economies, 33*(Supplement_2), ii39–ii61.

Chuku, C., Samal, P., Saito, J., Hakura, D., Hakura, M. D. S., Chamon, M., d Chamon, M. M., Cerisola, M., Cerisola, M. M. D., & Chabert, G. (2023). *Are we heading for another debt crisis in low-income countries? Debt vulnerabilities: Today vs the pre-HIPC era*. International Monetary Fund.

Committeri, M., Alves, I., Arthur, J., De Marchi, R., Essers, D., Keeney, M., Kosterink, P., Lieber, A., Martinez-Resano, J. R., & Osińska, J. (2021). *The IMF's role in sovereign debt restructurings.* https://repository.uantwerpen.be/docstore/d:irua:12969

Commodore, R., & Awuah, G. B. (2024). The changing nature of debt in Africa. https://acetforafrica.org/?smd_process_download=1&download_id=64880

Coulibaly, I., Gnimassoun, B., Mighri, H., & Saadaoui, J. (2024). International reserves, currency depreciation and public debt: New evidence of buffer effects in Africa. *Emerging Markets Review, 60*, 101130.

Dalio, R. (2022). *Principles for navigating big debt crises.* Simon and Schuster.

De Kluiver, J. (2023). *Africa's debt dilemma: China's role and implications for development.* Institute for Security Studies. http://issafrica.s3.amazonaws.com/site/uploads/PB-185.pdf

De Marchi, R. (2022). Public debt in low-income countries: Current state, restructuring challenges and lessons from the past. *Bank of Italy Occasional Paper, 739.* https://papers.ssrn.com/sol3/papers.cfm?abstract_id=4463139

Dzawu, M. M. (2024). Ghana Eurobonds exit default as new bonds issued to investors. https://www.bloomberg.com/news/articles/2024-10-10/ghana-eurobonds-exit-default-as-new-bonds-issued-to-investors

Egiyi, M. A. (2025). *Today's reckless borrowing: Economic incarceration and infertility for tomorrow.* https://gouni.edu.ng/new/wp-content/uploads/2025/07/17-INAUGURAL_LECTURE-CORRECTED-COPY.pdf

Epaphra, M., & Mesiet, W. (2021). The external debt burden and economic growth in Africa: A panel data analysis. *Theoretical & Applied Economics, 28*(2) http://www.ebsco.ectap.ro/Theoretical_&_Applied_Economics_2021_Summer.pdf#page=175

Essers, D., & Cassimon, D. (2023). Towards HIPC 2.0? Lessons from past debt relief initiatives for addressing current debt problems. *Journal of Globalization and Development, 13*(2), 187–231.

Fatima, F., & Olasunkanmi, O. (2023). Debt crisis and Nigerian economy: An assessment of the Buhari administration (2015-2021). *Journal of Economics, Management and Trade, 29 (3), 65, 72.*

Ferry, M., & Raffinot, M. (2019). Curse or blessing? Has the impact of debt relief lived up to expectations? A review of the effects of the multilateral debt relief initiatives for low-income countries. *The Journal of Development Studies, 55*(9), 1867–1891.

Fitch. (2023). Final terms of Ghana's sovereign domestic debt restructure to still hurt banks' capital. https://www.fitchratings.com/research/banks/final-terms-of-ghanas-sovereign-domestic-debt-restructure-to-still-hurt-banks-capital-15-02-2023

Fosu, A. K., & Gafa, D. W. (2023). Governance and debt accumulation in Africa. In *Handbook of public management in Africa* (pp. 151–168). Edward Elgar Publishing. https://www.elgaronline.com/abstract/book/9781803929392/chapter9.xml

Gelpern, A. (2016). Sovereign debt: Now what? *Yale Journal of International Law, Forthcoming.* https://papers.ssrn.com/sol3/papers.cfm?abstract_id=2820626

Gelpern, A., & Powell, A. (2023). *Sovereign debt restructuring: The need for a newapproach.*https://publications.iadb.org/en/sovereign-debt-restructuring-need-new-approach

Gerretsen, I. (2020). The deal that saved Seychelles' troubled waters. https://www.bbc.com/future/article/20200803-the-deal-that-saved-seychelles-troubled-waters

Grigorian, D. A., & Bhayana, A. (2024). *Zambia: A case study of sovereign debt restructuring under the G20 common framework.* Center for Global Development. https://www.cgdev.org/sites/default/files/zambia-case-study-sovereign-debt-restructuring-under-g20-common-framework.pdf

Grigorian, D. A., & Vessereau, L. (2024). *Ghana: A case study of sovereign debt restructuring under the G20 common framework.* Center for Global Development. https://www.cgdev.org/sites/default/files/ghana-sovereign-debt-restructuring-under-g20-common-framework.pdf

Gumel, B. I., & dos Santos Chivurre, A. L. (2024). *The impact of sovereign debt and currency depreciation on the Mozambican economy.* https://hal.science/hal-04754813/

Gwaindepi, A. (2025). The solution for Africa's debt lies in economic resilience. https://www.diis.dk/en/research/the-solution-africas-debt-lies-in-economic-resilience

Horas, Y., Morra, F., & Wiedenbrüg, A. (2025). *Debt relief for resilience*. https://www.iisd.org/system/files/2025-04/debt-relief-for-resilience.pdf

Igberi, C. O., Odo, S. I., Anoke, C. I., & Nwachukw, U. G. (2016). The implications of rising public debt on unemployment in Nigeria: An auto regressive distributed lag approach. *Asian Research Journal of Arts & Social Sciences, 1*(1), 1–15.

IMF. (2019). Heavily indebted poor countries (Hipc) initiative and multilateral debt relief initiative (MDRI). https://www.imf.org/-/media/Files/Publications/PP/2019/PPEA2019028.ashx

IMF. (2023). IMF managing director welcomes debt treatment agreement reached by Zambia and its official creditors under the G20 common framework. https://www.imf.org/en/News/Articles/2023/06/22/pr23235-imf-welcomes-debt-treatment-agreement-reached-by-zambia

Imosemi, A., & Taiwo, A. (2016). Child marriage and abduction in Nigeria: Exploring the Ese Oruru Saga and the legal implications. *University of Jos Law Journal, 5*(4), 70–73.

James, H. (2024). *The IMF and the European debt crisis*. International Monetary Fund.

Jose Maliakal, S. (2024). *Debt relief initiatives: HIPC and MDR*. https://open-docs.ids.ac.uk/articles/report/Debt_Relief_Initiatives_HIPC_and_MDR/29314733?file=55369832

Joseph, F. I., Nwankwo, K. C., & Ihuoma, W. E. (2024). Effect of external debt on economic growth in Nigeria. *International Journal of Economics and Financial Management (IJEFM), 9*(9), 53–83.

Kaluba, C. C. (2025). *Measuring systemic risk for Zambia's banking institutions: A proactive approach*. [PhD Thesis, The University of Zambia]. https://dspace.unza.zm/handle/123456789/9182

Loewald, C., Steinbach, R., & Rakgalakane, J. (2025). *Less risk and more reward revising South Africas inflation target*. https://www.resbank.co.za/content/dam/sarb/publications/working-papers/2025/less-risk-more-reward.pdf

Makin, A. J., & Layton, A. (2021). The global fiscal response to COVID-19: Risks and repercussions. *Economic Analysis and Policy, 69*, 340–349.

Marcelino, M. S., & Hakobyan, M. I. (2014). *Does lower debt buy higher growth? The impact of debt relief initiatives on growth*. .

Masamba, M. L. (2024). Examining the interconnection between debt, climate change, and conservation: The potential role of state-contingent debt instruments in Africa. *Development, 67*(3–4), 305–314. https://doi.org/10.1057/s41301-025-00430-0

Mathebula, N. (2025). *Debt crises and sovereign risk in Africa*. Taylor & Francis.

Mathebula, N. C. (2023). *The Indicators of sovereign risk for South Africa's Imf loan*. University of Johannesburg (South Africa). https://search.proquest.com/openview/550c0d35c7d2447e3dd93b335b441900/1?pq-origsite=gscholar&cbl=2026366&diss=y

Mbalyohere, C., & Lawton, T. C. (2018). Engaging stakeholders through corporate political activity: Insights from MNE nonmarket strategy in an emerging African market. *Journal of International Management, 24*(4), 369–385.

Ministry of Finance. (2023). The government announces successful results of its domestic debt exchange with approximately 85% Participation rate and a new settlement date. https://mofep.gov.gh/press-release/2023-02-14/the-government-announces-successful-results-of-its-domestic-debt-exchange-with-approximately-85-participation-rate-and-a-new-settlement-date

Mizes, J. C., & Donovan, K. P. (2022). Capitalizing Africa: High finance from below. *Africa, 92*(4), 540–560.

Mohamud, K. M. (2025). *Transforming Somalia's public financial management: Reforms, federalism, and economic resilience in a post-conflict state*. https://www.researchsquare.com/article/rs-6803842/latest

Morrissey, B., & Kleiman, G. (2025). *Emerging economies and financial markets: A career-tested approach to analyzing the markets. Springer Nature Switzerland*. https://doi.org/10.1007/978-3-031-85669-3

Mosley, L., & Rosendorff, B. P. (2023a). Government choices of debt instruments. *International Studies Quarterly, 67*(2), sqad030.

Mosley, L., & Rosendorff, B. P. (2023b). The unfolding sovereign debt crisis. *Current History, 122*(840), 9–14.

Nadabo, Y. S., & Alkasim, S. (2025). Decolonizing debt: A critical analysis of neocolonial structures in international debt agreements and institutional sovereignty in Sub-Saharan Africa. *International Journal of Integrative Research, 3*(5), 343–364.

Narnor, A. D. (2023). *Macroeconomic policies and external debt in Ghana: Lessons from the Latin American countries* [Master's Thesis, University of Lethbridge (Canada)]. https://search.proquest.com/openview/cd9aa14df0f063c42083bd8493f4b782/1?pq-origsite=gscholar&cbl=18750&diss=y

Naseer, S., Khalid, S., Parveen, S., Abbass, K., Song, H., & Achim, M. V. (2023). COVID-19 outbreak: Impact on global economy. *Frontiers in Public Health, 10*, 1009393.

Nchake, M. A. (2025). Green transition, trade policy and sustainable development: An African perspective. *Mohd Nayyer Rahman Nida Rahman, 125*.

Note, L. D. G. (2024). *Public debt coverage*. https://www.elibrary.imf.org/downloadpdf/view/journals/002/2024/350/article-A002-en.pdf

Nwankwo, A. (2023). Sustainability of the debt relief: Nigeria's case. https://ecdpm.org/work/debt-relief-where-do-we-stand-where-do-we-go-

volume-2-issue-1-january-2013/sustainability-of-the-debt-relief-nigerias-case

Ocampo, J. A., & González, K. D. (2025). Current debt challenges and proposals for an enhanced international debt architecture. *Journal of Globalization and Development*. https://doi.org/10.1515/jgd-2024-0044

Okonjo-Iweala, N. (2007). Nigeria's fight for debt relief: Tracing the path. *Global development, 2.*

Okorie, O. (2023). Addressing the impending sovereign debt crisis in Nigeria: Strategies for prevention and sustainable management. Available at SSRN 4949609. https://papers.ssrn.com/sol3/papers.cfm?abstract_id=4949609

Owusu, O. J. (2019). *Debt sustainability of emerging economies in sub-Saharan Africa* [PhD Thesis, University of Ghana]. https://ugspace.ug.edu.gh/items/238384a2-3aa5-4feb-bb24-a8a8c91df78c

Petrukha, N., Petrukha, S., & Miakota, R. (2024). Debt policy in the conditions of the war economy and post-war recovery. *Publishing House "Baltija Publishing."* http://www.baltijapublishing.lv/omp/index.php/bp/catalog/download/467/12558/26248-1

Póra, A. (2021). Policy proposal trends in sovereign debt restructuring. *Law and Financial Markets Review, 15*(1–2), 164–180. https://doi.org/10.1080/17521440.2022.2063569

Prenestini, F. (2021). The importance of being bound: Bondholders' vote and workouts in the US and in Italy. *Am. Bankr. LJ, 95*, 313.

Radhakrishnan, H., Patel, S., Kelly, L., & Steele, P. (2025). Aligning debt relief for climate and nature with the principles of effective development cooperation. *Economics.* https://www.iied.org/sites/default/files/pdfs/2025-02/22608iied.pdf

Rodriguez Torres, M. C. (2023). *Impacts of social spending, economic freedom and Institutional factors on poverty in Latin American countries. Impact analysis of free school policy in Colombia.* http://elea.unisa.it/handle/10556/7893

Sandra, A. (2025). Gov't makes US$346 million Eurobond coupon payment. https://propartners.com.gh/govt-makes-us346-million-eurobond-coupon-payment/

Savage, R. (2023). Ghana and Zambia's debt restructurings going in diverging directions. https://www.reuters.com/world/africa/ghana-zambias-debt-restructurings-going-diverging-directions-citi-2023-03-17/

Sembene, D. (2021). Mobilizing external financing for Africa's crisis recovery. *CGD Policy Paper, 206.* https://www.cgdev.org/sites/default/files/mobilizing-external-financing-africas-crisis-recovery.pdf

Smith, G. (2021). *Where credit is due: How Africa's debt can be a benefit, not a burden.* Oxford University Press.

Sokpoh, A., & Kessler, M. (2023). African perspectives on the current debt situation and ways to move forward. https://findevlab.org/african-perspectives-on-the-current-debt-situation-and-ways-to-move-forward/

Steadman, S., Gençsü, I., Mustapha, S., Colenbrander, S., & Tyson, J. (2023). *Indebted: How to support countries heavily reliant on oil and gas revenues to secure long-term prosperity.* ODI Report. https://www.econstor.eu/handle/10419/280303

Tang, X., & Pan, S. (2024). Impact of market-based financing on Africa's debt and development. *China International Strategy Review, 6*(1), 122–138. https://doi.org/10.1007/s42533-024-00164-7

The Commonwealth. (2020). Case study: Innovative financing – Debt for conservation swap, Seychelles' conservation and climate adaptation trust and the blue bonds plan, Seychelles (on-going). https://thecommonwealth.org/case-study/case-study-innovative-financing-debt-conservation-swap-seychelles-conservation-and

Thegeya, A. (2025). *Public debt in Kenya: An economic history.* Taylor & Francis.

Tyson, J. (2021). Financial-sector development and inclusive and sustainable economic growth in sub-Saharan Africa. *Joint FSDA and ODI Working Paper.* http://cdn-odi-production.s3.amazonaws.com/media/documents/ODI_Working_Paper_1_Financial_sector_development_FINAL.pdf

Vague, R. (2023). *The paradox of debt: A new path to prosperity without crisis.* University of Pennsylvania Press.

Valadier, C., Jonveaux, B., Vigato, A., Le Goff, M., Hemar, M., Torrellio, L., Puloc'h, M., Terrieux, M., Monat, E., & Duquesnay, C. (2021). Endemic uncertainties in developing countries: Issues arising from an increased interdependence between banks and the state. *AFD MacroDev, 37*, 1–37.

Van Mourik, S. (2025). Globalizing neoliberalism: The IMF, the Paris Club, and the political economy of sovereign default in Africa after 1982. *Global Perspectives, 6*(1), 131862.

Xafa, M. (2023). Sovereign debt restructuring: The way forward. *Journal of Globalization and Development, 13*(2), 435–474. https://doi.org/10.1515/jgd-2021-0070

CHAPTER 6

# Global Economic Shocks and Debt Vulnerability in African Economies

*Khadijah Iddrisu*

## 6.1 Introduction

Over the years, African economies have become more deeply integrated into global financial and trade systems (Iddrisu et al., 2025). This integration is reflected in trade linkages, where many African countries, particularly resource-rich ones, including Ghana, Nigeria, Algeria, and Congo, primarily export raw materials while simultaneously relying on imports of finished goods from advanced economies (Kyereboah-Coleman et al., 2024). It is also evident in the continent's efforts to attract international engagement through policies including the African Continental Free Trade Area (AfCFTA) (Iddrisu et al., 2024; Opoku & Boachie, 2020). The reliance on multilateral development agencies such as the United Nations, the International Monetary Fund (IMF), and multilateral development banks (MDBs) underscores the deep interconnectedness of Africa with the global system. While this integration offers opportunities for growth, technology transfer, and financing, it also increases exposure to

K. Iddrisu (✉)
Department of Finance, Islamic University College, Accra, Ghana
e-mail: khadijahiddris@iug.edu.gh



I. N. Yakubu (ed.), *Public Debt and Economic Resilience in Africa*, Palgrave Studies in African and Development Economics,
https://doi.org/10.1007/978-3-032-25835-9_6

external shocks, over which governments have little control. These external shocks are mostly referred to as global economic shocks. Examples of these shocks include the outbreak of the Coronavirus Disease 2019 (COVID-19), vulnerabilities in the Middle East and North Africa (MENA), ongoing trade wars, and recent coup d'états in several African countries.

Global economic shocks can affect multiple areas of a country's economy, often increasing the risk of debt vulnerability. Debt vulnerability is a situation in which a country faces an elevated risk of debt distress due to its limited capacity to manage and sustainably repay public debt (Elkhishin & Mohieldin, 2021). Given the limited domestic resources of most African governments, managing such shocks often compels them to increase borrowing. For instance, the COVID-19 pandemic and the Russia-Ukraine war forced the Ghanaian government to resort to unprecedented levels of borrowing, marking the highest in the country's history. The United Nations Conference on Trade and Development (UNCTAD, 2025) revealed that, most African countries spend more on interest payments than health and education. Zambia defaulted on its external debt in 2020 as a result of the COVID-19 crisis, and by 2023, its debt-to-GDP ratio had surpassed 100%, leaving the country with limited fiscal space for recovery (Ndwaru, 2024). It is therefore essential to analyse how global economic shocks influence debt vulnerability in Africa. The central objective of this chapter is to examine the ways in which such shocks interact with African economies' debt profiles, thereby amplifying their vulnerability.

Unlike some existing studies that focus exclusively on external debt vulnerability (Elkhishin & Mohieldin, 2021; Leykun, 2024; Muhanji & Ojah, 2011), or examine factors unrelated to global economic shocks (Leykun, 2024), this chapter considers overall debt vulnerability and how it is shaped by global economic shocks. While it does not employ inferential statistical methods to establish causality, it relies on empirical data to conduct descriptive analysis and draws on practical examples from diverse African countries to illustrate the realities beyond what the data alone may reveal. This paper is significant in several respects. First, it helps policymakers understand the vulnerability of African debt to global shocks. Second, it provides insights on building resilience through policies that reduce overdependence on other continents. Third, it serves as a guide for policymakers on effective debt management, even in the face of global economic shocks.

The remainder of this chapter is organized as follows: Section 6.2 examines debt evolution and associated vulnerabilities. Section 6.3 explores the impact of global economic shocks on debt vulnerabilities in Africa. Section 6.4 discusses coping mechanisms and policy responses, while Section 6.5 considers the future outlook of global economic shocks and debt vulnerabilities in Africa. The chapter concludes with final remarks.

## 6.2 Debt Evolution and Vulnerabilities in Africa

In the late twentieth century, many African countries faced unsustainable debt due to heavy external borrowing, weak exports, and macroeconomic instability, with debt-to-GDP ratios often exceeding 100% and debt service consuming over 30% of revenues (Dawelbait, 2015). In response, the international community launched two major initiatives such as the Heavily Indebted Poor Countries (HIPC) and Multilateral Debt Relief Initiative (MDRI). The HIPC Initiative of 1996 provided debt relief tied to structural reforms, while the MDRI of 2005 offered full cancellation of eligible debts to the IMF, World Bank, and African Development Bank (AfDB) for countries completing the HIPC process (see Box 6.1). While 34 African countries have been deemed eligible, 3 of them such as Somalia, Sudan, and Eritrea have not completed the process (Box 6.1).

**Box 6.1 HIPC Initiative and MDRI**

The Heavily Indebted Poor Countries (HIPC) Initiative, launched in 1996 by the World Bank, IMF, and other multilateral, bilateral, and commercial creditors, was designed to restore debt sustainability for the world's poorest nations. It sought to prevent countries from being trapped in unsustainable debt while freeing resources for development. To qualify, a country had to demonstrate unsustainable debt even after traditional relief mechanisms, rely primarily on highly concessional financing from the International Development Association (IDA) and the IMF's Poverty Reduction and Growth Trust (PRGT), and establish a credible track record of reforms under IMF and World Bank supported programmes. In addition, countries were required to prepare a Poverty Reduction Strategy Paper (PRSP) with civil society participation.

(*continued*)

**Box 6.1 (continued)**

The Multilateral Debt Relief Initiative (MDRI), launched in 2005, complemented the HIPC Initiative by providing full cancellation of eligible debts owed to the IMF, IDA, and African Development Bank (AfDB) for countries that had completed the HIPC process. Its primary objective was to create fiscal space for achieving the Millennium Development Goals, particularly poverty reduction. By 2024, 37 countries worldwide had benefited, including 34 in Africa, together receiving more than US$100 billion in relief. Of these African cases, 31 have completed the process, though Sudan faces delays due to political instability, and Eritrea remains potentially eligible but has not engaged. Somalia reached completion in December 2023, unlocking US$4.5 billion in savings. These 31 countries are Benin, Burkina Faso, Burundi, Cameroon, the Central African Republic, Chad, Comoros, Republic of Congo, Democratic Republic of Congo, Côte d'Ivoire, Ethiopia, The Gambia, Ghana, Guinea, Guinea-Bissau, Liberia, Madagascar, Malawi, Mali, Mauritania, Mozambique, Niger, Rwanda, São Tomé and Príncipe, Senegal, Sierra Leone, Tanzania, Togo, Uganda and Zambia.

Source: IMF (2025c) and World Bank (2024)

The composition and structure of Africa's debt have changed significantly since the HIPC/MDRI era, reflecting new financing sources and instruments (see Table 6.1). Although most African countries borrow both domestically and externally, external borrowing tends to dominate. World Bank data indicate that Mozambique holds the highest external debt stock at 192%, while Botswana records the lowest at 11% (Fig. 6.1).

Debt vulnerability is the extent to which a country's debt position is exposed to risks of distress under adverse economic or financial conditions, determined not only by the absolute level of debt, but also by the fragility of its fiscal and external position shaped by both domestic and global factors (Doemeland et al., 2022). Emerging markets and developing economies, in particular, face heightened debt vulnerabilities due to evolving financing challenges and shifts in creditor composition (IMF, 2025a). Assessing vulnerability through indicators such as credit ratings, liquidity risks, and external debt-service burdens is therefore critical for identifying countries at risk of debt distress (Jensen, 2021). As of 2024, a record number of low-income countries are grappling with debt distress

**Table 6.1** Current public debt landscape in Africa

| *Debt landscape* | *Focus* |
|---|---|
| External vs. domestic debt | External debt dominates low-income African countries, while middle-income states increasingly use costly domestic bonds due to high interest rates. |
| Concessional vs. commercial loans | After HIPC/MDRI, concessional loans from institutions like IMF, World Bank, and AfDB dominated, but the past decade saw rising costly Eurobonds and syndicated loans. |
| Eurobond | Since Ghana's 2007 debut Eurobond, over 20 African states have issued sovereign bonds, expanding financing but creating refinancing risks tied to volatile global financial conditions. |
| Multilateral and bilateral creditors | Despite diversification, IMF, World Bank, and AfDB remain vital in crises, while emerging bilateral creditors like India, Turkey, and Gulf states grow but lack coordination |
| Chinese lending and South–South financing | China has become a key bilateral lender funding infrastructure, but concerns remain over opaque terms, collateralised loans, and concentrated repayment risks burdening African borrowers. |

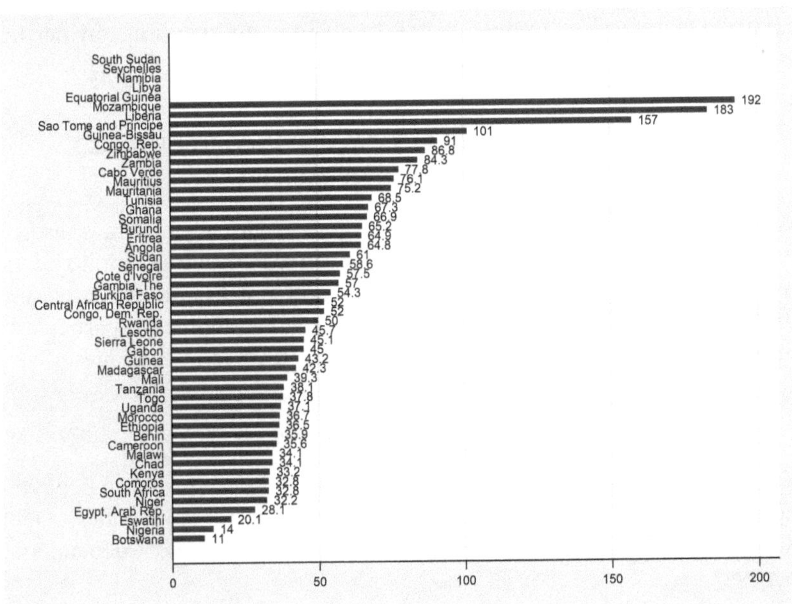


**Fig. 6.1** External debt (% GNI) in Africa, 2000–2023, by country. (Source: Authors' Construct based on data from World Development Indicators of the World Bank)

or are at heightened risk. The IMF's latest debt sustainability analysis shows that 10 countries are already in debt distress, while another 52 face moderate to high risk. Notably, 40 of these 62 countries are in Africa (United Nations Department of Economic and Social Affairs (UNDESA), 2024).

Debt vulnerability in Africa is aggravated by narrow revenue bases, high dependence on commodity exports, weak domestic capital markets, and governance challenges (Moreira, 2023). For instance, the 2008 global financial crisis, commodity price shocks in the 2010s, and easy access to global capital markets encouraged a new wave of borrowing, which finance deficits and development needs. Pandemics and some geopolitical shocks also cause debts vulnerability. COVID-19 triggered Africa's worst recession in 50 years, exacerbate debt vulnerabilities (Moreira, 2023). The war in Ukraine and global monetary tightening further strained fiscal space and raised borrowing costs (Coulibaly, 2024). For example, the IMF approved Mongolia's US$99 million Rapid Financing Instrument to address COVID-19 impacts, supporting urgent budget and balance needs while protecting vulnerable groups and hardest-hit sectors (Utsunomiya, 2020). Debt service burdens began crowding out spending on health, education, and climate resilience (Commodore & Awuah, 2024).

## 6.3 Evidence on Global Economic Shocks and Debt Vulnerability

While global economic shocks affect economies globally, Africa is disproportionately impacted due to its reliance on commodities, limited economic diversification, high debt levels, and weak infrastructure and institutions. Examining their effect on debt vulnerabilities is particularly important given the structural characteristics of African economies.

### *6.3.1 Theoretical Linkages*

Various theories show how global economic shocks can promote debt vulnerability. This chapter focuses on the following key theories: Debt Sustainability Analysis (DSA) and structuralist and dependency perspectives.

*Debt Sustainability Analysis*

DSA is the conventional framework used by the IMF and World Bank to evaluate debt dynamics (IMF, 2025b; World Bank, 2022a). Rooted in the work of Domar (1944) and further developed in the debt sustainability literature (Blanchard, 1990), the model assesses whether a country can manage its debt over time. Debt is deemed sustainable when the real growth rate of the economy ($g$) exceeds the real interest rate on public debt ($r$), provided that primary fiscal balances remain under control. Conversely, when $r$ surpasses $g$, debt ratios increase, particularly in the presence of persistent fiscal deficits, leading to risks of unsustainable accumulation.

However, this balance is highly vulnerable to external shocks beyond domestic control. Growth shocks, such as falling global demand or declining commodity prices, reduce export revenues and fiscal space, thereby constraining debt servicing capacity (UNCTAD, 2021). Interest rate shocks, often triggered by monetary tightening in advanced economies such as the U.S. Federal Reserve rate hikes, increase borrowing costs and debt service burdens (Eichengreen & Hausmann, 1999). Exchange rate shocks, such as dollar appreciation, further amplify risks by raising the local currency cost of servicing foreign-denominated debt (Reinhart & Rogoff, 2010). Consequently, even seemingly sustainable debt can quickly become distress-prone under adverse global conditions.

*Structuralist and Dependency Theories*

While classical models emphasise mathematical debt dynamics, structuralist and dependency theories underscore the systemic vulnerabilities embedded in Africa's global economic position. Scholars such as Frank (1967) and Singer (1975) argue that African economies are structurally dependent on the export of a narrow range of primary commodities, such as oil, minerals, coffee, and cocoa, leaving them highly exposed to volatile price swings beyond their control. Their reliance on external borrowing, often denominated in foreign currency, further entrenches a cycle of peripheral dependence on global creditors and investors (Amin, 1976; dos Santos, 1985). From this perspective, the debt problem is not merely cyclical but fundamentally structural, rooted in global inequalities in trade, finance, and technology. For instance, Zambia's dependence on copper exports or Nigeria's reliance on oil revenues demonstrates how sudden global downturns or price collapses can translate almost immediately into fiscal crises and debt distress (Baskaran & Pearson, 2023; Ernest, 2024).

Thus, debt vulnerability in Africa is reframed less as a product of domestic policy mismanagement and more as a systemic feature of global capitalism, shaped by enduring asymmetries between the core and the periphery (Amin, 1976).

### 6.3.2 Channel Mechanism

Global economic shocks transmit into sovereign debt distress in Africa through multiple, often overlapping, channels. These mechanisms transform external disturbances into fiscal fragility and heightened default risks. Five of the most significant channels are discussed below.

*Exchange Rate Depreciation and External Debt Service Burdens*
Contemporary analyses of debt dynamics highlight the growing influence of global financialisation in a highly interconnected economy. Sovereign debt is no longer shaped solely by fiscal balances and economic growth but also by global investor sentiment, credit ratings, and portfolio shifts driven by changing risk perceptions (Al-Amine & Willems, 2020). Sudden changes in global risk appetite can trigger abrupt reversals in capital flows, known as "sudden stops", which leave African governments struggling to refinance maturing obligations. In Ghana, the inability to refinance maturing obligations forced the government to postpone Eurobond issuances and suspend payments on some selected external debts (Moses-Ashike, 2022). In addition, geopolitical shocks such as conflicts, sanctions, or pandemics can undermine investor confidence. The increasing role of non-traditional creditors adds complexity, making debt management and restructuring more challenging.

*Revenue Volatility and Fiscal Fragility*
Many African economies remain highly dependent on commodity exports such as oil, copper, and cocoa, making them particularly vulnerable to external shocks. When global demand weakens or prices fall, export earnings decline sharply, leading to reduced fiscal revenues and limited capacity to service debt obligations. This dependence exposes governments to significant repayment challenges, as their revenue bases are not sufficiently diversified to absorb sudden downturns. A clear example is the 2014–2016 oil price collapse, which severely undermined the fiscal and debt positions of Nigeria and Angola, forcing both countries into greater borrowing and macroeconomic instability (Grigoli et al., 2017; Stocker et al., 2018).

Burkina Faso's reliance on gold and cotton exports made it vulnerable to COVID-19, and the 2022–2023 inflation surge cut export revenues, strained fiscal space, and increased debt dependence, heightening exposure to external shocks (Federal Ministry for Economic Cooperation and Development, 2024).

*Refinancing and Rollover Risks*

A key feature of Africa's recent borrowing trend is the growing reliance on short- to medium-term commercial instruments like Eurobonds and syndicated loans. While these provide access to large-scale financing, they expose countries to significant refinancing and rollover risks. Several governments now face "maturity walls", where large Eurobond redemptions fall due within tight timeframes, as seen in Kenya and Nigeria during the mid-2020s (Obulutsa, 2024). Global shocks, including US interest rate hikes or investor risk aversion, can abruptly shut markets, making refinancing difficult or only possible at sharply higher costs. This dynamic creates a vulnerability trap, heightening risks of arrears or restructuring.

*Political Economy Dimensions*

Debt vulnerability in Africa is shaped not only by macroeconomic conditions but also by the political economy of borrowing and debt management. Weak governance and opaque loan agreements, such as Mozambique's "hidden debt" scandal, undermine accountability and heighten repayment risks, while fragile public financial systems compound the problem (Gebregziabher & Sala, 2022). Creditor fragmentation adds complexity, as the mix of Eurobond holders, China, Gulf States, and multilateral lenders complicates restructuring and requires strong institutional capacity and diplomatic skill. Political incentives also drive risky borrowing, with governments often increasing debt to finance election-related spending. Limited technical expertise further weakens debt management, turning fiscal challenges into systemic crises.

*Crowding Out of Development Spending*

Rising debt service costs in African economies impose severe opportunity costs by diverting resources away from essential development priorities. In many countries, debt servicing now exceeds spending on health, education, or infrastructure (UNDESA, 2024). For instance, Nigeria spends more on interest payments than on health and education combined, while Kenya allocates nearly half of its revenues to debt servicing (Amadala,

2025; Bahuli & Bala, 2020). This forces governments to cut capital expenditure, undermining long-term growth and perpetuating cycles of debt dependence. The burden also carries intergenerational consequences, as delays in public investment weaken human capital and infrastructure development. Thus, debt distress functions not just as a fiscal challenge but as a fundamental developmental constraint.

## 6.4 Coping Mechanisms and Policy Responses

### *6.4.1 Domestic Resource Mobilisation and Revenue Reforms*

A central strategy for reducing Africa's dependence on external borrowing is strengthening domestic revenue generation. Many countries have pursued tax policy reforms, such as broadening tax bases, digitising administration, and expanding value-added taxes (VAT). Rwanda modernised its tax systems to improve compliance (Rwanda Revenue Authority, 2023), while Nigeria increased VAT to boost non-oil revenues (Alli, 2025). Resource-rich states have also sought to enhance transparency and capture more rents through revised regimes, as seen in Botswana's diamond revenues, Nigeria's Petroleum Industry Act, Zambia's mining tax regime and among others (African Forum and Network on Debt and Development, 2021; Ndlovu & Vandome, 2024). However, most African economies still collect under 20% of GDP in taxes due to informality, weak enforcement, and political resistance. Sustainable progress requires stronger institutions and firm political will.

### *6.4.2 Role of Multilateral Institutions*

Multilateral institutions remain central to Africa's debt management and crisis response. The IMF provides emergency financing, such as the Rapid Credit Facility during COVID-19, and conducts debt sustainability assessments that guide restructuring negotiations, though its austerity-linked programmes often raise social tensions. The World Bank, through the International Development Association (IDA), supplies concessional lending and technical support for debt management and fiscal reforms. The AfDB offers countercyclical budget support and project financing, while its African Development Fund (ADF) provides concessional financing for low-income states. For instance, Ghana benefited from the IMF and World Bank during COVID-19 (Quarm et al., 2020). Despite criticism over delays, conditionalities, and rigid policy prescriptions, these institutions remain indispensable in supporting Africa's debt resilience.

### 6.4.3 *Debt Restructuring Mechanism*

When debt becomes unsustainable, restructuring is essential, though processes are often slow and fragmented. The G20's Common Framework, launched in 2020, sought to unify restructuring efforts, but progress in cases like Ethiopia, Chad, and Zambia has been delayed by creditor disagreements and procedural ambiguities (Georgieva & Pazarbasioglu, 2021). Private creditors, particularly Eurobond holders, complicate negotiations by resisting significant relief, as Zambia's prolonged default shows (Chen et al., 2020). Innovative tools, such as Seychelles' 2015 debt-for-nature swap, highlight alternatives, yet global restructuring mechanisms remain reactive and inadequate.

### 6.4.4 *Green and Sustainable Finance as a Buffer Against Shocks*

Africa is increasingly turning to innovative financing tools to address the dual challenge of rising debt and climate change. Countries such as South Africa, Nigeria, Tunisia, and Egypt have issued green bonds to fund renewable energy and climate-resilient infrastructure (Lwesya, 2025). Island states like Seychelles and Mauritius pioneered debt-for-climate swaps that reduce debt burdens while supporting environmental protection (Elmahdi & Jeong, 2024). Multilateral climate funds, including the Green Climate Fund (GCF),[1] Global Environment Facility (GEF),[2] and Climate Investment Fund (CIF)[3], provide additional resources for adaptation projects. For example, GEF has financed adaptation projects across

[1] GCF is the world's largest dedicated climate finance mechanism, established in 2010 under the United Nations Framework Convention on Climate Change (UNFCCC). As of 2023, GCF had a portfolio of US$13.5 billion, mobilizing over US$51.9 billion including co-financing.

[2] GEF is a multilateral financial mechanism established in 1991, just ahead of the 1992 Rio Earth Summit, to help tackle the world's most pressing environmental challenges. Since inception, the GEF has provided over US$26 billion in grants and mobilized more than US$150 billion in co-financing, supporting over 5,000 projects globally.

[3] CIF, established in 2008 by MDBs, mobilized US$7.4 billion and US$64.6 billion co-financing to support low-carbon, climate-resilient development in emerging economies.

countries like Malawi, Tanzania, and Burkina Faso, focusing on agriculture, water security, and climate-resilient infrastructure (Aleksandrova et al., 2025; Michaelowa et al., 2021).

### 6.4.5 *Regional Approaches*

Regional initiatives seek to strengthen Africa's financial resilience by pooling risks and building buffers against shocks. The AfCFTA aims to boost intra-African trade, reducing dependence on volatile global commodity markets, though its benefits depend on infrastructure and gradual implementation (Samunderu, 2024). Regional financial institutions like African Export–Import Bank (Afreximbank) have provided countercyclical support, as seen during COVID-19 (Afreximbank, 2024). The proposed African Monetary Fund symbolises aspirations for financial sovereignty but remains unrealised (Box 6.2). Currency unions in West African Economic and Monetary Union (WAEMU) and the Communauté Financière Africaine (CFA) zone offer exchange rate stability but limit monetary policy autonomy (AU, 2014; Dagah et al., 2019).

**Box 6.2 African Monetary Fund a Means to Minimise Debt Vulnerability in Africa**

The African Monetary Fund (AMF) is a proposed financial institution of the African Union (AU) intended to advance monetary cooperation, macroeconomic stability, and deeper economic integration across the continent. Formally established through the AU Protocol adopted at the Malabo Summit in June 2014, the AMF will become operational once at least 15 member states ratify the treaty. With its headquarters planned in Yaoundé, Cameroon, the Fund is envisioned as a key pillar of Africa's financial architecture, alongside the African Central Bank and the African Investment Bank under the Abuja Treaty. Its mandate includes harmonising monetary policies, reducing trade restrictions, and laying the foundation for a future common African currency. The AMF is projected to operate with a paid-up capital of US$23 billion, positioning it as one of Africa's largest regional institutions. However, it remains non-operational due to limited ratification and governance concerns, raising questions about its feasibility and role.

Source: AU (2014) and Dagah et al. (2019)

## 6.5 Future Outlook

Africa's debt vulnerability depends on global financing shifts, national and regional policies, and structural transformation capacity, with innovation offering resilience but persistent risks of recurrent distress.

### *6.5.1 Trend in Global Financing Conditions*

Global financing conditions are shifting in ways that will heavily influence African debt sustainability. Post-COVID borrowing has elevated debt ratios, forcing governments to balance growth with consolidation. For example, a clear example is Cabo Verde, where post-COVID borrowing led to a sharp rise in public debt, peaking at over 150% of GDP in 2021 (Laws et al., 2025). Geopolitical fragmentation such as US-China rivalry and Russia West tensions is altering trade, aid, and investment patterns, which could either broaden financing options or deepen dependencies. Persistently, high global interest rates tighten liquidity, raising borrowing costs and restricting Eurobond access mainly to stronger rated economies. For instance, Kenya, facing high global interest rates in 2023–2024, postponed Eurobond issuance, shifted to syndicated loans and concessional financing, while rising bond yields signalled investor concerns and costly refinancing (Cytonn, 2024). At the same time, growing momentum for climate finance, including green bonds, carbon markets, and concessional funds, offers opportunities.

### *6.5.2 Risks of Debt Distress Cycles Without Structural Transformation*

Despite opportunities, Africa faces a high risk of recurring debt crises if structural weaknesses persist (Ndung'u et al., 2021). Heavy dependence on commodities leaves fiscal revenues vulnerable to global price shocks, while weak tax systems and large informal sectors constrain domestic resource mobilisation. Rising debt service ratios already divert funds from health, education, and infrastructure, threatening a "lost decade" of development (Atingi-Ego et al., 2021). For example, Kenya has seen its debt service costs rise to nearly 60% of revenues, forcing budgetary reallocations away from public investment (Global Development Policy Center, 2025). A fragmented creditor landscape complicates future restructurings, slowing recovery. Climate vulnerability further compounds risks, as unintegrated adaptation strategies may trigger simultaneous environmental and fiscal crises. Without structural transformation, Africa risks repeating pre HIPC cycles of borrowing, distress, and delayed recovery.

### 6.5.3 *Opportunities for Resilience*

Despite ongoing challenges, African economies have significant opportunities to strengthen resilience and reduce debt vulnerability. Economic diversification through industrialisation, value addition, and expansion of services can stabilise fiscal revenues, with Ethiopia's manufacturing drive and Kenya's ICT sector providing encouraging examples. Regional integration under the AfCFTA could expand intra-African trade, reduce exposure to external shocks, and attract investment, with potential GDP gains of US$450 billion by 2035 (World Bank, 2022b). Innovative financing tools such as debt-for-climate swaps, green and blue bonds, and blended finance platforms can simultaneously ease debt burdens and mobilise sustainable investment. Countries like Seychelles, Cabo Verde, Nigeria, and Egypt are already piloting these instruments (Aleksandrova et al., 2025; Elmahdi & Jeong, 2024; Lwesya, 2025; Michaelowa et al., 2021). Additionally, some African countries are gradually deepening domestic financial systems by expanding local bond markets and leveraging pension funds, insurance, and diaspora bonds, which can reduce reliance on volatile external capital (Box 6.3).

**Box 6.3 Some Examples of Financial Market Deepening in Africa**
Nigeria provides a strong example of progress in deepening domestic financial markets. In 2017, the government successfully issued a US$300 million diaspora bond, oversubscribed by 130%, which highlighted strong demand from Nigerians abroad and investor confidence in the country's regulatory environment. Listed on the London Stock Exchange, the bond offered international legal protections while diversifying Nigeria's funding sources beyond volatile external capital markets. Alongside this, Nigeria has broadened its local bond market, with the Debt Management Office issuing Federal Government Bonds, Sukuk, and Green Bonds to attract domestic investors such as pension funds and insurance companies. The country's pension sector, holding assets above ₦17 trillion

(*continued*)

**Box 6.3 (continued)**

(about US$22 billion), has emerged as a significant financier of government borrowing, enhancing fiscal stability. Similarly, Kenya has strengthened its domestic bond market through infrastructure bonds, retail-oriented products like M-Akiba, and pension reforms that boosted retirement fund participation in long-term government securities.

Ethiopia provides another example, having issued local bonds to mobilise domestic financing for the Grand Ethiopian Renaissance Dam (GERD). This demonstrate how local instruments can reduce reliance on external borrowing while supporting nationally significant infrastructure projects. Ghana is leveraging domestic financing tools as in 2020, it announced a US$3 billion diaspora bond after studies showed strong investor interest. By 2023, pension funds held GH¢29 billion in government securities, achieving a 94% exchange rate under DDEP, while Treasury bills, ESLA, and infrastructure bonds remain central to local financing.

Source: Abtew and Dessu (2019), Mensah (2019), Papadavid (2025) and Taylor and Opoku-Bossman (2020)

## 6.6 Conclusions

Achieving sustainable development in Africa requires substantial financing, yet limited domestic revenues force many governments to rely heavily on borrowing, with external debt becoming the primary source. Historical debt challenges peaked in the late twentieth century, prompting initiatives such as the HIPC Initiative and MDRI. Today, global economic shocks continue to heighten debt vulnerabilities, exposing deeper structural fragilities, including dependence on volatile commodity revenues, weak fiscal institutions, limited economic diversification, and fragile financial systems. These vulnerabilities amplify the effects of exchange rate depreciation, rising debt service obligations, revenue volatility, refinancing risks, political constraints, and the crowding out of development spending. Addressing these risks requires short-term strategies such as strengthening domestic resource mobilisation, engaging multilateral institutions, advancing debt restructuring, adopting green finance, and fostering regional debt management approaches, alongside long-term structural reforms to build resilience. Without such transformation, Africa risks repeated debt distress, highlighting that sustainable development depends on tackling the structural drivers of debt vulnerability.

The chapter outlines several practical recommendations for policymakers. Policymakers should prioritise the balance of the pursuit of development goals with the need to safeguard debt sustainability. This requires strengthening tax systems, enhancing digital revenue collection, and reducing fiscal leakages to lessen reliance on external borrowing. At the same time, diversifying financing sources through sustainable and green instruments can bolster resilience while supporting climate objectives. Additionally, policymakers should strengthened regional and multilateral cooperation in order to expand access to concessional financing and facilitate effective debt restructuring. Ultimately, advancing structural economic transformation, adopting proactive debt management strategies, and implementing institutional reforms will be critical for building long-term resilience against future shocks.

## References

Abtew, W., & Dessu, S. B. (2019). *Financing the grand Ethiopian renaissance dam* (pp. 161–169). https://doi.org/10.1007/978-3-319-97094-3_11

Afreximbank. (2024). *African trade report 2024: Climate implications of the AfCFTA implementation.* https://media.afreximbank.com/afrexim/African-Trade-Report_2024.pdf

African Forum and Network on Debt and Development. (2021). *state of mineral resources governance in Southern African development community.*

Al-Amine, R., & Willems, T. (2020). *Investor sentiment, sovereign debt mispricing, and economic outcomes* (WP/20/166; IMF Working Paper).

Aleksandrova, M., Kanyangi, W. O., Atchadé, A. J., Atela, J., & Tonui, C. (2025). *Allocating international loss and damage finance through national climate funds: Prospects for African LDCs* (6/2025; IDOS Policy Brief). https://www.econstor.eu/bitstream/10419/315215/1/1921344652.pdf

Alli, W. (2025, August 29). *Non-oil sector powers Nigeria's tax revenue to N17.4trn.* Business Day. https://businessday.ng/business-economy/article/non-oil-sector-powers-nigerias-tax-revenue-to-n17-4trn/#google_vignette

Amadala, V. (2025, July 9). *Kenya among nations spending more on servicing debt than on health or education - UNCTAD.* The Star.

Amin, S. (1976). *Unequal development: An essay on the social formations of peripheral capitalism.* Monthly Review Press.

Atingi-Ego, M., Timuno, S., & Makuve, T. (2021). Public debt accumulation in SSA: A looming debt crisis. *Journal of African Economies, 30*(Supplement_1), i103–i139. https://doi.org/10.1093/jae/ejab023

AU. (2014). *Protocol on the establishment of the African monetary fund.* https://au.int/sites/default/files/treaties/36417-treaty-0046_-_protocol_on_the_establishment_of_the_african_monetary_fund_e.pdf

Bahuli, A. S., & Bala, I. M. (2020). Impact of external debt servicing on health outcomes in Nigeria 1995–2017. *IDOSR Journal of Arts and Humanities, 5*(1), 1–20.

Baskaran, G., & Pearson, W. (2023, July 12). *Tripling Zambia's copper production: A way out of the debt crisis.* Brookings. https://www.brookings.edu/articles/tripling-zambias-copper-production-a-way-out-of-the-debt-crisis/

Blanchard, O. J. (1990). *Suggestions for a new set of fiscal indicators (No. 79).*

Chen, Y., Raga, S., Calabrese, L., & Mustapha, S. (2020, October 15). *Four lessons from Zambia's emerging debt default.* ODI Global. https://odi.org/en/insights/four-lessons-from-zambias-emerging-debt-default/

Commodore, R., & Awuah, G. B. (2024, November 19). *The changing nature of debt in Africa.* African Center for Economic Transformation.

Coulibaly, S. (2024). Russia–Ukraine war and the cost of borrowing in the west African economic and monetary union sovereign debt market. *African Development Review, 36*(S1). https://doi.org/10.1111/1467-8268.12780

Cytonn. (2024, January 14). *Sub-Saharan Africa (SSA) Eurobonds performance in 2023.* Cytonn. https://cytonn.com/topicals/sub-saharan-africa-ssa-4?utm_source=chatgpt.com

Dagah, H. G., Kring, W. N., & Bradlow, D. (2019). *Jump-starting the African Monetary Fund* (008; GEGI Policy Brief). https://www.chr.up.ac.za/images/publications/centrepublications/documents/jumpstating_the_african_monetary_fund.pdf

Dawelbait, O. Y. M. (2015). Debt crisis in Africa. *Journal of Economics and Sustainable Development, 6*(8), 21–29.

Doemeland, D., Estevão, M., Jooste, C., Sampi, J., & Tsiropoulos, V. (2022). *Debt vulnerability analysis: A multi-angle approach* (9929; Policy Research Working Paper). https://documents1.worldbank.org/curated/en/514551644261687296/pdf/Debt-Vulnerability-Analysis-A-Multi-Angle.pdf

Domar, E. D. (1944). The "burden of the debt" and the national income. *The American Economic Review, 34*(4), 798–827.

dos Santos, T. (1985). The structure of dependence. In A. Seligson Mitchell (Ed.), *The gap between rich and poor: Contending perspectives on the political economy of development (First).* Routledge.

Eichengreen, B., & Hausmann, R. (1999). *Exchange rates and financial fragility.* https://doi.org/10.3386/w7418

Elkhishin, S., & Mohieldin, M. (2021). External debt vulnerability in emerging markets and developing economies during the COVID-19 shock. *Review of Economics and Political Science, 6*(1), 24–47. https://doi.org/10.1108/REPS-10-2020-0155

Elmahdi, A., & Jeong, J. (2024). From debt to sustainability: Advancing wastewater projects in developing countries through innovative financing mechanisms—The role of debt-for-climate swaps. *Climate, 12*(8), 122. https://doi.org/10.3390/cli12080122

Ernest, B. (2024, June 14). *Copper mining and Zambia's debt crisis.* African Leadership Magarzine. https://www.africanleadershipmagazine.co.uk/copper-mining-and-zambias-debt-crisis/

Federal Ministry for Economic Cooperation and Development. (2024, February 15). *Great dependency on gold and cotton.* Federal Ministry for Economic Cooperation and Development. https://www.bmz.de/en/countries/burkina-faso/economic-situation-51424

Frank, A. G. (1967). *Capitalism and underdevelopment in Latin America* (Vol. 93). NYU Press.

Gebregziabher, F. H., & Sala, A. P. (2022, April 19). *Mozambique's "hidden debts": Turning a crisis into an opportunity for reform.* World Bank. https://blogs.worldbank.org/en/africacan/mozambiques-hidden-debts-turning-crisis-opportunity-reform

Georgieva, K., & Pazarbasioglu, C. (2021, December 2). *The G20 common framework for debt treatments must be stepped up.* IMF Blog. https://www.imf.org/en/Blogs/Articles/2021/12/02/blog120221the-g20-common-framework-for-debt-treatments-must-be-stepped-up

Global Development Policy Center. (2025, May 15). *Diverting development: The G20 and external debt service burden in Africa.* Global Development Policy Center. https://www.bu.edu/gdp/2025/05/15/diverting-development-the-g20-and-external-debt-service-burden-in-africa/

Grigoli, F., Herman, A., & Swiston, A. J. (2017). *A crude shock: Explaining the impact of the 2014–16 oil price decline across exporters* (2017/160; IMF Working Papers).

Iddrisu, K., Abor, J. Y., & Banyen, K. T. (2024). Financial development, globalisation and foreign direct investment nexus: an empirical study from Africa. *SN Business & Economics, 4*(6), 69. https://doi.org/10.1007/s43546-024-00667-w

Iddrisu, K., Asongu, S. A., & Boadi, E. K. (2025). Mediation role of economic freedom in the nexus between financial integration and inclusive growth in Africa. *Humanities and Social Sciences Communications, 12*(1), 1163. https://doi.org/10.1057/s41599-025-04762-7

IMF. (2025a). *Debt vulnerabilities and financing challenges in emerging markets and developing economies—An overview of key data* (20; IMF Policy Paper).

IMF. (2025b, June 24). *Debt sustainability analysis.* IMF. https://www.imf.org/external/pubs/ft/dsa/

IMF. (2025c, June 24). *Multilateral debt relief initiative—Questions and answers.* IMF. https://www.imf.org/external/np/exr/mdri/eng/index.htm

Jensen, L. (2021). *Sovereign debt vulnerabilities in developing economies: Which countries are vulnerable and how much debt is at risk?* (Development Futures Series Working Papers). https://www.developmentaid.org/api/frontend/cms/file/2021/04/5424120-20UNDP20WP20Debt20Vulnerability-web.pdf

Kyereboah-Coleman, A., Boumbouya, R. K., Marimo, M., & Latif, N. (2024). Structure, composition, and trends in African trade. In M. K. Ocran & J. Y. Abor (Eds.), *The Palgrave handbook of international trade and development in Africa* (pp. 71–88). Springer International Publishing. https://doi.org/10.1007/978-3-031-65715-3_5

Laws, A., Lemaire, T., & Spatafora, N. (2025, July 8). *How to stabilize Africa's debt.* IMF. https://www.imf.org/en/News/Articles/2025/07/08/cf-how-to-stabilize-africas-debt

Leykun, F. (2024). Climate change and external debt vulnerability: The case of Sub-Saharan Africa. *Journal of Innovation and Entrepreneurship, 13*(1), 81. https://doi.org/10.1186/s13731-024-00416-1

Lwesya, F. (2025). Green finance in Africa: mapping progress, challenges and prospects. *Future Business Journal, 11*(1), 195. https://doi.org/10.1186/s43093-025-00596-6

Mensah, L. (2019). Prospects and feasibility of diaspora bond: The case of Ghana. *International Journal of Financial Research, 10*(4), 25. https://doi.org/10.5430/ijfr.v10n4p25

Michaelowa, A., Hoch, S., Weber, A.-K., Kassaye, R., & Hailu, T. (2021). Mobilising private climate finance for sustainable energy access and climate change mitigation in Sub-Saharan Africa. *Climate Policy, 21*(1), 47–62. https://doi.org/10.1080/14693062.2020.1796568

Moreira, E. P. (2023). *Debt dynamics and financial stability in Africa* (25/23; Policy Brief). https://www.policycenter.ma/sites/default/files/2023-06/PB_25-23_EmmanuelPinto Moreira Final.pdf

Moses-Ashike, H. (2022, December 19). *Financial crisis: Ghana suspends Eurobond, bilateral debt service payment.* Business Day. https://businessday.ng/news/article/financial-crisis-ghana-suspends-eurobond-bilateral-debt-service-payment/

Muhanji, S., & Ojah, K. (2011). External shocks and persistence of external debt in open vulnerable economies: The case of Africa. *Economic Modelling, 28*(4), 1615–1628. https://doi.org/10.1016/j.econmod.2011.02.020

Ndlovu, X. A., & Vandome, C. (2024). *Mineral resource governance in Botswana.* https://doi.org/10.31752/idea.2024.117

Ndung'u, N., Shimeles, A., & Manda, D. K. (2021). Growing with debt in African economies: Options, challenges and pitfalls. *Journal of African Economies, 30*(Supplement_1), i3–i13. https://doi.org/10.1093/jae/ejab019

Ndwaru, J. (2024, April 26). *Visualising the state of debt in Africa 2024*. The Exchange. https://theexchange.africa/countries/debt-crisis-in-africa-2024/

Obulutsa, G. (2024, February 7). *Kenya can repay $2 billion bond, says central bank governor*. Reuters. https://www.reuters.com/world/africa/kenya-central-bank-governor-gdp-growth-be-slightly-faster-2024-2024-02-07/?utm_source=chatgpt.com

Opoku, E. E. O., & Boachie, M. K. (2020). The environmental impact of industrialization and foreign direct investment. *Energy Policy, 137*, 111178. https://doi.org/10.1016/j.enpol.2019.111178

Papadavid, P. (2025, July 31). *From remittances to bonds: mobilising diaspora finance in African economies*. ODI Global. https://odi.org/en/insights/from-remittances-to-bonds-mobilising-diaspora-finance-in-african-economies/

Quarm, R. S., Sam-Quarm, R., & Sam-Quarm, R. (2020). The ramifications of the treasury single account, the Ifmis platform, and government cash management in developing economies in the wake of the Covid-19 pandemic: Ghana's empirical example. *Journal of Economics and Business, 3*(4), 1654–1672. https://doi.org/10.31014/aior.1992.03.04.311

Reinhart, C. M., & Rogoff, K. S. (2010). *Debt and growth revisited*.

Rwanda Revenue Authority. (2023). *New changes in tax laws*. https://www.rra.gov.rw/fileadmin/user_upload/CHANGES_IN_TAX_LAWS_Oct_2023.pdf

Samunderu, E. (2024). Liberalisation of trade regime under AfCFTA: A perspective analysis on Africa's single market. In E. Samunderu (Ed.), *The economic effects of air transport market liberalisation. Advances in African economic, social and political development* (pp. 641–730). Springer. https://doi.org/10.1007/978-3-031-61864-2_7

Singer, H. W. (1975). The distribution of gains between investing and borrowing countries. In S. A. Cairncross & M. Puri (Eds.), *The strategy of international development: Essays in the economics of backwardness* (pp. 43–57). Palgrave Macmillan UK. https://doi.org/10.1007/978-1-349-04228-9_3

Stocker, M., Baffes, J., & Vorisek, D. (2018, January 18). *What triggered the oil price plunge of 2014–2016 and why it failed to deliver an economic impetus in eight charts*. World Bank. https://blogs.worldbank.org/en/developmenttalk/what-triggered-oil-price-plunge-2014-2016-and-why-it-failed-deliver-economic-impetus-eight-charts

Taylor, D., & Opoku-Bossman, M. (2020, August 8). *Revisiting Ghana's financing requirement: The case of diaspora bonds*. GhanaWeb. https://www.ghanaweb.com/GhanaHomePage/features/Revisiting-Ghana-s-financing-requirement-The-case-of-diaspora-bonds-1028944

UNCTAD. (2021). *Economic development in Africa report 2021: Reaping the potential benefits of the African continental free trade area for inclusive growth.* https://unctad.org/system/files/official-document/aldcafrica2021_en.pdf

UNCTAD. (2025, February 10). *Africa's vulnerability to global shocks highlights need for stronger regional trade.* UNCTAD. https://unctad.org/news/africas-vulnerability-global-shocks-highlights-need-stronger-regional-trade

UNDESA. (2024). *Debt sustainability challenges in Africa: The role of domestic debt* (108; Monthly Briefing: World Economic Situation and Propects). https://policy.desa.un.org/sites/default/files/publications/2024-04/mb180.pdf

Utsunomiya, H. (2020). *IMF executive board approves US99.4 million emergency support for Mongolia's COVID-19 response.*

World Bank. (2022a). *International debt report 2022.* https://thedocs.worldbank.org/en/doc/6e72b0ded996306fa01f5db7a0c38b19-0050052021/related/IDR2022-Appendix-About-the-Data.pdf

World Bank. (2022b, June 30). *Free trade deal boosts Africa's economic development.* World Bank. https://www.worldbank.org/en/topic/trade/publication/free-trade-deal-boosts-africa-economic-development

World Bank. (2024, May 9). *Heavily indebted poor countries (HIPC) initiative.* World Bank. https://www.worldbank.org/en/topic/debt/brief/hipc

CHAPTER 7

# Evaluating the Effectiveness of Concessional Loans in Reducing Debt Stress in Africa

*Khadijah Iddrisu*

## 7.1 Introduction

To promote sustainable development and strengthen climate resilience, many governments have increased investments in infrastructure and other public goods. In Africa, this focus has increasingly shifted toward critical sectors such as energy, water and sanitation, transportation, information and communication technology (ICT), and social infrastructure (Cromwell & Peprah, 2025; Iddrisu et al., 2025b). With limited domestic revenue, many African governments increasingly rely on borrowing to finance essential public goods. The continent's average tax-to-GDP ratio stands at only 16.5%, well below the global average. As a result, external loans have become a common source of funding. For example, Uganda owed the World Bank approximately US$4.5 billion in 2022, while Egypt secured a US$12 billion facility from the International Monetary Fund (IMF) in 2016. However, heavy reliance on debt has fuelled widespread debt stress across many African countries. For example, Zambia defaulted in 2020

K. Iddrisu (✉)
Department of Finance, Islamic University College, Accra, Ghana
e-mail: khadijahiddris@iug.edu.gh



I. N. Yakubu (ed.), *Public Debt and Economic Resilience in Africa*, Palgrave Studies in African and Development Economics,
https://doi.org/10.1007/978-3-032-25835-9_7

after struggling to service its substantial external obligations (Mbewe et al., 2024). Ghana followed in 2022, burdened by a high debt-to-GDP ratio (Atuahene, 2024). More recently, in 2023, both Ethiopia and Nigeria also fell into default (Africanews, 2024).

Although rising debt stress calls for urgent action, the limited domestic revenue base leaves African governments with little choice but to continue borrowing. This raises a critical question: To what extent can concessional loans help alleviate debt stress in Africa? A concessional loan, also called a soft loan, is financing provided on more favourable terms such as very low or below-market interest rates, longer repayment periods, and grace periods before repayment begins (Teng, 2021). Often tied to development projects, those loans are mainly offered by multilateral institutions like African Development Bank (AfDB), World Bank, IMF, among others as well as bilateral partners. The features of concessional loans make them a preferable option for reducing debt stress. Their below-market interest rates and extended grace periods ease immediate debt servicing pressures, thereby expanding fiscal space for development spending. The significance of concessional loans, as illustrated in some countries, such as Greece (Louka, 2020), has contributed to their growing use in Africa. However, despite this reliance, several African countries continue to experience debt stress. This chapter therefore examines whether concessional lending alone is sufficient to ensure debt sustainability, or if structural and institutional weaknesses limit its effectiveness.

The chapter is important because it highlights how African countries can leverage concessional loans to better manage or even avoid debt stress. Unlike earlier studies that broadly examined external borrowing and its implications for debt sustainability and development (see Atingi-Ego et al., 2021; Ndung'u et al., 2021), this chapter specifically focuses on concessional loans, recognizing their unique features and potential benefits. In doing so, it adds to ongoing policy debates and complements existing initiatives such as the G20 Common Framework for Debt Treatments, the African Union (AU)'s Debt Management Reform Agenda, the IMF's Sustainable Development Finance Policy, as well as innovative financing mechanisms like blended finance and green bonds, all of which aim to support Africa's efforts in addressing debt challenges.

The remainder of the chapter is organised as follows: Section 7.2 examines the nature and extent of debt stress in Africa, while Section 7.3 provides an overview of concessional loans. Section 7.4 evaluates their effectiveness, and Section 7.5 discusses key challenges alongside potential solutions. The chapter concludes with final remarks.

## 7.2 Debt Stress in Africa

Debt stress is a situation where a country experiences difficulty in meeting its debt obligations without compromising economic growth and development priorities. It often arises when debt servicing consumes a significant share of government revenues, leaving little fiscal room for other expenditures (Table 7.1). The concept is closely linked to debt sustainability, which assesses a country's ability to meet its current and future debt service obligations without resorting to exceptional financing or arrears accumulation.

Debt stress is not a new phenomenon in Africa, as the governments in the continent have low domestic revenue. Twenty-one African countries are currently either in debt stress or at high risk of it (AU, 2025). Among the 36 SSA countries eligible for the Poverty Reduction and Growth Trust (PRGT) with available debt sustainability analyses (DSAs) are classified as either in debt stress or at high risk. SSA countries in debt distress or high risk rose from 31% (11 countries) in 2011 to 44% (16 countries) in 2018, and further to 56% (20 countries) by 2020. The drivers of debt stress in Africa are discussed in the sub-section.

**Table 7.1** Proxy of debt stress

| *Proxy* | *Meaning* |
|---|---|
| Debt-to-GDP ratio | Reflects the size of debt relative to the economy's output. High ratios suggest limited capacity to service debt without growth trade-offs. |
| Debt service-to--revenue ratio | Captures the proportion of government revenue devoted to debt repayment, with higher levels indicating reduced fiscal flexibility. |
| Debt service-to--exports ratio | Highlights the burden of external debt in relation to a country's foreign exchange earnings. |
| Arrears accumulation | Persistent inability to service debt on schedule signals stress. |
| Default events | The most extreme form of debt stress, where a government fails to honour its debt commitments. |

### 7.2.1 Drivers of Debt Stress

*Fiscal Management Challenges*

African economies frequently run persistent budget deficits, mainly due to high recurrent expenditures such as wages, subsidies, and administrative costs, which reduce fiscal space for investment. Weak public financial management, including poor expenditure tracking and low revenue mobilisation, worsens the problem and undermines resource allocation. To cover financing gaps, governments often rely on domestic borrowing. However, excessive reliance on such debt raises interest costs and crowds out private sector credit, limiting investment and constraining broader economic growth. For example, Nigeria has faced decades of fiscal deficits, driven by high recurrent spending on wages, subsidies, and overheads (Asogwa, 2013). Over 75% of its 2023 budget went to recurrent costs, limiting investment (BusinessTrumpet, 2022).

*Rising Development and Infrastructure Needs*

African countries face immense pressure to expand infrastructure, including energy generation, transport networks, and digital connectivity, to support rapid urbanisation, population growth, and economic transformation. Africa's infrastructure needs are between US$130 billion and US$170 billion annually (United Nations Economic Commission for Africa (UNECA), 2025). However, Africa's infrastructure receives about US$80 billion in investment annually, yet the continent still faces a financing shortfall estimated at US$70–90 billion each year (UNECA, 2025). Limited domestic revenue mobilisation often makes external borrowing the primary financing option. In addition, climate change heightens vulnerabilities, creating urgent demands for adaptation and resilience investments in agriculture, water management, and disaster preparedness.

*Geopolitical and Security Pressures*

Many African countries grapple with ongoing conflicts, insurgencies, and political instability, all of which significantly strain public finances. Heightened insecurity often necessitates increased military and security spending, diverting resources away from social and developmental priorities. In addition, instability disrupts trade routes, reduces foreign direct investment, and discourages private sector activity. Cross-border tensions and regional instability can also undermine economic cooperation and integration efforts, further weakening growth prospects. These combined pressures intensify debt stress by eroding revenues while raising expenditure needs. Ezeoha et al. (2023) revealed that, conflict-affected provinces contributed 40–60% less in formal mining royalties compared to stable regions.

*Global Uncertainties and Shocks*
Global shocks such the COVID-19 pandemic caused Africa's sharpest economic disruption in decades, slashing revenues and raising health and social spending, leading to record fiscal deficits and a 1.9% contraction in 2020. The advent of the Covid-19 pandemic further accelerated the debt burden across Africa where the median debt-to-GDP ratio is expected to reach close to 70% (AfDB, 2021). Limited relief came from the G20 Debt Service Suspension Initiative (DSSI) and IMF Special Drawing Rights (SDRs), with Africa receiving only US$33 billion (Gallagher, 2025). The Russia-Ukraine war and global trade tensions further increased commodity prices, disrupted supply chains, and reduced export earnings (Baffes & Nagle, 2022). Rising interest rates and tighter financial conditions intensified debt vulnerabilities, while slow, uneven debt restructuring constrained fiscal flexibility.

*Structural Economic Weaknesses*
Many African economies remain heavily dependent on primary commodities such as oil, minerals, and agricultural products, leaving them vulnerable to price volatility and external demand shocks (Kyereboah-Coleman et al., 2024). Limited export diversification constrains resilience and undermines sustainable growth. Fiscal fragility is further compounded by narrow tax bases and persistently low tax-to-GDP ratios, which restrict governments' ability to generate stable domestic revenue (United Nations Conference on Trade and Development (UNCTAD), 2022). As a result, many countries rely extensively on external financing, both concessional and commercial, exposing them to exchange rate risks, higher debt servicing costs, and cyclical debt stress (Ndung'u et al., 2021).

## 7.3 Overview of Concessional Loans

Concessional loans differ from non-concessional loans by offering terms that are deliberately more favourable to the borrower as shown in Table 7.2.

**Table 7.2** Difference between concessional and non-concessional loans

| *Feature* | *Concessional loans* | *Non-concessional loans* |
|---|---|---|
| Interest rate | Below market rate (subsidised) | Market-based or higher |
| Grace period | Often included (borrowers delay repayment for some years) | Usually shorter or none |
| Maturity period | Long-term (can extend 20–40 years) | Shorter (often 5–15 years) |
| Source | Multilateral institutions (IMF PRGT, World Bank IDA, AfDB ADF) or bilateral donors | Commercial lenders, capital markets, export credit agencies, non-concessional windows of MDBs |
| Purpose | Development financing, poverty reduction, social sectors, infrastructure | General budget financing, large--scale infrastructure, refinancing debt |
| Eligibility | Low-income and lower-middle--income countries | Middle- and high-income countries; sometimes available to LICs in stress but at higher cost |
| Debt sustainability impact | Intended to reduce burden and promote sustainability | Can increase debt stress if not managed well |

Source: Bhattacharya and Rashmin (2020) and Potts and Chung (2008)

The history of concessional loans in Africa is closely tied to the continent's post-independence development path, debt challenges, and the shifting global financial architecture. Concessional lending gained momentum after independence, with Ghana and Sudan joining the IMF in 1957, followed by a surge of new African members (Camdessus, 2000). By 1969, 44 of the IMF's 115 members were African. Egypt was among the earliest borrowers, accessing IMF resources after the Suez Crisis (1956–57) (Ikram, 2007). By 1975, 19 African countries had IMF credits, though these accounted for only 8.4% of the Fund's total portfolio. At this stage, loans were mainly for balance-of-payments support and macroeconomic stabilisation rather than long-term development. The 1980s debt crisis marked a turning point, as many African countries adopted IMF and World Bank structural adjustment programmes (SAPs), often financed through concessional lending (Logan & Mengisteab, 1993). The World Bank's International Development Association (IDA) became a key source of such financing, offering loans with low interest rates, long maturities, and extended grace periods. Concessional lending was later reoriented toward Poverty Reduction Strategy Papers (PRSPs), aligning loan disbursement with national development plans. Financing increasingly targeted sectors such as health, education, infrastructure, and governance reforms.

Over time, concessional borrowing became central to Africa's efforts to finance infrastructure and public goods. World Bank data covering 39 African countries between 2000 and 2023 show that most countries relied primarily on concessional loans from the Regional Development Banks (RDBs). Ethiopia was the largest recipient, with average inflows of about US$122 million, while Egypt recorded the lowest net receipt at US$2.5 million (Fig. 7.1).

In 2023, Tanzania received the highest inflow of RDB concessional loans (about US$89 million), whereas Ghana registered the lowest (around US$10 million). Ghana's comparatively limited access reflects its lower-middle-income classification, ongoing debt stress and restructuring, preference for non-concessional borrowing, and governance challenges such as weak fiscal discipline and delayed reforms that constrained eligibility (Fig. 7.2). In contrast to data on RDBs, the flow of concessional loans from the IMF has limited data as only 8 African countries have consistent data from 2000 to 2023 (Fig. 7.3). Among the eight countries, Mozambique received the highest flow of IMF concessional loans

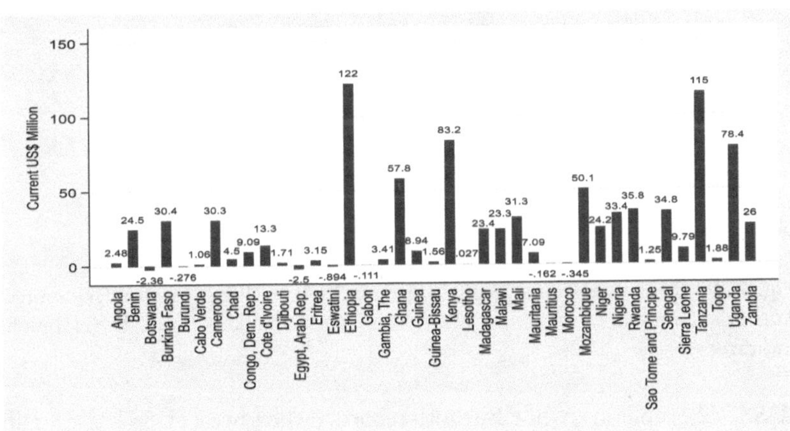


**Fig. 7.1** RDB concessional loans in Africa, 2000 to 2023, by country. Notes: RDB is Regional Development Banks. Source: Author's Construct based on data from World Bank's World Development Indicators

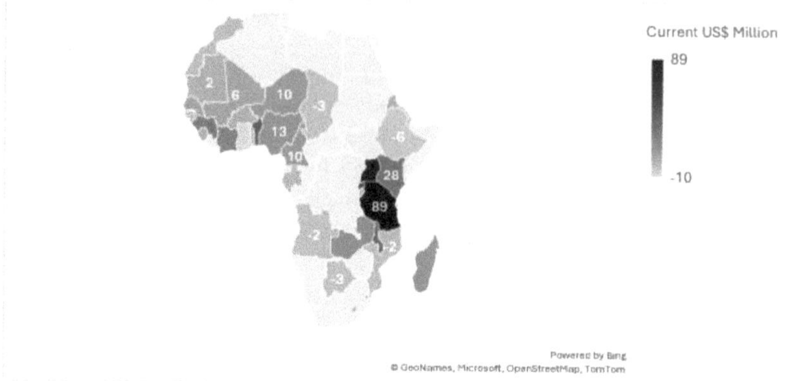


**Fig. 7.2** RDB concessional loans in Africa 2023, by country. Notes: RDB is Regional Development Banks. Source: Author's Construct based on data from World Bank's World Development Indicators

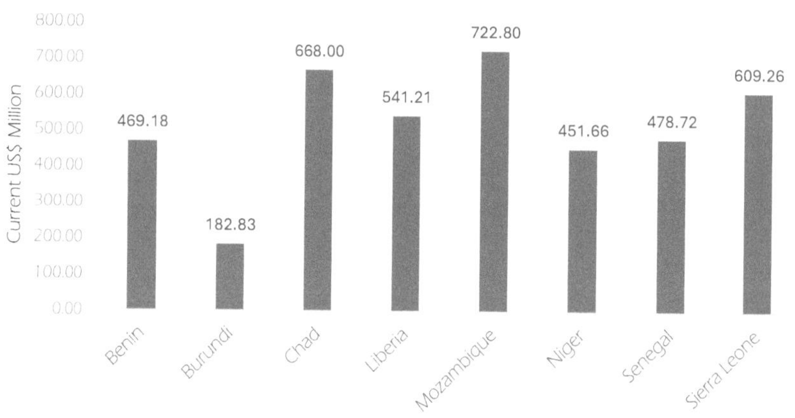


**Fig. 7.3** IMF concessional loans in Africa, 2000 to 2023, by country. Source: Author's Construct based on data from World Bank's World Development Indicators

(US$772.8 million), while Burundi recorded the lowest (US$182.83 million) (Fig. 7.3).

More recently, a significant share of concessional resources has been directed toward climate adaptation and mitigation. In 2022, over 60% of

Africa's climate-related official development assistance (ODA) was delivered in the form of loans, with the IDA accounting for 83% of climate adaptation ODA loans (Bekele & Miller, 2024). Bilateral lenders have also emerged as Africa's third-largest source of concessional climate loans, though often at higher interest rates than those offered by multilateral institutions in 2022 (Bekele & Miller, 2024).

### 7.3.1 Importance of Concessional Loans from Theoretical Perspective

From a theoretical standpoint, concessional loans hold significant importance, as highlighted by the following theories.

*Debt Overhang Theory*

Debt overhang theory suggests that when debt reaches unsustainable levels, investors expect that future resources will primarily be used for repayment rather than productive investment, thereby discouraging both domestic and foreign investment (Krugman, 1988; Sachs, 1988). Concessional loans, by reducing repayment burdens, can mitigate the debt overhang and restore growth incentives provided borrowing is channelled productively. The relevance of this theory in the context of concessional lending has been substantiated by empirical evidence. For example, Ezeaku et al. (2019) found that concessional loans improved living standards across 29 SSA countries between 1999 and 2017. The positive impact was most pronounced when such loans were allocated to social infrastructure and public services rather than to recurrent expenditures. Nwakoby and Ezeaku (2021) also supported Ezeaku et al. (2019) and concluded that concessional loans have remarkable impact on standard of living.

*Fiscal Space Theory*

Fiscal space theory emphasises a government's capacity to mobilise and allocate resources for development without compromising long-term fiscal sustainability. The concept was initially advanced by Heller (2005), who described fiscal space as the budgetary room that allows governments to fund desired priorities without undermining fiscal stability. Ostry et al. (2010) later broadened this perspective by identifying key avenues for creating or expanding fiscal space, including concessional borrowing, domestic revenue mobilisation, and expenditure reprioritisation. This framework is particularly relevant for developing countries that face pressing needs in infrastructure, health, and education but are constrained by narrow revenue bases and high debt burdens. Concessional loans, by lowering near-term debt service costs, play a vital role in expanding fiscal space and enabling governments to channel resources into priority investments such as infrastructure, education, and healthcare (Ostry et al., 2010). The theoretical insights are reflected in practical examples from several African countries. In 2022, Ethiopia received 18.01% of its climate-related ODA as concessional loans, enabling investments in rural electrification, transport, renewable energy, climate adaptation, and expanded education and healthcare access, particularly benefiting underserved regions (Bekele & Miller, 2024).

*Two-Gap Theory*
Two-gap model of development finance developed by Chenery and Strout (1966), highlights the structural financing challenges faced by developing economies. The model identifies two main deficits: the savings-investment gap, which arises because many low-income countries have insufficient domestic savings to finance the level of investment required for growth, and the foreign exchange gap, which occurs when shortages of foreign exchange restrict the ability to import capital goods, technology, and essential inputs. To bridge these gaps, external financing becomes necessary, and concessional loans are particularly relevant in this context because they provide resources at below-market terms, enabling countries to address deficits without exacerbating debt vulnerabilities. Concessional loans expand the pool of investable resources for infrastructure, education, and health, while also providing foreign currency inflows that ease balance-of-payments constraints and allow for the importation of critical goods and services. Unlike commercial borrowing, they achieve this at lower cost and with longer maturities, thereby reducing repayment pressures and better aligning with the long-term nature of development projects.

## 7.4 Evaluating the Effectiveness of Concessional Loans

### 7.4.1 *Evidence of Debt Relief and Reduced Repayment Burdens*

One of the primary advantages of concessional loans is their ability to ease immediate debt servicing pressures. With below-market interest rates, extended maturities, and grace periods, these loans are structured to

**Box 7.1 Senegal Secured a Concessional Loan from the IMF**
Senegal faced rising post-COVID debt servicing pressures, with external debt exceeding 70% of GDP by 2022 and interest payments consuming an increasing share of domestic revenue, constraining fiscal space for development and climate initiatives. In 2023, the country secured a concessional loan under the IMF's Resilience and Sustainability Trust (RST), featuring below-market interest rates, extended maturities of up to 20 years, and 10-year grace periods, which smoothed repayment schedules and reduced near-term debt pressures. Senegal strategically allocated these funds to climate adaptation, renewable energy expansion, and public financial management reforms, demonstrating how concessional finance can enhance debt sustainability and support long-term resilience.

Source: UNECA (2023)

reduce the short-term repayment obligations of borrowing countries. This design theoretically provides relief by lowering the cost of borrowing compared to commercial debt and by smoothing out repayment schedules. Senegal provides a practical example, leveraging a concessional IMF loan to support infrastructure development while easing its debt repayment obligations (Box 7.1).

However, while concessional loans reduce repayment burdens in the short run, their long-term impact depends on how effectively borrowed funds are invested to generate growth and revenue. For example, although Zambia has received concessional loans from the IMF and World Bank, these have not translated into significant economic growth. The Link Zambia 8000 road project, financed partly through concessional and semi-concessional loans, has faced criticism for low traffic volumes and inadequate maintenance, limiting its ability to generate expected revenue[1].

### 7.4.2 *Contribution to Fiscal Space and Development Spending*

Concessional loans also play a critical role in expanding fiscal space by reducing immediate debt servicing requirements, thereby freeing resources

[1] Read more here: https://2009-2017.state.gov/e/eb/directline/2013/206322.htm

**Box 7.2 Concessional Loans Contribute to Fiscal Space in Rwanda**
In Rwanda, concessional financing has played a central role in advancing infrastructure and economic resilience. A notable example is the Scaling Up Electricity Access Programme Phase II (SEAP II), supported by the African Development Bank and its concessional arm, which mobilised €229 million in concessional loans and grants. This programme facilitated over 300,000 new electricity connections while also upgrading key infrastructure. Additionally, Rwanda developed a US$257.5 million blended finance package to support micro, small, and medium enterprises (MSMEs), combining concessional loans from the International Development Association and the Asian Infrastructure Investment Bank to bolster pandemic recovery and strengthen debt sustainability.

Source: World Economic Forum (WEF) (2018) and World Bank (n.d.)

for development expenditure. These loans allow governments to allocate a greater share of their budget to priority sectors such as health, education, and infrastructure development. Countries such as Rwanda have utilised concessional loans to finance large-scale infrastructure and social sector programmes, enabling higher public investment without excessive reliance on domestic borrowing (Box 7.2). Nonetheless, the extent of this contribution varies significantly across countries, as weak public financial management and corruption can dilute the developmental impact of concessional borrowing. For example, Mozambique obtained concessional loans for maritime security and infrastructure via state-owned enterprises. However, in 2016 it emerged that over US$2 billion in undisclosed borrowing from foreign banks had bypassed parliamentary approval (Gebregziabher & Sala, 2022). This revelation precipitated a sovereign default, the suspension of IMF and donor assistance, and a sharp decline in investor confidence, ultimately eroding fiscal space and reversing development progress (Gebregziabher & Sala, 2022).

### 7.4.3 *Short-Term vs. Long-Term Impact on Debt Stress*

The short-term benefits of concessional loans are relatively straightforward: lower debt service obligations and greater budget flexibility. However, the long-term effects are more nuanced. If concessional loans finance projects that boost productive capacity, they can enhance growth and expand the tax base, thereby improving debt sustainability over time. Conversely, if such loans are poorly managed, misallocated, or used for non-productive spending, they may add to future repayment burdens without generating sufficient returns. The long-term effectiveness of concessional loans thus hinges not only on their favourable terms but also on governance, absorptive capacity, and economic resilience in recipient countries.

## 7.5 Challenges of Using Concessional Loans: What Can Be Done

### 7.5.1 *Challenges and Limitations*

*Persistent Vulnerabilities Despite Concessional Loans*
Although concessional loans provide favourable terms that reduce borrowing costs, African economies remain highly vulnerable to both domestic and external shocks. Commodity price volatility continues to expose resource-dependent countries to revenue instability. For instance, sharp declines in oil and mineral prices have significantly reduced export earnings in countries such as Nigeria, Angola, and Zambia, undermining their capacity to service even concessional debt (Agbetiloye, 2025; Doemeland et al., 2022). External shocks such as the COVID-19 pandemic, global inflationary pressures, and geopolitical disruptions further exacerbate debt vulnerabilities by constraining fiscal revenues and increasing financing needs (Iddrisu et al., 2025a). These persistent risks highlight that concessional loans, while helpful, cannot by themselves resolve structural fragilities in African debt management.

*The Debt-Growth Paradox in Africa*
Another limitation is the so-called debt growth paradox. In theory, concessional loans should stimulate growth by financing infrastructure, social services, and productive investment, thereby improving debt sustainability in the long term. Yet, in practice, many African countries continue to experience sluggish growth despite significant inflows of concessional financing (Ndung'u et al., 2021). This paradox is often attributed to weak absorptive capacity, inefficiencies in project implementation, and low returns on public investment. Moreover, excessive borrowing, even at

concessional terms, can discourage private sector investment if it raises concerns about future taxation or debt sustainability. As a result, the expected virtuous cycle of cheap borrowing leading to investment, growth, and stronger repayment capacity has not consistently materialised, leaving many countries in a cycle of repeated debt accumulation and restructuring.

*Over-Reliance on External Concessional Finance*

A further challenge lies in Africa's heavy dependence on external concessional financing (Bekele & Miller, 2024). While concessional loans provide critical fiscal space, an over-reliance on them can undermine efforts to build domestic resource mobilisation and strengthen local capital markets. Many African governments face low tax-to-GDP ratios, weak financial intermediation, and limited ability to raise long-term financing domestically. This dependence creates vulnerabilities to shifts in donor priorities and conditionalities, leaving fiscal planning exposed to the policies of external partners. Moreover, concessional resources are often insufficient to meet Africa's large infrastructure and social sector financing needs, prompting governments to complement them with non-concessional borrowing, sometimes at unsustainable levels. This dual dependence can trap countries in a cycle where concessional loans provide temporary relief but fail to build lasting financial resilience.

*Coordination Problems Among Creditors*

The growing diversity of creditors poses a major limitation in managing concessional lending. Traditionally, African countries borrowed mainly from multilateral institutions such as the World Bank and IMF, whose concessional terms were coordinated under established frameworks. However, the creditor landscape has expanded to include bilateral partners (such as China, India, and Gulf states) and private bondholders (Wu & Chen, 2024). This diversification complicates debt management, as different creditors apply varying terms, transparency standards, and restructuring approaches. The lack of coordination was evident in Zambia's protracted restructuring negotiations, where securing agreement among multilateral, bilateral, and private lenders proved challenging (ChinaFile, 2017; Knowledge at Wharton, 2019). Such fragmentation weakens the effectiveness of concessional loans, since relief from one group of creditors can be offset by more onerous obligations to others. Without improved coordination, concessional financing risks being undermined by inconsistent lending practices across creditors.

*Weak Governance and Institutions*
Weak governance and institutions reduce the growth and development impact of concessional loans in Africa by creating leakages, inefficiencies, and distortions in how funds are used (Manasseh et al., 2022). Instead of being invested in high-return infrastructure or productive sectors, resources are often misallocated to prestige projects or diverted through corruption, leaving rising debt but limited new capital. Poor project appraisal, procurement fraud, and weak oversight inflate costs and delay outcomes, while limited institutional capacity constrains absorptive ability. These weaknesses also discourage private investment, turning concessional borrowing from a potential growth catalyst into recurring debt stress without sustainable productivity or development gains. For instance, Namibia filed lawsuit against two ministers who were implicated and jailed in the "Fishrot" corruption scandal (Zenda, 2020).

### 7.5.2 The Way Forward

*Strategic Approaches in the Use of Concessional Loans*
African governments need to adopt more strategic approaches in the use of concessional loans. Beyond accessing financing on favourable terms, governments should ensure that such resources are directed toward high-impact investments that enhance productive capacity and generate long-term growth. Priority should be given to infrastructure, education, health, and climate resilience projects that not only stimulate economic activity but also improve human capital and social outcomes. Furthermore, strengthening project appraisal and monitoring mechanisms can help maximise the developmental returns of concessional borrowing. Governments should also integrate concessional loans into medium-term debt management strategies, ensuring that new borrowing aligns with repayment capacity and broader fiscal objectives.

*Role of International Financial Institutions and Lenders*
International financial institutions (IFIs) and bilateral lenders play a central role in shaping the effectiveness of concessional financing. These institutions can enhance their impact by designing concessional loan facilities that are more responsive to the specific needs and vulnerabilities of African economies. Flexibility in repayment structures, countercyclical lending, and stronger support for capacity building in debt management are

critical. In addition, creditors should improve coordination to avoid fragmented lending practices that undermine sustainability. Initiatives like the G20 Common Framework represent steps in this direction but require more robust implementation and inclusivity. IFIs can help concessional loans serve as a true tool for resilience rather than a temporary relief measure.

*Debt Transparency and Accountability*
A recurring challenge in Africa's debt landscape is the lack of transparency in loan contracting and management. Hidden debts and opaque loan terms have undermined public trust and complicated debt sustainability assessments, as demonstrated by the Mozambique debt scandal. To fully realise the benefits of concessional borrowing, governments should commit to publishing comprehensive, timely, and accurate data on debt stocks, terms, and repayment schedules. Stronger parliamentary oversight, civil society engagement, and independent audits can enhance accountability and ensure that concessional loans are used for intended developmental purposes. Transparency not only strengthens domestic governance but also improves relations with creditors and investors, reducing borrowing costs in the long run.

*Strengthening Domestic Resource Mobilisation*
While concessional loans provide important fiscal space, they cannot serve as a permanent solution to Africa's financing needs. Strengthening domestic resource mobilisation is essential for reducing dependency on external finance and building long-term debt sustainability. This requires broadening the tax base, improving revenue collection systems, and curbing illicit financial flows that drain public resources. Deepening domestic capital markets can also provide governments with alternative sources of long-term financing, reducing reliance on external concessional or non-concessional borrowing. African countries can build resilience, finance development priorities more sustainably, and reduce vulnerability to external creditor conditions.

## 7.6 Conclusion

African governments increasingly rely on borrowing to finance infrastructure and public goods due to weak domestic revenue bases, with concessional loans offering short-term relief through low interest rates and extended repayment terms. However, persistent debt stress in countries such as Zambia, Ghana, Ethiopia, and Nigeria raises concerns about their long-term sustainability. This chapter first outlines the drivers of Africa's debt stress, including fiscal mismanagement, rising infrastructure demands, geopolitical and security pressures, global shocks, and structural economic weaknesses. It then examines concessional loans, noting that almost all African countries have benefitted from them, and situates their role within debt overhang, fiscal space, and two-gap theoretical frameworks. The analysis highlights that concessional loans can ease repayment burdens, expand fiscal space, and support development spending, though their effectiveness is shaped by both short- and long-term dynamics. Despite their potential, the following challenges exist: vulnerabilities persist even with concessional support, many countries face the debt-growth paradox, and over-reliance on external finance, weak governance, and creditor coordination issues further undermine sustainability.

The chapter provides some practical implications. First, African governments should link concessional borrowing to well-structured, high-return projects that directly support growth, such as energy, transport, and ICT, rather than dispersing funds into politically motivated or low-impact initiatives. To achieve this, ministries of finance and central banks should build stronger institutional frameworks for debt sustainability analysis, ensuring that concessional loans are integrated into medium- and long-term fiscal strategies rather than used as stop-gap financing. Second, improving transparency and accountability is also critical; publishing loan contracts, repayment schedules, and project performance reports can reduce corruption and mismanagement while boosting investor and citizen confidence, helping to avoid scandals like those witnessed in Zambia and Mozambique. Third, over-reliance on concessional loans increases vulnerability, making it essential for governments to balance external financing with domestic resource mobilisation through tax reforms, digital tax systems, and broadening the tax base to create sustainable fiscal space. Fourth, collaboration with international lenders should go beyond financing, with multilateral institutions and bilateral partners coordinating lending terms, supporting debt restructuring when necessary, and providing technical assistance for governance and capacity-building. Finally, since concessional loans alone cannot resolve debt stress, governments must address structural weaknesses by diversifying exports, enhancing industrial competitiveness, and building resilience to global shocks so that borrowed funds translate into transformative and sustainable development outcomes.

## References


AfDB. (2021). *African economic outlook 2021: From debt resolution to growth: The road ahead for Africa.*

Africanews. (2024, August 13). *Ethiopia defaults on $33 Million bond payment.* Africanews. https://www.africanews.com/2023/12/27/ethiopia-defaults-on-33-million-bond-payment/

Agbetiloye, A. (2025, April 26). *Africa's second-largest oil exporter may turn to the IMF amid oil price slump.* Business Insider Africa. https://africa.businessinsider.com/local/markets/africas-second-largest-oil-exporter-may-turn-to-the-imf-amid-oil-price-slump/kqsdze1

Asogwa, F. O. (2013). The crowding out effect of budget deficits on private investment in Nigeria. *European Journal of Business and Management, 5*(20).

Atingi-Ego, M., Timuno, S., & Makuve, T. (2021). Public debt accumulation in SSA: A looming debt crisis. *Journal of African Economies, 30*(Supplement_1), i103–i139. https://doi.org/10.1093/jae/ejab023

Atuahene, R. A. (2024, December 4). *The public debt crisis and debt overhang: No easy way out.* Business & Financial Times. https://thebftonline.com/2024/12/04/the-public-debt-crisis-and-debt-overhang-no-easy-way-out/

AU. (2025, May 19). *With 21 African countries either at high risk or in debt distress, continental leaders unite to demand reform & equitable systems.* AU. https://au.int/en/pressreleases/20250519/continental-leaders-unite-demand-reform-equitable-financial-systems

Baffes, J., & Nagle, P. (2022, May 5). *Commodity prices surge due to the war in Ukraine.* World Bank. https://blogs.worldbank.org/en/developmenttalk/commodity-prices-surge-due-war-ukraine

Bekele, M., & Miller, A. (2024). *Concessional loans for Africa's climate crisis: Whose fiscal effort?* https://devinit.org/files/documents/1500/concessional_loans_for_africas_climate_crisis_whose_fiscal_effort.pdf

Bhattacharya, D., & Rashmin, R. (2020). Financial flows from China and India: How concessional are they? *Forum for Development Studies, 47*(1), 181–199. https://doi.org/10.1080/08039410.2019.1672780

BusinessTrumpet. (2022, December 29). *Breakdown of the 2023 federal government budget in charts.* BusinessTrumpet. https://businesstrumpet.com/breakdown-of-the-2023-federal-government-budget-in-charts/

Camdessus, M. (2000). *Looking to the future: The IMF in Africa.* IMF. https://www.imf.org/external/pubs/ft/history/2012/pdf/c14.pdf

Chenery, H. B., & Strout, A. M. (1966). Foreign assistance and economic development. *The American Economic Review, 56*(4), 679–733.

ChinaFile. (2017, November 17). *China and the United States are equals. Now what?* ChinaFile. https://www.chinafile.com/reporting-opinion/viewpoint/china-and-united-states-are-equals-now-what

Cromwell, R. S., & Peprah, J. A. (2025). Banking business models and sustainable development: Challenges and opportunities. In I. N. Yakubu (Ed.), *Strategic approaches to banking business and sustainable development goals* (pp. 3–22). Springer. https://doi.org/10.1007/978-3-031-80744-2_1

Doemeland, D., Estevão, M., Jooste, C., Sampi, J., & Tsiropoulos, V. (2022). *Debt vulnerability analysis: A multi-angle approach* (9929; Policy Research Working Paper). https://documents1.worldbank.org/curated/en/514551644261687296/pdf/Debt-Vulnerability-Analysis-A-Multi-Angle.pdf

Ezeaku, H. C., Nwakoby, I. C., Egbo, O. P., & Onwumere, J. U. J. (2019). On the dynamic effect of bilateral concessional debts on living standards in Sub-Saharan Africa. *Sage Open, 9*(3). https://doi.org/10.1177/2158244019877879

Ezeoha, A., Igwe, A., Okoyeuzu, C., & Uche, C. (2023). The fiscal effects of armed conflicts in Africa. *African Development Review, 35*(4), 444–456. https://doi.org/10.1111/1467-8268.12720

Gallagher, K. (2025). *The international financial architecture and sustainable prosperity* (14/25; WIDER Working Paper). https://www.econstor.eu/bitstream/10419/315170/1/1920595007.pdf

Gebregziabher, F. H., & Sala, A. P. (2022, April 19). *Mozambique's "hidden debts": Turning a crisis into an opportunity for reform.* World Bank. https://blogs.worldbank.org/en/africacan/mozambiques-hidden-debts-turning-crisis-opportunity-reform

Heller, P. S. (2005). *Understanding fiscal space* (PDP/05/4; IMF Policy Discussion Paper). https://www.imf.org/external/pubs/ft/pdp/2005/pdp04.pdf

Iddrisu, K., Abor, J. Y., Issah, O., & Gyebi, F. O. (2025a). Monetary policy and inclusive growth in the era of economic uncertainty: Navigating challenges and opportunities. In I. Yakubu (Ed.), *Strategic approaches to banking business and sustainable development goals. Sustainable development goals series* (pp. 263–283). Springer. https://doi.org/10.1007/978-3-031-80744-2_16

Iddrisu, K., Camara, B., & Oppong, F. (2025b). Resource financed infrastructure. In J. Y. Abor, J. Macomber, & V. Murinde (Eds.), *The Routledge handbook of infrastructure finance.* Routledge.

Ikram, K. (2007). *The Egyptian economy, 1952–2000* (1st ed.). https://doi.org/10.4324/9780203014462

Knowledge at Wharton. (2019, September 19). *Chinese investments in Africa: Four anti-corruption trends to watch.* Knowledge at Wharton. https://knowledge.wharton.upenn.edu/article/chinese-investments-africa-four-anti-corruption-trends-watch/

Krugman, P. (1988). Financing vs. forgiving a debt overhang. *Journal of Development Economics, 29*(3), 253–268. https://doi.org/10.1016/0304-3878(88)90044-2

Kyereboah-Coleman, A., Boumbouya, R. K., Marimo, M., & Latif, N. (2024). Structure, composition, and trends in African trade. In M. K. Ocran & J. Y. Abor (Eds.), *The Palgrave handbook of international trade and development in Africa* (pp. 71–88). Springer International Publishing. https://doi.org/10.1007/978-3-031-65715-3_5

Logan, I. B., & Mengisteab, K. (1993). IMF-world bank adjustment and structural transformation in Sub-Saharan Africa. *Economic Geography, 69*(1), 1. https://doi.org/10.2307/143887

Louka, E. (2020). Case study: The Greek debt crisis (2009–2018). In E. Louka (Ed.), *The global economic order: The international law and politics of the financial and monetary system*. Edward Elgar Publishing. https://doi.org/10.4337/9781839102684.00030

Manasseh, C. O., Abada, F. C., Okiche, E. L., Okanya, O., Nwakoby, I. C., Offu, P., Ogbuagu, A. R., Okafor, C. O., Obidike, P. C., & Nwonye, N. G. (2022). External debt and economic growth in Sub-Saharan Africa: Does governance matter? *PLOS ONE, 17*(3), e0264082. https://doi.org/10.1371/journal.pone.0264082

Mbewe, M., Masilokwa, I., Humann, T., Kalikeka, M., Kessler, M., & Mwamba, S. (2024). *The road to Zambia's 2020 Sovereign debt default*. https://findevlab.org/wp-content/uploads/2023/12/The-Road-to-Zambias-2020-Sovereign-Debt-Default-vf.pdf

Ndung'u, N., Shimeles, A., & Manda, D. K. (2021). Growing with debt in African economies: Options, challenges and pitfalls. *Journal of African Economies, 30*(Supplement_1), i3–i13. https://doi.org/10.1093/jae/ejab019

Nwakoby, I. C., & Ezeaku, H. C. (2021). Effects of concessional debt on economic development: A multilateral and bilateral perspective on the West African monetary zone. *European Journal of Economic and Financial Research, 5*(2), 10.46827/ejefr.v5i2.1104.

Ostry, J. D., Ghosh, A., Kim, J. I., & Qureshi, M. S. (2010). *Fiscal space* (10/11; IMF Staff Position Note). https://www.imf.org/external/pubs/ft/spn/2010/spn1011.pdf

Potts, D., & Chung, W. Y. (2008). How concessional is aid lending? *The Journal of Development Studies, 44*(7), 1023–1036. https://doi.org/10.1080/00220380802150797

Sachs, J. (1988). The debt overhang of developing countries. In G. A. Calvo, R. Findlay, P. J. K. Kouri, & J. B. de Macedo (Eds.), *Debt, stabilization and developing: Essay in memory of Carlos Diaz Alejandro*. Blackwell Publishing.

Teng, L. (2021). Do foreign aid and concessional debts attract FDI flows into recipient countries? *The Journal of Developing Areas, 55*(4), 49–59. https://doi.org/10.1353/jda.2021.0078

UNCTAD. (2022). *Economic development in Africa report 2022: Rethinking the foundations of export diversification in Africa- The catalytic role of business and financial services.* https://unctad.org/system/files/official-document/aldcafrica2022-summary_en.pdf

UNECA. (2023, March 27). *Africa urgently needs concessional financing to build resilience against shocks, experts say.* UNECA. https://www.uneca.org/stories/africa-urgently-needs-concessional-financing-to-build-resilience-against-shocks%2C-experts-say

UNECA. (2025, March 21). *Infrastructure demand boosts investment opportunities.* UNECA. https://www.uneca.org/stories/infrastructure-demand-boosts-investment-opportunities

WEF. (2018, January 1). *Concessional loans.* WEF. https://initiatives.weforum.org/playbook-of-solutions/case-study-details/concessional-loans/aJYTG0000000IOL4A2

World Bank. (n.d.). *Mobilizing more money for small businesses in Rwanda through innovative blended finance.* Retrieved September 10, 2025, from https://thedocs.worldbank.org/en/doc/86721f41f40ef7529c929dd6baf1d5dd-0340012022/original/Case-Study-Rwanda-Blended-Finance.pdf

Wu, T., & Chen, Y. (2024). *China's creditor diversification in Africa: Impacts and challenges of infrastructure debt-financing by Chinese commercial creditors.*

Zenda, C. (2020, November 6). *Fish-rot' scandal stink reaches far beyond Namibia's shores.* Fair Planet. https://www.fairplanet.org/story/'fish-rot'-scandal-stink-reaches-far-beyond-namibia's-shores/

CHAPTER 8

# Islamic Sovereign Bonds (Sukuk) and Debt Sustainability in Africa: Emerging Trends and Policy Options

*Abdul-Hamid Abdul-Wahab and Ibrahim Nandom Yakubu*

## 8.1 Introduction

Africa stands at a critical juncture in its development trajectory. While the continent possesses immense potential for growth and transformation, it faces persistent and escalating fiscal pressures (United Nations Economic Commission for Africa, 2025). Public debt levels across many African nations have surged in recent years, driven by factors including infrastructure deficits, commodity price volatility, the economic fallout from the COVID-19 pandemic, tightening global financial conditions, and the impacts of climate change. For instance, public debt-to-GDP ratios in Sub-Saharan Africa, rose significantly since 2020 due to the COVID-19 pandemic (see Fig. 8.1) (Were, 2025; IMF, 2023; World Bank, 2023). This rising debt burden threatens macroeconomic stability, constrains

A.-H. Abdul-Wahab (✉) • I. N. Yakubu
School of Business, University for Development Studies, Tamale, Ghana
e-mail: abdulhamid@uds.edu.gh



I. N. Yakubu (ed.), *Public Debt and Economic Resilience in Africa*, Palgrave Studies in African and Development Economics,
https://doi.org/10.1007/978-3-032-25835-9_8

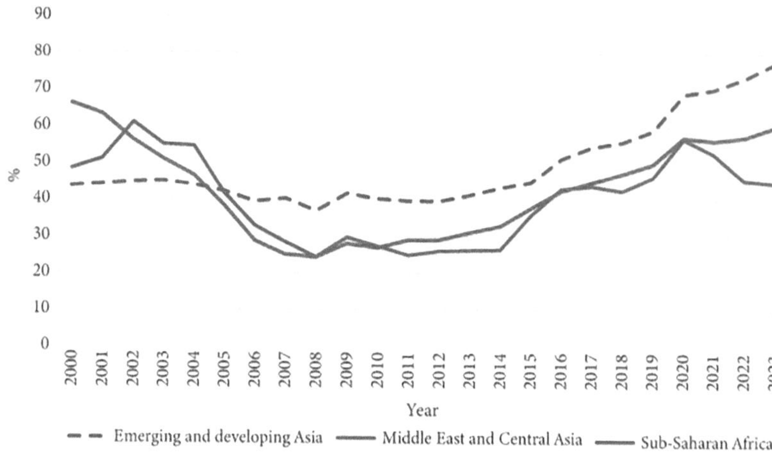


**Fig. 8.1** Trends in public debt-to-GDP ratios in developing economies. Source: Were (2025)

fiscal space for essential social and development spending, and heightens vulnerability to external shocks, placing the imperative of debt sustainability firmly at the center of the continent's economic policy agenda (AfDB, 2022).

Islamic finance, which is based on *Shariah* principles and thus bans interest (*riba*), excessive risk and uncertainty (*gharar*), as well as gambling (*maysir*), has become an important part of the global financial market. At the core of the Islamic capital markets are the well-known Islamic bonds (*sukuk*). Whereas traditional bonds are essentially debt securities, which yield interest, *sukuk* are asset-based certificates of equitable ownership in an asset, usufruct, service or project. The returns that accrue to the investor come from the earnings or cash flow generated from the asset or transaction, thereby satisfying the *Shariah* principles of risk sharing as well as asset backing (AAOIFI, 2017). This structural and ethical distinction represents a potential positive aspect, as it unlocks an enormous and growing source of *Shariah* compliant capital, largely from the Middle East and Asia, as well as the potential to diversify the investor base (Naz et al., 2025; IFSB, 2023).

For African states dealing with the huge costs associated with high debt and looking for alternative means of finance, *sukuk* provide one such avenue that is relatively unexplored. Several African nations have successfully tapped into the international and domestic *sukuk* markets (World Bank, 2017). These are evidence of the technical viability and the will by investors to patronize African sovereign *sukuk*.

It is in this context of growing public debt and limited fiscal space that innovative and sustainable financing instruments should be seen not just as a favorable alternative but as a necessity for African economies. Islamic bonds, or *sukuk*, with their asset-backing and risk-sharing principles as well as ability to mobilize vast pools of ethical capital, represent an important opportunity for addressing the challenge of enhancing debt sustainability in Africa. This chapter critically examines this proposition by first explaining the core principles and structures of *sukuk*, before analyzing global and African issuance trends. It goes on to evaluate the actual contribution of *sukuk* as an instrument for funding infrastructure and debt portfolio diversification, provides a comparative analysis with conventional bonds, and outline the regulatory and institutional frameworks required. The chapter ends by balancing the opportunities with the trade-offs and providing a pragmatic set of policy recommendations for African sovereigns that are considering this emerging and alternative financing option.

The chapter is structured as follows. Section 8.2 outlines the foundational principles and contractual structures underpinning sukuk, clarifying their distinguishing features relative to conventional debt instruments. Section 8.3 examines global and African trends in sukuk issuance, highlighting recent developments and market dynamics. Section 8.4 assesses the role of sovereign sukuk in infrastructure financing and debt portfolio diversification, while Section 8.5 provides a comparative analysis between sukuk and conventional bonds. Section 8.6 discusses the regulatory and institutional prerequisites for effective sovereign sukuk issuance. Section 8.7 evaluates the key opportunities and risks associated with sukuk adoption in Africa. Section 8.8 concludes the chapter and presents policy recommendations aimed at integrating sukuk into sustainable public debt strategies.

## 8.2 Principles and Structures of Sukuk

### *8.2.1 Key Shariah Principles Underlying Sukuk*

The design of any *sukuk* instrument is governed by several key Islamic finance principles:

*Prohibition of* Riba *(Interest)*
The most fundamental principle is the strict prohibition of *riba*, which refers to any predetermined, guaranteed interest on a loan or debt (Usmani, 2002). Money alone cannot generate more money. Financial returns must be linked to tangible assets, services, or projects that generate value, making finance a tool for real economic activity. Thus, returns to investors must not be fixed or predetermined regardless of asset or project performance. Instead, *sukuk* income are driven from rents, profits, or revenues generated by the underlying assets (Iqbal & Mirakhor, 2011).

*Asset-Backing and Materiality*
Every *sukuk* must represent an undivided ownership interest in an underlying asset, usufruct (right to use), service, or project. This asset-backing requirement ties the instrument to the real economy and ensures that investors hold ownership rights (legal or beneficial) and participate in the risks and rewards of a tangible venture, rather than unsecured debt claims (AAOIFI, 2017).

*Risk-Sharing (*Al-Ghunm bil-Ghurm*)*
The principle of "no gain without risk" is central. *Sukuk* holders, as owners of the underlying asset, are entitled to a share of the profits generated but must also bear a proportionate share of any losses incurred. This risk-sharing mechanism aligns the interests of the issuer such as the government, and the investors more closely than a conventional debtor-creditor relationship. This differentiates sukuk from risk-transferring conventional bonds (Ghazali et al., 2024; Askari et al., 2014; El-Gamal, 2006).

*Prohibition of* Gharar *(Excessive Uncertainty)*
Contracts must be clear and transparent, avoiding excessive uncertainty, ambiguity, or speculation about the fundamental terms of the transaction. This principle mandates precise definitions of the underlying asset, costs, and profit-sharing ratios (Iqbal & Mirakhor, 2011; Usmani, 2002).

Shariah *Compliance and Governance*
Issuance requires oversight by *Shariah* boards or supervisory authorities to ensure conformity with Islamic jurisprudence, enhancing ethical integrity and investor trust. Thus, *sukuk* financing cannot be used for activities deemed harmful or non-compliant with Islamic ethics, such as gambling, alcohol production, or pornography (Bennett & Iqbal, 2013; Fadzil,

2024). These principles collectively ensure that *sukuk* are not merely "Islamic" in name but are structured as asset-based and asset-backed securities that facilitate risk-sharing and promote a direct link between finance and productive economic activity.

### 8.2.2 Common Sukuk Structures

Below are descriptions of the most prevalent sukuk structures. The accompanying figures illustrate the nodes representing the flow of assets and cash at each phase of the sukuk transactions: (1) the fund-raising stage during sukuk issuance, (2) periodic payments to investors throughout the sukuk's duration, and (3) the maturity or dissolution stage. Following the figures, a summary of the common sukuk structures is presented in Table 8.1. It should however be noted that these phases are summarized into three for ease of understanding. In actual fact, a more detailed presentation will include more than three phases. In the following descriptions and diagrams, the term "obligor" is employed broadly to denote the financed party in the sukuk transactions. The terms "originator" and "obligor" are frequently used synonymously (Kusuma & Silva, 2014).

*Ijara Sukuk*

The basis for this kind of *sukuk* is leasing agreements (Fig. 8.2). In this framework, an issuer (SPV) issues *sukuk* to fund the acquisition of one or more assets belonging to the obligor. After that, a lessee will lease the assets, and the lessee's lease payments will represent the investors' (*sukuk* holders) regular payouts. Upon maturity, the assets will be reacquired by an obligor at an agreed-upon price; the proceeds from this transaction will be allocated to the sukuk holders. For sovereigns, *Ijara* is popular because it can mimic predictable cash flows in the form of regular coupon payments while an underlying asset is linked to the lease. At maturity the asset is usually repatriated to the sovereign or sold at pre-established conditions. *Ijara* has been a key structurer for most sovereign sukuk issuances and infrastructure sukuk (Kusuma & Silva, 2014).

*Murabaha Sukuk*

This sukuk is established on the basis of sale-and-purchase agreements with fixed profit and cost margins. Using the sukuk funds, the issuer (SPV) buys an asset or assets in this structure. The assets are promptly sold for a higher price, which includes the cost-plus profit, but the payment is made

**Table 8.1** Common *sukuk* structures

| *Underlying structure based on* | *Type* | *Short description* |
|---|---|---|
| Lease agreement | Ijara (Lease) | Sukuk is issued to finance the purchase of certain assets which are leased out to a lessee, whose rent payments are used for the periodic payments to the investors (sukuk holders). At maturity, the assets are repurchased by an obligor, and the proceeds of this sale are transferred to the investors |
| Sales agreement | Murabaha (Mark-up Sale) | The proceeds of the sukuk are used to purchase commodities or other assets from a supplier. They are then on-sold at a deferred price, which includes a mark-up on the purchase price. The installments from the on-sale are then used to pay the periodic distribution amount due to investors under the sukuk |
| | Istisna'a (supply agreement) | The proceeds from issuance are passed on to a contractor for future delivery of a manufactured or constructed asset, which is then to be on-sold after delivery to pay back the investors. This is often combined with a forward-lease agreement for the asset, and the fees received from this advance rental are used for periodic payments |
| | Salam (futures contract) | The proceeds are used as spot payment for future delivery of a commodity, which is then sold to pay back the sukuk holders. The commodity must be a standardized one, and its quality, quantity, place, date, and time of delivery must be well defined in advance |
| Agency agreement | Wakala | An appointed agent (the wakeel) uses the sukuk proceeds to invest in a pool of permissible investments or assets. Periodic payments to investors are made from the profits derived from the investment |
| Partnership agreement | Mudaraba | Proceeds of the sukuk issuance are used by the issuer as capital to finance a business in partnership with an entrepreneur, who contributes his labor and expertise. Profit generated from the business is distributed in pre-defined proportions between the business entrepreneur and the issuer, who then uses them for periodic payments to the sukuk holders |
| | Musharaka | Proceeds are utilized to finance a business, but on a joint-venture basis, where both parties contribute capital to the business. Periodic payments and payment at maturity are generated in a manner similar to those in a mudaraba structure |

Source: World Bank (2017)

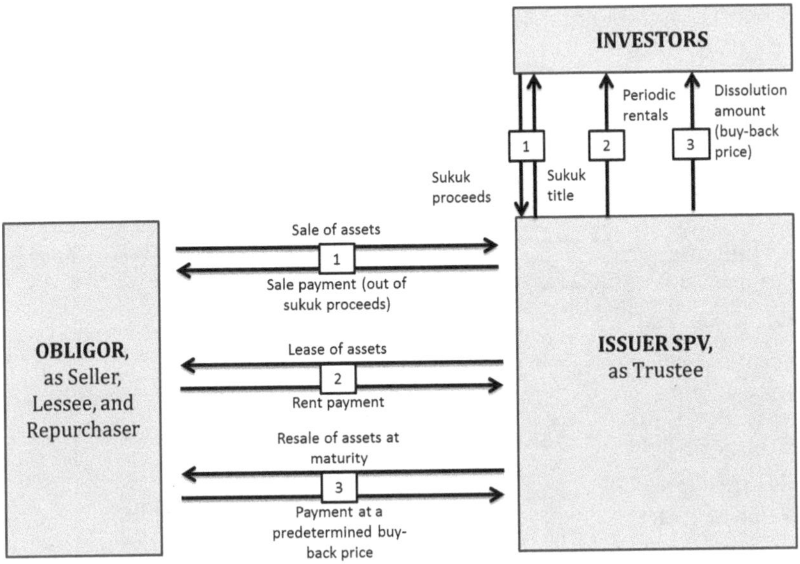


**Fig. 8.2** Structure of *Ijara sukuk*. Source: Kusuma and Silva (2014)

in installments, typically, at a later date. Payments to sukuk holders will be made on a recurring basis based on the installments. The assets are often resold to a final buyer in sukuk structures (Fig. 8.3) (Kusuma & Silva, 2014).

*Mudaraba Sukuk*

In this type of sukuk, the investors form a partnership with the issuer (SPV), who in turn lends the money to the entrepreneur (obligor), according to a profit-sharing arrangement. The issuer uses the funds from the sukuk issuance to fund a project in this structure. Periodic payments to the holders of sukuk are made by the issuer, who has previously agreed upon a split of the project's profits with the entrepreneur. In accordance with the sale or purchase undertaking, the entrepreneur will acquire the issuer's participation stake in the commercial enterprise at maturity or in the case of default. The sukuk holders will get the funds from this sale (Fig. 8.4). For sovereigns funding revenue-generative projects such as toll roads, ports, among others, Mudaraba can be used to link investor returns to the performance of the project, but with these also come more variability in

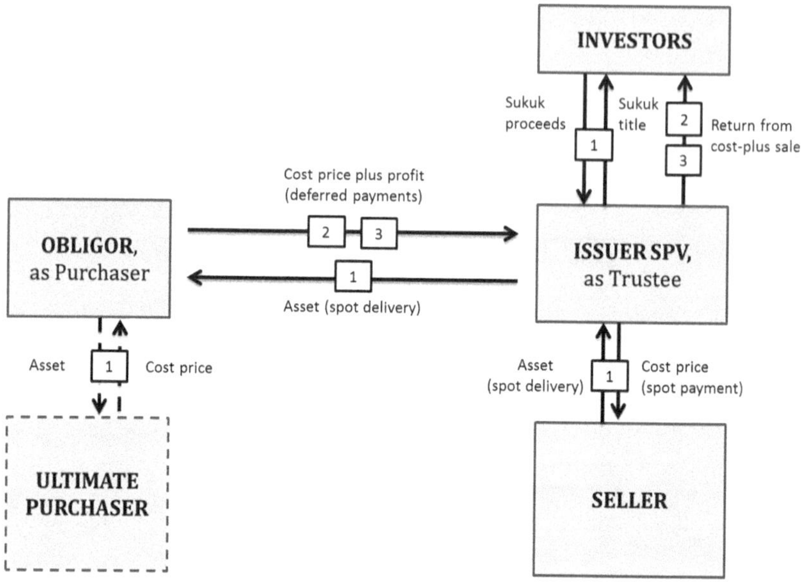


**Fig. 8.3** Structure of *Murabaha sukuk*. Source: Kusuma and Silva (2014)

cash-flows and a need for more stringent project governance and revenue transparency (Kusuma & Silva, 2014).

*Musharaka Sukuk*

The foundation of Sukuk al-Musharaka is a partnership with an obligor. Similar to al-mudaraba, sukuk al-musharaka is utilized to fund a commercial initiative, but operates on a joint-venture framework with the obligor. The obligor and the issuer both provide funds to the project, which will be managed by the obligor. Periodic payments and payments at maturity are produced in a manner analogous to that of the mudaraba structure (Fig. 8.5) (Kusuma & Silva, 2014).

*Wakala Sukuk*

Sukuk al-Wakala is founded on an investment agency agreement, wherein the agency allocates the funds into a collective pool of permissible investments or assets. The investment pool is often first possessed by the obligor. The obligor, acting as an agent, will oversee the investment in

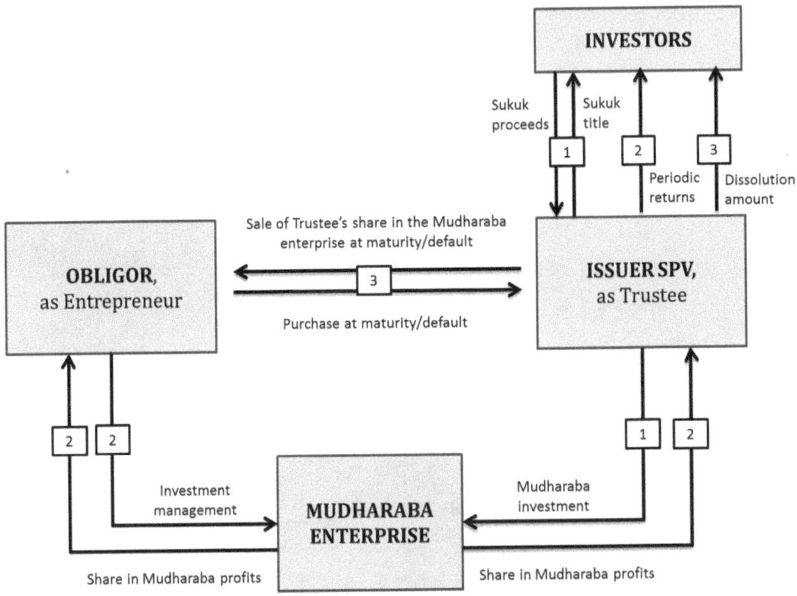


**Fig. 8.4** Structure of *Mudaraba sukuk*. Source: Kusuma and Silva (2014)

accordance with the agreement established between the principal (investors, through SPV) and the agent, which stipulates the anticipated return (profit) and fees (often performance-based). A sale/purchase undertaking agreement regulates the obligor's purchase obligation at maturity and the associated exercise price (Fig. 8.6) (Kusuma & Silva, 2014).

*Salam Sukuk*

This type of sukuk is based on a forward contract, typically involving commodities, where the seller (obligor) agrees to provide the buyer (investor) with an asset (via a special purpose vehicle, SPV) at a future date in return for a complete payment made on the spot (see Fig. 8.7). Obligor shall pay SPV the relevant proportionate amounts of salam assets prior to each date on which investor periodic distribution amounts are due and at maturity. The investors will get their money back from the sale of the asset, which will typically go to the obligor, since they do not plan to keep it. Because the underlying assets' (commodity's) prices tend to fluctuate quite a bit,

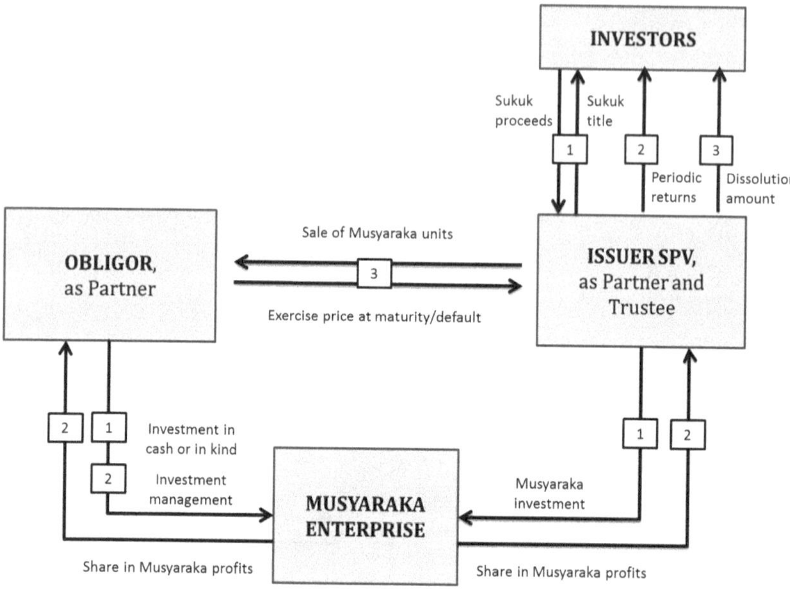


**Fig. 8.5** Structure of *Musharaka sukuk*. Source: Kusuma and Silva (2014)

this contract is best suited for managing liquidity or providing short-term funding (Kusuma & Silva, 2014).

*Istisna Sukuk*

Similar to al-salam, sukuk al-istisna are based on a contract for the future delivery of an asset or assets that have been constructed. The obligor will deliver the asset or assets at the delivery date or dates, which can be single or multiple. Like al-salam, sukuk al-istisna investors do not intend to hold the assets but rather sell them to an ultimate buyer, who may or may not be the obligor. The investors will then receive the proceeds from this sale. A forward lease arrangement is often combined with sukuk al-istisna to allow investors to receive a return before the delivery of the asset or assets (Fig. 8.8) (Kusuma & Silva, 2014).

*Hybrid* Sukuk

Hybrid *sukuk* is a type of sukuk which combines several contracts into the sukuk structure. One good example of hybrid sukuk is the Malaysian

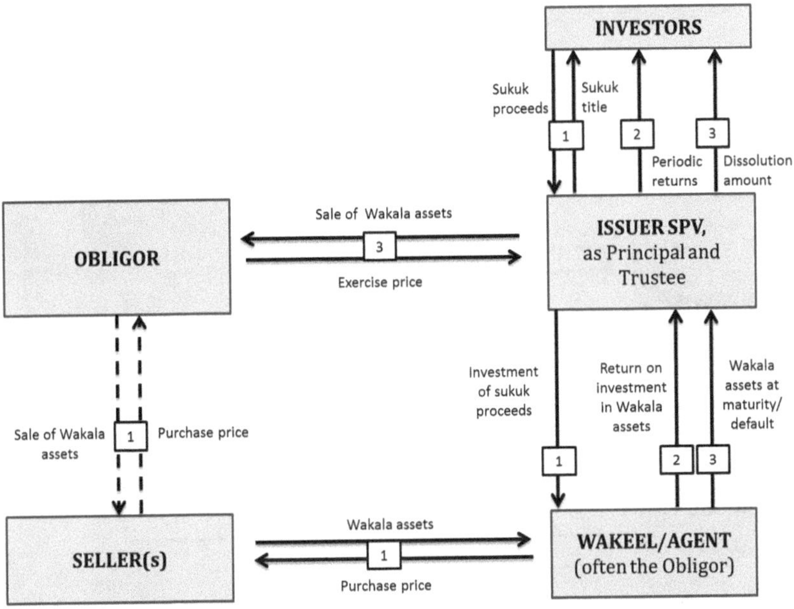


**Fig. 8.6** Structure of *Wakala sukuk*. Source: Kusuma and Silva (2014)

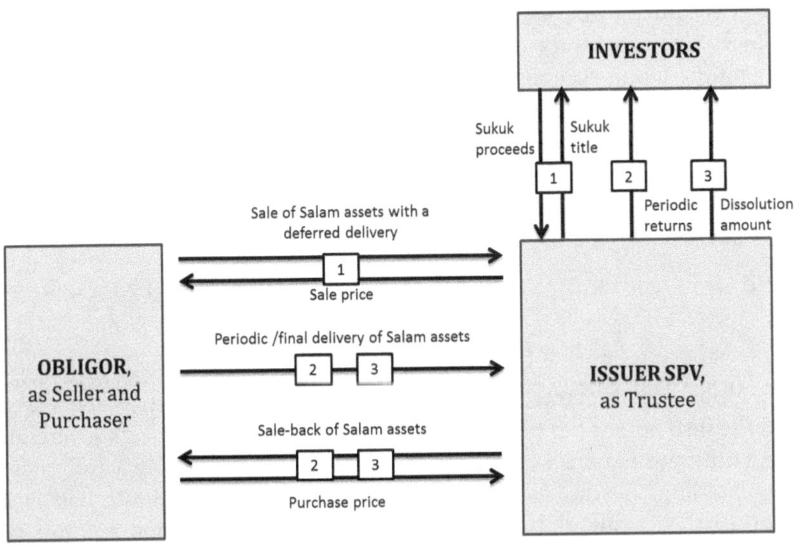


**Fig. 8.7** Structure of *Salam sukuk*. Source: Kusuma and Silva (2014)

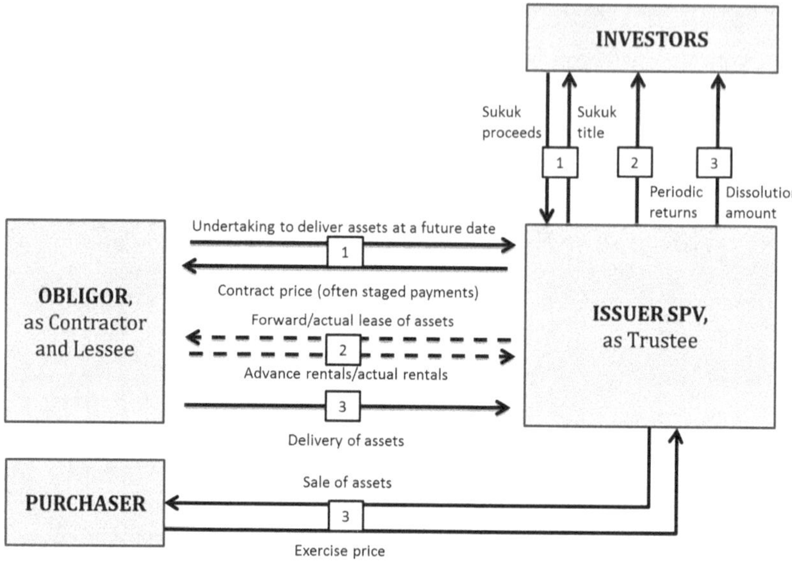


**Fig. 8.8** Structure of *Istisna sukuk* (combined with a forward lease arrangement)

government's Government Investment Issues (GII). In this sukuk, first, the government will sell its Shariah-compliant assets, such as stocks, to financial institutions for quick cash payments in order to raise the necessary funds. Upon completion of the transaction, financial institutions will sell the assets back to the government at a profit that is paid later. The government will then issue GII as proof of the debt. Proceeds from the sale will be disbursed periodically in accordance with the GII coupon. The structure of hybrid sukuk is presented in Fig. 8.9.

## 8.3 Global and African Trends in Sukuk Issuance

### *8.3.1 Global Trends in Sukuk Issuance*

The global sukuk markets have grown significantly in the past ten years, and the instrument has become a viable asset class that connects sovereign and corporate issuers with a large pool of investors looking to diversify their holdings beyond traditional assets, not just in the Middle East and Southeast Asia but globally (World Bank, 2017). The total amount of

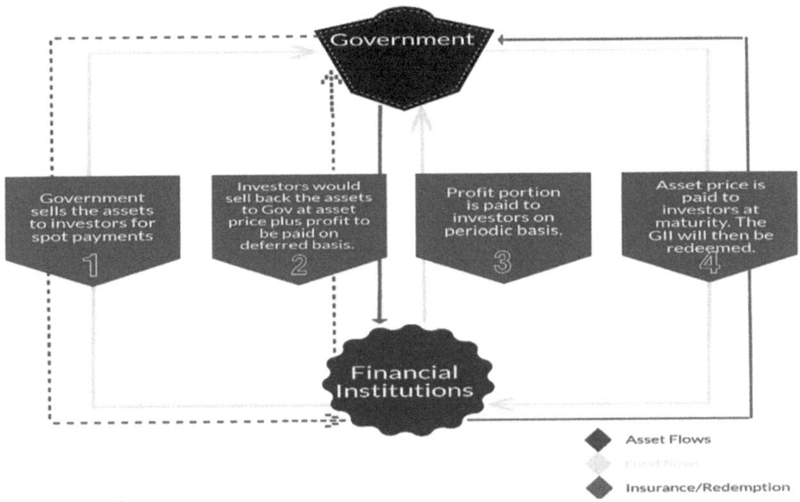


**Fig. 8.9** Structure of hybrid *sukuk*. Source: Razak et al. (2019)

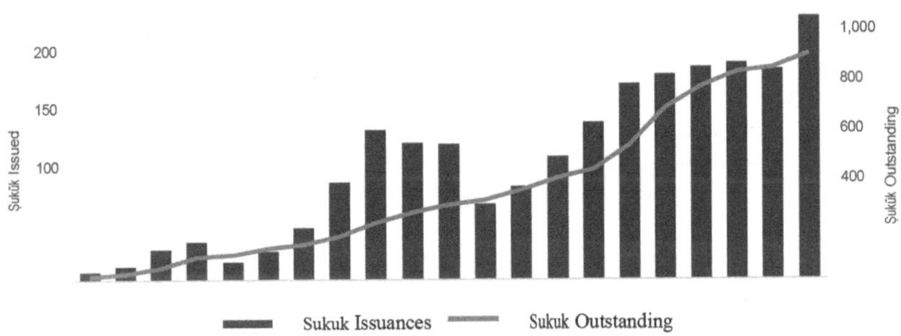


**Fig. 8.10** Global sukuk issuances and outstanding (2004–2024) (USD in billion). Source: IFSB (2025)

outstanding sukuk surpassed USD 900 billion, while new sukuk issuances increased by 25.6% to USD 230.4 billion as at 2024 (see Fig. 8.10). Falling interest rate expectations, along with sufficient global liquidity and tightened credit spreads, established favorable financing conditions, prompting issuers to access the sukuk market for refinancing and project funding. Governments and corporations in prominent Islamic finance regions expanded sukuk issuance to fund extensive infrastructural and economic diversification projects. Corporate issuers have become more active in the sukuk market, but public sector issuers still dominate issuance activity. Sovereign and quasi-sovereign entities comprised around 52.9% of total issuances (IFSB, 2025).

Nevertheless, corporate sukuk issuance increased by 21.2% to USD 87.7 billion, indicating greater private sector participation and acceptance of sukuk as a legitimate alternative to traditional debt (Fig. 8.11). In 2024, issuances by international institutions, particularly the Islamic Development Bank and the International Islamic Liquidity Management Corporation, surpassed USD 20 billion, fueled by initiatives to mobilize development financing and enhance cross-border liquidity management. Although these advancements indicate more engagement from issuers, the market structure continues to be concentrated in specific industries and sectors (IFSB, 2025).

Another trend in the global sukuk market is the increase in foreign currency-denominated sukuk. In 2024, foreign currency-denominated sukuk rose, indicating enhanced interaction with international capital markets, which suggests market advancement but also introduces potential vulnerabilities. Foreign currency sukuk constituted 34% of total issuances, an increase from 26% in 2023. The rise was fueled by issuers aiming to diversify their investor base, access overseas markets, and capitalize on favorable global financing conditions. The greater utilization of foreign currencies indicates a deeper connection of the sukuk market with global capital

**Fig. 8.11** Sukuk issuances by issuer type (2024). Source: IFSB (2025)

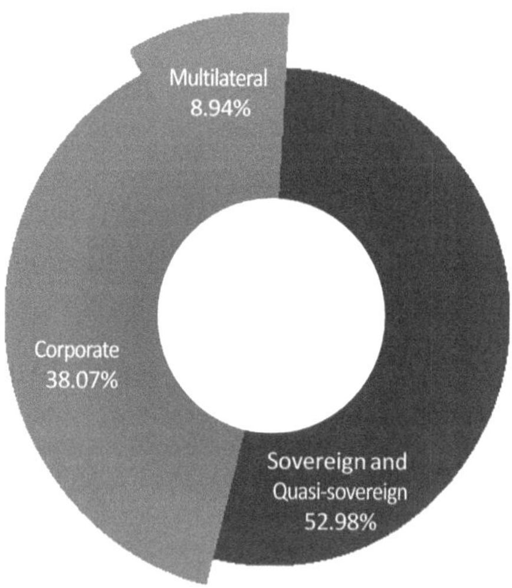

markets. Nevertheless, it also presents increased vulnerability to foreign exchange risks and possible currency mismatches, especially for issuers whose revenues are predominantly in local currency. A sudden depreciation of the domestic currency may substantially elevate debt servicing expenses and exert pressure on fiscal or corporate balance sheets. Consequently, it necessitates vigilant oversight and enhanced risk management to ensure financial stability, especially during times of market distress (IFSB, 2025).

Sukuk issuance continue to remain concentrated in mature markets such as Gulf Cooperation Council (GCC) and East Asia and Pacific (EAP), exhibiting varied issuance trends across regions and categories of issuers. Sukuk issuances were predominantly led by the EAP area and the GCC, with 51.2% and 42.1% of total issuances, respectively, while other regions made little contributions (Fig. 8.12). The EAP area dominated sovereign

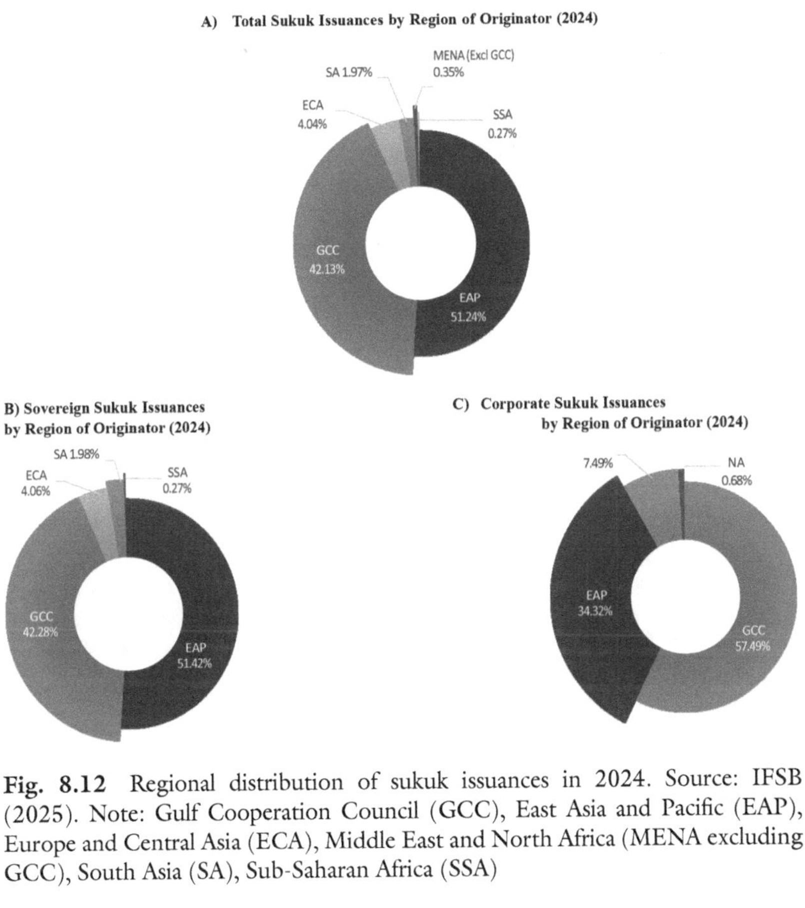


**Fig. 8.12** Regional distribution of sukuk issuances in 2024. Source: IFSB (2025). Note: Gulf Cooperation Council (GCC), East Asia and Pacific (EAP), Europe and Central Asia (ECA), Middle East and North Africa (MENA excluding GCC), South Asia (SA), Sub-Saharan Africa (SSA)

sukuk issuance, accounting for 51.4% of the global total, indicative of sukuk's application in public financing and monetary operations, especially in Malaysia and Indonesia. The GCC recorded 42.2%, propelled by rising fiscal needs and infrastructure financing. Corporate sukuk issuances in the GCC rose, comprising 57.5% of global corporate sukuk, indicating the region's increasing dependence on sukuk as a financing mechanism amidst economic diversification initiatives. The EAP region represented 34.3% of corporate sukuk, whereas the Europe and Central Asia (ECA) constituted 7.5%. Engagement from other regions remained constrained across both groups of issuers. These trends emphasize the concentration of sukuk activity in a restricted number of primary markets and the underdevelopment of sukuk markets in other regions, indicating the necessity for more geographical diversification to enhance the market's long-term depth and robustness (IFSB, 2025). Nevertheless, the inaugural sovereign issuances from nations lacking overwhelming Muslim populations, such as the UK, South Africa, and Luxembourg, underscored the importance of the sukuk market (World Bank, 2017).

The sustainable sukuk market experienced steady expansion in 2024, while its growth was unsteady and minor compared to the overall trends in the worldwide sustainable bond market. Total sustainable sukuk issuances amounted to USD 15.3 billion in 2024, representing a 27.9% increase from the prior year and constituting 5.8% of worldwide sukuk issuances (Fig. 8.13). This expansion was chiefly propelled by corporate issuers in the GCC and EAP areas, bolstered by government-initiated sustainability frameworks and increasing demand for ESG-linked

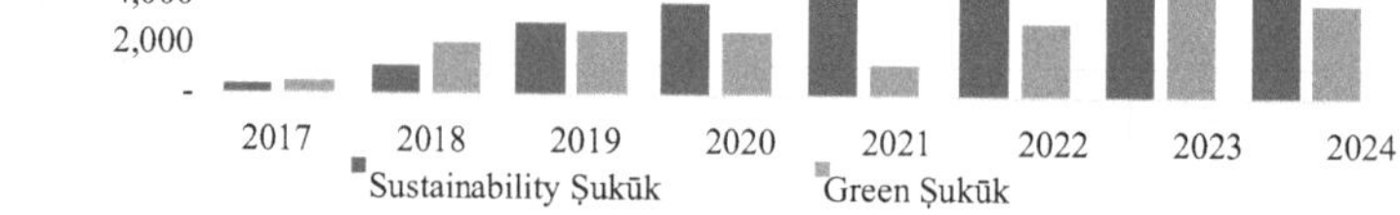


**Fig. 8.13** Sustainability and green sukuk issuances (2017–2024). Source: IFSB (2025)

instruments. The composition of sustainable sukuk however had a significant shift, as green sukuk issuances fell to USD 4.81 billion from USD 7.75 billion in 2023. This decrease indicates structural difficulties, such as a constrained pipeline of qualifying green projects and a transition in issuer preference towards more comprehensive sustainability sukuk. Despite the sustainable sukuk segment exhibiting encouraging momentum, its proportion of the total sukuk market remains relatively small, highlighting the necessity for enhanced governmental assistance to link sukuk markets with the global sustainable finance agenda (IFSB, 2025).

### *8.3.2 African Trends in Sukuk Issuance*

The African sukuk market remains small compared to the GCC and ASEAN ones. However, some sovereigns have showcased progress of issuances both internationally and in local currency. The Gambia, Sudan, South Africa, Egypt, Morocco, Nigeria, Senegal, Ivory Coast, among others, have all utilized sukuk to finance various projects. For example, the Republic of South Africa issued its first sovereign 5.75-year Sukuk in September 2014, raising $500 million on the international capital market. This made it the first sovereign Sukuk issuer in Africa and among Muslim-minority states. The Ijara framework served as the basis for the Sukuk. A total of 2.2 billion US dollars were ordered for this deal, which was more than four times oversubscribed (Abdul-Wahab & Yakubu, 2026; National Treasury, 2014). The government finally issued its second sovereign Sukuk in 2023 after more than a decade of waiting. The $1,084.99 million was raised in a four-tranche transaction with different tenors, volumes, and profit rates to be paid to the holders of the Sukuk (Abdul-Wahab & Yakubu, 2026; DDCAP, 2023).

In 2013, the government of Osun State in Nigeria issued the country's first sukuk to finance educational infrastructure projects. Subject to approval by the Osun State Government in 2013, the offering was valued at N11.4 billion naira, or approximately US$73 million (Abubakar & Baba, 2020). According to the Debt Management Office (2017), ₪100 billion, or approximately US$270 million, was the initial value of the first Sovereign Sukuk, which are seven-year Ijara sukuk. Revenues were earmarked for massive road construction projects (Abdul-Wahab & Yakubu, 2026; Abubakar & Baba, 2020). As of the middle of 2019, Nigeria's outstanding Sovereign Sukuk were worth ₦200 billion (Abubakar & Baba, 2020). The eighth sovereign sukuk issued by the Nigerian government in May 2025 was seven times oversubscribed, indicating strong demand. As of the middle of 2025, there were 2.2 billion USD worth of sukuk in Nigeria (Abdul-Wahab & Yakubu, 2026; Fitch Ratings, 2025).

Moreover, in 2015, the Republic of the Ivory Coast issued CFA150 billion worth of Sukuk. The amount, expressed in dollars, was approximately $253.34 million, and the maturity period was 5 years. The purpose of this was to broaden the pool of potential funders for infrastructure projects in regional and global capital markets (IFN, 2016; IFN, 2022; Mapenzauswa, 2015; Abdul-Wahab & Yakubu, 2026). This contract, which was structured under the Ijara framework, was based on two Abidjani government buildings. The profits went toward supporting various social and economic initiatives run by the government. Participating investors came from the Middle East (38%), North Africa (6%), and West Africa (56%), all of which were facilitated by the Islamic Corporation for the Development of the Private Sector (ICD) (IFN, 2016; Abdul-Wahab & Yakubu, 2026).

Similarly, in August 2016, the Togolese government put out its inaugural sukuk, totaling 150 billion CFA francs ($251.40 million), in a bid to broaden the country's budget funding base. Sukuk with a face value of CFA10,000 were issued through the Joint Receivables Securitization Fund (FCTC) in a total of fifteen million units. The Ijara structure served as the basis for the arrangement. The Sukuk with a yield of 6.5% matured after 10 years. The profits were used to finance significant national programs for economic and social development (Abdul-Wahab & Yakubu, 2026; Peyton & King, 2016; Togo First, 2025; IMF, 2017).

## 8.4 Sukuk for Infrastructure and Debt Diversification

Sovereign sukuk have the ability to diversify government debt portfolios and help finance Africa's massive infrastructure gap, which is one of the main reasons for their emerging popularity in the region (Parker, 2025). According to the African Development Bank (AfDB) Africa needs between $130 and $170 billion worth of infrastructure per year. That is a lot more than the commonly accepted annual estimate of $93 billion (AfDB, 2018). Several countries have utilized sukuk to fund infrastructure and to diversify government debt portfolios including Malaysia, Indonesia, Pakistan,

Nigeria, Ivory Coast, among others (World Bank, 2017). The purpose of most initial sukuk offerings in various countries were mainly meant for infrastructure and debt diversification as demonstrated in Table 8.2.

From the early 2000s onwards, Malaysia has been in the forefront of using sovereign and corporate sukuk to finance infrastructure, positioning itself as a global leader in the sukuk market (Bank Negara Malaysia, 2008). With the goal of becoming a high-income nation, Malaysia issued a variety of infrastructure sukuk to fund projects like the Kuala Lumpur International Airport, Maju Expressway, Pan-Borneo Highway, and Klang Valley Mass

**Table 8.2** Sovereign sukuk issuances from select countries

| *Country* | *Year of first issue* | *Structure used* | *Purpose* | *Key outcomes* |
|---|---|---|---|---|
| Malaysia | 2002 | Ijara, Musharaka | Infrastructure financing (e.g., airports, roads) | Established largest sukuk market globally |
| Indonesia | 2008 | Sukuk Negara (Ijara) | Infrastructure, SDG-aligned projects | Supports fiscal needs while promoting Shariah compliance |
| Pakistan | 2004 | Ijara | Budgetary support, infrastructure | Diversified funding, attracted Islamic investors |
| Nigeria | 2017 | Ijara | Road construction, infrastructure | Over ₦360 billion raised in multiple rounds, oversubscribed |
| UK | 2014 | Ijara | General government funding | £200 million sukuk; first by non-Muslim-majority country |
| HKSAR (Hong Kong) | 2014 | Ijara, Wakala | Infrastructure, green finance | Positioned as gateway for Islamic finance in East Asia |
| South Africa | 2014 | Ijara | Infrastructure funding | $500 million sukuk; successful debut in Africa |
| Luxembourg | 2014 | Ijara | Portfolio diversification, Islamic investor base | Enhanced Islamic finance footprint in Europe |
| Ivory Coast | 2015 | Ijara | Road and infrastructure projects | Financed government's social and economic projects |
| Togo | 2016 | Ijara | Development projects | Diversified debt strategy; growing market appetite |

Source: Abdul-Wahab and Yakubu (2026)

Rapid Transit system (Abdul-Wahab & Yakubu, 2026; Bennett & Coyle, 2025; AbdulKareem & Mahmud, 2019; Malikov, 2017). Tadau Energy Sdn Bhd of Malaysia raised MYR250 million ($59 million) in 2017 to fund a 50MW solar photovoltaic power plant, making it the first green sukuk issued globally. This sukuk was issued in compliance with the Shariah Advisory Council's approval, in line with Malaysia's SRI sukuk structure, and it received the top grade from the Center for International Climate and Environmental Research Oslo (CICERO) (Bennett & Coyle, 2025; Abdul-Wahab & Yakubu, 2026).

From 2014 to 2024, the government of Indonesia utilized sovereign sukuk to fund infrastructure projects totaling approximately $14.96 billion. These projects encompassed roads, trains, airports, seaports, schools, and hospitals (Abdul-Wahab & Yakubu, 2026; The Jakarta Post, 2024). To finance hydroelectric, renewable, and climate resilience initiatives, Indonesia issued the first sovereign green sukuk in March 2018 with a face value of $1.25 billion. The issuance confirmed Indonesia's dedication to sustainable fiscal tools and financing that aligns with the SDGs, while also attracting diverse global investments (Abdul-Wahab & Yakubu, 2026; UNDP, 2018). Similarly, Pakistan's historic first sovereign domestic green Sukuk issuance in May 2025 demonstrated the country's commitment to utilizing Islamic financing for long-term sustainable development (Abdul-Wahab and Yakubu, 2026; IFN, 2025).

In the case of Africa, Nigeria issued Sovereign Sukuk worth about US$270 million in 2017 (Debt Management Office, 2017). Proceeds were used for major road infrastructure projects (Abubakar & Baba, 2020; Debt Management Office, 2017). The Republic of the Ivory Coast issued Sukuk in 2015 worth about $253.34 million to diversify infrastructure funding sources in international and regional capital markets (IFN, 2016; IFN, 2022; Mapenzauswa, 2015). The Togolese government also issued *sukuk* in 2016 for about $251.40 million to diversify sources of deficit funding. Important national economic and social development initiatives were funded by the earnings (Peyton & King, 2016; Togo First, 2025; IMF, 2017).

When structured carefully, sukuk issuance for productive infrastructure can contribute positively to debt sustainability. The most important thing is to make sure that the projects that are funded bring in enough money, either from toll roads or other direct sources, or from indirect sources like increased economic output and larger tax bases, to pay back the sukuk. Rather than focusing solely on debt accumulation, sukuk can encourage economic activity by funding growth-enabling infrastructure. This, in turn, helps to keep debt-to-GDP ratios at sustainable levels.

## 8.5 Comparative Analysis with Conventional Bonds

Bonds and *sukuk* exist in the same markets, yet they are governed by different *Shariah* requirements. This is an undeniable reality. *Sukuk* are structured according to *Shariah* principles, however their execution is often modeled after traditional bond procedures (Cakir & Raei, 2007). This makes a number of scholars (Miller et al., 2007; Wilson, 2008; Cakir & Raei, 2007) consider *sukuk* to be similar to conventional bonds. Cakir & Raei, (2007) for instance, are of the opinion that contract execution for *sukuk* typically follows the pattern of traditional bonds, with the underlying *Shariah* principles guiding the various sukuk structures. According to research by Miller et al. (2007) and Wilson (2008), *sukuk* returns are designed to mimic characteristics of traditional bonds.

Notwithstanding the above assertions, several studies also documented notable differences between sukuk and conventional bonds. Sukuk, differ structurally from conventional bonds by emphasizing asset-backing, risk-sharing, and prohibition of interest (riba), while conventional bonds rely on debt obligations with fixed interest payments (Ariff et al., 2013; Arif & Safari, 2012; Uddin et al., 2022). This fundamental distinction influences their risk profiles, returns, market performance, and appeal to investors (Alam et al., 2013; Godlewski et al., 2013). Specific value-at-risk (VaR), yield curves, stock market reactions, and determinants of issuance can be found in the empirical literature and point that sukuk are unique securities with diversification benefits (Bhuiyan et al., 2020; Boujlil et al., 2020).

Studies on risk assessment (Nasir & Farooq, 2017; Billah et al., 2024; Bhuiyan et al., 2020) show that sukuk have usually lower VaR than conventional bonds, indicating a higher stability. For example, in a VaR-based comparison study of world sukuk and bond indices between January 2010 and December 2015, it is identified that sukuk indices have a VaR well below bond indices, and if combined with bond indices can decrease the portfolio risk to about 30-50% in bond indices (Bhuiyan et al., 2020). In Pakistan as well, sukuk had a lower VaR than conventional bonds, which imposed a lower downside risk for investors, Nasir and Farooq (2017). The forms of connectedness are further distinguished by tail-risk connectedness. In particular Sukuk markets have exhibited time-varying and event-induced connectedness, such as during the COVID-19 crisis, lower spillovers across frequencies than conventional bonds (Billah et al., 2024). These findings imply sukuk's resilience in volatile markets, attributed to their asset-linked nature.

In terms of returns and yields, sukuk often provide competitive or superior performance, though influenced by market conditions. An analysis of yields to maturity (YTM) for sukuk and conventional bonds traded on the Indonesia Stock Exchange in October 2011 showed significant differences, with sukuk YTMs exceeding those of bonds in certain groups, recommending greater attention to *Shariah* compliance in pricing (Fathurahman & Fitriati, 2013). Primary market evidence from 2004 to 2020 indicates sukuk issuances at lower coupon rates (11–28 basis points less) than conventional bonds, due to high demand from Islamic investors (Almaskati, 2022). However, yield curves vary whereby sukuk yields are significantly different from conventional bonds of the same issuer, rating, and term from 2005 to 2012, with no Granger causality between the two, confirming distinct pricing dynamics (Ariff et al., 2013).

Stock market reactions to issuances also diverge, often favoring sukuk under specific conditions. Announcements of sukuk issuances elicit negative stock returns in Malaysia, linked to adverse selection where lower-quality firms prefer sukuk (Godlewski et al., 2013). In contrast, international evidence from 2004 to 2012 shows negative market reactions to sukuk before and during the 2007–2009 crisis, but positive for conventional bonds pre-crisis and negative thereafter, with bond size negatively impacting sukuk cumulative abnormal returns (Alam et al., 2013). Shareholder wealth effects in Malaysia from 2000 to 2015 reveal that stocks in Malaysia reacted abnormally to sukuk issuances in terms of return following the global financial crisis, in comparison to conventional bond issuances (Sherif & Erkol, 2017). These reactions highlight sukuk's role in signaling firm quality and market sentiment.

Sovereign issuance choices emphasize sukuk's appeal in developed markets. Governments in OIC countries, including those in Africa, prefer sukuk over conventional bonds when financial markets are advanced, credit quality is high, and macroeconomic indicators are strong, with sukuk often larger and longer-tenured (Boujlil et al., 2020). This supports sukuk's potential for debt sustainability in emerging economies by diversifying funding and aligning with ethical finance.

Pricing models further underscore differences in a sense that sukuk require distinct frameworks due to risks like market volatility and information asymmetry, unlike conventional bonds benchmarked to LIBOR (Uddin et al., 2022). Empirical tests confirm sukuk's unique yield curves and causal independence from bonds (Arif & Safari, 2012; Ariff et al., 2013). Some common distinguishing characteristics of sukuk as compared to conventional bonds are presented in Table 8.3.

**Table 8.3** Conventional bonds vs. sukuk

| *Features* | *Conventional bonds* | *Sukuk* |
|---|---|---|
| Form of entitlement | Debt | Undivided, pro-rata ownership rights to the underlying assets. However, sukuk holders do not necessarily have recourse to the assets in case of default |
| Form of return or compensation | Coupon | Beneficial interest (e.g., profits) of the underlying assets/transactions. However, many sukuk are structured in such way that they closely resemble conventional bonds in terms of risk-return profile. For example, in profit-sharing sukuk, return is predetermined at a certain level under which the obligor would cover the gap. In a case where there is excess profit, the obligor retains it. This has been a source of major debate |
| Form of payment at maturity | Repayment of debt | Repurchase of assets by the obligor or sponsor or sale of assets to a third party, the proceeds of which will be distributed to investors ("redemption" by investors) |
| Issuer | Sovereign or corporate entity | An SPV (e.g., trust or company-based) |
| Documentation | Capital market documentation (e.g., prospectus) | • Capital market documentation<br>• Sharia transaction documents depending on the structure (e.g., lease agreement in *al-ijara*) |
| Regulatory process | Typical capital market approval or issuance process | Typically, in addition to the same regulatory approval process as in conventional bonds, the issuer must retain a Sharia adviser (or Sharia board) whose principal role is to ensure all aspects of transaction comply with Shariah rules. The regulatory approval includes a review of the transaction's Shariah compliance |

(*continued*)

**Table 8.3** (continued)

| *Features* | *Conventional bonds* | *Sukuk* |
|---|---|---|
| Primary risk | Credit risk of the issuer | Usually credit risk of the ultimate obligor. Except in case of asset-backed sukuk (where investors have the legal title of the assets, thus subject to asset/price risk), the primary risk in sukuk is the credit risk of the obligor, i.e., the entity who has the obligation to make payments, delivery, and/or repurchase of the assets in maturity or in case of default |
| Cost | Typical | In theory should be higher due to additional regulatory and documentation requirements but typically not prohibitive |
| Length of time needed to issue | Typical | Possibly longer, but experience shows that it is not necessarily so except for first-time issuers |

Source: Adapted from Kusuma and Silva (2014)

## 8.6 Regulatory and Institutional Requirements

Successful issuance of sovereign sukuk is not just a financing issue, but requires that the legal, regulatory and institutional framework are consistent with Shariah principles as well as regulations regarding public debt management, market infrastructure, investor protection and fiscal sustainability (World Bank, 2017). Thus, the absence of a supportive enabling environment represents a major barrier not only for the development of sovereign sukuk but also the potential contribution of sovereign sukuk to sustainable public finance in emerging countries (Zulkhibri, 2015). The following are some of the key regulatory and institutional requirements for effective sovereign *sukuk* issuance.

### *8.6.1 Legal-Enabling Framework and Statutory Authorization*

Sovereign sukuk require explicit statutory authority or clear amendments to existing public debt statutes to permit asset-ownership structures, special purpose vehicles (SPVs), and transfer of title mechanisms that underpin most sukuk structures (Mohamed et al., 2022; Zulkhibri, 2015). Absent enabling legislation, issuances rely on ad hoc arrangements that raise legal uncertainty for title transfer, investor recourse and tax treatment, risks that raise sovereign funding costs or deter international sukuk investors (Jobst et al., 2008). Empirical and review studies emphasize that a direct legal mandate (specified in debt management, public finance or capital markets law) reduces transactional frictions and enhances investor confidence (Jobst et al., 2008; World Bank, 2017; Mohamed et al., 2022; Zulkhibri, 2015).

### *8.6.2 Governing-Law, Dispute Resolution and Cross-Jurisdictional Certainty*

Choice-of-law and dispute resolution clauses are particularly critical for sovereign sukuk because many structures involve cross-border investors, assets located in different jurisdictions, or English-law style trust or assignment constructs. Regulators and sovereign drafters must therefore resolve whether domestic courts will respect SPV or ownership transfers, or whether English or common-law contract provisions and arbitration clauses will be used, and how those choices interact with sovereign immunity, public-asset protection and enforcement regimes (World Bank, 2017; Oseni & Hassan, 2015). Legal scholarship demonstrates that poorly drafted governing-law clauses and uncertainty over remedial rights are a recurring structural weakness in sukuk transactions that regulators must correct through model documentation and clarifying statutes (Mohamed et al., 2022; Oseni & Hassan, 2015; World Bank, 2017; Jobst et al., 2008).

### *8.6.3 Shariah Governance and Harmonization of Standards*

A consistent Shariah governance regime (standards for certification, monitoring and post-issuance compliance) reduces idiosyncratic rulings that fragment demand and increase structuring costs. Comparative reviews find divergence across jurisdictions in how Shariah boards, national Shariah review bodies, and market regulators interact, with implications for cross-listing, secondary market liquidity and investor eligibility. Harmonization (or at least mutual recognition) of Shariah rulings, combined with transparency on the Shariah opinion and on the structure's economic substance, is repeatedly recommended in the literature as necessary for scaling sovereign sukuk markets (Hasan, 2011; Alkhamees, 2013; Al-Twairesh, 2021; Zulkhibri, 2015).

### 8.6.4 Taxation, Bankruptcy and Investor Protections

Sovereign sukuk are sensitive to tax neutrality (no double taxation on transfers or income) and to predictable bankruptcy and insolvency treatment. Tax exemptions or clarifying rulings on VAT or stamp duties for asset transfers to SPVs, and explicit rules on the treatment of sukuk assets under insolvency (including carve-outs for true sale or ownership models), are essential. Comparative analyses of issuance jurisdictions show that tax or insolvency uncertainty materially increases issuance costs or leads issuers to adopt less Shariah-pure structures to avoid tax or insolvency risks. Regulatory guidance and tax rulings thus function as practical enablers of viable sovereign sukuk programs (Mohamed et al., 2022; World Bank, 2017; Paltrinieri et al., 2023; Jobst et al., 2008).

### 8.6.5 Institutional Arrangements: Debt Management and Market Infrastructure

Successful sovereign sukuk programs typically rest on institutional capacity within (a) the sovereign debt management office (DMO) or treasury to design instruments consistent with fiscal rules and debt sustainability objectives, (b) the securities regulator/stock exchange to admit and list alternative structures, and (c) payment/settlement systems able to handle ownership registers for asset-backed or lease-based sukuk. Cross-institutional coordination—DMO, Ministry of Finance, central bank, tax authority, securities regulator and national Shariah board—is a recurring theme in the comparative literature; weak coordination creates operational delays, uneven documentation and mismatch with investor workflows. Studies on market development stress the need for a whole-of-government roadmap for sovereign sukuk programs (World Bank, 2017; Zulkhibri, 2015; Ulusoy & Ela, 2025).

### 8.6.6 Transparency, Reporting and Alignment with Debt-Sustainability Frameworks

To ensure that sovereign sukuk serves as a positive contribution to debt sustainability and not just an additional layer of liability complexity, it should be introduced with (i) clear ex-ante disclosures about the use of proceeds, cashflows and ownership of the assets; (ii) post-issuance reporting tracking project-level performance (in the case of project-linked sukuk); and (iii) integrated into existing debt sustainability frameworks, such as debt limits, fiscal rules, and medium-term debt strategies. Among the emerging good practices are explicit ties to revenue generating projects or ring-fenced assets and adherence to consistent reporting to reduce moral hazard and preserve market access (Surachman et al., 2023; Boujlil et al., 2020; World Bank, 2017).

### *8.6.7 Market-Making, Secondary Markets and Investor Base Development*

Regulators can foster a domestic investor base (pension funds, Islamic mutual funds, TA local banks) via clear eligibility rules and market conventions, while simultaneously working to reduce barriers for international Islamic investors (tax treaties, withholding tax exemptions, custodial arrangements). Bibliometric and empirical studies highlight that sovereign sukuk issuance is most sustainable when complemented by measures to deepen secondary markets, improve liquidity and standardize documentation—outcomes that depend on both regulatory reforms and private market development (Paltrinieri et al., 2023; Jobst et al., 2008; Kusuma & Silva, 2014; World Bank, 2017).

## 8.7 Opportunities and Risks in Sukuk Adoption

The adoption of sovereign Sukuk in Africa presents a dual landscape of opportunities and risks that shape its role in advancing debt sustainability and financial sector development (Abdo, 2014). On one hand, *sukuk* offers African governments innovative financing avenues aligned with *Shariah* principles, while on the other hand, structural and regulatory weaknesses raise significant concerns for long-term sustainability (UNDP, 2024).

### *8.7.1 Opportunities*

First, Sukuk enhances infrastructure financing by mobilizing long-term capital from both domestic and international Islamic investors. Unlike conventional bonds, Sukuk is asset-backed or asset-based, linking financing to tangible projects such as energy, transport, or housing. This feature reduces speculative activity and encourages greater fiscal discipline, making it particularly suitable for African economies facing infrastructure deficits (Aassouli et al., 2018; Sylla, 2023; Khokher, 2021; World Bank, 2019).

Second, Sukuk broadens the investor base, attracting liquidity from Islamic finance hubs in the Gulf Cooperation Council (GCC) and Southeast Asia. Sukuk issuance improves portfolio diversification opportunities for institutional investors, thereby enhancing financial resilience (World Bank, 2017; Baita et al., 2023; Svoboda, 2024). For African countries seeking access to new forms of capital, Sukuk provides an instrument to tap into the rapidly growing Islamic capital markets.

Third, Sukuk may strengthen financial inclusion by appealing to Muslims who prefer Shariah-compliant investments. This could foster domestic savings mobilization and deepen capital markets in Africa (Ahmed et al., 2015). Effective deployment of Sukuk in social sectors, such as education, agriculture, and poverty alleviation, may also align with the Sustainable Development Goals (SDGs) while reducing reliance on short-term commercial borrowing (Naz et al., 2025; UNDP, 2024).

### *8.7.2 Risks*

Despite these benefits, Sukuk adoption carries several risks that warrant critical attention. One prominent challenge is legal and regulatory uncertainty. African jurisdictions differ significantly in their legal frameworks, and the enforceability of Sukuk contracts can be problematic without harmonized standards. Conflicts between Shariah principles and existing common law systems have undermined investor confidence in some emerging markets (Alam et al., 2013; Ulusoy & Ela, 2017; Adeyemo et al., 2018).

Another concern is sovereign credit risk. Although sovereign Sukuk is often marketed as less risky due to asset-linkage, in practice many issuances have been structured as asset-based rather than asset-backed, meaning that investors primarily rely on the sovereign's repayment capacity rather than direct recourse to the underlying assets (Noor & Shahimi, 2013; Godlewski et al., 2013). In African issuances, this could exacerbate debt vulnerabilities if Sukuk replicates the risk profile of conventional Eurobonds.

Liquidity and secondary market development present further risks. Limited depth in Sukuk markets constrains investors' exit options and undermines price discovery. Studies (Cakir & Raei, 2007; Haque et al., 2017; Ariffin, 2012) reveal that Sukuk markets remain less liquid compared to conventional bonds globally, exposing investors to rollover and marketability risks (Smaoui & Nechi, 2017). For African issuers, this illiquidity can translate into higher costs of capital and reduced attractiveness to foreign investors.

Finally, the issue of Shariah compliance risk cannot be overlooked. Divergence in interpretation among Shariah scholars may deter cross-border investors if the Sukuk structure used in one country is not recognized elsewhere. This risk is amplified by the limited availability of local expertise in Islamic finance across the African continent (Alswaidan et al., 2017; Hasan et al., 2019; Mohd Noor, 2024).

## 8.8 Conclusion and Recommendations

### *8.8.1 Conclusion*

This chapter has analyzed the possibility of Islamic sovereign bonds (sukuk) as a mechanism for strengthening debt sustainability in Africa. Given the increasing public debt, infrastructure financing gaps, and fiscal space that is constrained in many African economies, there are legitimate reasons to explore a more diversified approach to public financing. Sukuk provide a mechanism for funding productive infrastructure that avoids some of the pitfalls of debt-creation.

The sukuk market has evolved as a significant global asset class, showing stability and growing interest from a variety of investors. But, its confined geographical area in the GCC and East Asia draws attention to the fact that one of the most promising and untapped regions in the world is Africa. Despite the fact that groundbreaking issuances by countries such as South Africa, Nigeria, Ivory Coast and Togo have proven the technical possibility and investor appetite, the sukuk market in Africa is still nascent. The comparison with traditional bonds shows that sukuk present lower value-at-risk, can access ethical funds, and add diversification to sovereign debt portfolios. Nevertheless, these benefits are not inherent. They rely heavily on the sukuk structure itself and the productivity of the funded projects, and the enabling environment.

The constraints to scaling the sukuk market in Africa are essentially structural and institutional. The lack of well-defined legal structure, tax and bankruptcy implications, underdeveloped secondary markets, and lack of local expertise are serious barriers. Also, there is a risk that sukuk would neutralize and copy debt like characteristics of conventional bonds as opposed to genuinely reflecting the principles of risk-sharing. This threatens the sustainability benefits of these tools.

Thus, to minimize risks and to look at sukuk as a tool for African sovereign debt sustainability, an effective way is through a well thought out planned approach. So, the following are the proposed policy recommendations.

### 8.8.2 *Policy Recommendations*

In order for African governments to strategically position sukuk as a means towards debt sustainability, a gradual, well-planned approach is necessary. The number one issue is the harmonization of legislation and regulation. This involves enacting enabling legislation to amend public debt management acts and capital markets regulations, thereby explicitly recognizing sukuk structures, Special Purpose Vehicles (SPVs), and asset-transfer mechanisms to reduce legal uncertainty. Concurrently, governments must ensure tax neutrality through clear rulings or legislation to avoid double taxation, and strengthen Shariah governance by establishing national advisory boards aligned with international standards to facilitate cross-border investment.

Following the establishment of a supportive framework, governments should adopt a strategic and phased approach to issuance. It is prudent to begin with simple, well-understood structures like *Ijara* (leasing) to build market confidence. Crucially, sukuk proceeds should be strategically linked to revenue-generating projects to ensure the obligations are serviced by productive economic activity. Furthermore, developing a domestic yield curve by starting with local currency sukuk is vital for deepening the domestic capital market and mitigating foreign exchange risk.

To ensure that sukuk contribute genuinely to fiscal health rather than complicating the debt portfolio, it is imperative to enhance transparency and integrate sukuk into debt sustainability frameworks. This entails mandating clear disclosure in issuance documents regarding underlying assets and use of proceeds, complemented by robust post-issuance reporting on project performance. Most importantly, Debt Management Offices (DMOs) must fully integrate sukuk into their medium-term debt strategies, subjecting them to the same sustainability analyses and fiscal rules as conventional debt.

Underpinning all these efforts must be a commitment to building institutional capacity and developing markets. This requires investing in targeted training for officials in finance ministries and DMOs on sukuk structuring and risk management. Alongside capacity building, governments should actively foster investor relations with Islamic capital pools and promote secondary market liquidity by working with stock exchanges to improve trading platforms and price discovery.

Finally, African nations should explore innovative applications for sustainable development. A promising avenue is to pioneer green and sustainable sukuk, leveraging their asset-specific nature to finance climate-resilient infrastructure and SDG-aligned projects, thereby tapping into the growing global demand for ESG-compliant investments.

## References


Aassouli, D., Asutay, M., Mohieldin, M., & Nwokike, T. C. (2018). Green sukuk, energy poverty, and climate change: A roadmap for Sub-Saharan Africa. *World Bank Policy Research Working Paper*, (8680). https://papers.ssrn.com/sol3/papers.cfm?abstract_id=3303597

Abdo, A. (2014). A critical review of the Sukuk market: A qualitative study to identify current risks and opportunities. Dublin Business School. https://esource.dbs.ie/server/api/core/bitstreams/66bc2da3-696a-4a14-a9fb-30a341cc8ed6/content

AbdulKareem, I. A., & Mahmud, M. S. B. (2019). Infrastructure project financing through sukuk as an alternative to conventional bond financing. *Journal of management and operation research, 1*(19), 1–11.

Abdul-Wahab, A., & Yakubu, I. N. (2026). Debt without usury: How Islamic finance can reshape Sovereign borrowing in developing nations. In C. Paldi, P. Lieberman, M. Kabir Hassan, & I. Lifshitz (Eds.), *Legal and regulatory aspects of Abrahamic finance* (pp. 93–130). IGI Global Scientific Publishing. https://doi.org/10.4018/979-8-3373-1887-5.ch003

Abubakar, A. M., & Baba, I. M. (2020). Sukuk and nation-building: A theoretical analysis of sukuk financing in Nigeria. *Ikonomika, 5*(1), 76–87. https://ejournal.radenintan.ac.id/index.php/ikonomika

Accounting and Auditing Organization for Islamic Financial Institutions (AAOIFI). (2017). *Shari'ah Standard No. (17): Investment Sukuk*. AAOIFI. https://aaoifi.com/shariaa-standards/?lang=en

Adeyemo, L. W., Aunurra'him, A. A. S. M., & Masa'ad, A. Z. S. (2018). Jurisdictional conflicts between Shariah courts and common law courts in the application of Islamic banking and finance in Nigeria. *International Journal of Business Society, 2*(8), 12–21. https://doi.org/10.30566/ijo-bs/2018.282

African Development Bank (AfDB). (2018). *African economic outlook 2018.* AfDB. https://www.icafrica.org/fileadmin/documents/Knowledge/GENERAL_INFRA/AfricanEconomicOutlook2018.pdf

African Development Bank (AfDB). (2022). *African economic outlook 2022: Supporting climate resilience and a just energy transition in Africa.* AfDB. https://www.afdb.org/en/documents/african-economic-outlook-2022

Ahmed, H., Mohieldin, M., Verbeek, J., & Aboulmagd, F. (2015). On the sustainable development goals and the role of Islamic finance. *World Bank policy research working paper*, (7266). http://documents.worldbank.org/curated/en/442091467999969424

Alam, N., Hassan, M. K., & Haque, M. A. (2013). Are Islamic bonds different from conventional bonds? International evidence from capital market tests. *Borsa Istanbul Review, 13*(3), 22–29. https://doi.org/10.1016/j.bir.2013.10.006

Alkhamees, A. (2013). The impact of Shari'ah governance practices on Shari'ah compliance in contemporary Islamic finance. *Journal of Banking Regulation, 14*(2), 134–163. https://doi.org/10.1057/jbr.2012.12

Almaskati, N. (2022). Sukuk versus bonds: New evidence from the primary market. *Borsa Istanbul Review, 22*(5), 1033–1038. https://doi.org/10.1016/j.bir.2022.06.005

Alswaidan, M. W., Daynes, A., & Pasgas, P. (2017). Understanding and evaluation of risk in Sukuk structures. *Journal of Islamic Accounting and Business Research, 8*(4), 389–405. https://doi.org/10.1108/JIABR-05-2015-0021

Al-Twairesh, E. (2021). Shariah governance framework for local banks operating in Saudi Arabia: Theoretic jurisprudential study. Available at SSRN 4262677. https://doi.org/10.2139/ssrn.4262677

Arif, M., & Safari, M. (2012). Are sukuk securities the same as conventional bonds? *Afro Eurasian Studies, 1*(1), 101–125. https://dergipark.org.tr/en/pub/afes/issue/44785/557059

Ariff, M., Safari, M., & Mohamed, S. (2013). Sukuk securities and conventional bonds: Evidence of significant differences. *Pertanika Journal of Social Sciences & Humanities, 21*(2), 621–638. https://papers.ssrn.com/sol3/papers.cfm?abstract_id=2360914

Ariffin, N. M. (2012). Liquidity risk management and financial performance in Malaysia: Empirical evidence from Islamic banks. *Aceh International Journal of Social Science, 1*(2).

Askari, H., Iqbal, Z., & Mirakhor, A. (2014). *Introduction to Islamic economics: Theory and application.* John Wiley & Sons. ISBN: 9781118732984.

Baita, A. J., Malami, H. U., & Al-Faryan, M. A. S. (2023). Fiscal policy and sukuk market development in OIC countries. *Journal of Islamic Accounting and Business Research, 14*(8), 1216–1231. https://doi.org/10.1108/JIABR-06-2022-0159

Bank Negara Malaysia. (2008). *Financial Stability and Payment Systems Report 2007*. Bank Negara Malaysia. Kuala Lumpur. https://www.bnm.gov.my/documents/20124/856398/cp02.pdf

Bennett, M. S., & Iqbal, Z. (2013). How socially responsible investing can help bridge the gap between Islamic and conventional financial markets. *International Journal of Islamic and Middle Eastern Finance and Management, 6*(3), 211–225. https://doi.org/10.1108/IMEFM-Aug-2012-0078

Bennett, M. & Coyle, H. (2025). *State of the Sukuk Market and Prospects for Growth*. World Bank Blogs. https://blogs.worldbank.org/en/allaboutfinance/stateof-the-sukuk-market-and-prospects-for-growth

Bhuiyan, R. A., Puspa, M., Saiti, B., & Ghani, G. M. (2020). Comparative analysis between global sukuk and bond indices: Value-at-risk approach. *Journal of Islamic Accounting and Business Research, 11*(6), 1245–1256. https://doi.org/10.1108/JIABR-02-2018-0019

Billah, S. M., Kapar, B., Hassan, M. K., Pezzo, L., & Rabbani, M. R. (2024). Tail-risk connectedness between sukuk and conventional bond markets and their determinants: Evidence from a country-level analysis. *Borsa Istanbul Review, 24*(1), 137–163. https://doi.org/10.1016/j.bir.2023.11.005

Boujlil, R., Hassan, M. K., & Grassa, R. (2020). Sovereign debt issuance choice: Sukuk vs conventional bonds. *Journal of Islamic Monetary Economics and Finance, 6*(2), 275–294. https://doi.org/10.21098/jimf.v6i2.1104

Cakir, S., & Raei, F. (2007). Sukuk vs. Eurobonds: Is there a difference in value-at-risk? IMF Working Paper No. 07/237. https://doi.org/10.5089/9781451868012.001

DDCAP. (2023). Sovereign Sukuk – South Africa ZAR20.4bn Sukuk Ijarah. DDCAP Group. https://www.ddcap.com/sovereign-sukuk-south-africa-zar20-4bn-sukuk-Ijarah/

Debt Management Office. (2017). *Nigeria offers its first sovereign Sukuk*. Central Bank of Nigeria (CBN). https://www.dmo.gov.ng/fgn-bonds/sovereign-sukuk/2095-new-advert-on-sukuk/file

El-Gamal, M. A. (2006). *Islamic finance: Law, economics, and practice. Cambridge University Press*. https://doi.org/10.1017/CBO9780511753756

Fadzil, M. H. I. (2024). Beyond traditional Sukuk: Unveiling the potential of social impact Sukuk. https://doi.org/10.2139/ssrn.4845776.

Fathurahman, H., & Fitriati, R. (2013). Comparative analysis of return on sukuk and conventional bonds. *American Journal of Economics, 3*(3), 159–163. http://journal.sapub.org/economics

Fitch Ratings. (2025). Nigeria's Islamic finance industry to benefit from Sovereign Sukuk; New Liquidity Tools. Fitch Ratings. https://www.fitchratings.com/research/islamic-finance/nigerias-islamic-finance-industry-to-benefit-from-sovereign-sukuk-new-liquidity-tools-03-06-2025

Ghazali, N. M., Sawari, M. F. M., Alhabshi, S. M. S. J., & Ghalia, B. (2024). Fiqh maxim of "al-ghurm bi al-ghunm": A critique on the interpretation of the maxim relating to risk-return concept in Islamic banking and finance. *ISRA International Journal of Islamic Finance, 16*(2), 4–19. https://hdl.handle.net/11159/703302

Ghezal, M., Hassan, R., & Lahsasna, A. (2021). Legal and regulatory requirements to implement Sukuk in Algeria: Learning from Malaysian experience. *Journal of Islamic Finance, 10*, 030–044. https://journals.iium.edu.my/iiibf-journal/index.php/jif/article/view/525/226

Godlewski, C. J., Turk-Ariss, R., & Weill, L. (2013). Sukuk vs. conventional bonds: A stock market perspective. *Journal of Comparative Economics, 41*(3), 745–761. https://doi.org/10.1016/j.jce.2013.02.006

Haque, M. M., Chowdhury, M. A. F., Buriev, A. A., Bacha, O. I., & Masih, M. (2017). *Who drives whom-sukuk or bond? Review of Financial Economics.* https://doi.org/10.1016/j.rfe.2017.09.002

Hasan, R., Ahmad, A. U. F., & Parveen, T. (2019). Sukuk risks–a structured review of theoretical research. *Journal of Islamic Accounting and Business Research, 10*(1), 35–49. https://doi.org/10.1108/JIABR-06-2015-0026

Hasan, Z. (2011). A survey on Shari'ah governance practices in Malaysia, GCC countries and the UK: Critical appraisal. *International Journal of Islamic and Middle Eastern Finance and Management, 4*(1), 30–51. https://doi.org/10.1108/17538391111122195

IFN. (2016). Ivory coast's maiden Sukuk: A landmark deal for the West African nation. Islamic Finance News (IFN). https://www.islamicfinancenews.com/ivory-coasts-maiden-sukuk-a-landmark-deal-for-the-west-african-nation-2.html

IFN. (2022). Islamic finance in the ivory coast: Timid enthusiasm. Islamic Finance News (IFN). https://www.islamicfinancenews.com/islamic-finance-in-the-ivory-coast-timid-enthusiasm.html

IFN. (2025). Pakistan marks milestone in sustainable Islamic finance with debut sovereign green Sukuk. Islamic Finance News (IFN). https://www.islamicfinancenews.com/pakistan-marks-milestone-in-sustainable-islamic-finance-with-debut-sovereign-green-sukuk.html

IMF. (2017). Togo context and recent developments. IMF eLibrary. https://www.elibrary.imf.org/view/journals/002/2017/127/article-A001-en.xml?ArticleTabs=fulltext

International Monetary Fund (IMF). (2023). *Regional economic outlook for Sub-Saharan Africa: The big funding squeeze.* IMF. https://www.imf.org/en/Publications/REO/SSA/Issues/2023/04/14/regional-economic-outlook-for-sub-saharan-africa-april-2023

Iqbal, Z., & Mirakhor, A. (2011). *An introduction to Islamic finance: Theory and practice* (Vol. 687). John Wiley & Sons. ISBN 978-0-470-82810-6.

Islamic Financial Services Board (IFSB). (2023). *Islamic financial services industry stability report 2023*. IFSB. https://www.ifsb.org/pub.php?id=6670

Islamic Financial Services Board (IFSB). (2025). *Islamic financial services industry stability report 2025*. Islamic Financial Services Board. May 2025. Kuala Lumpur. https://www.ifsb.org/press-releases/islamic-financial-services-industry-stability-report-2025-need-for-coordinated-action-to-deepen-markets-and-sustain-growth-momentum/

Jobst, A., Kunzel, P., Mills, P., & Sy, A. (2008). Islamic bond issuance: What sovereign debt managers need to know. *International Journal of Islamic and Middle Eastern Finance and Management, 1*(4), 330–344. https://doi.org/10.1108/17538390810919637

Khokher, Z. U. R. (2021). The role of Islamic financial system in building sustainable infrastructure. In M. K. Hassan, M. Saraç, & A. Khan (Eds.), *Islamic finance and sustainable development*. Palgrave Macmillan. https://doi.org/10.1007/978-3-030-76016-8_8

Kusuma, K. A., & Silva, A. C. (2014). Sukuk markets: A proposed approach for development. *World Bank Policy Research Working Paper*, (7133). https://hdl.handle.net/10986/20702

Malikov, A. (2017). How do sovereign Sukuk impact on the economic growth of developing countries? An analysis of the infrastructure sector. In *Critical issues and challenges in Islamic economics and finance development* (pp. 1–37). Cham: Springer International Publishing.

Mapenzauswa, S. (2015). Ivory coast to issue 150 billion CFA francs worth of 5-year sukuk. Reuters. https://www.reuters.com/article/ivorycoast-sukuk-idAFJ8N12101Y20151120/

Miller, N. D., Challoner, J., & Atta, A. (2007). UK welcomes the Sukuk-how the UK finance bill should stimulate Islamic finance in London, much to the delight of the City's banks. *International Financial Law Review, 26*, 24. https://heinonline.org/HOL/LandingPage?handle=hein.journals/intfinr26&div=135&id=&page=

Mohamed, G., Hassan, R., & Ahcene Lahsasna, D. (2022). Legal and regulatory approaches in Ṣukūk issuance: A comparative analysis. *UUM Journal of Legal Studies, 13*(1), 249–281. https://e-journal.uum.edu.my/index.php/uumjls/article/view/15619

Mohd Noor, N. F. (2024). Shariah non-compliance risk and its management techniques: Empirical evidences in selected wakalah sukuk documents issued in Malaysia jurisdiction. *Qualitative Research in Financial Markets, 16*(4), 803–829. https://doi.org/10.1108/QRFM-10-2022-0171

Nasir, A., & Farooq, U. (2017). Analysis of value at risk of Sukuk and conventional bonds in Pakistan. *Journal of Islamic Accounting and Business Research, 8*(4), 375–388. https://doi.org/10.1108/JIABR-01-2014-0004

National Treasury. (2014). South Africa concludes debut sukuk bond. National Treasury, Republic of South Africa. https://www.treasury.gov.za/comm_media/press/2014/2014091701%20-%20Sukuk%20Statement.pdf

Naz, A., Ali, M., & Barut, A. K. (2025). Sukuk and corporate governance: Ethical foundations, economic impact, and global relevance in Islamic finance. In *Islamic finance and corporate governance: Synergies for sustainable growth* (pp. 147–173). Emerald Publishing Limited. https://doi.org/10.1108/978-1-83662-346-520251022

Noor, N. M., & Shahimi, S. (2013). Credit risk management for Sukuk: A case study of debt based Sukuk. *Prosiding PERKEM viii, jilid, 3*, 1259–1271. https://www.ukm.my/fep/perkem/pdf/perkemVIII/PKEM2013_5A1.pdf

Oseni, U. A., & Hassan, M. K. (2015). Regulating the governing law clauses in Sukuk transactions. *Journal of Banking Regulation, 16*(3), 220–249. https://doi.org/10.1057/jbr.2014.3

Osun State Government. (2013, October 11). *Osun successfully completes N11.4 billion Sukuk bond, Aregbesola commended for exploring new development options.* Osun State Government. https://www.osunstate.gov.ng/2013/10/osun-successfully-completes-n11-4-billion-sukuk-bond-aregbesola-commended-for-exploring-new-development-options/

Paltrinieri, A., Hassan, M. K., Bahoo, S., & Khan, A. (2023). A bibliometric review of Sukuk literature. *International Review of Economics & Finance, 86*, 897–918. https://doi.org/10.1016/j.iref.2019.04.004

Parker, M. (2025). Sukuk popularity growing in Africa. African Business. https://african.business/2025/08/african-banker/sukuk-popularity-growing-in-africa

Peyton, N. & King, L. (2016). Togo issues first $251 MLN, 10-yr Sukuk bond with 6.5 PCT yield. Reuters. https://www.reuters.com/article/business/finance/togo-issues-first-251-mln-10-yr-sukuk-bond-with-65-pct-yield-idUSKCN1071OC/

Razak, S. S., Saiti, B., & Dinç, Y. (2019). The contracts, structures and pricing mechanisms of Sukuk: A critical assessment. *Borsa Istanbul Review, 19*, S21–S33. https://doi.org/10.1016/j.bir.2018.10.001

Sherif, M., & Erkol, C. T. (2017). Sukuk and conventional bonds: Shareholder wealth perspective. *Journal of Islamic Accounting and Business Research, 8*(4), 347–374. https://doi.org/10.1108/JIABR-09-2016-0105

Smaoui, H., & Nechi, S. (2017). Does Sukuk market development spur economic growth? *Research in International Business and Finance, 41*, 136–147. https://doi.org/10.1016/j.ribaf.2017.04.018

Surachman, E. N., Hermawan, R. P., Handayani, D., & Astuti, E. (2023). Evaluation of sovereign Sukuk as a government financing instrument with stakeholder theory: A moving forward policy from Indonesia's experience.

*Journal of Islamic Accounting and Business Research, 14*(2), 315–338. https://doi.org/10.1108/JIABR-03-2022-0066

Svoboda, A. (2024). Investing in the Islamic world: Opportunities, challenges, and implications. *Economics and Finance, 12*(1), 13–21. https://economics-and-finance.com/archive/EF_2024_1.pdf#page=13

Sylla, M. (2023). The role of Sukuk (Islamic bonds) in financing infrastructure. *Uluslararası Öğrenci Sempozyumu.* https://www.researchgate.net/publication/371724438

Tan, Y. L., & Mohamad Shafi, R. (2021). Capital market and economic growth in Malaysia: The role of Ṣukūk and other sub-components. *ISRA International Journal of Islamic Finance, 13*(1), 102–117. https://doi.org/10.1108/IJIF-04-2019-0066

Togo First. (2025). *Togo prepares to repay CFA12.1 billion on Islamic Sukuk loan by August 2025.* Togo First. https://www.togofirst.com/en/economic-governance/2307-16815-togo-prepares-to-repay-cfa12-1-billion-on-islamic-sukuk-loan-by-august-2025

Uddin, M. H., Kabir, S. H., Kabir Hassan, M., Hossain, M. S., & Liu, J. (2022). Why do Sukuks (Islamic bonds) need a different pricing model? *International Journal of Finance & Economics, 27*(2), 2210–2234. https://doi.org/10.1002/ijfe.2269

Ulusoy, A., & Ela, M. (2017). Lack of standardization in Sukuk market. *Journal of Islamic Economics, Banking and Finance, 13*(1), 147–169. https://platform.almanhal.com/Reader/Article/128755

Ulusoy, A., & Ela, M. (2025). Sukuk and public debt management: General assessment and the way forward. *Bilimname, 53*, 665–696. https://doi.org/10.28949/bilimname.1489395

UNDP (2018). Indonesia's green bonds & sukuk initiative. UNDP Climate Promise. https://climatepromise.undp.org/research-and-reports/indonesias-greenbond-sukuk-initiative

UNDP. (2024). The potential growth and future trends of Green Sukuk as a tool for sustainable financing. United Nations Development Programme (UNDP). https://www.undp.org/publications/potential-growth-and-future-trends-green-sukuk-tool-sustainable-financing

United Nations Economic Commission for Africa. (2025). Economic report on Africa 2025: *Advancing the implementation of the agreement establishing the African continental free trade area: Proposing transformative strategic actions.* United Nations Economic Commission for Africa. https://www.uneca.org/economic-report-on-africa-2025

Usmani, M. T. (2002). *An introduction to Islamic finance* (Vol. 20). Kluwer Law International.

Were. (2025). Public debt challenges in sub-Saharan Africa. In *The domestic savings shortfall in sub-Saharan Africa: What can be done about it?* (pp. 117–142).

Oxford University Press. https://doi.org/10.1093/oso/9780198932482.003.0006

Wilson, R. (2008). Innovation in the structuring of Islamic sukuk securities. *Humanomics, 24*(3), 170–181. https://doi.org/10.1108/08288660810899340

World Bank. (2017). *Establishing a legal framework for sovereign sukuk issuance: A public debt management perspective.* MFM Discussion Paper No.18. World Bank. https://hdl.handle.net/10986/27536

World Bank. (2019). Reference guide: Islamic finance for infrastructure PPP projects. International Bank for Reconstruction and Development / The World Bank. https://ppp.worldbank.org/public-private-partnership/sites/ppp.worldbank.org/files/2022-02/REFERENCE_GUIDE_ISLAMIC_FINANCE_FOR_INFRASTRUCTURE_PPP_PROJECTS.pdf

World Bank. (2023). *International debt report 2023.* World Bank. https://openknowledge.worldbank.org/handle/10986/40670

Zulkhibri, M. (2015). A synthesis of theoretical and empirical research on sukuk. *Borsa Istanbul Review, 15*(4), 237–248. https://doi.org/10.1016/j.bir.2015.10.001

PART III

# Innovative Financing, Social Dimensions, and Governance in Debt Management

CHAPTER 9

# Climate Financing: Innovative Tool for Debt Management in Africa

*Khadijah Iddrisu*

## 9.1 Introduction

Over the past two decades, Africa has witnessed a steady increase in public debt, driven by infrastructure financing needs, declining revenues, and external shocks such as the coronavirus disease 2019 (COVID-19) pandemic and global commodity price volatility. In 2022, Africa's public debt climbed to US$1.8 trillion, representing a 183% increase since 2010, a pace nearly four times faster than the continent's GDP growth in dollar terms (United Nations Conference on Trade and Development (UNCTAD), 2023). While debt relief initiatives such as the Heavily Indebted Poor Countries (HIPC) programme and the Multilateral Debt Relief Initiative (MDRI) provided temporary fiscal space (World Bank, 2024b), many African states have since re-entered cycles of high indebtedness. For instance, Ghana, despite receiving HIPC debt relief in 2006 (Merotto et al., 2015), faces renewed debt challenges, losing eligibility for the U.S. Millennium Challenge Corporation's 2026 candidate list due to

K. Iddrisu (✉)
Department of Finance, Islamic University College, Accra, Ghana
e-mail: khadijahiddris@iug.edu.gh



I. N. Yakubu (ed.), *Public Debt and Economic Resilience in Africa*, Palgrave Studies in African and Development Economics,
https://doi.org/10.1007/978-3-032-25835-9_9

arrears and default (Ali, 2025). Rising interest rates in global capital markets have further constrained borrowing capacity, placing additional strain on debt servicing obligations (UNCTAD, 2023).

Climate change intensifies Africa's debt vulnerabilities by acting as a fiscal shock amplifier. The continent is highly exposed to climate-related disasters such as droughts in the Horn of Africa, floods in Southern Africa, and cyclones along the Indian Ocean coast (LeComte, 2021; Tedla et al., 2025). These events destroy infrastructure, disrupt agricultural production, and displace populations, forcing governments to increase emergency spending while simultaneously experiencing decline in tax revenues. For example, Cyclone Idai inflicted about US$1.4 billion in direct damages and US$1.39 billion in economic losses on Mozambique, amounting to a total impact of US$2.79 billion that severely strained fiscal stability (United Nations Development Programme (UNDP), 2019). Long-term adaptation costs, including climate-resilient infrastructure, food security, and renewable energy, intensify Africa's fiscal pressures. The continent needs about US$579 billion for adaptation by 2030 but mobilises only US$11.4 billion annually (Richmond et al., 2022). Rwanda, allocating over half its budget to adaptation, still faces a major financing gap, underscoring Africa's urgent climate finance challenge (Richmond et al., 2022). As such, climate change not only worsens fiscal gaps but also reduces governments' capacity to service existing debt, creating a climate debt trap.

Traditional debt instruments such as Eurobonds and syndicated loans often come with high interest rates and limited flexibility, making them unsuitable for countries already at or near debt distress. Against this backdrop, innovative climate financing is emerging as a viable alternative (Abor et al., 2025; Koh, 2018). These instruments provide access to capital that is not only cost-competitive but also explicitly linked to climate adaptation and mitigation projects. Debt for nature and debt for climate swaps, green sovereign bonds, and blended finance schemes are particularly promising for African economies seeking to diversify their debt portfolios while meeting global commitments under the Paris Agreement and the Sustainable Development Goals (SDGs). Morocco mobilised approximately US$200 million in climate financing from the World Bank, alongside US$97 million from the Clean Technology Fund (CTF) and additional climate-related resources, to support the development of the Noor-Ouarzazate solar power complex (World Bank, 2024a). This chapter explores the role of climate financing as innovative tools for managing Africa's rising debt challenges.

The chapter provides a policy framework for African governments on leveraging climate finance to address escalating debt challenges. Unlike some existing studies that primarily examine green and climate finance as tools for addressing climate change or improving living standards (Abor et al., 2025; Cudjoe et al., 2023; Iddrisu et al., 2025a, b, c), this chapter takes a different approach by exploring their potential for debt management, while still acknowledging their importance for climate action and development. Its relevance lies in advancing the SDGs, specifically SDG 7 (affordable and reliable energy), SDG 9 (industry, innovation, and infrastructure), SDG 13 (climate action), and SDG 17 (partnerships for the goals). It further contributes to Agenda 2063, particularly Aspiration 1, which emphasises inclusive growth and sustainable development.

The rest of the chapter is organised as follows: Section 9.2 examines the state of climate finance in Africa. Section 9.3 analyses mechanisms linking climate finance to debt management, while Sect. 9.4 highlights opportunities and benefits for the continent. Section 9.5 discusses challenges and future prospects, with concluding remarks provided in Sect. 9.6.

## 9.2 Climate Finance in Africa

Climate finance is more specific, focusing on initiatives that directly address climate change, such as mitigation efforts to reduce greenhouse gas emissions and adaptation measures to build resilience against climate-related shocks (Abor et al., 2024, 2025; Cromwell & Peprah, 2025; Wachira et al., 2023). Climate finance employs financial instruments such as green bonds, concessional loans, blended finance mechanisms, and grants to support environmentally friendly initiatives and projects that enhance climate resilience. Data indicate that Africa received an average of US$29.5 billion in climate finance during 2019/2020, which rose to US$43.68 billion in 2021/2022 (see Fig. 9.1). While total flows remain relatively modest compared to the continent's needs, the increase reflects a clear upward trend, with climate finance expanding by more than US$14 billion in just two years.

Out of the total, US$25.3 billion and US$36 billion, respectively, were contributed by public sources, with the balance coming from the private sector. Public sources include development finance institutions (bilateral, multilateral, and national), export credit agencies, government budgets, multilateral climate funds,[1] and other public channels. Private sources comprise commercial banks, other financial institutions,

[1] Multilateral climate funds include Adaptation Funds, Climate Investment Funds, Green Climate Fund, Global Environment Facility, Least-Developed Countries Fund, German IKI Initiative, UNEP Enlighten Energy Efficiency Initiatives, UNDP Low Emission Capacity Building Programme.

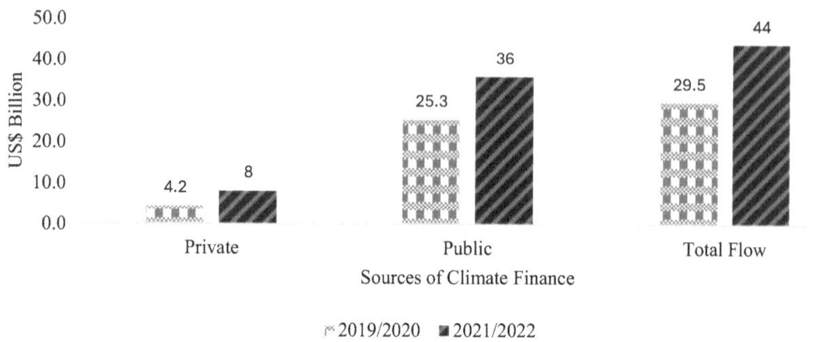


**Fig. 9.1** Climate finance flow in Africa, 2019/2020 and 2021/2022, by actor. Source: Author's Construct based on Data from Meattle et al. (2022, 2024)

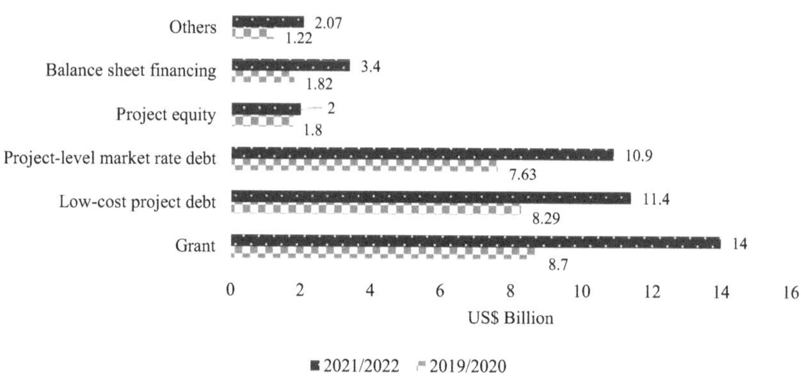


**Fig. 9.2** Instrument of climate finance in Africa, 2019/2020 and 2021/2022. Source: Author's Construct based on Data from Meattle et al. (2022, 2024)

corporations, households and individuals, institutional investors, and additional private entities.

Climate finance is primarily directed towards mitigation rather than adaptation or dual purposes. For example, in 2019/2020, climate finance was distributed as 49% for mitigation, 39% for adaptation, and 12% for cross-cutting projects. By 2021/2022, allocations amounted to US$19.9 billion for mitigation, US$13.8 billion for adaptation, and US$9.3 billion for projects addressing both objectives (Meattle et al., 2022, 2024). In Africa, grants are the most widely used instrument for scaling up climate finance. On annual averages i.e., 2019/2020 and 2021/2022, grants accounted for US$8.75 billion and US$14 billion in climate finance, making them the largest source of support (see Fig. 9.2).

This is further reflected in various grant programmes across Africa, such as the African Development Bank's (AfDB) initiative, which provides grants ranging from US$260,000 to US$1.3 million (Box 9.1).

**Box 9.1 Climate Action Window at COP29 to Promote Fight Against Climate Change**

The African Development Fund (ADF-16) has launched the Third Call for Proposals under the Climate Action Window (CAW) at COP29, inviting eligible beneficiaries to apply for grant funding through the Technical Assistance (TA) sub-window. The CAW was established to address Africa's climate vulnerabilities, particularly in low-income countries, by accelerating adaptation and promoting Paris-aligned climate projects. Approximately US$56 million has been allocated for this TA call, with grants ranging from US$260,000 to US$1.3 million. Resources will support project preparation, capacity building, and the development of long-term climate strategies, Nationally Determined Contributions (NDCs), National Adaptation Plans (NAPs), and climate diagnostics. Eligible activities include consultant fees, proposal development, training, consultations, advocacy, and communications, while operating costs must remain below 15% and staff remuneration below 25% of total grants. Funding will focus on priority areas such as Paris alignment, gender and youth inclusion, biodiversity, climate governance, capacity development, and disaster risk management. Eligible beneficiaries include ADF governments, AfDB departments, regional bodies, NGOs, community-based organisations, UN agencies, and consortia, but not private sector entities. Target sectors include agriculture, water, energy, transport, sustainable finance, and resilient infrastructure. The initiative aims to enhance Africa's climate resilience, mobilise additional finance, and strengthen governance for sustainable development.

Source: https://www.afdb.org/en/topics-and-sectors/initiatives-and-partnerships/adf-climate-action-window/call-proposals-climate-action-window accessed September 13, 2025.

**Table 9.1** Trend in international sources of climate finance in Africa, 2011 to 2021

| *Year* | *Bilateral* | *Multilateral development banks* | *Climate funds* | *Other international organisation* | *Philanthropic funder* | *South-South* |
|---|---|---|---|---|---|---|
| 2011 | 3.6 | 0 | 0 | 0 | 0 | 0 |
| 2012 | 6 | 0 | 0 | 0.2 | 0 | 0 |
| 2013 | 7 | 3.2 | 0.2 | 0.3 | 0 | 0.1 |
| 2014 | 6.3 | 4.4 | 0.3 | 0.3 | 0.1 | 0.1 |
| 2015 | 7.2 | 2.7 | 0.4 | 0.4 | 0 | 0.1 |
| 2016 | 11 | 0 | 0.6 | 0.2 | 0.1 | 0.2 |
| 2017 | 8.5 | 7.3 | 1.5 | 0.2 | 0.2 | 0.2 |
| 2018 | 8.2 | 7.2 | 1.3 | 0.3 | 0.1 | 0.1 |
| 2019 | 9 | 9.5 | 0.8 | 0.2 | 0.2 | 0.2 |
| 2020 | 10.5 | 12.3 | 0.9 | 0.3 | 0.2 | 0.2 |
| 2021 | 11.3 | 13.6 | 1.2 | 0.4 | 0.3 | 0.3 |
| Total | 88.6 | 60.2 | 7.2 | 2.8 | 1.2 | 1.5 |

Note: all the sources were measured in US$ billion

Source: Author's Construct based on Data from Freitas and Mwaniki (2024)

Additionally, between 2011 and 2021, bilateral sources provided approximately US$88.6 billion in climate finance to Africa, representing the largest overall contribution. However, from 2019 to 2021, multilateral development banks (MDBs) emerged as the leading source, channelling US$9.5 billion, US$12.3 billion, and US$13.6 billion respectively (see Table 9.1).

Credit rating agencies have also played an important role in enhancing the flow of climate finance in Africa, as their role gives investors greater assurance that their funds are being allocated to sound and reliable projects. For instance, the AfDB's 200 million South African rand (ZAR) green bond was oversubscribed due to strong ratings from Moody's (Aaa), Standard & Poor's (AAA), Fitch (AAA), and the Japan Credit Rating Agency (AfDB, 2022).

## 9.3 Mechanism of Climate Financing for Debt Management

### *9.3.1 Structure and Process of Debt-for-Climate/Nature Swaps*

Debt-for-climate (or debt-for-nature) swaps allow debtor countries to restructure part of their external debt in exchange for commitments to invest in climate or environmental projects (Naumenkova et al., 2023). Typically, an external creditor agrees to reduce, cancel, or refinance a portion of sovereign debt. In return, the debtor government commits to channel the freed fiscal space into climate-resilient infrastructure, renewable energy, biodiversity protection, or adaptation programmes (Nedopil et al., 2024). The process usually involves three actors: creditors (bilateral or multilateral), the debtor government, and an intermediary such as a conservation trust fund, which ensures transparency and accountability in project implementation. A practical example in Africa is Seychelles, where external creditors restructured US$21.6 million of debt to support marine conservation efforts (Box 9.2).

**Box 9.2 Seychelles Used Debt-for-Climate Swap to Manage High Public Debts**

In response to a severe debt crisis in 2008, Seychelles entered a five-year IMF-supported economic reform programme aimed at restoring fiscal stability. At the time, public debt reached 151% of GDP, with external debt accounting for 98% and large arrears owed to Paris Club creditors. In 2009, the Paris Club agreed to cancel 45% of debt in two phases and reschedule the remainder over 18 years with a five-year grace period. By 2014, debt had fallen to 60% of GDP, economic indicators had improved, and Fitch upgraded Seychelles to B+ with a positive outlook. Building on this progress, Seychelles negotiated the world's first debt-for-nature swap in 2015, restructuring US$21.6 million of external debt in exchange for a commitment to protect 30% of its Exclusive Economic Zone. The swap established the Seychelles Conservation and Climate Adaptation Trust (SeyCCAT) and laid the groundwork for the pioneering Blue Bonds initiative.

Source: Dogley (2024).

### 9.3.2 *Issuance Strategies and Fiscal Implications of Sovereign Green Bonds*

Sovereign green bonds enable governments to raise capital from domestic and international investors specifically for climate-related projects. The issuance process typically involves:

- Establishing a green bond framework aligned with recognised standards (e.g., ICMA's Green Bond Principles).
- Defining eligible sectors such as renewable energy, climate-smart agriculture, and resilient infrastructure.
- Independent verification or certification to enhance investor confidence.

For debtor governments, sovereign green bonds offer dual fiscal benefits: they diversify funding sources and can lower borrowing costs due to ESG-driven investor appetite. Nigeria, as Africa's first sovereign green bond issuer, leveraged the instrument as a debt management strategy (Box 9.3).

**Box 9.3 Nigeria Issued Africa's First Sovereign Green Bonds**

In 2017, Nigeria became the first African country to issue a sovereign green bond, raising ₦10.7 billion (about US$29 million) certified under the Climate Bonds Standard and financing projects in afforestation, solar energy, and climate-resilient agriculture. A second issuance in 2019 raised ₦15 billion (about US$42 million), expanding investments to off-grid solar, energy efficiency, and gas flaring reduction. Both issuances were aligned with Nigeria's Nationally Determined Contributions (NDCs) under the Paris Agreement and coordinated by the Federal Ministry of Environment in collaboration with the Debt Management Office (DMO), marking a pioneering effort in linking sovereign debt with climate action.

Source: Green Finance Platform (2017).

### 9.3.3 *Leveraging Concessional Finance to Crowd in Private Capital Using Blended Finance*

Blended finance combines concessional resources from development partners with commercial capital to reduce investment risk in climate projects. In the African context, multilateral institutions such as the AfDB and the Green Climate Fund (GCF) play catalytic roles by providing first-loss guarantees, subordinated debt, or interest rate subsidies (Belianska et al., 2022; Iddrisu et al., 2025a, b, c). This de-risking makes it more attractive for private investors to finance projects that would otherwise appear too risky, such as off-grid renewable energy or climate-resilient agriculture. In terms of debt management, blended finance reduces reliance on expensive Eurobonds and fosters sustainable investment without overburdening public balance sheets. For instance, Gabon leveraged blended finance to develop the Kinguélé Aval Hydropower Plant, thereby reducing pressure on the public balance sheet (Box 9.4).

**Box 9.4 Gabon Applied Blended Finance for Kinguélé Aval Hydropower**

The Kinguélé Aval Hydropower Plant, located on the Mbéi River about 90 kilometers from Libreville, is a 35-megawatt renewable energy project expected to generate around 205 gigawatt hours annually. It is designed to replace thermal power generation and avoid approximately 150,000 tonnes of carbon dioxide emissions each year. Developed under a public–private partnership, the project is managed by Asonha Énergie, jointly owned by Meridiam (60 percent) and Gabon Power Company (40 percent), a subsidiary of Gabon's sovereign wealth fund. With a total cost of about €179 million, financing was structured through a blend of debt and equity. Shareholders provided €44 million in equity, while debt financing totalled €131 million. Climate-focused blended finance was critical: the International Finance Corporation contributed a €33 million senior loan and €23 million concessional loan under the Canada–International Finance Corporation Renewable Energy Programme; the African Development Bank added €20 million senior debt, €10 million from the Africa Growing Together Fund, and €9 million concessional funding from the Sustainable Energy Fund for Africa. Additional support came from the Development Bank of Southern Africa and the Emerging Africa Infrastructure Fund.

Source: Meridiam (2019).

### *9.3.4 Linking Green Instruments to National Debt Sustainability Frameworks*

For climate financing tools to be effective in addressing debt pressures, they must be integrated into national debt sustainability strategies. This requires debt management offices (DMOs) and finance ministries to explicitly consider climate-related risks and opportunities in their fiscal frameworks. Governments can ensure that new borrowing not only avoids worsening debt vulnerabilities but also contributes to building climate resilience by aligning sovereign green bonds, swaps, and blended finance with long-term debt sustainability analyses (DSAs). Moreover, integrating climate instruments into Medium-Term Debt Strategies (MTDS) allows policymakers to diversify financing sources, improve debt transparency, and strengthen investor confidence. Regional institutions such as the African Union (AU) and AfDB are increasingly advocating for this alignment, recognising that climate financing should not be treated as parallel to, but rather embedded within, broader debt management policies (Freitas & Mwaniki, 2024).

## 9.4 Opportunities and Benefits for Africa

### *9.4.1 Access to Cheaper and Diversified Capital Markets*

Green and climate-linked instruments offer African governments access to pools of capital that prioritise environmental, social, and governance (ESG) criteria. These investors are often willing to accept lower yields in exchange for the environmental impact of their investments, thereby lowering borrowing costs compared to conventional Eurobonds. For example, Egypt's US$750 million sovereign green bond in 2020 attracted bids worth nearly five times the issue size (Box 9.5). Diversification also reduces overreliance on a few high-cost instruments and opens up alternative financing channels that are less vulnerable to global interest rate fluctuations.

**Box 9.5 Egypt's Green Bond Was Oversubscribed**
In 2020, Egypt issued the Middle East and North Africa's first sovereign green bond, raising US$750 million to finance a US$1.9

(*continued*)

**Box 9.5 (continued)**

billion portfolio of green projects, such as clean transportation, renewable energy, and sustainable water management. The five-year US dollar bond, priced at a 5.25 percent yield 50 basis points below the initial target and was nearly five times oversubscribed, attracting US$3.7 billion in orders. The offering drew strong global interest, including first time investors, despite market concerns linked to COVID-19 and heavy new issuance. Egypt's debut marks a milestone in sustainable finance, reflecting surging global demand for climate friendly investments and green securities.

Source: English (2020).

### 9.4.2 *Strengthening Climate Adaptation and Mitigation Investments*

Climate financing enables governments to channel resources into priority areas such as renewable energy, sustainable agriculture, climate-smart infrastructure, and coastal protection. These investments directly reduce the long-term economic damages of climate shocks, thereby protecting public finances from unplanned expenditures. For instance, Gabon debt-for-nature supported marine conservation and fisheries management, strengthening climate adaptation while securing livelihoods (Box 9.6).

### 9.4.3 *Enhancing Creditworthiness and Investor Confidence*

Successfully issuing and managing green or climate bonds signals strong governance, transparency, and commitment to sustainability, all of which are valued by credit rating agencies and global investors. Over time, this can translate into improved sovereign credit ratings, which reduce borrowing costs across the board. Countries that demonstrate credible reporting, monitoring, and alignment with international standards (e.g., ICMA Green Bond Principles) are better positioned to attract repeat investors. This is demonstrated by Gabon and Egypt, which have strengthened investor confidence through the issuance of green bonds (see Boxes 9.5 and 9.6). This reputational dividend is particularly important for African countries that have historically faced higher risk premiums in international markets.

**Box 9.6 Gabon Debt-for-Nature Swap Protect the Climate and Biodiversity**

In 2023, Gabon completed Africa's first multilateral debt-for-nature swap, reducing its sovereign debt while funding marine conservation. The US$500 million, 15-year blue bond maturing in 2038 repurchased about 4 percent of Gabon's older debt at a discount, generating US$125 million in savings earmarked for ocean conservation in local currency. Backed by insurance from the U.S. International Development Finance Corporation, the bond's credit rating rose from Caa1/B- to Aa2, lowering its coupon rate to 6.097 percent and drawing strong investor demand. The Nature Conservancy advised and oversaw the deal, ensuring environmental milestones are met, with penalties for non-compliance. Funds will expand marine protected areas, strengthen fishing regulations, and support Gabon's 30×30 conservation target, vital for protecting biodiversity such as one-third of the world's leatherback turtles. Despite political upheaval, Gabon has honoured payments and advanced marine planning with The Nature Conservancy. This innovative swap highlights the role of sustainable finance in climate and biodiversity protection.

Source: Simeth (2025) and Zorn and Ntabeni (2025).

### 9.4.4 *Building Local Green Capital Markets and Institutional Capacity*

Issuance of sovereign and corporate green bonds stimulates the development of domestic capital markets by setting standards for verification, disclosure, and investor protection. It also builds technical expertise within finance ministries, DMO, and regulatory agencies. Kenya have already used sovereign and corporate green bonds to deepen their local markets (Box 9.7). This institutional capacity not only strengthens climate finance but also improves broader debt management systems, encouraging better fiscal discipline and transparency.

**Box 9.7 Corporate Green Bond Innovation Boost Domestic Capital**
In 2020, Acorn Holdings issued Kenya's first corporate green bond, raising Kenya Shillings (KES) 4.3 billion (approximately US$40 million) to finance green-certified student housing for 5000 students. The bond, Climate Bonds Certified, was listed on the Nairobi Securities Exchange and later cross-listed on the London Stock Exchange, signalling Kenya's ambition to globalise its green finance ecosystem. Moody's rated Acorn's medium-term note programme B1, one notch higher than Kenya's sovereign rating, making it the first non-governmental green bond in Africa rated by Moody's. Supported by the Green Bonds Programme Kenya, involving Financial Sector Deepening (FSD) Africa, the Netherlands Development Finance Company (FMO), the Kenya Bankers Association (KBA), the Nairobi Securities Exchange (NSE), and the Climate Bonds Initiative, it marked a milestone in East Africa's sustainable finance development.

Source: FSD Africa and Climate Bonds Initiative (2020).

### *9.4.5 Advancing Africa's Agenda 2063, SDGs, and Paris Agreement Commitments*

Climate-linked debt instruments can help African countries align their financing strategies with continental and global development goals. Agenda 2063 emphasises inclusive growth, resilience, and environmental sustainability, while the SDGs and Paris Agreement require significant investment in climate adaptation and mitigation. Green financing offers a pathway for African states to meet these commitments while simultaneously addressing fiscal constraints. African governments can turn financial vulnerability into an opportunity for long-term structural transformation by linking debt management with sustainable development. For example, Boxes 9.5 to 9.7 illustrate how green bonds and other financial instruments are being used to support the implementation of Agenda 2063, the SDGs, and the objectives of the Paris Agreement.

## 9.5 Challenges and Future Prospects for Africa

### *9.5.1 Challenges*

1. **Risk of Greenwashing Without Robust Verification**
   One of the most pressing concerns in Africa's green finance landscape is the risk of greenwashing, where funds raised through green instruments are not genuinely applied to climate or environmental projects (Cromwell & Peprah, 2025; Iddrisu et al., 2025b). In 2023, the Daily Nation reported that several carbon credit projects in Kenyan community forests exaggerated their climate impact and delivered minimal benefits to local communities (Mbuthia, 2025). Weak monitoring frameworks, inadequate data systems, and limited third-party verification raise questions about accountability. If investors perceive that proceeds are misused or projects fail to deliver measurable climate outcomes, market credibility could erode, deterring future investment (Riedl, 2022).
2. **Weak Institutional and Technical Capacity in Some States**
   Issuing and managing climate finance instruments requires specialised skills in structuring, monitoring, and reporting. Many African DMOs, ministries of finance, and central banks face institutional and technical constraints, including shortages of trained personnel and limited financial infrastructure. Mooldijk and Lütkehermöller (2021) noted that, for Kenya's market to scale, issuing entities and intermediaries required training in areas such as structuring, taxonomies, and post-issuance reporting. Without adequate capacity, governments may struggle to design credible green frameworks, negotiate effectively with creditors, or maintain investor trust through transparent reporting.
3. **Limited Investor Appetite due to Perceived High Risk**
   Despite rising global demand for green assets, African issuers still contend with investor concerns about sovereign risk, currency volatility, and political instability. These perceptions often lead to higher risk premiums on African debt, offsetting the potential cost advantages of green instruments. For smaller economies with limited market visibility, attracting large-scale ESG investors remains particularly challenging. A feasibility study on developing a green bond market in Ghana revealed several challenges, including limited understanding of green-eligible assets, uncertainty around pricing, a perceived lack of pipeline,

and the absence of supportive policies or guidelines (FSD Africa, 2021). These issues can undermine investor confidence, leading local investors to favour the stability of foreign currency issuances over domestic ones.

4. **High Transaction and Reporting Costs**
   Green financing instruments typically require rigorous pre-issuance frameworks, third-party certifications, and ongoing impact reporting. These processes involve substantial administrative and financial costs, which can be prohibitive for smaller or resource-constrained countries. In some cases, the cost of verification and reporting has accounted for 2 to 5 percent of total issuance, significant for countries with narrow fiscal space. Such expenses may discourage participation or reducing the net fiscal benefit of these instruments. For instance, ACEP Burkina Faso struggled with high verification costs, limited internal expertise requiring consultants, and weak digital infrastructure, making green finance pilots costly, capacity-constrained, and difficult to scale effectively (Carrillo, 2024).
5. **Danger of Worsening Debt Distress if Green Finance Is Poorly Designed**
   While green instruments can unlock new financing avenues, they remain debt obligations. If poorly structured or issued in already distressed contexts, they can exacerbate debt vulnerabilities rather than easing them. For instance, if sovereign green bonds are used to refinance short-term liabilities without clear climate benefits, they may simply add another layer of fiscal risk. The challenge lies in ensuring that green borrowing directly enhances resilience and contributes to long-term sustainability, rather than providing short-lived liquidity relief.
6. **Lack of Harmonised African Taxonomy for Green Finance**
   Currently, Africa lacks a continent-wide taxonomy or standardised definition of what qualifies as "green" or "climate-aligned" investment. This absence leads to inconsistencies across countries, reduces investor confidence, and limits cross-border capital flows. While the EU, China, and other regions have advanced taxonomies, Africa is still in the early stages of developing a harmonised framework. Regional institutions such as the AfDB and the AU are working towards standardisation, but progress remains uneven, leaving space for ambiguity and potential misuse.

### 9.5.2 *Future Prospects*

1. **Emerging Innovations**
Africa is well-positioned to benefit from the next wave of climate financing instruments. Blue bonds, pioneered by Seychelles in 2018, channel resources into the sustainable use of ocean and marine resources, a model that could be scaled across coastal states (Meattle et al., 2024). Resilience bonds link borrowing to disaster risk reduction measures and could help highly climate-vulnerable countries finance infrastructure that lowers future recovery costs. Sustainability-linked bonds (SLBs) go further by linking interest rates to the achievement of measurable climate or development targets. An increasing number of African countries, including Ghana and Burkina Faso, are undertaking pilot tests for green bond issuance (FSD Africa, 2021). These instruments broaden the menu of financing options beyond traditional green bonds, offering African issuers flexible tools tailored to diverse development contexts.
2. **Potential of Digital Finance**
Digital technologies present opportunities to strengthen trust and efficiency in climate finance. Blockchain platforms can provide transparent, tamper-proof tracking of how green bond proceeds are allocated and whether financed projects deliver their intended environmental impacts. This level of traceability could reduce greenwashing risks, enhance investor confidence, and lower verification costs. Pilot projects in Africa's fintech sector suggest that blockchain-enabled green finance could be particularly effective in contexts with weaker institutional oversight, ensuring that funds reach climate-resilient projects at both national and community levels. Sun Exchange, a Cape Town–based fintech, uses blockchain and cryptocurrency to finance small-scale solar projects (Box 9.8).

**Box 9.8 The Sun Exchange Enhance Trust in Climate Finance**
The Sun Exchange, founded in Cape Town in 2015, is a blockchain-based platform pioneering solar micro-leasing in Africa. It enables individuals worldwide to purchase solar cells that are leased to schools, hospitals, businesses, and community organizations, making clean energy more accessible and affordable. With over 13,000

(*continued*)

**Box 9.8 (continued)**

members across 180 countries and 68 completed projects, the platform democratises solar investment while fostering global collaboration. Sun Exchange ensures transparent, efficient transactions and optimized project management by leveraging blockchain, AI, and big data. Its triple impact approach reduces carbon emissions, lowers energy costs, and empowers communities. The initiative supports SDG 7 by driving renewable energy adoption, economic inclusion, and sustainable development.

Source: Spooner (2024).

3. **Role of African Climate Funds and Regional Pooled Financing**
   Regional climate financing platforms such as the Africa Climate Change Fund[2] (ACCF) and the Africa Adaptation Acceleration Programme[3] (AAAP) offer opportunities to pool resources, standardise frameworks, and support member states in accessing global climate finance. Regionalised green debt instruments can help Africa to attract investors who might otherwise be deterred by the small scale of individual issuances. Pooled financing also allows risk-sharing among countries, reducing the burden on fiscally weaker states and increasing bargaining power when negotiating with creditors.
4. **Prospects for Mainstreaming Debt-for-Climate Swaps Across High-Risk States**
   While debt-for-climate swaps in Africa have so far been limited in scale, the success of the Seychelles debt-for-nature swap has demonstrated proof of concept, as shown in Box 9.2. There is growing momentum to expand such instruments across other high-risk states such as Mozambique, Madagascar, and island economies in the Indian Ocean. With stronger engagement from bilateral and multilateral creditors, these swaps could be structured at a greater scale, directly linking debt restructuring to measurable climate adaptation and biodiversity conservation outcomes.

[2] The ACCF, created by AfDB in 2014, provides small grants for climate-resilient, low-carbon development. Now a multi-donor trust fund, it supports project preparation, capacity building, and access to global climate finance for capacity-constrained countries.

[3] The AAAP, led by AfDB and GCA, targets US$25 billion for climate adaptation through food security, resilient infrastructure, youth entrepreneurship, and finance. It has already influenced US$19 billion in investments across 40 African countries.

5. **Scaling Up Regional Cooperation for Greater Bargaining Power** A fragmented approach to climate finance weakens Africa's ability to secure favourable terms. African states can negotiate collectively with global investors and climate funds by pursuing regional cooperation through the AU, AfDB, and UNECA. Regional frameworks for taxonomy, reporting, and verification could create consistency and reduce transaction costs. Moreover, a unified African green finance agenda would amplify the continent's voice in global forums such as COP negotiations, ensuring that debt sustainability and climate finance are treated as interlinked priorities.

## 9.6 Conclusion

Africa faces twin challenges of rising debt and climate vulnerability, prompting the search for integrated solutions. Climate finance has emerged as a specialised instrument to address both debt pressures and climate concerns. With limited domestic resources, African governments often borrow to fund expenditures, but climate finance, typically tied to infrastructure and resilience projects, offers opportunities for sustainable debt management. This chapter explores the role of climate finance, beginning with trends that show Africa receives only a small share of global flows, though these are steadily increasing. Most funding is directed towards mitigation, with grants being the dominant instrument. Public actors, particularly MDBs, provide more climate finance than private sources. The chapter identifies four key mechanisms linking climate finance to debt management: debt for climate or nature swaps; sovereign green bonds; blended finance that leverages concessional funds to crowd in private capital; and integrating green instruments into national debt sustainability frameworks. Beyond debt management, climate finance provides opportunities such as access to cheaper and diversified capital, enhanced creditworthiness, stronger adaptation and mitigation investments, and progress towards Agenda 2063, the SDGs, and the Paris Agreement. Challenges include risks of greenwashing, weak institutional capacity, limited investor appetite, high costs, and a lack of harmonised taxonomy. Future prospects lie in digital finance, African climate funds, pooled regional approaches, and mainstreaming climate debt instruments across vulnerable states.

There are several practical implication for stakeholders. First, African policymakers should design climate finance strategies that simultaneously strengthen fiscal sustainability and advance resilience goals. This means embedding debt-for-climate swaps, green bonds, and blended finance into national debt management frameworks to avoid worsening debt distress while attracting concessional and private capital. Second, governments need to build institutional capacity for transparent project selection, monitoring, and reporting to reduce greenwashing risks and reassure investors. Last, the continent should prioritise regional cooperation and unified harmonised taxonomies to lower transaction costs, standardise green finance instruments, and expand market depth. Ultimately, aligning climate finance with debt management provides African states an avenue to diversify financing sources, improve creditworthiness, and unlock resources for climate-resilient infrastructure, thereby addressing debt pressures while progressing towards Agenda 2063, the SDGs, and Paris Agreement commitments.

## References


Abor, J. Y., Donkor, G. N. A., & Ofori-Sasu, D. (2024). Climate finance, international trade and inclusive growth in Africa. *Journal of Sustainable Finance and Accounting, 4*, 100016. https://doi.org/10.1016/j.josfa.2024.100016

Abor, J. Y., Murinde, V., & Iddrisu, K. (2025). Green infrastructure financing. In J. Y. Abor, J. Macomber, & V. Murinde (Eds.), *The Routledge handbook of infrastructure finance*. Routledge.

AfDB. (2022). The African Development Bank issues inaugural Green Bond in South African rand market. In *AfDB*. https://www.afdb.org/en/news-and-events/press-releases/african-development-bank-issues-inaugural-green-bond-south-african-rand-market-54722

Ali, M. (2025, September 9). *Why Ghana has been excluded from US Millennium Challenge list for 2026*. Graphic Online. https://www.graphic.com.gh/news/general-news/why-ghana-has-been-excluded-from-us-millennium-challenge-list-for-2026.html

Belianska, A., Bohme, N., Cai, K., Diallo, Y., Jain, S., Melina, G., Mitra, P., Poplawski-Ribeiro, M., & Zerbo, S. (2022). *Climate change and select financial instruments: An overview of opportunities and challenges for Sub-Saharan Africa* (2022/009; Staff Climate Notes).

Carrillo, N. R. (2024). *Green Inclusive Finance in Sub-Saharan Africa: Enabling environments, challenges, and opportunitie*. https://www.oxfamnovib.nl/Redactie/Downloads/English/publications/GreeninclusivefinanceinSub-SaharanAfrica_July2024.pdf

Cromwell, R. S., & Peprah, J. A. (2025). Banking business models and sustainable development: Challenges and opportunities. In I. N. Yakubu (Ed.), *Strategic approaches to banking business and sustainable development goals* (pp. 3–22). Springer. https://doi.org/10.1007/978-3-031-80744-2_1

Cudjoe, M. A., Abor, J. Y., & Volschenk, J. (2023). Environmental and climate finance in developing countries. In J. Y. Abor (Ed.), *Sustainable and responsible investment in developing markets* (pp. 172–189). Edward Elgar Publishing. https://doi.org/10.4337/9781803927060.00020

Dogley, D. (2024). *The Seychelles debt-for-nature swap: A case study.* https://seyccat.org/wp-content/uploads/2025/03/SeychellesDebtSwapCaseStudy_webversion.pdf

English, A. A. G. (2020, September 30). *Egypt sold $750 mn in green bonds, maiden issuance was 5x oversubscribed.* Amwal Al Ghad. https://en.amwalalghad.com/egypt-sold-750-mn-in-green-bonds-maiden-issuance-was-5x-oversubscribed/

Freitas, A. S., & Mwaniki, G. (2024). *Climate finance in Africa: An overview of climate finance flows, challenges and opportunities.* https://au.int/sites/default/files/documents/44101-doc-Climate_Finance_in_Africa_Report.pdf

FSD Africa. (2021). *Feasibility study for development of a green bonds market in Ghana.* https://fsdafrica.org/wp-content/uploads/2025/05/Ghana-Green-Bonds-Scoping-Report-22.04.21.pdf

FSD Africa, & Climate Bonds Initiative. (2020). *Africa Green Bond Toolkit: A practical guide to issuing green bonds for Africa.* https://fsdafrica.org/wp-content/uploads/2020/08/Africa_GBToolKit_Eng_FINAL.pdf

Iddrisu, A. G., Donkor, G. N. A., & Abor, J. Y. (2025a). Green finance, financial inclusion and agricultural productivity in Africa. *Development and Sustainability in Economics and Finance, 7*, 100060. https://doi.org/10.1016/j.dsef.2025.100060

Iddrisu, K., Boadi, E. K., Giamporcaro, S., & Doku, J. N. (2025b). Ethical banking and growth of small and medium enterprises in emerging economies. In I. Yakubu (Ed.), *Strategic approaches to banking business and sustainable development goals. Sustainable development goals series* (pp. 157–178). Springer. https://doi.org/10.1007/978-3-031-80744-2_10

Iddrisu, K., Yakubu, I. N., & Abor, J. Y. (2025c). Green finance initiatives in banking institutions. In I. Yakubu (Ed.), *Strategic approaches to banking business and sustainable development goals. Sustainable development goals series* (pp. 35–62). Springer. https://doi.org/10.1007/978-3-031-80744-2_3

Koh, J. M. (2018). *Green infrastructure financing.* Springer International Publishing. https://doi.org/10.1007/978-3-319-71770-8

LeComte, D. (2021). International weather highlights 2020: Record Atlantic Tropical Season, Historic Flooding in Asia and Africa. *Weatherwise, 74*(3), 26–35. https://doi.org/10.1080/00431672.2021.1896936

Mbuthia, W. (2025, April 30). *Greenwashing: How environmental falsehoods are undermining Africa's climate action.* Daily Nation. https://nation.africa/kenya/health/greenwashing-how-environmental-falsehoods-are-undermining-africa-s-climate-action-5021546

Meattle, C., Balm, A., Diaz, J. E., Miao, G., Stout, S., Gupta, I., Abraham, S., Sloley, A., & Wignarajah, D. (2024). *Landscape of climate finance in Africa 2024.* https://www.climatepolicyinitiative.org/wp-content/uploads/2024/10/Landscape-of-Climate-Finance-in-Africa-2024.pdf

Meattle, C., Padmanabhi, R., de Aragão Fernandes, P., Balm, A., Wakaba, E., Chiriac, D., & Tonkonogy, B. (2022). *Landscape of climate finance in Africa.*

Meridiam. (2019, October 24). *Meridiam signs Kinguele Hydropower plant concession contract in Gabon.* Meridiam. https://www.meridiam.com/news/meridiam-signs-kinguele-hydropower-plant-concession-contract-in-gabon/

Merotto, D., Stucka, T., & Thomas, M. R. (2015). *African debt since HIPC: How clean is the slate?* (2; MFM Global Practice).

Mooldijk, S., & Lütkehermöller, K. (2021). *SNAPFI case study Kenya: Transforming the finance sector with technical assistance.* https://newclimate.org/sites/default/files/2021/06/SNAPFI.-Transforming-Kenyas-Financial-Sector.pdf?utm_source=chatgpt.com

Naumenkova, S., Mishchenko, V., Chugunov, I., & Mishchenko, S. (2023). Debt-for-nature or climate swaps in public finance management. *Problems and Perspectives in Management, 21*(3), 698–713. https://doi.org/10.21511/ppm.21(3).2023.54

Nedopil, C., Yue, M., & Hughes, A. C. (2024). Are debt-for-nature swaps scalable: Which nature, how much debt, and who pays? *Ambio, 53*(1), 63–78. https://doi.org/10.1007/s13280-023-01914-4

Richmond, M., Tonkonogy, B., Padmanabhi, R., Pastor, A. O., Chin, N., & Hebbale, C. (2022). Adaptation finance flows in Africa. In Global Center on Adaptation (Ed.), *State and trend in adaptation report 2022: Adaptation at the core of a prosperous Africa in an uncertain and warming world.* Global Center on Adaptation. https://gca.org/wp-content/uploads/2023/01/GCA_State-and-Trends-in-Adaptation-2022_Adaptation-Finance-Flows-in-Africa.pdf

Riedl, D. (2022). Why market actors fuel the carbon bubble. The agency, governance, and incentive problems that distort corporate climate risk management. *Journal of Sustainable Finance & Investment, 12*(2), 407–422. https://doi.org/10.1080/20430795.2020.1769986

Simeth, N. (2025). Debt-for-nature swaps: A case study of Gabon. *Emerging Markets Review, 65*, 101244. https://doi.org/10.1016/j.ememar.2024.101244

Spooner, D. (2024, August 23). *The sun exchange: Empowering solar energy with blockchain.* Scrums.Com. https://www.scrums.com/blog/the-sun-exchange-empowering-solar-energy-with-blockchain

Tedla, M. G., Cho, Y., & Rasmy, M. (2025). Exploring the dynamics of flood and drought hazards and adaptation strategies in the horn of Africa. *Water International, 50*(3–4), 225–234. https://doi.org/10.1080/02508060.2025.2463797

UNCTAD. (2023). *Africa*. UNCTAD. https://unctad.org/publication/world-of-debt/regional-stories

UNDP. (2019, May 30). *Mozambique cyclone Idai Post-disaster needs assessment (PDNA)DNA*. UNDP. https://www.undp.org/publications/mozambique-cyclone-idai-post-disaster-needs-assessment-pdnadna

Wachira, M. M., Iddrisu, K., Abban, G., & Abor, J. Y. (2023). Sustainable financing in developing economies. In J. Y. Abor (Ed.), *Sustainable and responsible investment in developing markets* (pp. 159–171). Edward Elgar Publishing. https://doi.org/10.4337/9781803927060.00019

World Bank. (2024a, May 2). *Morocco: Noor Solar Power Project*. https://projects.worldbank.org/en/projects-operations/project-detail/P131256

World Bank. (2024b, May 9). *Heavily indebted poor countries (HIPC) Initiative*. World Bank. https://www.worldbank.org/en/topic/debt/brief/hipc

Zorn, G., & Ntabeni, B. (2025, July 22). *Innovative climate finance in Africa: Lessons from Gabon's debt-for-nature swap and the Central African Forest Initiative*. ACET. https://acetforafrica.org/research-and-analysis/insights-ideas/case-study/innovative-climate-finance-in-africa-lessons-from-gabons-debt-for-nature-swap-and-the-central-african-forest-initiative/

CHAPTER 10

# Economic Globalization, Institutions, and Debt Dynamics: Evidence from Sub-Saharan Africa

*Mohammed Ridwan Saani, James Atta Peprah, Mark Armah, and Kwadwo Ankomah*

## 10.1 Introduction

Over the past two decades of the twenty-first century, the world economy has been marked by an unprecedented wave of economic globalization, evidenced in the accelerated integration of markets, massive surges in international capital flows, and an extraordinary expansion of global trade (Halili, 2024). This phenomenon has redefined the global economic order, simultaneously creating vast opportunities and generating complex challenges for advanced and developing nations alike. For Sub-Saharan

M. R. Saani (✉)
Department of Economics, University of Cape Coast, Cape Coast, Ghana
e-mail: msaani@uds.edu.gh

J. A. Peprah • M. Armah • K. Ankomah
Department of Applied Economics, University of Cape Coast, Cape Coast, Ghana
e-mail: jpeprah@ucc.edu.gh; marmah@ucc.edu.gh



I. N. Yakubu (ed.), *Public Debt and Economic Resilience in Africa*, Palgrave Studies in African and Development Economics,
https://doi.org/10.1007/978-3-032-25835-9_10

Africa (SSA) with structural deficiencies and institutions often weak, the consequences of globalization have been multifaceted and transformational (Wondim & Chang, 2024). The region's exposure to globalization can be traced to the policy reforms imposed by the Bretton Wood Institutions through the structural adjustment programs (SAPs). This was in response to the debt crisis of the 1980s that engulfed many developing economies. Under these arrangements, governments were obliged to liberalize trade, open their economies to foreign direct investment (FDI), and remove restrictions on portfolio investment in order to restore macroeconomic stability (Honde, 2024). These reforms have since brought the interaction between globalization, institutional capacity, and public debt to the forefront of academic and policy discourse. Within the framework of the sustainable development goals (SDGs), economic globalization has implications for global cooperation (SDG17), debt sustainability is crucial for inclusive growth and employment (SDG 8) and inequality reduction (SDG 10) while the quality of institutions is indispensable for advancing peace, justice, and effective governance (SDG 16).

While some scholars maintain that globalization fosters positive externalities such as knowledge diffusion, better opportunities for consumption smoothing, greater access to capital, and stronger financial systems (Kaufmann, 2021), others emphasize the negative outcomes. Critics argue that globalization has reinforced global inequalities through skill-based competition, entrenched core-periphery relationships, and heightened exposure of developing countries to external vulnerabilities (Rodríguez-Pose & Bartalucci, 2024). Despite these divergent views, the KOF globalization index (Gygli et al., 2019) documents notable improvements in the degree of economic globalization achieved by Sub-Saharan Africa over the past two decades. This makes it crucial to delve into how these developments shape economic outcomes, especially the dynamics of public debt. The region's debt trajectory highlights a matter of concern. Over the past decade, external debt has expanded at a faster rate than economic growth. According to the World Bank debt statistics (2023), the external debt of Sub-Saharan Africa doubled between 2012 and 2022, increasing from USD 425.9 billion (26.8% of GNI) to USD 832 billion (42.2% of GNI). Debt as a share of GNI peaked at 46.8% in 2020 while the debt to GDP ratio averaged 45% that year. In extreme cases, such as Mozambique and Zambia, external debt exceeded 100% of GDP while in South Africa, Ghana, Zambia and Tanzania, more than 60% of the eternal debt originated externally. Tanzania's external debt alone accounted for 72% of its total public debt in December 2020. Such figures cast serious doubts on the sustainability of public borrowing and highlight the limits of fiscal policy as vehicle for long term growth and poverty alleviation. To mitigate this alarming trend in debt evolution in the region, it is pertinent to continuously research into the determinants of debt in order to proffer strategies to inform policy decisions. Besides, the consensus in the literature is that debt outcomes are significantly shaped by the institutional environment to foster prudent management and effective use of public debt (Jarju & Njie, 2023; Mehmood et al., 2024; Sani et al., 2019). The quality of institutions like good legal frameworks, transparency in governance, and efficient policy implementation is critical in using public debt properly for infrastructure and development projects (Okine et al., 2023; Ogbaro et al., 2022). Thus, institutional quality remains pivotal to determining whether public debt translates into development opportunities or entrenches vulnerabilities. Critically, although strong institutions are envisaged to foster efficient fiscal management, they may puzzlingly facilitate an economy's credit worthiness on the international financial markets and possibly boost their external borrowing due to globalization. Consequently, this study seeks to explore these dynamics in the globalization and debt nexus.

Several theoretical approaches explain how globalization interacts with debt in the literature. Barro's (1979) tax smoothing hypothesis suggests that, governments confronted with globalization induced shocks may rely on borrowing rather than sudden tax hikes to stabilize welfare. Yared (2019) also highlights that debt under financial globalization and uninsurable income risk serves as a welfare enhancing mechanism through consumption smoothing. However, Swamy (2020) cautions that excessive dependence on borrowing can generate imbalances and stifle long term growth. Together these viewpoints underscore both the stabilizing function and the inherent vulnerabilities of debt within a globalized economy. Moreover, empirical investigations on this nexus between economic globalization and public debt yield mixed and inconsistent findings. Some studies confirm a positive association between economic globalization and public debt (Alabi et al., 2024; Moeng & De Jongh, 2023), while others report a negative correlation (Ain, 2020). Such discrepancies largely stem from methodological differences, sample heterogeneity, and variations in measurement indicators. Given this background, an underexplored area of enquiry concerns the simultaneous role of economic globalization, debt, and institutional quality. To the best of our knowledge, limited attention has been given to the moderating role of institutional quality on the link between economic globalization and public debt, especially in the Sub-Saharan Africa context. The study fills this gap by applying dynamic panel techniques and using a system GMM estimator to analyze the relationship between economic globalization and public debt. Thus, this study is novel as it explores how institutional quality modifies the effect of the components of economic globalization (trade and financial) on public debt in Sub-Saharan Africa. The study advances knowledge and offers policy insight through employing institutional quality as a moderator for purposes of debt sustainability in Sub-Saharan Africa.

## 10.2 Literature Review

The relationship between globalization and public debt has generated intense scholarly debate, with two principal theories dominating the discourse. The compensation hypothesis (Rodrik, 1997, 1998) posits that greater openness to the global economy exposes domestic markets to external shocks such as commodity price volatility, import competition, and sudden capital reversals that destabilize local industries and increase unemployment. In response, governments often expand social spending through subsidies, safety nets, and stimulus programs. In contexts with limited fiscal capacity, these expenditures are financed by borrowing, thereby escalating public debt (Lammers et al., 2018; Sener et al., 2015). This argument is especially relevant in developing economies, where structural weakness and low diversification magnify the adverse effects of globalization. Complementing this theory, Barro's (1979) tax smoothing framework suggests that governments borrow in the short run during globally induced shocks to avoid abrupt tax hikes, with the expectation of repayment once growth recovers. By contrast, the efficiency hypothesis (Cerny, 1994) contends that globalization pressures compel states to enhance competitiveness in order to attract and retain mobile capital. This typically involves corporate tax reductions, labor market deregulation, and restrained public spending, all of which act to constrain debt accumulation (Kaufman & Segura; Mayer & Schnabl, 2023; Fourie & Blom, 2022). This perspective presumes strong institutional capacity and political will to enforce fiscal discipline conditions that are often absent in many developing countries.

Beyond these foundational theories, the literature highlights several other channels linking globalization to debt. Trade liberalization may undermine tariff revenues critical in countries where custom duties constitute a large share of fiscal receipts leading to financing gaps filled by borrowing (Eleni, 2024; Bataka, 2023). On the other hand, trade openness can enhance productivity through technology transfers, expand export revenues, and improve fiscal sustainability (Ahmed et al., 2025; Sishchuk,

2024). Similarly, inflows of foreign direct investment (FDI) can ease debt dependence by supplying alternative financing for infrastructure and production. However, in weak institutional settings, FDI may be accompanied by profit repatriation and capital flight, which worsen external balances and add to debt burdens (Joseph et al., 2019; Swamy, 2020). Empirical evidence on this nexus is extensive but far from conclusive. For Sub-Saharan Africa, Bataka (2023) employed the KOF index on panel data covering 38 countries from 1980 to 2017 and found that economic globalization increases debt in the short run but reduces it in the long run. Disaggregated results show that financial globalization consistently increased debt while trade globalization had a short-term positive effect but long-term negative effect on debt. Similarly, Alabi et al. (2024), using FMOLS (Fully Modified OLS), DOLS (Dynamic OLS), and CCR (Canonical Cointegration regression) for Nigeria for the period 1981 to 2022, revealed a significant positive long run relationship between economic globalization and public debt. Specifically, they argue that a one unit rise in globalization is associated with a 26% increase in debt. According to Kim et al. (2018), trade openness and financial liberalization spurred public borrowing in both advanced and developing economies. Other studies such as Çolak and Özkaya (2021) on transition economies, and Moeng and de Jongh (2023) for South Africa corroborated the debt increasing effect of globalization. Likewise, Zafar and Butt (2008) confirmed a positive long run relationship between trade globalization and external debt using the ARDL approach in Pakistan. By contrast, some other studies yielded conflicting results. For instance, Pirtea and Nicolescu (2013) and Sinha et al. (2011) observed that FDI inflows reduced debt burdens in Romania across a panel of 31 countries. Swamy (2015) showed that trade openness tends to increase debt while FDI inflows reduced it especially in middle- and high-income economies. Pyeman et al. (2016) found that FDI lowered debt in Malaysia, although exports contributed to debt accumulation. A study by Waheed (2017) concluded that higher globalization increased debt in oil importing but reduced it in oil exporting countries. Distinguishing between de jure and de facto globalization, Bataka (2023) suggested that while de facto trade globalization correlates negatively with debt, de facto financial globalization increased it in Sub-Saharan Africa. Obviously, previous studies provide no consensus on whether globalization increases or reduces debt and the arguments are highly context dependent. Although studies such as Bataka (2023) and Alabi et al. (2024) offer valuable insights for Sub-Saharan Africa and

Nigeria respectively, no attention has been paid to the moderating role of institutional quality in this relationship. More crucially, they fail to capture the mechanisms through which this relationship is altered by institutions but rather analyzed primarily the direct effect. None of the studies highlight the interactive dynamics to determine whether strong institutions control borrowing induced by globalization or enhance borrowing by promoting credit access of nations in Sub-Saharan Africa.

Recent literature also confirms that institutional quality plays a pivotal role in shaping these outcomes. Weak governance manifested in corruption, and ineffective regulation tends to divert globalization's benefits into unproductive channels, facilitating capital flight and intensifying debt dependence (Swamy, 2020; Bataka, 2023). For instance, in Sub-Saharan Africa financial liberalization has often coincided with capital outflows, rather than productive investment fueling recurrent borrowing cycles. On the contrary, strong institutions can ensure that globalization driven inflows are directed towards productive uses, improve tax efficiency, and uphold fiscal discipline thereby mitigating debt risk (Ostadi & Ashja, 2014). Moreso, capital account liberalization without effective oversight will increase exposure to speculative flows and external shocks, whereas sound governance can transform such flows into long term growth and fiscal sustainability. By incorporating the interactive term, this study broadens the discourse beyond the direct effect analysis to test clearly whether institutions are an enabling or mitigating variable in the globalization and debt nexus in Sub-Saharan Africa. The study seeks to fill this gap by applying dynamic panel techniques, and the system GMM estimator to examine whether institutional quality can influence economic globalization and debt dynamics in Sub-Saharan Africa.

## 10.3 Methodology

### *10.3.1 Sources of Data*

For this study annual panel data covering 43 Sub-Saharan Africa countries (see Appendix 1, Table 10.5) from 1996 to 2023 were considered. The data sources include the World Bank's Development Indicators (WDI), International Monetary Fund (IMF), and the KOF Swiss Economic Institute (KOFSEI).

### 10.3.2 Theoretical Framework

The theoretical framework is grounded in dependency theory, Keynesian finance, debt over hang, and institutional theory. The Dependency theory posits that globalization can reinforce debt dependence in developing economies (Prebisch, 1950; Antunes De Oliveira & Kvangraven, 2023). By contrast the Keynesian and debt over hang theories highlight that external borrowing may foster growth when productively utilized but could also generate fiscal imbalances when mismanaged (Krugman, 1988; Sachs, 1989). Institutional theory emphasizes the importance of governance quality, transparency, and the rule of law in determining fiscal outcomes (Mehmood, 2023; Arslan & Alqatan, 2020). Building on these perspectives, the framework assumes that economic globalization influences public debt but the magnitude and direction of this influence also hinge on institutional quality (Nguyen & Luong, 2021). Moreover, Ojeka et al. (2024) posit that effective institutions help ensure debt sustainability through sound resource management, while weak institutions intensify the debt risk associated with globalization. This rationale underpins the study's empirical focus on institutional quality as a moderating factor in the economic globalization debt relationship in Sub-Saharan Africa.

### 10.3.3 Model and Estimation Method

The study employs a dynamic panel approach and the general functional form of the model can be expressed as:

$$Y_{it} = \alpha + \beta' X_{it} + \varepsilon_{it} \tag{10.1}$$

In this study the panel structure is defined such that $i$ represents the cross-sectional units while the time dimension is $t$. The dependent variable is denoted by $Y$ while the explanatory variables are $X$. The parameter estimates are $\beta$, $\alpha$, and $\varepsilon$ is the error term. To account for potential endogeneity and the persistence of the dependent variable, the study applies the dynamic generalized method of moment (GMM) developed by Arellano and Bond (1991) and further refined by Blundell and Bond (1998).

The dynamic model can be expressed as follows:

$$Y_{it} = \theta + \alpha Y_{it-1} + \beta' X_{it} + \mu_{it} + \varepsilon_{it} \tag{10.2}$$

The empirical model can be specified as below:

$$PD_{it} = \alpha + \beta_1 PD_{it-1} + \beta_2 Glob_{it} + \beta_3 INSQ_{it} + \beta_4 \left(Glob_{it} \times INSQ_{it}\right) + \beta_5 X_{it} + \mu_i + \varepsilon_{it} \tag{10.3}$$

Where:

$PD_{it}$ = Public debt of country $i$ at time t
$PD_{it-1}$ = Lag of public debt
$Glob_{it}$ = (economic globalization index constituting financial globalization index and trade globalization index)
$INSQ_{it}$ = Institutional quality index
$X_{it}$ = Vector of independent variables
$\varepsilon_{it}$ = Error term

## 10.4 Discussion of Empirical Results

### *10.4.1 Descriptive Statistics*

Table 10.1 display the descriptive statistics of the variables. Public debt, averages 55.5% of GDP but highly variable, with extreme outliers indicating severe debt burdens in some countries. Economic globalization (EGI), financial (FGI), and trade (TGI) have moderate averages (approximately 40–45) with maximum values above 80, indicating that while most countries are moderately globalized some are highly integrated into the global system. Institutional quality (INSQ) varies widely, highlighting sharp contrasts in the quality of governance. Government expenditure (GOE) averages 14.6% of GDP but varies considerably, whereas economic growth (ECG) is extremely volatile, averaging 4.4% but with extreme boom and bust phases. Inflation (INF) is most unstable, with hyperinflationary shocks pushing values to levels around 4.145%. Urbanization (URB) is relatively stable at an average of 39.5% but still showing regional disparities. Overall, the evidence presents substantial heterogeneity in Sub-Saharan Africa, with urbanization and globalization having more stable patterns, but growth, debt, and inflation being marked by outliers and sharp fluctuations.

**Table 10.1** Descriptive statistics of variables

| *Statistic* | *PD* | *EGI* | *FGI* | *TGI* | *INSQ* | *GOE* | *ECG* | *INF* | *URB* |
|---|---|---|---|---|---|---|---|---|---|
| Mean | 55.519 | 42.796 | 45.166 | 40.646 | 0.000 | 14.598 | 4.402 | 15.093 | 39.510 |
| Median | 46.900 | 42.150 | 45.503 | 37.943 | −0.163 | 13.773 | 4.371 | 5.101 | 38.335 |
| Maximum | 278.300 | 85.137 | 86.523 | 84.787 | 5.486 | 46.262 | 149.973 | 4145.106 | 91.029 |
| Minimum | 0.000 | 20.794 | 20.242 | 12.719 | −5.975 | 2.047 | −36.392 | −16.860 | 7.412 |
| Std. Dev. | 38.559 | 11.522 | 11.888 | 14.091 | 2.232 | 6.904 | 6.987 | 130.934 | 16.110 |
| Skewness | 1.861 | 0.780 | 0.468 | 0.957 | 0.313 | 1.344 | 8.361 | 29.067 | 0.508 |
| Obs. | 1087 | 1150 | 1161 | 1135 | 1072 | 1045 | 1204 | 1090 | 1204 |

Source: Author's Construct, 2025

### 10.4.2 *Correlation and Multicollinearity Analysis*

In Table 10.2, the association of the independent variables is depicted in the correlation matrix. The analysis suggests that the correlation coefficients are low with the highest being 0.602. Kennedy (2003) posits that a correlation coefficient of more than 0.80 shows strong evidence of greater correlation and thus a multicollinearity issue. Therefore, based on Kennedy's (2003) assertion, it can be said that no multicollinearity exists in this study. Variance inflation factor results (VIF) tests also validate the free multicollinearity problem in the research. The rule of thumb is that if a VIF is more than 10 and a tolerance value is less than 0.1, it indicates multicollinearity. Because all VIF values for the variables are less than the threshold and their tolerance values are more than 0.1, the tests reveal no multicollinearity with the explanatory variables.

### 10.4.3 *Regression Results*

Table 10.3 presents the GMM results focusing on the direct effect of economic globalization on public debt. The Wald Chi-square tests and the probability values demonstrate the joint significance, validity, and overall model fitness. The Hansen J-test probabilities confirm valid instruments. The AR (2) tests show no second-order serial correlation, which confirms robustness. Overall, the results indicate that the type of globalization is crucial for public debt dynamics. In Sub-Saharan Africa, economic globalization correlates negatively with public debt. This suggests that higher

**Table 10.2** Correlation matrix with variance inflation factor analysis

| *Variable* | *PD* | *EGI* | *INSQ* | *GOE* | *ECG* | *INF* | *URB* |
|---|---|---|---|---|---|---|---|
| PD | 1.000 | | | | | | |
| EGI | 0.050 | 1.000 | | | | | |
| INSQ | −0.115 | 0.602 | 1.000 | | | | |
| GOE | 0.086 | 0.439 | 0.425 | 1.000 | | | |
| ECG | −0.221 | −0.034 | 0.043 | −0.146 | 1.000 | | |
| INF | 0.237 | −0.049 | −0.156 | −0.106 | −0.136 | 1.000 | |
| URB | 0.032 | 0.416 | 0.245 | 0.091 | −0.159 | −0.053 | 1.000 |
| *Multicollinearity diagnostics* | | | | | | | |
| VIF | | 1.947 | 1.703 | 1.384 | 1.098 | 1.058 | 1.273 |
| Tolerance | | 0.513 | 0.587 | 0.723 | 0.911 | 0.945 | 0.785 |

Source: Author's Construct, 2025

**Table 10.3** GMM results: effect of globalization on public debt

| *Variable* | *Model 1* | *Model 2* | *Model 3* |
|---|---|---|---|
| PD(−1) | 0.837*** (0.0036) | 0.837*** (0.0032) | 0.826*** (0.0041) |
| EGI | −0.259*** (0.0516) | | |
| FGI | | 0.131*** (0.0415) | |
| TGI | | | −0.409*** (0.0343) |
| GOE | 0.991*** (0.0473) | 0.923*** (0.0589) | 0.975*** (0.0233) |
| ECG | −0.871*** (0.0313) | −0.910*** (0.0239) | −0.845*** (0.0267) |
| INF | −0.009 (0.0064) | −0.025*** (0.0029) | −0.012** (0.0052) |
| URB | 0.170** (0.0683) | −0.142** (0.0648) | 0.228*** (0.0734) |
| J-statistic | 35.49 | 34.24 | 33.98 |
| Prob (J-statistic) | 0.398 | 0.456 | 0.469 |
| Arellano-Bond AR (2) (Prob) | −0.62 (0.535) | −0.68 (0.4934) | −0.31 (0.758) |
| Wald Chi-square | 1654003.0*** | 3875887.0*** | 2151863.0*** |

Source: Author's Construct, 2025

economic integration lowers the amount of debt, possibly by encouraging growth-stimulating trade and investment flows. The finding supports the efficiency hypothesis, which posits that globalization compels governments to become more efficient in public spending and resource management. While the result confirms the conclusion of Bataka (2023), Ain (2020), it contradicts other findings (Alabi et al., 2024; Moeng & de Jongh; 2023), who assert that the association between economic globalization and public debt is positive and significant in Nigeria and South Africa. Financial globalization exhibits a positive and significant effect on public debt in Sub-Saharan Africa. Thus, greater financial integration raises public debt, possibly due to higher external borrowing and capital inflows. The positive result is in congruence with the findings of Bataka (2023; Kim et al. 2018) for Sub-Saharan Africa as well as developed and developing countries respectively. Trade globalization exerts a significant negative influence on public debt, suggesting that trade openness contributes to the reduction of public debt, possibly through export revenues and optimal resource allocation. This is consistent with the long-run effect of trade globalization observed by Bataka (2023) for Sub-Saharan Africa.

The result revealed that it reduces public debt in the long run after increasing it in the short run. Government expenditure is positive and highly significant, meaning that increased government expenditure contributes directly to rising debt levels. This is supported by Bataka (2023), who suggests a positive and significant association between public debt and government consumption expenditure. The increase in public debt due to increase in government expenditure shows that Sub-Saharan African countries often run budget deficits and hence they borrow more. Economic growth exhibits a significant negative effect implying that higher growth alleviates debt burdens, consistent with the growth-debt sustainability nexus. This result is confirmed by Bataka (2023) and Saani et al. (2024), who report that GDP reduces debt burdens in Sub-Saharan Africa and Ghana, respectively, in both short and long run. This finding is expected since strong growth generates resources through taxation and domestic savings, reducing the need to rely on external borrowing to fund programs. Inflation is significant and negative suggesting that inflation reduces debt burdens. This result is confirmed by Saani et al. (2024) who suggest a negative correlation between inflation and public debt in Ghana. This could be possible because high inflation reduces the debt burden for creditors. This contradicts Bataka (2023), who concludes that inflation is positively associated with public debt in Sub-Saharan Africa. Urbanization has mixed signs but is significant. This indicates that urbanization's effect on debt depends on whether it creates productive economic activity (debt-reducing) or higher fiscal burdens (debt-increasing)

In Table 10.4, financial globalization continues to increase public debt perhaps through increased external borrowing while trade globalization reduces debt through trade related gains. Institutional quality has significant and negative coefficient implying that stronger institutions lower public debt in Sub-Saharan Africa by improving governance, fiscal discipline, and debt management. The interactive effect (EGI × INSQ) is positive and highly significant, which means that when economic globalization is supported with strong institutions, it actually increases debt. This is perhaps because stronger institutions improve credit rating and trust, which enhance access to foreign credit. Similarly, the interaction term (TGI × INSQ) is positive and significant, suggesting that in countries with better-quality institutions, trade globalization can also lead to more debt. This may be possible due to governments borrowing to finance trade-related integration and infrastructure initiatives. Government Expenditure (GOE) remains positive and significant across models, confirming that

**Table 10.4** GMM results: Effect of institutional quality on globalization and debt nexus

| *Variable* | *Model 4* | *Model 5* | *Model 6* |
|---|---|---|---|
| PD(−1) | 0.837*** (0.0140) | 0.800*** (0.0148) | 0.808*** (0.0146) |
| EGI | 0.014 (0.1069) | | |
| FGI | | 0.393*** (0.0953) | |
| TGI | | | −0.239*** (0.0624) |
| INSQ | −3.185*** (0.9658) | 1.920 (2.2779) | −2.978** (1.4688) |
| EGI* INSQ | 0.086*** (0.0199) | | |
| FGI* INSQ | | 0.013 (0.0584) | |
| TGI* INSQ | | | 0.091** (0.0382) |
| GOE | 0.764*** (0.2106) | 0.609*** (0.2079) | 0.927*** (0.1746) |
| ECG | −1.089*** (0.0396) | −0.962*** (0.1054) | −0.888*** (0.1078) |
| INF | −0.035 (0.0469) | −0.049 (0.0381) | −0.041 (0.0398) |
| URB | 0.022 (0.2253) | 0.243 (0.2301) | 0.356 (0.2802) |
| J-statistic | 33.41 | 32.20 | 32.82 |
| Prob (J-statistic) | 0.399 | 0.457 | 0.427 |
| Arellano-Bond AR (2) (Prob) | −0.11 (0.916) | −0.002 (0.998) | 0.02 (0.987) |
| Wald Chi-square | 32866.84*** | 16134.04*** | 27012.38*** |

high expenditure drives debt upwards. Economic Growth (ECG) is negative and significant, confirming that higher growth consistently reduces debt burdens. The Hansen J-test probabilities suggest valid instruments. The AR (2) tests show no serial correlation. Wald Chi-square is highly significant, implying strong explanatory power of the models. Overall, the results indicate that institutional quality is a determining factor in how economic globalization affects public debt. Stronger institutions directly reduce debt but also change how economic globalization affects debt dynamics. Specifically, while financial globalization continues to increase debt regardless of institutional strength, both economic and trade globalization have debt-increasing effects when coupled with strong institutions, reflecting easier access to international markets and external finance. This highlights a paradox in Sub-Saharan Africa. Sound institutions decrease debt on their own, but can amplify debt pressures when combined with economic globalization as governments utilize institutional credibility to borrow more. At the same time, in Sub-Saharan Africa, consistent results across specifications show that government spending is the main driver of debt, while growth is the most effective debt-reducing factor.

## 10.5 Conclusions and Policy Recommendations

Economic and trade globalization reduces debt while financial globalization increases debt burdens in Sub-Saharan Africa. Good institutions while ideal for reducing debt, can paradoxically encourage more borrowing when combined with economic and trade globalization in Sub-Saharan Africa. Consistently, government spending drives debt upward while economic growth plays a strong debt reducing role in Sub-Saharan Africa. The effect of inflation on public debt is generally debt reducing while the impact of urbanization on public debt is mixed, increasing borrowing needs when it drives fiscal pressure and reducing debt when it boosts production and revenue capacity. The study recommends that policy makers should prioritize trade and economic globalization over financial globalization and implement prudent controls to manage capital flows. Secondly, while strengthening institutions is crucial, the focus should be on ensuring they channel borrowing into productive capacity rather than facilitating access to more credit. Moreover, governments in Sub-Saharan Africa should focus on productive investment, sustained growth, and stable inflation to ensure debt sustainability. Finally, strategic urban planning by governments and policy makers is required to enhance debt reduction in Sub-Saharan Africa.

## Appendix 1 (Table 10.5)

**Table 10.5** List of countries covered in the sample

| *No.* | *Country* |
|---|---|
| 1 | Angola |
| 2 | Benin |
| 3 | Botswana |
| 4 | Burkina Faso |

(*continued*)

**Table 10.5** (continued)

| *No.* | *Country* |
|---|---|
| 5 | Burundi |
| 6 | Cabo Verde |
| 7 | Cameroon |
| 8 | Central African Republic |
| 9 | Chad |
| 10 | Comoros |
| 11 | Congo, Dem. Rep. |
| 12 | Congo Republic |
| 13 | Cote Devoir |
| 14 | Equatorial Guinea |
| 15 | Eswatini |
| 16 | Ethiopia |
| 17 | Gabon |
| 18 | Gambia The |
| 19 | Ghana |
| 20 | Guinea |
| 21 | Guinea -Bissau |
| 22 | Kenya |
| 23 | Lesotho |
| 24 | Madagascar |
| 25 | Mali |
| 26 | Mauritania |
| 27 | Mauritius |
| 28 | Mozambique |
| 29 | Namibia |
| 30 | Niger |
| 31 | Nigeria |
| 32 | Rwanda |
| 33 | Senegal |
| 34 | Seychelles |
| 35 | Sierra Leone |
| 36 | Somalia |
| 37 | South Africa |
| 38 | Sudan |
| 39 | Tanzania |
| 40 | Togo |
| 41 | Uganda |
| 42 | Zambia |
| 43 | Zimbabwe |

Source: Author's Construct, 2025

## References

Ahmed, N., Shahzada, N., & Mubarik, H. (2025). Buoyancy, elasticity and stability of custom duty: Evidence from Pakistan. *Journal for Current Sign, 3*(2), 537–555.

Ain, N. T. (2020). *Globalization and public debt: Evidence from Pakistan* [PhD Thesis, Pakistan Institute of Development Economics]. https://file-thesis.pide.org.pk/pdf/mphil-economics-2018-namra-tul-ain%2D%2Dglobalization-and-public-debt-evidence-from-pakistan.pdf

Alabi, M. K., Ojuolape, A. M., Egbewole, A. B., & Sanjo, O. A. (2024). Economic globalization and public debt in Nigeria. *Lapai Journal of Economics, 8*(2), 34–43.

Antunes De Oliveira, F., & Kvangraven, I. H. (2023). Back to Dakar: Decolonizing international political economy through dependency theory. *Review of International Political Economy, 30*(5), 1676–1700. https://doi.org/10.1080/09692290.2023.2169322

Arellano, M., & Bond, S. (1991). Some tests of specification for panel data: Monte Carlo evidence and an application to employment equations. *The Review of Economic Studies, 58*(2), 277–297.

Arslan, M., & Alqatan, A. (2020). Role of institutions in shaping corporate governance system: Evidence from emerging economy. *Heliyon, 6*(3) https://www.cell.com/heliyon/fulltext/S2405-8440(20)30365-0

Barro, R. J. (1979). On the determination of the public debt. *Journal of Political Economy, 87*(5, Part 1), 940–971. https://doi.org/10.1086/260807

Bataka, H. (2023). Economic globalization and public debt in SUB-SAHARAN Africa. *International Journal of Finance & Economics, 28*(2), 1756–1771. https://doi.org/10.1002/ijfe.2506

Blundell, R., & Bond, S. (1998). Initial conditions and moment restrictions in dynamic panel data models. *Journal of Econometrics, 87*(1), 115–143.

Cerny, P. G. (1994). The dynamics of financial sus harmonization in European Company Law. In Globalization: Technology, market structure, and policy response. *Policy Sciences, 27*(4), 319–342.

Çolak, O., & Özkaya, M. H. (2021). The nexus between external debts and military expenditures for the selected transition economies: A panel threshold regression approach. *Defence and Peace Economics, 32*(7), 882–898. https://doi.org/10.1080/10242694.2020.1736779

Eleni, D. (2024). Theoretical review of the impact of customs duties revenue on economic growth. *Предприемачество, 12*(1), 1–7.

Fourie, D. J., & Blom, P. P. (2022). Challenges, strategies and solutions to manage public debt in South Africa. *African Journal of Public Affairs, 13*(1), 27–53.

Gygli, S., Haelg, F., Potrafke, N., & Sturm, J.-E. (2019). The KOF globalization index – revisited. *The Review of International Organizations, 14*(3), 543–574. https://doi.org/10.1007/s11558-019-09344-2

Halili, N. (2024). *Global challenges in the XXI century*. Prishtinë: Lena. https://www.researchgate.net/profile/Nijazi-

Honde, G. (2024). Botswana: Challenges and policy responses to avoid the trap. In E. Pinto Moreira (Ed.), *Avoiding the middle-income trap in Africa* (pp. 207–258). Springer Nature. https://doi.org/10.1007/978-3-031-69248-2_7

Jarju, S., & Njie, M. (2023). The determinants of public debt in The Gambia: Estimates using the autoregressive redistributed lag (ARDL) bound cointegration technique. *Journal of Economics and International Finance, 15*(2), 46–55.

Joseph, F. I.-O., Onyinyechi, C., & Ihendinihu, J. U. (2019). Effect of capital flight on foreign direct investment: Evidence from multinational corporations in developing African Countries. *Themes in Applied Sciences Research, 2*(1), 9–19.

Kaufmann, L. (2021). *Tanzania's perception of Scandinavian investments in Tanzanian SMEs*. https://www.diva-portal.org/smash/record.jsf?pid=diva2:1562969

Kennedy, P. (2003). A guide to econometrics 5th edition. Malden, Massachusetts: Blackwell.

Kim, D., Seun, Y., Lin, S., & Hsieh, J. (2018). Government size, government debt and globalization. *Applied Economics, 50*(52), 2729–2803. https://doi.org/10.1080/00036846.2017.1409418

Krugman, P. (1988). Financing vs. Forgiving a debt overhang. *Journal of Development Economics, 29*(3), 253–268.

Lammers, I., Van Gerven-Haanpää, M. M.-L., & Treib, O. (2018). Efficiency or compensation? The global economic crisis and the development of the European Union's social policy. *Global Social Policy, 18*(3), 304–322. https://doi.org/10.1177/1468018118790957

Mayer, T., & Schnabl, G. (2023). How to escape from the debt trap: Lessons from the past. *The World Economy, 46*(4), 991–1016. https://doi.org/10.1111/twec.13382

Mehmood, S. (2023). *The rule of law approach for more resilient institutions: Judicial accountability and independence, and global economic activities*. ADBI Working Paper. https://www.econstor.eu/handle/10419/296810

Mehmood, W., Mohd-Rashid, R., Ullah, A.-A., Patwari, A. K., & Aman-Ullah, A. (2024). High public debt in Japan: The institutional quality perspective. *International Journal of Business and Technopreneurship (IJBT), 14*(1), 1–20.

Moeng, M., & De Jongh, J. (2023). Economic globalisation and public debt: What implications does an integrated South African economy hold for fiscal policymakers? *Forum Scientiae Oeconomia, 11*(4), 35–62. https://www.ceeol.com/search/article-detail?id=1254808

Nguyen, T. A. N., & Luong, T. T. H. (2021). Fiscal policy, institutional quality, and public debt: Evidence from transition countries. *Sustainability, 13*(19), 10706.

Ogbaro, E. O., Young, A. O., & Bank-Ola, R. F. (2022). Revisiting the threshold effect of corruption in the link between public debt and economic growth in Nigeria. *Economic Journal of Emerging Markets*, 151–161.

Ojeka, O. J., Egbetunde, T., Okoduwa, G. O., Ojeyode, A. O., Jimoh, M., & Ogunbowale, G. O. (2024). Moderating effect of institutional quality on the influence of debt on investment in sub-Saharan Africa. *Future Business Journal, 10*(1), 76. https://doi.org/10.1186/s43093-024-00362-0

Okine, C. K. R., Appiah, M., & Tetteh, D. (2023). The linkage between fiscal policy and financial development: Exploring the moderating role of institutional quality in emerging economies. *Organizations and Markets in Emerging Economies, 14*(3), 670–695.

Ostadi, H., & Ashja, S. (2014). The relationship between external debt and foreign direct investment in D8 member countries (1995-2011)'. *WALIA Journal, 30*(S3).

Pirtea, M. G., & Nicolescu, A. C. (2013). An empirical study on public debt's determinants: Evidence from Romania. *Transylvanian Review of Administrative Sciences, 9*(38), 144–157.

Prebisch, R. (1950). *The economic development of Latin America and its principal problems.* https://repositorio.cepal.org/bitstreams/08ac817a-864c-4df6-961c-7745a3b2fae9/download

Pyeman, J., Noor, N. H. H. M., Mohamad, W. M. F. W., & Yahya, A. A. (2016). Factors affecting external debt in Malaysia: An empirical investigation. In Proceedings of the 1st AAGBS international conference on business management 2014 (AiCoBM 2014) (pp. 449–455). Singapore: Springer Singapore.

Rodríguez-Pose, A., & Bartalucci, F. (2024). The green transition and its potential territorial discontents. *Cambridge Journal of Regions, Economy and Society, 17*(2), 339–358.

Rodrik, D. (1997). *Has globalization gone too far?* Institute for International Economics.

Rodrik, D. (1998). Why do more open economies have bigger governments? *The Journal of Political Economy, 106*(5), 997–1032.

Sachs, J. D. (1989). *Social conflict and populist policies in Latin America.* National Bureau of Economic Research Cambridge, MA. https://www.nber.org/papers/w2897

Sani, A., Said, R., Ismail, N. W., & Mazlan, N. S. (2019). Public debt, institutional quality and economic growth in Sub-Saharan Africa. *Institutions and Economies*, 39–64.

Saani, M. R., Abdulai, A. M., & Salifu, M. (2024). Inflation, public debt and unemployment nexus in Ghana. An ARDL analysis. *Cogent Economics & Finance, 12*(1), 2345296.

Sener, S., Bayrakdar, S., & Hacioglu, V. (2015). The analysis for the validity of compensation and efficiency hypotheses in Turkey between 1975 and 2013. *Procedia-Social and Behavioral Sciences, 195*, 624–631.

Sinha, P., Arora, V., & Bansal, V. (2011). *Determinants of Public Debt for middle income and high income group countries using Panel Data regression.* https://mpra.ub.uni-muenchen.de/id/eprint/32079

Sishchuk, M. (2024). Ways to improve the administration of local taxes and fees in Ukraine. *Икономика и Управление, 21*(2), 1–12.

Swamy, V. (2015). *Government debt and its macroeconomic determinants–an empirical investigation.* Available at SSRN 2601875. https://papers.ssrn.com/sol3/papers.cfm?abstract_id=2601875

Swamy, V. (2020). Debt and growth: Decomposing the cause-and-effect relationship. *International Journal of Finance & Economics, 25*(2), 141–156. https://doi.org/10.1002/ijfe.1729

Waheed, A. (2017). Determinants of external debt: A panel data analysis for oil & gas exporting and importing countries. *International Journal of Economics and Financial Issues, 7*(1), 234–240.

Wondim, A., & Chang, C. L. (2024). The impact of globalization on economic growth: Insights from Sub-Saharan Africa (1971-2019). *African Journal of Food, Agriculture, Nutrition and Development, 24*(7), 23999–24019.

World Bank. (2023). *World development indicators.* Retrieved from https://databank.worldbank.org/source/world-development-indicators (accessed 10 October 2024).

Yared, P. (2019). Rising government debt: Causes and solutions for a decades-old trend. *Journal of Economic Perspectives, 33*(2), 115–140.

Zafar, S., & Butt, M. S. (2008). *Impact of trade liberalization on external debt burden: Econometric evidence from Pakistan.* https://mpra.ub.uni-muenchen.de/id/eprint/9548

CHAPTER 11

# Public Debt, Corruption Control, and Economic Growth Dynamics in Africa

*Mohammed Ridwan Saani, Abdul-Malik Abdulai, and Munira Muhammed Alhassan*

## 11.1 Introduction

The nexus between public debt and economic growth has long occupied a central place in macroeconomic theory, public policy and global development discourse. Classical debt sustainability models suggest that robust economic growth serves as a natural mechanism for reducing public debt burdens. A growing economy raises national income and broadens the tax base, thereby enhancing government revenues and improving the capacity of states to service debt without resorting to excessive borrowing (Blanchard, 2019; Yamin et al., 2023). Moreover, higher growth mechanically reduces the debt to GDP ratio, making the stock of debt more sustainable. This logic has historically underpinned fiscal consolidation strategies recommended by institutions such as the International Monetary Fund (IMF) and World Bank, which often frame growth-oriented reforms

M. R. Saani (✉) • A.-M. Abdulai • M. M. Alhassan
Department of Economics, University for Development Studies, Tamale, Ghana
e-mail: msaani@uds.edu.gh; abdulai.abdul-malik@uds.edu.gh; amunira@uds.edu.gh



I. N. Yakubu (ed.), *Public Debt and Economic Resilience in Africa*, Palgrave Studies in African and Development Economics,
https://doi.org/10.1007/978-3-032-25835-9_11

as essential for maintaining debt sustainability (Dalmer, 2019).There is considerable evidence in advanced economies to support such conventional perspective. For instance, post-World War II reconstruction in Europe demonstrated how rapid economic expansion could dramatically reduce debt ratios (Berend, 2023). Similarly, the United States and Japan experienced significant debt reduction during prolonged periods of high growth in the 1950s and 1960s. These demonstrate how strong institutional frameworks, effective fiscal management, and broad-based growth can enable economies escape the debt trap (Wood, 2024). However, this optimistic scenario does not easily translate to developing economies, where weak fiscal institutions, volatile growth patterns, and governance challenges complicate the issue.

In Africa, the recent evidence highlights the severity of the debt challenge despite periods of growth. The continent's average public debt to GDP ratio has risen sharply over the past decade, increasing from about 31% in 2010 to 64.3% in 2023. Projections show a slight moderation to 67.5% in 2024 and further decline to 64.3% by 2025. This trend manifests ongoing fiscal challenges and effort towards fiscal discipline in African economies (AFDB, 2024). This sustained upward trend reflects structural fiscal weaknesses and the impact of external shocks, including COVID-19 pandemic, global commodity volatility, and higher global interest rates. The debt level remains substantially above the pre-2000 averages, suggesting that Africa's debt burden has become a structural rather than a cyclical concern (Yi, 2023). Africa's external debt servicing burden is substantial but expected to ease slightly in 2025, with payments projected to drop 13% to about $88.7 billion from $102.6 billion in 2024. Despite this decline, debt servicing still consumes a large portion of government revenues estimated at 16.7% and export earnings 14.8% in 2023 limiting funds available for development priorities such as health and education (Heel, 2025).The implications for development are profound. According to Shabalala et al. (2025) the diversion of resources from long-term investment into debt repayment undermines structural transformation and affects progress towards the sustainable development goals. This is particularly troubling given that Africa still requires significant investment to meet SDG 3 on health, SDG 4 on education and SDG 9 on infrastructure and innovation.

Together these trends demonstrate that while Africa has enjoyed episodes of growth, debt has continued to rise and service obligations have expanded at an even faster pace. The paradox of growth co-existing with rising debt is therefore not just a regional issue but a continental challenge conditioned by structural fiscal weakness and governance failures (Omulo, 2023). Unless institutional reforms are prioritized alongside growth strategies, Africa risk remaining trapped in a cycle of high borrowing and limited fiscal space for development financing (Amaka, 2024). One of the most decisive factors shaping this relationship is corruption. Athari (2021) suggests that in well-governed settings where fiscal institutions are strong, economic growth tends to yield fiscal dividends. This implies that revenues are efficiently mobilized, expenditures are strategically allocated and debt sustainability is achieved. On the contrary, in contexts by systemic corruption the debt-reducing potential of growth is eroded. Corruption facilitates tax evasion, weakens revenue administration and distorts expenditure towards unproductive projects, while also fostering fiscal indiscipline and hidden liabilities (Omotehinse et al., 2023). Consequently Vague (2023) posits that even periods of robust growth fail to translate into improved debt outcomes, creating the paradoxical coexistence of growth and escalating debt. Country level experiences illustrate the severity of this issue. Ghana for example recorded an impressive 8.4% GDP growth rate in 2008, yet the debt stock continued to rise surpassing 60% of GDP by 2019 (Owusu-Nantwi & Owusu-Nantwi, 2023).Corruption in procurement and inefficiencies in public financial management diluted the potential benefits of growth. Zambia fueled by a copper boom, also recorded strong growth, but widespread corruption and cost of inflation in infrastructure projects led to unsustainable borrowing and ultimately debt default in 2020 (Ndikumana et al., 2024). According to Okonjo-Iweala (2018) Nigeria, despite benefitting from oil windfalls, has faced persistent fiscal deficits and rising debt levels due to corruption -driven revenue leakages and poor expenditure control. This evidence highlights that Africa's debt challenges cannot be solved by growth alone but require strong governance and anti-corruption measures (Mkhize et al., 2024).

This study is relevant since it examines contemporaneously the complex nexus between economic growth, corruption and public debt in Africa. A region that continues to experience rising debt levels despite periods of growth (Ibrahim, 2021). While previous studies have extensively explored growth and debt nexus emphasis is mostly placed on investigating the impact of public debt on economic growth (Cibulskienė, 2025; Kamanda Espoir, 2024; Swamy, 2020; Lim, 2019; Siddique et al., 2016) with little attention paid to the effect of economic growth on public debt. Moreover, limited attention has been given to the moderating role of corruption in this link, especially in the African context. This paucity in the literature remains striking in Africa, where weak institutions and governance challenges are widespread. Thus, the novelty of this study lies in the integration of corruption into the growth and debt relationship, thereby filling a significant gap in the literature. By so doing, the study does not only advance theoretical insight but also has practical implications for policy reforms in Africa.

## 11.2 Literature Review

The link between economic growth, corruption and public debt has been widely explored in both theoretical and empirical literature. Traditional debt sustainability theory asserts that robust growth reduces public debt by increasing fiscal revenues and lowering debt to GDP ratios (Shi et al., 2025).Keynesian perspectives emphasize that growth-induced fiscal space allows governments to run primary surpluses (Parui, 2024), while neoclassical and endogenous growth theories highlight how economic expansion enhances long-term debt carrying capacity(Angulo Bustinza, 2024). In contrast, the Ricardian equivalence hypothesis (Barro, 1974) argues that debt financed spending is neutral because rational agents save more in anticipation of future taxes. However, Ricardian neutrality has limited relevance in developing economies where capital markets are imperfect, fiscal capacity is weak and corruption undermines fiscal discipline (Egiyi, 2025). Empirical evidence across countries demonstrates that the growth-debt relationship is highly context dependent. In advance economies such as Germany and South Korea, growth has historically facilitated fiscal consolidation by expanding tax revenues and controlling debt accumulation (Heimberger, 2025). In developing countries however, especially in Sub-Saharan Africa growth has often coincided with rising debt burden, suggesting the influence of government-related factors (Manasseh et al., 2022). Otovwe (2023) asserts that, Ghana, Zambia, and Nigeria illustrate this paradox, where robust growth periods failed to reduce debt levels due to fiscal mismanagement and corruption. Corruption is widely recognized as a critical factor undermining the debt reducing effect of growth. It affects revenue mobilization by eroding tax compliance, facilitates illicit financial flows and reduces efficiency in tax collection (Owusu-Nantwi & Owusu-Nantwi, 2023). It also distorts public expenditure through rent seeking and inflated contracts, thereby reducing the growth impact of fiscal spending. Furthermore, corruption undermines fiscal transparency, leading to hidden debts and off budget liabilities (Park, 2018). Asteriou et al. (2021) argue that issues regarding debt are common issues to the developing and the developed world. Several alternative empirical methods have been used in studying the connection between public debt and growth. Results may be highly dependent on the period covered, country selection and method of estimation. According to Panizza and Presbitero (2013) the theoretical level models yield ambiguous findings about the nature of the relationship between public debt and economic growth and therefore the link between the two is fundamentally an empirical issue.

While the debt–growth nexus has been extensively studied, the vast majority of the available literature has examined the impact of public debt on growth (Hameed & Quddus, 2020; Gómez Puig & Sosvilla Rivero, 2017; Owusu-Nantwi & Erickson, 2016), often emphasizing debt stocks, crowding out, or fiscal sustainability concerns (Shi et al., 2025; Hameed & Quddus, 2020; Baret & Menuet, 2024). Surprisingly little empirical effort has been devoted to the reverse connection particularly how growth affects debt when it is arguably as important for policy consideration. This is an underexplored view that signifies an important literature gap. Strong economic growth can potentially alter debt trajectories by raising government revenues, improving the ability to service debt, or, conversely, by causing governments to borrow more as a result of expected permanent growth (Bohn, 1998; Barro, 1979). For instance using data from 1980 to 2018 and employing the ARDL technique Yusuf and Mohd (2021) suggest that while external debt correlated positively with growth in the short run it was detrimental to it in the long run in Nigeria. Additionally, domestic debt was growth enhancing in the long run but negatively affected it in the short run. Other evidence across Africa highlights the overall debt–growth nexus, although country- and region-specific differences are also present. Mhlaba and Phiri (2019) using quarterly data for South Africa demonstrated that gross and net public debt actually significantly constrained long-term growth, with smaller effects in the short term. Similarly, Saungweme and Odhiambo (2019) found in Zambia that debt accumulation had been prompted by economic growth itself, verifying the hypothesis of reverse causality in the debt–growth nexus. Elom-Obed et al. (2017) illustrated how domestic and foreign debt negatively affected growth by employing the vector error correction model, while Akhanolu et al. (2018) reported mixed findings that external debt had a significant negative impact on economic growth but domestic debt positively affected growth. Udeh et al. (2016) further reported that debt servicing and external debt reduced growth, even as movement in the exchange rate correlated positively with economic growth. In East Africa, however Babu et al. (2015) established a positive contribution of domestic debt to growth in East African countries to show that debt management and debt structure matter for the result. In the rest of the world, cross-country evidence contributes richness to this discussion. Gómez-Puig and Sosvilla-Rivero (2017) revealed that unsustainable public debt dampened long-run growth in Euro Area economies, but with some short-run positive effects depending on the country. Thao (2018) using an analysis of six ASEAN countries, learnt that government debt, foreign direct investment, and capital formation stimulated growth, but population growth correlated negatively with growth rates of those countries. Using data from 1969 to 1998 and a panel of 93 countries, Pattillo et al. (2004) emphasized that debt has non-linear effects. Thus, small levels can enable growth, but above certain thresholds, debt reduces growth mainly by constraining investment efficiency and productivity, ultimately constraining long-term growth.

The corruption-public debt nexus has been thoroughly researched. For instance, Apergis and Apergis (2019), using a smooth transition regression model on a large panel of countries, demonstrated that the accumulation of debt is accelerating faster in more corrupt governments compared to less corrupt governments. Similarly, Cooray et al. (2017), employing different estimation techniques for 106 countries, showed that corruption not only increases government debt but also government spending, and the shadow economy increases this effect. Liu et al. (2017), on U.S. states and local governments, also identified higher levels of debt in settings where corruption was more entrenched. Benfratello et al. (2018) suggested similar findings, where corruption positively linked to sovereign borrowing, particularly in high-income countries where it is severe and weaker in less developed countries. The theoretical underpinnings for these results are found in previous research. Tanzi and Davoodi (1997) argued that corruption in government spending corrupts investment decisions, encouraging overpriced and unnecessary projects that balloon fiscal deficits and end in higher borrowing. Kaufmann et al. (2009) noted that corrupt officials often use rent-seeking strategies in large-scale capital projects, which are primarily financed through debt, thereby reinforcing indebtedness. Velasco (2000) similarly suggested that corruption-driven increases in public investment expenditure benefit narrow interest groups while shifting the tax burden onto society, ultimately expanding debt issuance. Another channel operates through public revenues. Corruption in tax and customs administration reduces government revenues by encouraging bribery, tax evasion, and underground economic activity (Tanzi, 1998; Friedman et al., 2000; Johnson et al., 1997). Revenue erosion undermines the government's capacity to provide public goods, worsens fiscal balances, and forces greater dependence on borrowing. Gupta et al. (2001) and Shleifer and Vishny (1993) also argued that corruption tendencies divert public funds into non-productive and secretive activities rather than essential sectors like health and education, making debt less efficient in development outcomes. Overall, the literature implies that corruption raises public indebtedness both by decreasing revenue and by increasing expenditure. More significantly, it also distorts how borrowed money is being spent, leading to mismanagement, inefficiency, and negative development impacts. Despite this background, significant gaps remain (Owusu-Nantwi & Owusu-Nantwi, 2023). Much of the existing literature treats corruption, growth, and debt as separate issues rather than examining their interaction within a unified framework. Cross-country studies often overlook country-specific dynamics and institutional heterogeneity. Moreover, few studies explicitly connect this debate to the SDGs, even though the implications for development financing and social investment are profound. This study addresses these gaps by investigating how corruption moderates the relationship between economic growth and public debt in Africa. By situating the analysis within the SDG framework, the study underscores the importance of governance reforms and anti-corruption measures in ensuring that growth translates into fiscal sustainability and broader developmental outcomes. The study also advances literature both theoretically and empirically whiles offering policy relevant insights for managing debt and governance challenges in Africa.

## 11.3 Methodology of the Study

This study investigates the moderation effect of corruption on the public debt and GDP dynamics. The dataset consists of annual data for ten (10) countries[1] over the 2000 to 2024 period and was sourced from the World Bank and IMF database. The countries selected for the study are the top ten countries in Africa with the highest debt to GDP ratio. These

[1] These countries are Angola, Cameroon, Ivory Coast, Egypt, Ethiopia, Ghana, Democratic Republic of the Congo, Kenya, Senegal and Tanzania.

countries were selected because they are representative of the mass of African countries which makes the study relevant to the debt sustainability phenomenon in the region. Data obtained is analyzed using series of procedures. First and foremost, a statistically descriptive analysis of the variables was carried out. Secondly, a test for stationarity was conducted by employing the Augmented-Dicky-Fuller (ADF) (Dickey & Fuller, 1979) and Phillips and Perron (1988) (PP) test for all the series. The ARDL method was then applied after the bound test for cointegration was completed. The advantage of this technique lies in its ability to estimate the long-run cointegration relationship among variables even when the variables are integrated of different orders, whereas the Johansen cointegration approach requires the variables to be integrated of order 1. In addition, ARDL considers the dynamic heterogeneity of the adjustment process and detects possible convergence toward the long-run equilibrium. The PMG estimator of Pesaran et al. (1999) is used to estimate the panel ARDL. This approach adapts the simple ARDL model to a panel setting by allowing cointegrating terms to differ across cross-sections. The advantage of the PMG ARDL method is that it provides consistent coefficients in the presence of country heterogeneity. Lastly, the lags of all variables were selected using the Akaike Information Criterion (AIC).

To examine the moderation effect of corruption on the dynamic relationship between public debt and GDP the panel ARDL model is estimated and the general form is specified as follows:

$$Y_{it} = \sum_{j=1}^{p} \alpha_{ij} \Delta y_{i,t-1_0} + \sum_{z=1}^{k} \sum_{j=1}^{q} \beta_{ij} \Delta X_{z,i,t-j} + \varepsilon_{it} \tag{11.1}$$

Where the dependent variable is public debt, measured by general government gross debt (% of GDP). The main regressor is economic growth measured as gross domestic product per capita (annual %). The symbol $\Delta$ is the difference operator, i represents the country, and t represents time. $X_{z,i,t-j}$ is the vector of regressors with k regressors. $\alpha_{ij}$ is the coefficient of the lagged dependent variable and $\beta_{ij}$ represents the coefficients of the lagged regressors. $\varepsilon_{it}$ represents the error term.

Reparameterization of the PMG ARDL estimation into the error correction model (ECM) based on Pesaran et al. (1999), we have:

$$\Delta Y_{it} = \sum_{j=1}^{p-1} \alpha_{ij} \Delta y_{i,t-1} + \sum_{z=1}^{k} \sum_{j=1}^{q-1} \beta_{ij} \Delta X_{z,i,t-j} + \varphi_i ECM_{it} + \varepsilon_{it} \tag{11.2}$$

Where $ECM_{it}$ is the error correction term that results from the long-term relationship. $\varphi_i$ represents the speed of adjustment toward that equilibrium. Δ is the difference operator. In examining the moderation effect of corruption on the relationship between public debt and GDP, we applied Eq. (11.2) for the PMG ARDL estimation as specified in Eq. (11.3).

$$\begin{aligned} \Delta PD_{it} &= \alpha_i PD_{i,t-1} + \beta_{1i} GDP_{i,t-j} + \beta_{2i} CORR_{i,t-j} + \beta_{3i} GGE_{i,t-j} + \beta_{4i} INF_{i,t-j} \\ &+ \beta_{5i} TRAD_{i,t-j} + \beta_{6i} GDP * CORR_{i,t-j} + \sum_{j=1}^{n} \gamma_{1ij} \Delta PD_{i,t-j} \\ &+ \sum_{j=1}^{q} \gamma_{2ij} \Delta GDP_{i,t-j} + \sum_{j=1}^{q} \gamma_{3ij} \Delta CORR_{i,t-j} + \sum_{j=1}^{q} \gamma_{4ij} \Delta GGE_{i,t-j} \\ &+ \sum_{j=1}^{q} \gamma_{5ij} \Delta INF_{i,t-j} + \sum_{i=1}^{q} \gamma_{6ij} \Delta TRAD_{i,t-j} + \sum_{j=1}^{q} \gamma_{7ij} \Delta GDP * CORR_{i,t-j} \\ &+ \varepsilon_t \end{aligned} \tag{11.3}$$

Where Δ refers to the difference operator and $\beta_1$ to $\beta_7$ are the long-run parameters to be estimated. The $\gamma$ terms denote the short-run parameters. The description of the variables is presented in Table 11.1.

**Table 11.1** Definitions of variables

| *Variable* | *Description* |
|---|---|
| Public debt (PD) | General government gross debt (% of GDP) |
| Economic growth (GDP) | Gross domestic product per capita (annual %) |
| Corruption CORR | Control of corruption index |
| Government expenditure (GGE) | General government expenditure (percentage of GDP) |
| Inflation (INF) | Inflation, consumer prices (annual %) |
| Trade (TRAD) | Trade (percentage of GDP) |

Source: Authors' Own

**Table 11.2** Descriptive statistics of variables

| *Variable* | *Observation* | *Mean* | *Maximum* | *Minimum* | *Std. dev.* |
|---|---|---|---|---|---|
| GDP | 211 | 2.122 | 11.337 | −9.850 | 3.135 |
| GGE | 211 | 20.088 | 47.201 | 2.489 | 6.780 |
| PD | 211 | 51.063 | 164.086 | 11.153 | 26.103 |
| TRAD | 211 | 55.756 | 122.446 | 20.598 | 20.054 |
| CORR | 211 | 0.159 | 0.330 | 0.124 | 0.031 |
| INF | 211 | 12.431 | 513.907 | −2.248 | 36.909 |

Source: Authors' construct, 2025

## 11.4 Data Analysis and Discussion

### *11.4.1 Descriptive Statistics of Variables*

This study was conducted based on annual data spanning from 2000 to 2024 on the top 10 indebted African countries. Table 11.2 presents the descriptives of the secondary data collected, showing the averages, deviations, minimum, and maximum levels of the various variables. The statistics shows that control of corruption (CORR) has the least mean value of 0.159, followed by gross domestic product (GDP) with a mean of 2.122. This signals a very low level of corruption control and GDP over the period. On the other hand, trade (TRAD) has the highest mean value of 55.756, followed by public debt (PD) of 51.063 mean. Public debt has the second highest volatility ranging from 11.153 to 164.086. The volatility level shows how unstable public debt has been over the period and a potential mismanagement or wrong policy implementations by governments of these indebted countries in sustaining their debt levels. Moreover, inflation (INF) has the highest volatility, fluctuating between −2.248 and 513.907 with a mean value of 12.431. This could be attributed to many factors including increment of salaries coupled with underproductivity among workers. The statistics also shows the gross government expenditure (GGE) which fluctuated moderately between 2.489 and 47.201 with 20.088 mean value, signaling a moderate expansionary fiscal policy by various governments over the period. Overall, corruption control and gross domestic product was found to be relatively stable over the period with standard deviations of 0.031 and 3.135 respectively.

**Fig. 11.1** Trend graphs of public debt and GDP for the top 10 indebted countries in Africa

### *11.4.2 Trend Analysis of GDP and Public Debt*

To understand the pattern of movement of the variables of interest over time, a comprehensive visualized trend graph of both gross domestic product and public debt was obtained for analysis. In Fig. 11.1, public debt increased in the year 2000 to 2001 from 74.3512% to 79.8481 whilst gross domestic product also increased from −0.3288 to 0.5830. Public debt decreased after the year 2001 at a decreasing rate until 2003 where the value was 65.4262, but GDP was relatively stable. At this point, public debt then increased from 65.4262 to 67.5415 in 2004 whilst GDP also moved in same direction from 0.2697 to 3.9301 respectively. Moving forward from 2004, a similar reduction of the public debt was observed for a period of three years until 2007, where public debt decreased greatly to 40.1182, while GDP was still stable relatively. Again, these countries experience fluctuations in their debt for the next four years (2008 to 2012), where public debt increased from 2008 to 2009, then decreased in 2010. Public debt increased by a margin of 0.1488 in 2011 and then decreased to 33.5344 in 2012. But these fluctuations seemed to have affected the GDP, as it also experienced a downward trend from 2008 to 2009 and then bouncing back to its initial relatively stable trend in 2012. These fluctuations could be related to many factors, including change of governments, policy challenges and the global financial crisis of 2008. Moreover, from 2012 to 2019 (a period of seven years), the countries experienced year-on-year increase of public debt but GDP remained relatively stable over that period. A sharp interesting hike of public debt was experienced among these countries from 2019 to 2020 with a contrary sharp decreased in GDP. While public debt had skyrocketed from 56.4324 to 65.4341, GDP dipped from 2.2899 to −1.5277 from 2019 to 2020 respectively. These surprising trends can be attributed to the global pandemic (COVID-19) that placed many economies on their knees. Finally, public debt decreased from 65.4 in 2020 to 60.5 in 2024 and GDP increased from −1.5277 in 2020 to 2.19 in 2023 and remained relatively stable till date. Overall, public debt has been unsustainable over the past decade whilst GDP has been relatively sustainable.

### *11.4.3 Discussion of Regression Results*

*Stationarity Tests*

To avoid producing spurious regression results which could be used for analysis and consequently for making economic decisions, it is desirable to conduct stationarity test of the series. Therefore, the unit root test was conducted and the results are as presented in Table 11.3.

Results of the panel units root tests revealed that except PD, GGE and TRAD all other variables were stationary at levels. They all however became stationary after first differencing, supporting the use of panel ARDL for this analysis.

**Table 11.3** Panel unit root tests

| *Variable* | *Test of stationarity at level* | | *Test of stationarity at first difference* | |
|---|---|---|---|---|
| | *ADF test statistic* | *PP test statistics* | *ADF test statistic* | *PP test statistics* |
| Debt | 18.989 | 17.115 | 55.623*** | 109.096*** |
| GDP | 48.896*** | 91.110*** | 142.892*** | 456.165*** |
| GGE | 16.006 | 14.729 | 89.397*** | 166.737*** |
| INF | 69.636*** | 335.415*** | 161.410*** | 310.819*** |
| TRAD | 18.502 | 16.712 | 128.978*** | 201.240*** |
| CORR | 46.943*** | 91.523*** | 71.578*** | 99.141*** |
| GDP*CORR | 64.238*** | 92.877*** | 151.862*** | 580.818*** |

**Table 11.4** Moderation effect of corruption on the GDP and debt relationship

| *Variable* | *Coefficient* | *Std. error* | *T-stats* | *Prob.** |
|---|---|---|---|---|
| *Long-run equation* | | | | |
| GDP | 0.992 | 0.289 | 3.431 | 0.001 |
| CORR | 16.260 | 6.302 | 2.580 | 0.011 |
| GDP*CORR | −6.785 | 1.903 | −3.566 | 0.001 |
| GGE | 0.116 | 0.025 | 4.567 | 0.000 |
| INF | −0.006 | 0.009 | −0.654 | 0.515 |
| TRAD | −1.309 | 0.268 | −4.891 | 0.000 |
| *Short run equation* | | | | |
| CointEq(−1) | −0.161 | 0.029 | −5.517 | 0.000 |
| D(PD(−1)) | 0.060 | 0.115 | 0.524 | 0.602 |
| D(GDP) | −0.099 | 0.026 | −3.795 | 0.000 |
| D(CORR) | 4.701 | 2.793 | 1.683 | 0.095 |
| D(GDP*CORR) | 0.556 | 0.185 | 3.007 | 0.003 |
| D(GGE) | 0.006 | 0.008 | 0.684 | 0.496 |
| D(INF) | −0.007 | 0.005 | −1.498 | 0.137 |
| D(TRAD) | 0.217 | 0.094 | 2.303 | 0.023 |
| C | 0.672 | 0.128 | 5.250 | 0.000 |

Source: Authors' construct, 2025

The study also examined how corruption control moderates the relationship between gross domestic product and public debt. The key finding is that corruption control significantly alters this relationship in both the long and short run, but in alternate ways. The presence of an error correction term CointEq(−1) confirms a stable long-run relationship between the variables, which is adjusting over time, as presented in Table 11.4.

### *11.4.4 Long-Run Regression Results Analysis*

The coefficient for GDP is positive and statistically significant. This suggests that, a 1% increase in GDP growth is associated with a nearly 1% increase in public debt in the long run, holding other variables constant. This finding is consistent with Musah (2023), who found public debt to increase as economies grow. This positive relationship could be due to countries, especially developing countries financing their development projects, including roads, industries, and health facilities through debt accumulation. Corruption control is positive and statistically significant, suggesting that a unit increase in corruption control increases public debt by 16.260, holding all other variables constant. This result is in line with the study by Adekunle (2025), who concluded that an increase in control of corruption increases public debt in South Africa, but at variance with Cooray and Özmen's (2024) finding, which found a negative relationship between corruption control and debt accumulation among EU countries. This may be attributed to heavy borrowing by governments to fund initiation of robust systems that will reduce or eliminate corruption which will end up by accumulating debt. Moderated effect of control of corruption and GDP has a negative and highly significant coefficient. This means that a unit increase in the composite GDP and corruption control will induce a 6.785 reduction in public debt in the long-run. This means that the composite GDP corruption control is an effective mechanism for debt reduction in an economy. Government expenditure is positive and significant, showing that a unit increase in government spending is associated with a 0.116 increase in public debt, all other thing being equal. This is intuitive because government spending requires more funds and borrowing is one of the major sources of securing funds. This result is consistent with the study by Ciaffi et al. (2024), who found government spending as a key driver of debt dynamics. Trade is negative and significant. A unit increase in trade is associated with a 1.309 reduction in public debt in the long-run. This could possibly be due to higher revenues from tariffs, economic diversification, and efficiency gains from other countries. This result support the study by Suryandaru (2023) and Edo (2024) who concluded that trade openness lowers public debt in the long-run.

### *11.4.5 Short-Run Dynamics*

The error correction term CointEq(−1) has a negative coefficient and it is statistically significant. This negative sign is expected and a confirmation for long-run cointegration. The coefficient −0.161 reflect the speed at which the system returns to long-run equilibrium after a short-term shock or disturbance. Control of corruption is positive and marginally significant. A unit increase in corruption control will induce a 4.701 increase in debt, which is similar to the long-run result. This means that a fight against corruption alone significantly increases the level of debt, until it is coupled with GDP to have a significant reduction in public debt, but only in the long-run. Moderated effect of control of corruption and GDP is positive and significant in the short-run. This is the opposite of the long-run result. Here, a unit increase in the composite GDP and control of corruption will induce a 0.556 increment in public debt. This in the short run suggest that growth in a corrupt environment might be fueled by large, debt-financed projects that are susceptible to corruption control which might spike debt levels at least in the short-run. GDP appeared as negative and significant. A unit increase in GDP will render a 0.099 reduction in public debt. This indicates that a positive growth shock is associated with a short-run decrease in the rate of debt accumulation. This is consistent with Abubakar and Mamman (2020), who found that economic upturn can lead to sustainable debt ratio. Finally, trade is positive and significant, meaning that in the short-run, a unit increase in trade is associated with a 0.217 increase in debt. Trade is found by Musah (2023) to be positively related to public debt which coincides with the result of this study. This short-run effect is the opposite of its long-run effect, which could be due to costs of trade adjustment. According to Musah (2023), it is caused by heavy reliance on external trade.

## 11.5 Conclusions and Recommendations

This study explored the moderation effect of corruption control on the public debt and GDP relationship in Africa. Annual data was sourced from the World Bank Development indicators' website and the IMF database spanning from 2000 to 2024 and used for analysis. Using the panel ARDL bound test of cointegration to examine the long-run relationship, the study revealed that public debt has both short and long-run relationship with gross domestic product, corruption control, general government expenditure, the interaction between corruption control and gross domestic product and trade openness.

In the long run, GDP is positive and significantly contributing to public debt, which means that when economies expand, governments borrow to cater for developmental projects. Similarly, government expenditure has a positive and significant effect on debt, providing evidence that fiscal stimulus is the cause of debt accumulation. Corruption control also has a positive effect on public debt, suggesting that the improvement in anti-corruption policy is associated with more borrowing. This is supposedly due to the expense of implementing governance reforms. However, when corruption control moderates the effect of GDP on public debt, the combined impact sharply lowers public debt, highlighting the role of good governance in fostering sustainable growth and debt relief in the long-run. Trade openness appears to lowers public debt in the long term, highlighting the role of foreign competitiveness and diversification in advancing relief from debt.

Contrary to the long-run results, GDP has a significant and adverse impact on public debt in the short-run suggesting that economies debt burden reduces as they witnessed short-run economic growth. The interaction between GDP and corruption control raises debt in the short term, implying the cost of rebuilding governance as well as credit from growth. Trade openness significantly raises public debt in the short term, perhaps as a result of dependence on imports. The study recommends that African governments should not only be concerned with simply stimulating GDP growth but also ensuring that the growth is accompanied by good governance and strong anti-corruption institutions. Thus, governments in Africa should promote growth strategies which are simultaneously implemented together with anti-corruption institutions. Specifically, debt-financed projects must be subjected to enhanced publicly audited procurement processes to propel growth and ultimately mitigate the debt burden. The long-term record is that employing economic growth together with stemming corruption is at the heart of lowering the debt levels of nation states. Also, as trade openness lowers debt levels in the long run, African economies need to diversify exports, enhance regional integration, and exercise maximum restraint on import dependence. This will create sustainable revenues, enhance balance of payments, and ease debt pressures. Lastly, since government spending is one of the significant determinants of accumulating debt, fiscal policy must focus on productive spending like infrastructure, industrialization, and human development.

## References

Abubakar, A. B., & Mamman, S. O. (2020). Permanent and transitory effect of public debt on economic growth. *Journal of Economic Studies, 48*(5), 1064–1083. https://doi.org/10.1108/JES-04-2020-0154

Adekunle, A. O. (2025). *New applied studies in management, economics & accounting control of corruption, public debt and economic growth: An empirical investigation from South Africa. 8.*

African Development Bank. (2024). *African Economic Outlook: Driving Africa's Transformation.* The reform of the global financial architecture. Online Publication.

Akhanolu, I. A., Babajide, A. A., Akinjare, V., Oladeji, T., & Osuma, G. (2018). The effect of public debt on economic growth in Nigeria: An empirical investigation. *International Business Management, 12*(6), 436–441.

Amaka, E. M. (2024). *The politics of borrowing in Nigeria: Balancing short-term gains and long-term risks.* https://www.researchgate.net/profile/Modesta-Egiyi/publication/388629409

Angulo Bustinza, H. D. (2024). Economic growth theory. In *International trade and inclusive economic growth: A case study of Peru and China* (pp. 3–18). Emerald Publishing Limited. https://www.emerald.com/insight/content/doi/10.1108/978-1-83753-470-82024002/full/html

Apergis, E., & Apergis, N. (2019). New evidence on corruption and government debt from a global country panel: A non-linear panel long-run approach. *Journal of Economic Studies, 46*(5), 1009–1027.

Asteriou, D., Pilbeam, K., & Pratiwi, C. E. (2021). Public debt and economic growth: Panel data evidence for Asian countries. *Journal of Economics and Finance, 45*(2), 270–287. https://doi.org/10.1007/s12197-020-09515-7

Athari, S. A. (2021). The effects of institutional settings and risks on bank dividend policy in an emerging market: Evidence from Tobit model. *International Journal of Finance & Economics, 26*(3), 4493–4515. https://doi.org/10.1002/ijfe.2027

Babu, J. O., Kiprop, S., Kalio, A. M., & Gisore, M. (2015). Effect of domestic debt on economic growth in the East African community. *American Journal of Research Communication, 3*(9), 73–95.

Baret, M., & Menuet, M. (2024). Fiscal and environmental sustainability: Is public debt environmentally friendly? *Environmental and Resource Economics, 87*(6), 1497–1520. https://doi.org/10.1007/s10640-024-00847-0

Barro, R. J. (1974). Are government bonds net wealth? *Journal of Political Economy, 82*(6), 1095–1117. https://doi.org/10.1086/260266

Barro. (1979). On the determination of the public debt. *Journal of Political Economy, 87*(5), 940–971.

Benfratello, L., Del Monte, A., & Pennacchio, L. (2018). Corruption and public debt: A cross-country analysis. *Applied Economics Letters, 25*(5), 340–344. https://doi.org/10.1080/13504851.2017.1321831

Berend, I. T. (2023). *Decades of crisis: Central and eastern Europe before world war II.* University of California Press.

Blanchard, O. (2019). Public debt and low interest rates. *American Economic Review, 109*(4), 1197–1229.

Bohn, H. (1998). The behavior of US public debt and deficits. *The Quarterly Journal of Economics, 113*(3), 949–963.

Ciaffi, G., Deleidi, M., & Di, L. (2024). Fiscal policy and public debt: Government investment is most effective to promote sustainability. *Journal of Policy Modeling, 46*(6), 1186–1209. https://doi.org/10.1016/j.jpolmod.2024.07.002

Cibulskienė, D., Garšvienė, L., Butkus, M., Šeputienė, J., & Leach, N. (2025). The impact of public debt on economic growth: determining of factors and their interactions. *Journal of Business Economics and Management, 26*(4), 941–957. https://doi.org/10.3846/jbem.2025.24703

Cooray, A., & Özmen, I. (2024). The role of institutions on public debt: A quantile regression approach. *International Review of Economics and Finance, 93*(March), 912–928. https://doi.org/10.1016/j.iref.2024.03.065

Cooray, A., Dzhumashev, R., & Schneider, F. (2017). How does corruption affect public debt? An empirical analysis. *World Development, 90*, 115–127.

Dalmer, N. K. (2019). Considering the local and the translocal: Reframing health information practice research using institutional ethnography. *Aslib Journal of Information Management, 71*(6), 703–719.

Dickey, D. A., & Fuller, W. A. (1979). Distribution of the estimators for autoregressive time series with a unit root. *Journal of the American Statistical Association, 74*(366a), 427–431.

Edo, S. (2024). Comparative performance of trade openness and sovereign debt accumulation in fostering economic growth of sub-Saharan African Countries. *Foreign Trade Review, 59*(1), 98–116. https://doi.org/10.1177/00157325221145452

Egiyi, M. A. (2025). *Today's reckless borrowing: Economic incarceration and infertility for tomorrow*. https://gouni.edu.ng/new/wp-content/uploads/2025/07/17-INAUGURAL_LECTURE-CORRECTED-COPY.pdf

Elom-Obed, F. O., Odo, S. I., Elom-Obed, O., & Anoke, C. I. (2017). Public debt and economic growth in Nigeria. *Asian Research Journal of Arts & Social Sciences, 4*(3), 1–16.

Friedman, E., Johnson, S., Kaufmann, D., & Zoido-Lobaton, P. (2000). Dodging the grabbing hand: The determinants of unofficial activity in 69 countries. *Journal of Public Economics, 76*(3), 459–493.

Gómez Puig, M., & Sosvilla Rivero, S. J. (2017). *Nonfinancial debt and economic growth in euro-area countries.* Instituto Complutense de Estudios Internacionales (ICEI). https://docta.ucm.es/entities/publication/67cc884e-c4fc-4d47-a843-670a6cc356d6

Gómez-Puig, M., & Sosvilla-Rivero, S. (2017). *Public debt and economic growth: Further evidence for the euro area.* ICEI WP09/17. https://papers.ssrn.com/sol3/papers.cfm?abstract_id=3041117

Gupta, S., De Mello, L., & Sharan, R. (2001). Corruption and military spending. *European Journal of Political Economy, 17*(4), 749–777.

Hameed, M. R., & Quddus, M. A. (2020). Impact of high and growing public debt on economic growth in SAARC countries: An econometric analysis. *Journal of Political Studies, 27*, 125.

Heel, A. A. (2025). *The Gambia Public Debt.* https://documents1.worldbank.org/curated/en/099070125072566070/pdf/P507238-70f99bb6-2c49-421c-955a-95ba67e6c5f7.pdf

Heimberger, P. (2025). Fiscal consolidation and its growth effects in euro area countries: Past, present and future outlook. *Review of Evolutionary Political Economy.* https://doi.org/10.1007/s43253-025-00146-4

Ibrahim, C. (2021). Corruption, public debt and economic growth–evidence from developing countries. *International Journal of Development Issues, 20*(1), 24–37.

Johnson, S., Kaufmann, D., Shleifer, A., Goldman, M. I., & Weitzman, M. L. (1997). The unofficial economy in transition. *Brookings Papers on Economic Activity, 1997*(2), 159–239.

Kamanda Espoir, D. (2024). Investigating the dynamic impacts of public debt on economic growth in the Democratic Republic of Congo: a case of quantile on quantile regression. MPRA Paper 122415, University Library of Munich, Germany.

Kaufmann, D., Kraay, A., & Mastruzzi, M. (2009). *Governance matters VIII: Aggregate and individual governance indicators, 1996–2008.* World Bank Policy Research Working Paper, 4978. https://papers.ssrn.com/sol3/papers.cfm?Abstract_id=1424591

Lim, J. J. (2019). Growth in the shadow of debt. *Journal of Banking & Finance, 103*, 98–112. https://doi.org/10.1016/j.jbankfin.2019.04.002

Liu, C., Moldogaziev, T. T., & Mikesell, J. L. (2017). Corruption and state and local government debt expansion. *Public Administration Review, 77*(5), 681–690. https://doi.org/10.1111/puar.12711

Manasseh, C. O., Abada, F. C., Okiche, E. L., Okanya, O., Nwakoby, I. C., Offu, P., Ogbuagu, A. R., Okafor, C. O., Obidike, P. C., & Nwonye, N. G. (2022). External debt and economic growth in Sub-Saharan Africa: Does governance matter? *Plos One, 17*(3), e0264082.

Mhlaba, N., & Phiri, A. (2019). Is public debt harmful towards economic growth? New evidence from South Africa. *Cogent Economics & Finance, 7*(1), 1603653. https://doi.org/10.1080/23322039.2019.1603653

Mkhize, N., Moyo, S., & Mahoa, S. (2024). African solutions to African problems: A narrative of corruption in postcolonial Africa. *Cogent Social Sciences, 10*(1), 2327133. https://doi.org/10.1080/23311886.2024.2327133

Musah, I. (2023). An empirical investigation of macroeconomic determinants of public debt in Ghana. *Cogent Economics and Finance, 11*(2). https://doi.org/10.1080/23322039.2023.2285625

Ndikumana, L., Mudenda, D., & Gurara, B. (2024). *The state, corporations, or the people: Who benefits from mining in Zambia?* PERI Working Paper 601. Political Economy Research Institute. https://peri.umass.edu/wp-content/uploads/joomla/images/publication/WP601.pdf

Okonjo-Iweala, N. (2018). *Fighting corruption is dangerous: The story behind the headlines.* Mit Press.

Omotehinse, T., Esenohor, E. T., & Okoh, G. A. (2023). *The impact of taxation in combating corruption and promoting sustainable development goals in Nigeria.* https://cognizancejournal.com/vol3issue9/V3I914.pdf

Omulo, A. G. (2023). Towards an assessment of the legacy of Kenya's Uhuru Kenyatta: Pan-Africanist or subtle Western lackey? *Cogent Social Sciences, 9*(1), 2221970. https://doi.org/10.1080/23311886.2023.2221970

Otovwe, E. (2023). *The implication of public debt and financial instability on economic growth: A case study of selected West African countries* [PhD Thesis, Anglia Ruskin Research Online (ARRO)]. https://aru.figshare.com/articles/thesis/The_implication_of_public_debt_and_financial_instability_on_economic_growth_A_case_study_of_selected_West_African_countries/23764236

Owusu-Nantwi, V., & Erickson, C. (2016). Public debt and economic growth in Ghana: Public debt and economic growth in Ghana. *African Development Review, 28*(1), 116–126. https://doi.org/10.1111/1467-8268.12174

Owusu-Nantwi, V., & Owusu-Nantwi, G. (2023). Public debt, corruption and shadow economy in Africa: An empirical analysis. *Journal of Economic and Administrative Sciences, 39*(1), 184–202.

Panizza, U., & Presbitero, A. F. (2013). Public debt and economic growth in advanced economies: A survey. *Swiss Journal of Economics and Statistics, 149*, 175–204.

Park, S. (2018). Understanding public sector debt: Financial vicious circle under the soft budget constraint. *Public Organization Review, 18*(1), 71–92. https://doi.org/10.1007/s11115-016-0358-y

Parui, P. (2024). Fiscal expansion, government debt and economic growth: A post-Keynesian perspective. *Journal of Post Keynesian Economics, 47*(1), 117–154. https://doi.org/10.1080/01603477.2023.2221444

Pattillo, C., Poirson, H., & Ricci, L. (2004). *What are the channels through which external debt affects growth?* International Monetary Fund.

Pesaran, M. H., Shin, Y., & Smith, R. J. (1999). Pooled mean group estimation of dynamic heterogeneous panels. *Journal of the American Statistical Association, 94*(446), 621–634. https://doi.org/10.1080/01621459.1999.10474156

Phillips, P. C. B., & Perron, P. (1988). Testing for a unit root in time series regression. *Biometrika, 75*(2), 335–346. https://doi.org/10.1093/biomet/75.2.335

Saungweme, T., & Odhiambo, N. M. (2019). Government debt, government debt service and economic growth nexus in Zambia: A multivariate analysis. *Cogent Economics & Finance, 7*(1), 1622998. https://doi.org/10.1080/23322039.2019.1622998

Shabalala, G., Magazi, N., & Manamela, A. (2025). *Ensuring debt sustainability for low-income countries.* https://p20.parliament.gov.za/storage/app/media/p20/Research%20Papers/Debt%20sustainability%20for%20low-income%20countries%2025%20Aug.pdf

Shi, H., Song, D., & Ramzan, M. (2025). Institutional quality, public debt, and sustainable economic growth: Evidence from a global panel. *Sustainability, 17*(14), 6487.

Shleifer, A., & Vishny, R. W. (1993). Corruption. *The Quarterly Journal of Economics, 108*(3), 599–617.

Siddique, A., Selvanathan, E.A. & Selvanathan, S. (2016). The impact of external debt on growth: Evidence from highly indebted poor countries. *Journal of Policy Modeling, Elsevier, 38*(5), 874–894.

Suryandaru, R. A. (2023). *The relationship between public debt, trade openness, and economic growth in Indonesia: Symmetric and asymmetric analysis.* April, 35–60.

Swamy, V. (2020). Debt and growth: Decomposing the Cause and Effect relationship. *International Journal of Finance & Economics, 25*, 141–156. https://doi.org/10.1002/ijfe.1729

Tanzi, V. (1998). Corruption around the world: Causes, consequences, scope, and cures. *Staff Papers - International Monetary Fund, 45*(4), 559. https://doi.org/10.2307/3867585

Tanzi, V., & Davoodi, H. (1997). *Corruption, public investment, and growth.* Working paper No. 97/139, International Monetary Fund, available at:www.imf.org/en/Publications/WP/Issues/2016/12/30/Corruption-Public-Investment-and-Growth-2353

Thao, P. T. P. (2018). Impacts of public debt on economic growth in six ASEAN countries. *Ritsumeikan Annual Review of International Studies, 17*(3), 63–88.

Udeh, S. N., Ugwu, J. I., & Onwuka, I. O. (2016). External debt and economic growth: The Nigeria experience. *European Journal of Accounting Auditing and Finance Research, 4*(2), 33–48.

Vague, R. (2023). *The paradox of debt: A new path to prosperity without crisis.* University of Pennsylvania Press.

Velasco, A. (2000). Debts and deficits with fragmented fiscal policymaking. *Journal of Public Economics, 76*(1), 105–125.

Wood, R. E. (2024). *From Marshall Plan to debt crisis: Foreign aid and development choices in the world economy* (Vol. 15). University of California Press.

Yamin I., Al_Kasasbeh, O., Alzghoul, A., & Alsheikh, G. (2023). The influence of public debt on economic growth: A review of literature. *International Journal of Professional Business Review, 8*(4), e01772.

Yi, F. (2023). *Essays on sovereign risk* [PhD Thesis, Princeton University]. https://search.proquest.com/openview/f4aa25b6afe2489f6dbaf8b4493a164d/1?pq-origsite=gscholar&cbl=18750&diss=y

Yusuf, A., & Mohd, S. (2021). The impact of government debt on economic growth in Nigeria. *Cogent Economics & Finance, 9*(1), 1946249. https://doi.org/10.1080/23322039.2021.1946249

CHAPTER 12

# Driving Inclusive Development Through Borrowing in Africa: The Urgency for Asymmetric Analysis

*Emmanuel Issifu Fuseini, Muazu Ibrahim, and Ustarz Yazidu*

## 12.1 Introduction

Prudent and productive means of boosting global inclusive development through investment using sovereign or public debt is a renewed, debatable issue for economic managers, development agencies, and scholars, especially in low- and middle-income countries in regions like sub-SA. This discourse diverges from the initial income-led development argument (Matekenya et al., 2021).

Most developing economies, like those in sub-SA, finance their developmental programmes and projects by enhancing quality education, good healthcare, social services, and infrastructure through domestic and

E. I. Fuseini (✉) • M. Ibrahim • U. Yazidu
Department of Finance, School of Business, University for Development Studies, Tamale, Ghana
e-mail: emmamuelfuseini1962@uds.edu.gh; imuazu@uds.edu.gh; uyazidu@uds.edu.gh



I. N. Yakubu (ed.), *Public Debt and Economic Resilience in Africa*, Palgrave Studies in African and Development Economics,
https://doi.org/10.1007/978-3-032-25835-9_12

foreign borrowing. This is due to these economies' inability to generate enough tax revenue, as well as their heavy reliance on the exportation of raw materials and minerals without value addition (see World Bank, 2024), limiting the opportunity to generate sufficient revenue and foreign exchange for development and growth. Conversely, this channel of financing projects is also associated with the risk of economic hardship because of the potential for repayment challenges, if not utilised prudently.

However, empirical evidence on how this source of funding promotes inclusive human development (focusing on education, healthcare, and standard of living) is limited. Motivated by empirical studies like Adegboye et al. (2025) and Dianda et al. (2024), this study defines inclusive human development through the lens of the "Inequality-Adjusted Human Development Index" (IHDI), as espoused by the UNDP (2010–2025). The IHDI estimates human development by concentrating on education, healthcare, and living standards after eliminating inequality (UNDP, 2025).

The IHDI indicates that in 2022, there was a 22.1% global loss in human development due to inequality being accounted for in these three key dimensions, with the highest inequality in living standards (30.3%), followed by education (21.1%) and healthcare (13%). The IHDI for 2022 stood at 57.6%, reflecting a modest 0.4% increase from 2021, suggesting persistent global inequality in key sectors. In sub-SA, the IHDI in 2022 was 36.3%, indicating a 33.9% loss when adjusted for inequality in the "Human Development Index (HDI)" of 54.9% (UNDP, 2010–2025). Inequality levels in sub-SA were 33.6% in education, 27.9% in healthcare, and 39.4% in living standards (UNDP, 2025).

These statistics on inclusive human development in sub-Saharan African countries and other developing economies underscore the need for strong policies guided by empirical evidence to promote inclusive HuD. One such robust policy could involve how fiscal policies regarding sovereign debt and its servicing costs translate into growth and development. However, despite the unsatisfactory performance of inclusive HuD, there is a notable increase in sovereign borrowing by developing countries (International Monetary Fund, 2024, 2025). Specifically, the estimates for sovereign borrowing for 2024 and beyond stand at $100 trillion globally, representing about 93% of global GDP (International Monetary Fund, 2024). What is more concerning is that the IMF further argued that this current estimate may reach 100% of global GDP by the end of 2030, the year the Sustainable Development Goals (SDGs) set by the United Nations (UN) are expected to be achieved.

Therefore, with the prevailing economic uncertainty and fiscal sustainability risk (see International Monetary Fund, 2025; World Bank, 2025b), there is an urgency to gain insight into the asymmetric effects of this massive sovereign borrowing and its servicing costs on fostering inclusive HuD. Especially, as the empirical literature backing policymaking and practice to support sovereign borrowing-inclusive development relationships focuses on the linearity effect, threshold effect, and transmission channels (see, e.g. Abubakar et al., 2025; Colak et al., 2025; Fosu et al., 2025). Previous studies argue that sovereign borrowing has a profoundly contradictory and symmetric influence on economic growth (see, e.g. Amowine et al., 2023; Otieno, 2024; Singh & Kumar, 2024), under the assumption that the relationship is linear.

Conversely, numerous financial and economic variables have been shown to exhibit nonlinearity (e.g. asymmetric effects—where changes in sovereign borrowing and debt servicing costs have different impacts on growth and development), which are often overlooked in traditional estimation models like the ARDL (Kripfganz & Schneider, 2023). Also, the existing literature is heavily focused on establishing the threshold effect of sovereign debt on economic growth (see, e.g. Alsamara et al., 2024; Elkhalfi et al., 2024; Shah et al., 2024), as well as the transmission channels of the debt-economic growth nexus (see, e.g. Apeti et al., 2024; Gaiya et al., 2024). The few studies that explored the asymmetric effect of debt primarily concentrated on sovereign borrowing's asymmetric effect on economic growth, proxied by GDP growth (see, e.g. Amoh et al., 2024), with little or no attention given to inclusive development that focuses on key sectors like education, health, and social welfare.

Furthermore, the existing literature on debt-human development nexuses has failed to significantly factor in how positive and negative changes in sovereign borrowing and its servicing costs influence inclusive development, particularly from the perspective of sectoral-specific effects (i.e. education, health, and social services) amid unsustainable debt levels in sub-SA. The existing empirical evidence assumes that both positive and negative changes in sovereign borrowing would have the same magnitude of effect on growth and development (see, e.g. Amaechi, 2023; Beyene, 2024; Nwokoye et al., 2024).

Based on the asymmetric adjustment effect theory by Shin et al. (2014) and empirically used by Ibrahim and Alagidede (2020), this study argues that a variation in inclusive HuD arising from a change (positive or negative) in sovereign borrowing and its servicing costs would not lead to the same magnitude of effect in the short and long run. Consequently, the unanswered question in the prevailing literature is: what is the asymmetric effect of sovereign debt and servicing costs on education, health, and social welfare in sub-Saharan Africa for both short- and long-term periods?

Therefore, this study aims to respond to this question within the existing empirical studies to uncover empirical evidence that strengthens the current literature guiding policymaking and practice regarding debt sustainability-inclusive development interlinkages. To achieve this, the study employed the panel nonlinear autoregressive distributed lag (PNARDL) model, an extension of the NARDL model by Shin et al. (2014), controlling for the symmetric influences of fiscal policy, inflation, trade, and population growth.

The major findings are as follows: first, positive changes in sovereign debt significantly improve inclusive HuD in the long run. Second, adverse changes in sovereign borrowing significantly hinder inclusive HuD in the long run but substantially enhance inclusive HuD in the short run. Third, both positive and negative changes in debt servicing costs significantly constrain inclusive HuD in the long run. Fourth, only positive changes in debt servicing costs significantly improve inclusive HuD in the short run. Fifth, there is an asymmetric effect of sovereign borrowing and debt servicing costs on inclusive HuD in the long run. Sixth, there is an asymmetric effect of debt servicing costs on the standard of living in both the long run and the short run. Finally, there is a symmetric effect of sovereign borrowing and debt servicing costs on education and healthcare in the long run and the short run.

The rest of the study is sectioned as follows: Sect. 12.2 Literature review, Sect. 12.3 Methodology, Sect. 12.4 Findings, and Sect. 12.5 Conclusion.

## 12.2 Literature Review: The Sovereign Debt and Development Prospects Relationship

### *12.2.1 Theoretical Perspective*

The concept of inclusive HuD originates from the argument made by Amartya Sen (1999). Amartya Sen argues that human development is accomplished by enhancing individuals' capabilities in areas such as health, education, and living standards. The effectiveness of these capabilities is influenced by fiscal policies concerning government spending. Governments typically borrow to finance this spending when there is a revenue shortfall to meet these expenditures. However, this borrowing does not ensure an improvement in inclusive HuD, as its application to foster growth and development is subject to numerous variables that can be either favourable or unfavourable.

Sen (1999) and the United Nations Development Programme (UNDP, 1990–2025) collectively assert that growth is not an end in itself but a means to promote human well-being. Hence, human development theory emphasises health, education, and income levels as critical dimensions of inclusive human development free from inequalities. Moreover, the most prevalent perspective in the empirical literature regarding the nonlinear relationship between debt, growth, and development (see, e.g. Elkhalfi et al., 2024; Otieno, 2024; Yusuf & Mohd, 2023) is the concept of debt overhang, introduced by (Krugman, 1988). The core argument of this concept is that increases in sovereign borrowing beyond a certain threshold negatively affect economic growth and development. This adverse effect extends to vital sectors like health, education, social services, and infrastructure (i.e. inclusive HuD).

Consequently, this study argues that variations in sovereign borrowing and servicing levels can yield different impacts on growth and development, particularly in human development, during varying time periods. Therefore, there is an urgent need to empirically provide these insights to inform policy and practice for enhancing the relationship between debt sustainability and development.

The concept of asymmetric effects, with theoretical reference to Shin et al. (2014), in their innovative Nonlinear Autoregressive Distributed Lag (NARDL) model, posits that finance and macroeconomic variables may be influenced differently by positive and negative shocks to causal variables over both the long and short run. This concept suggests that positive and negative changes in sovereign borrowing and servicing costs may have different effects on inclusive HuD in the short and long term.

Consequently, this study maintains the theoretical view that positive and negative changes in sovereign borrowing and servicing costs would differently impact education, health, and social welfare in the short and long run in sub-Saharan Africa.

### 12.2.2 *Empirical Literature: Sovereign Debt and Development Prospects Nexus*

Empirically, the key thematic areas for discussion in the extant literature on the debt-development nexus focus on determining the threshold effect, the transmission mechanisms, and the linearity effects of sovereign borrowing. The dialogue on the asymmetric effect is now emerging in contemporary literature, especially in the context of s-SA.

Starting with the symmetric (linearity) effect of sovereign borrowing on growth, existing studies generally agree that debt inhibits economic growth, although other studies contradict this, showing some evidence of a positive relationship. For example, with the positive symmetric effect of debt on growth and development, Taylor and Lokina (2024) conducted a case study on Tanzania using the Vector Error Correction Model (VECM) from 2005 to 2022, contending that there is a long-run positive symmetric effect of debt on economic growth. Similarly, the research by Yusuf and Mohd (2024) and Edo (2024) employed the Generalised Method of Moments (GMM) techniques on a panel of sub-Saharan Africa from 1980 to 2020.

Additionally, Roy and Sen (2024) examined 32 emerging economies and revealed similar findings supporting the positive symmetric impact on growth. Furthermore, Singh and Kumar (2024) utilised the Johansen cointegration, fully modified ordinary least squares, and Toda and Yamamoto's (1995) Granger causality test in the context of India for the period from 1980 to 2019. Conversely, regarding the negative symmetric effect of debt on economic growth, Edo (2024) argued that, except for domestic borrowing, sovereign bonds hinder economic growth in sub-Saharan Africa. This negative linearity effect of debt identified by Edo (2024) is consistent with similar studies, such as Otieno (2024), in the context of Eastern Africa for the period from 1992 to 2019 using the Durbin Fixed Effect (SDM-FE) model, and the research conducted by Amowine et al. (2023) concerning African economies from 2010 to 2019.

Regarding the asymmetric effect of sovereign debt, existing empirical evidence is limited and inconsistent for both the short and long runs across various contexts. The asymmetric effect emphasises time series estimation more than panel time series estimation. For instance, Sharaf et al. (2024) applied the NARDL approach in the context of Brazil. The authors argued that their findings indicate that, in the short run, changes to foreign debt increase inflation; however, in the long run, positive and negative changes to foreign debt also promote inflation. On economic growth, Amoh et al. (2024), based on their PNARDL analysis, assert that foreign debt asymmetrically influences economic growth in sub-Saharan Africa, regardless of the period. However, the study by Özmen and Mutascu (2024) contradicts that of Amoh et al. (2024). Özmen and Mutascu (2024) analyse the asymmetric causalities of debt in driving economic growth in the context of the United States, the United Kingdom, Sweden, and Japan from 1801 to 2011.

Regarding the symmetric effect of debt on human development, Nwokoye et al. (2024), using fully modified ordinary least squares and canonical cointegration regression in the context of Nigeria from 1990 to 2021, supports evidence that government debt significantly promotes human capital development. Similarly, Amaechi (2023) posits that in the short run, foreign debt significantly enhances human capital, while the long-run effect is insignificant based on their estimation using the ADF for unit roots and the ARDL approach. Conversely, Beyene and Kotosz (2023) employed seemingly unrelated regressions (SUR) and simultaneous equations models (SEMs) on a panel of selected heavily indebted poor countries (HIPCs) to examine the interaction between debt and human capital development. The findings of Beyene and Kotosz (2023) indicate that "the relationship between foreign debt and HCD is negative and non-linear".

These reviews highlight the need to investigate the asymmetric effect of sovereign borrowing on education, health, and living standards in sub-Saharan Africa. Uncovering these empirical insights will enrich the prevailing extant literature (Adegboye et al., 2025; Fuseini, 2025a, 2025b; Fuseini & Ibrahim, 2025), focusing on the African growth and development prospects. This need arises from the projected increase in sovereign borrowing levels without a corresponding improvement in the anticipated global growth beyond 2025 (International Monetary Fund, 2025; World Bank, 2025a). The existing literature reviewed above lacks significant empirical evidence to aid policymaking and practice regarding how positive and negative changes in sovereign borrowing and its servicing costs influence inclusive HuD in the short and long run. The expected empirical findings will yield valuable insights for developing policy guidelines aimed at facilitating robust debt sustainability strategies to enhance the unsatisfactory performance of inclusive HuD in sub-Saharan Africa and beyond. This is particularly crucial given the high levels of poverty, inequality, inadequate healthcare, and elevated illiteracy rates across the African continent amid unsustainable debt levels.

## 12.3 Methodology

### 12.3.1 *Data and Variable Definition*

A panel dataset of 41 countries in sub-SA was established, covering the period from 2010 to 2023. The choice of this sample size and period was constrained by adequate data availability from various sources, particularly the IHDI. The study employed secondary data sourced from reputable and robust databases, including the International Debt Statistics database (IDS) and the World Development Indicators (WDIs) of the World Bank, as well as the UNDP-United Nations Development Programme.

For the dependent variable of the study, the "Inequality-Adjusted Human Development Index"-IHDI is used to represent inclusive HuD as the explained variable. The IHDI is developed by the UNDP to estimate human development in three key areas: education, health, and standard of living, after removing inequalities in each dimension (UNDP, 2010–2025). For sensitivity analysis, these three sub-dimensions are further utilised as dependent variables in the analysis to validate and ensure the reliability of the findings. The IHDI, as a proxy for inclusive HuD, is consistent with the prevailing literature on the measure of inclusive HuD in sub-SA (as empirically used works like Dianda et al., 2024; Stylianou et al., 2023).

There are two explanatory variables: sovereign debt and debt services. Sovereign borrowing is measured by "external debt stocks (% of GNI)", while debt servicing cost is represented by "debt service on external debt, total (current US$)", all sourced from the IDS-World Bank. The choice of these measurements for sovereign borrowing and servicing cost is empirically supported by existing studies (see, e.g. Amoh et al., 2024; Singh & Kumar, 2024; Yusuf & Mohd, 2024).

The control variables include fiscal policy, inflation, trade openness, and population growth (as used in empirical works like Fuseini, 2025a; Fuseini & Ibrahim, 2025). See Table 12.1 for further details on data and variable definitions, sources, and supporting empirical studies.

### 12.3.2 *Empirical Approach*

The PNARDL technique is employed in this study to unearth the asymmetric effect of sovereign borrowing and its servicing cost on inclusive HuD in sub-SA. The PNARDL approach is an extension of the ARDL

**Table 12.1** Summary of variables definition, measurement, and sources

| *Type* | *Variable* | *Construct* | *Measurement* | *Supporting literature* | *Source* |
|---|---|---|---|---|---|
| Dependent | Inclusive Human Development | Inclusive HuD | Inequality-Adjusted Human Development Index | UNDP (United Nations Development Programme) (2024) | UNDP-2010-2025 |
| Independent | Sovereign Debt | Sovdebt | External debt stocks (% of GNI) | Yusuf and Mohd (2024) | IDS-WB 2025 IDS-WB 2025 |
| Independent | Sovereign Debt Service | Debtserv | Debt service on external debt, total (TDS, current US$) | Singh and Kumar (2024) | |
| Control | Inflation | Infl | Inflation, consumer prices (annual %) | Chang and Fang (2024) | WDI-WB 2025 |
| | Population growth | Pgrowth | Population growth (Annual %) | Fuseini et al. (2024) | |
| | Fiscal policy | Fpo | General government final consumption expenditure (% of GDP) | Xie et al. (2024) | WBI-WB 2025 |
| | Trade openness | Trade | Trade (% of GDP) | Fuseini et al. (2024) | WDI-WB 2025 |

"Total external debt is debt owed to non-residents repayable in currency, goods, or services. It is the sum of public, publicly guaranteed, and private nonguaranteed long-term debt, short-term debt, and use of IMF credit". "Total debt service is the sum of principal repayments and interest paid in currency, goods, or services on long-term debt, interest paid on short-term debt, and repayments (repurchases and charges) to the IMF". Data are in current U.S. dollars. WB-World Bank, WDI-World Development Indicators

Source: Author's Compilations

(see Kripfganz & Schneider, 2023) by the theoretical argument of Shin, Yu, and Greenwood–Nimmo (2014) in their renowned NARDL technique. The key merit of the PNARDL approach, as opposed to the PARDL in this context, is the capacity of the PNARDL technique to differentiate between positive and negative shocks to macroeconomic variables. More significantly, the PNARDL method is robust in estimating asymmetrical linkages between the explained variable and the explanatory variables in the long and short runs. The PNARDL approach, as an extension of the NARDL model, is empirically used in similar studies like (Ibrahim & Alagidede, 2020; Ziaei, 2025).

Specifically, the PNARDL technique estimates the effects of changes in sovereign borrowing across sub-SA in determining inclusive HuD, when the change is positive versus when it is negative for both the short-run and long-run. The theoretical argument is that an increase (positive) and a decrease (negative) in sovereign borrowing will differently influence inclusive HuD.

Therefore, following an inspiration on the use of the PNARDL approach to finding answers to similar questions guiding this study, the PNARDL model for the long run, based on the variables of this study, is written as:

$$\begin{aligned} inclusive\,HuD_t = Sovdebt_{0,i} + \alpha^{+} Sovdebt^{+}_{i,t} + \alpha^{-} Sovdebt^{-}_{i,t} \\ + \alpha CO_{i,t} + \varepsilon_{i,t} \end{aligned} \tag{12.1}$$

$$\text{Where} : Sovdebt_{i,t} = \mu_{i,t-j} \tag{12.2}$$

$$Sovdebt^{+}_{i,t} = \sum_{j=1}^{t} \Delta Sovdent^{+}_{i,t} = \sum_{j=1}^{t} \max\left(\Delta XSovdebt_{i,t}, 0\right) \tag{12.3}$$

$$Sovdebt^{-}_{i,t} = \sum_{j=1}^{t} \Delta Sovdebt^{-}_{i,t} = \sum_{j=1}^{t} \min\left(\Delta Sovdebt_{i,t}, 0\right) \tag{12.4}$$

Therefore, empirically, following Iheanacho et al. (2023), Zamir et al. (2023), and Ziaei (2025) with theory grounded in Shin, Yu, and Greenwood–Nimmo (2014), the study's PNARDL model for the long run and short run asymmetries relationship between inclusive HuD and sovereign debt and servicing cost, as controlled by fiscal policy, trade, inflation, and population growth, is specified in Eq. (12.5).

$$\begin{aligned}\Delta inclusive\, HuD_{i,t} &= \mu + \varphi inclusive\, HuD_{i,t-1} + \vartheta_1^+ Sovdebt_{i,t-1}^+ \\ &+ \vartheta_1^- Sovdebt_{i,t-1}^- + \vartheta_2^+ Debtserv_{i,t-1}^+ \\ &+ \vartheta_2^- Debtserv_{i,t-1}^- \vartheta_3 \Delta Co_{i,t} \\ &+ \sum_{J=1}^{p-1} \omega \Delta inclusive\, HuD_{i,t-j} + \sum_{j=0}^{q-1} \pi_1 \Delta Sovdebt_{i,t-j}^+ \\ &+ \sum_{j=0}^{q-1} \pi_2 \Delta Sovedebt_{i,t-j}^- + \sum_{j=0}^{q-1} \pi_3 \Delta Debtserv_{i,t-j}^+ \\ &+ \sum_{j=0}^{q-1} \pi_4 \Delta Debtserv_{i,t-j}^- + \sum_{j=0}^{q-1} \pi_{52} \Delta Co_{i,t-j} + \varepsilon_{i,t}\end{aligned} \tag{12.5}$$

The "+" and "−" signs on the right side of each equation denote the partial sum of positive and negative effects. $i$ and $t$ indicate the cross-section and time respectively, $\vartheta$ the long-run relationship coefficient and $\omega$ and $\pi$ denote the short-run coefficients. Eq. (12.5) is estimated based on the mean group (MG) approach. This is because Table 12.11 shows the pre-diagnostic test on the panel dataset to be heterogeneous.

Equations (12.6) and (12.7) specify the models to test for the existence of either a symmetric effect or an asymmetric effect.

$$\varphi = \vartheta_1^+ = \vartheta_1^- = \vartheta_2^+ = \vartheta_2^- = \vartheta_3 = 0 \tag{12.6}$$

$$\theta^+ = \theta^- \tag{12.7}$$

Where $\theta^+ = -\vartheta^+/\varphi$ and $\theta^- = -\vartheta^-/\varphi$.

Equation (12.7) specifies the asymmetric coefficients test, where the Wald test would be employed to test this hypothesis.

## 12.4 Findings

### 12.4.1 *Descriptive Statistics*

Table 12.2 displays the descriptive statistics of the series used in this study. This statistic presents preliminary evidence about the state of inclusive HuD, sovereign debt, its servicing cost, and the control variables. From Table 12.2, the mean for inclusive HuD, sovereign debt, and debt servicing are 34.09%, \$49.19202 trillion, and \$10.45603 trillion, respectively.

The associated standard deviation is 8.47% for inclusive HuD. The significant preliminary implications from Table 12.2 are that, on average, inclusive HuD in sub-SA is very unsatisfactory amid high sovereign debts and also high servicing costs across sub-SA.

This descriptive statistic displayed in Table 12.2 inspires the need to re-explore how debt is a significant determinant of growth and development in the short and long runs.

### *12.4.2 Panel Cointegration and Stationarity of Variables*

The use of the PNARDL approach requires establishing the stationarity of the series under study and determining whether a long-run equilibrium exists. To illustrate this, Table 12.3 presents the panel cointegration test based on the three robust estimation approaches prevalent in the literature (i.e. Kao, 1999; Pedroni, 2004; Westerlund, 2007; Kao 1999). The selection of these three estimation techniques strengthens the case for the existence of long-run equilibrium (cointegration). Moreover, the Westerlund (2007) test is particularly preferred over the other two, as it effectively addresses issues of heterogeneity and multidimensional or cross-sectional mean dependence.

Therefore, Table 12.3 indicates that there is panel cointegration in the panel dataset for this study, as we reject the null hypothesis of no cointegration. This implies that when shocks to inclusive HuD, debt service costs, and sovereign debt lead to disequilibrium, the disequilibrium swiftly adjusts to restore equilibrium in the long term. Additionally, Table 12.10 in the appendices displays the stationarity of variables, evaluated using the Im et al. (2003), Levin et al. (2002), and Phillips and Perron (1988) approaches of unit root tests. Table 12.10 shows that some variables did not exhibit unit roots at either level or first difference, or both. For instance, inclusive HuD, sovereign debt, and debt service do not have unit roots at the level and first difference, as we reject the null hypothesis of the existence of unit roots at a 1% significance level.

The economic significance of achieving stationarity in the variables is that their influence from a threat is only temporary and "tends to mean-revert" (Ibrahim & Alagidede, 2020). From a statistical perspective, spurious findings in regression models are minimal, except in situations where the series are cointegrated and independent variables are perfectly exogenous. It is crucial to note that attaining perfect exogeneity in a practical experiment is nearly impossible.

**Table 12.2** Descriptive statistics

| | *Mean* | *Median* | *Maximum* | *Minimum* | *Std. Dev.* | *Skewness* | *Kurtosis* | *Jarque-Bera* | *P-value* | *Sum* | *Sum Sq. Dev.* | *Obs* |
|---|---|---|---|---|---|---|---|---|---|---|---|---|
| Inclusive HuD | 0.340930 | 0.334000 | 0.720000 | 0.184000 | 0.084666 | 1.511867 | 6.650038 | 498.9267 | 0.000000 | 181.7156 | 3.813576 | 533 |
| Sovdebt | 49.19202 | 37.21044 | 434.1945 | 8.392616 | 48.61119 | 4.919007 | 34.24748 | 23833.79 | 0.000000 | 26219.34 | 1,257,141. | 533 |
| Debtserv | 10.45603 | 7.626204 | 105.3570 | 0.540012 | 10.12165 | 3.065749 | 20.48129 | 7621.692 | 0.000000 | 5573.062 | 54502.24 | 533 |
| Education | 32.70685 | 34.17100 | 50.83100 | 6.656000 | 10.42614 | −0.25867 | 2.273678 | 17.65993 | 0.000146 | 17432.75 | 57830.69 | 533 |
| Healthcare | 27.98536 | 28.32700 | 46.78400 | 8.770000 | 8.418939 | −0.34272 | 2.885376 | 10.72573 | 0.004687 | 14916.20 | 37707.38 | 533 |
| St, living | 44.04657 | 44.58800 | 67.58800 | 16.56200 | 9.984512 | −0.24453 | 3.122736 | 5.646194 | 0.059422 | 23476.82 | 53035.34 | 533 |
| Fpo | 15.28622 | 14.88271 | 40.55353 | 3.587513 | 6.753518 | 1.249215 | 5.118048 | 238.2571 | 0.000000 | 8147.554 | 24264.53 | 533 |
| Infl | 9.667350 | 5.184247 | 557.2018 | −4.29487 | 32.73136 | 12.29771 | 179.5318 | 705523.7 | 0.000000 | 5152.698 | 569953.7 | 533 |
| Trade | 69.44091 | 65.48779 | 222.1783 | 2.698834 | 32.26442 | 1.572041 | 6.963727 | 568.4531 | 0.000000 | 37012.01 | 553808.0 | 533 |
| Pgrowth | 2.396861 | 2.538489 | 4.681011 | −2.62866 | 0.894257 | −1.24815 | 5.532049 | 280.7752 | 0.000000 | 1277.527 | 425.4379 | 533 |

Source: Author's computation

**Table 12.3** Panel cointegration test

| *Kao test* | *Statistic* | *p-value* |
|---|---|---|
| Augmented Dickey-Fuller t | 3.4342 | 0.0003 |
| Unadjusted Dickey-Fuller t | −1.66 | 0.0485 |
| *Pedroni test* | | |
| Modified Phillips–Perron t | 10.8214 | 0.0000 |
| Phillips–Perron t | −15.437 | 0.0000 |
| Augmented Dickey-Fuller t | −12.357 | 0.0000 |
| *Westerlund test* | | |
| Variance ratio | 2.1114 | 0.0174 |

H0: No cointegration, Ha: All panels are cointegrated, Kernel: Bartlett, Lags: Newey–West

Sources: Authors' compilations

The significance of using the ARDL framework is that its output remains valid regardless of whether the independent variables are stationary at [I(0)], [I(1)], or mutually cointegrated. Therefore, the results from Tables 12.4 and 12.11 further underscore the choice of the PNARDL approach rooted in the ARDL theory. Table 12.11 also supports the Westerlund (2007) test for heterogeneity and cross-sectional dependence, as it shows a test for slope heterogeneity or homogeneity. The test reveals that the models for sovereign debt and debt service cost slopes are heterogeneous, as we reject the null hypothesis that "slope coefficients are homogeneous" at a 1% significance level. This suggests that the models must be estimated using the mean groups (MG) option, rather than the pooled mean group (PMG).

In addition, Table 12.12 presents the test for the existence of cross-sectional dependence (CD) in the panel models. Specifically, we employed the CD Star (CD*) proposed by Pesaran and Xie (2024) and the weighted CD (CDw) test developed by Juodis and Reese (2022). The findings from Table 12.12 indicate that there is weak CD in the panel models, as we fail to reject the null hypothesis of the existence of weak cross-sectional dependence. The presence of strong CD in panel models can lead to spurious regressions, necessitating correction. However, our models do not exhibit weak CD, making them robust for valid and reliable regressions.

### 12.4.3 *Asymmetric Effect of Sovereign Borrowing on Inclusive Human Development*

This subsection discusses the symmetric and asymmetric effects of sovereign debt (Sovdebt) and debt services (Debtserv) on inclusive HuD and its sub-dimensions. The estimation of these effects using the PNARDL is displayed in Tables 12.4, 12.5, 12.6, 12.7, 12.8 and 12.9.

Starting with the error correction terms (EC Term) in Tables 12.4, 12.5, 12.6, 12.7, 12.8 and 12.9, the inference is that there exists a long-run equilibrium in the models, indicated by high negative coefficients with a statistical significance level of 1%. This EC term also supports the findings in Table 12.3 regarding the presence of panel cointegration.

Regarding the symmetric effects of Sovdebt and Debtserv, Table 12.4 shows that Sovdebt promotes inclusive HuD trivially for both the long-run (LR) and short-run (SR), significantly at 1% and 5% significance levels, respectively (see columns 1 and 2). Additionally, Table 12.4 indicates that Debtserv positively drives inclusive HuD for both LR and SR, but the LR effect is significant at 1% (columns 3 and 4).

Concerning the asymmetric effect, Table 12.5 presents the results. From columns (1) and (2), a percentage positive change in sovereign debt (Sovdebt+) would promote inclusive HuD in the LR by 0.342% significantly at 1%, whereas in the SR, the effect is a trivial, insignificant damping effect. Moreover, from columns (3) and (4), a percentage negative change in sovereign debt (Sovdebt--) would significantly decrease inclusive HuD in both LR and SR by 0.635% and 0.111% respectively, at 1% and 5% significance levels. Regarding the sub-dimensions, Tables 12.6 and 12.7 display the results of the symmetric effects. From columns (1) to (6) of Table 12.6, Sovdebt shows a mixed insignificant symmetric effect on education, healthcare, and standard of living for both LR and SR, except in column (5). In that column, a percentage increase in Sovdebt in the LR significantly hampers the standard of living by 7.82% at a 1% significance level, while the SR shows an adverse symmetric effect, which is insignificant.

Concerning sovereign debt services (Debtserv), Table 12.8 shows the estimation output. The inferences from Table 12.8 indicate that, from column (3), a percentage increase in Debtserv would significantly impede healthcare in the LR by 17.2% significantly at a 1% significance level. Similarly, from column (2), a percentage increase in Debtserv negatively influences education in the SR at a 10% significance level. The remaining

**Table 12.4** Symmetric effect of sovereign borrowing and servicing cost on inclusive human develoment

| | (1) | (2) | (3) | (4) |
|---|---|---|---|---|
| Variables | Sovereign debt Inclusive HuD | | Debt servicing cost Inclusive HuD | |
| | LR | SR | LR | SR |
| EC Term | | −0.128*** | | −0.148*** |
| | | (0.0431) | | (0.0431) |
| Sovdebt | 0.000318*** | 0.000739** | | |
| | (0.000111) | (0.000293) | | |
| Debtserv | | | 0.00574*** | 0.000656 |
| | | | (0.000394) | (0.000507) |
| Fpo | −0.0115*** | −0.00167 | −0.000151 | 0.00157* |
| | (0.00220) | (0.00285) | (0.00126) | (0.000931) |
| Infl | 0.000543*** | 0.000828 | 0.00107*** | 0.000508 |
| | (0.000132) | (0.000584) | (0.000310) | (0.000585) |
| Trade | 0.00580*** | −0.000585 | 0.00247*** | −9.35e-05 |
| | (0.000507) | (0.000413) | (0.000228) | (0.000150) |
| Pgrowth | | 0.00451 | 0.586*** | −0.0730*** |
| | | (0.00785) | (0.0956) | (0.0258) |
| Observations | 492 | 492 | 492 | 492 |
| 1795.673 | | 1795.673 | 1795.673 | 1795.673 |

Note: Standard errors in parentheses, *** $p < 0.01$, ** $p < 0.05$, * $p < 0.1$, LR = Long run, SR = Short run

Sources: Authors' compilations

columns of Table 12.8 show a mixed insignificant symmetric effect on education, healthcare, and standard of living for both LR and SR. Furthermore, concerning the asymmetric effects on education, healthcare, and the standard of living, Tables 12.7 and 12.9 provide the estimation results. From Table 12.7, columns (3) and (4) reveal that a percentage positive change in sovereign debt (Sovdebt+) in the LR would significantly (at 1%) negatively influence healthcare by 11.4%, but insignificantly affect healthcare in the SR.

Also, from columns (5) and (6) of Table 12.7, a percentage positive change in sovereign debt (Sovdebt+) in the LR would significantly constrain healthcare at a 1% significance level by 11.9%, whereas the effect in the SR is positively insignificant. For negative changes in sovereign debt (Sovdebt--), from columns (1) and (2), a percentage Sovdebt-- would significantly negatively influence education at a 10% significance level by a trivial effect of 0.0232% in the SR, while the LR positive effect is

**Table 12.5** The asymmetric effect of sovereign borrowing and debt servicing cost on inclusive human development

| | *(1)* | *(2)* | *(3)* | *(4)* |
|---|---|---|---|---|
| | *Sovereign debt* | | *Debt servicing cost* | |
| | *Inclusive HuD* | | *Inclusive HuD* | |
| *Variables* | *LR* | *SR* | *LR* | *SR* |
| EC Term | | −0.104** | | −0.140*** |
| | | (0.0404) | | (0.0459) |
| Sovdebt⁺ | 0.00342*** | −0.000414 | | |
| | (0.000437) | (0.000686) | | |
| Sovdebt⁻ | −0.00635*** | 0.00111** | | |
| | (0.000999) | (0.000512) | | |
| Debtserv⁺ | | | −0.00612*** | 0.00159** |
| | | | (0.000523) | (0.000625) |
| Debtserv⁻ | | | −0.00461*** | 0.000539 |
| | | | (0.000884) | (0.000944) |
| Fpo | −0.0138*** | 0.000639 | −0.00260*** | 0.00112 |
| | (0.00183) | (0.00118) | (0.00101) | (0.000983) |
| Infl | 0.000647*** | 0.000165 | 0.00116*** | 0.000888 |
| | (0.000141) | (0.000779) | (0.000165) | (0.000638) |
| Trade | 0.00621*** | −0.000192 | 0.00406*** | −0.000320 |
| | (0.000378) | (0.000240) | (0.000244) | (0.000301) |
| Pgrowth | −0.113*** | 0.0208** | 0.291*** | −0.0281* |
| | (0.00886) | (0.0100) | (0.0523) | (0.0162) |
| Observations | 492 | 492 | 491 | 491 |
| Log-likelihood | 1848.6 | 1848.6 | 1830.21 | 1830.21 |
| Asymmetric test: | | | | |
| Chip-square | 61.07 | 1.90 | 3.38 | 0.68 |
| p-value | 0.0000 | 0.1683 | 0.0662 | 0.4096 |

Note: Standard errors in parentheses, *** $p < 0.01$, ** $p < 0.05$, * $p < 0.1$

Sources: Authors' compilations

insignificant. Again, from columns (3) and (4), a percentage Sovdebt-- would lead to a significant improvement in healthcare in the LR at a 1% significance level by 10.1%, conversely, in the SR, a percentage Sovdebt-- would have a significantly negative effect on healthcare at 5%.

Regarding the standard of living, from columns (5) and (6) of Table 12.7, a percentage Sovdebt-- would result in a significant negative effect on the standard of living in the LR by 13.1% at a 1% significance

**Table 12.6** Symmetric effect of sovereign borrowing on inclusive human development dimensions

| | *(1)* | *(2)* | *(3)* | *(4)* | *(5)* | *(6)* |
|---|---|---|---|---|---|---|
| | *Education* | | *Healthcare* | | *St. of living* | |
| *Variables* | *LR* | *SR* | *LR* | *SR* | *LR* | *SR* |
| EC Term | | −0.279*** | | −0.0741*** | | −0.336* |
| | | (0.0303) | | (0.0255) | | (0.489) |
| Sovdebt | 0.000262 | −2.56e-05 | 0.00114 | 0.00872 | −0.0782*** | −0.106 |
| | (0.000187) | (0.000101) | (0.00248) | (0.00692) | (0.0145) | (0.0862) |
| Fpo | 0.00561** | −0.00152* | −0.104** | −0.0736 | 0.247*** | −0.0777 |
| | (0.00243) | (0.000789) | (0.0491) | (0.0711) | (0.0587) | (0.248) |
| Infl | −0.000324* | −2.00e-05 | 0.0157 | −0.00324 | −0.0358 | −0.0246 |
| | (0.000172) | (4.68e-05) | (0.0125) | (0.00609) | (0.0572) | (0.0788) |
| Trade | 0.000134 | −0.000267* | 0.00522 | 0.00708* | 0.246*** | 0.0595 |
| | (0.000537) | (0.000159) | (0.00857) | (0.00367) | (0.0172) | (0.0586) |
| Pgrowth | 0.00147 | 0.000409 | 9.588*** | −0.118*** | −660.7 | −220.3 |
| | (0.0133) | (0.00370) | (0.273) | (0.0342) | (530.0) | (322.9) |
| Observations | 492 | 492 | 492 | 492 | 492 | 492 |
| Log Likelihood | 309.04232 | 309.04232 | 309.0423 | 309.0423 | −827.6404 | −827.6404 |

Note: Standard errors in parentheses, *** $p < 0.01$, ** $p < 0.05$, * $p < 0.1$

Sources: Authors' compilations

**Table 12.7** The asymmetric effect of sovereign borrowing on Inclusive human development dimensions

| | *(1)* | *(2)* | *(3)* | *(4)* | *(5)* | *(6)* |
|---|---|---|---|---|---|---|
| | *Education* | | *Healthcare* | | *St, of living* | |
| *Variables* | *LR* | *SR* | *LR* | *SR* | *LR* | *SR* |
| EC Term | | −0.273*** | | −0.0283** | | −0.983 |
| | | (0.0302) | | (0.0143) | | (0.791) |
| $Sovdebt^{+}$ | −5.00e-05 | 8.02e-05 | −0.114*** | 0.00777 | −0.119*** | 0.0974 |
| | (0.000771) | (0.000149) | (0.0165) | (0.00641) | (0.0218) | (0.113) |
| $Sovdebt^{-}$ | 0.000724 | −0.000323* | −0.101*** | 0.0167** | −0.131*** | −0.438 |
| | (0.000928) | (0.000185) | (0.0231) | (0.00776) | (0.0329) | (0.334) |
| Fpo | 0.00554** | −0.00166** | −0.0785** | −0.0422 | 1.246*** | −0.0370 |
| | (0.00251) | (0.000788) | (0.0337) | (0.0438) | (0.0296) | (0.233) |
| Infl | −0.000284 | −2.31e-05 | 0.0516*** | −0.000387 | 0.0554*** | −0.0992 |
| | (0.000177) | (4.67e-05) | (0.0156) | (0.00747) | (0.00176) | (0.117) |
| Trade | 0.000165 | −0.000281* | −0.0200*** | 0.00545 | −0.0190* | 0.133 |
| | (0.000555) | (0.000160) | (0.00519) | (0.00343) | (0.0107) | (0.0895) |
| Pgrowth | −0.00159 | −0.000432 | 8.362 | −0.0887** | −116.1*** | 116.2 |
| | (0.0135) | (0.00368) | (0) | (0.0428) | (39.77) | (92.02) |
| Observations | 492 | 492. | 492 | 492 | 492 | 492 |
| Log Likelihood | 381.5656 | 381.5656 | 381.5656 | 381.5656 | −827.6404 | −762.408 |
| Asymmetric test: | | | | | | |
| Chi-square | 0.35 | 2.39 | 0.17 | 0.70 | 0.06 | 1.50 |
| *p-value* | 0.5556 | 0.1221 | 0.6823 | 0.4043 | 0.8009 | 0.2206 |

Note: Standard errors in parentheses, *** $p < 0.01$, ** $p < 0.05$, * $p < 0.1$

Sources: Authors' compilations

**Table 12.8** Symmetric effect of sovereign debt servicing cost on inclusive human development dimensions

| | *(1)* | *(2)* | *(3)* | *(4)* | *(5)* | *(6)* |
|---|---|---|---|---|---|---|
| | *Education* | | *Health* | | *St, of living* | |
| *Variables* | *LR* | *SR* | *LR* | *SR* | *LR* | *SR* |
| EC Term | | −0.277*** | | −0.0304** | | −0.312*** |
| | | (0.0295) | | (0.0125) | | (0.0977) |
| Debtserv | −0.00485 | −0.0111* | −0.172*** | −0.00662 | −0.0143 | 0.183 |
| | (0.0216) | (0.00567) | (0.0212) | (0.0157) | (0.00895) | (0.206) |
| Fpo | 0.159** | −0.0565** | 0.564*** | −0.0420 | 1.160*** | −0.101 |
| | (0.0739) | (0.0238) | (0.0532) | (0.0307) | (0.0265) | (0.246) |
| Infl | −0.00448 | −3.33e-05 | 0.0145*** | 0.00541 | 0.0759*** | −0.0415 |
| | (0.00529) | (0.00142) | (0.00540) | (0.00671) | (0.00815) | (0.0826) |
| Trade | 0.00129 | −0.00722 | −0.0947*** | 0.00302 | 0.143*** | 0.0556 |
| | (0.0168) | (0.00487) | (0.0126) | (0.00269) | (0.00432) | (0.0507) |
| Pgrowth | −0.117 | −0.0324 | 1.032 | −31.27** | −214.6 | 68.01*** |
| | (0.412) | (0.114) | (0) | (12.78) | (133.7) | (21.05) |
| Observations | 492 | 492 | 492 | 492 | 492 | 492 |
| Log-likelihood | 336.12585 | 336.12585 | 336.1907 | 336.1907 | −828.9562 | −828.9562 |

Note: Standard errors in parentheses, *** $p < 0.01$, ** $p < 0.05$, * $p < 0.1$

Sources: Authors' compilations

**Table 12.9** The asymmetric effect of debt servicing cost on inclusive human development dimensions

| | *(1)* | *(2)* | *(3)* | *(4)* | *(5)* | *(6)* |
|---|---|---|---|---|---|---|
| | *Education* | | *Health* | | *St, of living* | |
| *Variables* | *LR* | *SR* | *LR* | *SR* | *LR* | *SR* |
| EC Term | | −0.278*** | | −0.0667*** | | −0.825 |
| | | (0.0293) | | (0.00834) | | (0.594) |
| Debtserv⁺ | −0.0989** | 0.0298*** | 0.0199 | −0.00525 | −0.137* | 0.0640 |
| | (0.0479) | (0.0108) | (0.0968) | (0.00544) | (0.0750) | (0.267) |
| Debtserv⁻ | −0.211*** | 0.000375 | 0.192 | −0.00308 | −0.236*** | 0.114 |
| | (0.0617) | (0.0112) | (0.121) | (0.00571) | (0.0849) | (0.346) |
| Fpo | 0.154** | −0.0512** | −0.332** | −0.0117 | 0.857*** | −0.386** |
| | (0.0728) | (0.0235) | (0.154) | (0.0117) | (0.0913) | (0.196) |
| Infl | −0.00779 | 0.000883 | 0.0127 | −0.000820 | 0.0584*** | −0.0816 |
| | (0.00535) | (0.00144) | (0.0114) | (0.000714) | (0.00864) | (0.0683) |
| Trade | 0.00609 | −0.00829* | 0.0139 | 0.00202 | 0.0526*** | 0.0498 |
| | (0.0164) | (0.00483) | (0.0340) | (0.00241) | (0.0176) | (0.0383) |
| Pgrowth | −0.00836 | −0.00232 | 0.687 | 0.0458 | −6.102** | 7.593* |
| | (0.401) | (0.112) | (0.833) | (0.0564) | (2.384) | (4.060) |
| Observations | 491 | 491 | 491 | 491 | 491 | 491 |
| Log Likelihood | 481.31973 | 481.31973 | 491.31973 | 491.31973 | −768.4881 | −768.4881 |
| Asymmetric test: | | | | | | |
| Chi-square | 0.17 | 0.70 | 0.06 | 1.50 | 3.06* | 2.80* |
| *p-value* | 0.6823 | 0.4043 | 0.8009 | 0.2206 | 0.0800 | 0.0944 |

Note: Standard errors in parentheses, *** $p < 0.01$, ** $p < 0.05$, * $p < 0.1$

Sources: Authors' compilations

**Table 12.10** Panel stationarity test Variables

| | *Inclusive HuD* | *Education* | *Healthcare* | *St. Of living* | *Sovdebt* | *Debtserv* | *Fpo* | *Infla* | *Trade* | *Pgrowth* |
|---|---|---|---|---|---|---|---|---|---|---|
| *Method* | *Unit root test at level* | | | | | | | | | |
| | *Statistics* | *Statistics* | *Statistics* | *Statistics* | *Statistics* | *Statistics* | *Statistics* | *Statistics* | *Statistics* | *Statistics* |
| Levin, Lin & Chu t* | −56.01*** | −3.81*** | 0.223 | 3.2663 | −4.87*** | −6.84*** | −7.0*** | −0.572 | −2.44*** | −17.3*** |
| Im, Pesaran and Shin W-stat | −11.44*** | −0.19 | 3.234 | 3.6 | −0.51738 | −1.171 | −1.042 | 0.864 | 0.215 | −5.1*** |
| ADF - Fisher Chi-square | 134.0*** | 65.819 | 86.098 | 38.08 | 93.5161 | 97.52* | 90.32* | 98.898* | 81.759 | 149.5*** |
| PP - Fisher Chi-square | 184.52*** | 94.301 | 92.577 | 69.57 | 117.4*** | 186.35*** | 92.92* | 123.4*** | 70.55 | 113.0*** |
| **Unit root test at first difference** | | | | | | | | | | |
| Levin, Lin & Chu t* | −8.46*** | −9.55*** | −0.994** | −1.997** | −7.35*** | −8.46*** | −1.59** | −8.80*** | −10.2*** | −14.1*** |
| Im, Pesaran and Shin W-stat | −5.63*** | −4.47*** | −1.80** | 1.54** | −4.42*** | −5.63*** | −2.24** | −4.15*** | −3.5*** | −6.1*** |

| | | | | | | | | | | |
|---|---|---|---|---|---|---|---|---|---|---|
| ADF - Fisher Chi-square | 161.78*** | 125.37*** | 117.94** | 63.11** | 144.63*** | 161.78*** | 102.53** | 150.86*** | 128.0*** | 180.3*** |
| PP - Fisher Chi-square | 470.63*** | 326.82*** | 183.49** | 188.11** | 368.92*** | 470.63*** | 257.8*** | 328.29*** | 250.4*** | 180.2*** |

Newey-West automatic bandwidth selection and Bartlett kernel, probabilities for Fisher tests are computed using an asymptotic Chi-square distribution. All other tests assume asymptotic normality. Null: Unit root (assumes individual and common unit root process). Exogenous variables: Individual effects, individual linear trends. *** $p < 0.01$, ** $p < 0.05$, * $p < 0.1$, (+) and (−) denotes positive and negative respectively

Source: authors' compilation

**Table 12.11** Testing for slope heterogeneity

| *Sovereign debt* | | *Debt service* | |
|---|---|---|---|
| *Delta* | *p-value* | *Delta* | *p-values* |
| 7.788 | 0.000 | 6.139 | 0.000 |
| adj. 11.464 | 0.000 | adj. 9.037 | 0.000 |

Pesaran and Yamagata (2008) $H_0$: slope coefficients are homogeneous

**Table 12.12** Testing for weak cross-sectional dependence (CSD)

| | *Sovereign debt* | | *Debt service* | |
|---|---|---|---|---|
| | *CDw* | *CD** | *CDw* | *CD** |
| residuals | −1.20 | 1.57 | −1.20 | 0.64 |
| p-values | (0.230) | (0.116) | (0.229) | (0.525) |

CD*: by Pesaran and Xie (2024) with 4 PC(s), CDw: by Juodis and Reese (2022), $H_0$: weak cross-section dependence, $H_1$: strong cross-section dependence

level. In the SR, there is an insignificant adverse effect. Regarding the asymmetric effect of sovereign debt services, from columns (1) and (2) of Table 12.9, a percentage positive change in sovereign debt services (Debtserv+) would lead to a significant negative effect on education in the LR at a 5% significance level by 9.89%. In the SR, a percentage of Debtserv+ would result in a significant effect on education at a 1% significance level of 2.98%. Additionally, from columns (3) and (4), a percentage of Debtserv+ would have a mixed insignificant effect on healthcare in both LR and SR. In columns (5) and (6), a percentage of Debtserv+ would significantly lead to a negative effect on the standard of living at 10%, amounting to 13.7% in the LR. The SR effect is positively insignificant.

Furthermore, with the negative change in sovereign debt services (Debtserv--), from columns (1) and (2) of Table 12.10, a percentage of Debtserv-- would significantly negatively influence education by 21.1% at a 1% significance level in the LR. The SR effect is positively insignificant. From columns (3) and (4), a percentage of Debtserv-- would have a mixed insignificant effect on healthcare in the LR and SR.

For the standard of living, from columns (5) and (6), a percentage of Debtserv-- significantly constrains the standard of living in the LR by 23.6% at a 1% significance level. For the SR, the effect is insignificantly positive. Consequently, the Wald test for the existence of the symmetric or asymmetric effects of Sovdebt and Debtserv on inclusive HuD and its sub-dimensions is shown in Tables 12.5, 12.7, and 12.9. From Table 12.5, the coefficients of the asymmetric effect test indicate that there is an asymmetric effect of Sovdebt on inclusive HuD in the LR (column 1) at a 1% significance level, but a symmetric effect in the SR (column 2). Additionally, from column (3), the test shows an asymmetric effect of Debtserv on inclusive HuD in the LR at a 10% significance level and a symmetric effect in the SR. From Table 12.7, the Wald test indicates that there is a symmetric effect of Sovdebt on education, healthcare, and standard of living for both LR and SR (columns 1 to 6). From Table 12.9, the Wald test signifies that there is an asymmetric effect of Debtserv on the standard of living for both LR and SR.

The variables used to control these relationships exhibit a mixed effect, as shown in Tables 12.4, 12.5, 12.6, 12.7, 12.8 and 12.9. For instance, population growth as a control variable from Table 12.5 shows a mixed significant effect in controlling the relationship between sovereign debt, debt services, and inclusive HuD for both LR and SR.

Some findings presented in this subsection align with prevailing empirical evidence; however, in some instances, results contradict existing empirical findings. For instance, the uncovered findings that positive changes to sovereign debt significantly improve inclusive HuD in the long run are relatively consistent with the works of Yusuf and Mohd (2024) and Özmen and Mutascu (2024), which argue that debt drives economic growth, proxied by GDP. Additionally, negative changes in sovereign debt significantly enhance inclusive HuD in the short run, contradicting findings from Özmen and Mutascu (2024), but aligning with Amaechi (2023), which indicates that sovereign debt significantly enhances human capital.

The evidence that positive and negative changes in debt servicing costs significantly constrain inclusive HuD in the long run aligns with the findings of Yusuf and Mohd (2024) on the debt-economic growth nexus. Moreover, the study's findings that positive changes in debt servicing costs significantly improve inclusive HuD in the short run are inconsistent with similar studies like Yusuf and Mohd (2024) and Amaechi (2023).

Furthermore, the evidence that there is an asymmetric effect of sovereign debt and servicing costs on inclusive HuD in the long run aligns with the work of Yusuf and Mohd (2024) and Amoh et al. (2024). Amoh et al. (2024) findings argue that sovereign debt has an asymmetric effect on economic growth in both the short and long run. Moreover, some evidence of the positive effect of inclusive HuD is consistent with linearity studies such as Nwokoye et al. (2024), and Amaechi (2023), but contradicts other studies like Beyene and Kotosz (2023). Beyene and Kotosz (2023) findings show that "the relationship between foreign debt and HCD is negative and non-linear".

### 12.4.4 *Implication for Policy, Practice, and Theory*

This subsection discusses the implications of the main evidence unearthed in this study for policymakers, practitioners, and scholars. The study's findings on the asymmetric effect of sovereign borrowing and servicing costs on inclusive HuD have significant implications for sub-SA. Given sub-SA's high dependence on external borrowing for growth and development investments, prudent debt sustainability management is crucial to ensuring long-term inclusive HuD prospects.

The initial finding indicates that positive changes in sovereign borrowing drive inclusive HuD in the long run. This suggests that policymakers and practitioners can leverage debt to promote inclusive HuD by investing in long-term projects related to healthcare, education, infrastructure, and social welfare. Conversely, if sovereign borrowing is not managed prudently, it could lead to fiscal distress, undermining these benefits. Therefore, it is recommended to establish robust frameworks for sovereign borrowing sustainability to ensure that sovereign borrowing finances sectors that foster long-term inclusive HuD.

Additionally, there is a pressing need to promote sustainable debt management practices by prioritising concessional loans with favourable terms. This reinforces the urgency of directing debt towards financing human capital development through quality education, effective healthcare services, and infrastructure to maximise the developmental impact of sovereign borrowing. Furthermore, the finding that negative changes in sovereign borrowing impede inclusive HuD in the long term but enhance it in the short term implies that a reduction in sovereign debt can constrain long-term development due to inadequate fiscal capacity to implement inclusive HuD projects. Meanwhile, in the short term, reducing sovereign borrowing can free up resources for inclusive HuD programmes, creating a policy trade-off between fiscal consolidation and social expenditure.

As a result, it is recommended that sub-SA governments adopt balanced fiscal policies that safeguard social expenditure while effectively managing sovereign debt levels. It is also advisable for sub-SA to formulate and execute counter-cyclical strategies to ensure financing availability during economic downturns and to cut non-essential expenditure to prioritise critical sectors like health and education.

Moreover, the evidence that both positive and negative changes to debt servicing costs constrain inclusive HuD in the long run but improve it in the short run presents significant implications for policymakers and practitioners in sub-SA. This finding indicates that high debt servicing costs can crowd out resources for government services in the long term, limiting inclusive HuD. However, partial repayment of sovereign borrowing in the short term can stabilise finances and restore investor confidence.

Consequently, the recommendations suggest that sub-SA governments need to renegotiate sovereign borrowing terms to minimise the adverse impacts of debt servicing and create fiscal space for social spending. Additionally, sub-SA could advocate for debt-for-development barters to convert debt repayments into investments in inclusive HuD. Moreover, sub-SA should establish robust internal revenue mobilisation mechanisms to reduce reliance on foreign borrowing, ensuring sustainable domestic investment for inclusive HuD.

Furthermore, the finding that there is an asymmetric effect of sovereign borrowing and debt servicing costs on inclusive HuD in the long run suggests that the impact of sovereign borrowing is not uniform. Increases and decreases in sovereign debt have varying long-term influences on inclusive HuD. Traditional linear debt-development models often fail to capture these complexities. Thus, it is necessary to develop asymmetric debt models that accurately reflect the real-world performance of sub-SA economies.

Additionally, this evidence advocates the integration of inclusive HuD metrics into sovereign debt sustainability frameworks to ensure that debt strategies prioritise long-term welfare prospects. Furthermore, the finding that there exists an asymmetric effect of debt servicing costs on living standards in both the long run and short run indicates that debt servicing has a limited influence on living standards compared to its impact on education and healthcare. This suggests that debt servicing strategies should focus on sectors with the most direct effect on living conditions. Recommendations include targeting investments in living standards by addressing income inequality, housing, job creation, and other social welfare services. The formulation and implementation of social protection programmes are also crucial to ensure that the disadvantaged population is not adversely affected by debt servicing.

Finally, the finding that sovereign borrowing and debt servicing costs have symmetric effects on education and healthcare, both in the long run and the short run, indicates that sovereign debt and its associated servicing consistently impact these sectors. This underlines the importance of safeguarding education and healthcare from fiscal cuts to achieve sustainable inclusive HuD. Therefore, the study recommends prioritising education and healthcare expenditures when managing debt sustainability strategies to avoid unfavourable effects on inclusive HuD as a whole.

Additionally, exploring public-private partnerships (PPPs) can supplement public financing in education and healthcare, ensuring that debt sustainability measures protect investments in the social sector during fiscal adjustments. In summary, the empirical evidence uncovered emphasises the need for accountable debt management, improvements in financial and economic theory to account for the asymmetric and sector-specific effects of sovereign borrowing, and the necessity to prioritise human capital development while ensuring debt sustainability through transparent debt practices, debt renegotiation, and investment in critical sectors.

## 12.5 Conclusion

This study explored the asymmetric effect of sovereign borrowing and servicing costs on inclusive HuD and its three main dimensions. The debt-development literature has neglected this aspect, limiting effective and productive policy guidelines regarding the impacts of shocks to sovereign borrowing and its servicing costs on inclusive HuD in both the long and short run. The study employed the PNARDL technique to estimate a 41-panel time series of datasets covering 2010 to 2023 in sub-SA.

The major findings indicate that: first, positive shocks to sovereign debt significantly improve inclusive HuD in the long run (LR); second, negative shocks to sovereign debt hinder inclusive growth in the LR but significantly enhance inclusive HuD in the short run (SR). Positive and negative shocks in sovereign debt services significantly constrain inclusive HuD in the LR, but positive shocks in sovereign debt services significantly improve inclusive HuD in the SR. Fourth, an asymmetric effect exists between sovereign debt and debt services on inclusive HuD in the LR. Fifth, a weak asymmetric effect is observed from sovereign debt services on the standard of living in both the LR and SR. Sixth, there are symmetric effects of sovereign debt and debt services on education and healthcare in the LR and SR.

Consequently, the implications of the key findings for policy, practice, and theory are discussed along with recommendations to guide policy formulation and implementation in sub-SA. The main recommendations for policymaking and practice concern economic managers in sub-SA. These include renegotiating debt terms, promoting debt-for-development swaps, implementing asymmetric debt strategies, focusing on targeted investments in living standards, prioritising social spending, and encouraging public-private partnerships (PPPs). Additionally, the recommendations for theory emphasise the urgency of integrating asymmetric effects into debt models, redefining debt concepts to reinforce non-linear relationships, incorporating human development indicators into finance models, and assessing the sector-specific effects of debt policies.

Therefore, the empirical evidence provides significant insights for African economic and finance managers, suggesting that responsible borrowing and debt management are essential for achieving long-term inclusive HuD. Policymakers in sub-SA must balance the need for fiscal stability with investments in critical social sectors. Furthermore, there must be assurances that sovereign debt strategies do not undermine progress in education, healthcare, and living standards. Likewise, the evidence underscores the need to refine finance and economic theories to better capture the complex and asymmetric relationship between sovereign borrowing, debt servicing costs, and human development in sub-Saharan Africa.

## Appendix

### *Countries used*

| | | | |
|---|---|---|---|
| 1. Angola | 11. Congo, Rep. | 20. Liberia | 30. Rwanda |
| 2. Botswana | 12. Cote d'Ivoire | 21. Madagascar | 31. Sao Tome and Principe |
| 3. Burkina Faso | 13. Gabon | 22. Mali | 32. Senegal |
| 4. Burundi | 14. Gambia, The | 23. Malawi | 33. Seychelles |
| 5. Cabo Verde | 15. Ghana | 24. Mauritania | 34. Sierra Leone |
| 6. Cameroon | 16. Guinea | 25. Mauritius | 35. South Africa |
| 7. Central African Republic | 17. Guinea-Bissau | 26. Mozambique | 36. Sudan |
| 8. Chad | 18. Kenya | 27. Namibia | 37. Tanzania |
| 9. Comoros | 19. Lesotho | 28. Niger | 38. Togo |
| 10. Congo, Dem | | 29. Nigeria | 39. Uganda |
| | | | 40. Zambia |
| | | | 41. Zimbabwe |

Data sources

https://hdr.undp.org/inequality-adjusted-human-development-index#/indicies/IHDI

https://databank.worldbank.org/source/world-development-indicators

## References

Abubakar, A. B., McCausland, W. D., & Theodossiou, I. (2025). Do debt relief and fiscal rules improve public debt sustainability? The experience of sub-Sahara African countries. *Journal of Policy Modeling, 47*(1), 166–186. https://doi.org/10.1016/j.jpolmod.2024.06.007

Adegboye, A., Erin, O., & Asongu, S. (2025). Taxing Africa for inclusive human development: The mediating role of governance quality. *Journal of Economic and Administrative Sciences, 41*(1), 182–205. https://doi.org/10.1108/JEAS-03-2022-0061

Alsamara, M., Mrabet, Z., & Mimouni, K. (2024). The threshold effects of public debt on economic growth in MENA countries: Do energy endowments matter? *International Review of Economics and Finance, 89*. https://doi.org/10.1016/j.iref.2023.10.015

Amaechi, M. P. (2023). Analysing external debt impact on human capital development in Nigeria. *International Journal of Economics and Financial Management, 8*(1). https://doi.org/10.56201/ijefm.v8.no1.2023.pg70.86

Amoh, J. K., Abdul-Mumuni, A., & Amankwa Fosu, R. (2024). Revisiting the debt–growth nexus in sub-Saharan Africa: Fresh evidence from panel nonlinear ARDL approach. *International Journal of Emerging Markets*. https://doi.org/10.1108/IJOEM-04-2023-0598

Amowine, N., Balezentis, T., Zhou, Z., & Streimikiene, D. (2023). Transitions towards green productivity in Africa: Do sovereign debt vulnerability, eco-entrepreneurship, and institutional quality matter? *Sustainable Development*. https://doi.org/10.1002/sd.2857

Apeti, A. E., Bambe, B. W. W., Combes, J. L., & Edoh, E. D. (2024). Original sin: Fiscal rules and government debt in foreign currency in developing countries. *Journal of Macroeconomics, 80*, 103600. https://doi.org/10.1016/J.JMACRO.2024.103600

Beyene, A. B. (2024). Governance quality and economic growth in Sub-Saharan Africa: The dynamic panel model. *Journal of Economic and Administrative Sciences, 40*(2), 404–418. https://doi.org/10.1108/JEAS-08-2021-0156

Beyene, S. D., & Kotosz, B. (2023). The Impact of External Debt on Human Capital Development and GDP Growth in HIPCs: a Comprehensive Approach. *Statistika: Statistics and Economy Journal, 103*(3), 295–309. https://doi.org/10.54694/stat.2023.10

Chang, C., & Fang, M. (2024). Impact of a sharing economy and green energy on achieving sustainable economic development: Evidence from a novel NARDL model. *Journal of Innovation & Knowledge, 8*(1), 100297. https://doi.org/10.1016/j.jik.2022.100297

Colak, G., Habimana, T., & Korkeamäki, T. (2025). The effects of government debt on corporate borrowing in developing economies: Evidence from Africa. *Journal of International Business Studies*, 1–27.

Dianda, I., Ouedraogo, I., & Sawadogo, H. (2024). Inclusive human development effect of financial inclusion in sub-Saharan Africa: A gender perspective. *Journal of International Development, 36*(3). https://doi.org/10.1002/jid.3861

Edo, S. (2024). Comparative performance of trade openness and sovereign debt accumulation in fostering economic growth of Sub-Saharan African Countries. *Foreign Trade Review, 59*(1). https://doi.org/10.1177/00157325221145452

Elkhalfi, O., Chaabita, R., Benboubker, M., Ghoujdam, M., Zahraoui, K., Alaoui, H. E., Laalam, S., Belhaj, I., & Hammouch, H. (2024). The impact of external debt on economic growth: The case of emerging countries. *Research in Globalization, 9*, 100248. https://doi.org/10.1016/J.RESGLO.2024.100248

Fosu, P., Eshun, J., & Ankrah Twumasi, M. (2025). The linkage between economic growth, debt servicing, pollution and health expenditures: Panel evidence from 42 African countries. *African Journal of Economic and Management Studies, ahead-of-print* (ahead-of-print). https://doi.org/10.1108/AJEMS-01-2024-0039

Fuseini, E. I. (2025a). Entrepreneurial trend across Africa: Fresh evidence from the conditioning effect of governance quality on policy. *Journal of Small Business & Entrepreneurship, 1–29.* https://doi.org/10.1080/08276331.2025.2587475

Fuseini, E. I. (2025b). *Institutional quality-banking efficiency nexuses in Africa. How does ICT moderate?* (pp. 1–25). *Information Technology for Development.* https://doi.org/10.1080/02681102.2025.2460157

Fuseini, E. I., & Ibrahim, M. (2025). Fiscal policy cyclicality and inclusive growth outcomes in Sub-Saharan Africa: Identifying critical thresholds. *Macroeconomics and Finance in Emerging Market Economies, 1–22.* https://doi.org/10.1080/17520843.2025.2572169

Fuseini, E. I., Ibrahim, M., Adam, I. O., & Vinh, X. (2024). Re-examining the moderating role of ICT in the nexus between financial development and banking efficiency: Evidence from Africa. *Cogent Economics & Finance, 12*(1). https://doi.org/10.1080/23322039.2024.2325833

Gaiya, B. A., Akintola, A. A., Akpan, U., Abel, A., & Etudaiye, I. M. (2024). External debt, institutions, and economic growth: New evidence from emerging markets and low-income countries. *Journal of Social and Economic Development, 1–24.* https://doi.org/10.1007/S40847-024-00363-3/TABLES/10

Ibrahim, M., & Alagidede, I. P. (2020). Asymmetric effects of financial development on economic growth in Ghana. *Journal of Sustainable Finance and Investment, 10*(4). https://doi.org/10.1080/20430795.2019.1706142

Iheanacho, E., Okere, K. I., & Onoh, J. O. (2023). Nexus between financial integration, capital market development and economic performance: Does institutional structure matters? *Heliyon, 9*(1). https://doi.org/10.1016/j.heliyon.2023.e12827

Im, K. S., Pesaran, M. H., & Shin, Y. (2003). Testing for unit roots in heterogeneous panels. *Journal of Econometrics, 115*(1). https://doi.org/10.1016/S0304-4076(03)00092-7

International Monetary Fund. (2024). *FISCAL MONITOR: Putting a lid on public debt.* International Monetary Fund. https://www.imf.org/en/Publications/FM/Issues/2024/10/23/fiscal-monitor-october-2024

International Monetary Fund. (2025). *Fiscal monitor, April 2025: Fiscal policy under uncertainty.* International Monetary Fund (IMF). https://doi.org/10.5089/9798229002516.089

Juodis, A., & Reese, S. (2022). The incidental parameters problem in testing for remaining cross-section correlation. *Journal of Business & Economic Statistics, 40*(3), 1191–1203. https://doi.org/10.1080/07350015.2021.1906687

Kao, C. (1999). Spurious regression and residual-based tests for cointegration in panel data. *Journal of Econometrics, 90*(1). https://doi.org/10.1016/S0304-4076(98)00023-2

Kripfganz, S., & Schneider, D. C. (2023). ARDL: Estimating autoregressive distributed lag and equilibrium correction models. *Stata Journal, 23*(4). https://doi.org/10.1177/1536867X231212434

Krugman, P. (1988). Financing vs. Forgiving a debt overhang. *Journal of Development Economics, 29*(3). https://doi.org/10.1016/0304-3878(88)90044-2

Levin, A., Lin, C. F., & Chu, C. S. J. (2002). Unit root tests in panel data: Asymptotic and finite-sample properties. *Journal of Econometrics, 108*(1). https://doi.org/10.1016/S0304-4076(01)00098-7

Matekenya, W., Moyo, C., & Jeke, L. (2021). Financial inclusion and human development: Evidence from Sub-Saharan Africa. *Development Southern Africa, 38*(5), 683–700. https://doi.org/10.1080/0376835X.2020.1799760

Nwokoye, E. S., Dimnwobi, S. K., Onuoha, F. C., & Madichie, C. V. (2024). Does public debt matter for human capital development? Evidence from Nigeria. *Journal of Public Affairs, 24*(2). https://doi.org/10.1002/pa.2912

Otieno, B. A. (2024). Public debt, investment and economic growth dynamics: Do geographical proximity and spatial spillover effects matter? *Regional Science Policy & Practice, 16*(6), 100059. https://doi.org/10.1016/J.RSPP.2024.100059

Özmen, İ., & Mutascu, M. (2024). Public debt and growth: New insights. *Journal of the Knowledge Economy, 15*(2). https://doi.org/10.1007/s13132-023-01441-3

Pedroni, P. (2004). Panel cointegration: Asymptotic and finite sample properties of pooled time series tests with an application to the PPP hypothesis. *Econometric Theory, 20*(3). https://doi.org/10.1017/S0266466604203073

Pesaran, M. H., & Xie, Y. (2024). *How to detect network dependence in latent factor models? A bias-corrected CD test.* CESifo Working Paper.

Pesaran, M. H., & Yamagata, T. (2008). Testing slope homogeneity in large panels. *Journal of Econometrics, 142*(1), 50–93.

Phillips, P. C. B., & Perron, P. (1988). Testing for a unit root in time series regression. *Biometrika, 75*(2). https://doi.org/10.2307/2336182

Roy, S., & Sen, C. (2024). Role of debt in emerging economies: A re-examination of the debt-growth nexus. *Macroeconomics and Finance in Emerging Market Economies, 17*(2). https://doi.org/10.1080/17520843.2022.2028381

Sen, A. K. (1999). *Introduction—Development as freedom.*

Shah, S. S. A., Dickinson, D., Tao, K., Wang, C., & Zhang, L. (2024). The heterogeneous threshold effects of public debt on economic growth: Empirical evidence from developing countries. *Open Economies Review, 1–38.* https://doi.org/10.1007/S11079-024-09756-7/METRICS

Sharaf, M. F., Shahen, A. M., & Binzaid, B. A. (2024). Asymmetric and nonlinear foreign debt–inflation nexus in Brazil: Evidence from NARDL and Markov regime switching approaches. *Economies, 12*(1), 18. https://doi.org/10.3390/ECONOMIES12010018

Shin, Y., Yu, B., & Greenwood-Nimmo, M. (2014). Modelling asymmetric cointegration and dynamic multipliers in a nonlinear ARDL framework. In *Festschrift in Honor of Peter Schmidt.* https://doi.org/10.1007/978-1-4899-8008-3_9

Singh, B. P., & Kumar, S. (2024). Public debt and economic growth in India: The new evidence. *Millennial Asia, 15*(3), 429–446. https://doi.org/10.1177/09763996221136908/ASSET/IMAGES/LARGE/10.1177_09763996221136908-FIG1.JPEG

Stylianou, T., Nasir, R., & Waqas, M. (2023). Inclusive human development and governance nexus: Causality analysis of selected Asian Countries. *Economies, 11*(3). https://doi.org/10.3390/economies11030097

Taylor, R. S., & Lokina, R. (2024). The relationship between public debt and economic growth in Tanzania. *Review of Black Political Economy.* https://doi.org/10.1177/00346446241275134/ASSET/IMAGES/LARGE/10.1177_00346446241275134-FIG5.JPEG

UNDP (United Nations Development Programme). (2024). Human Development Report 2023–24. *UNDP (United Nations Development Programme).*

UNDP, (United Nations Development Programme). (2025). *IHDI adjusts the Human Development Index (HDI).* Human Development Report (1990 to Present). https://hdr.undp.org/inequality-adjusted-human-development-index#/indicies/IHDI

Westerlund, J. (2007). Testing for error correction in panel data. *Oxford Bulletin of Economics and Statistics, 69*(6). https://doi.org/10.1111/j.1468-0084.2007.00477.x

World Bank. (2024). Global Economic Prospects: 2024. In World Bank Group (Issue January). https://doi.org/10.2307/j.ctt183pb3w.5

World Bank. (2025a). *Global economic prospects, June 2025* (pp. 1–138). World Bank Group, Washington DC. https://openknowledge.worldbank.org/server/api/core/bitstreams/2baabfb0-d076-444b-9564-7935afab5ada/content

World Bank. (2025b). *Pulse, No. 31, Spring 2025: Improving Governance and Delivering for People in Africa.* © World Bank. http://hdl.handle.net/10986/42886

Xie, P., Xiao, W., Cai, Y., & Zhu, Z. (2024). Does decentralization improve natural resources and government efficiency? *Resources Policy, 91*. https://doi.org/10.1016/j.resourpol.2024.104865

Yusuf, A., & Mohd, S. (2023). Nonlinear effects of public debt on economic growth in Nigeria. *SN Business & Economics, 3*(4). https://doi.org/10.1007/s43546-023-00468-7

Yusuf, A., & Mohd, S. (2024). Investigating the asymmetric impact of public debt on economic growth in Nigeria. *Journal of the Knowledge Economy, 15*(2), 9452–9481. https://doi.org/10.1007/s13132-023-01362-1

Zamir, S., Abbasi, B. N., Yu, L., Sohail, A., & Yang, C. (2023). Transformative role of educational funding in shaping national development across SAARC countries in the 21st century: A panel NARDL approach. *Heliyon, 9*(10). https://doi.org/10.1016/j.heliyon.2023.e20417

Ziaei, S. M. (2025). Public spending on Energy innovations and CO2 impacts: Evidence from selected OECD countries. *Green Technologies and Sustainability, 3*(1), 100137. https://doi.org/10.1016/j.grets.2024.100137

CHAPTER 13

# Integrating ESG Considerations into Public Debt Management in Africa: A Pathway to Responsible and Sustainable Borrowing

*Osman Issah, Khadijah Iddrisu, and Ibrahim Nandom Yakubu*

## 13.1 Introduction

Over the past two decades, Africa has experienced a significant build-up of public debt, driven by the dual imperatives of financing economic growth and meeting urgent development needs (Commodore & Awuah, 2024; Selassie, 2018). Much of this borrowing has gone into infrastructure projects, social programmes, and efforts to close financing gaps, particularly as

O. Issah
Department of Accounting, University for Development Studies, Tamale, Ghana
e-mail: oissah@uds.edu.gh

K. Iddrisu (✉)
Department of Finance, Islamic University College, Accra, Ghana
e-mail: khadijahiddris@iug.edu.gh

I. N. Yakubu
School of Business, University for Development Studies, Tamale, Ghana
e-mail: ibrahim.yakubu@uds.edu.gh



I. N. Yakubu (ed.), *Public Debt and Economic Resilience in Africa*, Palgrave Studies in African and Development Economics,
https://doi.org/10.1007/978-3-032-25835-9_13

many countries contend with volatile commodity prices, recurrent fiscal deficits, and external shocks such as the coronavirus disease 2019 (COVID-19) pandemic (Were, 2024). However, rising debt levels have also heightened concerns about long-term debt sustainability, with several African countries currently at risk of or already experiencing debt distress. For instance, Ghana defaulted on its external debt in 2022, with its debt-to-GDP ratio peaking above 90%, prompting austerity measures, an IMF bailout, and debt restructuring negotiations (Kuwonu, 2025). This situation underscores the need for innovative approaches that go beyond traditional debt sustainability frameworks, which often emphasise fiscal and macroeconomic indicators without adequately accounting for broader environmental, social, and governance (ESG) dimensions.

The integration of ESG considerations into public debt management presents a promising pathway toward more responsible and sustainable borrowing (Collaborative Africa Budget Reform Initiative (CABRI), 2021). From an environmental perspective, climate risks such as droughts, floods, and rising temperatures directly affect economic performance, fiscal health, and repayment capacity. Mozambique was hit by Cyclones Idai and Kenneth in 2019, causing over US$3 billion in damages and devastating the country's infrastructure, agriculture, and livelihoods (United Nations Development Programme (UNDP), 2019). Socially, investments in education, health, and poverty reduction enhance human capital and social stability, creating conditions for stronger long-term growth and reduced vulnerability to crises (Šlaus & Jacobs, 2011). Governance factors such as transparency, accountability, and the rule of law remain central to attracting investor confidence, reducing borrowing costs, and ensuring that debt is used productively. Ignoring these dimensions not only weakens debt sustainability but also risks undermining Africa's broader development goals under the African Union's Agenda 2063 and the Sustainable Development Goals (SDGs) of the United Nations. This chapter aims to explore how African countries can integrate ESG considerations into their debt management strategies as a way of strengthening resilience, credibility, and long-term sustainability.

The chapter is structured as follows: Section 13.2 explores the concepts and significance of ESG in public finance. Section 13.3 examines the risks, opportunities, and existing gaps in integrating ESG within Africa's debt landscape. Section 13.4 highlights innovative ESG tools and ESG-driven debt management strategies. Section 13.5 presents key international case studies and discusses their relevance and potential applicability for African countries. Finally, Sect. 13.6 concludes the chapter and offers practical recommendations for policymakers and other stakeholders.

## 13.2 ESG in Public Finance: Concepts and Relevance

### *13.2.1 Concept of ESG*

The concept of "ESG" was formally introduced in the UN report Who Cares Wins, which called on financial institutions to integrate environmental, social, and governance factors into investment analysis and decision-making (Byrne, n.d.). This was followed by the launch of the UN-supported Principles for Responsible Investment (PRI), endorsed by institutional investors worldwide.[1] Over time, ESG investing evolved into a mainstream strategy for asset managers, pension funds, and sovereign wealth funds (Macesar, 2025). Governments also began enacting legislation to strengthen corporate governance and environmental accountability, such as the UK Companies Act of 2006 (Byrne, n.d.; Macesar, 2025). ESG principles, initially developed for the corporate and investment sectors, are increasingly critical in the context of sovereign debt management (Shilaho, 2021).

ESG extends beyond corporate compliance to encompass national policies, public infrastructure, social welfare programmes, and institutional governance (Sonko & Sonko, 2023), which can be useful for African governments. Environmental considerations include climate resilience, natural resource management, and disaster preparedness, which are especially relevant for countries vulnerable to extreme weather events such as cyclones and droughts (Oyugi, 2025) Social factors cover public health, education, poverty reduction, and inclusive economic growth, reflecting the impact of borrowing on citizens' well-being (CABRI, 2021). Governance entails transparency, accountability, anti-corruption measures, and sound fiscal management, all of which directly influence a country's ability to manage debt sustainably.

[1] https://www.unpri.org/about-us/what-are-the-principles-for-responsible-investment

### *13.2.2 Relevance of ESG*

1. **Promote Debt Sustainability**
   The linkages between ESG and debt sustainability are profound. Environmental shocks, such as climate-induced disasters or resource depletion, can strain public finances, increasing borrowing needs and heightening debt vulnerability (Barrage, 2025; Brownbridge & Canagarajah, 2024). Social challenges, including inequality, unemployment, or weak health systems, can reduce productivity and revenue generation, undermining a country's capacity to service debt (Ruckert & Labonté, 2017). Weak governance compounds these risks through mismanagement, corruption, or unsustainable fiscal practices. Embedding ESG considerations in debt management allows policymakers to anticipate and mitigate such risks, thereby supporting both financial stability and broader development objectives.
2. **Attracting Responsible Investors**
   The business case for ESG integration is equally compelling. African countries that demonstrate robust ESG practices are better positioned to attract a diverse pool of investors, including those seeking sustainable or impact-oriented assets (Carter & Ayres, 2024). ESG-aligned debt instruments, such as green bonds, social bonds, and sustainability-linked debt, can often secure funding at lower yields, reflecting enhanced investor confidence (Del Sarto, 2025a). Beyond cost savings, ESG integration strengthens resilience, helping nations withstand environmental shocks, social unrest, and governance crises that could otherwise trigger debt distress (Leung et al., 2025).
3. **Long-Term Fiscal Planning**
   ESG provides a strategic lens for long-term fiscal planning. Aligning borrowing and spending with SDGs allows governments to embed resilience into their debt portfolios, ensuring that public finance supports climate adaptation, social inclusion, and institutional reform (Elmahdi & Jeong, 2024). Rather than reacting to crises, ESG-informed debt management enables proactive strategies that transform public debt from a potential source of vulnerability into a tool for sustainable development, responsible borrowing, and economic growth across Africa (Vezér et al., 2021).

## 13.3 Debt Landscape in Africa: Risks, Opportunities, and ESG Gaps

### *13.3.1 Current Debt Trends and Post-pandemic Pressures*

Africa's debt trajectory has shifted significantly in the last decade, with many countries experiencing rapid debt accumulation. Public debt-to-GDP ratios have risen sharply, erasing much of the relief achieved through debt relief initiatives in the early 2000s (Arnone & Presbitero, 2016). As illustrated in Fig. 13.1, debt levels across Sub Saharan Africa (SSA) have been rising, with oil-importing countries experiencing particularly high public debt burdens.

The COVID-19 pandemic magnified fiscal stress by reducing government revenues, disrupting trade, and increasing spending on health and welfare (Makin & Layton, 2021). Many countries resorted to emergency borrowing, including issuance of Eurobonds and reliance on multilateral assistance, pushing debt service burdens to historic highs. Before COVID-19, debt levels were relatively low across all groups, including oil-exporting countries, oil-importing countries, and SSA as a whole, but they began rising again in 2020 (Fig. 13.1). Rising global interest rates and a strong U.S. dollar have further increased repayment costs, while

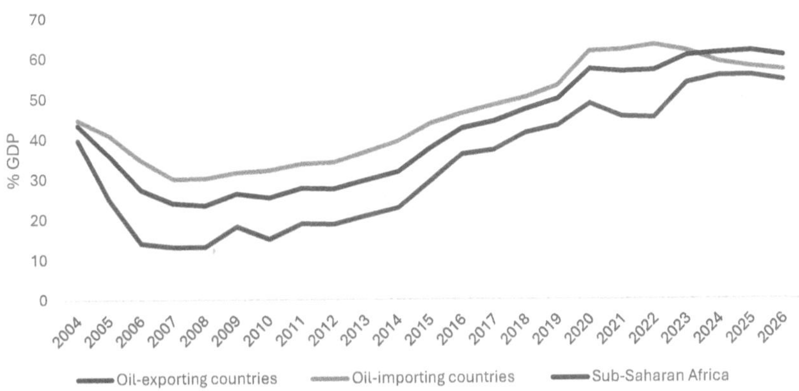


**Fig. 13.1** Trend in public debt in Sub-Saharan Africa (2004 to 2026) by subgroup. Source: Adapted from the IMF

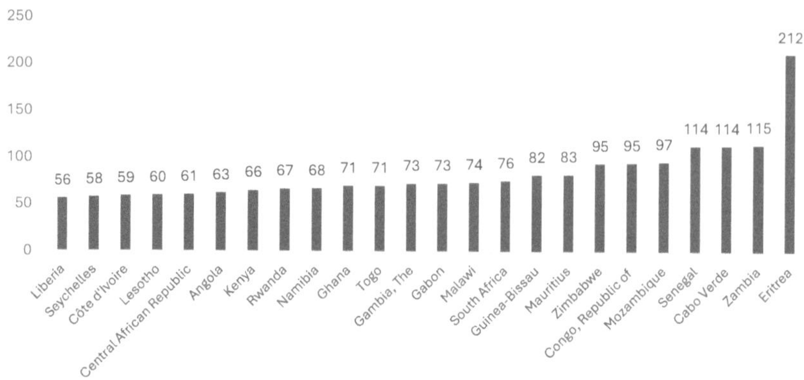


**Fig. 13.2** Sub-Saharan African countries with debt (% GDP) levels above 55% in 2024. Source: Adapted from the IMF

limited fiscal buffers have constrained governments' ability to absorb these shocks (Bocola & Lorenzoni, 2020). A growing number of African states either in or at high risk of debt distress, with debt service now crowding out essential social and infrastructure investments. For instance, in 2024, around 24 SSA countries recorded debt levels exceeding 55% of GDP, with Eritrea registering the highest at 212% (Fig. 13.2).

### 13.3.2 *Climate and Other Vulnerability*

Africa's debt sustainability is deeply affected by structural vulnerabilities. Climate shocks such as droughts in the Horn of Africa, cyclones in Mozambique, and flooding in West Africa destroy infrastructure, displace communities, and require costly reconstruction, adding fiscal pressure and increasing borrowing needs (Hove et al., 2025). Social inequality and weak human capital also undermine growth prospects: high unemployment, limited access to education, and fragile healthcare systems reduce productivity and constrain government revenue mobilisation (Cerf, 2023). Governance challenges including corruption, weak institutions, and low fiscal transparency further exacerbate debt risks by eroding investor confidence and enabling unsustainable borrowing practices.

While debt pressures are widespread across the continent, regional variations are notable. Resource-rich economies such as Angola and Nigeria face volatility tied to commodity price fluctuations (Ross & Werker, 2024), while low-income, fragile states such as Chad and Sudan remain dependent on concessional lending and vulnerable to conflict-related fiscal shocks (Hoeffler & Justino, 2024). Middle-income countries like Kenya and Egypt, with greater access to international bond markets, face rising exposure to commercial debt and foreign currency risk (UNCTAD, 2025a). Island states, including Mauritius and Seychelles, experience disproportionate climate-related risks due to reliance on tourism and vulnerability to extreme weather events (Doorga et al., 2023). Emerging patterns reveal a shift toward diversified creditors including China, Gulf states, and private bondholders, which complicates restructuring negotiations compared to the Paris Club dominated debt relief era.

### *13.3.3 Gaps in ESG Integration in Traditional Public Debt Management*

Despite the centrality of ESG risks to Africa's debt landscape, most public debt management frameworks on the continent remain narrowly focused on short-term financial indicators such as interest rates, maturities, and rollover risks. Several critical gaps can be identified:

1. **Overemphasis on financial metrics:** Traditional frameworks often concentrate on short-term fiscal indicators while neglecting the broader ESG risks that shape debt sustainability. For instance, Zambia's debt crisis highlights the limitations of traditional debt sustainability frameworks, which often focus too narrowly on fiscal indicators and overlook environmental and governance risks that weaken long-term repayment capacity (Were, 2024).
2. **Neglect of climate shocks:** Few debt strategies explicitly integrate climate-related risks, leaving countries vulnerable to natural disasters, resource depletion, and adaptation costs. For example, Madagascar's repeated exposure to cyclones and ongoing environmental degradation are risks that remain insufficiently captured in its debt sustainability frameworks (International Monetary Fund. African Dept., 2024).
3. **Political pressures:** Short-term political imperatives, such as election-related spending or prestige infrastructure projects, often override sustainable ESG-aligned borrowing strategies. For instance, Kenya borrowed over US$4.7 billion for the Chinese-financed Standard Gauge Railway before 2017 elections, prioritising prestige

**Box 13.1 Kenya Borrowed for Prestige Infrastructure Without Considering ESG**

In the run-up to the 2017 elections, Kenya accelerated borrowing for the Chinese-financed Standard Gauge Railway (SGR), one of the country's largest prestige infrastructure projects. The project cost over US$4.7 billion, mostly through external debt, despite concerns about commercial viability and weak returns. The political imperative to showcase rapid infrastructure delivery overshadowed considerations of fiscal sustainability and ESG alignment, including social displacement during land acquisition and environmental impact on Nairobi National Park and coastal ecosystems. This borrowing has contributed to Kenya's current high risk of debt distress, limiting fiscal space for climate adaptation, health, and social spending.

Source: Carrai (2021) and Shilaho (2021).

over fiscal and ESG concerns. The debt worsened distress risks, constraining spending on climate, health, and social needs (Box 13.1).

4. **Reactive rather than proactive management:** Traditional debt practices remain crisis-driven, leaving African economies poorly prepared to anticipate and withstand future ESG-related shocks. A practical example is how Mozambique resolve Cyclones Idai and Kenneth (Box 13.2).

In Sudan, debt strategy has been predominantly crisis-driven, with external borrowing used mainly to cover fiscal emergencies arising from conflict, humanitarian crises, and economic collapse (Box 13.3).

## 13.4 Innovative ESG Tools and ESG-Driven Debt Management Strategies

### *13.4.1 Innovative ESG Tools for Public Debt*

1. **Green, Social, and Sustainability-Linked Bonds**
   One of the most visible innovations in sovereign debt markets is the emergence of green, social, and sustainability-linked bonds (Volz, 2023). These instruments allow governments to raise funds for

**Box 13.2 Mozambique Allocates Funds to Address Crisis**

Following Cyclone Idai in 2019, Mozambique experienced acute economic and fiscal pressures, leading it to seek emergency financing from the IMF's Rapid Credit Facility to address budgetary and external shortfalls. The cyclone caused extensive damage, particularly to agriculture, which disrupted output and slowed growth. Reconstruction demands, combined with election-related spending, further strained fiscal stability. Successive shocks from Cyclones Idai and Kenneth deepened these challenges and delayed recovery. In response, international partners expanded emergency assistance, with the World Bank mobilising about US$700 million for affected countries, of which approximately US$350 million went to Mozambique, to rebuild infrastructure, restore livelihoods, sustain essential services, and safeguard macroeconomic stability in a highly fragile post-disaster environment.

Source: https://www.unocha.org/publications/report/mozambique/2018-2019-mozambique-humanitarian-response-plan-revised-following-cyclones-idai Accessed September 27, 2025.

**Box 13.3 Reactive Borrowing Amid Climate and Governance Fragility**

Sudan's debt strategy has been largely crisis-driven, relying on external borrowing to address fiscal emergencies linked to conflict, humanitarian crises, and economic collapse. Environmental vulnerabilities such as floods, droughts, and desertification further strain infrastructure, agriculture, and communities, yet climate adaptation remains absent from debt frameworks. Prolonged conflict and political instability have weakened institutions, limiting investment in health, education, and poverty reduction, while emergency borrowing crowds out social spending. Weak governance and opaque debt contracts undermine monitoring and transparency. Lacking ESG integration, Sudan faces persistent external debt distress, constrained access to concessional financing, and little resilience against recurrent shocks.

Source: UNCTAD (2025b).

projects that deliver environmental and social benefits while signaling responsible fiscal behaviour to investors. African countries such as Nigeria, Egypt, and Morocco have pioneered green bond issuances to finance renewable energy, clean transportation, and climate adaptation projects (CABRI, 2021). Social bonds, often tied to healthcare, education, or gender equity initiatives, are gaining momentum as a means of linking public borrowing directly to inclusive development outcomes. Sustainability-linked bonds, which tie interest rates to the achievement of measurable ESG targets, offer an additional layer of accountability. These instruments not only diversify financing sources, but also strengthen the credibility of the issuing countries with international investors seeking impact-driven assets.

2. **ESG Risk Assessment Frameworks for Sovereign Debt**
   Integrating ESG into debt management requires robust risk assessment frameworks that capture non-traditional fiscal risks (Abbood et al., 2025). Traditional debt sustainability analyses often overlook the long-term impacts of environmental shocks, social instability, or governance weaknesses. New frameworks are emerging to address this gap, including climate-adjusted debt sustainability models and ESG scoring systems developed by rating agencies and multilateral lenders (Macesar, 2025). Embedding ESG risk indicators such as climate vulnerability indices, social inclusion metrics and governance performance benchmarks into debt analysis enables policymakers to better anticipate fiscal pressures and adjust borrowing strategies accordingly. This approach enhances resilience and provides investors with greater confidence in the country's ability to manage long-term risks.
3. **Digital and Data-Driven Tools**
   Advances in digital technologies are reshaping the possibilities for transparent and efficient ESG integration in sovereign debt management. Blockchain platforms are being explored to track the use of proceeds from green or social bonds, ensuring that funds are directed to intended projects and reducing risks of misallocation or corruption (Chen & Volz, 2022). Artificial intelligence and big data analytics are enabling governments to model ESG risks more accurately, forecast debt sustainability under different climate or social

scenarios, and improve real-time monitoring of fiscal exposures (Mayegun & Chinonso Nwanevu, 2025). For African countries, where data gaps have long hindered effective debt management, these technologies represent an opportunity to leapfrog traditional systems and establish more credible, transparent reporting practices that meet investor expectations.

4. **Integrating Climate Stress Tests and Social Impact Analysis**
   Beyond financial metrics, innovative tools now include climate stress tests and social impact assessments as part of sovereign debt planning. Climate stress tests evaluate how extreme weather events, resource scarcity, or carbon transition risks could affect government revenues, expenditures, and debt repayment capacity (Acharya et al., 2023). Social impact analysis, meanwhile, examines how borrowing decisions affect inequality, employment, and access to essential services. Integrating these tools into debt strategy allows governments to identify vulnerabilities early and align borrowing with sustainable development objectives. For instance, linking borrowing to investments in climate-resilient infrastructure or health systems can reduce future fiscal shocks while promoting long-term social and economic stability.

### *13.4.2 ESG-Driven Debt Management Strategies*

1. **ESG Integration in Debt and Investment**
   Integrating ESG principles into borrowing strategies requires a shift from viewing debt purely as a financing mechanism to treating it as a tool for sustainable development. This involves embedding ESG considerations at each stage of debt management, from the design of borrowing strategies to the issuance of instruments and communication with investors (Lindner & Chung, 2023). Governments can, for example, link sovereign bond issuances to specific environmental or social outcomes, such as financing renewable energy projects, improving healthcare access, or promoting gender equity. Investor relations also play a critical role: proactive communication about ESG commitments and transparent reporting on the use of proceeds help strengthen credibility and attract a broader pool of

sustainable investors. By positioning debt issuance within a responsible borrowing framework, African governments can simultaneously improve financing terms and enhance their reputational standing in global capital markets.

2. **Sustainable Fiscal Policy and Debt Alignment**
   To be truly transformative, ESG-driven debt management should be aligned with broader national development agendas, particularly the SDGs (Del Sarto, 2025b). Fiscal policy and debt portfolio decisions should be guided by long-term priorities such as poverty reduction, education, healthcare, infrastructure development, and climate action. For instance, governments can design borrowing programmes that directly fund SDG-related projects or use sustainability-linked bonds tied to SDG performance indicators. Aligning debt with the SDGs not only ensures that borrowing contributes to inclusive and sustainable growth but also strengthens the case for concessional financing, blended finance, and other innovative instruments supported by multilateral institutions and impact-driven investors. This approach positions debt as a catalyst for development rather than a burden.
3. **Resilience to Climate, Social, Governance Risks**
   ESG-driven strategies also enhance resilience by reducing vulnerability to external shocks and internal instability. Climate shocks such as floods, droughts, and cyclones pose a growing threat to fiscal stability in many African countries. Incorporating climate risk assessments and adaptation measures into debt management helps governments plan borrowing around resilience-building projects, such as climate-smart agriculture or disaster-resistant infrastructure. Similarly, integrating social risk considerations ensures that borrowing supports employment generation, health services, and education systems, reducing the likelihood of unrest linked to inequality or exclusion. Strengthened governance mechanisms such as transparent procurement processes, independent audits, and citizen participation further safeguard debt management from misallocation and corruption.

## 13.5 Lessons from Other Continents and Implication for African Countries

This section discusses key cases from other continents and shows how it will be relevant for Africa.

### 13.5.1 Case Studies from Other Continents

*Case Study 1: Chile's Sovereign Green and Sustainability Bonds*
Chile provides one of the most advanced examples of integrating ESG principles into sovereign debt management through its Sustainable Bond Framework. The Ministry of Finance first issued a Green Bond Framework in 2019, which was later expanded into a Sustainable Bond Framework in 2020, enabling the issuance of green, social, and sustainability bonds. This framework aligns with international best practices, notably the ICMA Green Bond Principles, Social Bond Principles, and Sustainability Bond Guidelines, thereby enhancing credibility with global investors. Chile's first green bond was issued in June 2019, denominated in U.S. dollars, with exceptionally strong demand as investor bids totalled US$6.7 billion compared to the US$1.42 billion offered and achieved the lowest yield in Chile's history for that maturity, proving the financial advantages of ESG linked instruments. By early 2022, Chile had issued approximately US$31 billion in thematic bonds, representing about 28.3% of total central government debt. The country also launched a Sustainability Linked Bond (SLB) Framework in February 2022, linking coupon payments to sustainability targets, further embedding ESG commitments into fiscal policy. Support from the Inter-American Development Bank (IDB) helped design frameworks, identify eligible expenditures, and secure external reviews from entities such as Vigeo Eiris and the Climate Bonds Initiative. These innovations served debt management goals by diversifying Chile's investor base through ESG focused funds, lowering funding costs via yield advantages, optimizing maturity profiles through liability management, strengthening credibility on climate and governance risks, improving transparency through

mandatory reporting, and directly aligning debt servicing with national ESG objectives.

Source: IDA (2019) and Ministerio de Hacienda (2020, 2022).

*Case Study 2: France's Green Obligations Assimilables du Trésor*
France's experience with Green Obligations Assimilables du Trésor (OATs) illustrates how ESG instruments can be integrated into sovereign debt management while advancing environmental policy objectives. The first Green OAT, issued in 2017, attracted around 200 investors, including banks, pension funds, insurers, and ESG-focused asset managers, thereby diversifying the investor base and strengthening international demand. Issued as a benchmark bond with a long maturity of 22 years, the instrument was integrated into the OAT curve, managed like conventional OATs, and reopened through tap issues to maintain liquidity and market depth. The inaugural issuance was heavily oversubscribed, with bids of approximately €23 billion for €7 billion offered, underscoring strong investor appetite and favourable borrowing conditions. Proceeds are allocated to eligible green categories such as climate mitigation, biodiversity protection, and pollution control, explicitly aligning debt issuance with France's environmental and climate policies. Transparency is ensured through annual allocation and impact reporting, supported by an independent Green OAT Evaluation Council, which enhances credibility, reduces information asymmetries, and builds reputational capital. The introduction of inflation-linked Green OATs in 2022 further diversified the portfolio and provided protection against inflation risks. Collectively, Green OATs help France expand its investor base, optimise its maturity profile, reduce refinancing risks, and embed sustainability into public debt management.

Source: Agene France Trésor (2017) and Malecki (2021).

*Case Study 3: Canada's ESG Integration in Debt Strategy*
The Government of Canada's Debt Management Strategy (2025–26) outlines borrowing objectives, including the role of its Green Bond Programme. Guided by the Canada Green Bond Framework, which is aligned with ICMA's Green Bond Principles, the Programme defines eligible green expenditures, ensures proper management of proceeds, and mandates transparency through annual allocation and impact reports. Canada issued its inaugural green bond in March 2022, a $5 billion transaction, followed by additional issuances that brought the total

outstanding to around US$13 billion by 2023–24. In 2024, a reopening of a 10-year green bond added $2 billion more, reflecting strong investor demand. These issuances diversify the funding base by attracting ESG-focused investors, many of whom are distinct from conventional buyers of government bonds. They also provide benchmarks for green finance in domestic markets, helping deepen liquidity and support ESG standards. Annual reports, coupled with independent external reviews such as those by Sustainalytics, enhance transparency, credibility, and investor confidence, thereby reducing information asymmetries. Importantly, proceeds are integrated into the Consolidated Revenue Fund and linked to Canada's climate policy priorities, ensuring debt issuance supports decarbonisation, biodiversity protection, and clean growth, while remaining embedded in the broader cost- and risk-management framework of sovereign debt.

Source: Audet et al. (2025) and Department of Finance Canada (2024).

*Case Study 4: Indonesia's Green Sukuk*

Indonesia's 2018 sovereign green sukuk issuance of US$1.25 billion marked a pioneering step in aligning debt management with sustainability goals while diversifying its financing strategy. Structured under a Green Bond and Sukuk Framework, reviewed by CICERO, the issuance combined Shariah compliance with ESG objectives, creating a dual appeal to Islamic finance investors and environmentally focused funds. Approximately 29% of subscribers were "green investors," illustrating the ability to tap new investor segments and broaden the funding base. Investors appetite were strong, with the green sukuk oversubscribed 2.35 times, enabling Indonesia to secure more favourable pricing and reduce funding costs relative to initial guidance. Beyond financing, the sukuk established Indonesia as a benchmark issuer of thematic debt in emerging markets, building a track record for future ESG instruments. Proceeds were directed toward renewable energy, energy efficiency, and climate-resilient infrastructure, aligning borrowing with national emission reduction and renewable energy commitments. Transparent reporting requirements and independent reviews enhanced investor confidence, reducing information asymmetry and risk premiums. Additionally, issuance in U.S. dollars diversified the debt portfolio, smoothed the maturity profile, and provided instruments well-suited to market demand. Over time, Indonesia has institutionalised green sukuk as a regular issuance tool, reinforcing credibility while integrating sustainability into debt management.

Source: UNDP (2018) and Fitrah and Soemitra (2022).

### *13.5.2 Implications for African Countries*

1. **Broadening Investor Base and Lowering Costs**
   Chile and Indonesia provide useful lessons on how sovereigns can broaden their investor base through innovative financing. Chile successfully attracted ESG focused funds, while Indonesia appealed to both Shariah compliant and green investors, with both cases resulting in oversubscription and lower borrowing costs. African countries such as Nigeria and Senegal, which already issue sukuk (Hassan et al., 2022), could adopt Indonesia's green sukuk model to reach Islamic finance markets, while also drawing interest from ESG investors. At the same time, countries like Djibouti, Kenya, and Zambia, which have become vulnerable to debt pressures due to heavy reliance on loans from Chinese creditors (Knowledge at Wharton, 2019), could benefit from expanding and diversifying their investor base. Reducing reliance on a limited group of lenders, especially China, while incorporating ESG principles into debt management would enable these countries to enhance their financial resilience. Such an approach would not only reduce overreliance on traditional Eurobond markets but could also help achieve lower borrowing costs through robust and diversified demand from both ESG and Shariah compliant investors.
2. **Benchmarking and Market Development**
   The Green OAT was incorporated into the sovereign yield curve, reopened through tap issues, and served as a benchmark for ESG debt. Countries such as Kenya and Morocco, which are developing green finance ecosystems (Lwesya, 2025), can issue sovereign green bonds to establish pricing references for domestic corporate and municipal green bonds. This approach would strengthen local capital markets and encourage greater flows of sustainable private investment.
3. **Liability Management and Portfolio Diversification**
   Proceeds from Chile's ESG bonds were partly used for liability management through repurchasing shorter-term debt to smooth maturity profiles. Indonesia also diversified currency and maturity risk through US$ denominated sukuk. Countries such as Egypt and Côte d'Ivoire, with large refinancing needs, could strategically use ESG bond proceeds to refinance expensive short-term obligations,

extend maturities, and stabilise their debt portfolios while signaling commitment to sustainability.

4. **Enhancing Transparency, Credibility, and Governance**
   Chile and France both require annual allocation and impact reporting, supported by independent evaluation councils or external reviewers, which strengthens credibility and reduces risk premiums. Gabon's 2021 sustainability linked bond already tied debt costs to conservation targets in the forestry sector.[2] Replicating Chile's mandatory reporting and France's independent evaluation councils across African sovereign issuers could improve transparency, enhance investor trust, and reduce perceived governance risks, which are often a key challenge in African debt markets.
5. **Embedding ESG in Fiscal Policy and Debt Strategy**
   Green bonds are integrated into the broader Debt Management Strategy, with proceeds linked to climate policy priorities while remaining within fiscal risk management frameworks. South Africa and Kenya, despite existing debt pressures, can design green bond frameworks that channel proceeds into nationally determined contributions (NDCs) projects such as renewable energy, water resilience, and biodiversity protection, ensuring that borrowing directly supports long term development and climate goals.

## 13.6 Conclusion

ESG principles, though originally designed for corporate and investment decision-making, have become increasingly important in sovereign debt management. This chapter examines how Africa can integrate ESG considerations into its debt strategies. It begins by outlining the relevance of ESG in public finance, highlighting its potential to strengthen debt sustainability, attract responsible investors, and support long-term fiscal planning. The chapter also reviews Africa's debt landscape, noting that several countries face debt distress, often exacerbated by climate shocks and structural vulnerabilities. Challenges in embedding ESG into traditional debt management include overreliance on financial metrics, limited attention to climate and social risks, political pressures, and reactive rather than forward-looking approaches. To address these issues, the chapter evaluates innovative tools such as green, social, and

[2] https://unfccc.int/sites/default/files/resource/tar2021_GAB.pdf

sustainability-linked bonds, ESG risk assessment frameworks, digital and data-driven monitoring systems, and the integration of climate stress tests and social impact analysis. Broader strategies identified include aligning debt and investment decisions with sustainability goals, adopting resilient fiscal policies, and managing exposure to climate, social, and governance risks. Drawing lessons from successful experiences in other regions, the chapter shows that African countries could achieve similar outcomes through broadening their investor base, lowering borrowing costs, strengthening benchmarks and market development, diversifying debt portfolios, enhancing transparency, and embedding ESG into fiscal and debt policy frameworks.

African countries can strengthen debt management by embedding ESG principles into their borrowing strategies through several practical steps. First, governments should design national ESG debt frameworks aligned with international standards to enhance credibility, attract responsible investors, and ensure proceeds finance priority projects. Issuing instruments such as green, social, sustainability-linked bonds, or green sukuk would broaden the investor base by appealing to both ESG-focused and Islamic finance markets, reducing dependence on Eurobonds and bilateral loans while lowering borrowing costs. Transparency and accountability should be reinforced through mandatory allocation and impact reporting, supported by independent evaluation councils or external reviewers. Debt management offices also need to integrate climate stress tests, social impact assessments, and ESG risk indicators into borrowing decisions to better anticipate vulnerabilities and minimise refinancing risks. Proceeds from ESG bonds can be strategically applied to liability management, refinancing expensive short-term obligations, smoothing maturity profiles, and diversifying portfolios. Regional collaboration, for example through the African Union or African Development Bank, can help establish shared ESG taxonomies, pool expertise, and create benchmarks that deepen local capital markets. Crucially, all ESG debt issuance should be tied to national policy priorities such as NDCs, renewable energy, water resilience, and biodiversity protection, embedding sustainability into fiscal and debt strategies.

## References

Abbood, F. G., Jasim, B. F., & Dakhil, M. S. (2025). Analysing the role of non-traditional financial disclosures in enhancing corporate sustainability of high-risk sectors in Iraq. *Asian Journal of Economics, Finance and Management, 7*(1), 297–312. https://doi.org/10.56557/ajefm/2025/v7i1274

Acharya, V. V., Berner, R., Engle, R., Jung, H., Stroebel, J., Zeng, X., & Zhao, Y. (2023). Climate stress testing. *Annual Review of Financial Economics, 15*(1), 291–326. https://doi.org/10.1146/annurev-financial-110921-101555

Agene France Trésor. (2017, January 24). *24 January 2017: Launch of the green OAT 1.75% 25 June 2039.* https://www.aft.gouv.fr/en/publications/communiques-presse/24-january-2017-launching-green-oats

Arnone, M., & Presbitero, A. F. (2016). *Debt relief initiatives: Policy design and outcomes.* Routledge. https://doi.org/10.4324/9781315576060

Audet, N., Epp, A., Ning, J., & Gao, J. (2025). *The dynamic Canadian debt strategy model* (127; Technical Report/Rapport Technique). https://www.banqueducanada.ca/wp-content/uploads/2025/08/tr127.pdf

Barrage, L. (2025). Climate change impacts on public finances around the world. *Annual Review of Resource Economics.* https://doi.org/10.1146/annurev-resource-011624-035902

Bocola, L., & Lorenzoni, G. (2020). Financial crises, dollarization, and lending of last resort in open economies. *American Economic Review, 110*(8), 2524–2557. https://doi.org/10.1257/aer.20180830

Brownbridge, M., & Canagarajah, S. (2024). *Climate change vulnerability, adaptation and public debt sustainability in small island developing states* (10787; Policy Research Working Paper).

Byrne, D. (n.d.). *What is the history of ESG?* Corporate Governance Institute. Retrieved September 27, 2025, from https://www.thecorporategovernanceinstitute.com/insights/lexicon/what-is-the-history-of-esg/

CABRI. (2021). *Exploring environmental, social and governance (ESG) and sustainable finance solutions for African sovereigns.* https://www.cabri-sbo.org/uploads/files/Documents/Raising-and-managing-debt_ENGLISH_Final.pdf

Carrai, M. A. (2021). Adaptive governance along Chinese-financed BRI railroad megaprojects in East Africa. *World Development, 141*, 105388. https://doi.org/10.1016/j.worlddev.2020.105388

Carter, P., & Ayres, S. (2024). *Investing for impact in African private equity funds: Practical thinking on investing for development.*

Cerf, M. E. (2023). The social-education-economy-health nexus, development and sustainability: Perspectives from low- and middle-income and African countries. *Discover Sustainability, 4*(1), 37. https://doi.org/10.1007/s43621-023-00153-7

Chen, Y., & Volz, U. (2022). Scaling up sustainable investment through blockchain-based project bonds. *Development Policy Review, 40*(3). https://doi.org/10.1111/dpr.12582

Commodore, R., & Awuah, G. B. (2024, November 19). *The changing nature of debt in Africa*. Insight & Ideas. https://acetforafrica.org/research-and-analysis/insights-ideas/the-changing-nature-of-debt-in-africa/

Del Sarto, N. (2025a). *ESG Factors and financial outcomes in banks*. Springer Nature. https://doi.org/10.1007/978-3-031-87748-3

Del Sarto, N. (2025b). The European regulatory framework: Policies and regulations for sustainable finance. In *ESG Factors and financial outcomes in banks* (pp. 61–94). Springer Nature. https://doi.org/10.1007/978-3-031-87748-3_2

Department of Finance Canada. (2024, October 10). *Canada successfully re-opens 10-year green bond to raise an additional $2 billion*. https://www.canada.ca/en/department-finance/news/2024/10/canada-successfully-re-opens-10-year-green-bond-to-raise-an-additional-2-billion.html

Doorga, J. R. S., Pasnin, O., Dindoyal, Y., & Diaz, C. (2023). Risk assessment of coral reef vulnerability to climate change and stressors in tropical islands: The case of Mauritius. *Science of the Total Environment, 891*, 164648. https://doi.org/10.1016/j.scitotenv.2023.164648

Elmahdi, A., & Jeong, J. (2024). From debt to sustainability: Advancing wastewater projects in developing countries through innovative financing mechanisms—The role of debt-for-climate swaps. *Climate, 12*(8), 122. https://doi.org/10.3390/cli12080122

Fitrah, R., & Soemitra, A. (2022). Green Sukuk for sustainable development goals in Indonesia: A literature study. *Jurnal Ilmiah Ekonomi Islam, 8*(1), 231. https://doi.org/10.29040/jiei.v8i1.4591

Hassan, M. K., Muneeza, A., & Sonko, K. N. M. (2022). Islamic finance in Africa. In *The potential of cash waqf for poverty alleviation in Somalia* (pp. 2–13). Edward Elgar Publishing. https://doi.org/10.4337/9781802209907.00011

Hoeffler, A., & Justino, P. (2024). Aid and fragile states. In *Handbook of aid and development* (pp. 225–246). Edward Elgar Publishing. https://doi.org/10.4337/9781800886810.00020

Hove, S., Balma, L., & Simpasa, A. (2025). *Climate change risks and coping strategies in Mozambique: The role of climate-resilient infrastructure* (387; Working Paper Series).

IDA. (2019, May 31). *The IDB supports Chile in a sovereign green bond development*. https://www.iadb.org/en/news/idb-supports-chile-sovereign-green-bond-development

International Monetary Fund. African Dept. (2024). Republic of Madagascar: Request for an arrangement under the extended credit facility and cancellation of the current arrangement under the extended credit facility and request for an arrangement under the resilience and sustainability facility. *IMF Country Report*.

Knowledge at Wharton. (2019, September 19). *Chinese investments in Africa: Four anti-corruption trends to watch*. Knowledge at Wharton. https://knowledge.wharton.upenn.edu/article/chinese-investments-africa-four-anti-corruption-trends-watch/

Kuwonu, F. (2025, July 7). *Africa's debt dilemma: Turning crisis into reform: AU leaders push for reforms to fix global debt systems and strengthen fiscal sovereignty*. United Nations Africa Renewal. https://africarenewal.un.org/en/magazine/africas-debt-dilemma-turning-crisis-reform

Leung, C. K., Ko, J., & Chen, X. (2025). Economic crises and the erosion of sustainability: A global analysis of ESG performance in 100 countries (1990–2019). *Innovation and Green Development, 4*(2), 100226. https://doi.org/10.1016/j.igd.2025.100226

Lindner, P., & Chung, K. (2023). Sovereign ESG bond issuance: A guidance note for sovereign debt managers. *IMF Working Papers, 2023*(058), 1. https://doi.org/10.5089/9798400235047.001

Lwesya, F. (2025). Green finance in Africa: Mapping progress, challenges and prospects. *Future Business Journal, 11*(1), 195. https://doi.org/10.1186/s43093-025-00596-6

Macesar, A. F. (2025, April 26). *Sustainability: A brief history of ESG*. Akepa. https://thesustainableagency.com/blog/the-history-of-esg/

Makin, A. J., & Layton, A. (2021). The global fiscal response to COVID-19: Risks and repercussions. *Economic Analysis and Policy, 69*, 340–349. https://doi.org/10.1016/j.eap.2020.12.016

Malecki, C. (2021). *Corporate social responsibility in France* (S. O. Idowu (ed.); pp. 121–147). Springer. https://doi.org/10.1007/978-3-030-68386-3_7

Mayegun, K. O., & Chinonso Nwanevu. (2025). Harnessing big data and AI to revolutionize sustainability accounting and integrated corporate financial reporting. *International Journal of Computer Applications Technology and Research*. https://doi.org/10.7753/IJCATR1406.1008

Ministerio de Hacienda. (2020). *Sustainable bonds*. https://www.hacienda.cl/english/work-areas/international-finance/public-debt-office/esg-bonds/sustainability-linked-bonds

Ministerio de Hacienda. (2022, February 22). *Ministry of Finance publishes its sustainability-linked bond framework*. https://hacienda.cl/english/news-and-events/news/ministry-of-finance-publishes-its-sustainability-linked-bond-framework

Oyugi, E. C. A. (2025). Integration of ESG—Environmental, social, and governance policies in Africa. In G. Onyango & I. Jamil (Eds.), *Routledge handbook of public policy in the global south* (1st ed.). Routledge.

Ross, M. L., & Werker, E. (2024). Diversification in resource-rich Africa, 1999–2019. *Resources Policy, 88*, 104437. https://doi.org/10.1016/j.resourpol.2023.104437

Ruckert, A., & Labonté, R. (2017). Health inequities in the age of austerity: The need for social protection policies. *Social Science & Medicine, 187*, 306–311. https://doi.org/10.1016/j.socscimed.2017.03.029

Selassie, A. A. (2018, May 23). *The debt challenge to African growth.* World Bank Blog. https://www.imf.org/en/Blogs/Articles/2018/05/23/vc052318-the-debt-challenge-to-african-growth

Shilaho, W. K. (2021). Brics–Africa cooperation in perspective: The case of Kenya. In D. Monyae & B. Ndzendze (Eds.), *The BRICS order: Assertive or complementing the west?* (pp. 165–202). Springer International Publishing. https://doi.org/10.1007/978-3-030-62765-2

Šlaus, I., & Jacobs, G. (2011). Human capital and sustainability. *Sustainability, 3*(1), 97–154. https://doi.org/10.3390/su3010097

Sonko, K. N., & Sonko, M. (2023). *Demystifying environmental, social and governance (ESG).* Springer International Publishing. https://doi.org/10.1007/978-3-031-35867-8

UNCTAD. (2025a). *A world of debt: It is time for reform.* https://unctad.org/publication/world-of-debt

UNCTAD. (2025b, February 10). *Africa's vulnerability to global shocks highlights need for stronger regional trade.* UNCTAD. https://unctad.org/news/africas-vulnerability-global-shocks-highlights-need-stronger-regional-trade

UNDP. (2018, April 3). *Indonesia tackles climate change through the issuance of Green Sukuk (Islamic Bond) Issuance.* https://www.undp.org/indonesia/press-releases/indonesia-tackles-climate-change-through-issuance-green-sukuk-islamic-bond-issuance

UNDP. (2019, May 30). *Mozambique Cyclone Idai Post-Disaster Needs Assessment (PDNA)DNA.* UNDP. https://www.undp.org/publications/mozambique-cyclone-idai-post-disaster-needs-assessment-pdnadna

Vezér, M., Ferreira, R., Dobre, R., Grant, J., Huurdeman, T., & Kong, C. H. (2021). *10 for 2021: Investing in the circular food economy.*

Volz, U. (2023). On the Potential of Sovereign State-Contingent Debt in Contributing to Better Public Debt Management and Enhancing Sustainability Outcomes. *Journal of Globalization and Development, 13*(2), 379–409. https://doi.org/10.1515/jgd-2021-0071

Were, M. (2024). *Emerging public debt challenges in sub Saharan Africa* (2024/36; WIDER Working Paper). https://www.wider.unu.edu/sites/default/files/Publications/Working-paper/PDF/wp2024-36-emerging-public-debt-challenges-sub-Saharan-Africa.pdf

PART IV

# Risks, Volatility, and Debt Sustainability

CHAPTER 14

# Debt Overhang and Private Investment in Sub-Saharan Africa: Crowding Out or Complementarity?

*Emmanuel Issifu Fuseini*

## 14.1 Introduction

The importance of the private sector in an economy can never be underestimated, as it is regarded as the engine of growth and development prospects. However, the potential of this sector depends on the prevailing macroeconomic and fiscal policies in the country, particularly government borrowings. Yet, several global crises, such as the 2008 financial crisis, the Covid-19 pandemic, and the recent Russian-Ukrainian war, have prompted governments, especially in low- to middle-income countries, to increase their debt levels to improve growth and development prospects (International Monetary Fund, 2025b; World Bank, 2025b).

This has resulted in a rise in global sovereign debt, with recent forecasts indicating it will surpass \$100 trillion from 2024, representing roughly 93% of Gross Domestic Product (GDP), and projections suggest it could

E. I. Fuseini (✉)
Department of Finance, School of Business, University for Development Studies, Tamale, Ghana



I. N. Yakubu (ed.), *Public Debt and Economic Resilience in Africa*, Palgrave Studies in African and Development Economics,
https://doi.org/10.1007/978-3-032-25835-9_14

reach 100% by 2030 (International Monetary Fund, 2024, 2025a). Amid this increase in debt, recent policy reports suggest that developing economies are struggling with debt sustainability due to higher debt servicing costs and declining net inflows, even as they pursue infrastructural development projects (International Monetary Fund, 2025a).

Theoretically, linking debt to growth assumes that prudent use of government-borrowed funds for developmental projects can improve infrastructure. However, empirical studies show mixed results, raising questions about the benefits of debt-financed public infrastructure investments. Some insights indicate that governments, particularly in developing countries, can borrow continuously to boost liquidity and economic activity for consumption and investment (see Frimpong et al., 2024; Ogaga, 2025; Sala & Trivin, 2024). This points to government borrowing as a tool to address liquidity shocks and stimulate economic activities.

Furthermore, government borrowings are a vital channel for funding investment projects aimed at enhancing a country's productive capacity through improvements in private capital and labour (Islam & Nguyen, 2024). These financial measures tend to positively influence private sector investment and consumption, and this insight is supported by empirical studies like Frimpong et al. (2024), Ogaga (2025), and Sala and Trivin (2024). For example, Frimpong et al. (2024) argue that external debt supports infrastructure development in Ghana both in the short and long term.

Conversely, some empirical evidence suggests that at higher levels, government debt constrains investment opportunities (review Islam & Nguyen, 2024; Khan et al., 2025; Ojeka et al., 2024). For example, Ojeka et al. (2024) posit that higher public debt levels impair private sector investment. This aligns with the concept of debt overhang, which posits that once public debt exceeds a certain critical level, growth and development prospects are hindered, particularly in the private sector (Cordella et al., 2010; Islam & Nguyen, 2024; Reinhart et al., 2012).

These conflicting empirical understandings linking debt to growth outcomes raise concerns about the prudent and effective utilisation of public debt. The rationale for this adverse effect of public debt could be that increasing government borrowing might create a perception of high default risk, leading to rising real lending rates over time (Reinhart et al., 2012). Additionally, as Boskin (2020) suggests, a growing debt stock can trigger weak currencies, higher inflation, capital flight, and a monetised economy, increasing the likelihood of long-term financial and economic crises.

These phenomena are often described as the "crowding out" effect of excessive government borrowing (see Friedman, 1978; Islam & Nguyen, 2024), which correlates with the debt overhang concept (see Doruk & Gohore, 2025; Reinhart & Rogoff, 2010). Therefore, these conflicting perspectives on the impact of excessive government borrowing beyond a certain threshold—debt overhang—highlight an important area for further scholarly debate, especially regarding the specific effects of government borrowings exceeding policy thresholds and benchmarks (International Monetary Fund, 2025c; World Bank, 2025a).

Based on this debt overhang concept, seminal works such as Pattillo and Ricci (2011) and Reinhart et al. (2012) have identified various thresholds beyond which the debt-to-GDP ratio hampers growth. From a policy standpoint, the IMF and World Bank have jointly established thresholds and benchmarks indicating when government borrowings relative to GDP pose sustainability risks (International Monetary Fund, 2025c; World Bank, 2025c). Recognising the debt overhang theory, these institutions developed a debt sustainability framework in 2005, aimed especially at low-income countries, to maintain sustainable public debt levels. For example, these international bodies suggest that government borrowings exceeding 70% of the debt-to-GDP ratio constitute a high or significant risk to sustainability. This implies that beyond this threshold (70%), debt overhang may begin to crowd out private investment (International Monetary Fund, 2025c; World Bank, 2025c).

However, the empirical evidence is scant on how public debt stock beyond this threshold shapes private sector infrastructural development across low-to middle-income countries. Consequently, this study adopts this threshold to create an index of debt overhang and investigates its empirical influence—whether it results in "complements" or "crowding out"—on private sector investment within the SSA context. This subregion encompasses many low- and middle-income countries heavily reliant on debt-funded projects (International Monetary Fund, 2024, 2025b).

Therefore, the research question motivating this study is: does debt overhang across SSA complement or crowd out private sector investment? In this context, this study employed the IV-GMM technique, as extended by Kripfganz (2019), as its empirical strategy across a panel of SSA countries. The IV-GMM technique is highly recognised for its robustness in addressing critical regression issues such as endogeneity and heterogeneity in panel studies (Kripfganz, 2019).

Private sector infrastructural investment in this study is indicated by the World Bank measure of capital formation in the private sector. Debt overhang in this study is also estimated by creating an index of all government borrowings (comprising total debt stock plus debt servicing costs) exceeding 70% of debt-to-GDP (a threshold supported by the IMF-World Bank debt sustainability framework). This approach to measuring debt overhang is unique and robustly strengthens the literature. We argue that this method of defining debt overhang and its precise impact on investment Opportunities will reveal and reinforce valuable empirical facts to guide low- and middle-income countries, particularly in SSA, in their debt sustainability strategies and efforts to strengthen the private sector's role in national growth and development.

This study offers important contributions to policy, practice, and theoretical understanding. From a policy and practical perspective, the insights from this study's findings will support and reinforce existing strategies aimed at improving the government debt-private investment nexus, especially for SSA economies. This shifts the argument from debt sustainability analysis and reinforces its spillover empirical effects.

Furthermore, this study provides empirical evidence on how the government borrowings-to-GDP ratio exceeding the benchmark of 70% influences infrastructural investment in the private sector across SSA. Theoretically, by testing the concept of debt overhang at a threshold of 70%, the empirical evidence will either support or challenge the argument that debt overhang crowds out private investment, potentially warranting theoretical refinement.

Specifically, the contribution from the IV-GMM approach indicates that debt overhang at a threshold of 70% across the SSA crowd in private sector infrastructural investment, thereby refuting the concept of debt overhang. However, at this threshold, public sector infrastructural investment is dampened, which aligns with the concept of debt overhang. Moreover, without considering debt overhang at the 70% threshold, sensitivity analysis suggests that public debt as a percentage of GDP crowds in domestic infrastructural development (which includes both private and public capital formation).

The remaining sections of this study are organised as follows: Sect. 14.2 Literature review, Sect. 14.3 Methodology, Sect. 14.4 Findings, Sect. 14.5 Conclusion.

## 14.2 Literature Review

This section presents the theoretical and empirical perspectives connecting debt and development outcomes.

### *14.2.1 Theoretical Perspective*

This subsection focuses on the concepts related to debt overhang, threshold effects, and investment.

*Debt Overhang, Threshold Effect and Infrastructural Development Nexus*

The idea of debt overhang in growth and development is rooted in the seminal works of Myers (1997), at the micro-level, and Krugman (1988) and Sachs (1989), at the macro-level. The debt overhang hypothesis suggests that higher levels of debt can limit new investment returns by disproportionately benefiting lenders rather than borrowers (Krugman, 1988; Myers, 1997; Sachs, 1989).

Consequently, there is a demotivation to pursue prospective infrastructural development projects, even when these projects offer significant social and economic benefits. Specifically, at the firm or micro-level, Myers (1997) argues that higher levels of debt stock (debt overhang) lead to low infrastructural investment because shareholders lack motivation to undertake debt-financed projects. This is due to the perception that shareholders only gain residuals from debt after subtracting borrowing costs, while lenders or investors benefit mainly from marginal returns.

At the macro-level, Krugman (1988) and Sachs (1989) contend that economies with high sovereign debt stocks and increased risk to debt sustainability are less likely to invest further in growth and development projects if the returns are primarily used to service debt, as the projected net present value for the borrower becomes very small. These theoretical perspectives, rooted in the works of Myers (1997), Krugman (1988), and Sachs (1989), imply that beyond certain levels (threshold) of debt, development prospects such as infrastructural development through capital formation are hindered, reflecting the concept of debt overhang. Capital formation here refers to the process of accumulating physical capital assets through various channels.

The concept of debt overhang (rooted in seminal works like Aguiar et al., 2009; Cordella et al., 2010) also posits that servicing sovereign debt diverts fiscal resources away from infrastructural investments (Easterly, 2013; Pattillo et al., 2003). Moreover, an economy under debt sustainability stress signals a high likelihood of default, which leads to widening lending rate spreads and tighter lending conditions (Clements et al., 2003; Presbitero, 2012). This, in turn, creates uncertainty in macroeconomic performance due to the adoption of harsh fiscal measures, such as increasing taxes to meet debt obligations (Agenor, 2007).

As a result, infrastructural investment is suppressed by increased economic uncertainty and diminished lender confidence. Seminal works by Cecchetti et al. (2011), Panizza and Presbitero (2014), Reinhart et al. (2012), and Reinhart and Rogoff (2010) further expand the debt overhang concept by arguing that the relationship between debt and development outcomes, such as investment, is non-linear, specifically, there exists a threshold effect. This threshold hypothesis suggests that at moderate debt levels, the marginal impact on growth or infrastructural investment is negligible or positive. However, beyond a certain optimal point (threshold), the marginal effect becomes negative (Reinhart et al., 2012; Reinhart & Rogoff, 2010).

Contributing factors include financial market frictions and investor behaviour. The perspective on financial market frictions is that with lower sovereign debt levels, access to foreign borrowing is high, but once a critical debt-to-GDP ratio is exceeded, lenders impose stricter terms, limiting borrowing capacity (Cordella et al., 2010). Regarding market perception, the argument is that beyond a certain threshold, sovereign bond spreads widen disproportionately, reflecting perceived default risk (Greenlaw et al., 2013).

Consequently, the concept of the threshold effect in the nexus between debt and infrastructural investment can be argued in three phases. The first phase examines the relationship below the established threshold. This stage hypothesises that increases in debt stock levels foster infrastructural development. The second phase focuses on the effect at the threshold. This stage posits that sensitivity analysis shows debt stock increases sharply, as a unit increase in debt stock can raise risk premiums. The third phase, which is the concern of this study, concentrates on the effect above the threshold. This stage views that the borrower is overwhelmed with challenges in servicing debt obligations, thereby suppressing the flow of finance into infrastructural investments, with the associated effect of long-term low development prospects and debt sustainability stress.

Moreover, the concept of the debt Laffer curve reinforces the idea of debt overhang and the threshold effect (Krugman, 1988). The debt Laffer curve suggests that the repayment forecast to investors increases with borrowing up to an optimal level, beyond which repayment difficulties impair the ability to pay, thereby limiting opportunities to borrow for investing in infrastructural projects.

*Concept of Debt Sustainability Analysis and Development Prospects*

Based on the theoretical arguments of debt overhang and the threshold effect grounded in debt overhang relating to the relationship between debt and development outcomes, the concept of debt sustainability analysis has evolved (International Monetary Fund, 2025c; World Bank, 2025d).

Generally, the debt sustainability framework suggests that a borrower is in a sustainable debt position when the discounted projected primary surpluses are sufficient to service the outstanding debt stock without unduly restricting development-enhancing investment (Blanchard et al., 1991; International Monetary Fund, 2025c). Referencing the seminal work of Domar (1944), the concept of debt sustainability posits that a sustainable debt stock level requires the ratio of debt to GDP to converge to a stable level, evidenced by the rate of economic growth exceeding the lending rate by a significant margin, and when primary surpluses are sufficient to offset the excess of the lending rate over the growth rate.

Recent theoretical and policy debates on debt-finance projects have embraced various debt sustainability frameworks. For instance, the International Monetary Fund (IMF) and the World Bank Group developed a theoretical framework for analysing the sustainability of sovereign debt in April 2005 (International Monetary Fund, 2025c; World Bank, 2025d). This modern framework concentrates on low-income countries, which are known for having higher levels of sovereign debt stock. The IMF-World Bank sustainability framework assesses how challenging it is for an economy to maintain its debt stock by evaluating the debt trajectory under alternative economic scenarios, especially under shocks to lending rates, economic growth, and exchange rates (International Monetary Fund, 2025c; World Bank, 2025d).

Consequently, based on the perspective of debt overhang and the threshold effect, the IMF-World Bank debt sustainability framework introduced critical thresholds and benchmarks, above which the risk or stress of debt sustainability is considered weak (55%), moderate (55%), and high or strong (70%) for the public debt-to-GDP ratio in low-income countries (review International Monetary Fund, 2025c; World Bank, 2025c).

Aside from these policy thresholds and benchmarks, similar theoretical works such as Pattillo et al. (2003), Pattillo and Ricci (2011), and Reinhart et al. (2012) demonstrate that a public debt-to-GDP ratio exceeding 35–40% and 90%, respectively, hampers growth outcomes. Catherine A. Pattillo et al. (2003) further argue that "high debt appears to reduce growth mainly by lowering the efficiency of investment rather than its volume."

This established argument indicates that crossing these critical thresholds can hinder capital formation by reducing infrastructural investment through the concept of crowding out productive investment, due to the need to maintain debt sustainability. The crowding-out effect suggests that at higher debt levels, the economy becomes monetised, leading to inflation, a weak currency, capital flight, and financial stress, thereby constraining private sector infrastructural investment (Boskin, 2020; Friedman, 1978; Islam & Nguyen, 2024).

Therefore, based on the concepts of debt overhang and the threshold effect, particularly within the IMF-World Bank debt sustainability framework's highest threshold of 70% for the debt-to-GDP ratio, this study hypothesises that debt stocks exceeding this threshold may crowd out private sector infrastructural investment. Testing this hypothesis can generate important insights for devising fiscal and investment strategies to promote long-term infrastructural development, especially in the context of SSA.

### 14.2.2 Empirical Literature: Public Debt and Investment Relationship

This section presents the prevailing empirical insights on the relationship between debt and investment. The prevailing understanding of how public debt drives growth outcomes remains uncertain. Several studies have examined concepts such as debt overhang, threshold effects (Reinhart & Rogoff, 2010), and crowding-out effects in the nexus between debt accumulation and development prospects (see Carrington et al., 2025; Dawood et al., 2024; Islam & Nguyen, 2024). However, there is no consensus on the precise effect of excessive debt accumulation on development outcomes (see Chudik et al., 2017; Eberhardt & Presbitero, 2015; Islam & Nguyen, 2024). Specifically, the prevailing specific-country studies and cross-country studies show both positive and negative effects of debt overhang on investment opportunities.

Given the study's aim to uncover whether debt overhang at a threshold of 70% crowds out or crowds in private sector investment in SSA, the closest empirical work is that of Islam and Nguyen (2024), conducted in the context of developing economies, focusing on firm-level studies. Islam and Nguyen (2024) employed a panel dataset of 14,000 firms across 57 developing countries from surveys conducted between 2006 and 2019 to investigate how public debt influences private sector investment. Their fixed effects analysis shows that at higher debt levels, private investment diminishes. Also, the key earthed transmitting channels of this negative effect are regulatory quality and tax formalities (Islam & Nguyen, 2024).

Similarly, Huang et al. (2020), using firm-level data from China, support Islam and Nguyen's (2024) findings. They show that higher debt levels impair private investment mainly through tighter lending conditions, though their results also indicate that debt overhang does not crowd out public firms' investment. Moreover, Huang et al. (2018), using data from the Orbis firm database, report findings consistent with existing literature on debt overhang and private sector infrastructural investments. Doruk and Gohore (2025) argue that for over 20 years, debt overhang in the Chinese micro sector has not crowded in private investment, reinforcing the view that debt overhang tends to crowd out investment. They also find that financial openness and credit market regulations do not moderate the negative impact of debt overhang on private investment in non-financial firms.

With regard to country-level studies, Dawood et al. (2024) analysed a panel of 32 Asian countries from 1995 to 2020 with GMM and dynamic common correlated effects estimators. The findings posit that infrastructural investment is a key channel through which public debt influences growth. Their results also confirm the existence of debt overhang and crowding-out effects in these countries relating to growth outcomes.

In the African context, the relationship between debt, investment, and growth remains mixed (see e.g., Frimpong et al., 2024; Ogaga, 2025; Ojeka et al., 2024; Yimer & Geda, 2024). The available empirical evidence shows both positive and negative effects of public debt on infrastructural investment. For example, Frimpong et al. (2024), employing the NARDL (Non-linear Autoregressive Distributed Lag) approach, find that in Ghana, from 1983 to 2020, external debt supported infrastructural investment more than domestic debt in both short and long-term periods. This finding aligns with Ogaga (2025), in Nigeria, who discovered that external debt of the Nigerian government crowds in private sector infrastructural development using the ARDL method.

Conversely, Ojeka et al. (2024), from their panel studies between 1996 and 2021, argue that external debt in 47 SSA economies constrains domestic infrastructural investment. Regarding Ethiopia, Yimer and Geda (2024) used ARDL analysis to demonstrate that debt overhang hinders economic growth, although the total debt stock supports infrastructural development and other growth-enhancing projects.

Overall, this review of the literature highlights the necessity to re-examine the concept of debt overhang in relation to private sector infrastructural investment, particularly within SSA. This re-examination focused on constructing an index of debt overhang at a threshold of 70% of debt-to-GDP ratio, based on the IMF-World Bank debt sustainability framework.

The rationale for this investigation involves three main points in strengthening extant studies on Africa's growth and development trajectory (Adegboye et al., 2025; Fuseini, 2025a, 2025b; Fuseini & Ibrahim, 2025) First, existing studies on debt overhang and private investment predominantly focus on micro or firm-level analyses (see e.g., Islam & Nguyen, 2024; Huang et al., 2020; Doruk & Gohore, 2025) at the global level, with limited macroeconomic research, thereby weakening efforts to develop prudent debt sustainability and fiscal measures to foster infrastructural investment.

Second, in the SSA context, empirical insights mainly consist of time series studies (e.g., Frimpong et al., 2024; Ogaga, 2025; Yimer & Geda, 2024), with scarce work on macro-level panel studies, which limits the development of comprehensive subregional debt and fiscal strategies for infrastructure development. Third, and more significantly, the existing literature has yet to examine the impact of debt overhang specifically in the context of debt accumulation exceeding the 70% threshold as recommended by the IMF-World Bank debt sustainability framework (International Monetary Fund, 2025c; World Bank, 2025b). Conducting this study enriches the prevailing extant empirical insights on Africa's growth and development prospects (see e.g., Fuseini, 2025a; Fuseini & Ibrahim, 2025; Ibrahim et al., 2022).

## 14.3 Methodology

This section presents the discussion on the data, variables, and the study's empirical approach in the following subsections:

### *14.3.1 Data and Variables*

The study used a panel time series of 32 economies in sub-Saharan Africa spanning from 2009 to 2023. The study employed a secondary dataset sourced from reputable international organisations like the World Bank and the International Monetary Fund (IMF). The sample size and duration are affected by missing data for some countries and periods, and the use of an imputation approach might impair the robustness of the findings, since data for some countries were entirely missing for the specified period.

The rationale for starting from 2009 is based on the study argument that global crises since 2008, such as the 2008 global financial crisis, COVID-19, and the Russian-Ukrainian war, have pushed economies to borrow more, especially low-to-middle economies (International Monetary Fund, 2025a). Therefore, necessitating the need to gain empirical insights on how the increase in government debt stock translates into private sector infrastructural development, amid debt sustainability issues (International Monetary Fund, 2025a, 2025b).

The dependent variable of interest is private investment, measured by capital formation in the private sector. This estimation approach of private sector infrastructural investment is grounded in the World Bank's approach of measuring infrastructural development. According to the World Bank, this estimation approach is viewed as:

> *Private investment covers outlays by the private sector (including private non-profit agencies) on additions to its fixed domestic assets. Gross fixed capital formation includes acquisitions less disposals of fixed assets during the accounting period, including certain specified expenditures on services that add to the value of non-produced assets,* as sourced from the WDI (World Bank, 2025e).

For sensitivity and robustness purposes, the study also employed public sector infrastructural investment and overall domestic (private plus public) infrastructural investment as dependent variables (see Table 14.1).

**Table 14.1** Summary of data and variables

| *Variables* | *Construct* | *Measurement* | *Source* |
|---|---|---|---|
| Private investment | PrI | Gross fixed capital formation, private sector (% of GDP) | WDI, 2025 |
| Public investment | PuI | National investment minus private investment | Authors' estimation |
| Domestic investment (public and private) | NII | Gross capital formation (% of GDP) | WDI 2025 |
| Debt service | DS | Total debt service (% of GNI) | WDI 2025 |
| Public debt | PD | Debt instruments, Central government, percent of GDP | IMF 2025 |
| Total public debt | TPD | Debt service + public debt | Authors' estimation |
| Debt overhang | DO | Total public debt > 70% | Authors' estimation |
| Economic growth | Eco | GDP growth (annual %) | WDI 2025 |
| Fiscal policy | FP | General government final consumption expenditure (% of GDP) | WDI 2025 |
| Exchange rate | Excrate | Price level ratio of PPP conversion factor (GDP) to market exchange rate | WDI 2025 |
| Remittances | Remit | Personal remittances, received (% of GDP) | WDI 2025 |
| Economic openness | Trade | Trade (% of GDP) | WDI 2025 |

Source: Authors' compilation

The independent variable is debt overhang, indicated by an index of debt overhang that is measured as the residual of subtracting the World Bank-IMF debt sustainability threshold at 70% (percentage of public debt-to-GDP) (International Monetary Fund, 2025c; World Bank, 2025b). The decision to use 70% as the threshold beyond which the concept of debt overhang sets in is based on the World Bank debt sustainability framework for low-income countries, as the highest benchmark above which public debt becomes a risk for growth prospects, echoing the concept of debt overhang.

Public debt in this study is computed as total government (or central) debt plus total debt service as a percentage of GDP (see Table 14.1). Therefore, the study argues that debt overhang in this context represents the residual of public debt beyond this threshold of 70%. Besides utilising the estimated debt overhang as the key independent variable, public debt is also used as an explanatory variable for sensitivity and robustness purposes.

To mitigate omitted variable bias and endogeneity issues, the study used five control variables: economic growth, government expenditure, exchange rate at market price, economic openness, and remittances received. The rationale for employing these variables is that they are among the factors that influence private investment and public debt in an economy (see e.g., Ahmed et al., 2025; Fuseini & Ibrahim, 2025), hence the need to control their effects. For instance, it is both theoretically and empirically proven that economic growth determines private investment (Abaidoo, 2013). Additionally, government expenditure is a key factor influencing the government's taste for borrowing (see Anastasiou et al., 2024). Table 14.1 provides further details on the data sources, variable measurements, and definitions.

### *14.3.2 Empirical Approach*

The main purpose of this study is to empirically unearth insight into whether debt overhangs crowd out or complement private investment across sub–Saharan Africa. Therefore, we specify Eq. (14.1) as a functional model to argue that private investment (PriI) is a function (f) of debt overhang (DO) and the control variables (CV).

$$PriI = f\left(DO, CV\right) \tag{14.1}$$

Based on the goodwill of the IV-GMM technique (see Fuseini, 2025b; Kripfganz, 2019) in handling endogeneity and heterogeneity issues in panel time series, this study adopted it as its empirical strategy to empirically uncover the argument raised in Eq. (14.1). Consequently, Eq. (14.1) is modified into an econometric model to reflect the requirement for the IV-GMM approach as shown in Eq. (14.2).

$$PrI_{it} = \beta_0 + \beta_1 PriI_{it-1} + \beta_2 DO_{it} + \beta_3 CV_{it} + \varepsilon_{it} \tag{14.2}$$

Where $\beta_1 PriI_{it-1}$ denotes lag of PrI, suggesting the dynamic nature of the model, for individual country (i) at a given time (t), $\beta$ represents the coefficient and $\varepsilon_{it}$ indicates the disturbance term. It is worth noting that in the performance of the sensitivity analysis, Eq. (14.2) is altered to replace separately public infrastructural investment (PuI) and domestic infrastructure investment (NII) as dependent variables. Also, DO is replaced with total public debt (TPD) as an independent variable.

Econometrically, the determination of debt overhang (DO) is expressed in Eq. (14.3) to posit that DO is the excess of TPD when it is above the threshold of ∅, which is 70% for this study. From Eq. (14.3), the estimated output has the probability of including data on countries and periods where the concept of DO for the study's argument is absent. Therefore, to address this possibility, Eq. (14.4) is specified to show that DO must not exceed zero (0)

$$DO_{it} = \frac{TPD_{it}}{GDP_{it}} - \varnothing \tag{14.3}$$

$$\text{Where}: DO_{it} \geq 0 \tag{14.4}$$

As stated earlier, there are significant reasons or rationales for adopting the instrumental variable (IV) with the two-step system GMM approach, rooted in the work of Kripfganz (2019), which is widely applied in similar empirical studies like Fuseini (2025a, b) and Saeed et al. (2025). This study's methodological approach is to empirically evidence insights into whether the concept of debt overhang in government borrowing crowds out private investment or complements it, with a focus on the unique context of low- and middle-income economies in subregions like SSA.

Specifically, the IV-GMM technique has recently been extended by Kripfganz (2019). It is theoretically and empirically argued to address critical issues in regression estimation, like endogeneity and reversal causality, where the regressors can correlate with the error to give spurious regression results (see e.g., Fuseini, 2025a, b; Fuseini et al., 2024; Kripfganz, 2019) Also, the GMM approach efficiently tackles the issue of heterogeneity, where means in the panel series may not be homogeneous. The ability of the GMM technique to handle these critical issues, especially given the heterogeneous nature of Africa's economic condition, makes it superior to traditional approaches like the OLS.

However, Roodman (2009) highlights the issue of too many or weak instruments in the model specification as being one of the demerits of the IV-GMM technique. To address this weakness, the Kleibergen (2007) approach of addressing weak and under-identified instruments specification is applied. Moreover, with the issue of too many instruments or over-identification of instruments, the Hansen-Sargan technique (Kripfganz,

2019) is utilised. Following the guidelines of Kripfganz (2019), the panel series is transformed at first difference to address the possibility of the existence of unit roots. Finally, Eq. (14.2) is estimated based on the instrumental variable (IV) framework with the two-step system IV-GMM option (see Kripfganz, 2019).

## 14.4 Empirical Results

This section presents discussions on the preliminary findings from the descriptive statistics, the presentation and interpretation of the findings from the IV-GMM estimation and the diagnostic test.

### *14.4.1 Preliminary Findings*

The initial findings from the descriptive statistics (see Table 14.2) reveal that, firstly, the mean of private sector investment is 14.88% of GDP, indicating that, on average, the private sector is involved in SSA infrastructural development at 14.88% of GDP. This suggests unsatisfactory performance, but it remains better than the public sector, which has a mean of 7.9% of GDP. Overall, the combined average domestic infrastructural investment from both sectors is 22.82% of GDP, reflecting below-moderate performance by SSA economies in enhancing their infrastructural development.

**Table 14.2** Descriptive statistics

| *Variable* | *Obs* | *Mean* | *Std. dev.* | *Min* | *Max* |
|---|---|---|---|---|---|
| PrI | 480 | 14.88085 | 8.726419 | −74.5115 | 59.38664 |
| NII | 480 | 22.82953 | 8.93488 | 0 | 76.78232 |
| PuI | 480 | 7.94868 | 7.508813 | −27.3577 | 84.37321 |
| DO | 480 | 9.172006 | 31.20912 | 0 | 221.4599 |
| TPD | 480 | 55.99941 | 41.56936 | 4.336992 | 291.46 |
| CGD | 480 | 52.96654 | 41.10968 | 4.336992 | 290.386 |
| DS | 435 | 3.346609 | 4.959354 | 0.061478 | 46.34025 |
| Eco | 480 | 3.81588 | 5.060878 | −36.392 | 19.67541 |
| FP | 480 | 14.70347 | 6.598645 | 5.090562 | 36.14315 |
| Exchrate | 480 | 0.421679 | 0.098188 | 0.172549 | 0.868975 |
| Trade | 480 | 65.18094 | 33.7034 | 2.473729 | 222.1783 |
| Remit | 467 | 2.46477 | 3.508585 | 0 | 27.16029 |
| Countries | 32 | 32 | 32 | 32 | 32 |

Source: Author's own work

Additionally, Table 14.2 indicates that the mean for debt overhang (i.e., residual of total debt stock above 70% threshold) is 9.17% of debt-to-GDP, implying that the average debt sustainability stress faced by SSA is approximately 9.17%. Also, the range shows some critical debt sustainability stress issues, highlighting that some economies, particularly low-income countries, are in a critical debt sustainability crisis. Furthermore, the mean of 56.00 for total public debt (debt stock plus servicing cost) as a percentage of GDP exceeds the threshold of 55% for moderate or medium debt sustainability stress or risk.

Consequently, these descriptive statistics underscore the need for further investigation into the causal relationship between debt overhang (above the 70% threshold) and infrastructural investment, especially within the private sector. The key inference from Table 14.2 is that most SSA economies are indeed experiencing debt overhang or debt sustainability stress, yet there is scant empirical insight on how this crowds out or complements infrastructural development in the private sector across SSA.

### 14.4.2 *The Relationship Between Debt Overhang (Beyond a Threshold of 70%) and Sectoral Investment*

This subsection presents the discussion on the IV-GMM estimation output as shown in Table 14.3. The research question guiding this study is: Does debt overhang have a spillover effect in crowding out or complementing private sector infrastructural investment?

The empirical answer to this question is shown in Table 14.3. Therefore, from Table 14.3, column (1), the empirical evidence indicates that debt overhang (DO) has a spillover effect that complements private sector investment in infrastructural development in SSA. Specifically, Table 14.3, column (1), shows that a percentage change in DO will support private sector efforts to advance infrastructural investment by 0.0799% at a 1% significance level. This evidence suggests that debt overhang does not crowd out private investment across SSA. This established evidence contradicts the argument of Islam and Nguyen (2024) in the context of firm-level studies across developing economies. This finding also challenges the common theoretical view (by Cordella et al., 2010; Krugman, 1988) that debt overhang restricts private investment.

Additionally, columns (2) to (5) of Table 14.3 present sensitivity analyses that strengthen the findings from column (1). From columns (2) and (3), it can be inferred that DO crowds out infrastructural investment in

**Table 14.3** Relationship between debt overhang and sectoral infrastructural investment

| | *(1)* | *(2)* | *(3)* | *(4)* | *(5)* |
|---|---|---|---|---|---|
| *VARIABLES* | *PrI* | *PuI* | *NII* | *PrI* | *NII* |
| L.Dependent | 0.1193*** | 0.1732*** | 0.3514*** | −0.0981*** | 0.3422*** |
| | (0.0075) | (0.0079) | (0.0148) | (0.0138) | (0.0126) |
| DO | 0.0799*** | −0.1101*** | −0.0244*** | | |
| | (0.0059) | (0.0170) | (0.0056) | | |
| TPD | | | | 0.0258*** | 0.0153** |
| | | | | (0.0066) | (0.0066) |
| Eco | 0.0655*** | 0.0189 | 0.2070*** | 0.0244* | 0.1448*** |
| | (0.0100) | (0.0234) | (0.0135) | (0.0139) | (0.0135) |
| Remit | 0.0304 | 0.8162*** | 0.4797** | 0.1740 | 0.5194** |
| | (0.0595) | (0.0846) | (0.1877) | (0.1701) | (0.2235) |
| FP | −0.7826*** | −0.2585*** | −0.3476*** | −1.1365*** | −0.5084*** |
| | (0.0628) | (0.0454) | (0.0446) | (0.0963) | (0.0798) |
| Exchrate | 3.7870*** | 14.0768*** | 6.8518** | 10.9580*** | 5.7230*** |
| | (1.2772) | (1.0743) | (3.1242) | (1.7213) | (1.7571) |
| Trade | −0.0403*** | 0.0304*** | −0.0153 | −0.1472*** | 0.0356*** |
| | (0.0093) | (0.0112) | (0.0173) | (0.0253) | (0.0119) |
| Constant | 24.5968*** | 0.9193 | 15.7708*** | 35.6923*** | 14.0979*** |
| | (1.2599) | (0.8029) | (0.9371) | (2.0028) | (0.7443) |

Source: Author's own work

the public sector and overall domestic infrastructural development (i.e., private sector plus public sector), respectively. This sensitivity analysis indicates that the argument of DO crowding out infrastructural development holds in the public sector. Furthermore, the results in columns (4) and (5) show that total public debt, composed of total principal debt plus servicing costs as a percentage of GDP (TPD) without considering the 70% threshold, promotes or supports private sector infrastructural investment and total domestic infrastructural development significantly, respectively. This significant sensitivity finding reinforces and validates the initial uncovered argument that DO has a spillover effect in supporting private sector investment.

Therefore, regarding the lag of PrI, column (1) demonstrates that a lag in PrI significantly increases current DO. The control variables also show significant effects in the relationship between DO and PrI. For instance, across columns (1) to (5), economic growth exerts a significant positive control effect, as expected. Also, fiscal policy, consistent with theoretical expectations, shows a significant negative control effect across columns (1) to (5).

### 14.4.3 *Diagnostic Checks*

This subsection presents the discussion of the diagnostic tests performed to further verify the validity and reliability of the uncovered empirical evidence for generalisation and robustness. Table 14.4 displays several diagnostic checks on each estimated model.

First, as a rule of thumb for adopting the IV-GMM technique, the number of cross-sections (32) is greater than the time frame (15 years). Also, Table 14.5 shows there is low to moderate multicollinearity between the series under study, as no correlation coefficient exceeds the 0.8 threshold, except between TPD and DO, which is expected since DO is derived from TPD.

**Table 14.4** Diagnostic test

| *Diagnostic test* | *(1)* | *(2)* | *(3)* | *(4)* | *(5)* |
|---|---|---|---|---|---|
| Observations | 435 | 435 | 435 | 435 | 435 |
| Countries | 32 | 32 | 32 | 32 | 32 |
| Centred $R^2$ | 0.4224 | 0.5805 | 0.9230 | 0.8865 | 0.9192 |
| Uncentred $R^2$ | 0.6329 | 0.1430 | 0.3833 | 0.2551 | 0.2551 |
| F-Statistics | 523.69 | 371.98 | 4586.45 | 301.81 | 3911.42 |
| Prob > F | 0.0000 | 0.0000 | 0.0000 | 0.0000 | 0.0000 |
| AR1- Z statistics | −1.3549 | −1.7804 | −1.8234 | −1.9088 | −1.7690 |
| Prob > \|z\| | 0.1754 | 0.0750 | 0.0682 | 0.0563 | 0.0769 |
| AR2-Z statistics | −0.9000 | −1.3336 | −2.0467 | −0.9452 | −2.2495 |
| Prob > \|z\| | 0.3681 | 0.1823 | 0.1407 | 0.3446 | 0.2450 |
| AR3-Z statistics | 0.8159 | 0.8699 | −0.8563 | 0.1105 | −0.8993 |
| Prob > \|z\| | 0.4145 | 0.3843 | 0.3918 | 0.9120 | 0.3685 |
| Kleibergen-Paap rk LM-UIR: $X^2$ | 29.24 | 29.46 | 29.42 | 29.01 | 29.90 |
| Prob>$X^2$ | 0.2113 | 0.2031 | 0.2049 | 0.1446 | 0.1882 |
| Sargan-Hansen: OIR-2-step MF | 26.12 | 24.26 | 25.95 | 27.37 | 22.40 |
| Prob>$X^2$ | 0.2951 | 0.3896 | 0.3032 | 0.1589 | 0.4964 |
| Kleibergen-Paap rk Wald-WIR | 10.07 | 22.61 | 21.99 | 14.36 | 23.91 |
| Cragg-Donald Wald-WIR | 0.5920 | 0.4722 | 0.6388 | 0.5612 | 0.5410 |

Notes: All Models have robust standard errors in parentheses. * ** and *** denote significance at 10%, 5%, and 1%, respectively. Arellano-Bond test for autocorrelation of the first-differenced residuals; H0: no autocorrelation. Sargan-Hansen test of the overidentifying restrictions; H0: overidentifying restrictions are valid

Source: Author's own work

**Table 14.5** Correlation Matrix

| *Variables* | *PrI* | *NII* | *TPD* | *DO* | *PuI* | *DS* | *Eco* | *FP* | *Exchrate* | *Trade* | *Remit* |
|---|---|---|---|---|---|---|---|---|---|---|---|
| PrI | 1.0000 | | | | | | | | | | |
| NII | 0.6387 | 1.0000 | | | | | | | | | |
| TPD | 0.0347 | −0.1746 | 1.0000 | | | | | | | | |
| DO | 0.0177 | −0.2088 | 0.9149 | 1.0000 | | | | | | | |
| PuI | −0.4021 | 0.4476 | −0.2481 | −0.2690 | 1.0000 | | | | | | |
| DS | 0.0095 | −0.0197 | 0.1319 | 0.0001 | −0.0341 | 1.0000 | | | | | |
| Eco | 0.1098 | 0.1489 | −0.0240 | 0.0048 | 0.0496 | −0.1051 | 1.0000 | | | | |
| FP | 0.0627 | −0.0703 | 0.0429 | 0.0821 | −0.1565 | −0.0028 | −0.1181 | 1.0000 | | | |
| Exchrate | 0.0842 | 0.1855 | −0.1961 | −0.1864 | 0.1229 | 0.0636 | 0.0704 | 0.1794 | 1.0000 | | |
| Trade | 0.2397 | 0.2907 | −0.1504 | −0.1646 | 0.0673 | 0.3590 | 0.0314 | 0.3949 | 0.5063 | 1.0000 | |
| Remit | −0.0864 | −0.0641 | 0.0808 | −0.0084 | 0.0255 | −0.0278 | 0.1414 | −0.1394 | −0.1993 | −0.1379 | 1.0000 |

Source: Author's own work

Table 14.5 further demonstrates that the specified models are not over-, under-, or weakly identified. This is confirmed by the failure to reject the null hypothesis at all conventional levels in the Sargan-Hansen test for over-identification restrictions, based on the two and three-step weighting matrix (see Kripfganz, 2019), and the Kleibergen (2007) approach for testing weak and under-identification restrictions.

Additionally, there are no concerns regarding autocorrelation (AR), even up to the third order (AR3) from the Arellano-Bond approach, because the null hypothesis of autocorrelation in the first-differenced residuals cannot be rejected. The Fisher statistic further supports the models' goodness of fit, as the p-values are significant at the 1% level. The robustness of the models is enhanced by the utilisation of robust standard errors clustered around the countries (ids) in the two-step system IV-GMM estimation process.

### 14.4.4 Discussion of Findings' Implications

This subsection summarises the findings and their implications for policy and practice. The main findings of the study are: first, debt overhang at a threshold of 70% attracts private sector infrastructural investment in SSA. However, debt overhang prevents public sector infrastructural development. Additionally, total public debt, including both principal and servicing costs without considering the threshold at 70%, supports domestic infrastructural development (i.e., a blend of private and public sector investment).

These empirical findings failed to align with the empirical works like Islam and Nguyen (2024), Huang et al. (2020), and Doruk and Gohore (2025) in the context of firm-level studies in other developing economies. These empirical works uncovered that debt overhang crowds out private investment in economies like China, using micro-level datasets, contradicting this study's findings. However, these discovered findings support empirical findings from works like Frimpong et al. (2024) and Ogaga (2025) in the context of SSA economies like Ghana and Nigeria, respectively. Yet in the same SSA context, Ojeka et al. (2024) and Yimer and Geda (2024) show that debt overhang impedes domestic infrastructural development and economic growth. It must, however, be noted that most of these studies focused largely on foreign loans to the government, deviating from this study's argument of using total government debt stock plus servicing cost.

These empirical evidences in SSA present several implications for policy, practice, and theoretical refinement. Basically, the findings suggest that the effect of debt overhang in crowding in or out infrastructural investment above a threshold of 70% of debt-to-GDP is sector-specific and sensitive. Moreover, these findings challenge the well-documented theoretical and policy argument of the concept of debt overhang, specifically with the focus on the threshold effect (International Monetary Fund, 2025c; Krugman, 1988; Reinhart & Rogoff, 2010; World Bank, 2025c).

These concepts generally suggest that higher debt levels above a certain point hinder growth and development prospects, particularly related to investment, due to the expectation of tax increases by the government to service and pay off debt obligations, thereby indirectly impeding investment returns. However, this study shows that governments experiencing debt stress or debt overhang have a spillover effect that attracts private sector infrastructural investment.

The possible inferences are that, first, increasing government debt levels may be linked to growth stages, where private sector organisations have access to significant infrastructure and a robust macroeconomic environment. Also, despite high levels of public debt, SSA governments still enact policies like tax incentives and credit accessibility or enough liquidity, which indirectly enable private firms to perform better. Furthermore, government debt might signal fiscal inducements and economic reforms that support private sector investment.

Therefore, these findings suggest that, in the SSA context, private investors view public debt as a sign of financial deepening led by the state, with no expectation of higher future taxes to repay sovereign debt. The sensitivity analysis indicates that the relationship between the debt-to-GDP ratio and infrastructural investment is non-linear. Particularly in SSA, where this study shows that beneath a threshold of 70%, the relationship may be positive or neutral, but above this point, public debt hinders capital formation, especially in the public sector.

The potential causes could be that debt levels above the threshold may lead to fiscal stress, forcing governments to prioritise debt servicing and repayments at the expense of capital expenditure. Additionally, infrastructural investments might be hampered by high borrowing costs, discouraging government interest in such projects. Moreover, debt sustainability analyses may indicate future austerity measures, which could reduce government expenditure on infrastructure.

For policymakers and practitioners, based on the World Bank and IMF debt sustainability frameworks (International Monetary Fund, 2025c; World Bank, 2025d), the findings recommend that governments in SSA reaching the 70% threshold should focus on fiscal consolidation measures to avoid debt stress that could hinder government infrastructure investment. Policymakers must recognise that crossing this threshold shifts debt from being an engine of growth to a drag on domestic infrastructural development.

The finding that total public debt can boost infrastructural development without considering the 70% threshold, and based on the sensitivity analysis, suggests that: first, debt-servicing costs are critical, not just the debt stock. If debt servicing costs are sustainable, regardless of the debt level, governments can maintain credibility, stability, and a strong financial sector that benefits private investors. Additionally, improvements in private investment are likely because sustainable debt servicing reduces economic uncertainty, liquidity challenges in domestic markets due to financial deepening via T-Bills, and investors' perception of sound debt management as a sign of strong institutional quality.

Overall, these empirical findings suggest that when government debt is sustainable, it can indirectly promote private sector investment through financial deepening, infrastructural support, and economic stability. Also, excessive fiscal policy to go beyond this threshold might hinder domestic infrastructural development in the public sector. As questionable sustainability of debt reduces investor confidence and hampers infrastructural project funding. Subsequently, the need to prioritise measures that ensure debt servicing sustainability, focusing on debt management rather than just debt levels. Sustainable debt servicing costs can support infrastructural development even at higher debt levels.

Consequently, key policy implications are that: firstly, the composition of public debt and debt sustainability measures are more critical than mere debt levels. Policymakers in SSA should focus on sustainable debt servicing through credible, growth-oriented policies to reduce servicing costs. Additionally, governments must pay close attention to the established threshold effects, especially for public sector infrastructural investment. Crossing the 70% threshold could restrict investment opportunities in infrastructure, potentially hindering long-term growth and development prospects.

Lastly, the resilience of the private sector is notably demonstrated in this study, especially within SSA. Private sector investment in SSA tends to be more resilient to debt overhang at the threshold of 70% of debt-to-GDP than the public sector, possibly due to strong subregional savings, developed financial markets, and openness to foreign capital and remittances.

## 14.5 Conclusion

Global projections indicate uncertainty in economic prospects worldwide, amid high levels of sovereign borrowings, particularly in developing regions like Africa. This uncertainty and stress on debt sustainability have led to fiscal consolidation in most low- and middle-income countries. However, debt is theoretically argued to be a crucial source of economic growth and development, especially for developing nations, yet the existing empirical literature offers limited and mixed insight into how public debt crossing a policy threshold of 70% of debt-to-GDP impacts private sector investment.

Consequently, this study examined the relationship between public debt and private sector investment, focusing on testing the concept of debt overhang in SSA. The study employed the IV-GMM technique on a panel dataset of 32 economies across SSA, spanning 2009 to 2023.

The primary findings suggest that debt overhang in SSA has a spillover effect, crowding in private sector investment. Conversely, debt overhang crowds out economic infrastructural development within the public sector. Moreover, without considering the concept of debt overhang at a threshold of 70%, sensitivity analysis indicates that public debt as a percentage of GDP crowds in economic infrastructural development for both the private and public sectors.

The implications of these findings for policymaking and practice, aimed at strengthening the debt-investment nexus, are highlighted and discussed, with a focus on SSA. As a limitation, the study utilised a threshold of 70%, as supported by the IMF-World Bank debt sustainability analysis thresholds and benchmarks (review International Monetary Fund, 2025c; World Bank, 2025c), in testing the debt overhang concept within the SSA context, concentrating on the post-2008 global financial crisis era. Therefore, this study recommends that future researchers employ other well-established debt thresholds in different contexts to reinforce these findings, using the panel ARDL technique.

## References

Abaidoo, R. (2013). Private and public investment growth: Macroeconomic expectations and fiscal policy uncertainty. *International Business Research, 7* (1). https://doi.org/10.5539/ibr.v7n1p116

Adegboye, A., Erin, O., & Asongu, S. (2025). Taxing Africa for inclusive human development: The mediating role of governance quality. *Journal of Economic and Administrative Sciences, 41*(1), 182–205. https://doi.org/10.1108/JEAS-03-2022-0061

Agenor, P.-R. (2007). Fiscal policy and endogenous growth with public infrastructure. *Oxford Economic Papers, 60*(1), 57–87. https://doi.org/10.1093/oep/gpm018

Aguiar, M., Amador, M., & Gopinath, G. (2009). Investment cycles and sovereign debt overhang. *The Review of Economic Studies, 76*(1), 1–31. https://doi.org/10.1111/j.1467-937X.2008.00523.x

Ahmed, B., Dawood, M. N., Waheed, M., Ahmed, I., & Bibi, N. (2025). Investigating the relationship between government debt levels and fiscal policy outcomes, focusing on debt sustainability and growth. *International Journal of Business and Management Sciences, 6*(1), 554–571.

Anastasiou, A., Apergis, N., & Zervoyianni, A. (2024). Convergence of public expenditures and revenues in EU28 during 2002–2019: Evidence from club-clustering analysis before and after the European debt crisis. *International Journal of Finance and Economics, 29*(2). https://doi.org/10.1002/ijfe.2756

Blanchard, O. J., Chouraqui, J.-C., Hagemann, R., & Sartor, N. (1991). *The sustainability of fiscal policy: New answers to an old question.* NBER Working Paper, R1547. https://ssrn.com/abstract=227461

Boskin, M. J. (2020). Are large deficits and debt dangerous? *AEA Papers and Proceedings, 110*, 145–148. https://doi.org/10.1257/pandp.20201103

Carrington, S. J., Padilla, L., & Herrera Pozo, R. O. (2025). How much debt is too much? Debt-growth dynamics in commodity-dependent and non-commodity-dependent developing economies. *International Economics, 182*, 100597. https://doi.org/10.1016/j.inteco.2025.100597

Cecchetti, S. G., Mohanty, M. S., & Zampolli, F. (2011). *The real effects of debt, September 2011.* Bank for International Settlement Working Paper, 352(352).

Chudik, A., Mohaddes, K., Pesaran, M. H., & Raissi, M. (2017). Is there a debt-threshold effect on output growth? *Review of Economics and Statistics, 99*(1). https://doi.org/10.1162/REST_a_00593

Clements, B., Bhattacharya, R., & Nguyen, T. Q. (2003). External debt, public investment, and growth in low-income countries. *SSRN Electronic Journal, IMF Working Paper No. 03/249.* https://ssrn.com/abstract=880959

Cordella, T., Ricci, L. A., & Ruiz-Arranz, M. (2010). Debt overhang or debt irrelevance? *IMF Staff Papers, 57*(1), 1–24. https://doi.org/10.1057/imfsp.2009.20

Dawood, M., Feng, Z. R., Ilyas, M., & Abbas, G. (2024). External debt, transmission channels, and economic growth: Evidence of debt overhang and crowding-out effect. *SAGE Open, 14*(3), 21582440241263626. https://doi.org/10.1177/21582440241263626

Domar, E. D. (1944). The 'Burden of the Debt' and the National Income. *The American Economic Review, 34*(4), 798–827. JSTOR.

Doruk, Ö. T., & Gohore, B. I. C. M. (2025). The effect of debt overhang on investment under financial liberalization: An examination for an emerging market. *Macroeconomics and Finance in Emerging Market Economies*, 1–15. https://doi.org/10.1080/17520843.2025.2505341

Easterly, W. (2013). The role of growth slowdowns and forecast errors in public debt crises. In *Fiscal Policy after the Financial Crisis* (pp. 151–173). University of Chicago Press. https://doi.org/10.7208/chicago/9780226018584.003.0005

Eberhardt, M., & Presbitero, A. F. (2015). Public debt and growth: Heterogeneity and non-linearity. *Journal of International Economics, 97*(1), 45–58. https://doi.org/10.1016/j.jinteco.2015.04.005

Friedman, B. M. (1978). Crowding out or crowding in? The economic consequences of financing government deficits. *Brookings Papers on Economic Activit, 1*, 593–654. https://doi.org/10.3386/w0284

Frimpong, B., Fumey, A., & Nketiah-Amponsah, E. (2024). Effects of public debt on public infrastructure investment in Ghana. *Cogent Economics & Finance, 12*(1), 2363460.

Fuseini, E. I. (2025a). Entrepreneurial trend across Africa: Fresh evidence from the conditioning effect of governance quality on policy. *Journal of Small Business & Entrepreneurship, 1–29.* https://doi.org/10.1080/08276331.2025.2587475

Fuseini, E. I. (2025b). *Institutional quality-banking efficiency nexuses in Africa. How does ICT moderate?* (pp. 1–25). *Information Technology for Development.* https://doi.org/10.1080/02681102.2025.2460157

Fuseini, E. I., & Ibrahim, M. (2025). Fiscal policy cyclicality and inclusive growth outcomes in Sub-Saharan Africa: Identifying critical thresholds. *Macroeconomics and Finance in Emerging Market Economies, 1–22.* https://doi.org/10.1080/17520843.2025.2572169

Fuseini, E. I., Ibrahim, M., Adam, I. O., & Vinh, X. (2024). Re-examining the moderating role of ICT in the nexus between financial development and banking efficiency: Evidence from Africa. *Cogent Economics & Finance, 12*(1). https://doi.org/10.1080/23322039.2024.2325833

Greenlaw, D., Hamilton, J. D., Hooper, P., & Mishkin, F. S. (2013). *Crunch time: Fiscal crises and the role of monetary policy.* National Bureau of Economic Research.

Huang, Y., Panizza, U., & Varghese, R. (2018). *Does public debt crowd out corporate investment? International evidence* (Graduate Institute of International and Development Studies Working Paper Nos. HEIDWP08-2018). Graduate Institute of International and Development Studies. https://hdl.handle.net/10419/201691

Huang, Y., Pagano, M., & Panizza, U. (2020). Local crowding-out in China. *The Journal of Finance, 75*(6), 2855–2898. https://doi.org/10.1111/jofi.12966
Ibrahim, M., Aluko, O. A., & Vo, X. V. (2022). The role of inflation in financial development–economic growth link in sub-Saharan Africa. *Cogent Economics and Finance, 10*(1). https://doi.org/10.1080/23322039.2022.2093430
International Monetary Fund. (2024). FISCAL MONITOR: Putting a Lid on Public Debt. International Monitary Fund. https://www.imf.org/en/Publications/FM/Issues/2024/10/23/fiscal-monitor-october-2024
International Monetary Fund. (2025a). *Debt vulnerabilities and financing challenges in emerging markets and developing economies—An overview of key data* (Nos. 2025, 002; p. 24). International Monetary Fund (IMF). https://doi.org/10.5089/9798229002264.007
International Monetary Fund. (2025b). *Fiscal monitor, April 2025: Fiscal policy under uncertainty.* International Monetary Fund (IMF). https://doi.org/10.5089/9798229002516.089
International Monetary Fund. (2025c, June 24). *The debt sustainability framework for low-income countries.* https://www.imf.org/external/pubs/ft/dsa/lic.htm
Islam, A. M., & Nguyen, H. (2024). *Distributional crowding out effects of public debt on private investment in developing economies.* World Bank.
Khan, M. A., Rahman, A., & Tareen, B. A. (2025). Is Pakistan in a debt trap? Do domestic and foreign debts crowd-out private investment? *Journal of Policy Modeling.* https://doi.org/10.1016/j.jpolmod.2025.06.005
Kleibergen, F. (2007). Generalizing weak instrument robust IV statistics towards multiple parameters, unrestricted covariance matrices and identification statistics. *Journal of Econometrics, 139*(1). https://doi.org/10.1016/j.jeconom.2006.06.010
Kripfganz, S. (2019). Generalized method of moments estimation of linear dynamic panel data models. *London Stata Conference*, 1–128.
Krugman, P. (1988). Financing vs. forgiving a debt overhang. *Journal of Development Economics, 29*(3), 253–268. https://doi.org/10.1016/0304-3878(88)90044-2
Myers, M. D. (1997). Qualitative research in information systems. *MIS Quarterly: Management Information Systems.*
Ogaga, T. C. (2025). Effect of government external debt on private investment in Nigeria. *International Journal of Innovative Finance and Economics Research, 13*(1), 417–427. https://doi.org/10.5281/zenodo.15298096
Ojeka, O. J., Egbetunde, T., Okoduwa, G. O., Ojeyode, A. O., Jimoh, M., & Ogunbowale, G. O. (2024). Moderating effect of institutional quality on the influence of debt on investment in sub-Saharan Africa. *Future Business Journal, 10*(1), 76. https://doi.org/10.1186/s43093-024-00362-0
Panizza, U., & Presbitero, A. F. (2014). Public debt and economic growth: Is there a causal effect? *Journal of Macroeconomics, 41.* https://doi.org/10.1016/j.jmacro.2014.03.009
Pattillo, C., & Ricci, L. A. (2011). External debt and growth. *Review of Economics and Institutions, 2*(3) https://rei.unipg.it/rei/article/view/45

Pattillo, C. A., Catherine A., Poirson, H., & Ricci, L. A. (2003). Through what channels does external debt affect growth? *Brookings Trade Forum, 2003*(1). https://doi.org/10.1353/btf.2004.0013

Presbitero, A. F. (2012). Total public debt and growth in developing countries. *The European Journal of Development Research, 24*(4), 606–626. https://doi.org/10.1057/ejdr.2011.62

Reinhart, C. M., & Rogoff, K. S. (2010). Growth in a time of debt. *American Economic Review, 100*(2). https://doi.org/10.1257/aer.100.2.573

Reinhart, C. M., Reinhart, V. R., & Rogoff, K. S. (2012). Public debt overhangs: Advanced-economy episodes since 1800. *Journal of Economic Perspectives, 26*(3), 69–86. https://doi.org/10.1257/jep.26.3.69

Roodman, D. (2009). A note on the theme of too many instruments. *Oxford Bulletin of Economics and Statistics.* https://doi.org/10.1111/j.1468-0084.2008.00542.x

Sachs, J. D. (1989). Conditionality, debt relief, and the developing country debt crisis. In *Developing country debt and economic performance, volume 1: The international financial system* (pp. 255–296). University of Chicago Press.

Saeed, U. F., Kamil, R., & Wiredu, I. (2025). The roles of ICT and governance quality in the finance-growth nexus of developing countries: A dynamic GMM approach. *Cogent Economics & Finance, 13*(1), 2448228. https://doi.org/10.1080/23322039.2024.2448228

Sala, H., & Trivin, P. (2024). Household finances, debt overhang and consumption patterns. *Economic Modelling, 139*, 106836. https://doi.org/10.1016/j.econmod.2024.106836

World Bank. (2025a). *Debt: Management, transparency, statistics and sustainability.* World Bank. https://www.worldbank.org/en/topic/debt/overview#3. *Understanding Poverty.* https://www.worldbank.org/en/topic/debt/overview#3

World Bank. (2025b). *Global economic prospects, June 2025* (pp. 1–138). World Bank Group. https://openknowledge.worldbank.org/server/api/core/bitstreams/2baabfb0-d076-444b-9564-7935afab5ada/content

World Bank. (2025c). *New business density (new registrations per 1,000 people ages 15–64)* [Dataset]. World Bank's Entrepreneurship Database. https://data.worldbank.org/indicator/IC.BUS.NDNS.ZS

World Bank. (2025d). New debt sustainability analysis for low-income countries. *Interactive Guide for Debt Sustainability Analysis for Low-Income Countries.* https://www.worldbank.org/content/dam/LIC%20DSF/Site%20File/index.html

World Bank. (2025e). *World development indicators* [Dataset]. https://databank.worldbank.org/source/world-development-indicators

Yimer, A., & Geda, A. (2024). A two-edged sword: The impact of public debt on economic growth—The case of Ethiopia. *Journal of Applied Economics, 27*(1), 2398908. https://doi.org/10.1080/15140326.2024.2398908

CHAPTER 15

# Public Debt and Exchange Rate Volatility in Africa: Implications for Trade and Investment

*Khadijah Iddrisu, Simplice A. Asongu, and Richard Stephens Cromwell*

## 15.1 Introduction

Africa's debt trajectory has followed recurring cycles of crisis, relief, and renewed borrowing. In the 1980s and 1990s, unsustainable borrowing, commodity shocks, and high global interest rates triggered severe debt crises (Stein, 2015; UNCTAD, 2023; World Bank, 2024). This led to the Heavily Indebted Poor Countries (HIPC) Initiative in 1996 and the Multilateral Debt Relief Initiative (MDRI) in 2005 (World Bank, 2024).

K. Iddrisu (✉)
Accounting and Finance Department, Islamic University College, Accra, Ghana
e-mail: khadijahiddris@iug.edu.gh

S. A. Asongu
School of Economics, University of Johannesburg, Johannesburg, South Africa

R. S. Cromwell
Institute of Oil and Gas, University of Cape Coast, Cape Coast, Ghana
e-mail: richard.cromwell@stu.ucc.edu.gh



I. N. Yakubu (ed.), *Public Debt and Economic Resilience in Africa*, Palgrave Studies in African and Development Economics,
https://doi.org/10.1007/978-3-032-25835-9_15

These programmes restored fiscal space and enabled governments to expand social and infrastructure spending. However, from the 2010s, debt composition shifted, where concessional financing was increasingly replaced by Eurobond issuances, Chinese loans, and commercial credit, exposing countries to higher costs, rollover risks, and global market pressures (Fliss, 2022; Mutai, 2025). The coronavirus disease 2019 (COVID-19) pandemic marked a turning point, as governments borrowed heavily to address economic disruptions (Anyanwu & Salami, 2021). Coupled with global financial tightening and inflationary pressures, these dynamics have deepened debt-servicing difficulties and undermined fiscal sustainability across the continent.

Africa's exchange rate regimes have undergone significant transitions (Ali & Obaidy, 2019). In the immediate post-independence era, many countries operated fixed or pegged exchange rate systems, often tied to colonial currencies. Over time, however, structural adjustment programmes and domestic policy reforms prompted a gradual shift towards more flexible exchange rate arrangements. For commodity-dependent economies such as Nigeria, Angola, and Zambia, exchange rates have exhibited considerable volatility, often reflecting swings in global oil or copper prices (Fliss, 2022). By contrast, countries in the CFA franc zone, which maintain a peg to the euro, have experienced relative exchange rate stability (Daba, 2024; Meh et al., 2025). Yet this stability has come with trade-offs, including limited monetary autonomy and periodic concerns about external competitiveness.

Africa faces mounting challenges as debt sustainability risks intersect with exchange rate instability. Rising global interest rates have increased borrowing costs, while currency depreciation has inflated the local-currency burden of external debt. With much of Africa's debt denominated in foreign currencies, depreciation heightens debt-servicing costs, crowding out essential spending and raising default risks, as seen in Zambia and Ghana (International Monetary Fund. African Dept, 2024a, b). Uncertainty in currency markets can deter foreign direct investment (FDI), as investors perceive greater risks to profitability and returns. Similarly, volatile exchange rates increase transaction costs for traders, disrupt cross-border commerce, and undermine regional integration initiatives. For small, open economies in Africa, where imports and exports account for a significant share of GDP, this volatility can have outsized effects on macroeconomic stability. Therefore, this chapter discusses the nexus between public debt and exchange rate volatility and how they influence trade and investment in Africa.

Rather than developing new theoretical models or conducting econometric estimations, the analysis focuses on synthesising existing evidence, identifying observable patterns across countries, and interpreting how debt dynamics and exchange rate instability shape economic outcomes. The aim is to provide policymakers with a clear understanding of the key channels through which public debt influences exchange rate movements, and how these, in turn, affect trade competitiveness and investment flows. The African Continental Free Trade Area (AfCFTA), launched in 2021, aims to boost intra-African trade, but its success depends partly on currency stability and predictable macroeconomic conditions. Moreover, the dual challenges of rising debt and unstable exchange rates threaten progress towards the Sustainable Development Goals (SDGs), particularly those related to inclusive growth, industrialisation, and investment promotion. Understanding how these dynamics interact is therefore critical for designing effective policy responses.

The remainder of the chapter is structured as follows: Section 15.2 provides a brief overview of public debt and exchange rates. Section 15.3 discusses the interaction between public debt and exchange rate dynamics. Section 15.4 examines the implications of this interaction for trade and investment. The final section presents the conclusion, summarising the key findings and outlining relevant policy implications.

## 15.2 Public Debt and Exchange Rates in Africa

### *15.2.1 Public Debts Trends*

The trajectory of Africa's public debt has been shaped by both domestic financing needs and external global conditions. Following the debt relief initiatives of the late 1990s and early 2000s, many African countries experienced a period of relative debt sustainability. Debt-to-GDP ratios declined significantly, allowing governments to increase spending on social services and infrastructure. However, this progress proved short-lived. By the mid-2010s, debt levels began to rise again, driven by large-scale borrowing to finance infrastructure, declining commodity revenues, and the increasing availability of international capital markets. For instance, United

Nations Conference on Trade and Development (UNCTAD) data indicate that prior to 2009, Africa's debt levels remained relatively low, peaking at about US$510 billion. From 2009 onward, however, debt rose steadily, climbing from US$565 billion to US$1.83 trillion by 2022 (see Fig. 15.1).

While this is a fraction of the overall outstanding debt of developing countries, Africa's debt has increased by 183% since 2010, a rate roughly four times higher than the growth rate of GDP in dollar terms. In 2022, Northern African countries accounted for about 40% of Africa's total public debt. Many of these economies have faced rising food prices and shortages in the wake of the conflict in Europe. For example, Egypt had public debt amounting to US$421 billion (Fig. 15.2) as the country relied on Russia and Ukraine for over 75% of its wheat imports in 2021 (Gebeltová et al., 2023). This dependence, combined with an already heavy debt burden, has constrained Egypt's capacity to secure essential food supplies and other critical imports.

Unlike the concessional loans of earlier decades, much of this new debt came in the form of Eurobond issuances and bilateral loans from emerging creditors, especially China. As a result, African debt profiles shifted from long-term, low-interest concessional loans to shorter-maturity, higher-interest commercial debt, making debt burdens more sensitive to global market conditions. As illustrated in Fig. 15.3, Africa's borrowing patterns

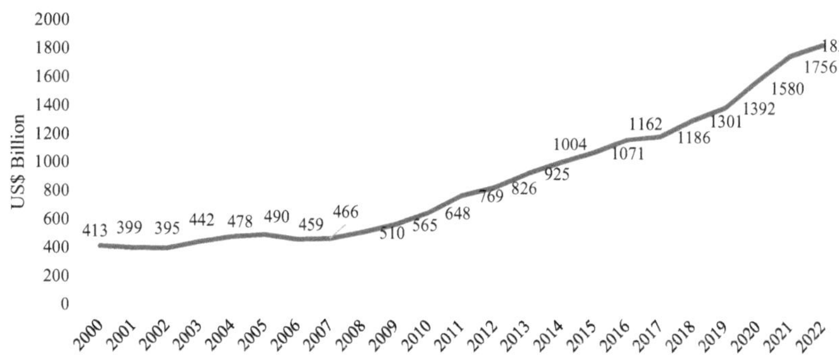


**Fig. 15.1** Trend in gross government debt (2000 to 2022). Source: Authors' construction based on data from UNCTAD (2023)

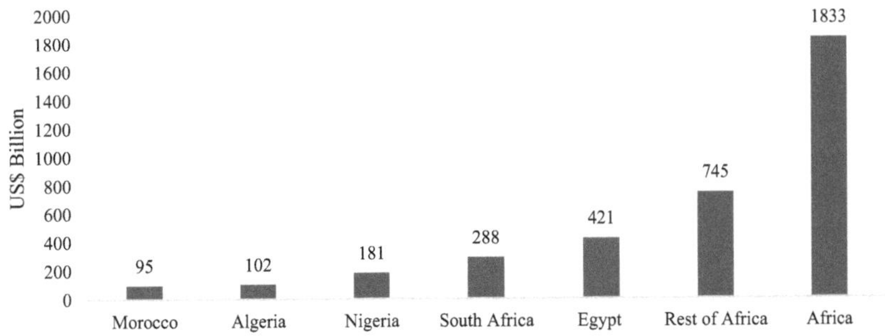


**Fig. 15.2** Gross government debt in Africa 2022, by country. Source: Authors' construction based on data from UNCTAD (2023)

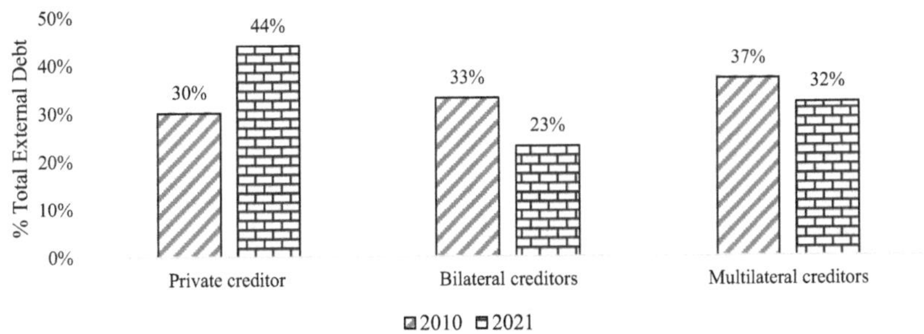


**Fig. 15.3** Creditor composition of external debt in Africa (2010 and 2021). Source: Authors' construction based on data from UNCTAD (2023)

have shifted significantly. In 2010, multilateral creditors accounted for 37% of total external borrowing, but by 2021, private creditors had become the dominant source, providing 44% of the continent's external debt.

Policy discussions on Africa's debt have traditionally centred on external obligations, yet domestic debt has gained growing importance in many countries over the past two decades. Most African countries have been involved in domestic borrowing. For instance, domestic debt of Kenya

**Box 15.1 Kenya's Involvement in Domestic Borrowing**

Kenya's rising budgetary needs, driven largely by infrastructure spending, have outpaced revenue collection, creating persistent fiscal deficits financed through both external and domestic borrowing. Domestic debt has mainly supported recurrent expenditure, with net domestic financing fluctuating between Ksh 167 billion in 2012/13 and Ksh 309 billion in 2016/17 before easing to Ksh 274 billion in 2017/18. Treasury bills and bonds dominate domestic debt, together accounting for over 95%, with commercial banks and non-bank financial institutions as the main holders. However, reliance on short-term instruments, particularly treasury bills, has shortened the debt maturity profile, exposing Kenya to refinancing risks. Average maturity fell from 5.14 years in 2012/13 to 4.4 years in 2017/18, while debt maturing within one year rose sharply to 37.7% of total debt. From the Medium Term Debt Management Strategy 2018/19–2020/21, the government envisages reducing the share of treasury bills in total net domestic financing ratio to around 13% in 2020/21 from the current 35% in a bid to lengthen the maturity profile of domestic debt.

Source: Kenya Institute for Public Policy Research and Analysis (KIPPRA, 2019).

rose to over 50% of total public debt, with Treasury bills and bonds dominating the portfolio (see Box 15.1).

In the aftermath of COVID-19 and heightened global financial volatility, many African countries turned increasingly to domestic borrowing as external financing options narrowed. For instance, countries including Ghana, Tunisia, Togo, Ethiopia, Côte d'Ivoire, Senegal, and Morocco have all expanded their domestic borrowing (Fig. 15.4).

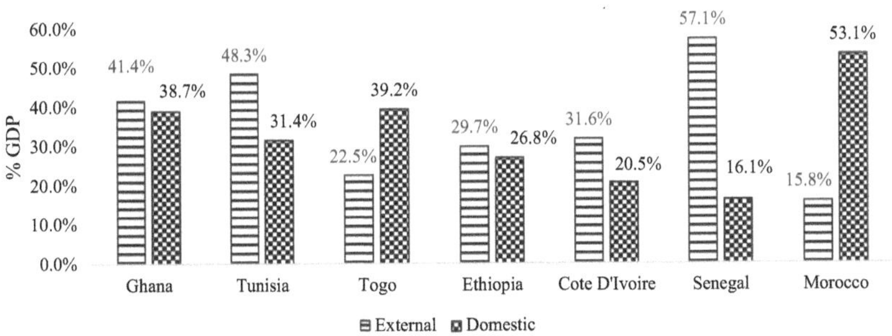


**Fig. 15.4** Public debt components in some African countries. Notes: The data reflect 2021 figures, except for Morocco and Senegal, where 2020 data is used. Source: Authors' construction based on data from Raga et al. (2022)

### *15.2.2 Exchange Rate Regimes and Volatility in Africa*

Exchange rate arrangements in Africa vary widely, reflecting historical legacies, institutional capacities, and policy choices. Broadly, three categories dominate:

(i) **Fixed Exchange Rate Regimes**: The most prominent example is the CFA franc zone, comprising 14 West[1] and the Central African countries[2] whose currencies are pegged to the euro and guaranteed

> **Box 15.2 CFA Franc Zone Reforms**
> The CFA franc's fixed-exchange-rate system, established in the mid-1940s, is one of the world's longest-running currency pegs, providing low nominal volatility but leaving member countries highly exposed to the economic cycles of the external anchors. Mounting policy misalignments and growing public debt eventually triggered the bloc's first major adjustment in January 1994, when the currency was devalued for the first time since 1948, marking a

(*continued*)

[1] The western countries include Benin, Burkina Faso, Guinea-Bissau, Côte d'Ivoire, Mali, Niger, Senegal, and Togo.

[2] Central African countries are Cameroon, Central African Republic, Chad, Republic of Congo, Equatorial Guinea, and Gabon.

**Box 15.2 (continued)**

shift from relying on "real side" adjustment to correcting the nominal anchor to restore competitiveness. In the euro era, the peg has at times led to CFA franc appreciation against the U.S. dollar, which has affected price competitiveness and external balances, particularly during periods of euro strength. Since 2020, global shocks from the pandemic to geopolitical tensions have renewed scrutiny of whether such a rigid regime supports diversification and resilient growth. While the peg offers predictability, credibility, and lower inflation that can attract investment, it also heightens vulnerability when public debt rises or when euro strength makes dollar-denominated imports and debt servicing more expensive. Sustained overvaluation risks undermining export performance and increasing import dependence, challenging trade-led growth strategies. Policy priorities, therefore, include maintaining macroeconomic consistency, improving supply-side infrastructure, strengthening fiscal anchors, managing currency composition of debt, building buffers, and adopting targeted industrial and trade facilitation measures to support competitiveness within a hard peg environment.

Source: Azam (1997) and Meh et al. (2025).

by the French Treasury (Nana, 2024). This arrangement has provided relative nominal stability and low inflation, but at the cost of reduced monetary policy autonomy and periodic competitiveness concerns. The CFA franc zone has implemented a series of reforms designed to strengthen its currency and improve trade performance (see Box 15.2).

(ii) **Managed Float Regimes**: Several African countries[3] operate managed floats, where central banks intervene periodically to smooth volatility. This allows countries to combine market mechanisms with heavy state involvement, often through foreign exchange restrictions and reserve interventions.

[3] Countries who have adopted regime are Angola, Ghana, Guinea, Malawi, Mozambique, Sierra Leone, Sudan, and Tanzania.

(iii) **Floating or Flexible Exchange Rate Regimes**: A growing number of African economies[4] have adopted more flexible exchange rate systems, allowing their currencies to adjust to market conditions. While this provides a shock absorber during external crises, it also exposes these economies to sharp fluctuations, especially when capital inflows are volatile or commodity prices collapse.

The choice of regime[5] has significant implications for debt sustainability. Economies with fixed exchange rates may enjoy stability but accumulate hidden vulnerabilities if debt is rising as in the case of Chad, while flexible regimes face more immediate market pressures when debt dynamics deteriorate, as in the case of Ghana (Box 15.3).

Exchange rate volatility describes the extent of fluctuations in the value of one currency against another over time. Put simply, it captures how strongly and unpredictably exchange rates shift (Alagidede & Ibrahim, 2017). High volatility reflects sharp, rapid movements such as sudden daily or monthly swings, while low volatility signals relative stability and

**Box 15.3 Debt Sustainability of Chad and Ghana Under Different Exchange Rate Regimes**

Chad and Ghana illustrate contrasting exchange rate regimes and debt dynamics. Chad, using the euro-pegged CFA franc, enjoyed monetary stability and low inflation but accumulated hidden vulnerabilities. Public debt exceeded 50% of GDP by 2023, with oil price shocks and limited fiscal space fueling pressures. The fixed regime masked risks by delaying currency depreciation, but debt service burdens forced Chad into IMF-backed restructuring under the G20 Common Framework. Ghana, with a managed float, faced vulnerabilities more openly. Its public debt rose to 85% of GDP by 2023, triggering sharp cedi depreciation, over 50% currency loss in 2022, and inflation surges. Market pressures led to an IMF bailout, aggressive interest rate hikes, and fiscal consolidation.

Source: The Conversation Africa (2024).

[4] Some examples include Liberia, Madagascar, Mauritius, Seychelles, Somalia, South Africa, and Uganda.

[5] It is important to note that countries may shift to a different exchange rate regime.

predictability (Bulut, 2024). These movements are shaped by factors including inflation, interest rates, capital flows, trade imbalances, commodity prices, political uncertainty, and market sentiment. Volatility directly influences import and export costs, the burden of servicing foreign-denominated debt, and broader investment and policy decisions.

Exchange rate volatility is a recurring feature of African economies, though its intensity varies by country. Nigeria's naira has faced repeated devaluations due to falling oil revenues and forex shortages. Multiple exchange rates undermined policy credibility, with the currency plunging from 430 NGN/USD in 2022 to nearly 1700 NGN/USD in 2024 (Box 15.4). Zambia's kwacha, among Africa's most volatile currencies, reflects copper price swings and debt distress. The 2020 Eurobond default triggered a sharp depreciation, while reliance on copper exports, over 70% of earnings, exposed the currency to external shocks and rising debt burdens (Mbewe et al., 2024). Angola's kwanza lost over 40% of its value between 2014 and 2018 after the oil price crash. The dollar peg was abandoned in 2018, with rates diverging to 430 Kz/USD unofficially versus 166 officially, worsening debt service and inflation (Paraskova, 2018). Kenya's shilling depreciated by 22% in 2023 to KSh 147.8/USD, with debt costs rising to KSh 131 billion in 2025 from Eurobond refinancing. Public debt reached KSh 10.9 trillion (67% of GDP), while exchange rate (FX) reserves fell below four months' import cover, intensifying pressures (Okoth, 2023). Since 2016, Egypt has repeatedly devalued the pound under IMF-backed reforms, most recently in March 2024 for a US$8 billion package. Devaluations, tied to subsidy cuts and privatisation, peaked inflation at 38%, doubled bread prices, and raised debt costs. By 2025, IMF obligations exceeded SDR 7.4 billion (Okoth, 2023).

**Box 15.4 Currency Depreciation and Debt Service Spira in Nigeria**

Nigeria's public debt, heavily denominated in U.S. dollars, made the economy highly vulnerable to currency depreciation. Between 2022 and mid-2024, the naira fell from ₦430/USD to over ₦1,700/USD, quadrupling external debt service costs. By 2024, debt service consumed over 45% of revenues, limiting funding for social programmes, infrastructure, and exchange rate stabilization. FX reserves fell below the three-month import benchmark, fueling imported inflation. Investor confidence weakened, triggering capital flight and further depreciation. Limited fiscal space and rising interest rates constrained policy responses, forcing budget revisions and delaying projects.

Source: Doshi (2024).

## 15.3 Channels Linking Public Debt and Exchange Rate Volatility

The relationship between public debt and exchange rate volatility in Africa is complex and multifaceted. Several transmission channels connect rising debt burdens to exchange rate instability, which in turn feeds back into debt dynamics. This section highlights four key channels through which these interactions occur.

### *15.3.1 Debt Service and Currency Depreciation*

A significant portion of Africa's external debt is denominated in U.S. dollars and euros, exposing countries to currency depreciation risks. When local currencies weaken, debt service costs surge. Depreciation pressures drain reserves, hinder exchange rate stabilisation, and worsen perceptions of debt sustainability. This often triggers further depreciation, creating a vicious cycle. The problem is acute when debt service already exceeds 30–40% of revenues, severely limiting fiscal space for stabilisation policies. This issue occurred in Nigeria, where dollar-denominated debt quadrupled in local-currency terms by 2024, consuming over 45% of revenues and fuelling depreciation, inflation and reserve losses (Box 15.4).

### *15.3.2 Investor Confidence and Sovereign Risk*

Rising public debt and weak fiscal transparency heighten perceptions of sovereign risk, undermining investor confidence and pressuring exchange rates. Nigeria's multiple exchange rate windows and opaque debt reporting, for example, weakened the naira. High risk premiums deter FDI and portfolio inflows, raising borrowing costs. When debt sustainability fears escalate, sudden capital reversals can trigger sharp depreciations. This is a vicious cycle, in which rising debt heightens investor scepticism and amplifies exchange rate volatility. This has affected several African economies. For example, the 2016 debt scandal involving US$2 billion in undisclosed loans for maritime projects in Mozambique, which led to depreciation of the metical, an inflation surge to 17.4%, and a collapse in donor confidence (Gebregziabher & Sala, 2022).

### 15.3.3 Monetary and Fiscal Policy Interactions

The interaction of fiscal and monetary policy strongly links debt to exchange rate volatility. High debt service may prompt domestic borrowing or central bank financing, boosting liquidity and inflation, which weakens the currency. Central banks may raise interest rates to stabilise the exchange rate, but this increases debt costs, especially for short-term or floating-rate debt. This policy trade-off, seen in Egypt, shows that defending the currency can temporarily restore investor confidence while exacerbating fiscal vulnerabilities through higher interest burdens and inflationary pressures (Alternative Policy Solutions, 2025; Crédit Agricole S.A., 2024).

### 15.3.4 Currency Mismatch

Currency mismatch is a major structural vulnerability in Africa, as governments collect revenues in local currency but service much debt in foreign currency. Depreciation forces more domestic revenue towards external obligations, reducing social and capital spending. The private sector is similarly exposed, with firms and banks facing higher external debt costs during depreciation, increasing financial instability. This dynamic amplifies fiscal and balance-of-payments stress and reinforces sovereign risk across the economy. A clear example is Ghana, where the country's cedi crash drove soaring debt costs, reserve losses, and an IMF bailout (Box 15.5).

**Box 15.5 Currency Mismatch and Fiscal Compression**

Ghana's heavy reliance on foreign-currency debt created severe vulnerabilities when the cedi depreciated by over 54% in 2022. Servicing external debt soon consumed more than 70% of revenues, far above the 30–40% stress threshold, forcing cuts to social and capital spending. Private firms and banks with foreign liabilities faced soaring costs, while import-dependent businesses collapsed under shrinking margins. Reserves fell below IMF adequacy levels, deepening balance-of-payments stress and fueling capital flight. To restore stability, Ghana entered a US$3 billion IMF programme in 2023, launched a domestic debt exchange of GH₵130 billion, and sought relief from external creditors.

Source: International Monetary Fund. African Dept (2024a, b).

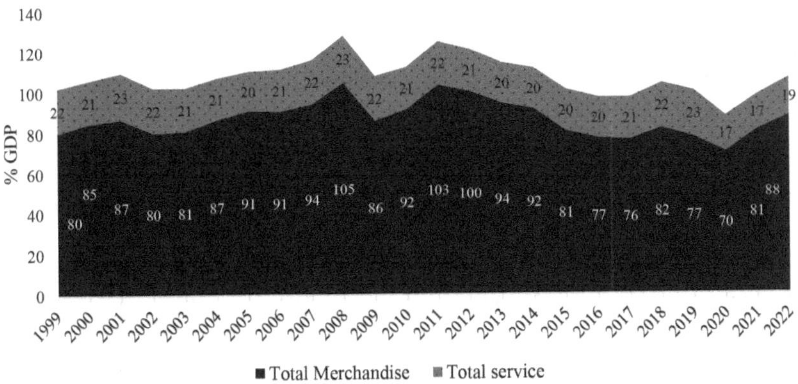


**Fig. 15.5** Trend in international trade in Africa (1999 to 2022), by components. Notes: Total merchandise and services were computed by the author using data for Eastern and Southern and Western, and Central Africa. Source: Authors' construction based on data from World Bank's World Development Indicators

## 15.4 Implications for Trade and Investment

### *15.4.1 Implications for Trade*

Although Africa has a long history of exporting goods dating back to the pre-colonial era, some trade patterns remain unchanged in the twenty-first century. The continent's primary exports continue to be oil, gas, minerals, and agricultural products, while its main imports are manufactured goods and machinery. This imbalance has contributed to persistent trade deficits, as unprocessed natural resources generate less value compared to higher-priced manufactured products and industrial machinery (AfDB, 2021). Data reveals that Africa trades more in merchandise (goods) than in services (Fig. 15.5). This underscores the reality that Africa exports more raw materials and natural resources than value-added products.

Trade in Africa emerges from both intra[6] and extra[7] trade. Intra-African trade has grown in absolute terms, rising from US$98 billion in 2013 to US$102 billion in 2022 (Africa Growth and Opportunity Act (AGOA), 2023). Intra-African trade peaked at 21% in 2015–2016 but stood at

[6] Trade among African countries.

[7] Trade between African countries and other continents.

about 15% (AGOA, 2023). In 2017, intra-African exports were 16.6% of total exports, far below Europe (68.1%), Asia (59.4%), and the Americas (55%). More recently, trade shares declined, with intra-African exports falling from 18.22% to 17.89% and imports from 12.81% to 12.09% between 2021 and 2022 (Economic Comission for Africa (ECA), 2024).

Africa's extra-continental trade spans Europe, Asia, the Americas, and the Middle East, but Asia and Europe dominate (ElGanainy et al., 2023). Exports to China and India rose from 5% in 2000 to 23% by 2019. After a 16.2% contraction in 2020, extra-African trade rebounded by 29.5%, largely driven by Asia's demand and improved commodity terms of trade (Afreximbank, 2022). Asia has since solidified its role as Africa's top trading partner, accounting for more than 32% of extra-African trade (African Union, 2020).

Among the various factors shaping trade, public debt and exchange rate volatility stand out, influencing it through the following channels:

1. **Exchange Rate Volatility and Export Competitiveness**
Exchange rate movements shape export competitiveness, but the benefits for African economies are limited. While depreciation should make exports cheaper, many countries rely on commodities like oil, copper, and cocoa whose international prices are unaffected. For manufactured or processed exports, heavy dependence on imported inputs offsets gains, as depreciation raises production costs (Kyereboah-Coleman et al., 2024). Moreover, volatility disrupts planning, pricing, and investment in export industries, creating uncertainty. Ghana's cocoa exports are globally priced, so cedi depreciation brings no competitiveness gains (Abukari & Cunfeng, 2021). Export earnings stay fixed internationally, while inflation-driven local costs like logistics and labour rise, squeezing profitability (Abukari & Cunfeng, 2021).
2. **Import Dependence and Pass-Through Effects on Inflation**
African economies depend heavily on imports of essentials like machinery, fuel, medicines, rice, and wheat (Mshomba, 2017). Currency depreciation raises import costs, fuelling inflation, eroding household purchasing power, and increasing business expenses (Afreximbank, 2025). Governments face widening trade deficits as import bills and foreign-currency debt servicing soar, creating a "double squeeze." In response, many resort to subsidies, trade

restrictions, or foreign exchange rationing (Afreximbank, 2025). While intended to stabilise markets, such measures often distort trade and reduce efficiency, further complicating long-term economic management and deepening vulnerabilities to external shocks.

3. **Regional Trade Integration Challenges**
   The AfCFTA aims to expand intra-African trade by cutting tariffs and aligning rules, but exchange rate volatility threatens progress (see Box 15.6). Divergent currency shifts create uncertainty in pricing and settlement, undermining trade predictability. Firms struggle with unstable relative prices and rising transaction costs from hedging or dollar-based settlement, weakening financial integration and limiting AfCFTA's potential to foster deeper, resilient cross-border trade across the continent. For instance, despite AfCFTA's promise, intra-African trade fell from US$18.6 billion in January to US$18 billion in February 2025, which is a sign that macroeconomic instability can offset integration gains (Afreximbank, 2025).

**Box 15.6 African Continental Free Trade Area (AfCFTA)**

The African Continental Free Trade Area (AfCFTA), signed in 2018 and operational since 2021, is one of the world's largest trade agreements, covering 1.4 billion people and a combined GDP of over US$3.4 trillion. Its core objective is to remove tariffs on 90% of goods, reduce non-tariff barriers, and create a unified African market. With 54 of 55 AU member states signed on, the agreement is expected to raise Africa's income by US$400–450 billion annually and increase intra-African trade by more than 50%, thereby fostering industrialisation, diversifying value chains, and reducing reliance on external markets. Protocols on women and youth in trade aim to promote social inclusion and support MSMEs. AfCFTA also strengthens Africa's collective bargaining power globally. However, challenges persist, including potential tariff revenue losses, inadequate infrastructure, uneven gains among countries, implementation gaps, and limited access to finance for women- and youth-led enterprises.

Source: Samunderu (2024) and UNCTAD (2017).

### *15.4.2 Implications for Investment*

This section discusses three main dimensions of investment, such as foreign direct investment (FDI), portfolio investment, and domestic investment and shows how public debt and exchange rate volatility affect it.

1. **Foreign Direct Investment**
   FDI in Africa has shown notable increases during periods of growth, although overall volumes remain comparatively small. SSA, in particular, records faster FDI growth than other continents, though at a modest scale. Africa's FDI trends show mixed resilience. After the 2008–2009 global financial crisis, Africa recovered faster than regions like East Asia, South Asia, and Europe (Iddrisu et al., 2024; UNCTAD, 2015). However, even before COVID-19, FDI had already fallen by 10% to US$45 billion in 2019 (UNCTAD, 2020). The pandemic and Middle East and North Africa (MENA) vulnerabilities worsened the decline, reducing flows by 23% in 2020. A strong rebound followed, with inflows reaching US$83 billion in 2021, raising optimism for sustained growth. Yet, FDI fell back to US$45 billion in 2022. By 2023, flows stabilised at US$44 billion, marking only a 1% decrease from the previous year (UNCTAD, 2023). FDI is often regarded as a stable source of external finance, yet exchange rate volatility can deter multinational corporations from committing capital to African economies. Investors prefer predictable macroeconomic conditions that allow for reliable projections of costs and returns. When exchange rates fluctuate unpredictably, investors face the risk that profits repatriated in hard currency will be eroded by depreciation. For instance, in Ethiopia, efforts to attract FDI into manufacturing under its industrial parks programme have been hampered by recurrent foreign exchange shortages and periodic devaluations of the birr.[8] Although lower exchange rates may improve export competitiveness, uncertainty about currency stability increases perceived risk, leading some investors to delay or scale down projects. In addition, countries with high debt burdens often face credit rating downgrades, which signal higher sovereign risk to potential investors. To compensate, foreign investors demand higher

[8] Read more here: https://research-api.cbs.dk/ws/portalfiles/portal/58452989/selamawit_berhe_woldekidan.pdf accessed September 10, 2025.

returns, effectively raising the cost of attracting FDI. This presents a clear paradox: the countries with the greatest need for stable, long-term investment are often the least capable of attracting such capital due to persistent debt distress and exchange rate volatility.

2. **Portfolio Investment**
   Portfolio flows, such as investments in government bonds, equities, and other financial assets, are particularly sensitive to debt and exchange rate dynamics. In African markets, these flows are often procyclical: they increase during periods of stability and rapidly withdraw during episodes of uncertainty. During debt distress episodes, investors tend to engage in sudden stops or reversals, withdrawing capital to avoid losses. This not only weakens financial markets but also exerts downward pressure on exchange rates, amplifying volatility. Such dynamics create a vicious cycle: portfolio outflows weaken currencies, which increases debt service burdens, which in turn fuels further investor scepticism. This self-reinforcing loop makes portfolio investment particularly fragile in African economies with high external debt exposure (Afreximbank, 2025).
3. **Domestic Investment**
   Exchange rate volatility also undermines domestic investment by raising the cost of imported capital goods. Many African countries rely heavily on imported machinery, equipment, and intermediate goods for production. Depreciation of local currencies inflates these costs, discouraging firms from expanding capacity. In Angola, for example, heavy dependence on oil revenues has made the kwanza highly volatile (World Bank, 2025). Sharp depreciations following oil price declines have increased the cost of imported machinery and spare parts, limiting investment in non-oil sectors such as agriculture and manufacturing. Domestic firms often delay or cancel investment plans due to uncertainty over future input costs, reinforcing structural dependence on resource exports. Furthermore, debt-financed public investment can crowd out private sector investment when governments dominate credit markets or when concerns about fiscal sustainability push up domestic interest rates. Exchange rate instability compounds this effect by increasing uncertainty in pricing, revenue forecasting, and input procurement.

## 15.5 Conclusions

This chapter has explored the intricate relationship between public debt dynamics and exchange rate volatility in Africa, showing how the two reinforce one another with broad implications for trade and investment. The historical review highlighted the transition from the debt crises of the 1980s and 1990s, through HIPC and MDRI debt relief in the 2000s, to renewed borrowing via Eurobonds, Chinese loans, and commercial debt in the 2010s. The post-COVID era has witnessed a sharp rise in debt-to-GDP ratios, with many countries again facing distress. Exchange rate analysis underscored three main patterns: commodity-dependent economies such as Nigeria, Angola, and Zambia experience pronounced volatility; the CFA franc zone benefits from relative stability but at the cost of reduced competitiveness; and more flexible regimes such as Kenya and Ghana struggle to anchor expectations amid global shocks. Together, rising debt and currency swings amplify risks for African economies by increasing debt service burdens, discouraging trade, and deterring investment. The channels of interaction, such as debt service pressures, investor confidence, fiscal monetary dynamics, and currency mismatches, demonstrate how macroeconomic fragility can spiral into financial instability.

The findings carry important lessons for multiple stakeholders: African governments need to adopt prudent debt management strategies, deepen domestic financial markets, diversify exports, and maintain credible exchange rate frameworks. Reducing foreign-currency debt exposure and enhancing transparency are critical steps towards resilience. Regional bodies such as the African Union, AfDB, and AfCFTA Secretariat should strengthen mechanisms for macroeconomic surveillance, promote regional financial safety nets, and coordinate currency stabilisation efforts to support integration. Regional initiatives could also foster shared reserves, cross-border payment systems, and coordinated debt restructuring platforms. Investors require better access to transparent information and risk-mitigation instruments. By promoting tools like local-currency bond markets, hedging facilities, and political risk insurance, policymakers can reduce the risk premiums that currently deter both trade and investments such as FDI and portfolio flows.

## References


Abukari, A., & Cunfeng, T. (2021). The export competitiveness of Ghana's cocoa industry in West Africa. *Journal of Agricultural Science, 13*(3), 80. https://doi.org/10.5539/jas.v13n3p80

AfDB. (2021). *African economic outlook 2021: From debt resolution to growth: The Road Ahead for Africa.*

Afreximbank. (2022). *African Trade Report 2022: Leveraging the Power of Culture and Creative Industries for Accelerated Structural Transformation in the AfCFTA Era.* https://media.afreximbank.com/afrexim/AFRICA-TRADE-REPORT-2022.pdf

Afreximbank. (2025). *Monthly developments in the African macroeconomic environment.* https://media.afreximbank.com/afrexim/monthly-developments-in-the-african-macro-environment-june-2025.pdf

African Union. (2020, November 18). *Documents African trade statistics 2020 yearbook.* African Union. https://au.int/en/documents/20201118/african-trade-statistics-2020-yearbook

AGOA. (2023, December 19). *Intra-Africa trade: Facts and figures 2022.* https://www.tralac.org/resources/infographic/16253-intra-africa-trade-facts-and-figures-2022.html

Alagidede, P., & Ibrahim, M. (2017). On the causes and effects of exchange rate volatility on economic growth: Evidence from Ghana. *Journal of African Business, 18*(2), 169–193. https://doi.org/10.1080/15228916.2017.1247330

Ali, A. A., & Obaidy, M. (2019). *Current account adjustments and exchange rate arrangements: What regime for African countries?* (RP-19/02; Research Paper). https://www.policycenter.ma/sites/default/files/PCNS-RP1902.pdf

Alternative Policy Solutions. (2025, February 10). *Inflation vs. investment: Egypt's struggle with interest rate policy.* Alternative Policy Solutions. https://aps.aucegypt.edu/en/articles/1469/inflation-vs-investment-egypts-struggle-with-interest-rate-policy

Anyanwu, J. C., & Salami, A. O. (2021). The impact of COVID-19 on African economies: An introduction. *African Development Review, 33*(S1). https://doi.org/10.1111/1467-8268.12531

Azam, J.-P. (1997). Public debt and the exchange rate in the CFA franc zone. *Journal of African Economies, 6*(1), 54–84. https://doi.org/10.1093/oxfordjournals.jae.a020923

Bulut, E. (2024). Market volatility and models for forecasting volatility. In J. C. Rouco & P. C. N. Figueiredo (Eds.), *Business continuity management and resilience: Theories, models and processes* (pp. 220–248). IGI Global. https://doi.org/10.4018/979-8-3693-1658-0.ch010

Crédit Agricole S.A. (2024). *EGYPT – Retrospective of a currency crisis: How to build confidence?* (24/195; Crédit Agricole Group Economic and Sector

Analysis). https://etudes-economiques.credit-agricole.com/en/previewPDF/181001

daba. (2024, August 18). *CFA Franc: A hedge against weak African currencies.* https://www.dabafinance.com/en/learn/blogs/cfa-franc-a-hedge-against-weak-african-currencies

Doshi, I. (2024, October 29). *Currency Conundrums: Volatile African exchange rates and what can be done.* MIT Management. https://mitsloan.mit.edu/centers-initiatives/ksc/currency-conundrums-volatile-african-exchange-rates-and-what-can-be-done

ECA. (2024, March 1). *African countries trading more outside the continent than amongst themselves.* ECA report. https://www.uneca.org/stories/african-countries-trading-more-outside-the-continent-than-amongst-themselves%2C-eca-report

ElGanainy, A., Hakobyan, S., Liu, F., Weisfeld, H., Allard, C., Balima, H. W., Bteish, C., Giri, R., Kanda, D. S., Meleshchuk, S., Ramirez, G., Zymek, R., Arora, V. B., Lall, S., Kett, B. R., & Pohl, M. M. (2023). Trade integration in Africa. *Departmental Papers, 2023*(003), 1. https://doi.org/10.5089/9798400232794.087

Fliss, L. (2022). *Eurobonds, Debt Sustainability in Africa and Credit Rating Agencies.* https://www.un.org/osaa/sites/www.un.org.osaa/files/docs/2118580-osaa-eurobonds_policy_paper_web.pdf

Gebeltová, Z., Hálová, P., Malec, K., Bartoňová, K., Blažek, V., Maitah, M., Koželský, R., Phiri, J., Appiah-Kubi, S. N. K., Tomšík, K., Severová, L., & Marušiak, J. (2023). Geopolitical risks for Egypt wheat supply and trade. *Frontiers in Sustainable Food Systems, 7.* https://doi.org/10.3389/fsufs.2023.1137526

Gebregziabher, F. H., & Sala, A. P. (2022, April 19). *Mozambique's "hidden debts": Turning a crisis into an opportunity for reform.* World Bank Blog.

Iddrisu, K., Abor, J. Y., & Banyen, K. T. (2024). Financial development, globalisation and foreign direct investment nexus: An empirical study from Africa. *SN Business & Economics, 4*(6), 69. https://doi.org/10.1007/s43546-024-00667-w

International Monetary Fund. African Dept. (2024a). Ghana: Second review under the arrangement under the extended credit facility, request for modification of performance criteria, and financing assurances review—Debt sustainability analysis. *IMF Staff Country Reports, 2024*(213).

International Monetary Fund. African Dept. (2024b). Zambia: Fourth Review Under the Arrangement Under the Extended Credit Facility and Financing Assurances Review—Debt Sustainability Analysis. *IMF Staff Country Reports*, 2024.

KIPPRA. (2019, December 22). *Composition of domestic debt in Kenya and implication on refinancing risk.* KIPPRA. https://kippra.or.ke/composition-of-domestic-debt-in-kenya-and-implication-on-refinancing-risk/

Kyereboah-Coleman, A., Boumbouya, R. K., Marimo, M., & Latif, N. (2024). Structure, composition, and trends in African trade. In M. K. Ocran & J. Y. Abor (Eds.), *The Palgrave handbook of international trade and development in Africa* (pp. 71–88). Springer International Publishing. https://doi.org/10.1007/978-3-031-65715-3_5

Mbewe, M., Masilokwa, I., Humann, T., Kalikeka, M., Kessler, M., & Mwamba, S. (2024). *The road to Zambia's 2020 sovereign debt default.* https://findevlab.org/wp-content/uploads/2023/12/The-Road-to-Zambias-2020-Sovereign-Debt-Default-vf.pdf

Meh, B. J., Kouam, J. C., Ngapmen, N. L., & Foretia, D. A. (2025). Impact of pegging the CFA franc to the euro on terms of trade and economic growth in the franc zone. *Discover Global Society, 3*(1), 22. https://doi.org/10.1007/s44282-025-00149-w

Mshomba, R. E. (2017). Africa and the global economy. In N. Cheeseman, D. Anderson, & A. Scheibler (Eds.), *Routledge handbook of African politics* (1st ed.). Routledge.

Mutai, N. (2025). *China's debt to Africa: A balancing act between development and dependency.* Democracy in Africa. https://democracyinafrica.org/chinas-debt-to-africa-a-balancing-act-between-development-and-dependency/

Nana, C. N. (2024). Currency relations between the global south and the global north: The case of the CFA France. *Beijing L. Rev., 15*, 35–53.

Okoth, J. (2023, September 29). *Kenya faces looming debt crisis as its first Eurobond matures in 2024.* Wallstreet Africa Technologies LTD. https://kenyanwallstreet.com/kenya-faces-looming-debt-crisis-as-first-eurobond-matures-in-2024/

Paraskova, T. (2018, January 5). Oil price rise not enough*: Angola Ditches U.S. Dollar Peg.* OilPrice.Com. https://oilprice.com/Latest-Energy-News/World-News/Oil-Price-Rise-Not-Enough-Angola-Ditches-US-Dollar-Peg.html

Raga, S., Ayele, Y., & te Velde, D. W. (2022). *Public debt profile of selected African countries* (ODI emerging analysis). https://odi.cdn.ngo/media/documents/Public_debt_profile_of_selected_African_countries_PDF_D9l4AzP.pdf

Samunderu, E. (2024). Liberalisation of trade regime under AfCFTA: A perspective analysis on Africa's single market. In E. Samunderu (Ed.), *The economic effects of air transport market liberalisation. Advances in African economic, social and political development* (pp. 641–730). Springer. https://doi.org/10.1007/978-3-031-61864-2_7

Stein, H. (2015). *Africa, Growth Sustainability and the Great Recession* (387; PERI Working Paper Series). https://peri.umass.edu/wp-content/uploads/joomla/images/publication/WP387_copy_1.pdf

The Conversation Africa. (2024, January 31). African countries are struggling with high debt, demands to spend more and collapsing currencies: The policy fixes that could help. *The Conversation Africa.* https://theconversation.com/african-countries-are-struggling-with-high-debt-demands-to-spend-more-and-collapsing-currencies-the-policy-fixes-that-could-help-221614

UNCTAD. (2015). *World investment report 2015: Reforming international investment governance.*

UNCTAD. (2017). *African continental free trade area: Challenges and opportunities of tariff reductions* (15; UNCTAD Research Paper).

UNCTAD. (2020). *World Investment Report 2020: International Production Beyond The Pandemic.* https://unctad.org/system/files/official-document/wir2020_en.pdf

UNCTAD. (2023). *Africa.* UNCTAD. https://unctad.org/publication/world-of-debt/regional-stories

World Bank. (2024, May 9). *Heavily indebted poor countries (HIPC) Initiative.* World Bank. https://www.worldbank.org/en/topic/debt/brief/hipc

World Bank. (2025, July 25). *Angola Economic Update - Boosting Growth with Inclusive Financial Development.* World Bank. https://www.worldbank.org/en/country/angola/publication/angola-economic-update-boosting-growth-with-inclusive-financial-development

CHAPTER 16

# The Role of Commodity Price Volatility in Public Debt Sustainability in Resource-Dependent African Countries

*Khadijah Iddrisu, Moses Dumayiri, Richard Takyi Opoku, and Felix Owusu Gyebi*

## 16.1 Introduction

Many African economies rely heavily on the extraction and export of natural resources, including oil, gas, minerals, and agricultural commodities. These are commonly referred to as resource-dependent countries,

K. Iddrisu (✉) • R. T. Opoku
Department of Banking and Finance, Islamic University College, Accra, Ghana
e-mail: khadijahiddris@iug.edu.gh; richard.takyi@iug.edu.gh

M. Dumayiri
School of Business, Simon Diedong Dombo University of Business and Integrated Development Studies, Wa, Ghana
e-mail: mdumayiri@ubids.edu.gh

F. O. Gyebi
Accountancy Department, Faculty of Business and Management Studies, Koforidua Technical University, Koforidua, Ghana
e-mail: felixo.gyebi@ktu.edu.gh



I. N. Yakubu (ed.), *Public Debt and Economic Resilience in Africa*, Palgrave Studies in African and Development Economics,
https://doi.org/10.1007/978-3-032-25835-9_16

meaning their economic performance is strongly tied to the production and sale of primary natural resources. Resource exports account for a significant share of foreign exchange earnings and government revenues in many African countries (Katoka & Dostal, 2022; Ross et al., 2019). Algeria's hydrocarbons make up 95% of export earnings and 60% of budget revenue (Bagshaw, 2025). Copper exports contribute about 70% of Zambia's total foreign exchange (Bagshaw, 2025). A high level of dependence results in vulnerability, where favourable commodity markets boost revenues, creating fiscal space and investment opportunities. However, during downturns, revenues collapse, often leading to fiscal deficits, balance-of-payments crises, and the need for external borrowing. Thus, resource dependence tends to reinforce fiscal procyclicality and heightens exposure to external shocks. For example, Nigeria's 2014 oil price crash cut revenues, causing deficits, currency depreciation, and borrowing. As of 2025, Nigeria's debt servicing consumes 45% of revenue, interest costs have doubled, and optimistic budget assumptions hide a 4.6% GDP deficit (Macheka et al., 2025).

Fiscal revenues and export earnings in resource-dependent African countries are tightly linked to commodity prices, making debt sustainability highly sensitive to global market shifts (Coulibaly, 2024; Da & Diarra, 2023). During price booms, governments often expand spending, invest in infrastructure, and accumulate external debt on the assumption of sustained revenues (Céspedes & Velasco, 2012). When prices decline, however, debt servicing becomes increasingly difficult, especially for countries that are reliant on commercial borrowing or Eurobond issuance. Ghana illustrates this vulnerability as a price decline pushed its debt-to-GDP ratio above 90% while Eurobond interest payments absorbed over 70% of government revenue, rendering debt servicing unsustainable (Ghana News Agency, 2024). Commodity price volatility represents a central challenge for debt sustainability. Prices of oil, copper, cocoa, and other key African exports are influenced not only by global supply and demand but also by geopolitical tensions, shifts in technology, financial speculation, and the global energy transition (Wanzala & Obokoh, 2024). The resulting price swings are often large, unpredictable, and persistent. For governments reliant on commodity rents, such volatility translates into unstable revenues, sudden financing gaps, and heightened borrowing needs (United Nations Conference for Trade and Development (UNCTAD), 2025). The "boom-and-bust" cycles lead to fiscal instability: during booms, governments may over-borrow and overspend, while in busts, they face fiscal contraction, rising debt distress, and in extreme cases, debt default or restructuring (United Nations Development Programme (UNDP) Regional Bureau for Africa, 2016). This chapter seeks to examine the role of commodity price volatility in shaping public debt sustainability in resource-dependent African countries.

The remainder of the chapter is organised as follows. Section 16.2 examines commodity price volatility in Africa, while Sect. 16.3 analyzes the channels through which it affects public debt sustainability. Section 16.4 explores policy and institutional responses, and Sect. 16.5 discusses the reasons why some of these measures have failed in practice.

## 16.2 Commodity Price Volatility in Africa

Africa's economic history has been deeply intertwined with the fluctuations of global commodity markets. From the colonial period, when African economies were integrated into the global economy as suppliers of raw materials, to the present, export earnings from oil, minerals, and cash crops have shaped macroeconomic trajectories. Commodity prices have typically followed boom-and-bust cycles, with periods of high demand and elevated prices followed by sharp downturns. Further discussion of the commodity prices in Africa is presented below:

1. **Pre-colonial and Early Colonial Period (Before 1900s):** Africa's commodity trade emerged through extensive trans-Saharan caravans and coastal maritime routes that connected to the North Africa, the Middle East, and Europe (History Rise, 2024). These networks facilitated the exchange of gold, ivory, kola nuts, salt, and enslaved people, embedding Africa in early global commerce. Distinct ecological zones shaped specialisation: the Sahara provided salt, West Africa's gold financed powerful empires, and the East African coast became a hub for ivory, spices, and maritime trade with Arab and Asian merchants (Maverick, 2025). This complementarity strengthened internal trade and global integration. The arrival of European and Arab traders intensified demand, shifting production toward exports and embedding extractive systems focused on foreign markets. Colonial expansion institutionalised this orientation, restructuring African economies around resource extraction for Europe's industrial needs. This legacy created enduring export dependence and vulnerability to global market

fluctuations, shaping structural economic challenges that continue into the present.

2. **Colonial Era (Late Nineteenth–Mid-Twentieth Century):** Under colonial rule, African economies were reshaped to serve Europe's industrial needs, with cash crops like cotton, cocoa, and coffee, and minerals such as gold and copper, dominating production (Hope, 2025). Subsistence farming and local industries were sidelined, creating export-dependent systems. Commodity price booms spurred infrastructure development such as railways, ports, and telegraphs, but these mainly facilitated extraction rather than domestic integration or industrialisation. Egypt during the U.S. Civil War illustrates the risks: cotton booms fuelled ambitious modernisation under Ismail Pasha, but falling prices led to unmanageable debts and foreign financial control (Toussaint, 2016). Such cycles of boom-driven borrowing followed by bust-induced crises entrenched dependency on external creditors and reinforced Africa's vulnerability to volatile global markets.
3. **Post-Independence Commodity Optimism (1960s–1980s):** In the decades following independence, many African governments nationalised mines, oil fields, and agricultural export sectors, believing that direct state control over resources would secure revenues for nation building, industrialisation, and social programmes (Andreasson, 2015). This optimism reflected a wider push for sovereignty and economic self-determination after years of colonial extraction. During the 1970s, countries such as Nigeria, Angola, and Zambia benefited from sharp increases in oil and copper prices, which financed ambitious development plans, large-scale infrastructure, and rapid public sector expansion (Cole et al., 2015; Falola & Heaton, 2012). Governments assumed high revenues would persist, embedding spending commitments that became unsustainable once global prices collapsed. The downturn of the 1980s devastated fiscal balances and created mounting external debts across Africa, forcing governments to seek assistance from the IMF and World Bank (Ghura et al., 1999). Structural adjustment programmes followed, reorienting economies toward liberalisation and austerity while reshaping development trajectories and reinforcing vulnerabilities tied to volatile global commodity markets.
4. **Commodity Supercycle and Globalisation (2000s–2014):** China's rapid industrialisation from the early 2000s generated unprecedented demand for oil, copper, iron ore, and other African commodities, driving prices upward and boosting export revenues and foreign exchange reserves across resource-rich states (Farooki & Kaplinsky, 2013). This

surge created optimism about sustained growth while deepening Africa's integration into global markets and reinforcing dependence on external consumption (Collier & Venables, 2010). During this boom, several countries including Ghana, Zambia, and Nigeria, tapped international capital markets by issuing Eurobonds, assuming that strong revenues from oil and minerals would cover debt obligations (UNCTAD, 2016, 2021). Although this strategy provided quick financing, it heightened exposure to global shocks and reduced fiscal flexibility during downturns (UNCTAD, 2016). High revenues also encouraged ambitious infrastructure expansion, with new roads, ports, power plants, and urban facilities launched to modernise economies and attract investment. Yet, limited fiscal buffers and weak institutional safeguards made spending unsustainable, leaving many countries vulnerable when global commodity prices collapsed and revenues declined.

5. **Post-2014 Decline and Debt Distress**: The sharp decline in global oil prices exposed the vulnerabilities of major producers such as Nigeria and Angola, where revenues fell dramatically, creating large fiscal deficits and foreign exchange shortages (The Conversation Africa, 2024). Both countries faced currency devaluations, rising inflation, and greater borrowing needs, underscoring the risks of heavy reliance on volatile oil exports. As commodity revenues weakened, debt burdens became increasingly difficult to manage, with Ghana defaulting on Eurobond repayments in 2022 and Zambia entering restructuring talks in 2020 after failing to meet obligations (Ekanem, 2025). These cases highlight how dependence on external commercial debt amplifies fiscal fragility during downturns, leading to crises of sustainability and credibility.

In many African countries, natural resources contribute more than half of government revenues, as seen in Angola, the Republic of Congo, and Nigeria. Data from 2000 to 2021 indicate that Africa remains highly dependent on income generated from natural resources, with natural resource rents serving as a proxy for resource revenues in their contribution to GDP. A regional breakdown shows that natural resources account for a larger share of GDP in Central and Western Africa compared to Eastern and Southern Africa. Overall, the trend reveals a gradual decline in resource rents over time, with the highest values recorded in 2000 and 2001 (see Fig. 16.1). At the country level, natural resource rents account for a substantial share of Libya's economy, contributing approximately 42.9% of GDP, while in Mauritius, their role is negligible, representing only about 0.03% of GDP (see Fig. 16.2).

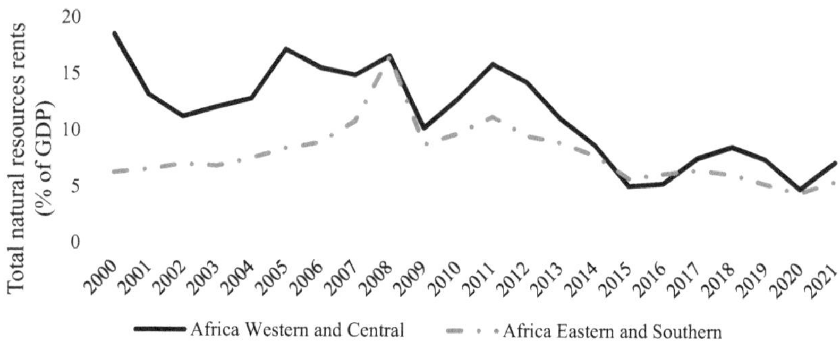


**Fig. 16.1** Trend in natural resource rent in Africa (2000 to 2021). Source: Authors' construct based on data from World Development Indicators

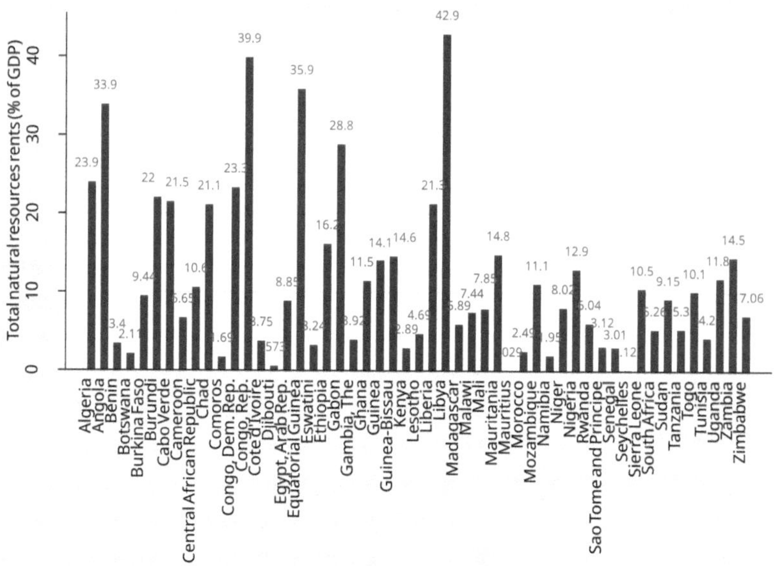


**Fig. 16.2** In-country natural resource rent in Africa (2000 to 2021). Source: Authors' construct based on data from World Development Indicators

This reliance creates extreme vulnerability to external shocks, since fiscal health depends on volatile global commodity prices, leaving budgets highly exposed to sudden downturns in demand or prices.

## 16.3 Channels of Transmission to Public Debt Sustainability

Commodity price volatility affects debt sustainability in resource-dependent African economies through multiple interrelated channels. These channels capture both direct fiscal impacts and broader macroeconomic spillovers that shape governments' capacity to manage debt over time. Some of these channels are discussed as follows:

### *16.3.1 Fiscal Revenues Tied to Commodity Cycles*

Resource-dependent economies often rely on commodity rents for a large share of government revenue. When global commodity prices rise, government coffers expand, allowing fiscal surpluses or increased spending. However, when prices collapse, revenues fall sharply, creating budget deficits and forcing governments to borrow in order to maintain basic expenditures. This volatility undermines predictable fiscal planning and weakens debt sustainability (Wanzala & Obokoh, 2024). In 2022, global shocks had a disproportionate impact on Africa's commodity-dependent economies (AfDB, 2025). Oil exporters experienced slower growth, while many struggled with fiscal pressures arising from shrinking revenues alongside increasing expenditure (AfDB, 2025). Oil accounts for more than 50% of fiscal revenues in Angola (see Fig. 16.3). Between 2015 and 2020, crude

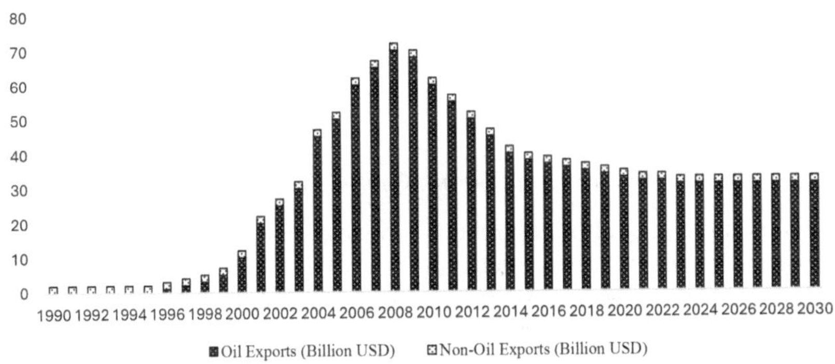


**Fig. 16.3** Trend and estimates in Angola's export (1990 to 2030). Notes: The dataset covers actual values for 1990–2020, while figures for 2021–2030 represent projections. Source: Authors' construct based on data from Cao et al. (2022)

oil and petroleum products accounted for roughly 96% of Angola's exports, generated 56% of government revenues, and contributed 34% to real GDP (Cao et al., 2022).

### *16.3.2 Procyclical Spending and Political Economy Pressures*

Governments in Africa often respond to resource booms with sharp increases in public spending, particularly on infrastructure, wages, and subsidies (Lledó et al., 2009). These policies are politically attractive, as they signal development progress and can consolidate political legitimacy. However, the expansion is typically procyclical: spending rises in good times but cannot easily be reduced during downturns because of rigid expenditure commitments, public sector wage bills, and political resistance (Carneiro & Kouame, 2020). The result is that, during commodity price collapses, governments resort to borrowing to maintain spending levels, thereby fuelling debt accumulation. Over time, these dynamics create a cycle of fiscal imbalances and debt vulnerabilities closely tied to commodity price swings. Procyclicality is more pronounced in resource-rich and resource-dependent economies. The averagely SSA has 0.31 unit of procyclicality, with resource-dependent countries recording 0.33 compared to 0.27 for other SSA economies (Fig. 16.4A). A cross-regional comparison further highlights this bias: SSA's resource-dependent countries exhibit a coefficient of 0.33, higher than the 0.23 observed in similar economies elsewhere (Fig. 16.5). The contrast is even sharper among resource-rich countries, where SSA registers 0.33 compared to just 0.08 in other regions (Fig. 16.5). This divergence reflects the closer overlap between resource-rich and resource-dependent groups in SSA, a pattern less evident in other regions.

### *16.3.3 Borrowing During Commodity Booms and Busts*

Commodity cycles also shape the borrowing behaviour of African states. During booms, countries often increase external borrowing, assuming that high export revenues will sustain debt repayment. Many governments issued Eurobonds in the 2000s and 2010s commodity boom, attracted by favourable global financial conditions. However, when prices later fell, debt service obligations became increasingly difficult to meet, as seen in Zambia's 2020 default (UNDP Regional Bureau for Africa, 2016). Conversely, during busts, governments may also turn to borrowing from

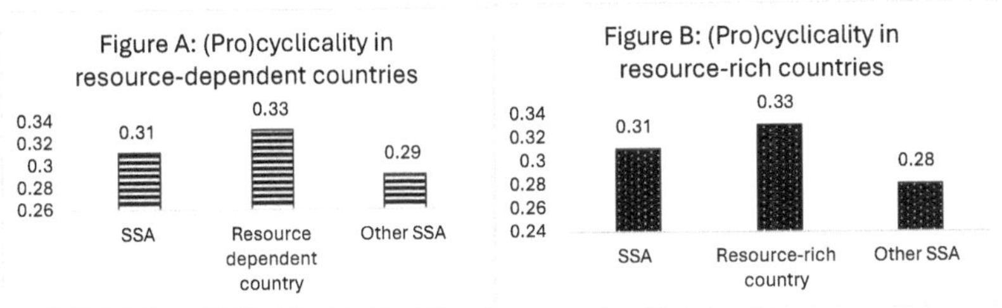


**Fig. 16.4** Average (pro)cyclicality in SSA, resource dependent and rich versus other countries (2000–2016). Source: Authors' construct based on data from Herrera et al. (2019)

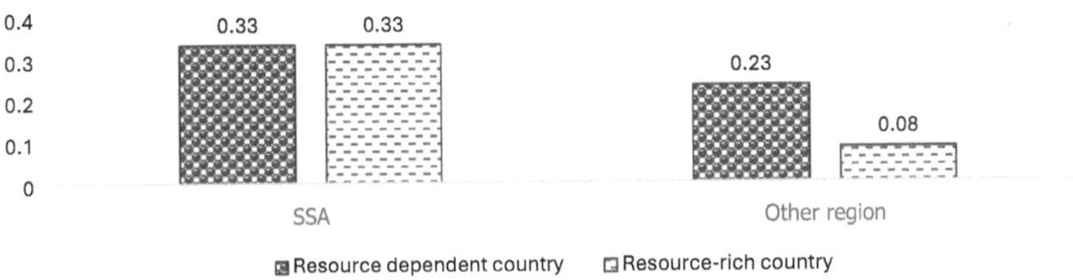


**Fig. 16.5** Average (pro)cyclicality in SSA versus other region (2009–2016). Source: Authors' construct based on data from Herrera et al. (2019)

multilateral institutions or bilateral creditors to fill financing gaps created by revenue shortfalls. Thus, both booms and busts can drive higher debt burdens, reflecting weak debt management strategies and over-optimism during price upswings.

### 16.3.4 *Currency Depreciation and External Debt Servicing*

Commodity price shocks often lead to significant exchange rate adjustments in resource-dependent economies. A fall in oil or copper prices typically reduces foreign exchange inflows, putting downward pressure on local currencies. Since much of Africa's public debt is denominated in foreign currencies (particularly U.S. dollars and euros), exchange rate depreciation amplifies debt burdens even if the nominal external debt stock remains unchanged. This "exchange rate pass-through" effect directly worsens debt sustainability and heightens rollover risks in international markets. For example, between June 2023 and June 2024, Nigeria's external debt in dollar terms changed little, but due to naira depreciation (from about ₦770.38/US$ in June 2023 to ₦1,470.19/US$ in June 2024), the naira-equivalent of that debt rose dramatically (by ~89.7%), making servicing that debt much more costly in local currency (Tunji, 2024). The Zambian kwacha traded as low as 26.47 per dollar in June 2024, marking one of its weakest performances, as commodity price volatility, depleted reserves, and fiscal stress worsened Zambia's ability to service external debt (Oluwole, 2024).

### *16.3.5 Macroeconomic Instability and Development Setbacks*

Commodity price volatility also undermines economic growth, which is a crucial determinant of debt sustainability. During booms, growth may accelerate as revenues finance infrastructure and social spending. But downturns often trigger recessions, investment slowdowns, and inflationary pressures. The uncertainty created by price swings discourages long-term private investment, reduces productivity, and weakens the structural transformation of African economies. Slower or negative growth reduces the revenue base available for debt servicing, raising debt-to-GDP ratios and pushing countries toward distress. Over the long term, persistent volatility can trap economies in a cycle of low diversification, unstable growth, and recurrent debt crises, as exemplified by many resource-dependent states. According to Copley (2016), commodity price slumps have in recent years led to weakened growth, fiscal deficits, currency depreciation, inflation, and difficulties in debt servicing in most African countries. An empirical study by Wanzala and Obokoh (2024) reveals that, commodity price volatility negatively affects long-term economic stability in 31 SSA countries.

## 16.4 Policy and Institutional Responses

Resource-dependent African countries have experimented with a variety of policy and institutional mechanisms to mitigate the effects of commodity price volatility on debt sustainability. These measures aim to smooth fiscal revenues, manage public debt more prudently, and provide buffers against external shocks.

### *16.4.1 Sovereign Wealth Funds and Stabilisation Funds*

Several African countries have established sovereign wealth funds (SWFs) or stabilisation funds to save excess revenues during commodity booms and provide buffers during downturns. SWFs are state-owned investment funds typically financed through resource rents, fiscal surpluses, government transfers, privatisation proceeds, official foreign currency transactions, and balance of payments surpluses (Gyeyir, 2019). Nigeria's Excess Crude Account (ECA), created in 2004, was intended to stabilise fiscal revenues by saving oil windfalls (Chioma, 2025). Ghana also created the Ghana Stabilisation Fund (GSF) to serve as a fiscal buffer to cushion public expenditure against unexpected petroleum revenue shortfalls (Box 16.1). Angola's Fundo Soberano de Angola (FSDEA) was designed both as a stabilisation and investment fund (Thomas, 2025). In principle, well-managed SWFs can reduce fiscal volatility and protect debt sustainability, but in practice, weak institutional frameworks and political interference have undermined their stabilising role.

**Box 16.1 Establishment of Stabilisation Fund in Ghana**

The Ghana Stabilisation Fund (GSF), created under the Petroleum Revenue Management Act (PRMA), serves as a fiscal buffer to cushion public expenditure against unexpected petroleum revenue shortfalls. It is funded by a portion of excess petroleum revenues channelled into the Ghana Petroleum Funds, with the goal of ensuring budget stability in times of volatility. The GSF's main function is to provide short-term fiscal relief, maintaining public spending when oil revenues fall below projections. To achieve this, it invests in highly liquid assets for quick accessibility during fiscal stress. The fund receives 70% of petroleum revenues allocated to the Ghana Heritage Fund (GHF) and excess revenues beyond the Annual Budget Funding Amount (ABFA). Governed under the PRMA, it operates within a three-tier structure where the Minister of Finance has discretion to cap its size, directing any excess resources to alternative accounts or uses.

Source: Bank of Ghana (2025) and Gyeyir (2019)

### 16.4.2 *Fiscal Rules and Debt Anchors*

Fiscal rules and debt anchors are another mechanism used to discipline fiscal policy in resource-dependent economies. Rules such as expenditure ceilings, budget balance requirements, or non-oil primary balance targets are meant to reduce procyclicality and ensure prudent borrowing. Several countries have experimented with debt ceilings as part of IMF-supported programmes. For example, Botswana's Mineral Revenues, Expenditure and Savings Policy is designed to ensure that recurrent or non-investment spending is funded exclusively from non-mineral revenues. This approach prevents the use of volatile mineral income to cover day-to-day government operations, reserving resource revenues for long-term development and investment purposes (Box 16.2).

**Box 16.2 Botswana's Mineral Revenues, Expenditure and Savings Policy**

Botswana's Mineral Revenues, Expenditure and Savings Policy is the country's disciplined approach to managing diamond revenues. Central to this policy is the principle that recurrent, or non-investment, expenditure should be financed solely from non-mineral revenue sources, ensuring that volatile mineral income is not used to sustain ongoing government operations. Instead, mineral revenues are directed toward investment in infrastructure, education, and development projects with long-term growth potential. This framework, known as the Sustainable Budget Index (SBI), acts as a fiscal rule to safeguard against overdependence on diamonds while promoting intergenerational equity. The approach has enabled Botswana to accumulate reserves, maintain relatively low debt levels, and strengthen economic resilience over the years.

Source: African Natural Resource Center (2016)

### 16.4.3 *Exchange Rate and Monetary Policies in Managing Shocks*

Exchange rate and monetary policy frameworks play an important role in mitigating the transmission of commodity shocks. Some African countries have historically used exchange rate controls and multiple exchange rate systems to shield their economies from volatility, though often with

**Box 16.3 Sudan Used Dual Exchange Rate System to Manage Scarce Foreign Exchange**

For years, Sudan maintained a dual exchange rate system with a wide gap between the official rate and the parallel market rate, largely to manage scarce foreign exchange under sanctions and declining oil revenues. This arrangement created major distortions, undermined investor confidence, and weakened economic efficiency. In February 2021, as part of an IMF-supported reform programme, Sudan unified its exchange rates to restore macroeconomic stability and improve transparency. The reform aimed to attract foreign investment and correct imbalances, with the IMF emphasising that the old system had distorted price signals and hindered sustainable economic growth.

Source: Logan (2021)

distortive consequences. For example, Sudan adopted a dual exchange rate system as a means of managing limited foreign exchange amid international sanctions and falling oil revenues (Box 16.3).

Others have allowed more flexible exchange rates, which absorb external shocks but can increase the local currency cost of external debt servicing. Monetary policy tools, such as interest rate adjustments and inflation targeting, are also employed to maintain macroeconomic stability. Yet, in highly resource-dependent economies, monetary authorities face difficult trade-offs between stabilising the exchange rate, preserving reserves, and sustaining debt repayment capacity.

### 16.4.4 *Regional Initiatives*

Regional institutions have increasingly recognised the need to support member states in managing commodity price volatility and its debt implications. The African Development Bank (AfDB) has provided countercyclical financing facilities, technical assistance in public financial management, and policy advice on resource governance. The African Union (AU) has also promoted initiatives, such as the African Mining Vision (AMV) to encourage transparent and sustainable resource

**Box 16.4 Establishment of the Africa Mining Vision Initiative**

The Africa Mining Vision (AMV), adopted at the 2009 African Union (AU) Summit, is a continent-wide framework to address the paradox of vast mineral wealth coexisting with poverty. It promotes a holistic, developmental approach that integrates mining into broader local, national, and regional policies. Beyond optimising tax revenues, the AMV ensures that communities and workers benefit directly from mining while protecting the environment. It also calls for fairer contracts with multinational companies, greater local participation in supply chains, and stronger industrial and trade linkages. By breaking mining's traditional enclave model, the AMV seeks to shift Africa from being a raw material exporter to building diversified economies anchored in manufacturing, innovation, and knowledge-based services for sustainable growth.

Source: https://au.int/en/ti/amv/about Accessed September 20, 2025

management (see Box 16.4). Regional economic communities (e.g., ECOWAS, SADC) have also engaged in policy harmonisation efforts, though with uneven implementation. While regional initiatives provide useful platforms for knowledge-sharing and technical support, their ability to enforce fiscal discipline or influence debt dynamics remains limited.

### *16.4.5 Role of International Institutions*

International financial institutions (IFIs) such as the IMF and World Bank have played a central role in helping African countries cope with commodity-driven debt crises. IMF programmes often include fiscal adjustment measures, debt restructuring, and technical assistance to strengthen debt management. For example, the IMF's Debt Sustainability Framework (DSF) provides guidance on borrowing limits based on countries' risk profiles. The G20 Debt Service Suspension Initiative (DSSI) and the Common Framework for Debt Treatments (CFDT) have provided temporary relief for some African states facing debt distress. Countries like Zambia, Ghana, Chad, and Mozambique have engaged extensively with international financial institutions, benefiting from programmes aimed at debt restructuring, fiscal stabilisation, and technical assistance (Box 16.5). However, reliance on IFIs has also raised concerns about conditionalities, social costs of austerity, and limited participation of private creditors in restructuring processes.

**Box 16.5 The Role of International Institutions in Some African Countries**

**IMF Debt Restructuring and Common Framework in Zambia:** Zambia defaulted on Eurobond payments in 2020 following copper price declines and debt pressures. In 2022, it secured a US$1.3 billion IMF Extended Credit Facility focused on fiscal consolidation, reforms, and technical support. Debt restructuring was pursued under the G20 Common Framework, making a crucial step toward restoring sustainability.

**IMF Programme and DSSI Participation in Ghana**: Amid falling gold and cocoa revenues, high external debt, and sharp currency depreciation, Ghana entered severe debt distress in 2022–2023. It benefited from temporary relief under the G20 DSSI. In 2023, Ghana secured a US$3 billion IMF bailout, centered on fiscal reforms, domestic debt restructuring, and comprehensive technical support.

**Common Framework and IMF Support in Chad**: Chad's oil-dependent economy was hit hard by price shocks and mounting debt. It became one of the first countries to request debt treatment through the G20 Common Framework. Alongside this, the IMF offered technical assistance and policy guidance, supporting fiscal adjustment efforts to stabilise the economy amid persistent vulnerabilities.

**IMF Technical Assistance Post-Debt Scandal in Mozambique**: Mozambique's hidden debt crisis in 2016, involving undisclosed loans tied to future gas revenues, triggered a suspension of IMF support. Assistance later resumed with a focus on strengthening debt transparency and public financial management. Technical guidance aimed to rebuild credibility, improve fiscal governance, and mitigate risks associated with resource-backed borrowing.

Source: Gebregziabher and Sala (2022) and IMF (2022a, 2022b, 2024)

## 16.5 Why Some of These Policy and Institutional Responses Fail?

### *16.5.1 Weak Institutional Capacity and Poor Governance*

Sovereign wealth funds or stabilization funds (e.g., Nigeria's Excess Crude Account) are often poorly designed and managed, and lack transparency, with weak enforcement of saving and withdrawal rules (Chioma, 2025). Institutions mandated to promote fiscal discipline frequently lack independence, adequate resources, or technical capacity. Instead of serving their intended purpose of smoothing revenue volatility and stabilising economies during downturns, these funds are often diverted for short-term political gains or populist spending. In many cases, rent-seeking elites capture resource revenues, undermining accountability and eroding fiscal buffers. As a result, countries remain exposed to commodity price swings and heightened debt vulnerabilities.

### *16.5.2 Political Economy Pressure*

During commodity booms, most African governments often face intense political and social pressure to ramp up spending on subsidies, public sector wages, and large-scale prestige projects intended to showcase economic progress. While saving excess revenues in stabilisation or sovereign wealth funds could provide long-term protection against downturns, such measures are politically unpopular. As a result, fiscal rules governing savings are frequently ignored, suspended, or manipulated, weakening fiscal discipline and leaving economies highly exposed when commodity prices eventually decline. For instance, fiscal rules like the Fiscal Responsibility Act (2018) guiding the Ghana Stabilisation Fund were suspended during downturns, leading to debt distress and an IMF bailout in 2023 (UNDP Regional Bureau for Africa, 2016).

### *16.5.3 Procyclicality of Fiscal Policy*

Even when formal fiscal rules are in place, governments in resource-dependent economies often spend aggressively during commodity booms, expanding subsidies, wages, and capital projects. However, when prices collapse, they find it politically and socially difficult to reduce expenditures, especially on entrenched commitments. This dynamic entrenches

**Box 16.6 Procyclicality in Zambia**

Zambia experienced a copper-driven boom that dramatically increased fiscal revenues, enabling the government to expand wages, sustain fuel and electricity subsidies, and embark on ambitious infrastructure projects such as roads, hospitals, and airports between 2004 and 2014. Despite the presence of a Medium-Term Expenditure Framework and fiscal rules, spending was highly procyclical and often politically motivated, particularly around elections. When copper prices collapsed in 2015 and again in 2020, revenues plunged, but entrenched expenditures proved difficult to cut. Fiscal rules were suspended, off-budget borrowing escalated, and debt soared, culminating in Zambia's 2020 Eurobond default and subsequent IMF-supported restructuring.

Source: IMF (2022b) and Rasmussen et al. (2015)

procyclical fiscal behaviour, locking countries into repeated boom and bust cycles. Such cycles undermine long-term fiscal stability, weaken debt sustainability, and increase the likelihood of borrowing, arrears, or debt restructuring during periods of economic downturn. Zambia's copper boom fuelled procyclical, politically driven spending; price collapses exposed fiscal rigidity, escalating debt and culminating in a 2020 Eurobond default and IMF restructuring (Box 16.6).

### 16.5.4 *Overdependence on External Solutions*

Reliance on IMF programmes or donor-driven reforms often results in temporary compliance focused on meeting conditionalities, rather than fostering deep, long-term structural change. Governments may adopt reforms to unlock external financing or debt relief, but once the flow of donor funds diminishes, political will and institutional commitment frequently weaken. As a result, reforms are either reversed, poorly implemented, or abandoned altogether. This cycle undermines credibility, perpetuates structural weaknesses, and leaves countries vulnerable to recurring fiscal and debt crises.

### 16.5.5 *Shallow Financial and Commodity Hedging Markets*

Instruments such as commodity hedging, designed to smooth revenue volatility and protect budgets from sharp price swings, require well-developed financial markets, strong institutional frameworks, and significant technical expertise (Liebenthal & Cheelo, 2020). Many African economies lack these prerequisites, making effective hedging difficult to implement. Past attempts at hedging have at times been poorly designed, politically manipulated, or excessively costly, leading to financial losses rather than stability. In some cases, misuse of hedging instruments has even fuelled controversy and eroded public trust in fiscal management.

### 16.5.6 *Exchange Rate and Monetary Constraints*

Many African economies are highly vulnerable to sharp currency depreciations during periods of commodity price declines, as reduced export revenues weaken foreign exchange inflows. This depreciation significantly raises the cost of servicing external debt, much of which is denominated in foreign currencies (Banking and Finance Magazine, 2024). At the same time, limited foreign reserve buffers constrain governments' ability to intervene and stabilise exchange rates. The combination of falling revenues, higher debt servicing costs, and weak reserve positions often amplifies fiscal stress and heightens debt vulnerabilities.

## 16.6 Conclusions

The chapter shows that commodity price volatility profoundly shapes public debt sustainability in resource-dependent African economies, and these effects are magnified by institutional weaknesses. Although boom periods generate temporary revenue surges from oil, mineral, or agricultural exports, inadequate fiscal rules, weak oversight, and political pressures often lead governments to adopt procyclical policies such as expanding spending, increasing subsidies and wages, and accumulating large debts for ambitious projects without building sufficient savings or stabilisation buffers. These responses reflect not only optimism about continued growth but also structural governance gaps that fail to restrain impulsive fiscal behavior. When commodity prices fall, revenues contract abruptly, revealing fragile budget systems and exposing the absence of effective stabilisation mechanisms. As buffers erode, deficits widen, borrowing costs rise, and countries slide toward debt distress. Volatility therefore affects fiscal sustainability through multiple interconnected channels including revenues, expenditures, debt management, exchange rates, and growth. However, weak institutions allow each shock to propagate more severely, deepening fiscal fragility and heightening long-term vulnerability.

For policymakers, development partners, and investors, the findings underscore the urgency of strengthening institutional frameworks that can insulate African economies from commodity price swings. Governments should prioritise building stabilization funds, enforcing fiscal rules, and improving transparency to prevent procyclical spending during booms. Development partners, including the IMF, World Bank, and AfDB, should support capacity building and design lending instruments that encourage countercyclical policies. Investors should recognise that resource dependence without governance safeguards increases sovereign risk, making due diligence critical. Ultimately, aligning fiscal discipline with inclusive growth strategies will be essential to convert resource wealth into sustainable prosperity.

## References


AfDB. (2025). *Africa's macroeconomic performance and outlook*. https://www.afdb.org/en/documents/africas-macroeconomic-performance-and-outlook-january-2025

African Natural Resource Center. (2016). *Botswana's mineral revenues, expenditure and savings policy: A case study*. https://www.afdb.org/fileadmin/uploads/afdb/Documents/Publications/anrc/Botswana_s_mineral_revenues_expenditure_and_saving_policy.pdf?utm_source=chatgpt.com

Andreasson, S. (2015). Varieties of resource nationalism in sub-Saharan Africa's energy and minerals markets. *The Extractive Industries and Society, 2*(2), 310–319. https://doi.org/10.1016/j.exis.2015.01.004

Bagshaw, J. (2025, July 22). *The top 10 African countries by export revenue, key commodities and innovations*. Export Focus Africa. https://exportfocusafrica.com/2025/07/22/the-top-10-african-countries-by-export-revenue-key-commodities-and-innovations/

Bank of Ghana. (2025). *Investment objectives of the Ghana petroleum funds*. Bank of Ghana. https://www.bog.gov.gh/ghana-petroleum-funds/investment-objectives/

Banking and Finance Magazine. (2024, December 9). Africa's currency crisis: A global problem. *Banking and Finance Magazine*. https://internationalfinance.com/magazine/banking-and-finance-magazine/africas-currency-crisis-a-global-problem/

Cao, Y., Mbogo, L. W., & Weiss, J. (2022). *Angola: Selected issues* (22/12; IMF Country Report). https://www.elibrary.imf.org/view/journals/002/2022/012/article-A001-en.xml

Carneiro, F. G., & Kouame, W. A. (2020). *Procyclicality trap in resource-rich countries and how to escape from it* (Africa Can End Poverty). https://blogs.worldbank.org/en/africacan/procyclicality-trap-resource-rich-countries-and-how-escape-it

Céspedes, L. F., & Velasco, A. (2012). Macroeconomic performance during commodity Price booms and busts. *IMF Economic Review, 60*(4), 570–599. https://doi.org/10.1057/imfer.2012.22

Chioma, U. (2025, May 3). From $20 billion to $475K: Nigeria's empty excess crude account stokes fears of fiscal collapse. *Business News*. https://thenigerialawyer.com/from-20-billion-to-473k-nigerias-empty-excess-crude-account-stokes-fears-of-fiscal-collapse/

Cole, O., Tse, T., & Esposito, M. (2015). Did Nigeria and Angola manage their oil windfalls well between 1970 and 2000: What lessons can be learned for new oil producers? *International Journal of Economic Policy in Emerging Economies, 8*(1), 1–19.

Collier, P., & Venables, A. J. (2010). Natural resources and state fragility. *European Economic Review, 54*(4), 401–412.

Copley, A. (2016, May 27). External risks to Africa's growth: Falling commodity prices, China's economic slowdown, and rising external debt. *Brookings*. https://www.brookings.edu/articles/external-risks-to-africas-growth-falling-commodity-prices-chinas-economic-slowdown-and-rising-external-debt/?utm_source=chatgpt.com

Coulibaly, Y. (2024). Resource-backed loans and ecological efficiency of human development: Evidence from African countries. *Ecological Economics, 224*, 108295. https://doi.org/10.1016/j.ecolecon.2024.108295

Da, D., & Diarra, M. (2023). Effect of international commodity Price shocks on public finances in Africa. *Public Finance Review, 51*(2), 236–261. https://doi.org/10.1177/10911421221137426

Ekanem, S. (2025, March 27). 4 African countries on the brink of debt default. *Business Insider Africa* https://africa.businessinsider.com/local/markets/4-african-countries-on-the-brink-of-debt-default/pfhwh84

Falola, T., & Heaton, M. M. (2012). Oil, state, and society, 1970–1983. In T. Falola & M. M. Heaton (Eds.), *A history of Nigeria*. Cambridge University Press.

Farooki, M., & Kaplinsky, R. (2013). The impact of China on global commodity prices. *Routledge*. https://doi.org/10.4324/9780203155912

Gebregziabher, F. H., & Sala, A. P. (2022, April 19). *Mozambique's "hidden debts": Turning a crisis into an opportunity for reform*. World Bank Blog.

Ghana News Agency. (2024, June 24). Ghana reaches agreement with Eurobond holders on US$13bn debt restructuring. *Ghana News Agency*. https://gna.org.gh/2024/06/ghana-reaches-agreement-with-eurobond-holders-on-us13bn-debt-restructuring/

Ghura, D., Basu, A., & Calamitsis, E. A. (1999). Adjustment and growth in sub-Saharan Africa. *IMF Working Papers, 99*(51), 1. https://doi.org/10.5089/9781451847093.001

Gyeyir, D. M. (2019). The Ghana stabilisation fund: Relevance and impact so far. *Energy Policy, 135*, 110989. https://doi.org/10.1016/j.enpol.2019.110989

Herrera, S., Kouame, W. A., & Mandon, P. (2019). *Why some countries can escape the fiscal pro-cyclicality trap and others cannot?* (8963; Policy Research Working Paper). https://documents1.worldbank.org/curated/en/510041565102137832/pdf/Why-Some-Countries-Can-Escape-the-Fiscal-Pro-Cyclicality-Trap-and-Others-Cannot.pdf

History Rise. (2024, September 11). The trans-saharan trade network and its role in African history. *History Rise*. https://historyrise.com/the-trans-saharan-trade-network-and-its-role-in-african-history/

Hope, K. N. (2025). Colonial rule and natural resources exploitation in post-colonial Africa. In D. N. Yuni, E. C. Iloh, & C. C. Ngang (Eds.), *Colonial heritage and the socio-economic development of Africa* (pp. 209–228). Springer Nature Switzerland. https://doi.org/10.1007/978-3-031-73695-7_11

IMF. (2022a). *IMF managing director welcomes debt treatment agreement reached by chad and its creditors under the G20 common framework* (22/379; Press Release). https://www.imf.org/en/News/Articles/2022/11/13/pr-22379-chad-imf-managing-director-welcomes-debt-treatment

IMF. (2022b, July 30). IMF managing director welcomes the statement by the creditor committee for zambia under the common framework for debt treatments. *IMF*. https://www.imf.org/en/News/Articles/2022/07/30/pr22282-Zambia-IMF-Managing-Director-Welcomes-Statement-Creditor-Committee-Zambia-Common-Framework

IMF. (2024). *IMF executive board completes the second review under the extended credit facility arrangement with ghana* (24/241; Press Release). https://www.imf.org/en/News/Articles/2024/06/28/pr24241-ghana-imf-exec-board-completes-2nd-rev-ecf-arr

Katoka, B., & Dostal, J. M. (2022). Natural resources, international commodity prices and economic performance in sub-Saharan Africa (1990–2019). *Journal of African Economies, 31*(1), 53–74. https://doi.org/10.1093/jae/ejab014

Liebenthal, R., & Cheelo, C. (2020). The boom–bust cycle of global copper prices, structural change, and industrial development in Zambia. In *Mining for change* (pp. 374–396). Oxford University PressOxford. https://doi.org/10.1093/oso/9780198851172.003.0017

Lledó, V., Yackovlev, I., & Gadenne, L. (2009). *Cyclical patterns of government expenditures in sub-Saharan Africa: Facts and factors* (WP/09/274; IMF Working Paper).

Logan, S. (2021). *Exchange rate reform in Sudan* (Policy Brief). https://www.theigc.org/publications/exchange-rate-reform-sudan?utm_source=chatgpt.com

Macheka, A., Nyathi, T., Matthee, R., & Acheampong, T. (2025, June 2). Fiscal prospects of sub-Saharan African states with debt vulnerability. *International Banker*. https://internationalbanker.com/finance/fiscal-prospects-of-sub-saharan-african-states-with-debt-vulnerability/

Maverick, C. (2025, January 23). Historic trade routes that connected africa to the world. *Africa-Interactive.Net*. https://africa-interactive.net/historic-trade-routes-that-connected-africa-to-the-world/

Oluwole, V. (2024, September 23). Worst performing African currencies: Zambian Kwacha, Angolan Kwanza, Nigerian Naira. *Business Insider Africa*. https://africa.businessinsider.com/local/markets/top-10-worst-performing-african-currencies/xghvplg

Rasmussen, T., Tsikata, T., Cui, Q., Jang, B., Rosales, M., & Tchaidze, R. (2015). *Zambia* (15/153; IMF Country Report).

Ross, A. G., Omar, M., Xu, A., & Pandey, S. (2019). The impact of institutional quality on Chinese foreign direct investment in Africa. *Local Economy: The Journal of the Local Economy Policy Unit, 34*(6), 572–588. https://doi.org/10.1177/0269094219882329

The Conversation Africa. (2024, January 31). African countries are struggling with high debt, demands to spend more and collapsing currencies: The policy fixes that could help. *The Conversation Africa*. https://theconversation.com/african-countries-are-struggling-with-high-debt-demands-to-spend-more-and-collapsing-currencies-the-policy-fixes-that-could-help-221614

Thomas, D. (2025, August 5). Angola's SWF chief on his second leadership stint. *African Business*. https://african.business/2025/08/finance-services/angolas-swf-chief-on-his-second-leadership-stint

Toussaint, E. (2016, June 6). *Debt as an instrument of the colonial conquest of Egypt*. CADTM. https://www.cadtm.org/spip.php?page=imprimer&id_article=13562

Tunji, S. (2024, December 5). Naira devaluation raises foreign debt by N30tn—Report. *PUNCH*. https://punchng.com/naira-devaluation-raises-foreign-debt-by-n30tn-report/?utm_source=chatgpt.com

UNCTAD. (2016). *Economic development in Africa report 2016: Debt dynamics and development finance in Africa*. https://unctad.org/system/files/official-document/aldcafrica2016_en.pdf

UNCTAD. (2021). *Commodities and development report 2021: Escaping from the commodity dependence trap through technology and innovation.* https://unctad.org/system/files/official-document/ditccom2021d1_en.pdf

UNCTAD. (2025, February 10). *Africa's vulnerability to global shocks highlights need for stronger regional trade.* UNCTAD. https://unctad.org/news/africas-vulnerability-global-shocks-highlights-need-stronger-regional-trade

UNDP Regional Bureau for Africa. (2016). *Primary commodity booms and busts: Emerging lessons from sub-Saharan Africa.* UNDP Regional Bureau for Africa.

Wanzala, R. W., & Obokoh, L. O. (2024). Sustainability implications of commodity Price shocks and commodity dependence in selected sub-Saharan countries. *Sustainability, 16*(20), 8928. https://doi.org/10.3390/su16208928

# Index[1]

**A**
Adaptation finance, 234–236, 249n3, 250, 334, 340
African Continental Free Trade Area (AfCFTA), 117, 160, 162, 385, 397, 400
Asset-backed financing, 219
Autoregressive Distributed Lag (ARDL) bounds testing, 91–108

**B**
Bilateral creditors, 120, 121, 124, 128, 134–137, 413
Blended finance, 162, 172, 182, 234, 235, 241, 250, 251, 342
Boom–bust cycles, 406, 407, 421
Borrowing, 3–7, 9–14, 16–21, 26, 29–32, 37, 39, 43–47, 53–55, 61, 62, 66, 67, 70–72, 74, 75, 80–85, 95, 99, 104, 116, 121, 127, 128, 130, 132, 133, 150–152, 154–158, 161–164, 171, 172, 174, 177, 179–187, 220, 234, 240, 242, 244, 247, 248, 256–261, 265, 266, 268, 275, 277, 280, 281, 288, 289, 297–325, 331–348, 355–361, 367, 368, 375, 377, 383–388, 393, 394, 400, 406, 408, 409, 412–413, 416, 418, 419, 421, 422

**C**
Capital markets, 7, 16, 25, 26, 32, 37, 38, 40, 44, 53, 62, 64, 108, 122, 127, 128, 131, 132, 154, 162, 184, 186, 194, 206, 209, 210, 212, 217, 220, 222, 234, 242–245, 278, 342, 346, 348, 385, 409

[1] Note: Page numbers followed by 'n' refer to notes.



I. N. Yakubu (ed.), *Public Debt and Economic Resilience in Africa*, Palgrave Studies in African and Development Economics,
https://doi.org/10.1007/978-3-032-25835-9

Climate adaptation, 75, 83, 84, 123, 124, 178–181, 234, 243–245, 249, 249n3, 334, 338–340
Climate bonds, 234, 244
Climate debt trap, 234
Climate finance, 161, 234–238, 244, 246, 248–251, 249n2
Commodity dependence, 106
Commodity price volatility, 183, 193, 233, 258, 405–423
Concessional loans, 4, 6, 17, 25, 73, 82, 171–187, 235, 241, 322, 386
Corruption control, 275–290
Crowding-out effect, 27, 362, 363

D

Debt accumulation, 37–38, 61, 62, 84, 93, 107, 184, 212, 258, 259, 278, 279, 287–289, 335, 362, 364, 412
Debt composition, 73, 85, 384
Debt crises, 6, 13, 20, 31, 71, 79, 86, 91, 116, 127, 132, 161, 383, 400, 414, 418, 421
Debt distress, 5, 16, 18–20, 26, 65, 66, 68–71, 75, 79, 115, 116, 130, 131, 150, 152, 154–156, 158, 161–164, 234, 247, 251, 332, 334, 336, 338, 339, 347, 392, 399, 407, 409, 418–420, 423
Debt dynamics, 37, 39–43, 56, 65, 68–69, 79, 92, 99, 103, 108, 155, 156, 255–268, 288, 385, 391, 393, 400, 418
Debt-for-climate swaps, 141, 159, 162, 239, 249, 251
Debt-for-nature swaps, 117, 239, 243–244, 249
Debt management, 5, 18, 30, 32, 71, 82–85, 103, 107, 116, 121, 141, 150, 156–158, 163, 164, 183–185, 216–218, 222, 233–251, 266, 280, 322, 324, 325, 331–348, 376, 400, 413, 418, 423
Debt overhang, 14, 15, 20, 28, 31, 126, 130, 179, 187, 301, 355–377
Debt relief initiatives, 6, 39, 233, 385
Debt restructuring, 5, 115–141, 159, 163, 164, 175, 187, 249, 332, 400, 418, 419, 421
Debt service burden, 26, 127, 131, 152, 154–156, 335, 391, 399, 400
Debt stress, 171–187, 375, 376
Debt sustainability, 5–10, 16, 26, 32, 61–86, 91–108, 115, 117, 119, 125, 129, 130, 141, 151, 155, 158, 161, 164, 172, 173, 181–184, 186, 193–223, 242, 250, 256, 258, 261, 268, 275–278, 282, 301, 303, 322, 324, 332, 334, 336, 337, 340, 341, 347, 356, 358–362, 364–366, 370, 376, 377, 384, 385, 391, 393, 405–423
Debt-to-GDP ratio, 3, 4, 7, 9, 14–16, 19, 62, 63, 65, 72, 73, 91, 93, 98, 99, 102, 103, 120, 126, 128, 130, 150, 151, 172, 175, 193, 194, 213, 332, 335, 357, 360–362, 364, 375, 385, 400, 406, 414
Demographic drivers, 38, 50, 54, 56
Domestic debt markets, 62

E

Economic globalization, 255–268
Economic growth, 6, 7, 43, 46, 48, 53, 56, 68, 95, 99, 103, 106,

116, 129–131, 156, 173, 174, 181, 256, 262, 266–268, 275–290, 299, 301–303, 321, 331, 333, 334, 361, 364, 367, 371, 374, 377, 414, 417
Emerging markets borrowing, 104
Environmental risk, 162, 337
Environmental, social and governance (ESG), 208, 223, 240, 242, 246, 331–348
Error correction model (ECM), 98, 279, 282
Exchange rate depreciation, 27, 156, 163, 413
Exchange rate regimes, 384, 389–392, 391n5
Exchange rate volatility, 6, 85, 383–400
External shocks, 3, 5, 7, 14, 20, 26, 27, 66, 130, 150, 155–157, 162, 183, 194, 233, 258, 260, 276, 332, 342, 392, 397, 406, 410, 414, 417

F
Financial globalization, 18, 257, 259, 262, 265–268
Fiscal discipline, 14, 45, 92, 94, 106, 107, 122, 127, 133, 177, 219, 244, 258, 260, 266, 276, 278, 418, 420, 423
Fiscal fragility, 156–157, 175, 409, 423
Fiscal governance, 5, 29, 91, 93, 106, 107, 117, 419
Fiscal policy, 24, 82–83, 92–96, 102, 119, 126, 284, 290, 300, 304, 306, 342, 343, 347, 372, 376, 394, 416, 420–421
Fiscal procyclicality, 406
Fiscal resilience, 5, 175
Fiscal rules, 12, 32, 47, 81, 82, 85, 91–108, 130, 218, 222, 416, 420–423
Fiscal space, 4, 5, 7, 15, 18, 20, 27, 29, 31, 54, 61, 84, 85, 99, 106, 107, 116, 120, 121, 123–126, 130, 131, 134, 141, 150, 152, 154, 155, 157, 172, 174, 179–182, 184, 186, 187, 193, 195, 221, 233, 239, 247, 277, 278, 323, 338, 384, 391–393, 406
Foreign direct investment (FDI), 37, 46, 50, 68, 174, 256, 259, 280, 384, 393, 398–400

G
G20 Common Framework, 12, 30, 84, 120, 124, 128, 129, 132, 172, 186, 391, 419
Ghana, 9, 11, 15, 17–19, 26, 27, 31, 39, 40, 48, 63, 68, 72, 91–108, 121–125, 128–129, 131, 132, 134, 137, 149, 152, 156, 158, 163, 172, 176, 177, 187, 233, 246, 248, 256, 266, 277, 278, 281n1, 332, 356, 363, 374, 384, 388, 390n3, 391, 394, 396, 400, 406, 409, 415, 418–420
Global economic shocks, 149–164
Governance, 4, 10, 30–32, 43, 48, 50, 55, 62, 79, 81, 82, 94, 116, 121, 124, 127, 130, 131, 133, 134, 154, 157, 160, 177, 183, 185, 187, 196–197, 200, 217, 222, 237, 244, 256, 257, 260–262, 266, 276–278, 281, 289, 290, 332–334, 336, 337, 339, 340, 342–343, 347, 348, 417, 420, 422, 423

Green bonds, 159, 161, 162, 172, 235, 240, 244, 245, 247, 248, 250, 251, 334, 346, 347
Green finance, 163, 240, 245–248, 250, 251, 345, 346
Green sukuk, 208, 209, 212, 345–346, 348

**H**

Heavily Indebted Poor Countries (HIPC) Initiative, 14–16, 18, 30, 31, 38–40, 46, 67, 73, 116, 118, 120, 121, 124–127, 130–133, 137, 151–152, 162, 163, 233, 303, 383, 400
Human development, 81, 84, 116, 290, 298, 300, 301, 303, 304, 325

**I**

Ijara sukuk, 197, 199, 209
Inclusive growth, 85, 235, 245, 256, 324, 385, 423
Inclusive human development, 298, 301, 311–320
Inequality-Adjusted Human Development Index (IHDI), 298, 304
Inflation, 11, 12, 14, 29, 46, 48, 50, 53, 56, 92–94, 96–99, 101–103, 105, 106, 128, 132, 157, 262, 264, 266, 268, 277, 284, 300, 302–304, 306, 344, 356, 362, 384, 390–394, 396–397, 409, 414, 417
Infrastructure financing, 118, 195, 208, 219, 221, 233
Institutional drivers, 46, 50
Institutional quality, 43, 44, 80, 81, 257, 258, 260–262, 266, 267, 376
International Monetary Fund (IMF), 3–5, 7, 11, 14, 15, 20, 26, 39, 47, 48, 66, 69–71, 80, 84, 91, 94, 96, 99, 103, 104, 116, 119, 120, 122, 125, 127, 129, 130, 132, 134, 149, 151, 152, 154, 155, 158, 171, 172, 175–178, 181, 182, 184, 185, 193, 210, 212, 260, 275, 281, 281n1, 289, 298, 299, 303, 305, 332, 335–338, 355–357, 361, 362, 365, 366, 375–377, 384, 391, 392, 394, 408, 417–421, 423
IV-GMM estimation, 369, 370, 374

**K**

KOF globalization Index, 256

**L**

Liability management, 108, 343, 346, 348
Long-run equilibrium, 92, 98, 103, 282, 288, 308, 311

**M**

Maastricht criteria, 62, 65
Macroeconomic stability, 5, 16, 29, 62, 116, 118, 160, 193, 256, 338, 384, 417
Multilateral creditors, 73, 120, 249, 387
Multilateral Debt Relief Initiative (MDRI), 15–16, 15n23, 18, 30, 31, 40, 116, 120–121, 124, 125, 127, 130, 137, 151–152, 163, 233, 383, 400
Multilateral development banks (MDBs), 30, 149, 159n3, 238, 250

**P**

Panel autoregressive distributed lag (ARDL), 282, 286, 289, 377
Panel generalized method of moment (GMM), 258, 260, 261
Panel nonlinear autoregressive distributed lag (PNARDL), 300, 303–306, 308, 310, 311, 324
Paris Agreement, 234, 240, 245, 250, 251
Paris Club, 15, 18, 28, 117–120, 124–126, 128, 132, 239, 337
Political drivers, 46, 50
Private creditors, 5, 12, 28, 41, 119–121, 133, 134, 141, 159, 387, 419
Private sector investment, 184, 356, 357, 363, 369–371, 375–377, 399
Procyclical spending, 412–413, 423
Public debt, 3–13, 26, 31, 37–38, 62, 63, 65, 66, 71, 80, 84, 85, 91, 92, 94, 96, 98, 103, 105, 115, 118, 122, 130, 150, 153, 155, 161, 193, 195, 216, 221, 233, 239, 256–259, 261, 262, 264–268, 275–290, 297, 331, 334, 335, 340–341, 356–358, 362–364, 366–368, 370, 371, 374–377, 383–400, 405–423
Public debt management, 216, 222, 331–348
Public expenditure, 278, 415

**Q**

Quintile method of moments, 56

**R**

Resource dependence, 406
Revenue volatility, 91, 95, 156–157, 163, 420, 422

**S**

Shariah governance, 217, 222
Social bonds, 334, 340, 341
Social sector investment, 182, 324, 325
Soft loans, 172
Sovereign bonds, 17, 69, 193–223, 234, 302, 342, 360
Sovereign borrowing, 66, 280, 298–304, 306, 311–320, 322–325, 377
Sovereign debt restructuring, 116, 117
Stress testing, 68
Structural transformation, 14, 61, 85, 117, 161–162, 245, 276, 414
Sukuk, 193–223, 345–348
Sustainability-linked bonds (SLBs), 248, 340, 342, 348
Sustainable development, 32, 163, 164, 171, 172, 187, 212, 223, 235, 334, 341
Sustainable Development Goals (SDGs), 4, 54, 75, 85, 116, 212, 220, 234, 235, 245, 250, 251, 256, 276, 281, 298, 332, 342, 385

**T**

Threshold effects, 46, 299, 302, 359–364, 375, 376
Time inconsistency problem, 93
Trade competitiveness, 385
Trade openness, 50, 258, 259, 265, 289, 290, 304
Two-gap theory, 180

**V**

Volatility, 6, 20, 72, 79, 85, 91, 95, 100, 103, 107, 129, 156–157, 163, 175, 183, 193, 215, 233, 246, 258, 276, 284, 336, 383–400, 405–423

FSC
www.fsc.org
MIX
Papier | Fördert
gute Waldnutzung
FSC® C083411

Kolibri 360 GmbH
Ferdinand-Jühlke-Straße 7
99095 Erfurt, Deutschland
produktsicherheit@kolibri360.de